CONTENTS

UPDATE NOTICE: We have taken every step to ensure that the contents of this guide are correct at the time of going to press. However, subsequent updates to *Breath of the Wild* may contain adjustments, gameplay balancing, and even feature additions that cannot be anticipated at the time of writing.

Foreword

「決められた道筋に沿って遊ぶ」という「ゼルダのあたりまえ」を見直して、「どこに行って、何をするのかはユーザーの自由」という、ゼルダ史上、類を見ない遊び方を実現したこの「ブレス オブ ザ ワイルド」は、その製作期間の大半を「遊びながら考える」という事に費やしました。それは、広大な世界の中に、プレイヤーが目指すべき「点」を無数に配置して、それを実際に遊びながら、大きくしたり、小さくしたり、位置を変えたりして、プレイヤーが感じることを遊びに取り入れていくという工程でした。この制作スタイルは、実の所、初代の「ゼルダの伝説」で宮本が行った手法とよく似ているのですが、ゲームが3Dになって、その世界に「リアリティー」が求められるようになってからは、最初に確実な「設計図」が求められた為に、次第に「プレイヤーには、こう遊んでもらう」という、制作者側の「都合」がゲームに反映される事になり、それが「決められた道筋に沿って遊ぶ」という「ゼルダのあたりまえ」を生むことになったのです。

ただ、この「遊びながら考える」という作り方は、時間と共に、ゲームを育てていくような作り方なので「終わり」をどこに定めるのかが非常に難しく、開発が終わった今でも、まだやり残したことがたくさんあるような気がしています。この「やり残し」という感覚は従来の制作でもあって、それは「残念」な感覚だったのですが、今作では、どちらかというと「もっと育てたい」という「希望」のような感覚となっている点も、大きな違いだと感じています。

未来のことはどうなるかわかりませんが、この「もっと育てたい」という感覚は、これからのゼルダを、また変えていくことの原動力となると思っているので、今後のゼルダにもどうかご期待を頂きたいと思っています。

In re-examining the convention that *Zelda* games are played on a set path, we decided to implement a groundbreaking new play style that would allow players to go wherever and do whatever they want. This has been achieved for the first time in the history of the series in its newest edition, *Breath of the Wild*. In order to attain this goal, we spent most of the production time creating the game as we played it.

The process of "creating while playing" went like this: first, we placed a countless number of "points" throughout the vast world of *Breath of the Wild*. Then, as we went through and actually played the game, we would make those "points" larger, smaller, or move them around, incorporating the things that we felt, while playing deeper into the game itself. In truth, this production style is very similar to the method Miyamoto used in the very first *The Legend of Zelda*. Nonetheless, as games became 3D and people wanted more realism from game worlds, it became necessary to have a concrete "blueprint" of our game world from the very start of development. In essence, what became known as the quintessential *Zelda* experience, following a path set by the developers from start to finish, ended up being a product of the demands placed on the developers by that blueprint.

However, since this approach of creating a game while actually playing it means that the game continues to grow and evolve over time, it makes it very difficult to decide where to place the ending. Even now, after development has finished, I still get the feeling that there are so many things left that we didn't get a chance to achieve. Although this feeling isn't new to this particular work, for past games, it was more a feeling of disappointment. For this game, in contrast, it's more of a desire to keep evolving and growing. I feel like that's a big difference between this Zelda game and previous versions.

I'm not sure what lies before us, but I'm positive that this feeling of wanting to keep on growing and changing will be a driving force for future *Zelda* games. I hope you'll keep your eye out for whatever comes next in *Zelda*.

Eiji Aonuma
Producer, *The Legend of Zelda: Breath of the Wild*

Thank you
for playing

青沼
英二

Breath of The Wildは、ゼルダ２５周年を機に、いままでのゼルダのあたりまえを見直した新しい基軸のゼルダを作りたいと考えて始まったプロジェクトでした。私自身、新ゼルダを制作する上で、今までにやっていない新しい遊び、新しいハード、新しい技術を使ったゼルダとは？に長い間悩み、スタッフと検討を重ねる毎日でしたが、その答えを、なかなか見つけることができませんでした。

そんな中、初心に帰りそもそもゼルダの面白さの源泉は何なのか？　と考えたとき、それは初代のゼルダの中にありました。フィールドの中を探索して回り、自分で想像して試行錯誤しうまくいくかどうか、いろんな事を試してみる・・・こうじゃないのか？　ここにあるんじゃないか？そのひとつ、ひとつのユーザーのアクションに丁寧に答えのあるゲームを、今この時に作ってみてはどうか？そのために必要なものは何か？を考えていくと完成したBreath of The Wildに実装されているすべての遊びの元となる"掛け算の遊び"に行き着いたのです。

Breath of The Wildの世界で起こる自然現象のほとんどは、物理法則をベースに、ゲームの中の登場物に影響を与えます。そして、プレイヤー自身の選択やアクション、道具を使った効果によって、様々なリアクションが返ってくるようになっています。これらの組み合わせ、すなわち掛け算によって、フィールド上では作った僕たちでさえ想像もつかない現象が起こるようになりました。そのため、本作をクリアするルートは１つではありません。みなさんの発想の数だけ、解法のある新ゼルダなのです。

広いフィールドには"ゼルダならでは"の謎や強敵、個性豊かなキャラタがたくさん待ち受けています。今回、主人公リンクがシーカーストーンというアイテムを手掛かりに冒険をして行く物語ですが、みなさんはこの本を片手に、掛け算の遊びがギッシリと詰まった広大なハイラルの大地を冒険し尽くしてみてください。

The *Legend of Zelda: Breath of the Wild* is a project that we started in an effort to completely re-imagine the conventions of *The Legend of Zelda* to commemorate the 25th anniversary of the series. I tried to imagine what that would look like: a new *Legend of Zelda*, utilizing new technology, new hardware, and new ways of playing that we had never done before. I contemplated this for a long time, and my staff and I spent day after day trying to come up with an answer, but for what seemed an age, we couldn't find one.

When we went back to the essence of what it was that originally made *The Legend of Zelda* so much fun, we realized the answer was in the very first *Zelda* game: venturing through wide open fields, using your imagination and trying out different approaches in order to overcome problems... Was this the answer? Was this the essence of *The Legend of Zelda*? What if we tried making a game where there was a response to every single one of the player's actions? What would we need in order to make that happen? After we started asking ourselves these questions, we came up with a vast variety of playstyles that served as the basis for everything that was implemented in the finished version of *The Legend of Zelda: Breath of the Wild*.

Most of the natural phenomena that occur in the world of *Breath of the Wild* are based on physics, and they affect all forms of life that appear in the game. In addition, depending on the choices and actions of the player or the effects from the items that they use, there are various kinds of reactions that can occur. Due to the mass of possible combinations, we have on occasion observed things happen in the field that not even we, who created the game, could have imagined. For this reason, there is no one way to beat this game. In *The Legend of Zelda: Breath of the Wild*, the number of ways that you can tackle and solve any problem is limited only by your imagination.

Unique characters, powerful enemies, and challenging puzzles that can only be found in the world of *The Legend of Zelda* are waiting for you. This time, our hero Link uses an item called the Sheikah Slate to aid him in his adventures, but with this strategy guide by your side, I hope that you too will be able to venture forth with confidence into the vast world of Hyrule and experience your own adventure to the fullest.

Hidemaro Fujibayashi
Director, *The Legend of Zelda: Breath of the Wild*

QUICKSTART

Breath of the Wild features a gigantic realm that you can explore at your leisure. After a brief introductory prologue, the full sandbox will be unlocked – a feature-packed, colorful world of outstanding scale and variety.

In this breathtaking environment, the game's narrative invites you to visit specific places and face set challenges. At any point in time, though, you can choose to go your own way. Opportunities to leave the main narrative path – either to roam freely or to attend to optional tasks – are quite literally *everywhere*.

Whether you are looking for step-by-step assistance, or instead intend to complete the adventure with minimal help, you will find that this book offers all the information you will need to support your playthrough. We have spared no expense to offer a primarily visual guide, where everything from puzzle solutions to prompts on where to go next can be absorbed with a simple glance at an annotated screenshot or map.

In this brief section, we draw your attention to points of entry in this guide that might be of interest to you.

GETTING STARTED › PRIMER CHAPTER

This guide begins with a short **PRIMER** (see page 8). This opening chapter introduces all game concepts of significance with one essential objective in mind: helping you to start the adventure with confidence. If you are a newcomer to *The Legend of Zelda* series, this should be your first port of call. Even long-time fans will learn a lot by reading this chapter, as *Breath of the Wild* has a huge number of new features that set it apart from its predecessors.

PLAYTHROUGH GUIDANCE › WALKTHROUGH CHAPTER

Our **WALKTHROUGH** (see page 32) has been designed to enhance your experience. If you wish, you can follow the main path that we recommend, honed over countless playthroughs. Alternatively, you can instead use it as a handy source of reference should you prefer to plot a more personal course through the adventure.

- A large map featuring key landmarks and points of interest illustrates each region that you visit during the main storyline. This is accompanied by a visual representation of the steps that you follow to complete main quests, and a list of the various optional objectives that you might feasibly complete while in the area. Essentially, the maps that preface each new area introduce the things that you *can* do while in the region – a welcome heads-up for players who would like to play under their own steam where possible, but do not want to miss any important opportunities.
- This is followed by a traditional step-by-step walkthrough where we detail how to overcome each challenge during that section of Link's journey.

SUPPLEMENTARY CHAPTERS

This Expanded Edition of the *Breath of the Wild* guide features four brand new, exclusive chapters. Two of these offer advanced information on the resources Link has access to throughout his adventure, while the other two are dedicated to the game's Expansion Pass content.

REFERENCE & ANALYSIS (see page 352): detailed guidance on how to optimize your playthrough by acquiring the best possible tools – weapons, armor upgrades, recipes and ingredients, horses, you name it.

MAPS (see page 374): a comprehensive collection of hi-res area maps showing the exact location of Hyrule's key points of interest and collectibles.

THE MASTER TRIALS (see page 410) & **THE CHAMPIONS' BALLAD** (see page 444): in-depth coverage of the game's two expansion packs.

3 SPECIFIC QUESTIONS → REFERENCE CHAPTERS

Whenever you have a question about a specific topic – shrines, items, enemies, optional quests – you have access to a wealth of reference material in the chapters that follow the main walkthrough.

You will also find a comprehensive index at the back of this book. Simply look for a key term to find a corresponding page reference, leading you straight to the answer you require.

SHRINE-RELATED QUESTIONS

Our **SHRINES CHAPTER** (page 112) offers a comprehensive directory of all shrines, sorted by regions. We use annotated screenshots and descriptive captions to show you the way to each altar, plus advice on how to plunder all hidden treasures.

SIDE-QUEST-RELATED QUESTIONS

Our **SIDE QUESTS CHAPTER** (page 214) explains how to find and complete all 76 side quests in the game. For ease of reference, we have sorted side quests by region, with maps detailing the positions of quest vendors and places you must visit in order to complete their objectives.

ITEM-RELATED QUESTIONS

The **INVENTORY CHAPTER** (page 278) is home to a full appraisal of all items, including where and how you can obtain them. If you are looking for better equipment or are in need of new cooking recipes to concoct decisive buffs, look no further.

MONSTER-RELATED QUESTIONS

This guide's **BESTIARY CHAPTER** (page 300) details every enemy that you may encounter over the course of your journey. Each species is analyzed with a data sheet revealing HP, habitats, drops, and other key pieces of information, along with essential combat strategies that will improve your performance against each foe.

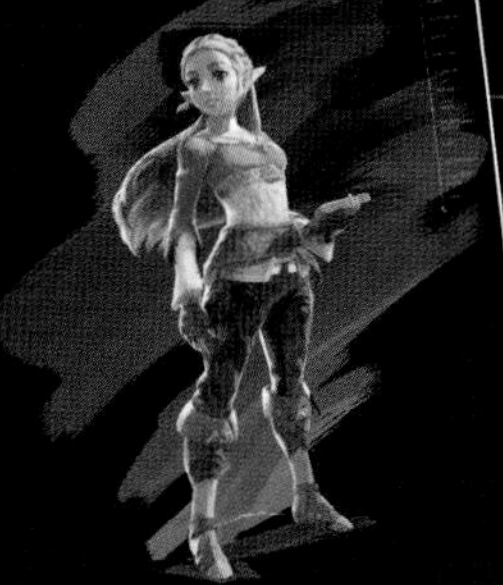

BONUS-RELATED QUESTIONS

Our **EXTRAS CHAPTER** (page 324) covers optional activities, challenges, and secrets that are not listed in your Adventure Log – some of which contribute to your overall completion rate.

PRIMER

This introductory chapter offers a general presentation of all primary features and concepts of significance in *Breath of the Wild*. As the adventure begins you are free, literally within seconds, to go where you want and do what you please. While this freedom is hugely enjoyable, it also means that there are countless traps that lie in wait for the unwary player: surprisingly tough opponents, complex puzzles, and the many challenges inherent in navigating a vast and varied game world.

Breath of the Wild does not coddle players with regular tutorials, or micro-manage movement with waypoints that map journeys on a step-by-step basis. Instead, you learn by observing, by attempting actions that seem logical, and – perhaps most importantly of all – by failing.

It's important to acquire a solid understanding of staple game features at an early stage in the story. If you would like to make a commanding start, digesting this Primer chapter will help you to get to grips with exploration, combat, character progression, equipment and many other core systems. For those relishing the opportunity to test their mettle against this world with minimal assistance, the chapter is also suited for occasional reference whenever you might like to learn more about a particular topic of interest.

GAME STRUCTURE

The Legend of Zelda: Breath of the Wild places your character, Link, in a breathtaking open world, and leaves you free to explore it as you please. While a main storyline quest is always available, reasons and opportunities to venture off the beaten track are seemingly countless in number.

The true joy of *Breath of the Wild* is that there is no right or wrong way to play. Some will choose to focus on advancing the story, while others may favor a more leisurely approach to completing critical missions in order to fully explore the lands of Hyrule.

Broadly speaking, there are three primary pursuits:

- **MAIN QUESTS:** These missions advance the main storyline upon completion. They are selected automatically by default, meaning that their waypoints are displayed in priority on your map and mini-map. These markers are very helpful to locate your next destination, but you can't expect to blindly follow them to complete objectives. Exploring each region on the way to your next destination is a large part of the challenge, where natural curiosity and a willingness to investigate the environment will enable you to find solutions on your own. Sometimes, you may not even receive a directional hint: certain main quest waypoints stay on the position of the quest giver. In such instances, you have no guidance other than the hints provided by the character in question to help you. It's up to you to decipher the meaning of their words and figure out what you are supposed to do next.

- **SIDE QUESTS & SHRINE QUESTS:** These assignments are generally shorter than main quests and involve a relatively simple objective – finding a specific item, revealing a hidden landmark, and so forth. Whenever you wish to complete one of these optional missions, be sure to select it in the Adventure Log menu: this will ensure that active waypoints on the map and mini-map point to relevant locations. In many cases, though, these waypoints will remain on the position of the quest vendor, making you directly responsible for figuring out what to do next. More often than not, optional missions do not involve intense combat, but instead test your wits and observation skills. If a character requires an elixir to heal a relative, you must use the clues at your disposal to infer which ingredients are required, and where these might be found. Our Walkthrough chapter offers selections of optional quests that are feasible and within the limits of Link's abilities for each stage in the storyline. As a general rule, we strongly encourage you to complete as many of these secondary quests as you can. Not only will they offer valuable rewards, but they will also enable you to see more of the wonders of Hyrule.

- **FREE ROAMING:** Even if you are not working on a quest there is still a lot that you can do in *Breath of the Wild*, such as exploring the spectacular environments, gathering resources or improved equipment, discovering secret areas, participating in mini-games, and facing ambient enemies. The world is *alive* with opportunities and rewards. Irrespective of the advantages that you'll gain by accumulating items, exploration is hugely rewarding in its own right: charting the vast expanses and discovering mesmerizing vistas can lead to many quietly profound moments.

DIFFICULTY

By modern gaming standards, *Breath of the Wild* is a relatively hard game. There are few tutorials or prompts to introduce even basic concepts and systems, waypoints deliberately offer limited visual guidance, battles can seem brutal if you are unprepared, the map you explore is gigantic, and the potential pitfalls numerous. It is, however, never unfair or cruel – quite the contrary, in fact. Every moment of failure teaches you something about how you could better approach a challenge or improve your preparations.

SKIPPING CUTSCENES

While most players will want to see every last story development, there are instances (particularly when triggering an event multiple times, or while replaying the game) where you may wish to avoid revisiting a cinematic sequence. To skip cutscenes, press (X). For important scenes, you will sometimes need to press (+) when the corresponding prompt appears. You can also speed up conversations with characters by pressing (B) every time they begin a new line of dialogue.

SAVING

Breath of the Wild employs an autosave system that automatically records your progress at regular intervals. This happens seamlessly (look for the autosave icon in the bottom-left corner of your screen) and means that you are taken back to a position mere minutes – or even seconds – prior to the moment that you hit the Game Over screen. There are five such autosave slots, offering plenty of flexibility if you would like to backtrack to an earlier point in time.

You can also create a manual save file via the System menu. Make a habit of using this feature to record your progress, especially before you attempt something dangerous. It is quick and painless, and will help you to avoid situations where you lose progress after a mistake or unanticipated difficulty spike in the rare instances when an autosave hasn't triggered for a while. You should note, though, that manual save functionality will occasionally be suspended when you visit particular locations.

Breath of the Wild offers frequent opportunities to venture off the beaten track, with your exploration and accomplishments all being of direct benefit to Link and your overall completion rate. Roaming the map is something that we strongly encourage – but until you have explored an area, you cannot be sure what lies in store. By saving regularly, you will insure yourself against sudden and decidedly unfavorable developments.

COMMANDS

The following table offers a handy recap of the main commands you will use throughout the adventure.

DEFAULT CONTROLS SUMMARY

SWITCH	WII U	SUMMARY
(L)	(L)	Used for basic movement and to navigate menus.
(R)	(R)	Used to control the game camera and to navigate pages in menus.
✚	✚	Used to select your current weapon/bow/shield/arrow/rune (hold a direction and navigate available items with (R)). Whistle to call your horse (✚). Also used to navigate menus.
(A)	(A)	Used to interact with the environment and to confirm selection in menus. During combat, press the button while holding a shield to perfect-guard. Used to mount a horse; while mounted, spur the horse to make it increase speed. With a shield drawn and Link airborne, tap this button to shield-surf.
(B)	(B)	Press to sheathe your current weapon or to put away the paraglider. Hold to sprint while running. Also used to cancel selection in menus, and to cancel charged attacks or bow shots.
(Y)	(Y)	Press to attack with a weapon in hand. Hold to perform a charged attack.
(X)	(X)	Press to jump while on a solid surface. While airborne, press to use the paraglider. While swimming, press to dash.
R	R	Press to draw your currently selected melee weapon. Hold to aim and release to throw that weapon. Also used to throw objects that you are carrying, such as jars or rocks.
ZR	ZR	Tap to draw your currently selected bow. Hold to aim and charge, and release to shoot.
L	L	Press to activate your currently selected rune. Press again to deactivate it.
ZL	ZL	Tap to instantly align the camera in the direction that Link is facing. Hold to focus (fixing Link in that direction), lock on to a nearby target, and draw your shield out. Press multiple times to change targets when applicable.
(L) click	(L) click	Used to crouch.
(R) click	(R) click	Press to use your scope, an item that you receive early in the main storyline.
(+)	(+)	Display the pause menu, where you can change tabs with L and R.
(−)	(−)	Display the Sheikah Slate, where you can change tabs with L and R.

On-screen Display

1 **HEARTS**
Hearts represent Link's health. The gauge is depleted every time he sustains damage, and you will hit the Game Over screen if it becomes fully empty. There are multiple methods to regain empty hearts, though the most common is to consume food. Starting with three hearts at the beginning of the game, you can increase your total permanently by completing dungeons and (albeit more gradually) shrines, or temporarily by eating appropriate cooked dishes. Temporary hearts are displayed in yellow and disappear when you lose them.

2 **LOADOUT**
This display reflects your current loadout. Press ✚ in the corresponding direction to access a shortcut: left to equip your shield, right to draw your melee weapon, up to ready your rune, and down to whistle for your horse. To change your current selection of shortcuts, either hold ✚ in the corresponding direction and choose a new one with ◉, or visit the Inventory menu.

3 **STAMINA WHEEL**
A green, circular bar will appear whenever you consume stamina while performing effortful actions such as sprinting or climbing. Once you curtail the activity, the gauge will refill automatically. If you fail to stop before the entire bar is exhausted, however, it will turn red and leave you unable to rely on stamina-fueled moves for several seconds until the gauge is fully restored. Worse still, if you run out of stamina while climbing or swimming, Link will lose his grip or drown.

4 **INTERACTIONS**
Objects or individuals that you can interact with in the game world using Ⓐ are highlighted by prompts such as "Talk" or "Activate" when you move within range.

5 **MINI-MAP**
This illustrates Link's immediate surroundings, including essential details such as waypoints, shrines, and assorted points of interactivity. See page 16 for details.

6 **SHEIKAH SENSOR**
At the beginning of the adventure, you will receive a Sheikah Slate, which gives you access to the in-game map. A little later in the adventure, a new function will be added: the Sheikah Sensor, which enables you to detect shrines nearby. This feature is represented by an antenna icon. Whenever a shrine is available in the current radius of the Sheikah Slate, the sensor will start glowing. The concentric circles light up when Link faces in the direction of the shrine; the better his alignment, the more circles glow. This enables you to locate shrines with a fairly high degree of precision, though you should note that the signal is three-dimensional, taking into account not just left and right, but also elevation.

7 **NOISE INDICATOR**
Whenever Link performs an action, this gauge reflects the amount of noise he makes. The louder he is, the greater the amplitude of the soundwaves on this display. This tool can prove helpful during stealth sequences. Whenever enemies or hunt targets are nearby, make sure you remain unseen and try to keep noise to a minimum. Crouch-walking is a great way to move while remaining quiet, especially if you tilt ◉ very gently. In addition, certain foods and pieces of armor can increase your ability to remain silent.

8 **TIME OF DAY**
The current time of day plays an important role in the game. For example:

- Various enemy types can only be encountered at night.
- Guards in outposts often sleep at some point after dusk, enabling you to either avoid conflict or plan sneak attacks if you visit in the evening.
- Certain flora and fauna specimens can only be found during specific time windows.
- Some optional quests and events are only available at night.

One second in real life translates into one minute in the game world – so a full day/night cycle in Hyrule corresponds to 24 actual minutes.

9 **WEATHER**
The glowing icon represents the current weather, while the icons to the right offer the forecast for the coming hours. All icons slowly scroll to the left as time passes by. The weather can have various practical gameplay consequences. For example, Link will slip and slide if you attempt to climb when it rains, and he can be struck by lightning during thunderstorms.

10 **TEMPERATURE**
The thermometer display represents the current temperature. If the meter enters the blue or red zones, you must consume appropriate food or elixirs, or to kit Link out with specific equipment that offers protection from cold or heat.

RUPEES

Rupees are the primary currency in the *Legend of Zelda* universe. Your current total funds will appear briefly in the top-right corner of the screen whenever you collect rupees, though you can also view a permanent tally of your wealth at the inventory menu. You need rupees to buy anything from a merchant. A rupee's color determines its value:

RUPEE	VALUE
	1
	5
	20
	50
	100
	300

NAVIGATION

Navigation is one of the primary challenges in *Breath of the Wild*. Though basic commands and movements are easy to execute, navigating complex environments and planning efficient trips can prove a little more demanding. With practice, though, these skills will soon become second nature. The key consideration here is that you should feel comfortable with every command. If any of them seem unclear or unnatural to you, practice them regularly and carefully read the corresponding explanations on these pages. Any traversal-oriented feature of importance that you choose to disregard will, at one point or another, hinder your progress during your travels.

BASIC MOVEMENT: Traveling from one destination to another on foot is extremely simple. You move Link around with Ⓛ and control the camera with Ⓡ. While running, hold Ⓑ to sprint and reduce the overall duration of your journeys. Sprinting will gradually deplete your stamina bar. Stop sprinting and the gauge will refill gradually. If you deplete the entire bar, Link will be left out of breath and temporarily unable to reach top speed until it has been fully replenished.

JUMPING: You can jump by pressing Ⓧ. This enables you to vault over obstacles or gaps. To leap over greater distances, prepare a suitable run-up and sprint in advance. Falling from great heights will cause damage, so be careful when you move close to noteworthy drops. Once you obtain the paraglider in the opening section of the game, however, you can avoid the effects of rapid descents by floating to kill your momentum just before you hit the ground.

SWIMMING: Link swims automatically when you tilt Ⓛ. Every movement he makes in deep water depletes a fraction of the stamina bar. If you cannot reach solid ground by the time the gauge is fully empty, he drowns and you return to your previous position on dry land with one heart fewer than before. You can dash over a short distance by pressing Ⓧ, though this removes a more substantial chunk from the stamina bar. Dashing has multiple applications, such as reaching the shore more quickly, catching fish, or putting distance between Link and an enemy.

CLIMBING BASICS: Link can scale virtually every single wall, cliff, and mountain available in the game, with the (common-sense) exception of perfectly smooth walls, typically found in shrines and ancient structures. To begin a climb, direct Link towards a solid, vertical surface. Use Ⓛ to ascend, traverse to the left or right, or descend. Every movement you make while climbing will take a toll on your stamina bar, so you must choose your route carefully. Employing Ⓡ to adjust the camera and plan ahead is a vital skill, as you will often need to find flat areas where you can take a break to refill your stamina during long ascents. Link will lose his grip and fall once the stamina wheel is fully depleted. You can jump with Ⓧ to reach a higher position quickly while climbing, but this will burn up a large portion of your stamina instantly – making it a move best left for low-risk situations.

DESCENT MOVES: To begin a descent from a standing position, head to the edge and press Ⓐ when the corresponding button prompt appears on your screen. While hanging, you can drop with Ⓑ, or back eject by holding Ⓛ down and pressing Ⓧ, causing Link to spring away from a surface. To grab a climbing position while in midair, simply move in its direction; you can do this easily once you have secured the paraglider.

ROUTE PLANNING: Before heading out on a long journey, make a habit of planning your route in advance. Following roads often presents a fast and direct path, but this is also where you will encounter the most enemies. Venturing through more remote areas will generally involve climbing and assorted detours, but will often lead to unexpected discoveries such as shrines. Whenever you espy elevated vantage points, it may be worth your while to climb up: standing on high ground gives you a better view of the region, and therefore enables you to adapt your journey based on what you observe. In the early hours of the adventure, though, your stamina will be very limited, so you can only climb for a short period of time. This means that more strenuous ascents are only possible if they feature flat areas for much-needed rest stops. Link's capacity for exploration (especially climbing) improves as he acquires better equipment and attributes throughout the adventure.

OPTIMAL APPROACH: When you decide to attack an enemy outpost, use your navigational skills to get an edge. Study your surroundings to get a clear sense of what dangers lie ahead. Eliminating a sentry on a lookout with an arrow headshot, for example, will prevent them from warning allies. Combat can be ruthlessly hard in *Breath of the Wild*, so advance preparation and creative thinking are vital skills. Watch out for situations that will enable you to avoid combat, or that will tip the odds in your favor. For example:

- Boulders on vantage points can be rolled down slopes to crush opponents below.
- A bomb thrown into the center of a close-formation pack of weak, early-game enemies might eliminate them all simultaneously.
- Raiding outposts at night while all local forces are sleeping might enable you to plunder certain rewards without once drawing a weapon.
- Stealing weapons that enemies have stowed in racks or left lying around may limit their offensive capabilities if a fight breaks out.

FAST TRAVEL: Every time you activate a tower or a shrine, it will instantly become a new fast travel position. Simply open the Map menu, move the cursor to one of these positions, and press Ⓐ to initiate the truncated journey. Given the gigantic size of Hyrule, this is an essential feature that you will come to use on a regular basis. Note that ancient tech labs, encountered a little later in the adventure, can also act as fast travel destinations.

PARAGLIDER: After you complete the main story objectives during the opening section of the game on the Great Plateau, you will receive the paraglider. This amazing tool enables you to glide over long distances when you jump from elevated positions such as towers and peaks, though the distances that you can travel are limited by Link's current stamina reserves. Press Ⓧ while airborne to initiate flight, then adjust your direction and speed with Ⓛ. This incredibly useful feature enables you to cross chasms and travel long distances much more quickly than you would on foot. Combined with the fast travel technique that gives you instant access to any tower that you have unlocked, this is one of the best ways to explore new regions.

ALTITUDE MANAGEMENT: While using the paraglider, you can put it away to deliberately fall, then draw it out again once you have reached the desired altitude. This trick is particularly handy if you are still high in the air with insufficient stamina to safely reach the ground: let yourself fall, then activate the paraglider just before you land to avoid taking any damage.

UPDRAFTS: Whenever you notice an upward gust of wind, you can use the paraglider to fly high in the air. Natural updrafts can be found in certain locations in Hyrule or inside shrines, but you can also utilize temporary updrafts that appear above large fires.

Landmarks & Points of Interest

Exploration is one of the most important activities in *Breath of the Wild*. The game world is quite astonishingly vast and features countless points of interest, characters to talk to, collectibles to acquire, and quests to complete. Scouring Hyrule for new experiences is utterly compelling, largely because your curiosity is so frequently rewarded. In this section, we describe the most important landmarks and features that you will discover during your travels.

TOWERS: As a general rule, a tower should be your first destination whenever you visit a new region. Climbing them is a challenge in the early game, when your stamina is limited, but this will become less of a concern later on. Certain towers are harder to beat than others, though, because of a heavy enemy presence, or due to environmental hazards or obstacles that hinder your progression. Reaching the top of a tower and interacting with its terminal will reveal the corresponding map portion, making navigation and exploration in the area much easier. Towers have a second application that is just as essential: once unlocked, they become fast travel positions, enabling you to warp to them whenever you please. As they are very tall, you can subsequently glide to any point of interest within range (such as a local shrine), then later warp back to the tower before floating off towards a new potential challenge in the vicinity.

ENEMY OUTPOSTS: You will encounter a great many outposts throughout the adventure. From rudimentary gatherings of enemies around a campfire, to elaborate bastions with multiple lookout towers, these should never be taken lightly. Defeating the enemies guarding an outpost will reward you with the weapons they were wielding in addition to item drops that can be used for crafting purposes. Many outposts also feature at least one treasure chest; occasionally, when accompanied by a purple hue, these can only be opened once all local troops have been eliminated. This does not mean that it is in your best interests to storm all outposts that you encounter, though. A hidden mechanic in the game gradually increases the level of your opponents as you defeat them – and so the more enemies you eliminate, the harder subsequent foes will be to beat. As a rule, it makes sense to prioritize only those outposts that provide noteworthy rewards.

SHRINES: Most shrines are small but perfectly formed "dungeons," challenging you to solve all sorts of physical or logical puzzles. Much like towers, shrines are high-priority targets in terms of exploration. Not only do they offer valuable rewards on completion (including spirit orbs – items that you can trade in for additional hearts or stamina segments), but they also turn into fast travel positions the moment you first interact with them. As the game features over a hundred shrines, these gradually form a network that enables you to warp to virtually anywhere on the map. Note that certain shrines will not be immediately available: you may need to complete specific shrine quests to make them appear.

VILLAGES: *Breath of the Wild* features a number of large villages where you will find assorted amenities including shops, quest vendors, cooking pots, and goddess statues where you can trade spirit orbs for heart containers or stamina vessels. Take the time to speak to all characters that you encounter. Most of them will have something useful to tell you, particularly hints that will help you to unlock or complete a quest.

STABLES: Stables are smaller settlements with one unique feature: they enable you to register any horse that you have tamed in the wild (see page 17). Once registered, a horse is available to you from any stable in Hyrule, even if you leave it in the middle of nowhere or at the opposite end of the world map. Conveniently, a shrine can usually be found a short walk from each stable, making them excellent starting points whenever you are ready to make a foray into an uncharted region.

GREAT FAIRY FOUNTAINS: Hidden in very specific locales throughout Hyrule, Great Fairy Fountains enable you to upgrade your pieces of armor in exchange for materials gathered in the wild. This is one of the most powerful ways to increase your resistance to damage. Eventually, you will enjoy unique benefits that are triggered when you wear complete sets of upgraded gear.

CAMPFIRES & COOKING POTS: You will frequently find campfires and cooking pots during your travels. These are a regular feature in villages, stables, and enemy outposts, but also appear in the wild. You can sit by campfires to pass the time, which is important if you would like to wait until dawn or dusk, or to sit out inclement weather. Cooking pots are campfires with the added functionality of enabling the preparation of various foodstuffs and the brewing of elixirs, which are important whenever you explore new regions or undertake quests. Note that you can light a fire yourself if required. This can be achieved in many ways, such as hitting a flint with a metallic weapon, or by using a fire arrow. Whenever you notice a plume of smoke in the distance, this indicates the likely presence of a character or point of interest near a corresponding campfire.

POINTS OF INTERACTIVITY: During your travels, you will happen upon dozens of different points of interactivity. These include characters you can speak to, treasure chests that you can open, devices you can activate, and objects that you can manipulate to solve puzzles. Interacting with certain characters (such as villagers) may initiate sidequests. Feel free to trigger as many of these as you can. There is no limit to how many quests you can have active at one time, and no obligation to complete them immediately. When you are ready to undertake a quest, select it from the list in the corresponding menu. Note that characters who have an important message for you can often be identified by the presence of a red exclamation mark next to their name.

COLLECTIBLES: As you explore Hyrule you will regularly stumble across items, including assorted fruits and vegetables, insects, and pieces of equipment. Collectibles such as these can be easily spotted over short-to-medium distances as they intermittently emit a shining light. Whenever you see this glow, it means the item in question can be picked up by pressing Ⓐ in close proximity – assuming you have an available slot in your inventory.

SHOPS: There are several types of shop in Hyrule, each offering unique varieties of goods or services. In *Breath of the Wild*, you do not shop via menus: instead, you should stand directly in front of a product you're interested in to buy it. **General stores** sell various sorts of goods, including cooking materials and arrows. **Armor shops** sell outfits that are unique from store to store. The **dye shop** in Hateno village enables you to customize the appearance of your clothes and armor sets. **Jewelries** sell head armor pieces called circlets. **Inns** offer an opportunity for Link to rest, regenerating hearts and providing further benefits if you opt for special services such as softer beds. In addition to traditional shops, you will regularly encounter wandering merchants, usually at stables or on the nearby roads, who sell a few goods and will happily buy your surplus inventory items.

MAPS & MARKERS

MAIN MAP: You can access the main map at any time by pressing ⊖ (and L / R if you need to change tabs). Link's position is represented by a triangular arrow that points in the direction that he is facing (▷). Once on the map screen, you can scroll with Ⓛ, zoom in or out as required with Ⓡ, and drop manual markers with Ⓐ.

Each map region is initially obscured, with its borders clearly visible: to reveal it, you must activate the terminal at the top of the local tower. This will unlock a full topographical representation of the area. Borders between neighboring regions that have been revealed will disappear. Select any activated tower or shrine if you wish to fast travel to it: this will warp you to the corresponding destination after a brief loading break.

MINI-MAP: The mini-map shows a small portion of the main map that corresponds with your immediate surroundings. The "N" icon on the outer edge always points north (note that you can fix the mini-map to north regardless of which direction Link is facing via the options menu). All other icons that appear here are identical to those found on the main map. These disappear once out of the mini-map's boundaries – with the exception of pins and your currently selected quest waypoint, which will remain visible at all times. The affected icons will appear either on the mini-map itself if you are close, or will otherwise rest on its outer rim to indicate their approximate location over longer distances.

Horses

TAMING HORSES: After you leave the Great Plateau during the opening hours of the game, you will often encounter wild horses. If you manage to move close to one of these by carefully crouch-walking during an approach from behind, you can then press Ⓐ to mount it. Depending on its temperament, the horse may try to throw you off, and will at least occasionally refuse to obey: in all such instances, soothe it with Ⓛ: when the command is successful, pink particles will appear next to the animal's head, representing the fact that it is getting more inclined to comply. Once your bond with a mount reaches 100 (a value that you can check at stables), a horse will unfailingly respond to your instructions.

RIDING HORSES: While riding a horse, steer with Ⓛ. To increase your speed, tap Ⓐ until you reach the appropriate gait: from a walk, to a trot, to a canter, and from there to a full gallop. Riding at top speed will consume one unit of the horse's energy every time you exhort it to greater effort (✺). These segments will refill automatically after a few seconds, and horses with a high stamina stat will have more available. If you fully deplete its energy reserves, your horse will slow down drastically and be temporarily incapable of faster speeds, so be sure to take this into account whenever possible. To slow down, tilt Ⓛ backwards. Note that you can fight while riding a horse, and strafe or move backwards by holding ZL.

REGISTERING HORSES: After you have tamed a horse, take it to a stable and register it by speaking to the manager (ZL + Ⓐ). Once a horse is registered, it is officially yours and you can subsequently summon it from any stable. When registering or summoning one of your horses at a stable you can check its attributes, which are represented by stars; the more of these you see, the better the stat. As a rule, speed and stamina are the most important characteristics, as they determine the horse's primary function: faster navigation. If you notice that a freshly recruited horse has poor stats, consider releasing it back into the wild before beginning a new search for a better mount.

MAP & MINI-MAP LEGEND

ANNOTATION	MEANING	ANNOTATION	MEANING
	Link		Tech Lab
	Link's current horse		Stable
	Quest waypoint		Village
	Pin		Other landmark
	Stamp (Example)		Armor Shop*
	Tower		General Store*
	Shrine (located, but not yet unlocked)		Inn*
	Shrine (unlocked, but not yet completed)		Dye Shop*
	Shrine (completed)		Jewelry*

* Shop icons only appear on the in-game map at the maximum zoom level.

MAP MARKERS: While observing the environment through your scope, you can manually drop "**pins**" with Ⓐ. This feature is very helpful when employed on high vantage points such as towers or mountain peaks: from here, you can survey the entire region through your scope and drop pins on any shrine or potential place of interest that you identify. You can also drop pins directly on the map, though you are limited to a maximum of five at a time. Pins remain visible on your mini-map at all times, making them very welcome navigational tools.

By contrast, "**stamps**" can only be dropped and consulted on the main map. They are primarily meant to be used as references or reminders. The fact that they do not appear on the mini-map at all times limits their effectiveness in terms of navigational support.

COMBAT

Fighting adversaries can be one of the most demanding challenges in *Breath of the Wild*. While early encounters may seem trivial, you will soon face opponents who can deplete most, if not all, of your hearts with a single bone-crunching blow. It is important to understand that combat in *Breath of the Wild* is highly strategic. Despite the game's focus on action, you cannot simply rush to engage assailants (or, worse, groups of hostiles) without running a high risk of failure. Instead, you must carefully consider your approach to each skirmish in advance, and prioritize defensive and counterattacking techniques once Link is engaged in a melee.

COMBAT INITIATIVE

STEALTH: By default, enemies are not automatically aware of your presence. As long as this is the case, you can observe them and plan your actions accordingly. To stay incognito, you must remain both silent (keeping soundwaves on your noise indicator to a minimum) and out of sight. To avoid making any noise, walk by tilting Ⓛ gently or, even better, crouch-walk by pressing Ⓛ. Note that jumping while being crouched enables you to slightly increase your movement speed while remaining silent. Where possible, use the environment: crouching in tall grass, for example, enables you to move fairly close to monsters without being detected. If there is a way to incapacitate or weaken opponents prior to an open brawl, always consider such opportunities before you draw your sword and charge. Naturally, eventualities where you can quietly eliminate individual adversaries without alerting their cohorts are always worthwhile.

ENEMY DETECTION: When not in combat mode, enemies will follow a general routine. Sentries on lookout towers, for example, will survey the environment; guards on patrol will focus their vigilance on their specific routes. If an enemy should hear or spot you from a distance, a question mark will appear above their head. Should you persist with noisy activities or impertinent displays of brazen visibility, the question mark will gradually fill with red. Once full, a yellow exclamation mark will appear, signifying that you have been detected. At this stage, all nearby forces will enter combat mode and start tracking you down. The moment you notice a question mark, crouch if you were noisy, or hide behind a solid surface if you were within a foe's field of vision. If you hide successfully, your enemies will soon lose interest and return to their routine. Whenever you are detected, pay attention to the tone and tempo of the background music. Should you choose a hiding spot that limits your ability to survey the area, a return to the ambient soundtrack will be your cue to – carefully! – emerge from your refuge and resume your infiltration.

SNEAKSTRIKE: Whenever you manage to stand right behind an enemy (generally by crouch-walking into position with Ⓛ), you can unleash a powerful blow known as a sneakstrike: press Ⓐ when the corresponding prompt appears on-screen. This deals massive damage that will often take down the target instantly, or at least weaken it severely. If you raid an outpost at night when all guards are sleeping, you can actually use this method to patiently clear the camp without ever engaging more than a single foe.

BOW OPENINGS: You can turn certain battles to your advantage through creative use of your bow. Fire arrows (or standard arrows that you set ablaze by bringing them into contact with fire) will cause explosive barrels to detonate. Alternatively, arrow shots can be used to sever ropes, perhaps causing a lantern to fall to the floor and causing nearby explosive barrels to detonate. Arrows can also be used to strike a solid surface close to enemies. These distractions offer a window of opportunity to approach opponents from behind and take them down with a sneakstrike.

DEFENSE

The ability to avoid injuries with astute use of defensive abilities is a critical skill. Enemies tend to inflict massive damage when their blows land, so instances where you can safely engage opponents with unfettered aggression are uncommon. Key defensive techniques act as a gateway to the best attacking opportunities, as evasive maneuvers and parries set up prime opportunities to quickly defeat your foes in open conflict. We strongly suggest that you take the time to practice all of the commands described here with comparatively weak early-game creatures to acquire a working familiarity of each technique. These training exercises will be of huge benefit during later encounters, where timing windows are tighter and enemies may possess intimidating strength.

BLOCKING: You can block enemy assaults by holding ZL while equipped with a shield. As long as you keep holding the button, all but the most powerful attacks will be deflected. Each hit will remove a portion of a shield's limited durability. The game will warn you when a piece is about to break, and its icon will flash in red in the inventory. Once durability is fully depleted, the shield will shatter and you must equip another. Hold + and make your selection with R if you have one stowed away for immediate use.

STRAFING & DODGING: Another very effective way to avoid incoming enemy attacks is to dodge them. To do so, hold ZL, which will enable you to strafe. While in this stance, jump either laterally to perform a side hop, or backward to perform a backflip. These moves will are useful not only to evade assaults, but also to rapidly move Link to a more advantageous position. If you are unsure of the timing or range of an imminent enemy assault, preemptive dodging is often the safest way to avoid injury. If executed a fraction of a second before an enemy attack connects (a feat called a "perfect dodge"), these moves trigger a slow-motion interval known as "flurry rush," where you can deal multiple counterattacks with total impunity – see overleaf for details.

SPRINTING: If you feel unprepared to defend against an incoming attack, elementary sprinting is often an effective solution. This is a reliable method to evade fast ranged attacks such as laser beams, or to move out of harm's way with area-of-effect assaults employed by large enemies (and, ideally, get into position to flank them and inflict damage). Turning tail and fleeing is also, naturally, the best recourse if you feel that you cannot win the current battle, or simply do not wish to engage an irrelevant group of adversaries.

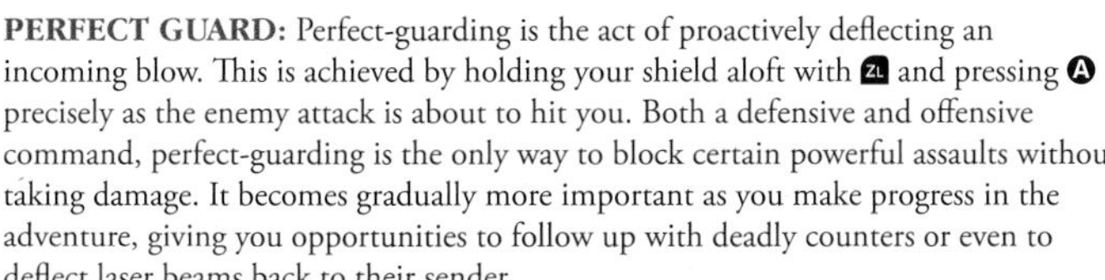

PERFECT GUARD: Perfect-guarding is the act of proactively deflecting an incoming blow. This is achieved by holding your shield aloft with ZL and pressing A precisely as the enemy attack is about to hit you. Both a defensive and offensive command, perfect-guarding is the only way to block certain powerful assaults without taking damage. It becomes gradually more important as you make progress in the adventure, giving you opportunities to follow up with deadly counters or even to deflect laser beams back to their sender.

CROWD MANAGEMENT: Your ability to defend is determined by your capacity not only to dodge, block, and perfect-guard, but also to keep track of all enemies. You will often face large groups of foes where attacks, including fast-moving projectiles, can potentially arrive from any direction. Make good use of R to monitor opponents in the surrounding vicinity, making a mental note of which opponents are weakened or could pose a grave threat. Whenever you face several assailants at once, it usually pays to keep moving and to use any environmental obstruction to your advantage, avoiding scenarios where you are completely surrounded or trapped in a corner. It is also, where possible, prudent to focus on eliminating foes one at a time. If you injure the combatants of a surrounding mob in a scattershot fashion, you will not reduce their combined damage-dealing potential – thus running the risk of protracted and unnecessarily dangerous fights.

RESTORING HEARTS: When Link has only one heart left, he will be highlighted by a flashing red hue to indicate that he is on the brink of collapse. The most practical way to restore his health is to consume food with healing properties: this can be achieved from the inventory menu at any time. All items in this category are clearly marked with a heart symbol. As a rule, raw ingredients offer limited health benefits, but this can be improved by cooking them in advance. Collecting small fairies during your travels will provide the boon of automatically restoring five hearts when Link is poised to keel over and stay down, forestalling a visit to the Game Over screen. During exploration, bathing in hot springs will gradually refill the entire gauge, while completing shrines and securing new heart containers will instantly regenerate all hearts.

OFFENSE

Defeating enemies is often a highly tactical process in *Breath of the Wild*, and mashing buttons will only get you so far. Trying to perform guileless extended combos will generally fail miserably: instead, you must make your attacks count. The best results will only be achieved by setting up counter opportunities, then unleashing brief but lethal assaults with your most powerful weapons.

LOCK ON/FOCUS: You can lock on to a target that you are currently facing by holding ZL. Locking on enables you to keep track of, and focus all your efforts on, one foe at a time. This will negate the need for constant directional adjustments and will simplify the process of thinning enemy numbers whenever you fight groups. A locked-on target will be clearly marked by a red downward arrow hovering overhead.

MELEE ATTACKS & COMBOS: Standard attacks are performed by pressing Y. Each button press leads to a unique attack, though you can also tap in rapid succession to perform combos. Mindlessly pressing the attack button will only enable you to defeat the weakest of enemies. It is vital that you pick up more advanced techniques early in the adventure to stand a chance against stronger foes.

CHARGED ATTACKS: Hold Y to initiate a charged attack. The blow will be unleashed when you release the button. The process of powering up will empty your stamina gauge at a rapid pace: once it is fully depleted, the attack will be triggered even if you continue to hold. You can cancel the charge process by pressing B to regain control of Link or to preserve a weapon's durability. The nature of a charged attack will depend on the weapon you wield. With one-handed weapons you perform a swirling, 360° blow that will hit all targets surrounding Link. With two-handed weapons, Link will start spinning, hitting nearby targets multiple times, and unleash a final blow that will strike the ground: this will cause a shockwave that can hit multiple enemies, also reducing the weapon's durability.

JUMP SLASH: If you press the attack button while airborne and sufficiently high above the ground, Link will dive down and slam the ground, causing a shockwave with an intensity proportionate to the total distance of the descent. A target directly within range of Link's strike will be hit by the attack itself, and then a second time by the shockwave. Though rarely feasible (or, for that matter, practical) during open conflict, this can be a powerful way to initiate a battle – you can even do so while gliding above enemy positions.

FLURRY RUSH: If you initiate a dodge (hold ZL and jump either sideways or backward) a fraction of a second before an incoming blow strikes Link, you will trigger a flurry rush. This is essentially a slow-motion time window during which you can unleash multiple attacks in a row with impunity. Mastering the timing of this move is absolutely essential: it is pivotal to your success in many of the more difficult battles, particularly tough bosses. Even if you struggle initially, be patient and persevere: practicing against weak foes will teach you the basic principles, which you can then adjust in accordance with the attack patterns of different opponents. By the time you leave the Great Plateau, you should aim to feel totally comfortable with this staple ability.

PERFECT GUARD: Much like the flurry rush, perfect guarding (press A while holding your shield aloft with ZL) is a critical move that you should quickly incorporate into your repertoire. It will enable you to deflect an incoming melee attack and, more importantly, to temporarily stagger your target. You can then follow up with a full combo, dealing massive damage. This is an indispensable technique against powerful bosses and sub-bosses. It is also employed to block and redirect laser beams emitted by Guardians. The timing window to successfully perform a perfect guard is tight, but it's definitely worthwhile to train as much as you can. Once you become accomplished in the use of this indispensable ability, some otherwise astonishingly hard battles can become almost routine by comparison.

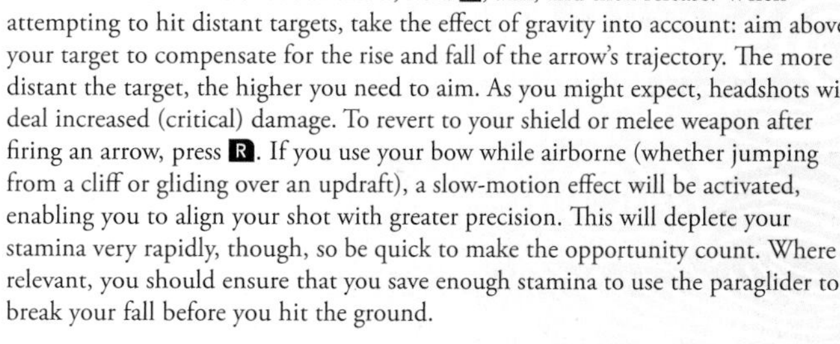

BOW ATTACKS: To shoot an arrow, hold ZR, aim, and then release. When attempting to hit distant targets, take the effect of gravity into account: aim above your target to compensate for the rise and fall of the arrow's trajectory. The more distant the target, the higher you need to aim. As you might expect, headshots will deal increased (critical) damage. To revert to your shield or melee weapon after firing an arrow, press R. If you use your bow while airborne (whether jumping from a cliff or gliding over an updraft), a slow-motion effect will be activated, enabling you to align your shot with greater precision. This will deplete your stamina very rapidly, though, so be quick to make the opportunity count. Where relevant, you should ensure that you save enough stamina to use the paraglider to break your fall before you hit the ground.

THROWING WEAPONS: You can throw any melee weapon by holding and then releasing R. Thrown weapons inflict critical damage on any target they strike, making this a potentially devastating form of attack. Boomerangs are particularly noteworthy in this respect: after you throw them via the method described here, you can catch them on their return flight with A. As long as you astutely pick targets in the open, and ensure that there is a low risk of the boomerang hitting a solid obstacle during flight, they offer the luxury of enhanced, repeatable long-range damage.

DAMAGE CALCULATION & WEAPON CATEGORIES: By default, your attacks will deplete the target's HP (health points) by an amount that corresponds to your weapon's power value. A sword with a power of 10, therefore, will remove 10 HP from the victim's health bar. A piece of armor that you will obtain later in the adventure reveals the exact health point total for each opponent you fight. As a rule, one-handed weapons do not offer noteworthy raw power, but instead provide alternative benefits. Notably, they enable you to wield your shield simultaneously, making it easy to switch to a defensive stance on the fly; their increased attack rate is also significant. Conversely, two-handed weapons are slower and incompatible with shield usage (you must sheathe your blade with B before you can block), but they are unparalleled in terms of brute force, range, and the sheer destructive potential of their devastating charged attacks.

SWITCHING WEAPONS & SHORTCUTS: You have access to two sets of combat gear during battle – your weapons and shields with R, and your bow and arrows with ZR. You can switch between these two "modes" at any time. To change your equipment without opening the menu, hold ✚ in the relevant direction (left for your shields or arrows, right for your melee weapons or bows).

BATTLE REWARDS

ITEM DROPS AND OUTPOST CHESTS: Every enemy that you defeat will yield at least one item, and sometimes more. Generally speaking, the stronger the adversary, the more valuable the rewards will be. Monster parts can be cooked with insects and other small animals to create powerful elixirs. Armed foes will also drop their current equipment when they collapse. If you notice that a hostile is carrying a noteworthy sword, for example, it will probably be worth your while to pick a fight. In addition to enemy-specific loot, most enemy outposts feature at least one treasure chest, in which you will often find a gemstone or piece of gear. Chests that emit a purple glow can only be opened once you have defeated all local troops; when the final associated enemy falls, the light will turn yellow.

ENEMY EVOLUTION & RESPAWNS: It's not immediately apparent, but there are consequences for defeating enemies. As you take down more and more foes, you will trigger the appearance of upgraded versions of the same archetypes. These can be identified by their colors, which are, in increasing order of difficulty: red, blue, black, white, silver. So: while killing adversaries will lead to immediate rewards, it will also gradually trigger the appearance of harder opponents.

Every full moon triggers the Blood Moon phenomenon, causing all defeated antagonists to respawn. This means that no matter how hard you try, you cannot rid the world of monsters: those that you kill will eventually be revived.

RESOURCES

There are many different types of resources in *Breath of the Wild*, most of which serve to make Link more powerful or adaptable by gradual increments – and even those that don't can be sold, funding useful or important purchases.

COMBAT ITEMS: Link can only expand his arsenal in the wild – weapons, bows, and shields are not available in shops. The primary method of acquisition is by appropriating them from defeated enemies, though you can also find equipment lying on the ground in many outposts. More valuable combat items can be obtained from high-value treasure chests, usually found in areas such as shrines, mazes, or forgotten ruins. All weapons, bows, and shields have limited durability. They will be damaged after a certain number of uses (at which point their icon will start flashing red), and ultimately break. Some items enjoy above-average durability, which is indicated by the ◆ icon next to their image. There are other such bonuses, for example increasing a weapon's strength or critical rate. When you are about to pick up a weapon, you can tell if its attack value is higher (⬆), lower (⬇), or equal (⬌) to your current one. However it's only by actually collecting it that you will find out about any special boon it might offer.

ARROWS: Arrows can be dropped by defeated enemies, particularly archers; you can also retrieve those that miss their target from your surroundings before you move on after a fight. They can also be found in treasure chests, or purchased from certain merchants and general stores. Arrows have countless applications: silently eliminating sentries, detonating explosives, cutting ropes, activating switches from range and – of course – dispatching opponents from a safe distance. It therefore makes sense to maintain a large stock of these projectiles at all times. Whenever you have an opportunity to purchase some, particularly in bundles, be sure to do so: the nominal rupee investment is well worth it. Elemental arrows are even more valuable than their standard counterparts. Their magical properties make them deadly in battle – for instance, enemies frozen by ice arrows will take higher damage, and most foes will be stunned by shock arrows. They also have a wide variety of applications when you need to solve puzzles or interact with your environment: fire arrows can light lanterns, bomb arrows can shatter destructible rocks, and so forth.

ARMOR: Link's armor determines how well he resists damage. This is represented by the numerical defense value of a garment (👕). The higher Link's armor-induced defense stat is, the less damage he will take from enemy attacks. Armor is primarily available in armor shops found throughout Hyrule. Certain valuable pieces can also be secured in treasure chests hidden in specific shrines. Many outfits provide bonus effects in addition to their defense attribute, such as resistance to an element or increased climbing speed, making them even more precious.

PLANTS: Many varieties of fruit, vegetables, and flowers are found in the wild, and they are all ripe for harvest. When these collectibles are out of reach, think creatively: *Breath of the Wild* allows for multiple solutions and rewards experimentation. To pick apples growing on high branches, for example, you could climb to the top of the tree, and then hit the trunk with a weapon to make the fruit drop. Alternatively, you could cut the tree with an axe, and then strike it again to obtain a bundle of wood. Or, you might simply hit an apple with an arrow and retrieve it from where it lands; the list goes on...

SMALL ANIMALS: You'll encounter numerous insects and lizards during your travels. To catch them, you must be in close proximity, which is most easily achieved by approaching quietly by crouch-walking (Ⓛ). As long as you remain in this stance, you will be virtually invisible to them. Sprinting to outpace them is also an option. You do not need to attack these creatures: simply press Ⓐ to collect them, as you would a plant.

LARGE ANIMALS: Hunting larger animals requires you to defeat them. They are generally weak and non-hostile. An arrow is sufficient for the smaller specimens, such as foxes and birds, though the more resilient creatures may require a little more effort. To sneak up on an animal, crouch-walk until you are behind them. Hunting animals will provide you with pieces of meat that offer strong healing properties, especially when cooked in advance.

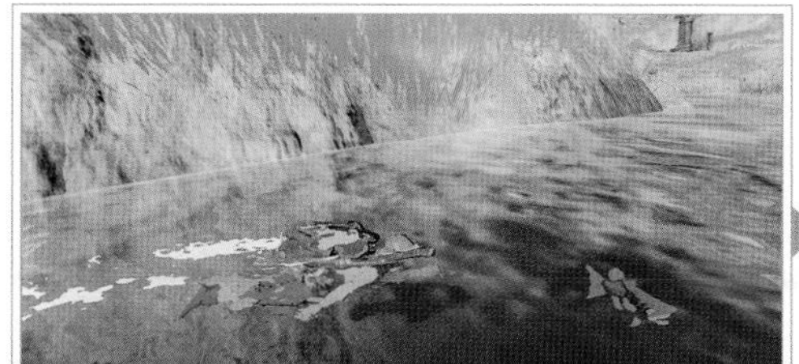

FISH: You can catch fish, though they are elusive targets. Either dash to outpace them in the water, or hit them if they are within range. A bomb can be a crude but effective way to prepare them for easy collection. As with meat obtained from animals, fish is used to regenerate Link's hearts.

MONSTER PARTS: These are the most common materials dropped by monsters when you defeat them. Of little value by themselves, they can be combined with lizards and insects in cooking recipes to create elixirs with potent effects.

RUPEES: Rupees are the primary currency in the Legend of Zelda universe. You need rupees in order to buy wares from a merchant. The color of a rupee collectible determines its value: green is worth one rupee, blue is worth five, red is worth 20, purple is worth 50, silver is worth 100, and gold is worth 300. Rupees can occasionally be obtained as collectibles, either when dropped by certain enemies or found inside treasure chests. The primary method of accumulating significant funds, though, is to sell items that you do not need to shopkeepers.

FAIRIES: Fairies are rare and precious creatures. They can be encountered in select locations, most commonly around Great Fairy Fountains. You will occasionally trigger the appearance of a fairy by cutting tall grass; a charged one-handed sword attack works well for this purpose. To catch one, proceed exactly as with insects: crouch-walk until you are within range to collect them, or sprint to outpace them. Once in your inventory, a fairy will automatically restore five of your hearts should your health be completely depleted. Their ability to bring Link back from the brink of death makes them extraordinarily valuable during the more challenging chapters of the adventure, but they can also be used as a cooking ingredient.

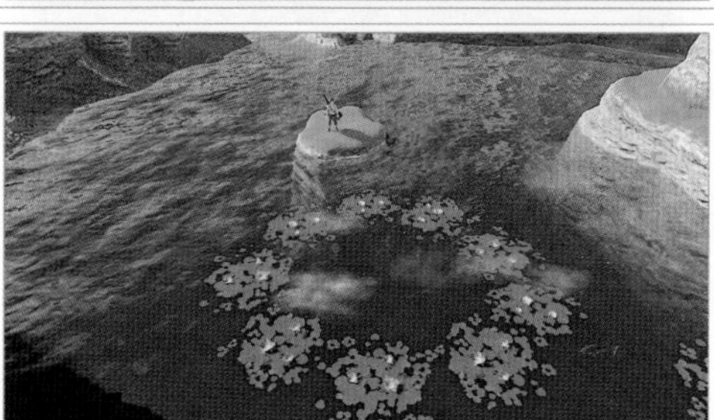

KOROK SEEDS: Korok seeds are special items that you obtain every time you find a Korok. These creatures are hidden everywhere in Hyrule, typically in positions that will attract your attention – for example, under a rock with a distinct placement that catches the eye at the top of a mountain peak. Essentially, whenever you notice something unusual in the environment, such as rocks aligned in a specific pattern, or water lilies forming a circle, you can be almost certain that a Korok awaits. In the two prior examples, you might solve the puzzles by adding a rock missing in the pattern, or by jumping from a nearby cliff to land inside the water lily circle. If you intuit and perform the correct action, the seed will be yours. There are many different configurations, and it is up to you to make sense of each of these puzzles. Taking the time to do so will pay off: a few hours into the adventure, you will encounter a character who will exchange your Korok seeds for additional equipment slots in your inventory.

GEMSTONES: The items with the best resale value tend to be gemstones such as amber and topaz. These can be farmed by destroying the ore deposits that jut out from cliffs and mountains. This can be achieved easily with heavy weapons such as sledgehammers, or with bombs. If you diligently collect all the gems that you find you'll never be short of a rupee or two when you need to make important purchases.

COOKING

Cooking is an essential feature of the adventure. Not only can cooked dishes offer powerful healing properties, they also provide additional effects with all sorts of applications.

COOKING POTS: The first component you'll need for cooking is a pot. These are found in many locations across Hyrule, but particularly in villages, outposts, and camps discovered in the wilderness. They cannot be moved or collected, so you must make use of them wherever you find them. Whenever you pass them, take the time to double-check your inventory to ensure that you have sufficient meals and elixirs to see you through to the end of your next objective; if not, a brief stop will enable you to resupply – assuming that you have the required materials in your inventory, of course (see page 296 for more details).

MAKING FIRE: A cooking pot can only be used if the fire beneath it is lit. If not, there are a number of ways to make fire: hitting a flint with a metallic weapon inches away from the wood; shooting a fire arrow; transferring fire from another source (such as a nearby lantern) with a wooden object; or dropping and striking red Chuchu jelly (an item obtained from enemies called fire Chuchus) to cause a small explosion.

THE COOKING PROCESS: Assuming you have a cooking pot at the ready, select a material from your inventory, then choose the Hold option to transfer it to Link's hands. You can then add more of the same (Ⓐ), or throw other materials into the mix. Once you are ready to proceed, press Ⓑ to return to the game, then Ⓐ to drop the ingredients in the pot. After a brief animation (which you can skip with Ⓧ), you can collect your new creation.

COMBINATIONS: There are many possible combinations of materials that will produce dozens of dishes and elixirs, each with unique properties. Many of these have healing powers, but they can also provide all sorts of special effects such as temporarily increasing stamina, improving your defense rating, or providing a brief resistance to extreme temperatures. For a complete presentation of this system, turn to our Inventory chapter on page 296. You should note, though, that you do not need an actual "recipe": items can be combined freely. Haphazard combinations can lead to unfortunate results, but the in-game descriptions of materials usually offer helpful suggestions and hints.

CHARACTER PROGRESSION

As you advance through the main storyline, Link will become stronger and more resilient in many ways. Understanding and optimizing his progression is critical if you wish to stay ahead of the game's difficulty curve.

EQUIPMENT: The most obvious way to improve Link's performance is by acquiring or upgrading equipment. As you advance in the storyline and explore the four corners of Hyrule you will gradually obtain more valuable gear, including powerful weapons, elemental arrows, and resilient armor. These acquisitions should be a priority whenever you have a chance to collect them.

ARMOR UPGRADES: Great Fairy Fountains are hidden in specific locations over Hyrule. Every time you find one, the great fairy it hosts will offer (after you pay an initial fee) to upgrade your existing armor, increasing its stats in exchange for materials. These improvements will substantially enhance Link's defense rating.

HEART CONTAINERS: You can obtain heart containers in two ways: by trading in four spirit orbs obtained in shrines to goddess statues found in villages, or by completing dungeons. Every container collected adds a permanent heart to Link's health bar, which can be upgraded to a maximum size of 30 heart containers.

STAMINA VESSELS: The only way to extend your stamina wheel is by trading in four spirit orbs with goddess statues found in villages. Each vessel adds a segment corresponding to a fifth of a full wheel. Securing many of these will eventually lead to a gauge made of multiple concentric circles. Such extensions are extremely valuable, enabling you to climb higher, glide further, and swim for longer.

EQUIPMENT SLOTS: Koroks are hidden in many places all over Hyrule. Whenever you find one of them, you will be rewarded with a Korok seed. Acquire as many of these as you can: by delivering them to a character called Hestu, you will have a chance to increase the size of your inventory. Having more slots to carry weapons, bows, and shields is always an important upgrade, and enables you to eventually be more strategic in your choice of equipment – such as having a full collection of elemental blades at the ready.

ENEMY PROGRESSION: Just like Link, enemies will become progressively stronger and more dangerous as you venture into the deeper and more hazardous areas of Hyrule. You can, however, slow down the general advancement of rank-and-file opponents by trying to avoid unnecessary confrontations. As higher-level variations of each species (distinguished by their different colors) only appear if you eliminate many of their peers, keeping optional confrontations to a minimum will delay the point in time when your foes "level up".

WEATHER & ELEMENTS

Weather conditions play a significant role in *Breath of the Wild's* sandbox, sometimes having a direct impact on what you might hope to accomplish at any given moment. It is therefore vital that you learn to identify what you can and cannot do under different meteorological circumstances. Elements and forces such as fire, wind, and electricity have a vital part to play in everything from combat to puzzles. In this section, we highlight the key principles that will help you make sense of the fundamental physical "laws" of the game world.

RAIN: Precipitation is probably the weather condition that you will encounter first – and certainly most often. Other than the fact that it somewhat limits general visibility, rain has one very annoying effect: it makes cliffs and walls slippery, preventing you from climbing efficiently. If you only have a short distance to scale, you can sometimes make it by taking a few steps up, then leaping vertically. In many cases, however, the fact that Link is prone to sliding makes climbing impractical during wet weather. In such circumstances, look for another way up, or simply wait for the shower to pass.

THUNDERSTORMS: During thunderstorms, the rain-induced impediments to climbing apply. More pressingly, though, lightning bolts can strike anywhere around you, or even directly on Link. Look for the cues that foreshadow this, particularly sparks that appear on his body at an incrementally faster rate. To reduce the probability that you will be struck by lightning, remove all equipment made of metal from your current loadout. If you fear that Link is at risk of an imminent strike, look for some sort of covered shelter, such as a cave or cliff overhang. Once the bolt has struck nearby, you will be free to proceed - until the next one!

LOW TEMPERATURES: Various locales in Hyrule have low temperatures, as indicated by the thermometer display on your screen. This applies to most snowy areas, the tallest mountain peaks, and regions at high altitudes, but also the Gerudo desert at night. By default, cold will cause Link to tremble. If you do not take any measures, he will begin to lose hearts gradually. To counter this, you have two options: either equip armor pieces with cold resistance (), or consume special cooked food or an elixir that will temporarily convey the same effect. Cold resistance effects are cumulative, so two appropriate armor pieces equipped simultaneously will grant a Level 2 resistance (), which is sometimes required to resist bitter cold.

HIGH TEMPERATURES: Hyrule also hosts regions where temperatures are so hot that they can prove harmful to Link. Just as with cold, you can negate the threat by equipping appropriate armor and consuming specific cooked dishes or elixirs. There are two distinct effects to be wary of, though, depending on the nature of the danger (sun-induced or lava-induced). You need heat resistance () during the day in the desert, whereas it's the flame guard effect () that will protect you near the volcano. Suffering the effects of heat gradually reduces your hearts, but being exposed to the volcano's flames is much more dangerous – and will cause Link's health to melt away in mere seconds.

FIRE: Fire is the element that you will likely encounter first – often found in camps, under cooking pots, or in lanterns. You can set wooden weapons ablaze, including arrows. This can be useful to cause additional damage to enemies, to solve puzzles, or to interact with the environment, though the item in question will eventually be consumed by the flames. Among many other possible applications, fire can burn dry grass, leaves, ivy, and bramble; create updrafts; cause explosive barrels to detonate; melt ice blocks; burn out-of-reach wooden platforms where a treasure chest rests; and so forth.

FROZEN INGREDIENTS: If you drop certain ingredients, such as pieces of meat, in the snow, they will freeze after a few seconds. Frozen food has one interesting application: it provides Link with heat resistance, which can make your life easier in the Gerudo Desert until you acquire armor that offers permanent protection against high temperatures.

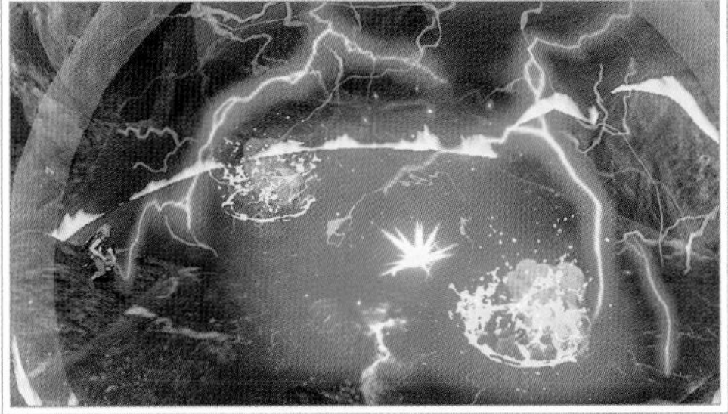

ELECTRICITY & CONDUCTORS: Electricity has two principal applications in the game. It can be used to shock enemies, which is particularly useful against ancient Guardians commonly encountered in shrines and dungeons, and it can electrify pools of water, momentarily stunning any entity that comes in contact with it. These are features that you can exploit, but be aware that certain enemies will employ similar techniques against Link. If you are hit by any form of electricity-conducting attack, or touch an opponent whose body is crackling with sparks, Link will not only be staggered, but will also drop his currently held weapon and shield.

WIND GUSTS & UPDRAFTS: You will often visit areas where the wind blows heavily. As a rule, if you can see thin white streams representing gust effects on your screen, it means that the wind is strong enough to send round items (such as bombs) rolling. You can actually use this to your advantage in specific situations, particularly to solve related puzzles. The wind will also affect Link while he is gliding, enabling him to cover surprisingly long distances when he has the wind behind him. Note that vertical, upward wind streams are called updrafts. If you open your paraglider while above an updraft, Link will fly high into the air. On a related note, if you ever find a Korok leaf, hang on to it. Every time you "attack" with this weapon, you will create a small but powerful burst of wind in the direction that Link is facing. This can be employed to propel a raft with a sail in the direction of your choice.

MAKESHIFT BRIDGES: When trees grow near cliffs or rivers, it is sometimes possible to chop them down to bridge a body of water or chasm. Be sure that you are facing the necessary direction, then set about them with an axe (or any suitable two-handed weapon). Tree trunks can also be used as floating platforms, enabling you to cross or navigate a river filled with ice-cold water that would otherwise harm Link.

ELEMENTAL ARROWS: You should find your first elemental arrows relatively early in the adventure. These work just like standard arrows, but provide the benefits of the element they are infused with. Fire arrows set what they touch ablaze, ice arrows freeze their targets (leaving them ripe for a finishing blow while they are incapacitated), and shock arrows electrocute enemies or activate certain mechanical devices.

ELEMENTAL WEAPONS: Much like arrows, there are also elemental weapons. These are very precious as they can be used to solve puzzles and to deal extra damage to enemies, especially those with an affinity for the opposite element. Striking an icy creature with a flameblade, for example, will often kill it instantly. Most elemental weapons need to recharge after each blow. This process takes no more than a few seconds and is clearly visible on your screen; when the weapon is ready, its blade will again shine with the characteristic color of its element.

CHUCHUS: Whenever you defeat Chuchus, they drop jelly of the element they are naturally imbued with. You can pick up jelly and drop it in specific positions before hitting it to cause a small explosion of the element in question. Red Chuchu jelly, for example, can light a fire under a cooking pot; the same principle applies to all variants. If you drop "neutral" blue Chuchu jelly in a particular environment, such as a snowfield, it will transform into the corresponding variant (in this instance, ice-elemental white Chuchu jelly).

RUNES

Runes are special commands with unique properties that become available in the opening sections of the game. You can change runes on the fly by holding ✚: once the corresponding menu is displayed, make your selection with Ⓡ. To use a rune, enter rune mode with L, then aim as required with Ⓛ and activate it with Ⓐ. Pressing L again will revert you to standard controls.

Runes are a pivotal feature in *Breath of the Wild*. Their primary function is to help you solve puzzles, but they have myriad other applications. They can be used to interact with the environment in unique ways, and can facilitate new strategies to defeat enemies. If you ever feel stuck in a shrine, a dungeon, or a particular environment, a quick study of your available runes may present the solution you are seeking.

REMOTE BOMB

PUZZLE APPLICATIONS: Remote bombs exist in round and cube versions: the round models will roll down hills and be propelled by gusts of wind, whereas cubic bombs tend to stay where you leave them. You can have one bomb of each type active simultaneously, enabling you to cause two consecutive explosions. The primary function of the remote bomb is to annihilate destructible objects. As a rule, you can easily recognize these objects by their gray, stone-like color, and the presence of telltale cracks. Once Link is holding a bomb above his head, press Ⓐ to drop it at his feet, or R to throw it a few feet in front of him (press Ⓑ if you have second thoughts and wish to put the explosive away). You can then trigger the detonation with L, though be careful to ensure that Link isn't caught in the blast. After you detonate a bomb, a cooldown begins: you can only summon a new bomb once this expires.

COMBAT APPLICATIONS: Bombs are powerful enough to defeat weaker enemies that you encounter in the early game. They also work very well against creatures that inhale before performing an attack, such as Octoroks. Wait until your quarry has ingested the explosive, then detonate it to cause massive damage.

EXPLORATION APPLICATIONS: Many caves and even certain shrines are blocked by destructible rocks. Use bombs liberally in all such instances to open the way forward. Bombs are also a great tool to blow up objects such as wooden crates (which often contain materials) and ore deposits that jut out from cliffs (which yield valuable gems). Bombs are also sometimes a handy way to "catch" fast-moving fish.

MAGNESIS

PUZZLE APPLICATIONS: Magnesis confers Link with the power to lift metal objects and move them (control basic motion with Ⓡ, and distance with ✚). Whenever you notice a metal slab or cube, this is often a cue that Magnesis will do the trick. Such objects are clearly highlighted in magenta while Magnesis is active; if they are within range, they will turn yellow when you aim at them. These objects can be used to create bridges across gaps, to stop wind streams, to arrange stepping stones, or to reveal new passages.

COMBAT APPLICATIONS: Magnesis can be used creatively in battle, most commonly to drop metal objects on enemies. You can push monsters back or propel them over ledges with this power. There are also boss and sub-boss battles where you will need to lift objects to protect yourself or to harm your opponent.

EXPLORATION APPLICATIONS: You will occasionally find metal slabs or cubes in the wild. These are generally located in useful positions, such as next to a river (enabling you to create a bridge). When you encounter metal treasure chests that are partially buried in the ground, you can use the rune to lift them up in order to plunder their contents.

STASIS

PUZZLE APPLICATIONS: Stasis grants you the ability to briefly stop time for an object; you might use it to temporarily freeze certain moving platforms to create a viable path, for example. This power has a second crucial application in that an object subject to Stasis will store energy acquired while it is immobilized, and release it afterwards. If you hit a boulder in Stasis with a sledgehammer multiple times, for instance, you will see a vector arrow appear. This illustrates the direction in which it will be propelled once the effect ends; the size and color of the arrow indicate how far it will go. This process is regularly required to remove heavy objects in your way, or to send them in the direction of another device. Each use of Stasis is followed by a brief cooldown period during which the ability is unavailable. You can reduce this cooldown by ending a Stasis prematurely: press Ⓐ while looking at the affected object.

COMBAT APPLICATIONS: Though not easy to engineer, you can sometimes use Stasis to propel a heavy object in the direction of enemies, which can kill them instantly. A more practical application becomes available once you upgrade this rune to Stasis+. At this juncture you can stop your adversaries in their tracks, literally freezing them in time, and pummel them with devastating combos.

CRYONIS

PUZZLE APPLICATIONS: With Cryonis you can summon a block of ice on flat water surfaces, creating makeshift stepping stones. These blocks are climbable, so it's possible to clamber on top even if you fall in the water. They can even be materialized on vertical streams, which you can exploit to form stairs. You can only summon three blocks of ice at a time; when you generate a fourth, the first in the series will be destroyed. You can also dismiss an existing block by pressing Ⓐ while looking at it. Note that Cryonis has another important use: you can summon a block of ice from underneath an object or entity to lift it up. This works on Link himself, but the most useful application of this feature is that it makes it possible to raise certain gates.

EXPLORATION APPLICATIONS: Whenever you encounter a river or pool of water in the wild, you can create blocks of ice to travel to the opposite site. If swimming is not an option (when the water is too cold, or the current too strong), Cryonis can get you where you want to be.

CAMERA

Unlocked at a later stage in the adventure, the camera is probably the most straightforward rune. Its principal application is that it enables you to fill your album with pictures (access the corresponding menu with ⊖ and R). Whenever a creature or object that you have not yet captured is on the camera's screen, it will appear in orange: take a picture to fill the corresponding entry in your compendium. The camera can also have an occasional use while you solve complex puzzles: when you need to memorize specific layouts or patterns for future reference, a picture can be a handy replacement for physical notes.

RUNE UPGRADES

A few hours into the story, you will visit your first tech lab. After completing specific steps, this will give you the opportunity to upgrade your runes. Upgrades improve their base effects (for example, increasing the explosion range and power of your bombs), making them very valuable.

QUICKSTART
PRIMER
WALKTHROUGH
SHRINES
SIDE QUESTS
INVENTORY
BESTIARY
EXTRAS
REFERENCE & ANALYSIS
MAPS
MASTER TRIALS
CHAMPIONS' BALLAD
INDEX
GAME STRUCTURE
COMMANDS
ON-SCREEN DISPLAY
NAVIGATION
LANDMARKS
MAPS & MARKERS
HORSES
COMBAT
RESOURCES
COOKING
CHARACTER PROGRESSION
WEATHER & ELEMENTS
RUNES
PUZZLES

Puzzles

Breath of the Wild features hundreds of varied puzzles. These are most commonly encountered in shrines and dungeons, but the world of Hyrule itself will often challenge your sense of logic, your perception of three-dimensional environments, and your ability to observe your surroundings closely.

Many puzzles in the game have multiple solutions. Depending on the tools at your disposal and your way of thinking, you may very well devise completely different solutions to those of a friend – or, indeed, this very guide. If you become stuck when faced with a real brain-teaser, think rationally: which runes or pieces of equipment might have an effect? What can you see in your surroundings that could help you? Are there any objects in the area with elemental properties? Asking these questions, and others in a similar vein, of yourself will always put you on the right path for the glorious "eureka" moment you seek. Puzzles in *Breath of the Wild* are remarkably considered and balanced, so persevering will almost always lead to a positive outcome.

RUNE-BASED PUZZLES: Many puzzles, particularly those found in shrines, rely on rune abilities. If you feel at a loss when facing a puzzle, try scanning the environment with Magnesis and Stasis active in search for highlighted objects, and look for water to use Cryonis on. More often than not, this should get you started.

PHYSICS PUZZLES: Many puzzles are physics-based, with those involving gravity in some sense being particularly common. Whether this means making boulders roll down hills, using objects to weigh down devices that function as scales, or activating floor panels with heavy items, a healthy dose of common sense is all you need to beat them.

TIMING PUZZLES: Certain puzzles involve precise timing. In these situations, you must trigger a chain of events (such as making an orb roll) and reach a specific position quickly (such as a moving platform that will be activated by the orb once it reaches its destination).

CEREBRAL PUZZLES: Various puzzles rely on your ability to carefully observe your environment and think creatively – for example, when you need to identify a pattern and replicate it somewhere else.

ELEMENT-BASED PUZZLES: Your innate, intuitive understanding of natural forces (evident in the very fact that you have lived a life that led to you being here, right now, with this book) is often the key to solving certain puzzles. Always think in terms of how objects in your environment might react. Can they burn? Would a strong gust of wind have an effect?

MOTION CONTROL PUZZLES: A handful of shrines will challenge your ability to use the gyroscopic features of your controller. In these cases, start from a neutral position, and methodically adjust your movements very carefully. This will soon become second nature once you get the hang of it.

RIDDLES: Various characters in Hyrule will offer you side quests with relatively vague objectives. You will only be able to solve these if you pay careful attention to the hints they offer. Interpreting such clues will become easier as you progress in the game and get more familiar with the world's many landmarks.

MAZES: You will find a handful of mazes in the deepest reaches of Hyrule. Each of these is a puzzle in its own right, challenging your perception of 3D environments. You will not waste your time even if you struggle to locate the entrance to the central room: many of their alleys feature treasure chests and valuable rewards.

ENVIRONMENT PUZZLES: Many discrete areas of Hyrule are puzzles in and of themselves. In the early game, for example, crossing a wide river can seem impossible – until you realize that cutting down a nearby tree will form a makeshift bridge once the current takes it downstream...

ORBS AND CONCAVE SLOTS: Many puzzles rely on the use of spherical, glowing balls called orbs. As a general rule, your goal is to drop each of these orbs in a specific concave slot, as illustrated in the accompanying screenshot. In many instances, this will require you to interact with environmental features, such as launchers that can propel an orb across a chasm. Orbs and concave slots are also occasionally encountered in the wild. In such cases, they will often lead to the appearance of a secret shrine.

CRYSTALS: These are switches that you can hit to trigger an effect in the environment: a door that will open or close, a platform that will rotate by 90 degrees with every activation, and so forth. Every time you hit a crystal, it will change color, alternating between blue and orange. You can strike them with any weapon, but also with arrows and remote bombs, making it possible to interact with them over a distance, or when your direct path is blocked.

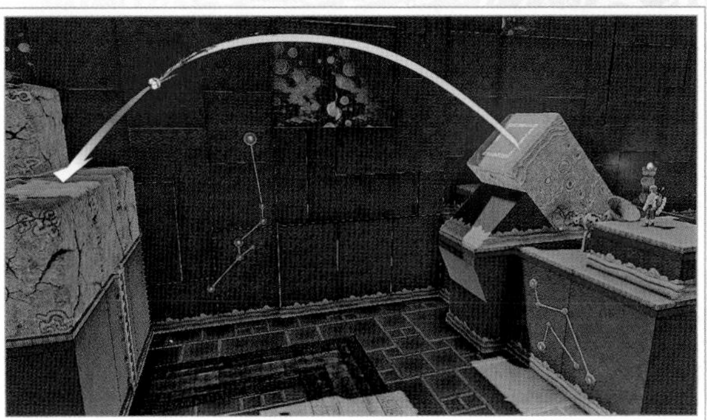

LAUNCHERS: These are piston-like devices that will propel Link (or, for that matter, any light object) in a specific direction. Puzzles relying on this mechanic can require you to time your flight correctly, or to combine multiple features at once. For example, you might hit a crystal that activates a launcher that sends a bomb flying to an otherwise inaccessible position, which you can then detonate to blow up destructible blocks.

WALKTHROUGH

This chapter will guide you through the full *Breath of the Wild* adventure. It provides a streamlined path that you can follow step by step to reach the ending credits, while also offering advice on when you might profitably venture off the beaten path to complete optional objectives.

The chapter's structure has been designed with flexibility in mind. It is suitable both for occasional reference and all-encompassing guidance.

Introduction

Breath of the Wild features a gigantic realm, known as Hyrule, that you can explore at your leisure. From very early in the adventure you are free to take your character, Link, to any place that he can physically reach.

At first, the play area is limited to a single region – the Great Plateau. This serves as a very welcome prologue, during which you will be introduced to most of the game's key mechanics. After you complete a handful of main story objectives, though, the full sandbox will be unlocked. The world is incredibly vast and varied. Virtually everything you see on your screen can be explored: every mountain peak, every valley, every snowfield. In short: if you see it, you can visit it.

In this breathtaking environment, the game's narrative invites you to visit specific places and face set challenges. At any point in time, though, you can choose to go your own way, either to roam freely in the wild or to attend to optional tasks unlocked during the course of the adventure. Opportunities to leave the main narrative path to complete secondary quests and challenges are quite literally *everywhere*.

To reflect the bountiful, feature-packed nature of this game, this walkthrough covers both main quests and a large selection of optional tasks that are within convenient range along the way. We've designed the chapter so that you can plot your own customized course through the adventure, should you wish, but always be able to refer to our guidance when it is needed.

- Each region that you visit during main missions is introduced in the guide with a double-page spread that features a large area map as its focal point. This highlights:
  - The key landmarks and points of interest for the area in question.
  - A visual representation of the steps that you must follow to complete the corresponding main quests. This information is displayed in orange.
  - A list of the various optional objectives that you might feasibly complete while in the area, taking your likely current level of proficiency and development into account. Call-outs detailing basic requirements and essential advice are printed in blue for shrines, and in green for side quests and all other similar activities.
- The pages that follow each map offer a traditional walkthrough for the main storyline events that occur in the corresponding map portion. This provides step-by-step guidance, with screenshots and captions detailing the actions you must take. For ease of reference, each entry is identified by a clear number icon that links to the area map.

If you would like to complete the adventure with minimal assistance, the map-oriented pages offer an essential directory of available activities. Expert gamers can use these to plan their path through the adventure, and therefore claim all major rewards, without fear of encountering spoilers or puzzle solutions.

Map Legend

The following legend details annotations and icons that you will encounter throughout the Walkthrough chapter. Our maps are oriented in accordance with the classic convention where "up" is always north, as with the main in-game map.

Note that most collectibles in the game vary in accordance with your current progression. In other words, a single, specific treasure chest can contain different items based on your accomplishments prior to opening it.

LEGEND

ANNOTATION	MEANING	ANNOTATION	MEANING
	Walkthrough path		Stable
1	Walkthrough step		Armor shop
	Player character movement		General store
	Interactive object movement		Inn
	Enemy movement		Dye shop
	Tower		Jewelry
	Shrine		Village
	Tech lab		Other landmark

Crash Course

Breath of the Wild offers little in the way of tutorials, waypoints, or any other form of in-game hand-holding. This is actually one of its most enjoyable features: as you learn from your experiences, you will obtain a powerful and genuine sense of accomplishment. The flipside of this is that there are many genuine challenges to overcome, particularly tough opponents, complex puzzles, and navigational conundrums. This is *not* an easy game.

We strongly suggest that you take the time to read our Primer chapter, starting on page 8, to learn about key concepts and acquire good habits that will serve you well throughout the adventure. That said, we completely understand that many readers will be eager to just dive in and begin playing. In recognition of this fact, the following concise summaries offer critical advice that will benefit anyone who would rather begin with minimal assistance or forewarning. When you're ready to learn more, you can refer back to the Primer at your leisure.

Navigation: Though basic commands and movements are easy to execute, navigating complex environments and planning efficient trips can prove more demanding. Stamina management is a massive part of the game. Sprinting, climbing, swimming, and gliding all consume Link's energy reserves, which are extremely limited at the start of the adventure. Overconfidence can be fatal, especially while climbing.

Combat: While early encounters may seem trivial and undemanding, you will soon face adversaries that can deplete most (if not all) of your hearts with a single blow. Combat in *Breath of the Wild* is highly strategic. You cannot simply rush your foes; many individual enemies, let alone groups, can make short work of Link in a guileless toe-to-toe melee. You must carefully consider your approach to each skirmish, and generally prioritize defensive tactics (especially oft-decisive counters).

Landmarks: *Breath of the Wild*'s massive game world is home to countless points of interest, characters to talk to, collectibles to acquire, and quests to complete. A working knowledge of the various types of landmarks you will come across can help you to make sense of the world you explore. There are three recurring destinations that are particularly important:

- **Towers** must be scaled to reveal regional maps as a matter of priority; they are also convenient fast travel points.
- **Shrines** are mini-dungeons that contain assorted treasures; they, too, serve as fast travel points.
- **Villages** are hubs for side quests, trading, and upgrades.

Resources: There are many different types of resources in *Breath of the Wild*. Ensuring that Link is suitably equipped for each encounter should always be a priority.

- A single weapon and shield will not suffice; they break over time. You need a varied stock of equipment to survive and thrive. Find Koroks and obtain their seeds to increase Link's carrying capacity.
- Gathering materials will enable you to create dishes or elixirs that grant temporary bonus effects such as enhanced stamina. Before you undertake any journey or trial of note, a brief stop at a cooking pot to prepare is always a good idea.
- You can *never* have too many arrows.

Weather & Elements: Weather conditions play a significant role in *Breath of the Wild*'s sandbox, sometimes having a direct impact on your gameplay possibilities: when it's wet, for instance, Link will struggle to climb. Elements such as fire, ice, and electricity also play a pivotal role, enabling you to exploit enemy weaknesses or to solve puzzles in creative ways.

Runes & Puzzles: *Breath of the Wild* features many hundreds of puzzles. These are most commonly encountered in shrines and dungeons, but the world of Hyrule itself will often test your ability to closely observe your surroundings and notice potential secrets or intriguing opportunities. Don't underestimate the runes that you receive in the opening region: these essential abilities are employed in countless different ways throughout the adventure.

Prologue: The Great Plateau

WALKTHROUGH SUMMARY (SEE OVERLEAF FOR DETAILS)

STEP	DESCRIPTION
1 → 4	From the Shrine of Resurrection where you begin, head to the terminal to the east to reveal the Great Plateau Tower.
5 → 10	Clear the Oman Au Shrine.
11 → 16	Clear the Ja Baij Shrine.
17 → 21	Make preparations in anticipation of a long climb and exposure to cold temperatures.
22 → 27	Clear the Owa Daim Shrine.
28 → 31	Clear the Keh Namut Shrine.
32 → 33	Interact with the goddess statue at the Temple of Time, then climb to the building's rooftop.

OPTIONAL CHALLENGES

ICON	ACTIVITY	NOTES
I	KOROK SEEDS	If you dive into the circle of waterlilies in the nearby pond after your very first encounter with the old man, you will obtain a Korok seed. These items can be traded a little later into the adventure for additional inventory slots for your weapons, shields, and bows. There are hundreds of Koroks to find in Hyrule in locations that will generally draw your attention; if a particular arrangement of objects catches your eye, it's usually a good idea to investigate. Refer to our Extras chapter for details (see page 330).
II	ENVIRONMENTAL PUZZLES	After you complete the Oman Au Shrine, your newly acquired Magnesis rune will enable you to interact with the environment in creative ways. You can experience this immediately as you leave the shrine: two treasure chests are submerged in the small pond adjacent to the building. Lift them with Magnesis to retrieve their contents. Scanning the pond will also reveal a thin metal slab, which you can use to reach the wooden ledge in the middle of the bog to the west, where two additional chests await. Get into the habit of studying your surroundings with Magnesis active, as the world is filled with similar opportunities.
III	ENEMY OUTPOSTS	You will come across a great many outposts throughout the adventure – some rudimentary, others much more elaborate. These should never be taken lightly and the approach you choose is always important. The outpost to the south of the Great Plateau Tower is a good example: if you are spotted by the sentry on the lookout tower, all local forces will attack you, making this a very tricky battle. If, on the other hand, you approach incognito from the north and use an arrow to cut the rope from which a lantern is hanging inside the skull-shaped building, the subsequent explosion will incapacitate or badly wound all foes inside, vastly simplifying the process of clearing the outpost.
IV	SUB-BOSS: TALUS (see page 314)	A Talus sub-boss awaits deep in the Forest of Spirits. You can defeat this enemy type by making it collapse with bombs, then climbing onto its back to attack its weak point, which looks like a dark crystal. Defeating it will reward you with numerous gems, which can be sold for hefty amounts of money. There are many other sub-bosses like this spread all over Hyrule.

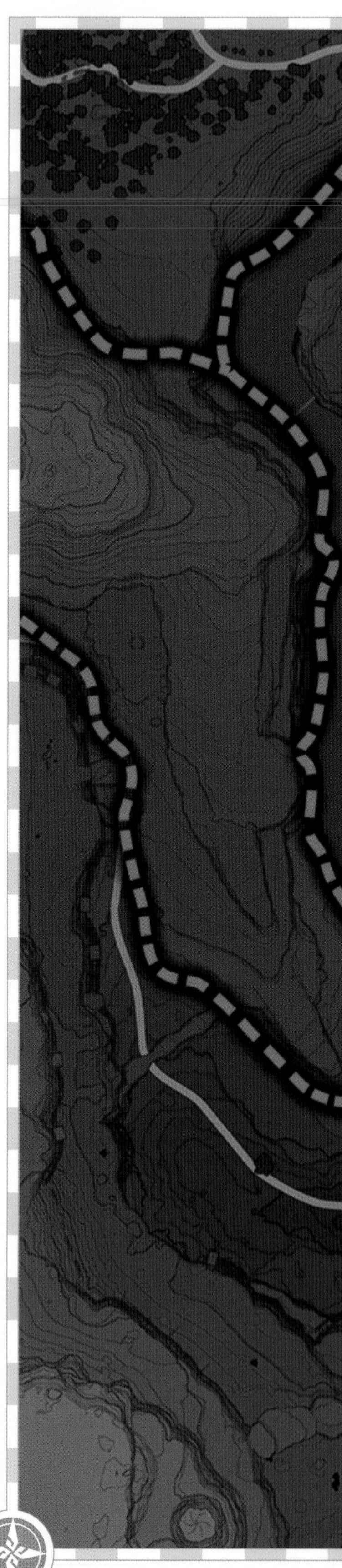

5 → 10 Oman Au Shrine

II

3 → 4

IV

GREAT PLATEAU TOWER

1 Shrine of Resurrection

2

I

III

12 → 16

27 → 31

32 → 33

17

11

Keh Namut Shrine

Temple of Time

Ja Baij Shrine

Owa Daim Shrine

20

18 → 19

26

21 → 25

1

After the introductory cutscene, you will gain full control over Link. You can move him around with Ⓛ and control the camera with Ⓡ. If you would like to adjust control settings, this is a good time to do so: open the System menu, then select Options. Interact with the first terminal with Ⓐ, then open the two treasure chests in the next room to receive your first pieces of armor. Equip these via the inventory menu, then activate the next terminal. You can now run outside, sprinting with Ⓑ if you wish. To climb the small cliff on the way, simply run into it and use Ⓛ to ascend. Both sprinting and climbing will deplete your stamina wheel. Link will be left out of breath and even lose his grip once his stamina is fully depleted.

2

Once outside, run down the slope, collecting your first resources on the way, and speak to the old man at the campfire. Shortly afterwards, you receive your first main quest: **"Follow the Sheikah Slate."**

3

Head to your objective, represented by a glowing yellow waypoint. Feel free to display the map with ⊖ if required. You will encounter your first enemy on the way, a lone Bokoblin. Use this opportunity to practice basic combat skills, particularly locking on to a target (hold ZL), strafing and dodging (hold ZL, then tilt Ⓛ and press Ⓧ), and attacking (Ⓨ). If you don't yet feel very comfortable with the combat system, avoid fights against multiple enemies for now and make your way directly to the waypoint shown on the mini-map: the Sheikah terminal found inside a small rock structure. This will raise the Great Plateau Tower (along with all the other towers in Hyrule) and reveal the regional map.

4

From the top of the tower, survey the surrounding region to locate the Great Plateau's four orange-glowing shrines. When you spot one, activate your scope by pressing Ⓡ, then align the reticle on the shrine and press Ⓐ to place a pin on it. This will add a colored icon to your map and mini-map at the position of a landmark, making it much easier to keep track of it. Two shrines are clearly visible to the west and northwest, while the other two (shown in the accompanying screenshot) are further away to the south and southwest. Once you have a pin on each of the four shrines, move between the ledges in a clockwise direction as make your way back down to ground level.

5

At the foot of the tower, you will receive your next main quest: **"The Isolated Plateau."** The old man asks you to visit your first shrine, to the north of your current position. Interacting with the terminal at the entrance will activate the building, turning it into a new fast travel destination. This means that you can simply select this shrine from anywhere in the world while looking at your map, and warp to it instantly. This applies to all towers and shrines that you activate. Step on the elevator platform inside the building and examine it to enter the shrine. Before you do so, consider making a brief detour to any pond in the area to catch a Hyrule bass, and to the nearby Forest of Spirits to the west to obtain raw meat from a fox or boar: this will come in handy very soon.

SHRINES

Shrines are miniature versions of dungeons, challenging you to solve all sorts of physical or logical puzzles. Much like towers, shrines are high-priority targets in terms of exploration. Not only do they offer valuable rewards on completion, but they also turn into fast travel positions the moment you first interact with them. As the game features over a hundred shrines, these soon form a network that enables you to warp to virtually anywhere on the map.

All shrines feature an altar – your goal. Examining the altar both completes the shrine and returns you to its entrance. The first four shrines you will encounter, all found on the Great Plateau, are mandatory and introduce key gameplay concepts. All future shrines, on the other hand, are *technically* optional. Finding and clearing as many as you can is extremely important, though, as the spirit orbs you obtain from altars can be exchanged for additional heart containers (that extend your health gauge) or stamina vessels (that add segments to your stamina wheel).

OMAN AU SHRINE

6

Once inside the Oman Au Shrine, interact with the terminal on the left to receive your first rune: **Magnesis**. This enables you to manipulate metallic objects. Test your new skills on the metal objects in the center of the room: trigger Magnesis mode with L, then align your cursor on one of the metal slabs and press A. With your grip on the object active, you can move it around freely with L and R, and adjust its distance relative to Link with ✚. For now, simply move one of the two metal slabs aside to reveal a hole in the ground leading to the other side of the fence.

7

Once on the other side, grab the metal cube in the wall with Magnesis and use it as a battering ram to knock down the pile of blocks. This will give you access to the next room. You can then use it to destroy the nearby Guardian Scout. These creatures can be dangerous at your current stage of progression. If you have a shield equipped, you can perfect-guard their laser beams to deflect them back for a one-hit kill, though this is a move that requires some practice to master. When the environment offers you an alternative (and easier) way to defeat opponents, it's wise to take it.

8

You will notice three platforms in the next section. Head to the middle one and cast Magnesis on the metal slab bridging the gap between the first two platforms, then move it over the next gap, so that it connects the second and third platforms.

9

Once on the third platform, grab the chest on the ledge to your left with Magnesis, then move it back to your position. You can now open the large metallic doors by pulling them in your direction with Magnesis.

10

Finally, head to the altar and examine it to complete the shrine and receive your first spirit orb – an item that you will soon be able to exchange (in bundles of four) to obtain additional heart containers and stamina vessels.

JA BAIJ SHRINE

11

From the Oman Au Shrine, head southeast to the Eastern Abbey. Go through the main entrance, to the west of the ruins. A few steps past the archway, a Decayed Guardian awakes from its slumber. This enemy type initially targets you with an aiming beam, then opens fire after a few seconds. This is currently lethal to Link, so you must be careful. Dash from one cover point to the next until you reach the wall with the cracked rocks. Thanks to the cover of the ruins behind you, you can scale the wall, behind which you will find the Ja Baij Shrine.

12

Once inside the shrine, examine the terminal on the left to receive a new rune: the **Remote Bomb**. Its primary function is to annihilate destructible objects. Remote bombs exist in round and cube versions; round bombs will roll when placed on slopes and if caught in the wind, whereas their cubic counterparts tend to stay where you place them. Choose one by holding ✚ and using ◉, then tap L for Link to hold the bomb above his head. Press Ⓐ to drop it at his feet, R to throw it, or Ⓑ to put it away. You can then trigger the detonation with L, though be careful to ensure that Link isn't caught in the blast. Try your new skill on the cracked blocks in front of you. Follow this by blowing up the two cracked blocks in the passage beyond. The opening on the right leads to a treasure chest, while the one on the left leads to the next room.

13

When you reach the moving platform, wait until it moves close to you then drop a cube bomb on it and backtrack to solid ground. Detonate the explosive when the moving platform touches the destructible wall on the far side. You can then step on the moving platform, which will take you to the final room.

14

Make your way to the launcher close to the left-hand wall: it will propel you to the treasure chest on the opposite ledge.

15

Head to the launcher on the right-hand side of the room. Drop a sphere bomb into the pipe so that it rolls onto the launcher. It will be propelled to the destructible rocks: detonate it to clear the path.

16

Finally, climb the ladder and run to the altar, which you can examine to complete the shrine.

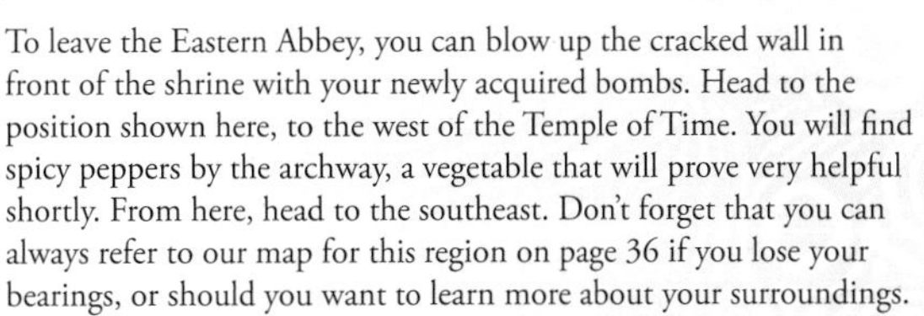

17

To leave the Eastern Abbey, you can blow up the cracked wall in front of the shrine with your newly acquired bombs. Head to the position shown here, to the west of the Temple of Time. You will find spicy peppers by the archway, a vegetable that will prove very helpful shortly. From here, head to the southeast. Don't forget that you can always refer to our map for this region on page 36 if you lose your bearings, or should you want to learn more about your surroundings.

18

In the far southeast of the Great Plateau, you will find the old man close to a hut. There are many collectibles in the area, including mushrooms with very interesting properties. Once cooked, stamella shrooms will restore some of your depleted stamina. Cook several in a single meal: the mushroom skewers you obtain can be profoundly helpful in a long and dangerous climb that awaits further ahead. The cooking process is easy. Select an item in your inventory, choose to hold it, add more copies or other items, then press Ⓑ to return to the field and Ⓐ to prepare the meal with the selected ingredients.

19

Next, you should try to cook spicy meat & seafood fry – a dish fancied by the old man, although he cannot recall the recipe. The diary inside the hut will put you on the right track. You must combine spicy pepper (look inside the hut, or see step 17), raw meat (obtained by hunting any large animal, such as a boar or a fox), and a Hyrule bass (available in the pond southeast of the Oman Au Shrine – see step 5). Cooking these three ingredients together will lead to the creation of spicy meat & seafood fry. Speak to the old man by the campfire and he will offer his thanks by giving you a warm doublet. This piece of armor bestows cold resistance, a bonus that you will greatly appreciate during a forthcoming challenge.

20

When you're ready, head to the southwest and cut a tree with a woodcutter's axe (there's one at the old man's hut): you can use the trunk as a makeshift bridge to cross the chasm. Eliminate any Bokoblins you encounter on the other side.

21

The next shrine is situated at the top of the cliff you are now facing. Your goal is to scale it, making regular stops at the horizontal ledges on the way to refill your stamina (press Ⓑ while above a ledge). You have little stamina available at this early stage, so aim straight for the closest ledge each time. Avoid jumping while climbing for now: this consumes a large chunk of the gauge. If you end up in a dire predicament, consume the food with stamina-boosting properties that you cooked at the hut. The Owa Daim Shrine awaits directly at the top.

OWA DAIM SHRINE

22

Interact with the terminal on your left to obtain the **Stasis** rune. Stasis grants you the ability to briefly stop an object in time – for example, to freeze a moving platform. This power has a second crucial application: an object subject to Stasis will store any kinetic energy accumulated while it is immobilized, and release it afterwards. If you hit a boulder in Stasis with a sledgehammer multiple times, for instance, you will see a vector arrow appear. This shows the direction in which it will be propelled once the effect ends. Each use of Stasis will be followed by a brief cooldown period during which the ability is unavailable. Try out your new power on the cogwheel in front of you: cast Stasis while the rotating platform is in a horizontal position, enabling you to cross the chasm.

23

Next, run to the bottom of the ramp. Observe the boulders that regularly roll down and fall into the abyss. Cast Stasis on one of them right as it passes your position. While it is frozen in time, sprint all the way up to the top of the ramp, letting your stamina refill once on the way. If you do not make it in time, come to a halt on the intermediate landing and stop the boulder when it passes in front of you.

24

From the chest, turn around, wait for a new boulder to roll, then sprint down the ramp. Take a right on the intermediate landing and collect the iron sledgehammer against the far wall.

25

Stand in front of the boulder blocking the way and cast Stasis on it. While it is frozen in time, hit it once with your sledgehammer. Once the effect ends, the boulder will roll forward and fall in the abyss, enabling you to make your way to the altar.

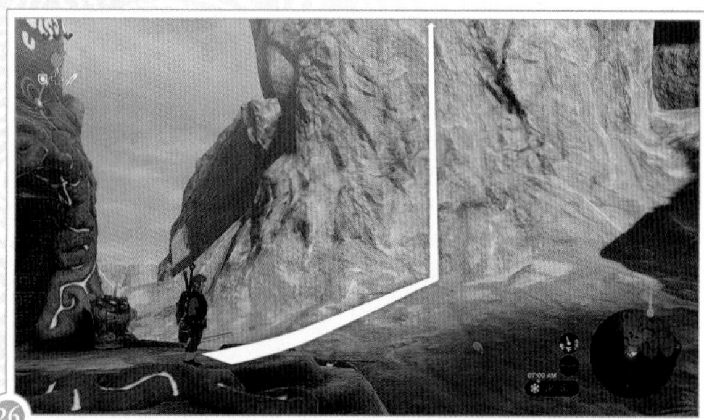

26

Back outside, climb the cliff directly west of the Owa Daim Shrine. There is a flat ledge where you can catch your breath midway through the ascent. Once at the top, you will reach an area with low temperatures. You will take gradual (and, in time, fatal) damage unless you trigger a cold resistance bonus. This can be induced in multiple ways: by equipping the warm doublet if you obtained this piece of armor from the old man at the hut; by cooking spicy pepper (available by the archway to the west of the Temple of Time); or by wielding a torch that you set ablaze, though this is a very temporary solution that will prevent you from sprinting, making it hard to recommend. The warm doublet is by far the best option as its effect is permanent. If you opt for food effects, note that you will need several minutes to reach the next shrine: cook at least four spicy peppers to be safe.

27

The path to the fourth shrine is relatively straightforward and uneventful, with only a few enemies standing in your way. The shrine lies to the northwest of Mount Hylia, on a small peak overlooking a pond. Examine its terminal and head inside once you're ready to proceed.

KEH NAMUT SHRINE

28

Interact with the terminal on the left to receive yet another vital rune. **Cryonis** enables you to summon blocks of ice on flat water surfaces, creating makeshift stepping stones. These blocks are climbable and can even be materialized on falling water. You can only summon three blocks of ice at a time, though; if you generate a fourth in succession, the first one in the series will be destroyed. You are also free to destroy an existing block by pressing Ⓐ while aiming at it. Note that Cryonis has another critical use: you can summon a block of ice under an object to lift it up. This works on Link himself, but the most valuable application of this feature is that it makes it possible to raise certain gates and access submerged items. For now, create a block of ice in the small pool and use this as a stepping stone to reach the corridor above.

29

In the next room, summon an ice block beneath the gate to open the way. This is a trick that is easy to forget, but will be key to solving multiple puzzles throughout the adventure.

30

You will encounter a Guardian Scout after you pass the gate. It should fall quickly to a few hits with your best weapon. Feel free to generate a block of ice in the middle of the area to enjoy a possible cover point if your enemy fires laser beams at you. When the battle ends, position an ice block at the base of the ledge with the treasure chest to access it.

31

Finally, summon an ice block beneath either end of the beam: once raised, it will form a ramp that you can use to make your way to the altar.

32

After the cutscene that ensues when you exit the shrine, head to your next destination. If you look on your map and draw two imaginary lines, one horizontal between the Keh Namut Shrine and the Ja Baij Shrine, and one vertical between the other two, the point where they intersect is the Temple of Time. Warp to the Shrine of Resurrection if you would like to shorten the journey. Once inside the Temple of Time, pray in front of the large goddess statue. You now have an important choice to make: this is your first opportunity to trade a bundle of four spirit orbs acquired from shrines for either a heart container or a stamina vessel. While the benefits of choosing heart containers should be obvious, extra stamina segments make a real difference to your ability to explore the world.

33

Now climb to the Temple of Time's rooftop to meet the old man. You can use the ladder on the building's east side to get there easily. This concludes **"The Isolated Plateau,"** and grants you the paraglider as a reward. This essential piece of equipment enables you to glide while airborne: press Ⓧ to draw the sail, and Ⓑ to put it away. Gliding consumes stamina, a factor that you must consider carefully when covering long distances.

Seek Out Impa

WALKTHROUGH SUMMARY (SEE OVERLEAF FOR DETAILS)

STEP	DESCRIPTION
1 → 4	Make your way to Kakariko Village and speak to Impa.
5 → 6	Head toward Hateno Village.

OPTIONAL CHALLENGES

ICON	ACTIVITY	NOTES
	SHRINES & SHRINE QUESTS	You can find step-by-step solutions for all shrines and shrine quests in our dedicated chapter: see page 118 for the shrines in the Dueling Peaks Tower region.
I	SIDE QUEST: MISKO, THE GREAT BANDIT (see page 220)	If you speak to Domidak at the Dueling Peaks Stable and agree to give him 100 rupees, you will trigger this side quest and obtain a riddle concerning a treasure. However, you can actually visit the cave in question without activating the quest: it is hidden behind destructible rocks, on the cliff at the south edge of Hickaly Woods.
II	SIDE QUEST: THE PRICELESS MARACAS (see page 220)	On your way to Kakariko Village, you can speak to a creature called Hestu. Retrieve his maracas from the outpost to the east and return them to him. He will then offer you additional inventory slots for your weapons, bows, or shields, in exchange for any Korok seeds that you take back to him.
III	WILD HORSES (see page 220)	When you reach the Dueling Peaks Stable, speak to Rensa, the man close to the counter. He will challenge you to mount a wild horse and take it back to him in under two minutes. You can find an introduction to this system on page 17.
IV	SIDE QUEST: FLOWN THE COOP (see page 221)	While visiting Kakariko Village at noon, speak to Cado, opposite the armor shop, to trigger this quest. Your goal is to round up seven cuccos within the village, including two that often stand on rooftops and one on the ledge overlooking the armor shop. Take them all back to the enclosure to complete the assignment.
V	SIDE QUEST: ARROWS OF BURNING HEAT (see page 221)	After completing the "Seek Out Impa" main quest, speak to Rola, the owner of the general store that sells arrows in Kakariko Village. She needs you to light the four candles behind the village's goddess statue. You can do so with fire arrows, or standard arrows set ablaze at the nearby campfire, or even with a fire-elemental melee weapon.
VI	SIDE QUEST: KOKO'S KITCHEN (see page 222)	Speak to Koko, a child that can be found by the cooking pot next to the general store in Kakariko Village every afternoon. Buy a swift carrot for her in the shop to complete this short assignment.
VII	SIDE QUEST: COOKING WITH KOKO (see page 222)	Speak to Koko again after completing her previous quest. This time she needs goat butter, which you can also purchase from the nearby general store.
VIII	SIDE QUEST: KOKO CUISINE (see page 222)	Speak to Koko again after completing Cooking with Koko. This time she needs raw meat, which you can obtain by hunting a mammal such as a fox, a boar, or a wolf.
IX	SIDE QUEST: KOKO'S SPECIALTY (see page 223)	Speak to Koko again after completing Koko Cuisine. You can help her by giving her some Courser bee honey (acquired by shooting a bee hive).
X	SIDE QUEST: PLAYTIME WITH COTTLA (see page 223)	Speak to Cottla between noon and 04:00 PM. She usually runs around near the armor shop. Choose to play tag with her. Once the game begins, sprint after Cottla and you should catch up in no time.
XI	MAIN QUEST: FIND THE FAIRY FOUNTAIN (see page 223)	Though considered a main quest, this mission is entirely optional. Speak to Pikango after you obtain the camera rune. Take a picture of the Great Fairy Fountain to the northeast of the village, then report back to Pikango.
XII	SIDE QUEST: BY FIREFLY'S LIGHT (see page 223)	This will become available after you complete the "Find the Fairy Fountain" and "Flown the Coop" quests. You receive this assignment from Lasli, the woman who stands outside Kakariko's armor shop during the day, but walks to her home at night, in the southeast corner of the village. Speak to her there from 10:00PM onwards to trigger this quest, then catch five sunset fireflies in the area. Once you have them, select them in your inventory, hold them in your hands, and release them in Lasli's house.
XIII	GREAT FAIRY FOUNTAIN	A short distance to the northeast of Kakariko Village, you will find your first Great Fairy Fountain. You must spend a set amount of rupees to unlock each fountain (100 rupees in this instance), but the investment is well worth the money: these fountains will enable you to upgrade your pieces of armor by spending materials gathered in the wild.

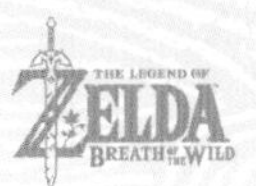

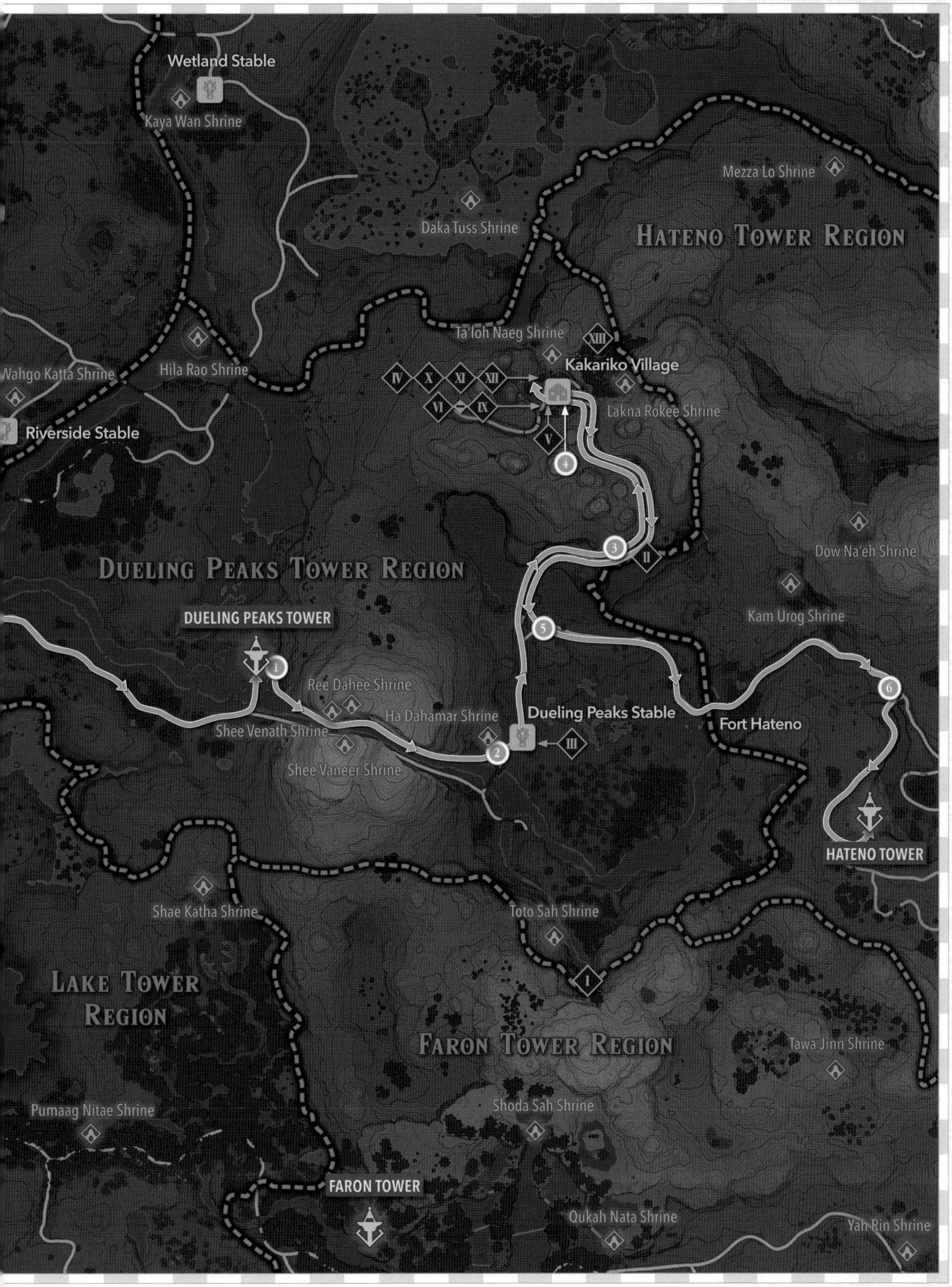
Wetland Stable
Kaya Wan Shrine
Mezza Lo Shrine
Daka Tuss Shrine
HATENO TOWER REGION
Ta'loh Naeg Shrine
XIII
Kakariko Village
Wahgo Katta Shrine
Hila Rao Shrine
IV
X
XI
XII
VI
IX
Lakna Rokee Shrine
Riverside Stable
V
4
3
II
Dow Na'eh Shrine
DUELING PEAKS TOWER REGION
Kam Urog Shrine
DUELING PEAKS TOWER
5
1
Ree Dahee Shrine
6
Ha Dahamar Shrine
Dueling Peaks Stable
Fort Hateno
Shee Venath Shrine
III
2
Shee Vaneer Shrine
HATENO TOWER
Shae Katha Shrine
Toto Sah Shrine
I
LAKE TOWER REGION
FARON TOWER REGION
Tawa Jinn Shrine
Shoda Sah Shrine
Pumaag Nitae Shrine
FARON TOWER
Qukah Nata Shrine
Yah Rin Shrine

1

Though you can, in principle, head to Castle Hyrule and attempt to destroy Ganon immediately, this would be suicidal. You will first need to greatly develop your gear and abilities. The first of many steps required to achieve this is to complete the **"Seek Out Impa"** main quest. From your starting position, glide to the east and keep going in the same direction until you reach the Dueling Peaks Tower. Activating this tower will add a new functionality to your slate: the Sheikah sensor, which is represented by an antenna icon on your screen. Whenever a shrine is available within its detection range, the sensor will start glowing. The concentric circles will light up when Link moves in the direction of the shrine. The better his alignment, the more circles glow, enabling you to locate shrines more easily.

2

Pass between the two Dueling Peaks to find a first stable, which will give you an opportunity to register a wild horse found in the area. You can find more details on how this works on page 17. There is also a very profitable side quest to complete in the vicinity (see **"Misko, the Great Bandit"** on the previous double-page spread). Once you're ready, head north and cross the bridge.

3

The rest of the path to Kakariko Village is entirely straightforward, following a linear canyon. One point of interest on the way is a creature called Hestu, who will trade any Korok seeds that you have gathered so far for additional inventory slots. Turn to the previous page for details on the connected side quest "The Priceless Maracas".

4

Once at Kakariko Village, we suggest you activate the local shrine that overlooks the village. This will act as a handy warp point whenever you need to return here. As a rule, this is something you should aim to achieve whenever you visit a new area or region. When you're ready, head for the largest building, inside which Impa awaits. Speaking to her completes the **"Seek Out Impa"** main quest and unlocks two new ones: **"Free the Divine Beasts"** and **"Locked Mementos"**. The former is a long-term task that you will make a start on soon. For now, prioritize the latter, which involves finding the Hateno Ancient Tech Lab.

5

Retrace your steps through the long canyon until you cross the Kakariko Bridge, then head east toward Hateno Village, following the main road. You will go through Fort Hateno on the way, with a cooking pot available should you need to replenish your stock of restoratives.

6

Keep following the main road until you reach the natural rock bridge shown here. Cross it and head south, alongside the river, until you are within climbing range of the Hateno Tower.

PRIMER RECAP

With the game's prologue now behind you, you have opportunities to venture off the beaten path at your leisure. If you simply follow the main storyline, you might get the impression that you have the situation very much under control and that the enemies you encounter pose no problem. While this is still true at this early stage of the primary quest, you will soon face more taxing challenges.

If you have read our Primer chapter, you should already know how adopting certain habits early and practicing the game's most demanding techniques is essential, and profoundly beneficial to your overall *Breath of the Wild* experience. If you haven't read it, or if you could use a concise summary to refresh your memory, the following points should help.

EXPLORATION (SEE PAGE 15)

- **Towers:** This is probably obvious to you at this point, but towers should be your first port of call every time you visit a new region. Navigating environments with no map is at best sub-optimal and at worst very dangerous, preventing you from identifying natural hazards. Towers are clearly recognizable thanks to their thin, tall shape. They also emit a distinct orange glow that is particularly visible at night. Reaching the top of a tower enables you to reveal the regional map. It also gives you a chance to spot landmarks in the vicinity, most notably shrines. Gliding from the top of a tower to a shrine, then warping back to the tower and repeating, is a very effective method to gradually conquer new territories.
- **Shrines:** Once you have unlocked a region's tower, shrines should be your second priority. Finding these enables you to develop a large network of fast travel positions, greatly shortening long journeys when you need to return to previously visited locations. Clearing shrines gives you access to important rewards: varied (and, on occasion, highly valuable) items from treasure chests, and spirit orbs that you can trade for physical upgrades (either additional hearts or extensions of your stamina wheel). Every stat boost that you can acquire makes a big difference, particularly in the early game. It therefore makes sense to complete as many shrines as you can before you undertake more demanding missions, as will be the case soon.
- **Korok seeds:** Gathering a large number of Korok seeds might seem like a very secondary objective, but is actually a vital activity. Every additional inventory slot that you can obtain from Hestu will be more than welcome once you reach the point where you find more weapons than you can carry. An expanded inventory will enable you to build a large and diversified arsenal, adapted to all sorts of situations.

COMBAT (SEE PAGE 18)

- **Strafe:** One of the most effective ways to avoid incoming enemy attacks is to dodge them. To do so while keeping your opponent in sight, hold ZL. While in this strafing stance, jump either laterally to perform a side hop, or backward to perform a backflip. These moves are useful not merely to evade assaults, but also to rapidly move Link to a more advantageous position.
- **Perfect dodge and flurry rush:** If executed a fraction of a second before an enemy attack connects, a sidehop or backflip will trigger a perfect dodge – a slow-motion interval during which your enemy is almost frozen in time while you can deal multiple "flurry rush" counterattacks with total impunity. This move is one of the most vital in the entire game. Even though you may not need to employ it right now, you soon will, and any effort you put into practicing sooner rather than later will pay off. We cannot stress this enough: mastering the perfect dodge/flurry rush combination is key to defeating most of the game's toughest creatures.
- **Perfect guard and counter:** Perfect-guarding is the act of proactively deflecting an incoming blow. Much like the previous command, perfect-guarding is also a demanding but indispensable combat move. This is achieved by holding your shield aloft with ZL and pressing A precisely as the enemy attack is about to strike. Both a defensive and offensive command, perfect-guarding is the only way to block certain powerful assaults without taking damage. Whenever you execute it successfully, this command will enable you to follow up with a counter while your target is temporarily stunned.
- **Charged attacks with two-handed weapons:** When you need to inflict massive amounts of damage, nothing can beat a two-handed weapon charged attack. Link starts spinning, hitting nearby targets multiple times, and unleashes a final blow that strikes the ground, causing a shockwave. With an extended stamina wheel, this type of attack can deal over a dozen blows in just a few seconds, potentially annihilating all but the most resilient enemies. This works wonderfully well against slow creatures such as Guardian Scouts.
- **Sub-bosses:** Sub-bosses can be found in various locations in Hyrule. These large-scale creatures pose challenges similar to those that you face against main quest bosses, but they spawn in the wild. Each type of sub-boss has its own behavior and attack patterns, as revealed in this guide's Bestiary chapter. As a general rule, defeating these giant enemies is worth the effort as they often drop valuable items, from gemstones to weapons of all kinds. Defeating sub-bosses will often require you to employ the techniques described above, making them excellent sparring partners.
- **Strategy:** If you struggle against an enemy type, take the time to observe and analyze its movements and the timing of its attacks. Once you've learned how to react accordingly, even the fiercest foe can be dominated with confidence. The important point is this: you should really be practicing any moves that you are uncomfortable with. Any of the commands detailed here that you choose to disregard *will* eventually cause you to struggle against certain creatures, especially bosses.

Locked Mementos & Captured Memories

WALKTHROUGH SUMMARY (SEE OVERLEAF FOR DETAILS)

STEP	DESCRIPTION
7 → 8	Make your way to the Ancient Tech Lab in Hateno Village.
9	Speak to Symin and Purah inside the tech lab, then light the furnace on the Tech Lab's outer wall with a blue flame.
10	Take a photo of Purah and show it to her, then return to Impa in Kakariko Village.
11	Find a captured memory spot to recall the events that occurred there, then return to Impa.
12	Choose which Divine Beast you want to conquer first.

OPTIONAL CHALLENGES

ICON	ACTIVITY	NOTES
	SHRINES & SHRINE QUESTS	You can find step-by-step solutions for all shrines and shrine quests in our dedicated chapter: see page 124 for the Hateno Tower region.
I	SIDE QUEST: THE STATUE'S BARGAIN (see page 226)	If you speak to a child called Teebo in Hateno Village, he will take you to a strange statue by Firly Pond. Speak to that statue to trigger the quest, then speak to it again to regain the essence it took from you. This is a simple introduction to a feature that enables you to turn a heart container you have acquired into a stamina vessel, or vice versa, for a mere 20 rupees.
II	SIDE QUEST: THE WEAPON CONNOISSEUR (see page 226)	Speak to Nebb, one of the children running in the streets of Hateno Village during daylight hours. He will ask you to show him a traveler sword. You can find one in the valley leading to Zora's Domain. He then has additional similar requests, making this is a long-term assignment that you will gradually complete as you progress in the adventure.
III	SIDE QUEST: A GIF FOR MY BELOVED (see page 228)	Speak to Manny, who is usually found between Hateno Village's dye shop and the local inn. Next, speak to Prima from behind the back of the inn's counter, and report the news of what she likes to Manny. You must then gather 10 restless crickets for him.
IV	SIDE QUEST: THE SHEEP RUSTLERS (see page 228)	Speak to Koyin, who watches over her flock outside the farm located between Hateno Village and the Tech Lab. She needs you to slay monsters that congregate at Hateno Beach, to the southeast of the village. After eliminating them, report to Koyin.
V	SIDE QUEST: ROBBIE'S RESEARCH (see page 229)	After showing Purah a picture of herself, speak to her again to trigger this quest. You first need to find Robbie at the Akkala Ancient Tech Lab, in the northeast corner of Hyrule. Once inside, speak to Robbie, remove all your armor pieces to show your scars, then speak to him again. Now pick up the torch leaning against the shelves and light it up with the blue flame found on Tumlea Heights, just west of the Tech Lab. After igniting the furnace with the blue flame, speak to Robbie again to complete the assignment.
VI	SIDE QUEST: SLATED FOR UPGRADES (see page 229)	After acquiring the camera rune from Purah at the Hateno Ancient Tech Lab, speak to her again to initiate this quest. If you give her three ancient screws, three ancient shafts, and three ancient cores, she will upgrade your Sheikah sensor, remote bomb, and Stasis runes respectively. The materials in question can be obtained by defeating guardians, commonly encountered in shrines and around Hyrule Castle.
VII	SIDE QUEST: SUNSHROOM SENSING (see page 230)	Once you've acquired the Sheikah Sensor+ rune upgrade, speak to Symin. Show him a picture of the sunshroom at the back of the Tech Lab, then find three of these for him. The sunshrooms are really easy to spot in Retsam Forest, just north of the Tech Lab.
VIII	SIDE QUEST: THE HERO'S CACHE (see page 230)	Speak to Kass on the tall rock, in the middle of Kitano Bay. If you interpret his clue ("17 of 24") as a clock position, the riddle means 5 o'clock. Looking at the group of rocks jutting out of the water as a circle, move to the ones in the bottom-right section, where a needle would point to show 5 o'clock. You will find a treasure chest hidden between the rocks.
IX	SIDE QUEST: HYLIAN HOMEOWNER (see page 231)	Speak to Bolson in Hateno Village. He and his men are at work around a house just south of Firly Pond. He will sell you the house in exchange for 3,000 rupees and 30 bundles of wood. You must then invest more rupees for furniture and other upgrades. This is a long-term task, though you can satisfy both initial objectives rather quickly by selling gemstones, and by felling trees with bombs.
X	SIDE QUEST: FROM THE GROUND UP (see page 232)	After you have purchased a house as part of the "Hylian Homeowner" side quest, speak to Bolson and Hudson. Once Hudson has departed for the Akkala region, meet him on the small island in the middle of Lake Akkala. He will require your help to gather more wood and to recruit people for his new village: Tarrey Town.

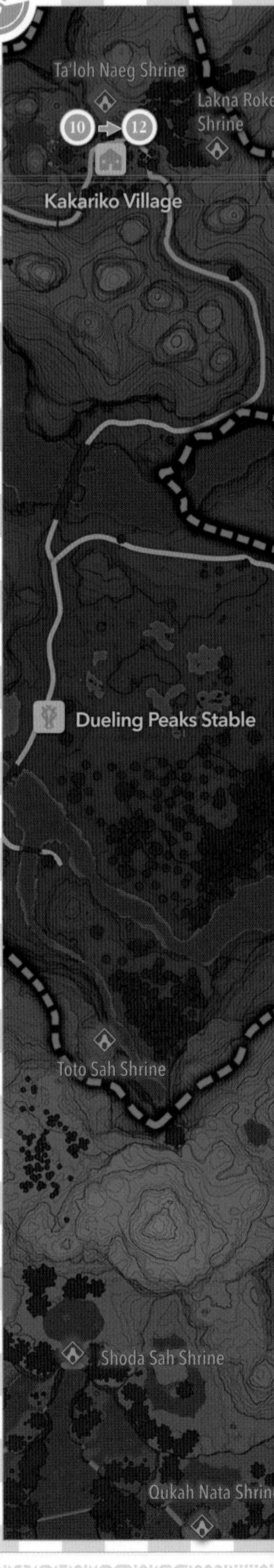

Hateno Tower Region
Dow Na'eh Shrine
Kam Urog Shrine
Jitan Sa'mi Shrine
Tahno O'ah Shrine
8
10
Hateno Village
7
HATENO TOWER
I
II
III
IV
V
VI
VII
Hateno Ancient Tech Lab
Myahm Agana Shrine
IX
X
VIII
Tawa Jinn Shrine
Chaas Qeta Shrine
Faron Tower Region

The Hateno Tower is overrun by brambles. While you can burn it, this is a waste of time and resources: it makes more sense to just carefully navigate the hazards. The southeast face of the tower's base is accessible, so start your ascent from there, stopping at each ledge on the way to refill your stamina bar. You must descend towards a ledge to your left approximately halfway through the climb. When you make it to the top, activate the tower, then glide directly to Hateno Village's entrance.

The Ancient Tech Lab is located at the far end of the village, at the top of a distinctive rock outcrop to the east. There are many points of interest on the way, including a local shrine; feel free to explore the town in search of equipment and side quest opportunities.

Speak to Symin inside the Tech Lab, then to Purah. She will ask you to light the furnace on the Tech Lab's outer wall with a blue flame. To do this, you must retrieve the blue flame from the ancient furnace, located a short distance to the west of your current position. Don't forget to pick up the torch inside the Tech Lab, as this will make your task much easier. Light your torch with the blue flame at the ancient furnace, then head back to the Tech Lab, making sure you light every lantern you encounter on the way. You can use these to retrieve the blue flame if, for example, your torch is destroyed, or should it start raining. Once the Tech Lab's furnace (to the left of the main entrance) is lit up with the blue flame, speak to Purah to activate the Guidance Stone.

Select your newly acquired camera rune and take a photo of Purah, then talk to her again. After the ensuing cutscenes, you will receive a new objective: speaking to Impa. You can fast travel to her almost instantly if you have activated the shrine overlooking Kakariko Village (Ta'loh Naeg Shrine). This completes the **"Locked Mementos"** main quest, and unlocks a new one: **"Captured Memories"**. Your objective here is to travel to one of the places shown in any of the 12 photos stored in your Sheikah slate album.

The easiest captured memory spot to reach is most likely the second from the left in the top row. Fast travel to the Oman Au Shrine on the Great Plateau (the very first shrine you completed, where you acquired Magnesis). From here, jump over the Great Plateau's edge and glide to the north. You will find the interaction point shown on the above screenshot in the woods, close to the lake's west shore. Press Ⓐ to recall the events that occurred at this location. After the cutscene, warp back to Impa at Kakariko Village.

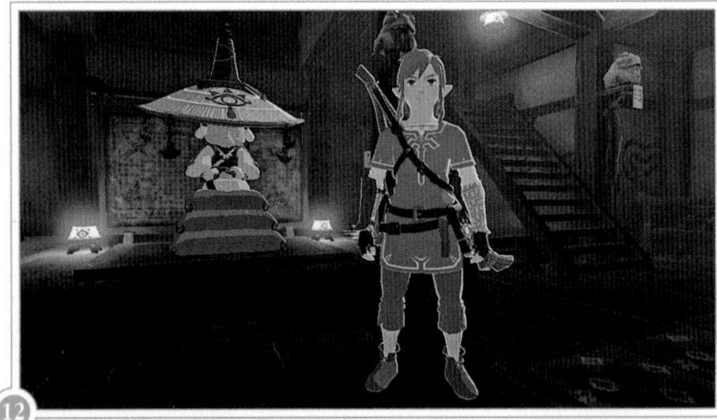

After Impa rewards you with the champion's tunic, a very useful armor piece that reveals enemy health points, speak to her again and ask about the four Divine Beasts. Each of these represents a main quest line that will take you to a specific region of the world and conclude with a difficult dungeon that you must clear. You can complete them in any order that you prefer, with the difficulty of their final bosses scaled to your current progress. In other words, if you complete the Divine Beast Vah Ruta dungeon first, its boss will be set at the easiest difficulty level. Once you defeat him, the other three will become harder to beat. After a second Divine Beast victory, the remaining two will become even more deadly; the last will be faced in its most perilous and pitiless configuration. For this reason, and based on the nature of each of these battles, we suggest that you begin with Divine Beast Vah Ruta (starting overleaf), then proceed in turn to Divine Beast Vah Naboris (see page 68), Divine Beast Vah Medoh (see page 80), and finally, Divine Beast Vah Rudania (see page 92). Our Walkthrough will follow this order, but feel free to proceed otherwise if you prefer; follow the page references listed here to jump to the appropriate sections of the chapter.

PRIMER RECAP (CONTINUED)

As you spend more time in the world of Hyrule, you will gather more and more resources. Soon, you will face situations where you cannot pick up new weapons, bows, or shields, because your inventory is full. This short section will help you to make informed decisions whenever you might need to leave equipment or items behind.

INVENTORY MANAGEMENT (SEE PAGE 22)

- **Durability:** Durability is a hidden attribute that determines how many times you can use a piece of equipment. Every weapon, bow, and shield has such a value. Each use reduces their durability, until the value reaches 0 – at which point, the item will break. This makes durability one of the key factors to take into account when managing equipment. If you have been using a sword for a while, for example, it is likely to break soon. Replacing it with a new one that you find can therefore make sense, even if the new blade has slightly lower stats. When an item is about to break, a message will appear on your screen as you wield it; it will also flash red in your inventory.

- **Special bonuses:** As you make progress in the adventure you will begin to receive equipment with special boons, such as bonuses to durability, damage, critical rates, and so forth. This will happen only occasionally at first, but becomes commonplace later on. These perks, which are represented by a small symbol in the top-left corner of an object's window, can be quite significant. As a general rule, items with a bonus are almost always preferable to those without.

- **Weapons:** There are many types of weapons, each with its own applications. You should ideally have a varied range at your disposal at all times. This is what makes collecting Korok seeds so important, expanding your tactical possibilities.

  - **One-handed weapons** tend to have limited power, but they enable you to hold your shield simultaneously; it's easily the most flexible option. Against enemy types that you are not familiar or comfortable with, these are always a safe bet.

  - **Two-handed weapons**, by contrast, can deal impressive amounts of damage, but are incompatible with shield usage. You must sheathe them before you can draw your shield. They are also slower, and therefore require more expertise to wield with the composed precision that is necessary to make best use of them.

  - **Spears** generally have low attack stats, but they compensate for this with their long reach and high attack rate. You can use them to hit enemies from greater distances, impeding their ability to retaliate. They are also helpful against tall or airborne adversaries. Like two-handed weapons, they must be sheathed before you can draw a shield.

  - **Elemental weapons** are imbued with fire, ice, or electricity. Even if their raw stats are unimpressive, these are often worth holding on to. Fire weapons can set things ablaze and kill ice-imbued enemies instantly. Ice weapons can freeze a target, with the subsequent attack inflicting triple damage. Shock weapons can temporarily stun susceptible opponents.

- **Bows:** There are two main types of bow.

  - **Standard bows** fire a single arrow at a time; they generally boast high damage values.

  - **Multiple-shot bows** have a lower base damage stat, but they shoot multiple arrows simultaneously (x2 means two arrows, x3 means three arrows – each inflicting the stated damage total), while consuming only one arrow. There are many situations where this can prove useful. You can, for example, employ these bows to cause an elemental effect multiple times, or to improve your chances of hitting a target.

- **Arrows:** Arrows are a key part of your arsenal throughout the adventure. You should ideally keep a large stock of them (at least 20) at all times. They are required for the completion of many puzzles in both shrines and dungeons, enabling you to cut ropes or to hit crystals, among other applications. Basic arrows can be farmed in large quantities on the path that runs alongside the Zora River, leading to Zora's Domain. Elemental arrows can be purchased in certain stores, found in treasure chests, and are dropped by specific enemy types.

- **Shields:** Shields are an integral part of your combat loadout. Their durability is such that they rarely break when you block melee attacks. On the other hand, charged laser beams fired by Guardians can destroy a shield instantly. Whenever you attempt to perfect-guard one of these attacks, you run the risk of losing your current shield if you fail, so consider equipping your weakest one in such instances.

- **Armor:** Link's armor determines how well he resists damage. The defense value of each piece of apparel he wears is cumulative, and the total corresponds to his overall defense. The higher Link's armor-induced defense stat is, the less damage he takes from enemy attacks. Armor is primarily available in armor shops found throughout Hyrule. Certain valuable pieces can also be secured in treasure chests hidden in specific shrines. Many outfits provide bonus effects in addition to their defense attribute, such as resistance to an element or increased climbing speed, making them even more precious.

- **Restorative Items:** Though many fruits and vegetables can be consumed raw, the best restorative items are those produced by cooking. Before you undertake any significant challenge, such as exploring a dungeon, you should ensure that you have a wealth of powerful dishes at your disposal, capable of replenishing most, if not all, of your health bar. Food or elixirs that grant special effects such as extra yellow hearts, enhanced movement speed, and increased defense can also prove very useful against bosses.

ZORA QUEST

WALKTHROUGH SUMMARY (SEE OVERLEAF FOR DETAILS)

STEP	DESCRIPTION
1 → 2	Activate the Lanayru Tower.
3 → 5	Trek along the Zora River until you reach Zora's Domain.
6	Speak with King Dorephan and Musu.
7 → 9	Retrieve 20 shock arrows on Ploymus Mountain, then glide to Sidon's position on the pier of East Reservoir Lake and speak to him.
10 → 12	Neutralize the Divine Beast.
13 → 34	Clear the Divine Beast Vah Ruta dungeon.

OPTIONAL CHALLENGES

ICON	ACTIVITY	NOTES
◈	SHRINES & SHRINE QUESTS	You can find step-by-step solutions for all shrines and shrine quests in the Lanayru Tower region on page 130.
I	SIDE QUEST: SPECIAL DELIVERY (see page 236)	After clearing the Divine Beast Vah Ruta dungeon, speak to Finley on the Bank of Wishes, in the valley leading to Zora's Domain. When she throws a letter down the river, follow it until it ends up in a small inlet at Mercay Island. Speak to the man making camp there, Sasan, then return to Zora's Domain where Finley and Sasan await.
II	SIDE QUEST: DIVING IS BEAUTY! (see page 237)	After initiating the Divine Beast Vah Ruta main quest, speak to Gruve near the stairs leading to the throne room in Zora's Domain. Dive from the edge of the platform next to him, then swim back up the waterfall with the aid of the Zora Armor.
III	SIDE QUEST: LYNEL SAFARI (see page 237)	After initiating the Divine Beast Vah Ruta main quest, speak to Laflat, a few steps to the east of the stairs leading to the throne room in Zora's Domain. She needs a picture of the Lynel that roams on Ploymus Mountain. The main quest in this region takes you there, so just take the photo in question on your way to Divine Beast Vah Ruta; you can return to Laflat later.
IV	SIDE QUEST: FROG CATCHING (see page 237)	Speak to Tumbo during the day at Zora's Domain – he's a child that runs around the statue opposite the shrine. He asks you to find five hot-footed frogs for him. During rainy weather, these frogs are usually plentiful near bodies of water such as Ralis Pond or the small pond to the south of Luto's Crossing.
V	SIDE QUEST: THE GIANT OF RALIS POND (see page 238)	After clearing the Divine Beast Vah Ruta dungeon, speak to Torfeau at the plaza underneath the throne room in Zora's Domain. Head to Ralis Pond, to the southwest, and eliminate the Hinox there.
VI	SIDE QUEST: LUMINOUS STONE GATHERING (see page 238)	After clearing the Divine Beast Vah Ruta dungeon, speak to Ledo, who needs 10 luminous stones. You can find multiple ore deposits with these minerals on the plateaus overlooking the northwest bridge of Zora's Domain.
VII	SIDE QUEST: A WIFE WASHED AWAY (see page 239)	After clearing the Divine Beast Vah Ruta dungeon, speak to Fronk. He can be found during the day on a round platform a short way east of the general store in Zora's Domain. You can find his wife at Lake Hylia, in the Lake Tower region, usually on the small islet east of Hylia Island.
VIII	SIDE QUEST: RIVERBED REWARD (see page 239)	Speak to Izra, on the shore of the river right by the Wetland Stable. He needs your help to lift a treasure chest out of the water – which is easily achieved with Magnesis.
IX	SIDE QUEST: ZORA STONE MONUMENTS (see page 240)	After clearing the Divine Beast Vah Ruta dungeon, speak to Jiahto, at the far end of the plaza underneath the throne room in Zora's Domain. He will ask you to search for 10 stone monuments in the surrounding area. You can find a map showing their positions on page 240.

Eldin Tower Region
ELDIN TOWER
...a Raym Shrine
Sah Dahaj Shrine
AKKALA TOWER
Tarrey Town
Mo'a Keet Shrine
Foothill Stable
Dah Hesho Shrine
Akkala Tower Region
Tah Muhl Shrine
IX
VI
II
V
III
Ke'nai Shakah Shrine
Ne'ez Yohma Shrine
7
8
Ploymus Mountain
IV
Dagah Keek Shrine
VII
Zora's Domain
9
Soh Kofi Shrine
6
4
2
3
10
34
I
East Reservoir Lake
LANAYRU TOWER
5
Lanayru Tower Region
Shai Yota Shrine
Mezza Lo Shrine
Rucco Maag Shrine
...a Tuss Shrine
...loh Naeg Shrine
Lakna Rokee Shrine
1
...akariko Village
Hateno Tower Region
Dow Na'eh Shrine
Jitan Sa'mi Shrine
Kam Urog Shrine

1

From Kakariko Village, you are very close to the Lanayru region. Make your way up to the shrine that overlooks the village and then glide to the north, in the direction of an archipelago of small islands (the closest of these featuring a shrine). You can then head to the northeast, in the direction of Lanayru Tower.

2

The easiest way to climb Lanayru Tower is to make your approach from the northwest. Climb up the long ladder leading to the top of the lookout platform, then glide from here to the tower itself. The rest of the ascent is undemanding. Activate the terminal at the top to reveal the map for this region. Once you are ready, glide down to Inogo Bridge, to the east, to trigger a cutscene and meet Sidon. This will trigger a new main quest: **"Reach Zora's Domain"**.

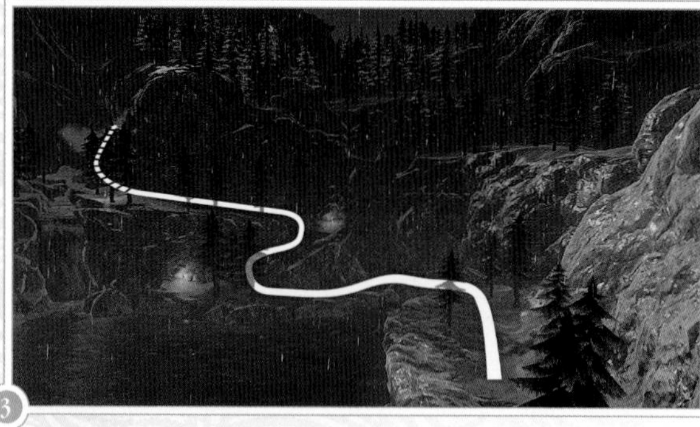

3

The trek along Zora River poses no great challenge, though you will experience occasional encounters with Octoroks. Eliminate these with bombs to spare your arrows. They will often drop octo balloons, a useful item that can simplify certain puzzles; it's a good idea to stockpile them when you can. There are zapshrooms growing at the foot of trees encountered along the way. Be sure to gather plenty of these: they can be cooked to provide protection against electricity.

4

When you reach the Tabahl Woods, be prepared to face multiple Lizalfos archers. These will fire shock arrows at you, so this might be a good time to drink the electro elixir that Sidon gave you at the bridge. Use cover points during your approach and eliminate each creature with quick melee combos. Your priority in this area should be to pick up as many arrows as possible. These will prove handy in a forthcoming challenge.

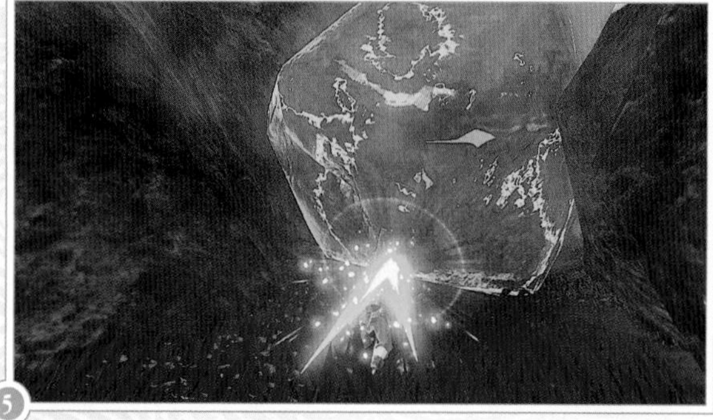

5

After you pass Oren Bridge, you must dodge boulders rolling in your direction, but you have plenty of time and space to do so. Shortly afterwards, a large boulder will block your path. You can either climb it, or cast Stasis on it and strike it multiple times, then sprint through before it rolls back down. A battle against multiple Lizalfos awaits on the other side. Lure them to your position in small groups if you can, or try to open hostilities with a sneakstrike. The rest of the journey to Zora's Domain is entirely straightforward.

6

When you reach the village, activate the local shrine, then visit King Dorephan in the throne room on the top floor. This completes the **"Reach Zora's Domain"** main quest, and triggers **"The Divine Beast Vah Ruta."** Your first objective in this mission is to speak to Muzu at the plaza just in front of the local shrine. After your first conversation with him, equip the Zora Armor received from the king and speak to Muzu again.

7

Your next goal is to retrieve 20 shock arrows on Ploymus Mountain. You can reach this area via the east exit of Zora's Domain. With the Zora Armor equipped, swim up the waterfalls by pressing Ⓐ until you make it to the top of the mountain. Run up the slope leading to the summit, collecting any shock arrows embedded in trees along the way.

8

On the plateau there are many more shock arrows. Try to grab as many as you can. You need 20 to move on to the next step of the quest, but any extra arrows will be more than welcome. The challenge here is that a fearsome Lynel roams the area. This enemy can be defeated, though doing so requires advanced equipment and skills (see page 320). Unless you are a true master of the perfect guard move, and in possession of powerful weapons, this is probably a fight you should leave for later. The Lynel has above-average detection capabilities, so stay out of sight and crouch-walk whenever required. Naturally, any stealth bonus you can trigger here will help. Don't forget to take a picture of it if you are working to complete the related side quest.

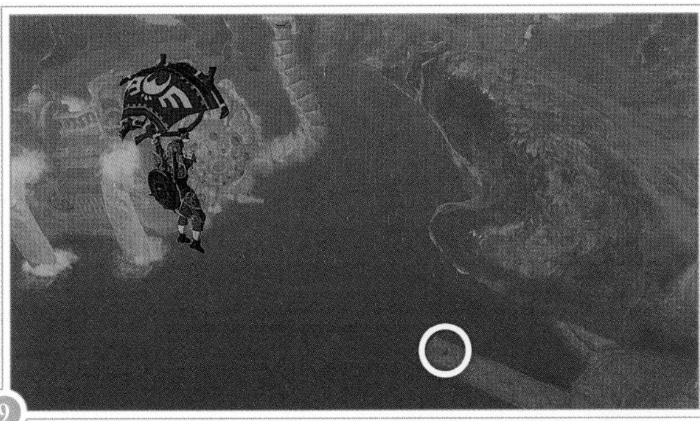

9

Once you're ready to proceed, head to the mountain's peak to the southwest: Shatterback Point. You can glide from here directly to Sidon's position on the pier at East Reservoir Lake. Speak to him and agree to begin your assault against the Divine Beast.

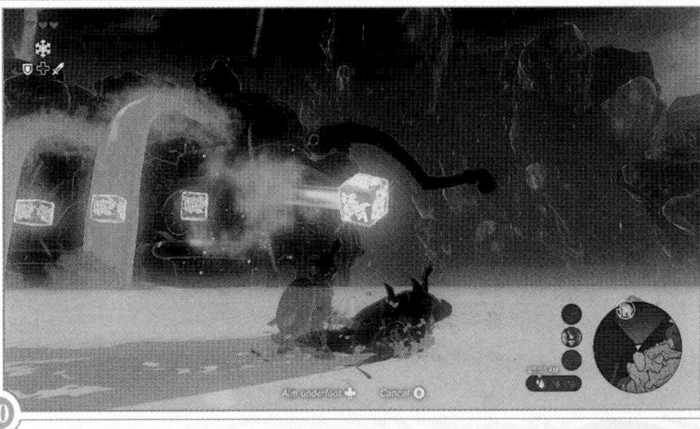

10

As you ride on Sidon's back, the Divine Beast will regularly hurl ice blocks in your direction. The best way to destroy these is with Cryonis. Activate this rune and look in the direction of the incoming projectiles; whenever you have one in your reticle, press Ⓐ to shatter it. If you struggle, a less-than-polished approach of pressing the button repeatedly while moving the camera can suffice.

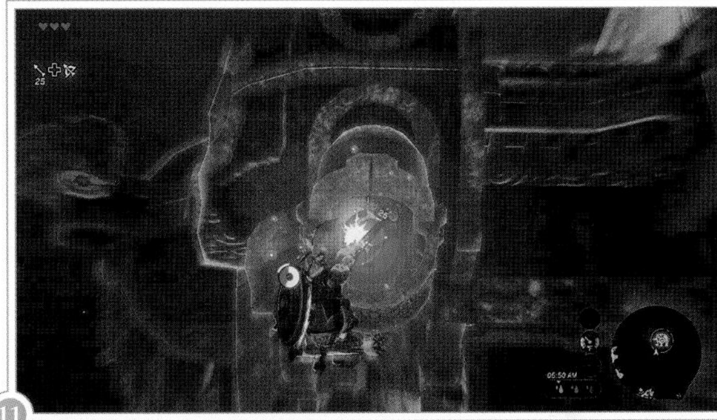

11

Every time you survive an ice block barrage, Sidon will take you to the monster. Press Ⓐ while passing close to a waterfall: this will enable you to swim upward and be propelled high in the air. At the peak of your flight, aim a shock arrow at one of the pink-glowing devices on Vah Ruta's back. If you're quick, you can hit two consecutively, but this is not easy. If in doubt, take them out one at a time.

12

There are four devices to hit in total. Every time you hit one with a shock arrow, a new loop will begin: you destroy the ice blocks thrown at you, swim up a waterfall, and shoot a glowing device. The sequences where you need to shatter ice projectiles become increasingly difficult, though. Each further series consists of more and more projectiles, and spiked ice boulders will be added to the mix. These behave differently: they are partly submerged during their approach, leaving less for your Cryonis reticle to aim at. Take your time and do not panic, tracking each one methodically and aiming just above the water's surface. After a few waves, you should get the knack of this maneuver. Once all four devices have been hit by a shock arrow, the sequence will end and you can finally enter the **"Divine Beast Vah Ruta"** dungeon.

This dungeon will become available as a fast travel position from the moment you reach it. This means that you can warp in and out of it at your leisure, which is useful if you lack a vital item or simply need to restock. Important resources to bring along in large quantities include dishes with healing properties, powerful weapons (with an attack value of at least 15), and arrows (ideally 30 or more). When you feel sufficiently prepared, fire an arrow at the glowing eyeball at the top of the ramp in front of you: this will remove the Malice goo that blocks the entrance. Some of these goo structures include a "mouth" that regularly releases flying skull enemies. Destroying the eyeball will rid you of the "mouth" as well. It therefore makes sense to eliminate these eyeballs as a matter of priority every time you encounter one.

FIRST TREASURE CHEST & MAP TERMINAL: There is a second eyeball waiting for you in the main room, just below the surface of the water. Move close to it, in the room's corner, and hit it with an arrow. This will free the nearby gate of Malice goo, enabling you to lift it with Cryonis. After you summon a block of ice beneath the gate, head through and activate the terminal to receive the dungeon's map. Note that you can find a first chest submerged in the water: grab it with Magnesis to retrieve its contents.

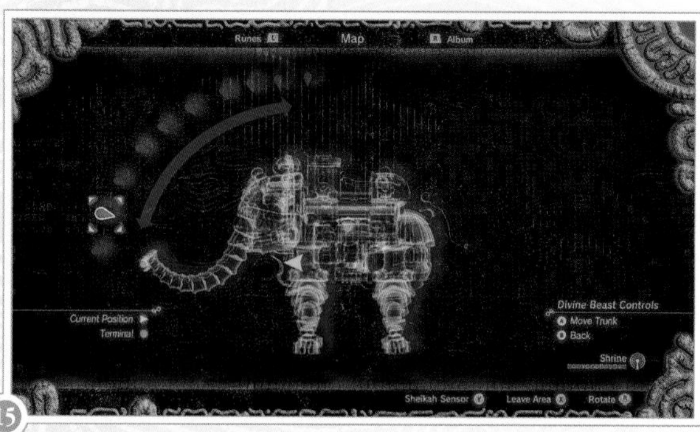

CONTROLLING DIVINE BEASTS: The Divine Beast's map is three-dimensional: you can rotate it as you please with Ⓡ. Your goal is to examine the dungeon's five terminals, represented by glowing orange dots (●). To do so, you must exploit one of the Divine Beasts' key features: they are articulated machines that you can partly control. In the case of Vah Ruta, you may freely move the elephant's trunk. The increments by which you can change the trunk's angle are represented with purple icons (●). Select one with Ⓛ and Ⓐ, then execute the command with Ⓑ. This is an important point that is easily overlooked: *it's only by pressing Ⓑ that you will make the trunk actually move.* It will then take a few seconds for the Divine Beast to react accordingly. This concept applies to all dungeons.

FIRST TERMINAL: Return to the first room you visited (where you eliminated the two eyeballs) and grab the cogwheel's handle with Magnesis. Rotate it clockwise until the terminal is fully out of the water. You can then walk over and activate it.

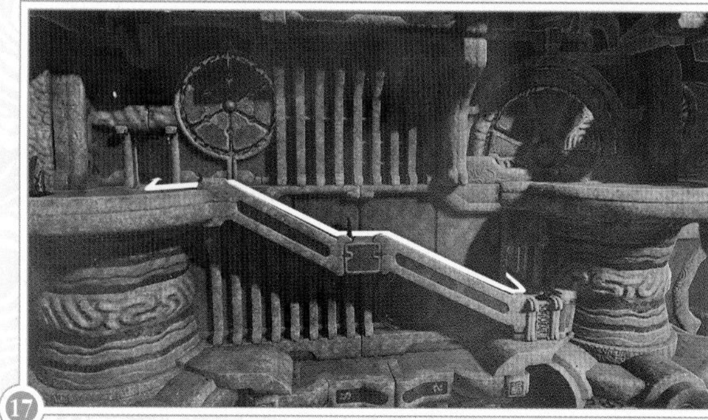

Go through the gate opposite the dungeon's entrance and run up the ramp. When you reach the top, take a right and defeat the Guardian Scout in the room with the watermill.

SECOND TERMINAL: If you look inside the rotating watermill, you will notice that it features a terminal. However, you cannot reach it because of the pool at the watermill's base. Wait until the terminal is close to the bottom of the wheel, then use Cryonis to summon a block of ice that will obstruct the flow of water from the fountain. This will stop the watermill and drain the pool, enabling you to access the terminal.

19

SECOND TREASURE CHEST: Free the flow of water from the fountain to make the wheel spin again. Step on one of the cogwheel's teeth, making sure that it and the tooth in front are free of Malice goo. When you are at the uppermost point of the cogwheel's rotation, glide to the top of the wall on which the fountain is built. This will give you access to a second treasure chest.

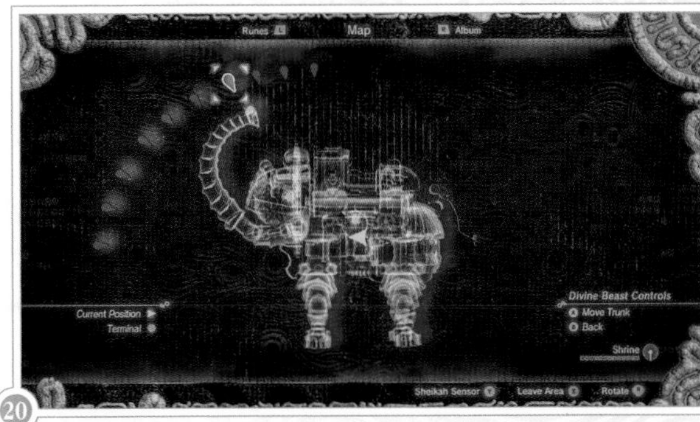

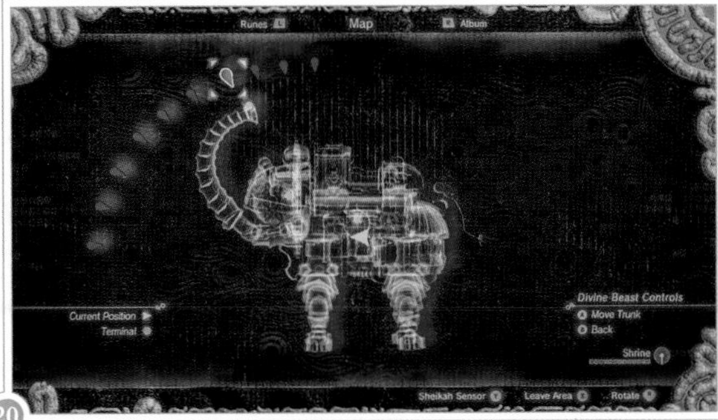

20

Move the Divine Beast's trunk to its fourth increment from the top. This will cause the water flowing from the trunk to make the second, larger watermill spin.

21

THIRD TREASURE CHEST: Standing between the two watermills, look in the direction of the larger one. When you notice a tooth with a treasure chest pass in front of you, hop on the next tooth and move forward until you are not pulled down by gravity anymore. Fire an arrow at the eyeball to remove the Malice goo and you can subsequently access the third treasure chest. Once the wheel's rotation has taken you to the platform on the other side, hop to it. Eliminate the Guardian Scout, then step on the nearby floor switch. This will create a waterfall that you can now use to swim back to the upper floor with the Zora Armor.

22

From the floor switch, glide to the walkway connected to the large watermill, and then look toward the watermill.

23

THIRD TERMINAL: This terminal lies behind a barred gate. The gate is temporarily unlocked when the nearby orb moves into the concave slot. You can extend this time window by casting Stasis on the orb just before it slides downwards – in other words, when it is to your left. This will enable you to wait for the terminal to pass right in front of you, with the gate still raised. Examine it and the gate will remain permanently open thereafter.

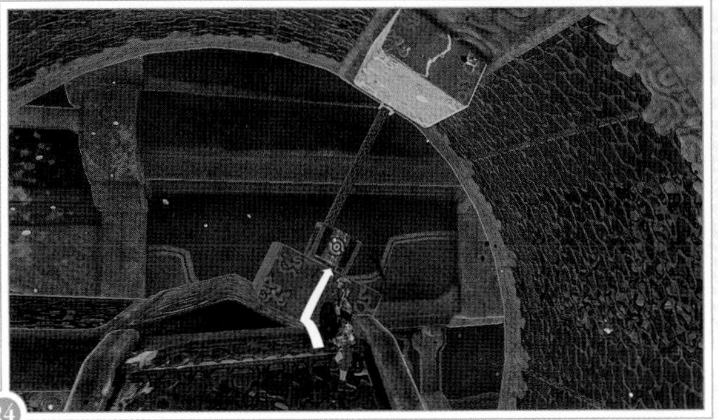

24

FOURTH TREASURE CHEST: Remain on the same walkway and observe the treasure chest that is sandwiched between two concrete blocks. The blocks will move along their slider under the effect of gravity. If you stop the farther of the two just in time as they are aligned horizontally to your right, only the other block will slide down, leaving you free to jump on it and retrieve the contents of the chest before Stasis ends.

Glide down to the pool on the bottom floor, then swim upward to return to the top of the waterfall. Head inside the corridor beyond it.

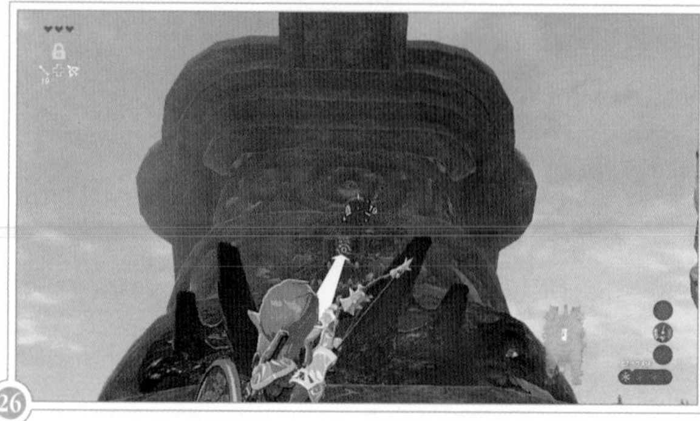

FIFTH TREASURE CHEST: At the end of the corridor, open the map menu and lower the Divine Beast's trunk to its lowest position. This will enable you to walk on the trunk itself. Shoot an arrow at the eyeball to remove the Malice goo and open the treasure chest. Now raise the trunk again and, once it is high enough, glide to return to the corridor from which you arrived.

Still in the corridor, move the trunk to its lowest position. Once it stops moving, glide to the small platform on the tip of the trunk.

FOURTH TERMINAL: From your position at the tip of the trunk, open the map menu and move the trunk again, this time to the fourth increment from the top. During the command's execution, readjust Link's position so as to remain at the top of the structure. When the trunk stops, you will end up in front of the fourth terminal. Examine it.

SIXTH TREASURE CHEST: From the fourth terminal, glide to the platform on your left, which features a treasure chest covered with Malice goo. Stand in the top-right corner of that platform, and aim an arrow at the eyeball on the opposite platform. Hitting it will remove the goo.

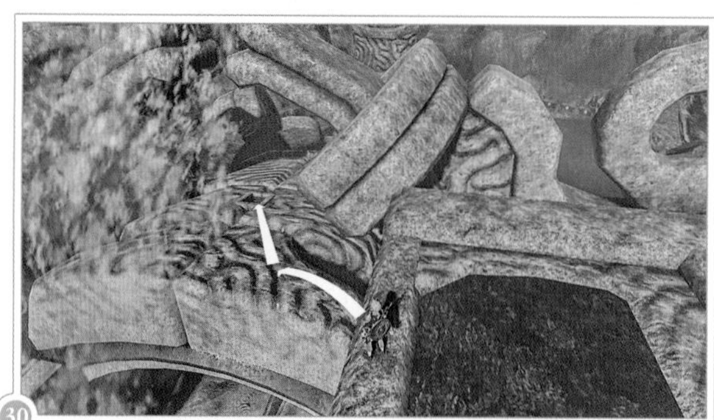

You can now glide to the nearby central platform – the top of the Divine Beast's head. Drop down through the small hole in the middle.

31

When you land on a semi-circular ledge, immediately eliminate the eyeball on the ceiling with an arrow. Once the Malice goo has disappeared, grab the nearby handle with Magnesis and rotate it clockwise until the hatch in the ceiling is completely open.

32

FIFTH TERMINAL: Open your map menu and move the trunk to the fifth increment from the top. This will cause the flow of water to extinguish the flames around the terminal directly below. Drop down and examine it.

33

SEVENTH TREASURE CHEST: From the fifth terminal, drop down to the ledge directly below to find this dungeon's final treasure chest.

34

MAIN CONTROL UNIT: The final step to clear this dungeon is to glide down back to the entrance. The main control unit is found in the only room that you haven't explored yet, opposite the waterfall. Interacting with it will trigger a boss battle, so make sure you are fully prepared before proceeding. Having a large stock of arrows and a selection of powerful weapons will definitely help here.

BOSS: WATERBLIGHT GANON

The fight against Waterblight Ganon has two distinct phases. The second begins when your opponent's health drops below 50%.

FIRST PHASE

Waterblight Ganon performs melee attacks with its spear. The size of this weapon is such that it can reach you over surprisingly long distances, so be ready to dodge or perfect-guard at all times.

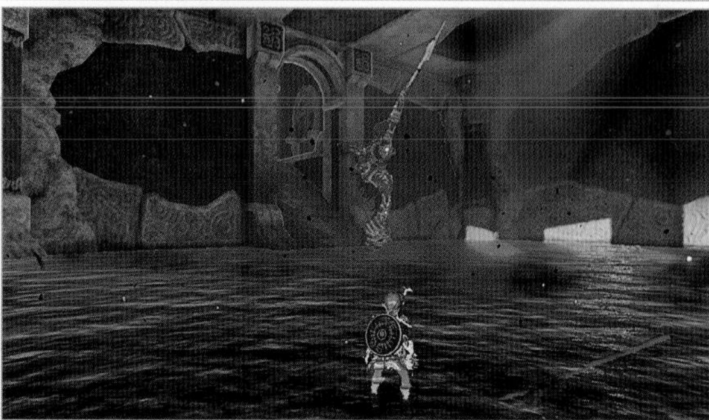

When you stand very far from Waterblight Ganon, it will often throw its spear at you. This is foreshadowed when the creature pulls its arm backward, as illustrated here. The best way to avoid the attack is with a side hop or by sprinting perpendicularly to the incoming projectile.

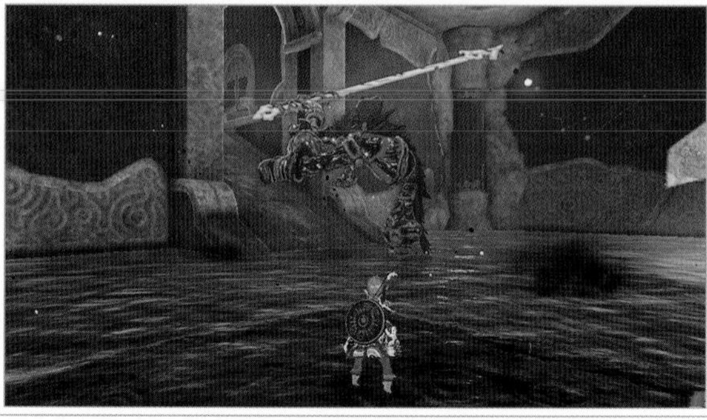

Over medium distances, Waterblight Ganon will often launch a sweeping attack – which you can identify when you see its arm moving far to the side. The best counter against this is to perfect-dodge the blow: execute a backflip a fraction of a second before the blade hits you. This will give you an opportunity to unleash a flurry rush. A spear-type weapon can prove very efficient here.

When you are within melee range, Waterblight Ganon will also regularly perform a thrust attack. Whenever you see the monster move its arm to its hip, be ready to side hop, ideally within perfect dodge timing requirements so as to follow up with a flurry rush.

At very close range, Waterblight Ganon will often plant its spear in the ground, causing a blue shockwave that is very hard to avoid. Sprinting away is the best course of action here.

After dealing significant amounts of damage, you will occasionally cause your foe to collapse. Use these opportunities to rush to it and unleash combos with your most powerful weapons.

SECOND PHASE

Once Waterblight Ganon's health reaches the 50% threshold, it will change strategy and switch to ranged attacks. The combat arena itself is modified, consisting of four square platforms surrounded by water.

Waterblight Ganon usually starts the second phase by hurling an ice block in your direction. Have your Cryonis rune at the ready: this will enable you to shatter the projectile before it reaches you.

The most obvious way to deal damage to this boss is with arrows. Aim at Waterblight Ganon's blue eye to reduce its health more rapidly. If you run out of ammo, throwing remote bombs is also a possibility, though they are less powerful and have a more limited range.

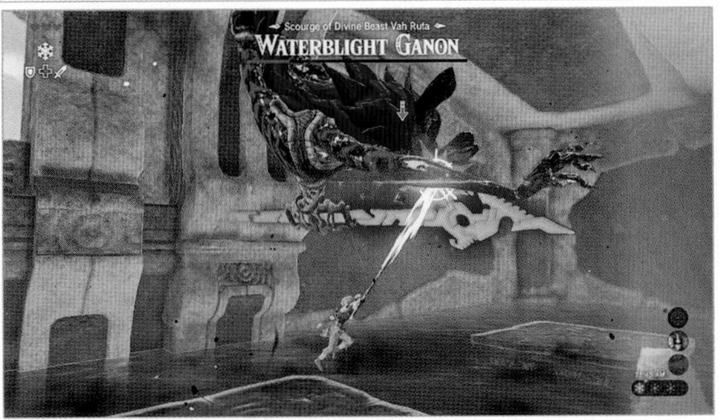

Alternatively, you can also try to swim to the monster's position and assail it with physical attacks. Swimming is a slow process, though, and the small size of the platforms means that this is not always a practical solution. This strategy works better with weapons with reach, such as spears; short blades will often fail to hit home. Overall, though, arrows are a much more reliable option for this battle.

Whenever Waterblight Ganon warps to another platform the loop is repeated, with one caveat: the lower its health, the more ice blocks it will throw at you. If you have Cryonis ready and sweep the screen with your reticle, destroying all projectiles should pose no particular problem. If you do struggle, consider diving in the water and seeking shelter behind a platform.

From time to time, Waterblight Ganon will target you with a red laser beam, just like Guardians. After a charging process, the beam soon reaches full power and is fired at you. The only efficient counter to this is to perfect-guard the beam precisely as it is about to hit you; this will deflect it back to the boss, causing significant damage and temporarily incapacitating your foe. As you are inevitably close to your enemy here, there's very little time to react. You must execute the parry command right as the beam of energy is about to be unleashed, as illustrated in the accompanying picture.

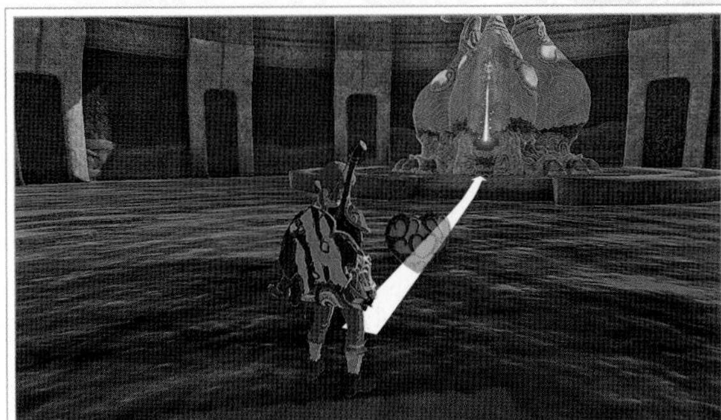

When Waterblight Ganon finally falls, be sure to collect the heart container. You should note that this is your last chance to open any treasure chests you may have missed in the dungeon, as you will not be able to return after you leave. Once outside, you will recieve Mipha's Grace ( ), a restorative power that resurrects Link with full health plus five temporary bonus hearts when he sustains critical damage. You should note, though, that every activation is followed by a long cooldown. Last but not least, you can collect a Lightscale Trident from the nearby chest after a final conversation with King Dorephan in the throne room. Once you have your rewards, you will be ready for the next major quest line. This takes place in the Gerudo Desert, situated in the southwest corner of Hyrule.

GERUDO QUEST

WALKTHROUGH SUMMARY (SEE OVERLEAF FOR DETAILS)

STEP	DESCRIPTION
1 → 8	Find a way to enter Gerudo Town and speak to Riju, the chief of the Gerudo.
9 → 23	Retrieve the Thunder Helm from the Yiga Clan Hideout and return it to Riju.
24 → 26	Make your way inside Divine Beast Vah Naboris.
27 → 57	Clear the Divine Beast Vah Naboris dungeon.

OPTIONAL CHALLENGES

ICON	ACTIVITY	NOTES
	SHRINES & SHRINE QUESTS	You can find step-by-step solutions for all shrines and shrine quests in the Wasteland Tower region on page 150.
I	SIDE QUEST: WANTED: GOOD-SIZED HORSE (see page 250)	Speak to Zyle in the Gerudo Canyon, northeast of the Wasteland Tower. If you have a spare registered horse, summon it from the Gerudo Canyon Stable and take it to Zyle.
II	SIDE QUEST: RUSHROOM RUSH! (see page 250)	Speak to Pirou at the Gerudo Canyon Stable. He requires 55 rushrooms, the purple fungi that grow on cliffs.
III	SIDE QUEST: MISSING IN ACTION (see page 250)	Speak to Sesami at the Gerudo Canyon Stable. He asks you to find four of his friends in the Koukot Plateau area. You can find them all on the elevated wooden walkways built on the cliffs of the canyon to the north of Koukot Plateau (north of the Wasteland Tower).
IV	SIDE QUEST: AN ICE GUY (see page 251)	Speak to Guy at Kara Kara Bazaar. He needs a chilly elixir, which you can cook by combining a winterwing butterfly and a monster part. These insects are common in the Gerudo Canyon and on the high plateaus surrounding the Wasteland Tower.
V	SIDE QUEST: TOOLS OF THE TRADE (see page 251)	Speak to Isha in Gerudo Town, outside the jewelry shop. She requires 10 pieces of flint to reopen her shop. You can acquire this resource by destroying ore deposits in mountainous regions.
VI	SIDE QUEST: MEDICINAL MOLDUGA (see page 252)	Speak to Malena in the west part of Gerudo Town. She requires Molduga guts, which you can obtain by defeating a Molduga. The one closest to your position roams in the Toruma Dunes, to the west of Gerudo Town.
VII	SIDE QUEST: THE EIGHTH HEROINE (see page 252)	Once you have bought the Gerudo outfit from Vilia during the main quest, equip it and speak to Bozai, a man who jogs around Gerudo Town during the day. If you ask for his boots, he will eventually trigger the quest. The statue he refers to can be found to the northwest of the Gerudo Summit, in the Gerudo Highlands. Stand on the statue's joined hands to photograph its torso, then show the picture to Bozai.
VIII	SIDE QUEST: THE FORGOTTEN SWORD (see page 252)	After completing "The Eighth Heroine," equip the Gerudo outfit and speak to Bozai again – he now waits under a canopy close to Gerudo Town's main entrance. This time he needs you to photograph the missing sword from the statue featured in his previous quest. The blade can be found at the top of the Gerudo Summit, at the heart of the Gerudo Highlands.
IX	SIDE QUEST: THE SECRET CLUB'S SECRET (see page 251)	If you examine the back door of Gerudo Town's armor shop, to the southeast of the premises, you will be asked for a password. You can learn this from the women in the bar in the north part of town. Head to the adjacent building and eavesdrop on them through the window. Return to the secret door with the password to open it.
X	GREAT FAIRY FOUNTAIN (see page 326)	A second Great Fairy Fountain lies to the southwest of Gerudo Town. Assuming you have freed the previous great fairy at Kakariko Village, you must offer 500 rupees to unlock her services.
XI	SIDE QUEST: THE THUNDER HELM (see page 253)	After clearing the Divine Beast Vah Naboris dungeon, interact with the Thunder Helm next to Riju inside her mansion. She will agree to give it to you once you have completed all other side quests in Gerudo Town.
XII	SIDE QUEST: THE MYSTERY POLLUTER (see page 253)	After clearing the Divine Beast Vah Naboris dungeon and starting the quest called "The Thunder Helm," speak to Dalia in the north corner of Gerudo Town. She will ask you to investigate the pollution of her water source. Head to the town's west corner and take to the rooftops. Talk to Calyban, a woman eating hydromelons. She will stop polluting the water if you give her 10 wildberries. The plateau directly north of the Gerudo Tower features a few trees; you will find sufficient wildberries at this location alone.
XIII	SIDE QUEST: THE SEARCH FOR BARTA (see page 253)	After clearing the Divine Beast Vah Naboris dungeon and beginning "The Thunder Helm," speak to Liana, the trainer in the courtyard in the west corner of Gerudo Town. Head to the Gerudo Great Skeleton, in the far southwest of the region, and you will find Barta under the fossil's head. Give her a hearty durian (which you can purchase from the fruit store in Gerudo Town) to save her, then return to Liana.

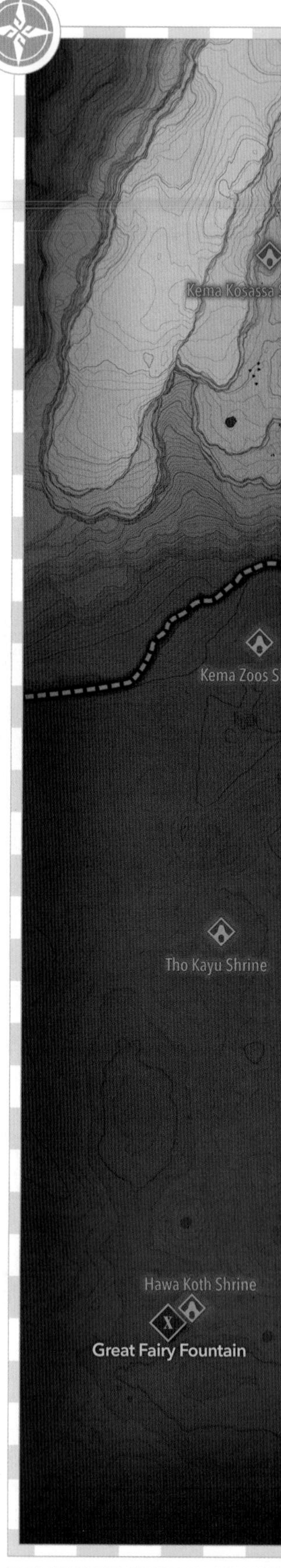

THE LEGEND OF
ZELDA
BREATH OF THE WILD

Mogg Latan Shrine
Keeha Yoog Shrine
Kuh Takkar Shrine
Outskirt Stable
Rota Ooh Shrine
Yiga Clan Hideout
GERUDO TOWER REGION
Sho Dantu Shrine
GERUDO TOWER
Dah Kaso Shrine
Joloo Nah Shrine
Keh Namut Shrine
Sasa Kai Shrine
Gerudo Canyon Stable
Dako Tah Shrine
Kay Noh Shrine
Kara Kara Bazaar
WASTELAND TOWER
Jee Noh Shrine
Dago Chisay Shrine
Korsh O'hu Shrine
Gerudo Town
Raqa Zunzo Shrine
Suma Sahma Shrine
Dila Maag Shrine
Misae Suma Shrine
WASTELAND TOWER REGION

1

The fastest way to begin your journey to the Gerudo Desert is to warp to the Keh Namut Shrine, at the western edge of the Great Plateau. Glide to the southwest (with the Jee Noh Shrine directly on your way), then head through the Gerudo Canyon. The path is entirely linear, with only occasional enemy encounters. Try to collect multiple winterwing butterflies and cold darners as you progress in the canyon: their heat resistance property when cooked will come in handy very soon.

2

Make a stop at the Gerudo Canyon Stable to assess your resources. The desert you are about to explore features extreme heat during the day and deadly cold at night. You should definitely have armor with cold resistance by this point, such as the warm doublet; if not, purchase suitable garb from the Hateno armor shop, or use the spicy peppers that grow behind the stable to cook appropriate dishes. Heat resistance is another matter entirely. You cannot count on suitable gear at this stage, so elixirs are your best choice. Cook any cold darners and winterwing butterflies that you collected along the way with monster parts: this will create chilly elixirs that provide heat resistance. Craft several of these before you depart. Other ingredients that will enable you to stay cool include chillshrooms and hydromelons.

3

From the Gerudo Canyon Stable, climb the cliff to the south until you reach the top of the scaffolding. From here, use the wooden ladders and bridges to make your way toward the Wasteland Tower, clearly visible in the distance.

4

The Wasteland Tower is surrounded by a bog. If you should fall in, you will be instantly taken back to your previous spot on dry land with one fewer heart. Gliding to reach the tower is not an option as strong winds seem to perpetually blow against you. The best solution, then, is to summon blocks of ice with Cryonis to make your way to the tower. Climb to the top and activate the terminal to reveal the regional map.

5

From the top of the Wasteland Tower, you have a clear view of your objectives in the distance: Kara Kara Bazaar to the west, and Gerudo Town beyond. Glide in their general direction. The length of your stamina wheel will determine how far you can go, and therefore how much of the journey you must complete on foot. Note that winterwing butterflies can often be found on the plateaus close to the tower. If you don't have any yet, make sure you collect a few to be able to cook chilly elixirs by combining these insects with monster parts.

6

You cannot enter Gerudo Town for now as only women are accepted. However, if you speak to Benja, between the city gate and the shrine, he will tell you about a man at Kara Kara Bazaar who found a solution to this problem. This will trigger the **"Forbidden City Entry"** main quest.

7

Head back to Kara Kara Bazaar and climb to the top of the rock peak above the inn. Speak to Vilia and tell her she's "very beautiful." She will then propose that you buy her clothes for 600 rupees. If you're short on funds, consider selling gems to any of the local vendors. This step is essential to advance the storyline.

8

Next, head back to Gerudo Town. Wearing the complete set of Gerudo clothes, you can enter the city without drawing any attention. This completes the **"Forbidden City Entry"** main quest. Make your way to the main building at the opposite end of the town and speak to Riju to trigger the **"Divine Beast Vah Naboris"** quest. Next, visit the courtyard in the town's west corner to speak to Teake.

9

Your new objective is to infiltrate the Yiga Clan Hideout, at the end of the Karusa Valley to the north of Gerudo Town. The most efficient way to complete the journey is to rent a sand seal for 20 rupees from the town's northwest gate. Sand seal controls are very similar to those for horses: you steer with Ⓛ and dash with Ⓐ. Once mounted, it's time to venture deep into the Karusa Valley.

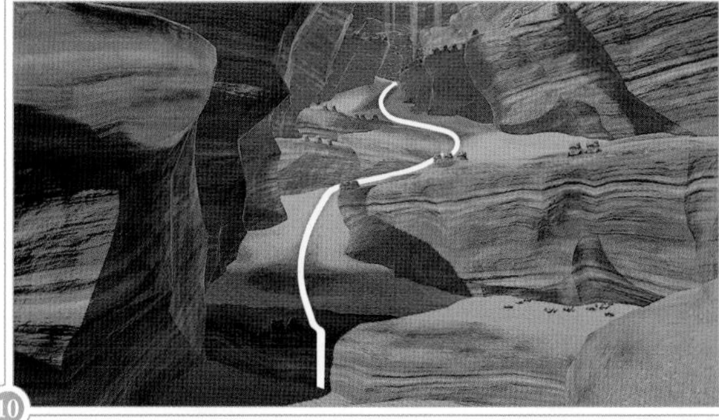

10

When you reach this cliff, your sand seal cannot proceed any further. Climb up, then go the rest of the way on foot. You will likely encounter your first enemy from the Yiga clan outside the hideout's entrance. Yiga Footsoldiers are relatively simple to defeat, either with arrows at long range or standard attacks up close. Their signature move is to disappear and reappear anywhere, though their laughs tend to clearly telegraph their approximate position. Consider a brief detour to the south to unlock the Sho Dantu Shrine before you proceed: this will create a handy fast travel position for future use.

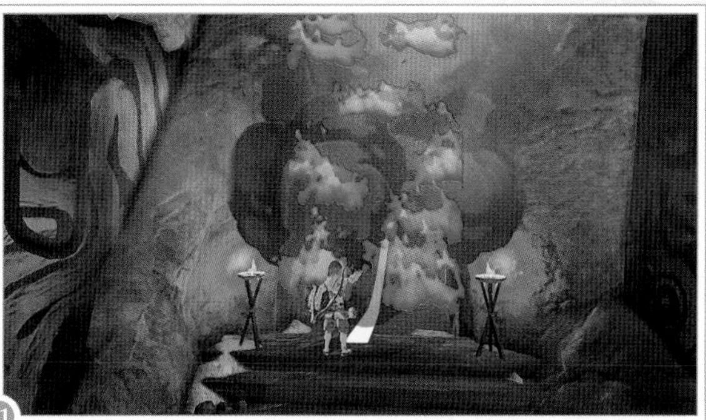

11

Once inside the large, round room, pick up a torch and light it using any of the nearby braziers. Now move to the top of each flight of stairs and set the wall hangings ablaze. This will reveal small hidden rooms, some containing weak Keese monsters, others featuring a treasure chest. One of them (at one o' clock relative to the entrance) is a secret passage leading to the Yiga Clan Hideout.

12

Stealth is highly recommended inside the Yiga Clan Hideout. If this is not your strong suit, we suggest that you take the most direct path and avoid taking risks with treasure chests (there will be an opportunity to return and open these without the complexity of potential combatants a little later). With a very well-developed Link it is possible to defeat the Yiga Blademasters that appear when you are spotted, but this is unlikely to be the case for you at the present stage. Favor infiltration tactics instead, starting with the first Blademaster that you encounter. Don't neglect to pick up the mighty bananas close to the cell, as these will prove useful for distractions. Wait until he disappears behind the passage to your left, then glide forward and walk down to the steps.

13

In the next room, hide behind the large block. Your task here is to go through the gate incognito. It is possible to crouch-walk along the left-hand wall and pass right by the Blademaster standing at the gate, especially if you have stealth bonuses you can secure through food or armor. Alternatively, you can draw the guard away from his position, either by briefly showing yourself (once a question mark appears above his head, be quick to get back behind cover), or by throwing a mighty banana into his line of sight (press ✚ to toss the fruit farther). As soon as he leaves his post, go around the block and walk through the gate.

APPROACH A

14

There are two completely different approaches to clearing the next main room, though both involve reaching the walkways overlooking the room. The first option (Approach A) is to climb the ladder at the end of the corridor. At the top, follow the walkway and you will find a large pile of mighty bananas and a treasure chest. You can now backtrack to the opening in the wall, just before the top of the ladder.

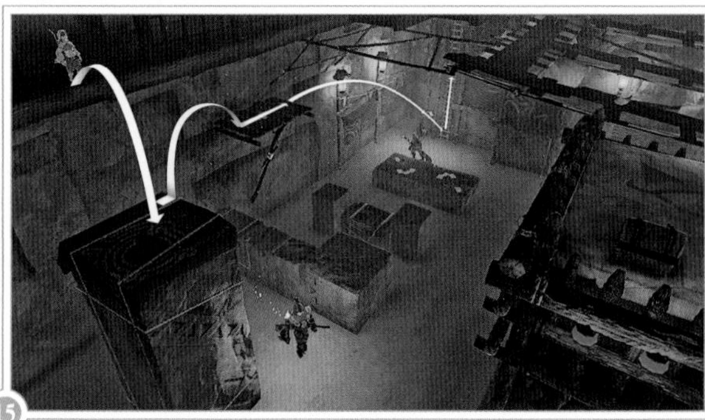

15

From the opening in the wall, drop down to the pillar just beneath your current position. The Blademasters on the ground floor cannot spot you here. Your objective is to reach the ladder in the nearby corner. To do so, sprint and jump to the wooden ledge against the wall. When the guard passes below your position, quickly glide to the ladder and you should remain completely unnoticed. Climb up to the walkways at the top.

APPROACH B

14

The second option for reaching the walkways overlooking the area is to enter the room from the ground floor, through the opening to your right as you come from the previous room. Hide behind the small pillars and look at the beige wall coverings on your right emblazoned with the Yiga Clan inverted eye emblem. If you shoot a fire arrow at the middle one, you will reveal a secret passage.

15

Observe the patrol route of the nearby Blademaster. When he turns his back on you, quietly walk into the secret passage. You will find two treasure chests inside, as well as a narrow opening leading to a ladder. Climb to the top of this to reach the upper walkways.

16

From the top of the ladder, move along the wall until you stand above the Blademaster guarding the exit. Throw a mighty banana so that it falls to the ground floor, in the Blademaster's field of vision. This will temporarily draw him away. Use this opportunity to drop down behind him and swiftly pass through the doorway. If you're interested, there are two chests that you can open before you drop down: one at the top of the room's central structure, and one in the alcove above the doorway.

17

In the final room, open the treasure chests (you will need to lift the ones partly buried in the ground with Magnesis). When you're ready, pull the metal wall slab with Magnesis to make it rotate. This will lead to a large arena where a boss battle will take place. Make sure you have a bow at the ready.

BOSS: MASTER KOHGA

18

Your opponent cannot be attacked at melee range unless you first stun him. From a distance, he will summon large boulders and throw them at you. These cannot be stopped, so just sprint sideways to dodge them. The most effective strategy is to hit Master Kohga with an arrow or a bomb while he is preparing his next assault, with a boulder held aloft. This will cause the boulder to fall on him, resulting in very significant damage. While you can run over and assail him with melee combos before he recovers, physical attacks actually inflict fairly negligible damage. You will, in essence, be wasting weapon durability for very little benefit.

19

After you remove one third of his health, Master Kohga will employ a new attack: he warps above the hole in the center of the arena and summons two boulders that rotate around him for a while, before he hurls them in your direction. Align an arrow shot and let fly at the precise moment when one of the boulders passes above his head. This will lead to the same result as in the previous phase.

20

Once he has lost two thirds of his health, your opponent will enter his final phase. This time, he will summon a spiked metallic boulder and try to hit you with it. Naturally, the solution is to reply in kind: grab the boulder with Magnesis, position it above your enemy's head, then drop it.

21

When Master Kohga falls, a treasure chest will appear. Open this to obtain the Thunder Helm, which you need to take back to Riju in Gerudo Town. Note that the entire hideout is now empty, so feel free to revisit prior areas to plunder any treasure chests that you may have left along the way. Warp to the shrine next to Gerudo Town's entrance once you're ready to continue.

22

Head to Riju's mansion. The chief of the Gerudo isn't in the throne room, but instead on the floor above. Climb the stairs and return the Thunder Helm.

23

You must now meet Riju at the lookout post, to the southeast of Gerudo Town. Taking a sand seal is the quickest way to reach your destination. You can either rent one, or grab a wild specimen outside the city's northeast gate. Climb the ladder to reach the top of the lookout platform where Riju awaits. She will give you 20 bomb arrows, which you will need to subdue the Divine Beast.

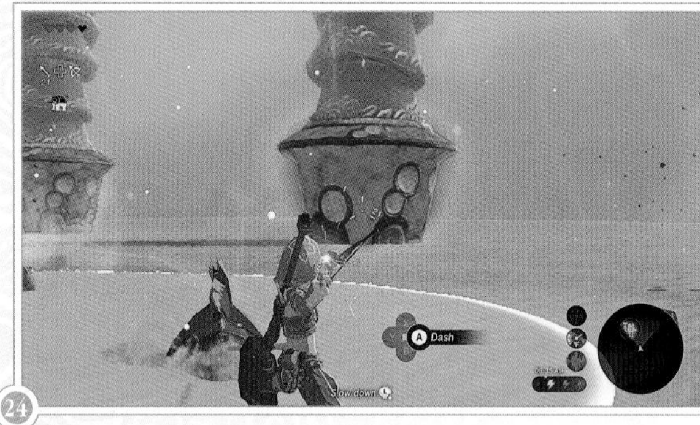

24

During the sand seal surfing sequence, your objective is to take down each of the Divine Beast's four hooves with bomb arrows. Be sure to move fairly close to them before you shoot to avoid wasting your precious ammo. Pressing Ⓐ to dash will help you to get within range. Each glowing hoof has an individual health bar. Whenever you fully deplete a gauge, the glow will disappear and you can move on to the next hoof until all four have been dealt with.

25

Throughout the sand seal surfing approach, the Divine Beast will regularly target you with lightning bolts. Whenever you notice a reticle on Link's body, be sure to remain inside the perimeter of your ally's protective aura. Once the bolt has struck, you will be safe to move out to aim your shots until the next lightning strike is imminent.

Divine Beast Vah Naboris

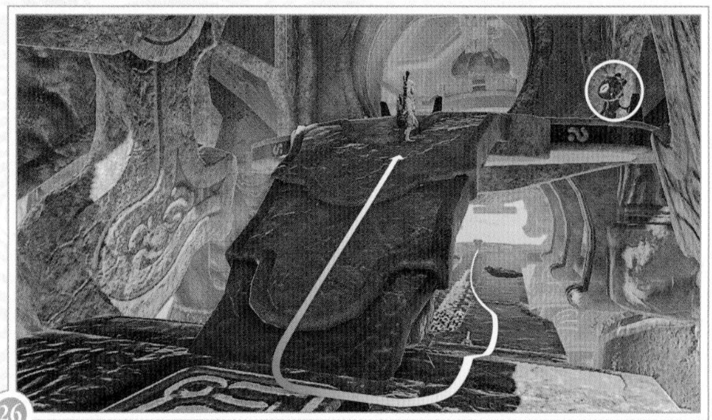

26

From the dungeon's warp point, eliminate the Guardian then head to the end of the walkway. You will find a glowing eyeball at the top of the ramp: shoot it with an arrow to remove the Malice goo and open the way to the dungeon's main room.

27

MAP TERMINAL: Run to the opposite side of the main room and climb up the ramp to your right. This will take you a terminal that provides you with the dungeon's map. As with the previous Divine Beast, your map documents terminals (●) that you must activate, and the mechanical parts of the dungeon's structure that you can manipulate. In this case, there are three circular sections of the main room that you can rotate by increments of 90 degrees. Each of these "rings" is marked with a purple icon (●): select one, press Ⓐ to initiate the command, and then Ⓑ to execute it. For the sake of clarity, we will refer to the ring closest to the beast's head as the **front ring**; the ring closest to the beast's tail as the **rear ring**; and the one in-between as the **middle ring**.

28 Open the map menu and rotate the front ring three times. When it stops moving, step on the (currently vertical) walkway that is to your right if you are facing the Divine Beast's head.

29 **FIRST TERMINAL:** From your position, open the map menu and rotate the front ring one more time: the walkway will be horizontal again, and you will end up with the first terminal a short distance in front of you. Sprint and leap over to it.

30 If you look in the gap that you jumped over before activating the first terminal, you will notice a glowing eyeball. Eliminate it with an arrow to get rid of the Malice goo that surrounds it.

31 **FIRST TREASURE CHEST:** Staying where you are, rotate the middle ring once and you will soon see a treasure chest within reach: glide to it.

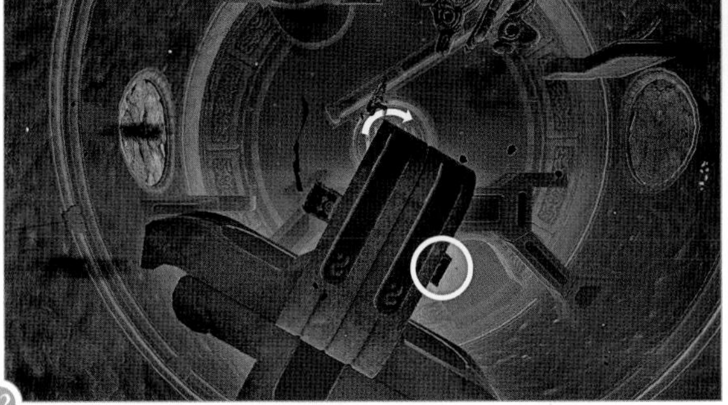

32 **SECOND TREASURE CHEST:** Standing at the edge of the platform with the first treasure chest, rotate the middle ring once more and walk around the edge of the moving surface before you fall. Now drop down on the other side, directly next to the second treasure chest. Rotate the middle disc again and you will end up with the chest right in front of you.

33 **THIRD TREASURE CHEST:** Head to the rear of the Divine Beast and you will notice a treasure chest hanging from a rope. Cast Stasis on it, then quickly cut the rope with an arrow and prepare your Magnesis rune. As soon as Stasis ends, grab the chest with Magnesis before it falls and pull it back to you.

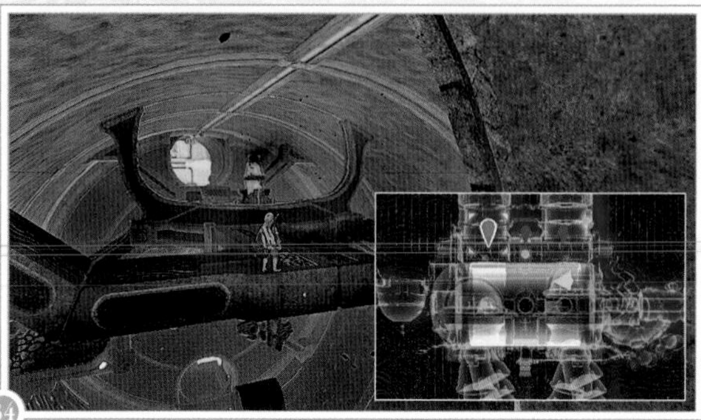
34

You must now rotate all three discs so that their power cables are aligned at the top of the structure. These cables are represented by a colored line segment on the in-game map: green when the cable is in its top position, and orange when not. This will trigger the rotation of a vertical disc adjacent to the front ring.

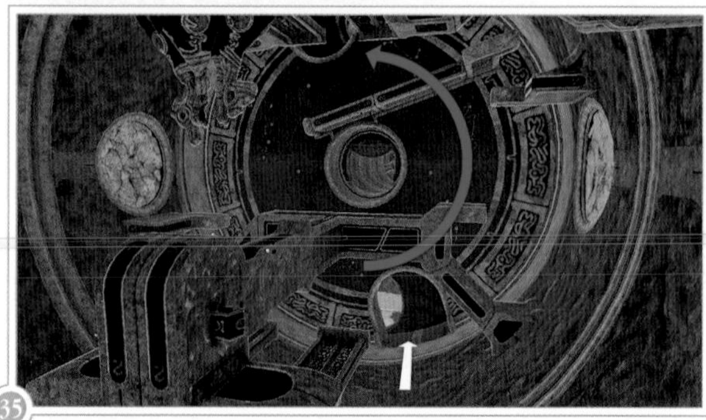
35

Head inside either opening on the rotating disc. Once the rotation has taken you to the top, you will have access to an exit overlooking the Divine Beast's neck portion. First, however, you can open a new treasure chest.

36

FOURTH TREASURE CHEST: From the top of the rotating disc, drop down and glide to the shaft at the center of the disc. Make your way to the end of the shaft, avoiding the various hazards on the way: spikes, goo, and laser beams. Shoot the eyeball to remove the Malice goo and open the treasure chest. You can now return to the top of the rotating disc.

37

Drop down to the platform with the cross-shaped lever. Pushing it clockwise will trigger the rotation of a small disc on the left; pushing it counterclockwise rotates the small disc on the right. Each disc features an electrode: your goal is to have both electrodes at the top of their respective discs aligned with the power cables on the floor. Deal with the electrodes one at a time. Push the lever slowly in one direction until the first electrode is activated, then repeat with the other by pushing the lever in the opposite direction. This will raise the Divine Beast's neck and activate an elevator platform.

38

SECOND TERMINAL: Step on the elevator and ride it all the way to the top to find the second terminal. You can now backtrack to the main room.

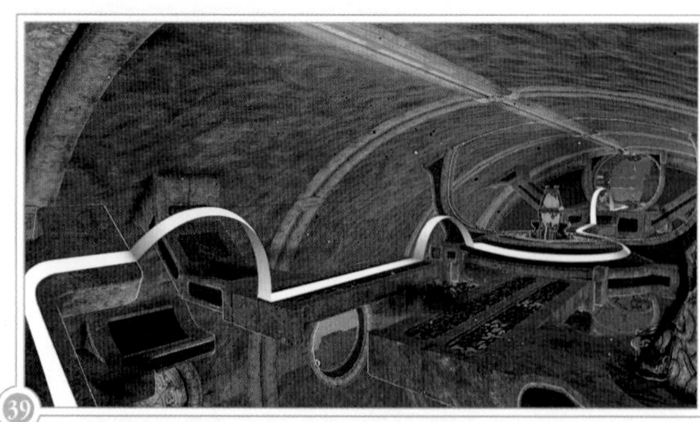
39

From the top of the rotating disc, drop down to the long ledge that runs across the disc when its longer side is on the right-hand side of the Divine Beast (facing its front, as usual). You can jump to the nearby walkway from the edge. Sprint and leap to the central platform with the green crystal, then keep going until you reach the shaft at the opposite side of the main room.

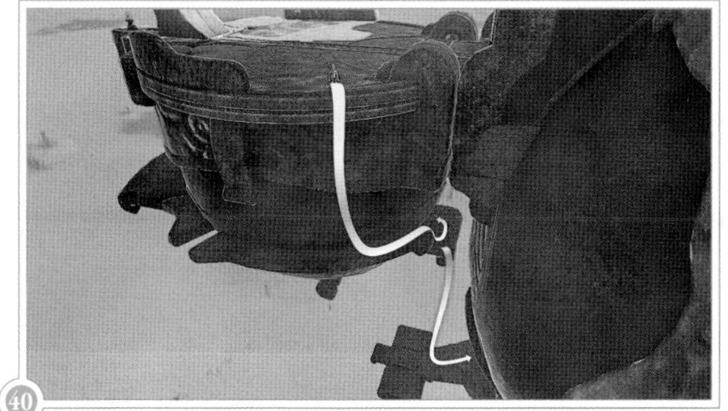

40

FIFTH TREASURE CHEST: Before you interact with the sliding power connectors, drop down on either side of the Divine Beast's tail. Draw your paraglider and you can glide to a treasure chest on a small ledge beneath your current position. Glide again to the walkway below, which is actually the dungeon's starting point. Return to the tail and the sliding power connectors when you're ready.

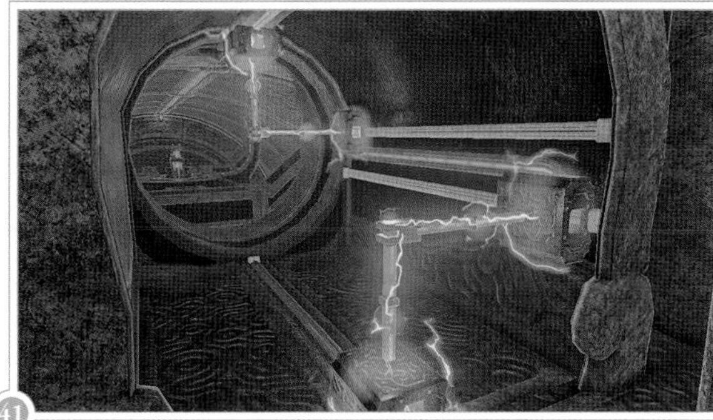

41

Adjust the position of the sliding power connectors with Magnesis as illustrated above. Essentially, you need one pair at each end of the sliders. This will cause the tail section of the Divine Beast to move upward.

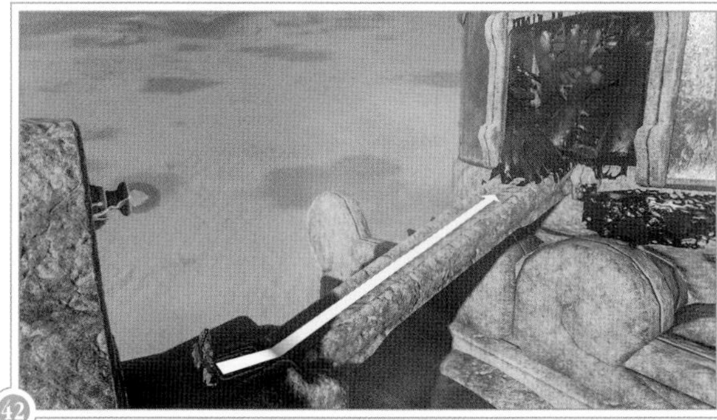

42

Rotate any of the three rings in the main room once to cut the power; the tail will move back in its original position. Head to the back of the pillar at the tip of the tail, close to an electrode. Now reposition the ring you just rotated in order to restore power: the tail will move upward again, but this time you end up on top of the pillar, which now acts as a bridge. This gives you access to the back hump of the Divine Beast. Note that you will need to move close to the glowing eyeball blocking your path before you can shoot it.

43

Inside the hump, shoot the glowing eyeball, then climb up the ladder to reach the ledge above the door you just went through. Rotate the cross-shaped lever until the power feeds the electrode. This will activate a sliding platform that will take you to the other hump – which we will come back to in a minute. For now, take the elevator down, and shoot another glowing eyeball in the room below.

44

SIXTH TREASURE CHEST: Stay on the elevator and pay attention to the two small ledges halfway between the floors. One of them features a treasure chest. You can either jump to it, or grab it with Magnesis. You can also cast Stasis on the elevator to make this easier.

45

The other ledge halfway between the two floors features an electric orb. Cast Stasis on the elevator when the orb is within reach and pull it to your position with Magnesis. You can now drop it to the lower floor: you will use it again in a few minutes.

Divine Beast Vah Naboris
(CONTINUED)

46

Ride the elevator back to the top room, and use the sliding platform to reach the other hump of the Divine Beast. Eliminate the Guardian Scout when you arrive.

47

THIRD TERMINAL: Hit the glowing eyeball just beneath the platform with an arrow. This will remove the Malice goo in which the third terminal was trapped, enabling you to activate it. With this achieved, take the elevator to the top floor.

48

SEVENTH TREASURE CHEST: Jump to the top of the sliding platform which you used a minute ago to reach the second hump. This will give you access to the treasure chest in the room with the cross-shaped lever, which you couldn't reach from the other side because of the Malice goo. After opening the chest, return to the previous room, pick up the second electric orb that lies there, then carry it to the elevator and ride all the way to the lowest floor.

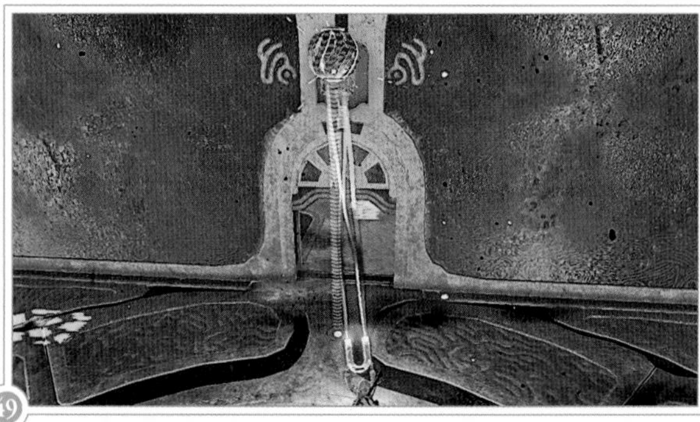
49

Eliminate the glowing eye in the corner of the room with an arrow, then lift the electric orb with Magnesis to put it into contact with the electrode above the sealed gate; this will open the gate and give you access to the adjacent room. Deal with the Guardian Scouts inside, ideally with an ancient weapon for maximum efficiency.

50

FOURTH TERMINAL: Pick up the electric orb and drop it on one of the two small pedestals in front of the large barred gate. Retrieve the first electric orb in the adjacent room and drop it on the second pedestal. This will raise the gate, giving you access to the fourth terminal.

51

Head back to the elevator room corresponding to the rear hump. Do not ride the elevator and exit the room instead. Jump to your left (the right side when facing the beast's head) and glide around its right hind leg: your goal is to land on the platform between its two right legs, as shown in the accompanying screenshot.

52

FIFTH TERMINAL: Walk into the right hind leg's structure and step inside the cube-shaped room. You will notice the fifth terminal positioned on the wall in front of you, though it is currently inaccessible. Rotate the rear ring once, however, and the terminal will end up upright, ready for you to activate. Rotate the rear ring three times afterwards to be able to leave the cube-shaped room.

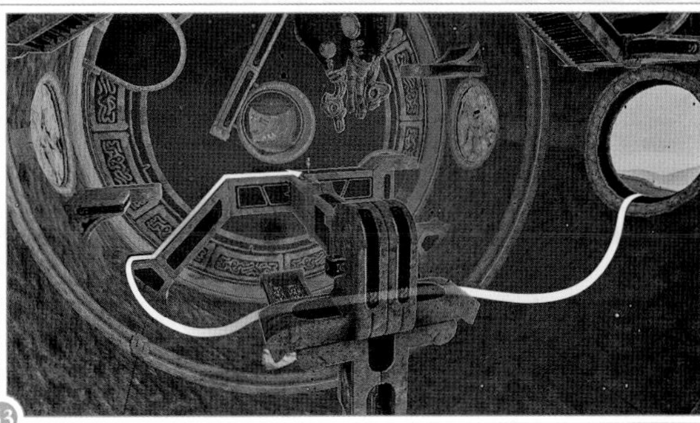

53

Move to left side (when facing the Divine Beast's head) of the front ring, and climb up to the walkway as illustrated here. You will notice two round openings that are blocked by destructible rocks on both ends of the walkway.

54

EIGHTH TREASURE CHEST: Throw a bomb at the opening on the right (when facing the Divine Beast's head). You can then sprint and jump through it to reach a new treasure chest. Return to the previous walkway once you have opened it.

55

Now detonate a bomb on the other destructible opening. Glide through it and eliminate the Guardian Scout.

56

NINTH TREASURE CHEST: Follow the walkway towards the Divine Beast's tail: it will lead to a small room inside the hind leg containing a treasure chest.

57

MAIN CONTROL UNIT: Finally, open your map and rotate the middle ring twice to align the main control unit in a horizontal position. Examine it to trigger this dungeon's boss fight.

BOSS: THUNDERBLIGHT GANON

FIRST PHASE

As long as Thunderblight Ganon has over 50% of its health bar remaining, it focuses on two types of attack.

Thunderblight Ganon regularly stands at a distance and propels three small lightning balls towards you. These are rather slow, and therefore easy to avoid. Run sideways or side hop, preferably to the right as your opponent casts the balls with its right arm. If you are far away, be careful: these balls can actually bounce when they reach the ground or a wall.

The boss's most dangerous attack occurs when he warps multiple times in your direction, quickly zigzagging to your left and right before he deals a powerful blow. Wield a one-handed weapon and keep your shield raised when this happens: you will block the attack automatically. Observe this technique a couple of times and you will soon become more familiar with its timing. As the monster warps to your right and readies its attack, poised to strike, perform a perfect dodge backflip: if successful, this will grant you an opportunity to unleash a full flurry rush combo. The creature will then collapse, giving you a chance to follow up with a second combo. Repeat this until you trigger the next phase of the battle.

SECOND PHASE

When your opponent's health reaches the 50% milestone, a much more dangerous second phase begins.

Thunderblight Ganon's first action in the second phase is to summon small metal pillars around your position in an attempt to electrocute you. It hides behind its shield and remains high in the air throughout this process, leaving you with no offensive options. Sprint away from the pillars and head to the upper walkways. As long as you stay clear of the pillars, you have nothing to fear.

Once you reach the upper walkways, wait at a safe distance until all the pillars have fallen, then grab one of them with Magnesis and position it close to the boss: the next lightning bolt that strikes in the area will electrocute your enemy. Rush over and attack with your best weapon.

From this point forward, the boss will resume his previous attack pattern, alternating between lightning balls and warp-based melee combos. One major difference, though, is that it now regularly infuses its weapon with electricity. This means that you cannot block or perfect-guard its blows unless you wield a wooden shield. The safest option is to sprint away until the effect ends. As soon as you notice the crackling effect vanish from the boss's weapon and shield, this is your cue to counter its next attack with either a perfect guard or a perfect dodge/flurry rush combination – exactly as you did during the first phase. When Thunderblight Ganon collapses, rush to its position and attack relentlessly.

Alternatively, you can hit the creature's shield with a weapon, preferably one with long range such as a spear. After a few hits, your opponent's shield will vanish, offering you an opportunity to follow up with a meaningful combo. This will take a serious toll on your weapon's durability, though, so you will need a large available arsenal to make this strategy viable.

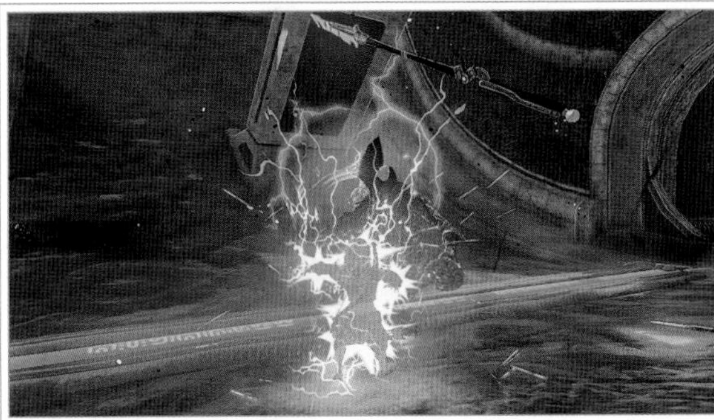

If you are struck by any lightning attack, you will drop the weapon, bow, or shield you are currently wielding. Collect your equipment as soon as you can and run away, as your opponent is likely poised to strike again. Expert players can attempt to perfect dodge even the thunder-infused melee blows with a backflip, and follow up with a flurry rush. This requires impeccable timing, though, and any error will lead you to drop your shield or weapon on the ground.

Ganon will occasionally target you with a red laser, focusing it for a few seconds until a powerful beam is released. This is the same technique employed by Guardians. If you successfully perfect-guard this and send the beam back to the monster it will be stunned, giving you an opportunity to unleash a full melee combo. If your timing is off, on the other hand, you will likely lose your shield. If you are not confident in your ability to perfect-guard, you can either sprint perpendicularly to the beam to dodge it, or hide behind a solid obstacle. Being able to redirect the beam back to your enemy makes the battle much more approachable, though, and is a skill that you will absolutely need to master sooner or later.

SUMMARY

This is clearly one of the harder boss battles in the game, particularly its second phase, but it becomes far less challenging once you know how to react appropriately to each of your opponent's attacks. After you've electrocuted Thunderblight Ganon with one of its own pillars, the monster will frequently infuse its weapon and shield with lightning: either perfect dodge your foe's blows with backflips if you're confident, or sprint away and wait until the effect ends to retaliate without having to worry about being shocked. Every flurry rush will take a toll on your enemy's health and create an opening for an additional combo. Perfect-guard its laser beam to send it back to it and you should be able to deliver the coup de grâce in relatively short order.

If you struggle, consider using the warp point to leave the dungeon and make specific preparations. Fill your inventory with fast weapons (either one-handed swords or spears), cook restorative dishes that will completely regenerate your HP gauge and others that will offer desirable effects (such as granting extra yellow hearts or increasing movement speed), and gather a few fairies from a Great Fairy Fountain. It may also be worth experimenting with the camera speed setting via the Options menu, as this may also be of benefit.

It's important to remain calm: if you start "tilting," take a short break. This boss moves quickly, but you have no reason to panic. Your priority is to keep it in sight at all times, and this is much easier to achieve if you avoid unnecessary movement. When you need to turn the camera, orient Link in the required direction and then tap ZL to instantly align it: this is far more effective than rotating the camera manually.

When you finally triumph, pick up the heart container in front of you. This is your last chance to open any treasure chests you may have missed in this dungeon, as you will not be able to return here after you leave. Once you're ready, activate the main control unit. When you return outside, you will receive Urbosa's Fury ( ) – a power that summons lightning around you when you unleash a charged attack. Report to Riju to complete the **"Divine Beast Vah Naboris"** quest. Open the two chests by her throne before you depart.

RITO QUEST

WALKTHROUGH SUMMARY (SEE OVERLEAF FOR DETAILS)

STEP	DESCRIPTION
1 → 6	Travel to Rito Village and speak to Kaneli.
7 → 10	Head to the Flight Range and pass Teba's test.
11 → 12	Make your way inside Divine Beast Vah Medoh.
13 → 36	Clear the Divine Beast Vah Medoh dungeon.

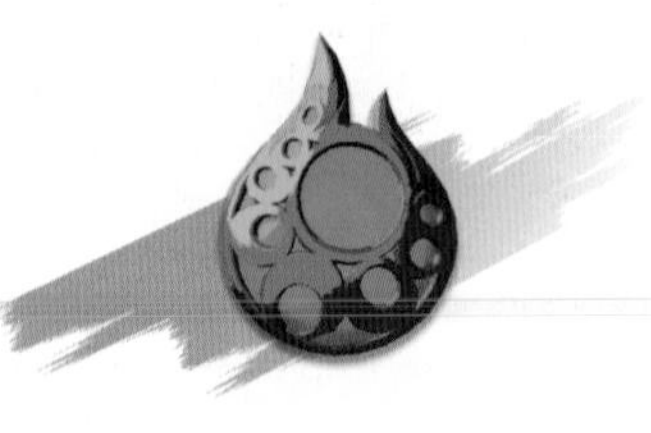

OPTIONAL CHALLENGES

ICON	ACTIVITY	NOTES
◇	SHRINES & SHRINE QUESTS	You can find step-by-step solutions for all shrines and shrine quests in the Gerudo and Tabantha Tower regions on pages 162 and 180 respectively.
I	SIDE QUEST: CURRY FOR WHAT AILS YOU (see page 256)	Lester, a man by the cooking pot at the Rito Stable, asks you to find Goron spice for him. This is an ingredient that can be purchased in Goron City's general store.
II	SIDE QUEST: THE APPLE OF MY EYE (see page 256)	Speak to Juney, next to Kaneli's hut in Rito Village. She requires a baked apple – an item that you may have in your inventory, enabling you to complete the quest instantly. If not, take a raw apple and drop it by a campfire: it will instantly transform into a baked apple.
III	SIDE QUEST: THE SPARK OF ROMANCE (see page 256)	Speak to Jogo during the day, inside Rito Village's inn. He needs some flint. If you don't have any, you can obtain it by destroying ore deposits in mountainous regions. As a rule, the land of the Gorons is a good place to farm for such materials.
IV	SIDE QUEST: FACE THE FROST TALUS (see page 257)	After completing the Divine Beast Vah Medoh dungeon, speak to Gesane, the Rito patrolling on the first wooden bridge leading to Rito Village. He will ask you to destroy a Frost Talus found in Coldsnap Hollow, at the heart of the Hebra Mountains to the north. Make sure you have fire arrows in stock before you attend to this challenge.
V	GREAT FAIRY FOUNTAIN (see page 326)	A third Great Fairy Fountain awaits you a short distance to the southeast of Tabantha Tower. If you have unlocked the previous two, you will need to pay 1,000 rupees to unlock the services of this great fairy.

GERUDO TOWER & TABANTHA TOWER REGIONS

Maka Rah Shrine
Hebra Tower Region
Flight Range
9
36
Sha Warvo Shrine
Gee Ha'rah Shrine
III
II
8
IV
Lanno Kooh Shrine
Rito Village
Hebra Tower
7
I
Voo Lota Shrine
Akh Va'quot Shrine
Rito Stable
Dunba Taag Shrine
Bareeda Naag Shrine
6
Tabantha Tower Region
Tabantha Tower
Toh Yahsa Shrine
5
Great Fairy Fountain
V
4
Tabantha Bridge Stable
Kah Okeo Shrine
Tena Ko'sah Shrine
Shae Loya Shrine
Ridgeland Tower Region
Mijah Rokee Shrine
3
Mogg Latan Shrine
Keeha Yoog Shrine
Kema Kosassa Shrine
Gerudo Tower Region
2
Kuh Takkar Shrine
Yiga Clan Hideout
Sho Dantu Shrine
Joloo Nah Shrine
1
Gerudo Tower
Kema Zoos Shrine
Sasa Kai Shrine

1

By now, you should be sufficiently familiar with the game and exploration in general to make your way to Rito Village on your own. An efficient route is to first stop by the Gerudo Tower, a relatively short distance to the north of Gerudo Town. If you activated the Sho Dantu Shrine on your way to the Yiga Clan Hideout, warp to it: you are then very close to the tower. Make your approach from the plateau to the northwest of the tower. This will enable you to glide to a very high point on the structure, well within range of the first ledge where you can catch your breath. Climb all the way to the top and unlock the regional map.

2

Resume your journey to the north by going through the Yiga Clan Hideout again. If you continue forward past the arena where you fought the clan leader, you will soon emerge in the Gerudo Highlands, where you will need Level 2 cold resistance. You can trigger this by equipping the warm doublet from Hateno Village and consuming appropriate food. When you reach the arch (a few steps from the Kuh Takkar Shrine) shown in the above picture, glide past it, then turn west.

3

Keep progressing to the west on the northern plateaus of the Gerudo Highlands, where the temperatures are frosty but tolerable. When you reach Mystathi's Shelf, glide to the northwest to land on the massif on the opposite side. You are now in Tabantha territory.

4

Keep moving north, alongside the western edge of the Hyrule continent. You will soon have Tabantha Tower in sight.

5

When you reach Tabantha Tower, Malice goo prevents you from making your way to the top. Scale the pillar southwest of the tower and look to the northeast: eliminate the glowing eyeball fixed to the pillar in that direction. This causes it to fall, creating a path to the tower – which you can now easily ascend to reveal the regional map.

6

From the top of Tabantha Tower, you can clearly see your next objective: Rito Village, with its distinctive rock "needle." Glide toward the wooden bridges just east of the village, then make your way to visit the village's chief, Kaneli. Consider purchasing the snowquill armor set at this point. You need at least two armor pieces granting cold resistance to be able to trigger this buff at Level 2 when required. This will be useful in various regions of Hyrule – not least in the dungeon that you are due to visit soon...

7

Kaneli, the elder of Rito Village, will trigger the **"The Divine Beast Vah Medoh"** main quest. Your first task is to speak to Saki in the adjacent hut. She will ask you to look for her husband, Teba, at the Flight Range.

8

Jump from Kaneli's hut and glide to the cliff north of Lake Totori. Follow the path to the north, through Dronoc's Pass. This leads directly to the Flight Range, where Teba awaits.

9

The Flight Range features a cooking pot. If you still do not own armor pieces with cold resistance (and by now, you really should), you could use the pot to prepare appropriate dishes. You need Level 2 cold resistance for the upcoming challenges, so make sure you combine appropriate ingredients in each recipe. However, purchasing at least two pieces of the snowquill outfit from the armor shop in Rito Village makes much more sense as a long-term investment. This is also a very good opportunity to cook dishes with restorative properties, as you will soon enter another dungeon. You should also collect the arrows close to the cooking pot. If you still have relatively few, buy some more from Rito Village's general store, as you'll need plenty. Once you are fully ready, speak to Teba to begin your archery skill test.

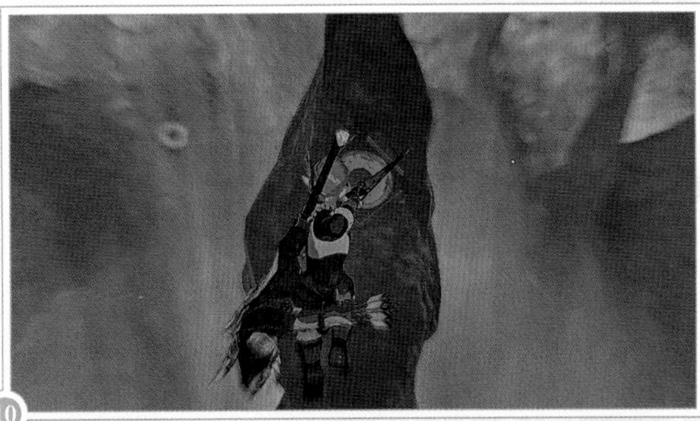

10

Your goal here is to navigate updrafts with the paraglider in order to hit five blue-glowing targets with arrows within three minutes. Your priority is to get close enough to these targets. Glide until you are within firing range, then aim to trigger the slow-motion effect and align your shot. The updrafts will keep you at a high elevation, so put your paraglider away whenever you need to lose altitude to hit low targets. After you pass the test, open the treasure chest next to Teba, then speak to him again if you're ready to proceed.

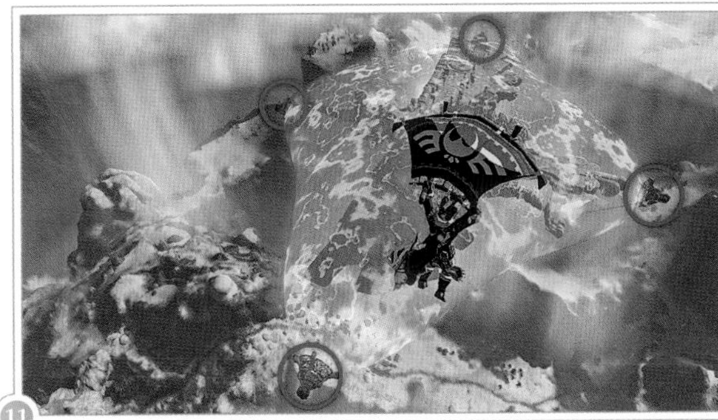

11

To access Divine Beast Vah Medoh, use bomb arrows to destroy the four cannons at the tip of the bird's head, tail, and both wings.

12

This sequence plays out very similarly to the earlier rehearsal at the Flight Range: you glide high in the air to move above targets (here, the four cannons), then put away your paraglider to free-fall close to each one (Ⓑ) and shoot bomb arrows. Unless you have a very powerful bow, it will likely take two shots to take down each cannon. Once all four have been destroyed, you will automatically land on the Divine Beast.

Divine Beast Vah Medoh

13

FIRST TREASURE CHEST: From your starting position, turn around and move to the edge of the Divine Beast's tail. Hit the glowing eyeball on the right with an arrow to remove the Malice goo and access the chest.

14

SECOND TREASURE CHEST: Head inside the dungeon and eliminate the glowing eyeball to your right as you enter. With the goo removed, you can catch the updraft to reach the wide ladder, at the top of which lies a second treasure chest.

15

MAP TERMINAL: From the second treasure chest, glide to the corridor featuring the map terminal. Get rid of the Guardian Scout II on the way before you unlock the dungeon's map. When you open it, you will notice the usual orange glowing points (●) corresponding to the terminals you need to activate, as well as three purple icons (●) that represent the increments at which you can tilt Vah Medoh.

16

THIRD TREASURE CHEST: Standing at the edge of the corridor with the map terminal, you should see a treasure chest in the corner to your right, on the walkway below: glide to it directly from your position. Even if something goes awry, you can still jump above the Malice goo to reach it.

17

FOURTH TREASURE CHEST: From the edge of the walkway with the third chest, look down again and shoot an arrow at the glowing eyeball. This will reveal yet another treasure chest.

18

Catch the updraft on the opposite side of the room. When you reach the ceiling, glide to the large ladder. Climb up to the platform where you found the second treasure chest, then eliminate the glowing eyeball and leap to the nearby doorway. This will lead to the first room in the Divine Beast's left wing.

19

Look to your left and fire an arrow at the glowing eyeball in the alcove to free the terminal it contains from Malice goo.

20

FIRST TERMINAL: Climb back up to the top of the ramp from which you entered this room. From this position, open your map and tilt the Divine Beast so that its right wing rises (top increment). In this new configuration, the alcove is lower than the ramp where you stand, enabling you to glide to it. Activate the terminal, then drop down to the floor.

21

FIFTH TREASURE CHEST: Run to the highest point of the walkway opposite the first terminal. Thanks to the incline, you can glide from here directly to the small ledge above the barred gate, where a chest awaits.

22

Drop a round bomb in the pipe to the right of the barred gate. The incline will take the bomb to the small stone arch beyond. Detonate the bomb to clear the way.

23

Now hit the nearby crystal to create a lateral wind stream, and drop another spherical bomb in the pipe. This time it will roll down to the wall, where the wind will propel it to the far corner: detonate it to release a large metallic boulder. Hit the crystal again to close the shutters.

24

Open your map and tilt the Divine Beast by selecting the lowest increment. This will cause the boulder to move in your direction. Grab it with Magnesis through the transparent energy field and move it to the right: drop it close to the pipe.

DIVINE BEAST VAH MEDOH
(CONTINUED)

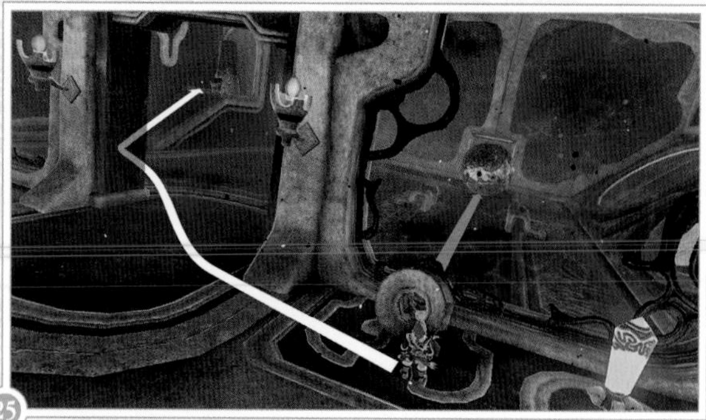

25

SECOND TERMINAL: Open your map and tilt the Divine Beast by selecting the highest increment. This will cause the boulder to roll down and press the switch against the wall. Once the gate is raised, you will be free to examine the terminal in that room.

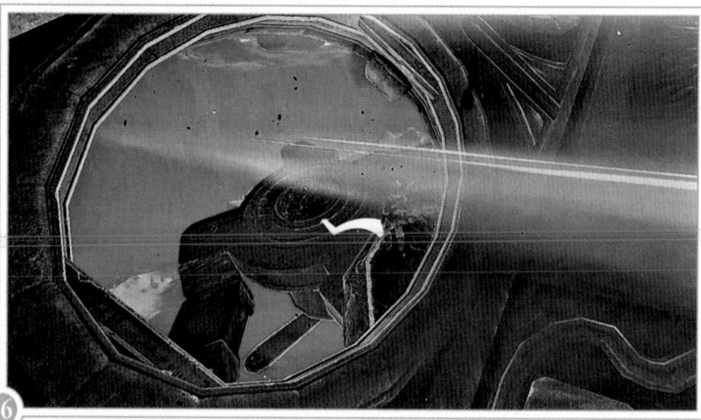

26

Return to the previous room. Hit the crystal once to reopen the shutters, then leap through the window opposite the first terminal. Glide to the platform below and eliminate the two glowing eyeballs: one blocking an updraft in front of your landing point, and one by the nearby doorway.

27

THIRD TERMINAL: Turn around and look toward the tip of Vah Medoh's left wing. Thanks to the incline, it is possible to glide to the room found there, which contains the next terminal.

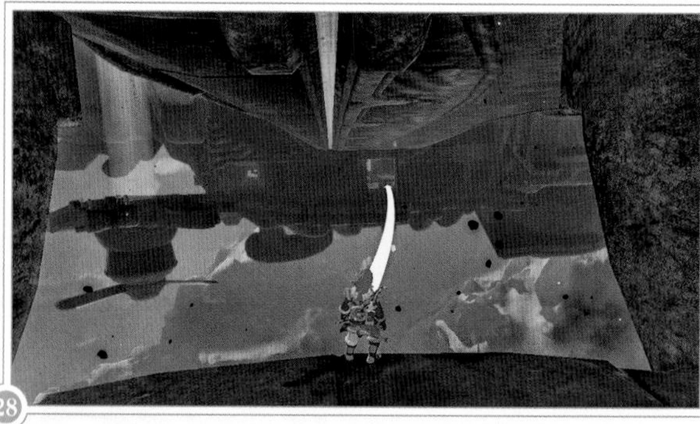

28

Open the map and tilt the Divine Beast by selecting the lowest increment. This will enable you to glide back to the central room.

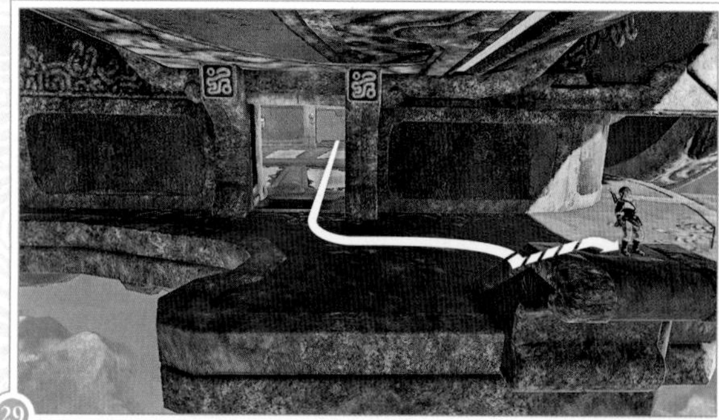

29

Remain on the lower level and go through the central room. When you emerge beneath the right wing, step on the small ramp.

30

From the small ramp, fire an arrow at the glowing eyeball fixed to the right wing. This will remove the Malice goo blocking the way, enabling you to glide to the room beyond.

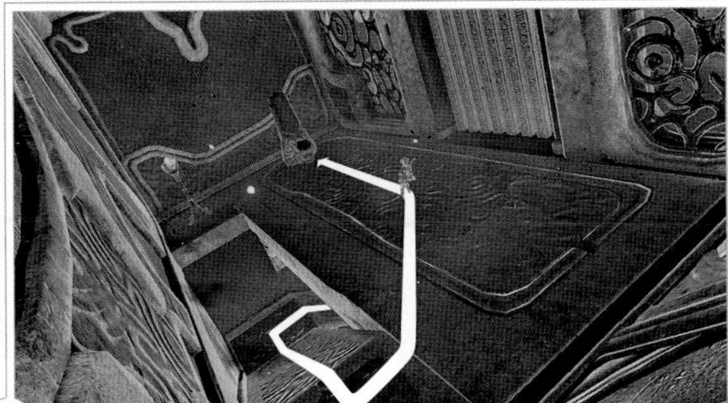

31

FOURTH TERMINAL: Walk up the ramp at the back of the room and activate the terminal at the top.

32

SIXTH TREASURE CHEST: With the nearby gate now open, head into the adjacent room. Turn around and shoot the glowing eyeball above the gate. This will release a treasure chest.

33

Hit the crystal to open the shutters on the wall. This will generate a wind stream that activates the two small windmills (one fixed, and another on a slider but already in the correct position thanks to the dungeon's current incline). With the two gates now lifted, the battering ram will slide to the bottom of the room.

34

FIFTH TERMINAL: Now open your map and tilt the Divine Beast by selecting the highest increment. Just as the dungeon reaches a horizontal position (and before its incline shifts), cast Magnesis on the windmill on the slider. As long as you maintain it in the wind stream, the gate will remain open, enabling the battering ram to hit the pressure switch at full speed. This will lift the nearby barred gate, giving you access to the final terminal.

35

SEVENTH TREASURE CHEST: Thanks to the current incline of the room, you can access the treasure chest on the ledge that overlooks the pressure switch. Standing at the opposite end of the room, on one of the two round windows beyond the crystal, you can glide directly to the chest.

36

MAIN CONTROL UNIT: Open your map and tilt the dungeon back to its neutral, horizontal position. Drop down in the central room and ride the updraft all the way to the top, where you can activate the main control unit to trigger the boss battle.

FIRST PHASE

As long as Windblight Ganon has over 50% of its health remaining, it will employ two types of attack.

When Windblight Ganon stands at ground level, it will usually unleash a tornado that will move slowly but rather unpredictably in your direction. This cannot be blocked, so your best bet is to sprint away from it.

When your opponent materializes higher in the air, it will generally fire a series of energy blasts at you. The best course of action is to perfect-guard each and every one of these, as they inflict significant damage when returned to sender. This requires a very good sense of timing, though. If you struggle, you can instead hide behind a solid object and wait until the barrage ends.

In terms of offensive moves, you have two main options here. The first is to fire arrows at the boss every time you have an opening; standard arrows will suffice. Feel free to use the numerous updrafts available in the arena. The slow-motion effect triggered when you aim while airborne will help you align clean shots at the beast's blue eye.

Another effective option is to sprint to Windblight Ganon when it appears at ground level. You can rapidly inflict great harm with melee combos, and remain out of range of its attacks by standing directly beneath or behind its body. This is a slightly more risky approach, but it's also much more efficient.

SECOND PHASE

Once Windblight Ganon's health is down to 50%, the battle will become significantly more difficult.

During the second phase, Windblight Ganon will regularly summon four small satellites that orbit its body. You can destroy all four with arrows (causing your opponent to temporarily revert to its attacks from the first phase) but they will eventually reappear. We would argue that it makes more sense to focus on your main enemy at all times.

With the satellites active, your opponent will occasionally charge wind energy in a vortex, then unleash it as a galestrike that moves at high speed in your direction. This is a very fast assault that cannot be blocked, so be prepared to sprint away from it, or hide behind a solid object.

During the second phase, the tornado attack is upgraded into a version with two whirlwinds. These cannot be blocked, so start dashing away from them as soon as they appear.

The energy blasts that the boss fires with its gun will now bounce off the satellites, making their movements unpredictable. Worse, perfect-guarding them is useless as they will not be redirected to your opponent's body. It therefore makes sense to avoid them.

As with its other forms, Windblight Ganon will occasionally target you with a red laser, focusing it for a few seconds until a powerful blue beam is released. If you successfully perfect-guard this and send the beam back to the monster it will be stunned, giving you an opportunity to unleash a full melee combo. If your timing is off, your shield will be destroyed. If in doubt, sprint perpendicularly to the beam to dodge it, or hide behind a solid obstacle.

Your offensive options in the second phase remain unchanged. You can either fire arrows at the creature's eye, preferably while riding updrafts to enjoy the slow-motion effect that makes aiming much easier. Alternatively, as before, you can rush to the monster whenever it materializes at ground level and assault it with your most powerful combos. The latter approach is by far the fastest, enabling you to end the battle quickly if you are suitably equipped.

Once Windblight Ganon falls, collect the heart container that appears. If you're ready to leave the dungeon permanently (there is no way to revisit it later), interact with the main control unit. After the following cutscene, you will receive Revali's Gale (X). This special power enables you to create an updraft by holding X, which can prove enormously useful for long climbs or particular puzzles. As with other similar powers, a cooldown will be triggered once you consume all available charges.

Report to Kaneli, the elder of Rito Village. This completes the **"Divine Beast Vah Medoh"** quest; claim a reward from the treasure chest on your left. You are now ready to visit the land of the Gorons and conquer the final Divine Beast.

Goron Quest

WALKTHROUGH SUMMARY (SEE OVERLEAF FOR DETAILS)

STEP	DESCRIPTION
1 → 7	Activate the Eldin Tower and make your way to Goron City, then speak to Bludo.
8 → 13	Free Yunobo at the Abandoned North Mine.
14 → 24	Team up with Yunobo to weaken Divine Beast Vah Rudania.
25 → 42	Clear the Divine Beast Vah Rudania dungeon.

OPTIONAL CHALLENGES

ICON	ACTIVITY	NOTES
◆	SHRINES & SHRINE QUESTS	You can find step-by-step solutions for all shrines and shrine quests in the Eldin Tower region on page 200.
I	SIDE QUEST: FIREPROOF LIZARD ROUNDUP (see page 272)	Speak to Kima at the Southern Mine. If you catch 10 fireproof lizards for him, he will reward you with a piece of armor granting the flame guard effect – a blessing in the Eldin region. Fireproof lizards are regularly encountered in the vicinity: when you spot one, approach slowly and quietly by crouch-walking to ensure that it will not run away.
II	SIDE QUEST: THE ROAD TO RESPECT (see page 272)	Speak to Fugo in Goron City. He needs you to defeat the Igneo Talus on the northwest shore of Darunia Lake. Freeze it with any ice-infused weapon or arrow, then attack its weak point as usual.
III	SIDE QUEST: DEATH MOUNTAIN'S SECRET (see page 273)	Speak to Dugby, a young Goron soaking in the Goron Hot Springs during the day. Head to the top of the middle lava waterfall, on the way to the Bridge of Eldin. You will find destructible rocks at the base of the small rock peak there. Shatter these with a bomb to find a drillshaft in a hiding spot. Report to Dugby to complete the mission.
IV	SIDE QUEST: THE JEWEL TRADE (see page 273)	After completing the Divine Beast Vah Rudania dungeon, speak to Ramella, a Gerudo found in Goron City. She needs 10 pieces of amber, which you will likely have in stock at this stage. If not, destroy ore deposits in the region until you meet the quota.

Shora Hah Shrine
Abandoned North Mine
Death Mountain
Shae Mo sah Shrine
Goron City
Bridge of Eldin
Daqa Koh Shrine
Maag Halan Shrine
Goron Hot Springs
Kayra Mah Shrine
Southern Mine
Ze Kasho Shrine
WOODLAND TOWER
ELDIN TOWER
Sah Dahaj Shrine
Qua Raym Shrine
Foothill Stable
Mirro Shaz Shrine
ELDIN TOWER REGION
Mo'a Keet Shrine
Woodland Stable
Tah Muhl Shrine
Namika Ozz Shrine
Sheh Rata Shrine
Soh Koli Shrine
LANAYRU TOWER

1

If you need assistance to find your way to Goron City, the easiest solution is probably to warp to the Lanayru Tower. Look to the north from here and you will see the Eldin Tower in the distance. Rather than aiming straight for it, though, you should consider making a small detour to the northeast: a brief stop at the Foothill Stable will give you a chance to purchase a very important item. You can follow the road marked on the in-game map, which will lead you straight to the stable.

2

Random encounters aside, the path leading to the Foothill Stable should be uneventful – though you are entirely free to briefly leave the main road to clear an enemy outpost or a shrine on your way.

3

Speak to Gaile at the Foothill Stable, who offers fireproof elixirs for sale. We suggest you buy three of these. The 150 rupee investment might sound like a lot, but this will remove any stress from your imminent foray into volcanic territory.

4

From the stable, keep following the road to the northwest. You will soon reach hot springs. The steam might suggest danger, but the contrary is true: bathing in the pools will actually replenish your hearts. Take a left after the springs and walk up the slope of igneous rock. You will find the Eldin Tower at the top.

5

Once you've activated the Eldin Tower, glide to the northwest. From this point forward, you need the flame guard effect to prevent Link from being set ablaze by the extreme temperature. Drink one of the fireproof elixirs you purchased at the Foothill Stable, and repeat this whenever the effect wears off. Going through the hot springs will enable you to replenish your hearts when required. Note that if you follow the main road instead, you will run into a dangerous Igneo Talus. If you choose to engage it, have your ice arrows at the ready to temporarily cool it down.

6

The final leg of the journey takes you through the Southern Mine. You can make a stop to complete a side quest here, which will reward you with a piece of gear providing the flame guard effect – refer to the previous double-page spread for details. Once you are ready, follow the path leading to Goron City to the north.

7

Once you reach Goron City, immediately head to the armor shop and purchase at least two pieces of armor that grant the flame guard effect. If you can afford the full set, do so. Upgrading it twice via great fairies (see page 326) will make you completely fireproof; at this level of resistance, Link could stand on the back of a Igneo Talus and not sustain heat-related damage. Once you are suitably equipped, speak to Bludo to initiate the **"Divine Beast Vah Rudania"** main mission. This requires you to find a Goron named Yunobo who has not yet returned from the Abandoned North Mine.

8

Make your way to the Abandoned North Mine by following the path to the north. Speak to Drak when you get there and mention that you were sent by "the boss." In the section that follows, a Level 1 flame guard effect will not be sufficient; you will need Level 2 protection to survive. As mentioned in the previous step, the best solution is to buy at least two pieces of armor from Goron City's shop, as these will prove useful many times in the future. If you really want to rely on elixirs alone, you will need to craft them with multiple effective ingredients, such as fireproof lizards.

9

You can navigate this entire area via a series of updrafts. However, you will encounter several enemy outposts on the way, where your opponents often occupy strategic vantage points. This significantly complicates your approach. To make things much easier, you need to use the cannons in the vicinity. Hit the handle to change the cannon's orientation, then drop a spherical bomb into the tube; detonate it to fire. A single direct hit from a cannon is sufficient to annihilate all creatures in an outpost.

10

After eliminating the first two groups of creatures to the west of your starting position, catch the updrafts to the east. A head-on assault is a risky approach as your foes shoot fire arrows at a fairly high rate. Instead, use the updrafts to reach the small island beyond their position. A cannon here will enable you to defeat both groups of monsters. There are also destructible rocks between the two enemy positions that yield resources; you can hit them by firing the cannon halfway through its rotation.

11

Follow the path to the north until you reach a new cannon. Rotate it to the far right to destroy the outpost with a skull-shaped building. To topple the two lookout towers, you'll need to fire the cannon midway through a rotation once again. Once the path is clear, head to the next cannon in line, to the southwest.

12

A single cannon shot is enough to blow up the entire outpost. You can then head to the final cannon position, to the northwest. You will need to climb to reach the top of the rock peak.

Drop a bomb in the pipe to load the final cannon, then hit the lever and be ready to open fire during the cannon's rotation. As soon as the bore is aligned with the destructible rocks that block the entrance to the cave in the background, detonate your bomb. Once a projectile hits home, head over and speak to Yunobo inside the cave. Don't forget to open the treasure chests before you return to Goron City (for example by warping to the local shrine).

After reporting to Bludo, your next objective is to head to the Bridge of Eldin. First, follow the path to the north of Goron City, which goes around the nearby mountain. This will take you to the Stolock Bridge, which overlooks Goron City.

Keep following the path represented on the in-game map until you run into Yunobo again. He is being attacked by Moblins. As the creatures are focusing on your ally, you can use this opportunity to stealthily approach one from behind and open hostilities with a powerful sneakstrike. Speak to Yunobo once the rescue is complete.

With Yunobo inside the cannon, use the same method as you did back in the Abandoned North Mine: drop a spherical bomb to load the cannon, then hit the lever to initiate the cannon's rotation; when it is directed at the Bridge of Eldin, detonate your explosive to open fire and cause the bridge to be lowered. Cross it to trigger a cutscene.

During the next sequence, you must make progress toward the summit without being spotted by the Sentries (which will trigger magma bombs to rain from the sky). With Yunobo following your lead, it is up to you to decide when he should stay close and when he should stop, in accordance with the dangers that lie ahead. You can give him orders with your whistle (✚). Every time you whistle, it will toggle Yunobo's current state between waiting and following. The first Sentry is relatively easy to avoid: follow it as it moves away from you and take shelter under the large rock that extends over a portion of the road; when the sentry moves back in the other direction, quickly head to the far end of the road to escape its detection range.

When you reach the next Sentry, whistle to tell Yunobo to stop moving, then climb up the cliff on your left. You will find rock boulders at the top, which you can push so that they fall on the sentry, destroying it instantly. Return to the path below and whistle to call Yunobo. You will need to push a boulder or two aside to clear the way for him.

19

When you reach the cannon, drop a round bomb to arm it, then hit the lever once to rotate the device to its leftmost position. Yunobo will hit the Divine Beast when you detonate your bomb.

20

When you reach the next Sentries, whistle to leave Yunobo behind you, then climb up the cliff to your left. You will find metallic cubes at the top. Grab one with Magnesis, then use it as a cudgel to destroy the first sentry. Move on to the next ledge and repeat this with the second sentry. Finally make your way to the third Sentry, climb on the nearby rock, and lift one of the metallic slabs from the ground to eliminate it in the same fashion.

21

Take a metallic cube with you and keep following the path up towards the volcano. When you run into another cannon, proceed exactly as you did before to hurl Yunobo into the Divine Beast after hitting the lever to realign the cannon to the left.

22

Get rid of the next two Sentries with the metallic object you've been carrying with you since the previous encounter. Cubes or slabs work equally well as blunt instruments, but cubes tend to be more stable when you put them down on the ground.

23

The next three Sentries are all high in the air. You can reach the first one by standing on the small rock spike on your right. The other two, on the other hand, will require you make use of the metallic cubes lying on a ledge on the cliff to your left. You can either climb there, or use the updrafts that the sentries are patrolling around. Once you have grabbed a cube with Magnesis, use it to eliminate the remaining sentries.

24

The final cannon is protected by a few enemies. Catch the updrafts and land on the cliff to your left. Grab one of the metal cubes with Magnesis and use it to bludgeon the hostiles into insensibility. Once the dust settles, rotate the cannon to the left and activate it with a bomb to strike the Divine Beast.

Divine Beast Vah Rudania

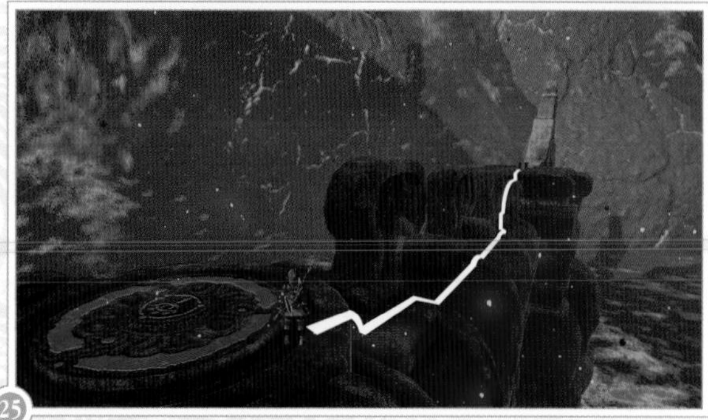

25

FIRST TREASURE CHEST: From your starting point in the dungeon, turn around and run in the direction of the Divine Beast's tail to open your first treasure chest. Backtrack to your original position and head inside when you're ready.

26

SECOND, THIRD, AND FOURTH TREASURE CHESTS: As you enter the dungeon's very first room, you will notice three glowing eyeballs – one on your left, one on your right, and one on the ceiling. Eliminate them with arrows and they will each drop a treasure chest. One of these contains a torch – a critical item for this dungeon. Light it up with one of the blue flames at the entrance to make it easier to find your way in the darkness.

27

FIFTH, SIXTH, AND SEVENTH TREASURE CHEST: Use your torch to light up the lantern by the barred gate. Once this is open, destroy the Guardian Scout and the two glowing eyeballs in the next room. There are two further eyeballs on your right as you go through the gate. When you have dealt with all of them, open the three treasure chests.

28

MAP TERMINAL: Light up your torch via the previous lantern, then head to the far corner of the room to find an unlit lantern: set it aflame with your torch. This raises the adjacent barred gate. Activate the terminal in the room beyond to unlock the dungeon's map and to flood the Divine Beast with light. As with all previous Divine Beasts, the map features terminals (●) that you need to activate, and purple icons (⬤) that represent two positions that enable you to tilt the whole dungeon by 90 degrees. To adjust the Divine Beast, visit the map screen, press Ⓐ to initiate a command, and Ⓑ to execute it.

29

FIRST TERMINAL: Set an arrow on fire with a blue flame (or use a fire arrow) and shoot at the ivy on the metal door close to the dungeon's entrance. Once the gates are free, open them with Magnesis and activate the terminal behind them.

30

EIGHTH TREASURE CHEST: Burn the ivy just above the first terminal. This will cause a treasure chest to fall from the ceiling.

31

If you look toward the entrance, you will notice a closed gate to the right of the blue flame lanterns. You can see an unlit lantern through a hole in that gate. Light an arrow with a blue flame, then fire through the opening to set it ablaze. This will open the gate.

32

Use the lantern you just lit to ignite an arrow, then shoot at the ivy on the ceiling, on the other side of the ramp. This will cause a large metal cube to fall.

33

SECOND TERMINAL: Position the metal cube next to the red flame streams, then open your map and tilt the dungeon by 90 degrees. The red flames are now horizontal. Move the metal cube against the devices that emit the flames to block them; with the streams neutralized, you can enter the room beyond. Open your map and tilt the dungeon again to interact with the terminal. The red flames are extinguished at this point, so you can return to the entrance immediately.

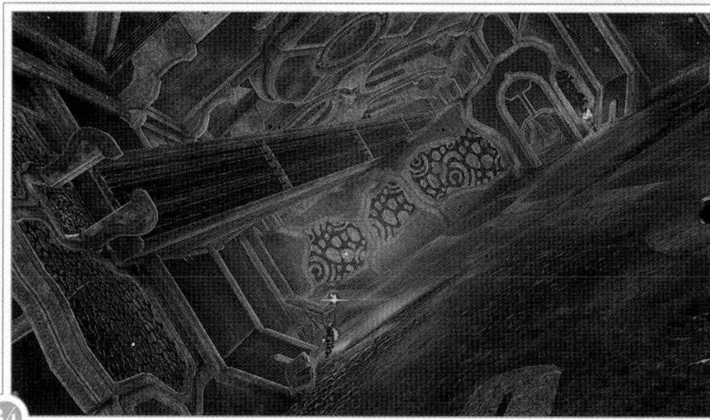

34

Light your torch with one of the blue flames, then stand against the wall opposite the metallic gates, beneath the long beam that runs diagonally across the room. Now open your map and tilt the dungeon by 90 degrees (selecting the bottom ●). As the whole dungeon rotates, the long beam becomes a ramp.

35

Jog all the way to the top of the ramp (do not sprint, as this will extinguish the torch's flame). Once outside, turn left.

36

Drop down to the unlit, open-air lantern just below. Once you are next to it, tilt the dungeon again, back to its original position, then light up the lantern with your torch.

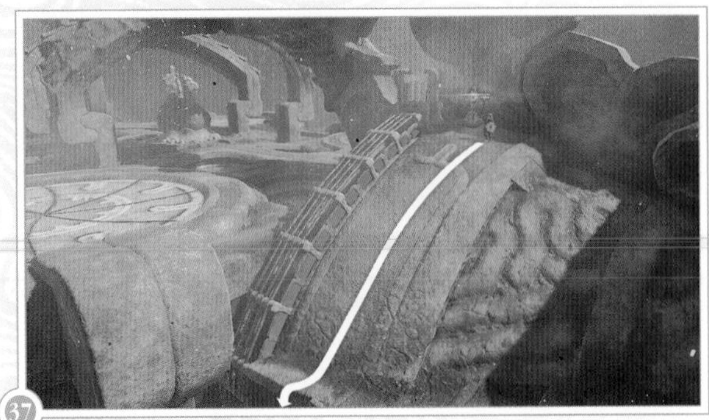

37

Lighting the torch will release an orb that rolls down the nearby caged track. Follow the orb until it stops, then tilt the dungeon once again.

38

THIRD TERMINAL: After the dungeon's rotation, the orb rolls down to the bottom of a ramp. For now, do not follow it: look down from the top of the ramp and you will see a terminal far below your position. Drop down and glide to it. Once you have activated it, return to the base of the long ramp, where the orb awaits.

39

FOURTH TERMINAL: Once you're at the base of the ramp, lift the metallic cube with Magnesis. This will cause the orb to fall into the concave slot – which raises the nearby gate. Activate the terminal behind it.

40

NINTH TREASURE CHEST: Open your map and tilt the dungeon back to its horizontal position to return to the entrance, then tilt it again while standing beneath the long beam to end up at the base of the ramp. Run to the top of the ramp and drop down to the open-air lantern that you lit up a few minutes ago. From your position next to the blue flame, shoot the nearby glowing eyeball to remove all the Malice goo. Take a few steps forward on your current ledge and you will notice a second glowing eyeball underneath the next ledge. Shoot it with an arrow as well. You can now use the walkway to your left to reach the treasure chest further along.

41

FIFTH TERMINAL: From your position by the ninth chest, stand against the small wall that separates the ledge from the walkway. Tilt the dungeon back to its default position and you will end up almost in front of the terminal.

42

TENTH AND ELEVENTH TREASURE CHESTS & MAIN CONTROL UNIT: With all terminals activated, you are now free to approach the main control unit. Before you do so, though, there are two remaining treasure chests that you may wish to open. The first is simple: just drop through one of the holes in the floor close to the main control unit, then glide to the long beam to open a tenth treasure chest. To reach the final container, head back to the top of the Divine Beast and tilt it vertically. You can then reach the dungeon's final optional reward by gliding through a hole on the left side of Vah Rudania's thorax that leads into the round room just below the beast's left foreleg, where the chest awaits. Now head back up to the main control unit and brace yourself for a boss battle when you examine the device.

BOSS: FIREBLIGHT GANON

FIRST PHASE

As long as Fireblight Ganon has over 50% of its health remaining it will focus mostly on melee attacks.

This boss often performs a swift sweeping attack. This has a very short wind-up, so be on your guard: perfect dodge or perfect guard as soon as the creature's elbow is level with its back, then follow up with a strong counter. Backflips are a safe option here as they will put you out of range of the blow even if you miss the perfect dodge/flurry rush timing window.

Fireblight Ganon's vertical sword slash has a longer preparation time. Sidehop or perfect guard precisely as its left hand moves above its eye when its palm is fully exposed. You can then retaliate with your best weapon.

The third melee technique is a swirling attack that completes three full rotations. Only one hit can be blocked with a shield, so you really need to perform a perfect dodge or perfect guard. The window of opportunity for this is approximately three seconds after the monster starts charging the attack. It takes practice to master the timing as there is no visual cue telling you when to execute your defensive move. As a rule, though, backflips tend to be preferable as they put you out of the sword's range if your input is too hasty.

Your enemy has a final trick up its sleeve in this initial phase: it throws a volley of fireballs at you. You can dodge these by sprinting away or by executing a sidehop.

The most effective way to defeat Fireblight Ganon's first stage is to focus on melee combat. Perfect dodge its assaults and follow up with flurry rushes. The rest of the time, strafe around your enemy and maintain a steady barrage of melee strikes. You can often flank it as it unleashes a blow and deal large amounts of damage completely unpunished. However, try to remain relatively close to the main control unit rather than the arena's edges, as a single hit could propel you into the lava.

If you struggle with melee combat against this powerful foe, consider shooting arrows at it instead. Whenever you manage to hit the creature's blue eye, it is temporarily stunned, enabling you to follow up with a quick combo. This can be repeated multiple times.

SECOND PHASE

When Fireblight Ganon loses 50% of its health, it will harness fire energy for offensive and defensive purposes.

As soon as the second phase begins, Fireblight Ganon will prepare a new technique. It now summons an impenetrable force field around its body: neither arrows nor physical attacks can break through it. After a charge time lasting a few seconds, the boss unleashes a slow but large fireball that homes in on you, causing a very large explosion on impact. You can try to sprint away from this, but the safest solution is to hide several steps behind a solid object to avoid splash damage. Alternatively, an ice arrow will freeze the fireball instantly.

The solution to breaking your opponent's seemingly unbreakable defense is hinted at when it charges the fireball attack: you can see that it absorbs particles and small objects in the area. Throw a bomb at your opponent during this stage and it will be admitted through the force field, at which point you can detonate it. This will stun your target, enabling you to run in and perform your best combos.

In this phase, the boss's small fireballs are replaced by a single large projectile – identical to the one employed during the force field sequence. Take shelter behind a solid object to avoid the blast. Alternatively, you can freeze a fireball with an ice arrow to eliminate the threat instantly.

Fireblight Ganon's melee attacks work identically in the second phase, though they now leave fire in their wake or at their point of impact, making them more dangerous. However the timing window for flurry rushes or parries remains unchanged. Using these counter opportunities and harassing your enemy at very close range, strafing in a circle at all times, is still the most effective strategy. If you wield suitably powerful weapons, this fight can end surprisingly quickly.

From time to time, Fireblight Ganon will target you with a red laser. Once the charge process is complete, an energy beam will be fired. Perform a perfect guard precisely as it is about to hit you, returning it to the boss. This will inflict damage and offer an opening for a melee combo.

After the battle, collect the heart container. Assuming you are finished with this dungeon and ready to leave (you cannot return afterwards), interact with the main control unit. Once outside, you will receive Daruk's Protection – a power that offers complete protection from attacks while you guard with ZL, with a cooldown after every three uses. Don't forget to speak to Bludo to formally complete the quest, and to open the treasure chest on his throne.

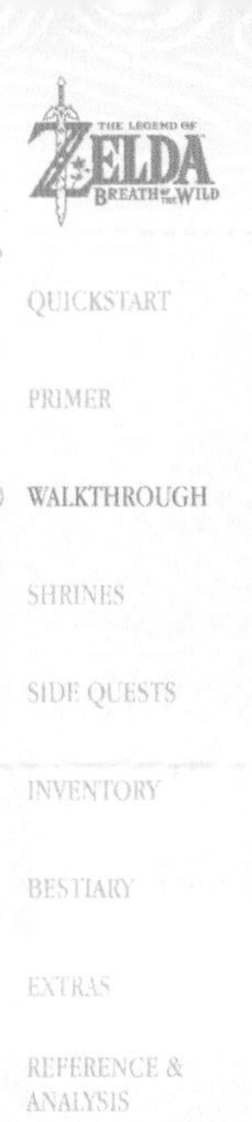

INTERMISSION

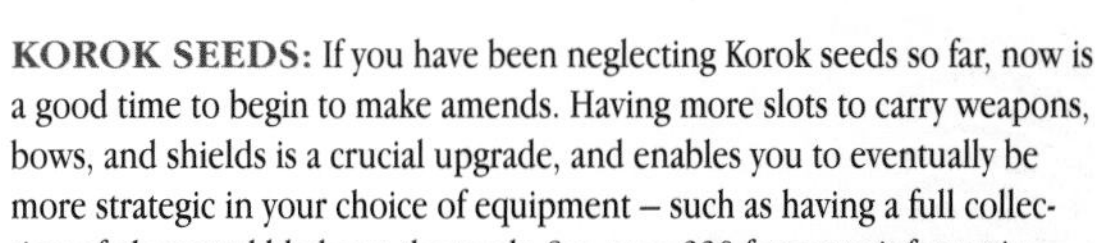

You can complete two optional main quests at this point in the story. These will not provide immediate benefits, but they will contribute to your enjoyment of the game's narrative by revealing important plot developments:

- Warp to Kakariko Village and speak to Impa to complete the **"Free the Divine Beasts"** main quest.
- You probably recall that Impa put you on the track of 12 **Captured Memories** earlier in your adventure. You may have stumbled across such memory positions by chance during your travels – but it's only by finding all of them that you will unlock the corresponding secret. See overleaf for details.

There are numerous tasks that you can perform at this point in the story before you head to the showdown against Calamity Ganon at Hyrule Castle. All of these activities are entirely optional, but completing any of them will improve your odds of success in the game's final challenges.

- **GREAT FAIRY FOUNTAINS:** These are hidden in specific locations in Hyrule. Every time you find one, the great fairy it hosts will offer to upgrade your existing armor, increasing its stats in exchange for materials. These improvements substantially enhance Link's defense rating, which can make a significant difference during tough encounters. See page 326 for details.
- **SHRINES:** You have hopefully been exploring as many shrines as possible during your travels – see page 112 for a comprehensive guide to all 120. Trading the spirit orbs they yield for additional heart containers will make a real difference in the run-up to the conclusion of the story. Stamina vessels matter mostly for world exploration, but this is also very important as you have yet to visit entire regions, with many landmarks, quests, and confrontations that you have yet to experience. An extended stamina wheel has combat applications as well, enabling you to increase the duration of charged attacks performed with two-handed weapons.
- **MASTER SWORD:** A specific quest enables you to obtain the legendary Master Sword. This blade is especially relevant when you commit to retaking Hyrule Castle, including the confrontation with the final boss. Refer to page 100 for guidance.
- **KOROK SEEDS:** If you have been neglecting Korok seeds so far, now is a good time to begin to make amends. Having more slots to carry weapons, bows, and shields is a crucial upgrade, and enables you to eventually be more strategic in your choice of equipment – such as having a full collection of elemental blades at the ready. See page 330 for more information.
- **ELEMENTAL WEAPONS:** Don't underestimate this vital part of Link's attacking repertoire, as elemental weapons can help you to end many battles before they really get going. Ice-imbued weapons are particularly powerful as they will freeze most targets. Not only is the victim temporarily paralyzed, but the next attack you inflict actually deals triple damage. Against all but the most powerful bosses and sub-bosses, this trick can be used to eliminate many opponents with great efficiency. Refer to page 285 for details.
- **COOKING:** Before you raid Hyrule Castle, you'll need to prepare a good stock of top-class restorative dishes. If your heart bar is well developed (and at this stage, it should be) we recommend that you now prioritize items that feature the "hearty" adjective. These will always completely heal Link, irrespective of the size of the health gauge. This will shorten the downtime required to heal during combat and, as a fringe benefit, enable you to carry more meals. Concoctions granting bonuses to your defense, attack and movement speed are also very useful. Consult our coverage of cooking on page 296 if you would like to learn more.
- **FAIRIES:** Their ability to bring Link back from the dead makes fairies extraordinarily valuable creatures, particularly for tough challenges such as the game's final quest. Fairies are most commonly found around Great Fairy Fountains, but you can also occasionally reveal one by cutting tall grass; charged two-handed sword attacks work well for this purpose.
- **RUNE UPGRADES:** If you have yet to do so, consider making a quick visit to the Hateno Ancient Tech Lab. By speaking to Purah, you can unlock upgrades for your runes in exchange for materials dropped by Guardians. Upgrading your bombs and Stasis will make a real difference. See page 229 for details.
- **OPTIONAL OBJECTIVES:** Finally, don't forget that there are dozens of side quests, mini-games, and other optional activities that you can complete and reap benefits from. Our Side Quests and Extras chapters, which start on pages 214 and 324 respectively, offer a convenient directory of all potential diversions.

Captured Memories

At the beginning of the game, Impa gave you the task of finding 12 locations corresponding to the memories that appear in your Album. However it is only now, with a well-developed Link and a much better knowledge of Hyrule's landmarks, that you are in a position to complete this quest.

We have numbered these locations based on the order of the pictures in your Album from left to right, starting with the top row:

If you find all 12 and return to Impa, she will show you a painting that offers a clue to the whereabouts of a 13th memory. Head to the corresponding location to complete the quest. This will also unlock a secret scene during the game's finale.

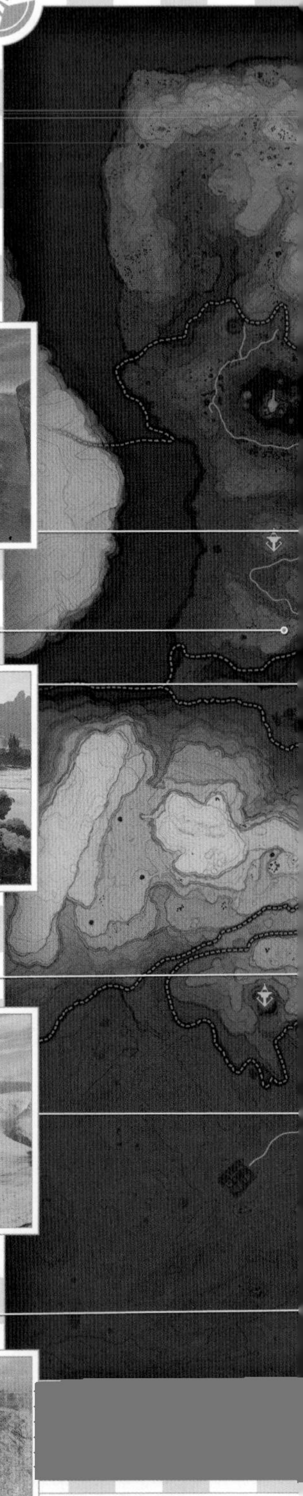

MEMORY 08

MEMORY 03

MEMORY 01

MEMORY 10

MEMORY 04

MEMORY 02

MEMORY 07

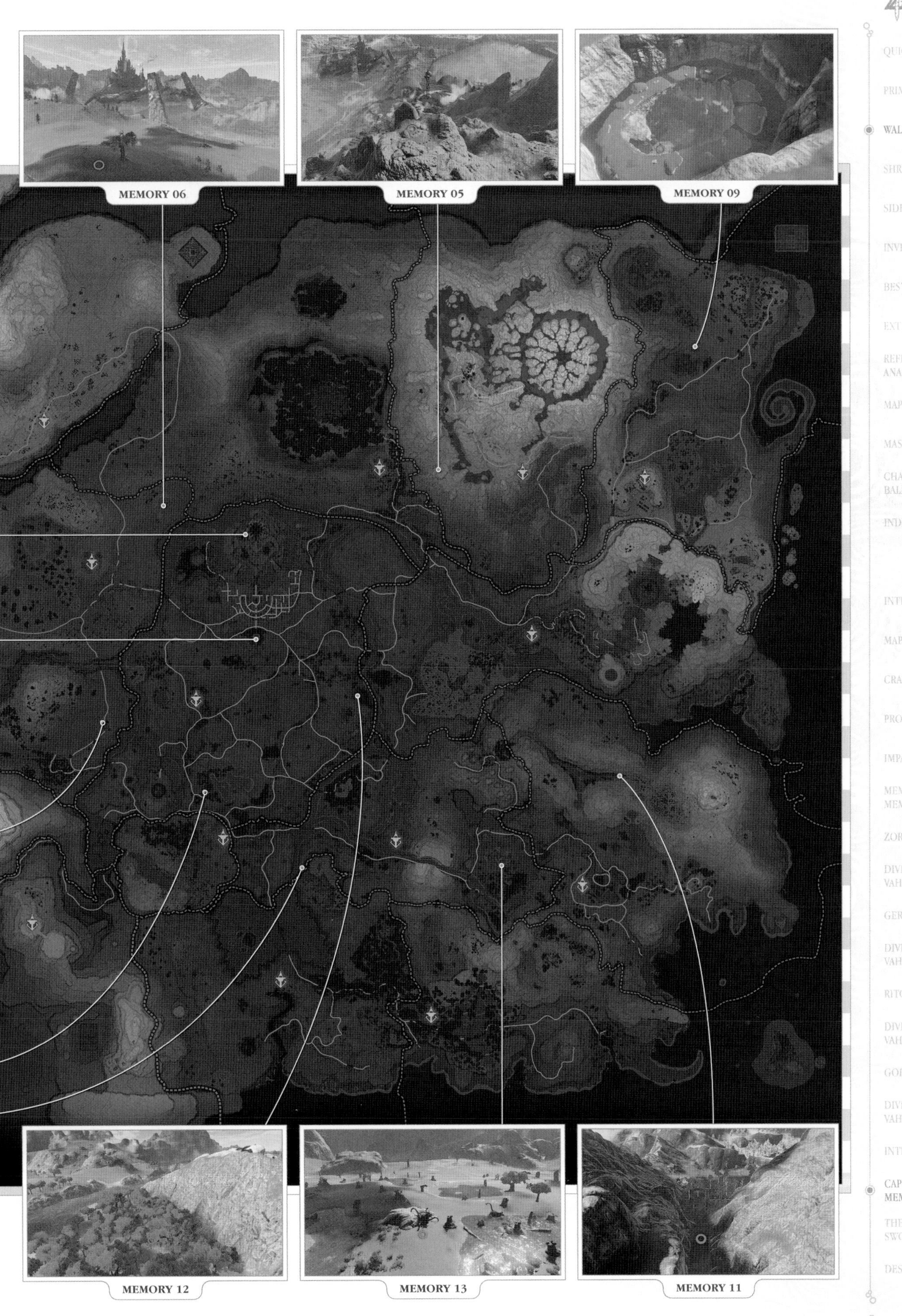
MEMORY 06
MEMORY 05
MEMORY 09
MEMORY 12
MEMORY 13
MEMORY 11

THE HERO'S SWORD

WALKTHROUGH SUMMARY (SEE OVERLEAF FOR DETAILS)

STEP	DESCRIPTION
1	Activate the Woodland Tower.
2 → 10	Make your way through the Lost Woods.
11 → 12	Explore the Korok Forest and retrieve the Master Sword.

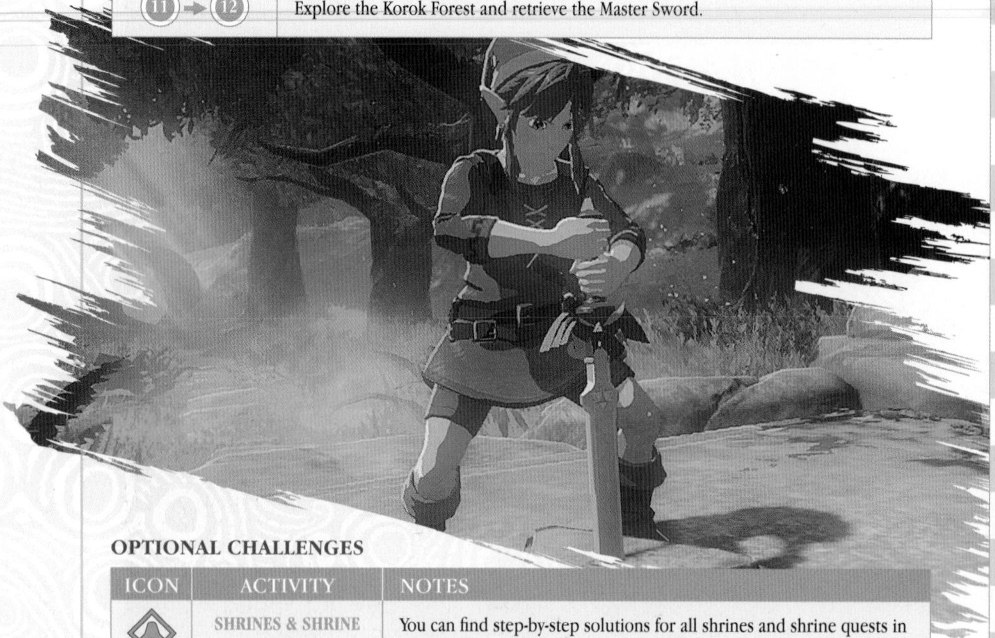

OPTIONAL CHALLENGES

ICON	ACTIVITY	NOTES
(Shrine icon)	SHRINES & SHRINE QUESTS	You can find step-by-step solutions for all shrines and shrine quests in the Woodland Tower region on page 194.
I	SIDE QUEST: BALLOON FLIGHT (see page 262)	Speak to Shamae at the Woodland Stable. Drop two octo balloons on one of the barrels in front of him so that it flies high into the air.
II	SIDE QUEST: FREEZING ROD (see page 262)	After initiating the "The Hero's Sword" main quest, speak to Kula in Korok Forest. He is usually found walking in the area where the Master Sword initially rests. He requires an ice-infused rod. You can obtain either an Ice Rod from an Ice Wizzrobe (there's one on the road between the Lanayru Tower and Foothill Stable, for example), or a Blizzard Rod from a Blizzrobe (you can find one in the round structures of Crenel Hills, to the east of Castle Hyrule).
III	SIDE QUEST: THE KOROK TRIALS (see page 263)	After initiating the "The Hero's Sword" main quest, speak to Chio in the Korok Forest, near the entrance leading to the local shops. He challenges you to complete three trials. These are actually shrine quests (see page 196 for guidance). Return to Chio after you've cleared all three.
IV	SIDE QUEST: LEGENDARY RABBIT TRIAL (see page 263)	After initiating "The Hero's Sword" (main quest) and The Priceless Maracas (side quest), speak to Peeks in the Korok Forest. He requires a picture of a Blupee – a glowing rabbit-like creature occasionally encountered in forests at night. The best location to find one is at the top of Satori Mountain, in the south part of the Ridgeland Tower region.
V	SIDE QUEST: LEVIATHAN BONES (see page 264)	Speak to the researchers at the Serenne Stable. They ask for pictures of a Leviathan skull. You can find one next to the Great Fairy Fountain to the southwest of Gerudo Town, one in the north of the Eldin region, and another inside an ice cave in the Hebra region.
VI	SIDE QUEST: RIDDLES OF HYRULE (see page 265)	If you climb to the top of the Great Deku Tree in Korok Forest, he will challenge you to take the ultimate trial. This is a series of riddles that you have to decipher. Whenever you have deduced the solution to a riddle, drop the corresponding item on the leaf in front of Walton to proceed to the next step.
VII	SIDE QUEST: A GIFT FROM THE MONKS (see page 264)	When you complete the final, 120th shrine by interacting with its altar, you will automatically trigger this quest. A reward awaits you at the Forgotten Temple. This is a secret landmark found at the north end of the Tanagar Canyon.

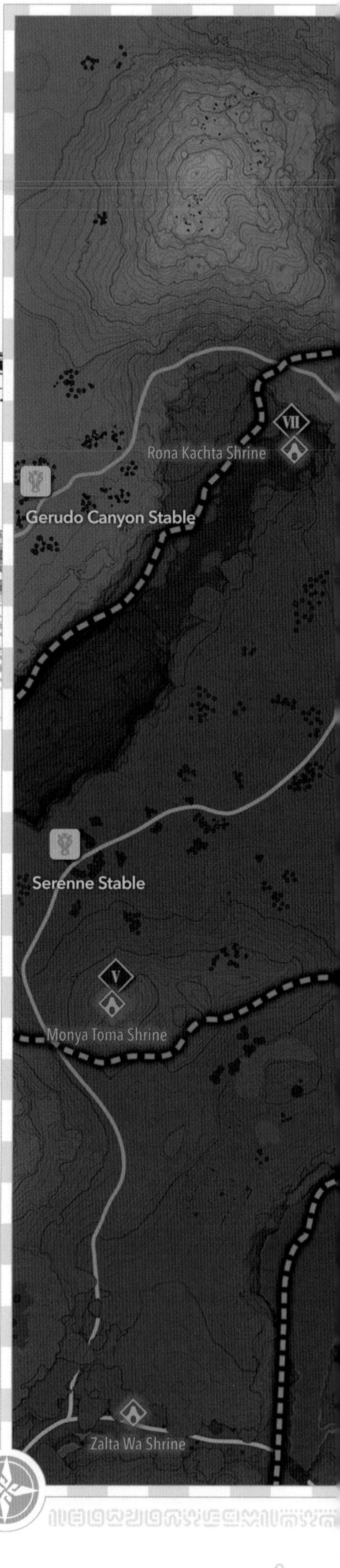

Ketoh Wawai Shrine

WOODLAND TOWER REGION

Daag Chokah Shrine

Maag Halan Shrine

Korok Forest

II III IV VI

Keo Ruug Shrine

Kuhn Sidajj Shrine

WOODLAND TOWER

Mirro Shaz Shrine

Woodland Stable

I

Saas Ko'sah Shrine

Namika Ozz Shrine

1

If you have not yet reached Woodland Tower by yourself, this can easily be accomplished from Lanayru Tower. Follow the road leading to the northwest. After you pass through the Woodland Stable, the tower itself a short distance away. It is surrounded by a large enemy outpost built on a bog, but this should pose no particular threat at this stage. Don't forget that ice-elemental weapons can freeze most creatures, enabling you to follow up with a strike inflicting triple damage. To cross the bog, summon as many ice blocks as you need with Cryonis.

2

Once you have activated the tower, glide to the northeast and land on the path leading to the entrance of the Lost Woods. You cannot glide directly to Korok Forest.

Important note: if you do not yet have 13 hearts, you cannot complete this quest. If this is the case for you, we suggest that you embark on a whirlwind tour of new shrines to gather the necessary resources for heart upgrades. Refer to our dedicated chapter on page 112 for guidance.

3

Navigating the Lost Woods can prove quite challenging. Whenever you step away from the only valid (but invisible) path, mist will surround you and return you to a previous position. In the first section, finding your way is actually easy: follow the trail of torches. The flames can be identified from a distance if you rotate the camera and carefully observe the environment.

4

When you reach the third flame in front of a large rock, make a 90-degree turn to your left and follow the trail of flames.

5

After another three flames, turn left again to find a lone flame.

6

From the lone flame, make a 90-degree turn to your right and head toward the two torches in the distance.

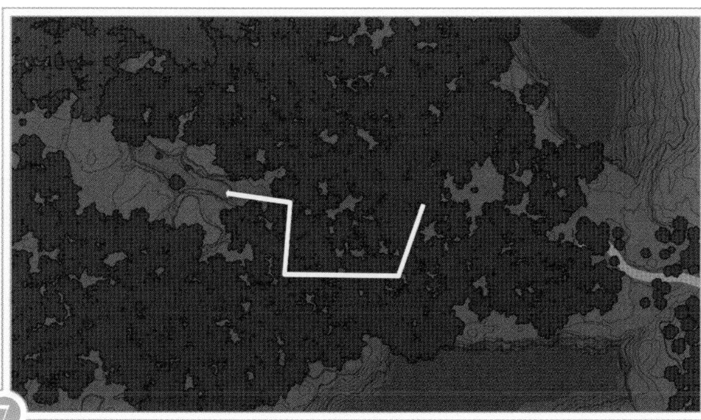

7

When you reach two torches side by side, the real challenge begins. You now need to find your way through the fog to reach the Korok Forest's entrance. If you stray from the correct invisible path, you will be taken back to the torches. The correct directions from the torches, if you just want a quick summary, are as follows: looking toward the nearby tree, take a left; halfway before you reach the shore, turn by 90 degrees to your right; when you reach a rock cliff, turn again by 90 degrees to your right; then turn by 90 degrees to your left to pass between the two rock cliffs. This is illustrated on the above map. The following three steps illustrate exactly when you are supposed to change direction.

8

From the two torches, take a left and head straight to the large tree shown here, barely visible through the fog. When you reach it, make a 90-degree turn to your right (west) and run straight forward.

9

When you reach a small hillock on your left, walk past it, then make a 90-degree turn to your right (north) and keep moving alongside the bottom of the cliff.

10

Running alongside the cliff, you will soon reach a small canyon on your left. Head through it and keep going straight: the rest of the path to Korok Forest is entirely safe and linear.

11

Your main objective in the Korok Forest is to pull the Master Sword from the stone. When you first interact with it, a cutscene will begin and the **"The Hero's Sword"** main mission is triggered. To obtain the weapon, you must fulfil a single condition: Link must have at least 13 full hearts. If you do, examine the Master Sword and it will be yours. If not, you must return here once your tally of heart containers reaches the required milestone. The Master Sword has a default attack value of 30, which is respectable but not spectacular for a one-handed blade. However, this value is doubled against enemies possessed by Calamity Ganon, which is the case of all those found in Hyrule Castle – including Ganon himself. Furthermore, the Master Sword cannot be broken: when it loses its charge, you just need to wait until a cooldown ends to begin using it again. Finally, the Master Sword can fire a projectile beam: hold then release R whenever Link is at full health.

12

In addition to the Master Sword, the Korok Forest is home to various interesting features: a shrine, three shrine quests, multiple side quests, and Hestu – the creature who will expand your inventory in exchange for your Korok seeds. If he has received a sufficient amount of Korok seeds from you at your previous encounters with him near Kakariko Village and at the Woodland stable, Hestu can be found a short walk east of the Master Sword.

DESTROY GANON

WALKTHROUGH SUMMARY (SEE OVERLEAF FOR DETAILS)

STEP	DESCRIPTION
	Make your way to the Sanctum and defeat Calamity Ganon.

OPTIONAL CHALLENGES

ICON	ACTIVITY	NOTES
	SHRINES & SHRINE QUESTS	You can find step-by-step solutions for all shrines and shrine quests in the Central and Ridgeland Tower regions on pages 168 and 174.
I	SIDE QUEST: A GIFT FOR THE GREAT FAIRY (see page 268)	Speak to Toren at the Tabantha Bridge Stable, at the west edge of the Ridgeland region. He asks you to find a Great Fairy Fountain for him by climbing Tabantha Tower and locating the fountain by using the tower's afternoon shadow. The fountain is located to the south of Tabantha Tower, at the base of Piper Ridge. It is in the small pond that is visible on your map.
II	SIDE QUEST: THE ROYAL GUARD'S GEAR (see page 268)	Speak to Parcy at the Riverside Stable. She asks you to find a piece of the "royal guard" series. You can find the royal guard's sword behind a doorway blocked by destructible rocks, in the corridor to the left when you reach the top of the stairs after the armory (see step 5 overleaf).
III	SIDE QUEST: A ROYAL RECIPE (see page 269)	Speak to Gotter at the Riverside Stable. You can find two recipes for him in Hyrule Castle's Library: a first on a large wooden table on the ground floor, and another on a small bookstand on one of the upper walkways. If you struggle to find these by yourself, we reveal their ingredients on page 269.
IV	SIDE QUEST: THE ROYAL WHITE STALLION (see page 269)	Speak to Toffa at the Outskirt Stable, in the far southwest of the Central Tower region. He asks you to find a specific white horse. Head to Safula Hill, across the river to the northwest. You can capture the horse in question like any other horse, though this one is warier and will require you to crouch-walk at the slowest possible speed over the final yards of your approach. Once the horse is under control, take it back to the stable to register it, then speak to Toffa again.
V	SIDE QUEST: A RARE FIND (see page 268)	Speak to Trott at the Outskirt Stable. He needs raw gourmet meat, which you can obtain from various large mammals, including wolves, bears, buffalos, and rhinos.
VI	SIDE QUEST: MY HERO (see page 268)	Speak to Aliza at the Outskirt Stable. All you need to complete this quest is to show her the Master Sword (see page 100).
VII	SUB-BOSS: STONE TALUS (RARE) (see page 314)	A rare version of the Stone Talus awaits in Hyrule Castle's East Passage, which you can access from the northeast shore. It is fast and aggressive. The best way to defeat it is to constantly remain close to its crystal weak point and attack it with a spear-type weapon from the ground.

CENTRAL & RIDGELAND TOWER REGIONS

CENTRAL TOWER & HYRULE CASTLE

If you haven't done so already, start by activating Central Tower to unfog the map in this region. This should pose no particular problems at this stage. There are a few Guardians in the area, including a Guardian Stalker, but you can either avoid them or eliminate them by perfect-guarding their laser beams. From the top of the tower, you are in a good position to observe Hyrule Castle. There are many points of entry and optional rooms with valuable rewards inside. We offer a "grand tour" of the castle overleaf, but you should feel absolutely free to explore on your own and choose whichever approach works best for you. The only mandatory step of this final mission is to reach the Sanctum in the center of the castle, where Ganon awaits the inevitable showdown with Link.

HYRULE CASTLE – THE STRAIGHT PATH

If you want to reach Ganon quickly and painlessly, there is a supremely easy way to do this. Equip the Zora Armor and use it to swim back up the river and to swim upward every time you reach a waterfall. This will lead you straight to the castle's Sanctum with practically no enemy encounters; you can just run past the few Guardians you cross paths with. The current in the river surrounding the castle is strong, so you should ideally jump to the first waterfall from the nearby walkway.

lonya Toma Shrine
Saas Ko'sah Shrine
Noya Neha Shrine
Zalta Wa Shrine
Hyrule Castle
Hyrule Castle Ruins
Katah Chuki Shrine
CENTRAL TOWER REGION
Wetland Stable
Kaya Wan Shrine
CENTRAL TOWER
Kaam Ya'tak Shrine
Wahgo Katta Shrine
Riverside Stable
Outskirt Stable
a Ooh Shrine

1

APPROACH: We suggest that you go on a grand tour of Hyrule Castle as it features many secrets and optional collectibles that are well worth the effort – including powerful weapons, shields, and bows that can prove immensely useful during the battle against Ganon. If you are already suitably equipped and do not wish to explore, feel free to take the straight path via the waterfalls as described on the previous double-page spread. Otherwise, approach the castle from the north. Standing on the cliff facing the back of the castle, you will see two cave entrances: first, go through the one on the right, leading to the Lockup (2); then head through the one of the left leading to the Docks (3).

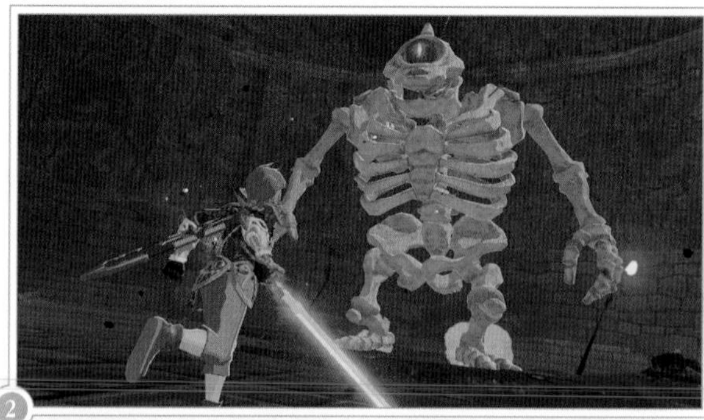

2

LOCKUP & HYLIAN SHIELD: The Lockup (which you can enter by lifting the entrance gate with Magnesis) features multiple cells behind which enemies are trapped. You can access them by opening the doors via levers or by blowing up destructible walls – they all lead to minor treasure. The grand prize, though, is found in the final room to the right. After eliminating a Stalnox sub-boss, you earn the right to collect the best shield in the entire game: Link's Hylian shield. This features unequaled stats, making it a fantastic asset for the showdown against Ganon. Defeating the Stalnox should pose no particular problem at this stage: just don't forget to hit its eye when it falls on the floor with only a fraction of its health left. Once the Hylian shield is yours, backtrack to the entrance and this time head through the main tunnel leading to the Docks.

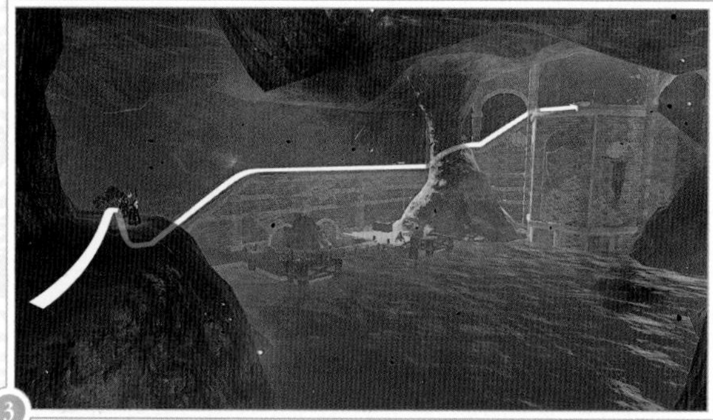

3

DOCKS: At the Docks, follow the ledge on the left-hand wall then go up the stairs. When you reach the upper floor, you can make the Saas Ko'sah Shrine appear by setting the brazier ablaze, though this is of course optional (see page 173). When you're ready to proceed, run up the long stairway that follows.

4

LIBRARY & KING'S STUDY: At the top of the stairs, grab the bookcase that blocks the path with Magnesis. This gives you access to the Library. You can use the bookcase or the nearby metallic cube as a cudgel to eliminate the few creatures in this room. You will find two recipes from open books: one on a large wooden table on the ground floor, one on a small bookstand on one of the upper walkways. These are involved in a specific side quest (see page 269). There are two other metallic bookcases that can be moved with Magnesis to reveal secret passages: one leads to a treasure chest and ore deposits, while the other leads to the King's Study. The King's Study is home to a note from King Rhoam and also contains the very sturdy royal guard's shield. Once you are satisfied with the current progress of your light pillaging, make your way to the exit on the opposite side via the upper walkway.

5

ARMORY: Follow the linear corridors until you make it to the armory. After defeating the few enemies in this room, pick up as many weapons as you can. There are very valuable and powerful pieces here. Climb to the floor above once you're done. Leaving the armory, you enter a corridor and come to a T-intersection: the door to the right leads to the Dining Hall (see next step). The dead end to the left features a doorway that is blocked by destructible rocks. Blow these up with bombs to obtain a royal guard's sword, which is required for the completion of a side quest.

6

DINING HALL: The next room you will come across is the Dining Hall. This features a few monsters and, more importantly, large quantities of ingredients that you can collect. A cooking pot in one corner of the room means that you can use this opportunity to prepare dishes with powerful restorative properties or other special effects if your supplies are low.

7

OBSERVATION ROOM: Your next destination is down the stairs close to the Dining Hall's wooden doors, at the end of the corridor in the opposite direction of the dead end with the royal guard's sword. On the Observation Room's upper landing you will find a treasure chest and collectible arrows. When you're ready to proceed, glide to your right from the balcony then reenter the castle via the door just before the waterfall. You will find a closed gate after a few steps: raise it with Cryonis to open the way. In the next corridor, you will soon reach a crossroads: the passage to the left leads to the Guards' Chamber (8), while the one to the right leads to a long corridor (9).

8

GUARDS' CHAMBER: From the corridor, take a left and pay a visit to the Guards' Chamber. In addition to a few opponents, this room is home to multiple advanced weapons, as well as hidden treasure chests with valuable contents: you will find one underneath both sets of stairs; you can climb to two additional ones on the upper deck. After you've plundered the weapon racks, backtrack to the previous corridor.

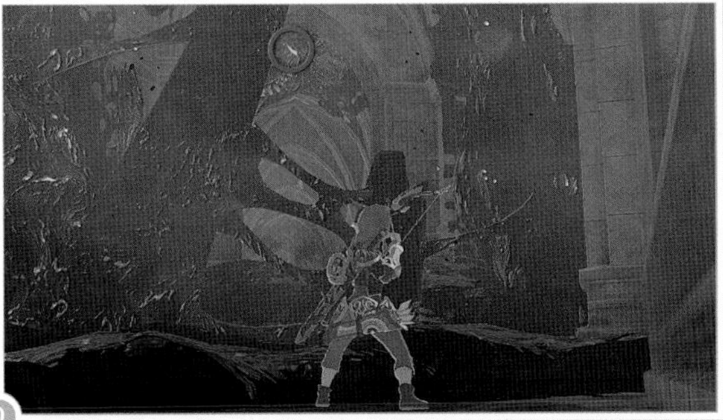

9

CORRIDOR: This time, take a right and head into the long corridor infested with Malice goo. When you reach the point where the goo completely blocks the way forward, peer through the opening in the toxic substance. Shoot an arrow at the glowing eyeball to clear the path, then exit the castle at the other end.

10

PRINCESS ZELDA'S ROOM & STUDY: Back in the open air, run up the nearby stairs. There are multiple flights and a small cliff to climb to reach Princess Zelda's Room. Inside you will find a powerful royal guard's bow above the fireplace, as well as Zelda's diary on a desk. Now climb up to the level above and cross the small bridge to reach Princess Zelda's Study in the small tower outside. This contains both Zelda's research journal and a silent princess flower.

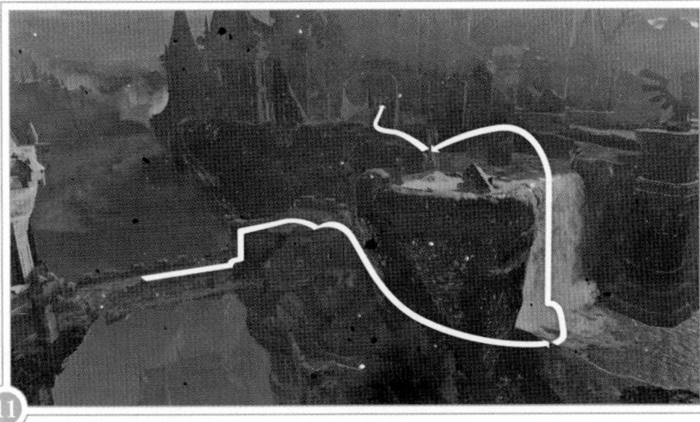

11

SANCTUM: From Zelda's Study, glide to the pool and use the Zora Armor to swim up the waterfalls until you reach the castle's main entrance. Once you enter the Sanctum beyond this doorway, you will hit a point of no return: the game's grand finale against Ganon will begin.

BOSSES: If you haven't freed all four Divine Beasts, note that you must face each undefeated boss inside the Sanctum before Calamity Ganon himself. If you haven't cleared the Vah Naboris dungeon, for example, you will find Thunderblight Ganon on your way, taking a toll on your resources before you even begin the battle against the main boss. In addition, you will enjoy neither the gift of the corresponding Champions (in this case, Urbosa's Fury) nor the health reduction applied to Calamity Ganon. This is why it is so important to complete all four dungeons prior to finishing the game, as described in this Walkthrough.

12

FIRST GATEHOUSE & SECOND GATEHOUSE: Optionally, note that you can visit the two round tower buildings on the main road, both within walking distance from Princess Zelda's Study. Each pits you against a high-level Lynel. These are extremely difficult battles, potentially harder than your imminent duel against Ganon himself. We suggest you confront these enemies only if you feel very confident in your perfect-guarding skills. The one in the First Gatehouse is a Blue-Maned Lynel, while the other one in the Second Gatehouse is an even more dangerous White-Maned Lynel. Feel free to use Revali's Gale to glide over the Malice goo separating the two buildings, though swimming also works. You can find more details concerning these creatures in our Bestiary chapter (see page 320). If you manage to defeat them, they will drop their remarkable weapons, shields, and bows; there will also be a treasure chest that offers an additional reward.

SUMMARY

OVERVIEW: After the battle's introduction, the champions of Hyrule that you rescued step in, unleashing the power of their Divine Beasts. Each one of them removes one eighth of Ganon's health bar. If you have conquered all four Divine Beasts, this means that the health of your enemy will be down by 50% when the battle begins. Calamity Ganon uses techniques derived from those of the four dungeon bosses, so you should be familiar with most of them.

STRATEGY: Arrows can be used to slowly chip away at Ganon's health, but the best way to cause large amounts of damage is via perfect dodges followed up by flurry rushes. Flurry rushes offer one very substantial benefit over perfect guard counters in this battle: the slow-motion effect they trigger means that Ganon cannot execute his area-of-effect attack every time you are within melee range. This makes flurry rushes the most efficient way to take down your opponent. If you are wielding the Master Sword (see page 100), you can inflict massive damage while keeping your shield at hand to perfect guard your enemy's laser beam attacks. Keep your target in sight at all times, defend against its long-range assaults and perform flurry rushes at close range.

FIRST PHASE: ATTACK OVERVIEW

The following captions illustrate the various types of assault that Calamity Ganon will use against you, and detail how to best defend against them or counter them.

At close range, Calamity Ganon will regularly perform melee attacks with his fire-infused sword, much like those executed by Fireblight Ganon (see page 95). These cause fire to spread at their point of impact, making them extremely dangerous. They require rather long preparation times, which makes them relatively easy to counter with a perfect dodge or perfect guard: initiate your command as soon as you notice the creature's arm start to move forward.

Calamity Ganon will also regularly attack with his blue-glowing Guardian blades. These are much swifter, and therefore harder to perfect dodge. Have your shield drawn at all times except when you are counterattacking to at least negate the damage of these blows.

Just like Windblight Ganon (see page 84), this boss frequently summons large tornadoes that move rather unpredictably in your direction. These cannot be blocked or stopped, so starting sprinting away from them as soon as they appear.

Your opponent also possesses the galestrike attack employed by Windblight Ganon. This technique cannot be blocked. Whenever you notice your foe point his weapon at you with a vortex of wind forming in front of it, sprint in a lateral direction to evade the incoming shot.

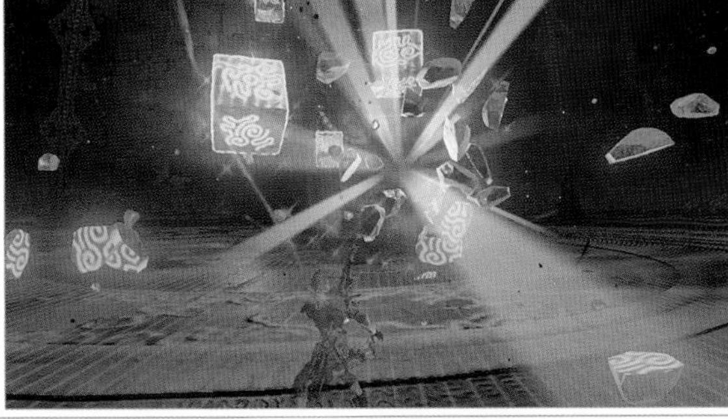

You will surely remember this attack from your encounter against Waterblight Ganon (see page 60). Whenever you notice that your enemy is summoning multiple ice blocks in the air, prepare your Cryonis rune and stand ready to press Ⓐ repeatedly while aiming at the incoming projectiles to shatter them. Sprinting away is also a possibility.

If your opponent summons pillars that fall close to you, be swift to sprint away. These will soon be struck by lightning, causing shock damage in the area.

When Ganon throws a fireball at you, you have two options: either running as far away as you can from the point of impact, or freezing it with an ice arrow.

Your opponent will regularly fire blue-glowing projectiles at you. These can be perfect-guarded. If you succeed, they will be redirected at Ganon and stun him – leaving him vulnerable to a full combo.

If you stay within melee range for more than a few seconds, Ganon will generally perform an area-of-effect attack, with blue energy striking everything around him. This is an unblockable technique, so you cannot afford to remain at close range unless you have stunned your foe beforehand.

Last but not least, your enemy will occasionally throw his spear at you. If you identify this in advance, you can easily dodge it with a sidehop or sprint away from its point of impact.

SECOND PHASE

After losing 50% of his starting health, Ganon will summon a fire energy field that protects him from all of your assaults. You can only inflict damage if you temporarily disable this protective barrier.

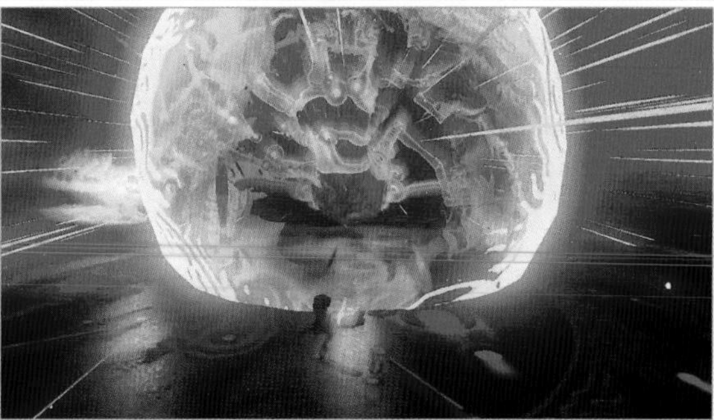

SUMMARY

OVERVIEW & STRATEGY: In the second phase, Ganon will regularly summon a field of fire energy that makes him invincible. As long as his body glows orange, none of your direct attacks can harm him. His assaults remain the same, with only a single addition to his repertoire, so you have no reason to panic: just defend calmly and consistently until you manage to create an opening. The following captions illustrate how you can achieve this. Every time you stun your enemy, rush to him and unleash your most powerful combo.

SECOND PHASE: POSSIBLE COUNTERS

The following captions illustrate the various methods you have at your disposal to counter your opponent, and therefore break his otherwise impenetrable defense.

GUN SHOTS: The easiest method to stun Ganon is probably to perfect guard his blue-glowing projectiles. He usually fires six of them at you, each one presenting a unique opportunity for a perfect guard counter. If you succeed, the beam will stun Ganon: rush to him and attack ferociously until a new cycle begins. Should you fail, the beams are not very powerful and will have a nominal effect on your shield's durability.

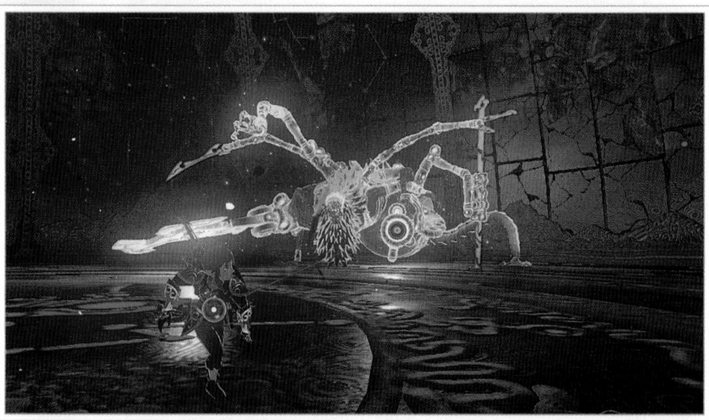

LASER BEAM: By now, you should be entirely familiar with this technique. Ganon directs a red laser at you. When his attack is fully charged, a powerful beam is fired. A successful perfect guard will redirect it back to Ganon and offer you an opportunity to attack. However, the timing here is particularly tricky: the charge delay is brief and the beam moves at very high speed. You therefore need to initiate the perfect guard a fraction of a second *before* the beam materializes. If your timing is off, your shield will be destroyed. Should you run out of shields, you will not be able to perfect guard either the blue projectiles or the laser beam, leaving you in a fairly dire predicament. If you are not confident in your ability to perfect guard the laser beam, sprint away from it and save your shield for the less effortful blue projectiles.

MELEE ATTACKS: Every time Ganon performs melee attacks, you have an opportunity to perform a perfect dodge or perfect guard by initiating your command at the last second. You can then follow up with a flurry rush or standard counter respectively, both of which will damage your opponent irrespective of its stalwart defense. As a rule, we recommend the perfect dodge/flurry rush combination, as its slow-motion effect leaves you less exposed to an immediate riposte when your opponent recovers.

BOSS: DARK BEAST GANON

1 After Calamity Ganon falls, you will regain control of Link outside the castle, facing a gigantic foe: Dark Beast Ganon. As soon as the final battle begins, collect and equip the nearby Bow of Light. This offers unparalleled power and infinite ammo. You do not need to get down from your horse: just gallop toward the bow and Link will pick it up automatically.

2 With the Bow of Light drawn, head to either side of the creature and wait for glyphs to appear on its body. As soon as they do, slow down, or even stop your horse if you are not currently under threat, and fire an arrow at all three of them: one at the top of each leg, and one on the flank. Feel free to fire liberally: your ammo is unlimited.

3 After eliminating the three light glyphs on one side of Dark Beast Ganon, gallop to the other side and repeat the process: fire an arrow at each of the three glyphs that appear.

4 When the first six glyphs have been hit, a seventh one will appear on the creature's belly. Gallop beneath it and look up: this is an easy shot at such close range.

5 Finally, gallop until you are in front of Dark Beast Ganon. You will soon see its weak point appear in the form of a large eyeball. If you fire an arrow at it from the ground, though, the eyelids will close and prevent you from dealing any damage. Instead, wait for your enemy to unleash a beam of energy, and use the updraft this generates to fly high in the air. This offers a cinematic opportunity for a *perfect* slow-motion finishing arrow...

POST-CREDITS PLAY

You may have reached the end of the main storyline, but your adventure in Hyrule is far from complete. After the credits roll, your game will be saved automatically. If you later load this save file from the title screen, you will be able to resume your playthrough at the entrance to Hyrule Castle's Sanctum with your equipment and parameters unchanged. This save file will feature a star icon, acknowledging the fact that you have defeated Ganon.

In addition to the main narrative, *Breath of the Wild* features dozens of side quests, mini-games, and optional challenges that you have probably yet to discover, let alone complete. Turn the page to read about these diversions, plus a variety of other enjoyable end-game activities…

SHRINES

This chapter has been designed to guide you through all shrines and, when applicable, the challenges required to reveal them. Throughout the chapter, we use sequences of annotated screenshots with accompanying captions. These highlight essential actions that need to be performed, providing at-a-glance solutions to all puzzles.

INTRODUCTION

Shrines are landmarks that you will encounter very regularly as you travel the vast expanses of Hyrule. Most of them are miniature versions of dungeons, challenging you to solve all sorts of physical or logical puzzles.

STRUCTURE

Every shrine in the game has the following features:

- An **entrance**: you can interact with this to leave a shrine prematurely if you wish, though fast travelling from any position in the shrine works just as well.
- At least one **treasure chest**: these can be directly in your path and easy to reach, or, instead, very hard to reach, offering a small puzzle of their own. Treasure chests are generally entirely optional: whether you open them or not has no influence on your ability to clear a shrine. The only exceptions to this rule are the few cases where a chest contains a small key required to open a locked door. Note that once you've cleared a shrine and opened all ist treasure chests on the way, a chest symbol will be displayed next to the shrine name on the map.
- An **altar**, easy to identify, thanks to the blue energy field that surrounds it: examining the altar completes the shrine and rewards you with a spirit orb.

PUZZLES

For most shrines, the path from the entrance to the altar features puzzles that rely on all sorts of mechanics, such as runes, your ability to carefully observe your environment and think creatively, your understanding of elements, to name but a few.

Throughout the chapter, we use sequences of annotated screenshots, with white arrows representing the path taken by Link, and blue arrows representing the movements of objects. These will guide you as you clear each dungeon, illustrating every key step of the way and enabling you to identify solutions in the blink of an eye.

Before you turn to our solutions, however, we strongly suggest that you attempt to solve puzzles by yourself. Every single one of them has been carefully designed and balanced by its creators. Many even offer multiple solutions, rewarding creative thinking. Puzzles in *Breath of the Wild* are both fun and fair, and clearing them can be one of the most enjoyable activities in the game.

To help you get started, here are a few recommendations that will enable you to develop the right habits:

- The most important point is that you should always try to think rationally. There is no magic trick to use, you don't need any specific knowledge or a degree in quantum physics to clear shrines: all you need is common sense and patience. More often than not, after solving a puzzle that initially seemed frustrating or insurmountable, you will realize that you had simply overlooked something obvious.
- One of the keys to solving puzzles is methodical observation: whenever you enter a new room, look around, heading to a vantage point if possible. Can you see any interactive objects such as floor switches, pedestals and orbs, launchers, crystals, or torches? These devices are always involved to some degree in the solution. Refer to our Primer on page 30 for a visual depiction of the most important of these puzzle components.
- If you can't spot anything of interest at first glance, scan the environment with your runes active. Potential targets appear in bright magenta for Magnesis and yellow for Stasis. If you spot one of these, the chances are that you can do something productive with it. An overwhelming majority of puzzles involve at least one rune, which makes this scanning process so pivotal. Likewise, if you notice a pool, or even a small puddle, keep in mind that you can create blocks of ice on top of water with Cryonis.
- Consider the possibility of using multiple runes at a time. For instance, you may need to stop a moving platform with Stasis, then drop a bomb on it while it's frozen in time. For a presentation of all runes, turn to page 28 in our Primer.
- Think logically in terms of the natural laws of physics. Dozens of puzzles are based on the game's physics engine, particularly gravity. This can mean, for instance, dropping a barrel on a seesaw to be propelled in the air, placing objects of various weights on balance scale devices, or activating floor panels with heavy items.

If you approach puzzles methodically, following the above points, you will very regularly experience "eureka" moments, significantly enhancing your enjoyment of the game.

AVAILABILITY

In the wild, most of the shrines are available by default. Standing at the top of a tower, you will frequently spot a couple of these: feel free to pin them with your scope, making the process to reach them far easier. The fact that towers are very tall enables you to safely glide toward the shrines that you have located in this manner, and thus reach them quickly. Once you have cleared one, you can warp back instantly to the tower and repeat. This is one of the most effective ways to scout new regions.

In addition to shrines that are blatantly visible in the open, many others are also available by default, but hidden: at the bottom of a pit, inside a small cave, or at the top of a mountain peak. This is why it makes so much sense to venture off the beaten path in this game. Your curiosity and perseverance will almost always pay off. Your Sheikah Sensor will help you track down these shrines. The sensor is represented by an antenna icon on your screen ( ). Whenever a shrine is available in the current perimeter, the sensor starts glowing. The concentric circles light up when Link moves in the direction of the shrine: the better his alignment, the more circles glow.

The hardest shrines to reach are those buried in the ground, as these are usually not detected by your sensor. To reveal them, you must carry out specific tasks, such as setting nearby lanterns ablaze or interacting with a pedestal in a specific way. You will generally find clues in the area to put you on the right track (a stone tablet with a riddle, for instance), and many of these challenges are actually part of shrine quests, which are listed in your adventure log once triggered.

REWARDS

Much like towers, shrines are high-priority targets in terms of exploration, as they offer valuable rewards on completion:

- A **spirit orb** – an item that you can trade in bundles of four for additional heart containers or stamina vessels. This is achieved by interacting with any of the goddess statues scattered in Hyrule.
- At least one **treasure chest** (and often more) with contents that tend to be worthwhile – gemstones, weapons, even special pieces of armor occasionally.
- Additionally, each shrine that you activate by interacting with the terminal at its entrance turns into a **fast travel position**. As the game features over a hundred shrines, these soon form a network that enables you to warp to virtually anywhere on the map. This proves particularly handy when carrying out side quests and optional objectives at the four corners of Hyrule.

SHRINE DIRECTORY

If you are looking for guidance for a specific shrine, this alphabetical list will enable you to find it in no time. The contents of most shrine chests are fixed, but note that the weapons you obtain can vary based on your progression. In this table, we reveal "base" weapons; the further you are in the adventure, the more likely you are to find better variants: either the same weapons but with bonuses, or stronger weapons within the same category.

SHRINE DIRECTORY

NAME	CHEST CONTENTS	PAGE
Akh Va'quot	Ancient Core, Sapphire, Feathered Spear	180
Bareeda Naag	Falcon Bow, Diamond	181
Bosh Kala	Amber, Soldier's Claymore	118
Chaas Qeta	Climbing Gear	126
Daag Chokah	Ancient Core	196
Dagah Keek	Silver Rupee	137
Dah Hesho	Giant Ancient Core	209
Dah Kaso	Ancient Core	170
Daka Tuss	Silver Longsword	135
Dako Tah	Moonlight Scimitar, Ancient Core, Silver Rupee, Radiant Shield	152
Daqa Koh	Silver Rupee	203
Daqo Chisay	Thunderblade	154
Dila Maag	Barbarian Armor	158
Dow Na'eh	Zora Sword, Amber, Opal	128
Dunba Taag	Falcon Bow, Great Thunderblade	192
Gee Ha'rah	Diamond	193
Goma Asaagh	Royal Claymore	188
Gorae Torr	Great Frostblade	203
Ha Dahamar	Purple Rupee	118
Hawa Koth	Ancient Core, Gold Rupee, Sapphire	157
Hia Miu	Sapphire	186
Hila Rao	Opal, Ice Arrow x5	119
Ishto Soh	Topaz, Ancient Core	148
Ja Baij	Traveler's Claymore, Amber	40
Jee Noh	Opal	150
Jitan Sa'mi	Frostspear	127
Joloo Nah	Golden Claymore, Gerudo Spear	166
Ka'o Makagh	Traveler's Bow, Gold Rupee, Opal	146
Kaam Ya'tak	Edge of Duality, Knight's Broadsword, Ancient Core, Silver Rupee, Diamond	169
Kah Mael	Diamond	132
Kah Okeo	Korok Leaf, Gold Rupee, Forest Dweller's Sword, Giant Ancient Core	184
Kah Yah	Knight's Claymore	141
Kam Urog	Opal, Soldier's Spear	129
Katah Chuki	Royal Halberd	172
Katosa Aug	Great Frostblade	209
Kay Noh	Gerudo Scimitar	151
Kaya Wan	Ancient Core, Knight's Broadsword	133
Kayra Mah	Ruby, Bomb Arrow x5	202
Keeha Yoog	Diamond	165
Keh Namut	Traveler's Spear	43
Kema Kosassa	Silver Rupee	163
Kema Zoos	Moonlight Scimitar	155
Ke'nai Shakah	Sapphire	212
Keo Ruug	Knight's Claymore	199
Ketoh Wawai	Ancient Core	195
Korgu Chideh	Gold Rupee	143
Korsh O'hu	Flamespear	160
Kuh Takkar	Frostblade	162
Kuhn Sidajj	Giant Ancient Core	197
Lakna Rokee	Edge of Duality	122
Lanno Kooh	Gold Rupee	191
Maag Halan	Giant Ancient Core	198
Maag No'rah	Silver Rupee	177
Maka Rah	Bomb Arrow x10, Diamond, Ancient Core	190
Mezza Lo	Thunderblade	125
Mijah Rokee	Frostblade	176
Mirro Shaz	Iron Sledgehammer x2, Giant Ancient Core	194
Misae Suma	Diamond	161
Mo'a Keet	Knight's Broadsword	204
Mogg Latan	Forest Dweller's Spear, Forest Dweller's Bow, Gold Rupee	179
Monya Toma	Thunderblade	194
Mozo Shenno	Diamond	187
Muwo Jeem	Knight's Bow	145
Myahm Agana	Phrenic Bow	124
Namika Ozz	Frostspear	172
Ne'ez Yohma	Zora Spear	130
Noya Neha	Knight Shield	170
Oman Au	Traveler's Bow	39
Owa Daim	Traveler's Shield	42
Pumaag Nitae	Boomerang	148
Qaza Tokki	Barbarian Leg Wraps	186
Qua Raym	Knight's Claymore	201
Qukah Nata	Rubber Tights	139
Raqa Zunzo	Radiant Shield	156
Ree Dahee	Climber's Bandana	121
Rin Oyaa	Ancient Core	191
Ritaag Zumo	Giant Ancient Core	213
Rok Uwog	Drillshaft	189
Rona Kachta	Great Flameblade	196
Rota Ooh	Feathered Edge	168
Rucco Maag	Opal, Silver Bow	131
Saas Ko'sah	Flameblade	173
Sah Dahaj	Knight's Bow	208
Sasa Kai	Frostblade	167
Sha Gehma	Royal Broadsword	188
Sha Warvo	Purple Rupee, Knight's Bow	182
Shada Naw	Great Frostblade	187
Shae Katha	Thunderspear	145
Shae Loya	Topaz, Falcon Bow	177
Shae Mo'sah	Stone Smasher, Ruby, Ice Arrow x10	205
Shai Utoh	Traveller's Sword, Ancient Core	144
Shai Yota	Great Flameblade	136
Shee Vaneer	Eightfold Longblade	120
Shee Venath	Serpentine Spear, Eightfold Longblade	120
Sheem Dagoze	Great Thunderblade	178
Sheh Rata	Opal, Giant Boomerang	134
Sho Dantu	Silver Rupee	164
Shoda Sah	Ice Arrow x5	140
Shoqa Tatone	Royal Broadsword	147
Shora Hah	Royal Bow, Great Flameblade, Giant Ancient Core, Forest Dweller's Sword, Silver Rupee, Ice Arrow x10	206
Soh Kofi	Knight's Bow	132
Suma Sahma	Moonlight Scimitar	153
Ta'loh Naeg	Shield of the Mind's Eye, Eightfold Blade, Opal	122
Tah Muhl	Ruby, Opal, Cobble Crusher	200
Tahno O'ah	Climbing Boots	126
Tawa Jinn	Great Thunderblade	142
Tena Ko'sah	Knight's Halberd	185
Tho Kayu	Golden Bow	159
To Quomo	Royal Claymore	189
Toh Yahsa	Rubber Armor, Opal	175
Toto Sah	Shield of the Mind's Eye	123
Tu Ka'loh	Barbarian Helm	213
Tutsuwa Nima	Flamespear	211
Voo Lota	Flameblade	183
Wahgo Katta	Amber	171
Ya Naga	Eightfold Blade	149
Yah Rin	Knight's Broadsword, Opal	138
Zalta Wa	Knight's Bow	174
Ze Kasho	Silverscale Spear	210
Zuna Kai	Flameblade	212

SHRINE MAP

This map shows the position of the 116 optional shrines that are covered in this chapter, as well as the four introduced in the Walkthrough chapter. Note that you can also find all shrines represented on area maps in the pages that follow, and on the guide's poster, enabling you to use both the poster and this chapter simultaneously if you wish.

Shrines are sorted by region – the very regions that are initially marked out on your in-game map and that will be "unfogged" when you activate the local tower. These regions appear in the following pages in an order that reflects the progression suggested in our Walkthrough.

A shrine icon can appear under different colors based on its current completion status. When you first reveal a shrine on your map, it is represented by a yellow icon (◈). Once you interact with the terminal at its entrance (turning it into a fast travel position), its icon outline turns blue (◈). Completing the shrine by examining the altar makes the icon entirely blue (◈). In addition, opening all treasure chests within a shrine triggers the appearance of a chest icon when you select the shrine in question on your map screen: this corresponds to 100% completion for each individual shrine.

GREAT PLATEAU SHRINES

Note that the four Great Plateau shrines visited during the main storyline act as simple introductions to the primary functions of each rune. These are covered in our Walkthrough chapter. Refer to page 38 if you need any guidance to complete them.

SHRINE QUEST OVERVIEW

Shrine Quest	Page
A Brother's Roast	202
A Fragmented Monument	141
A Landscape of a Stable	200
A Song of Storms	139
Cliffside Etchings	165
Guardian Slideshow	147
Into the Vortex	213
Master of the Wind	136
Recital at Warbler's Nest	183
Secret of the Cedars	126
Secret of the Snowy Peaks	153
Shrouded Shrine	195
Sign of the Shadow	167
Stranded on Eventide	143
Test of Will	166
The Ancient Rito Song	181
The Bird in the Mountains	187
The Ceremonial Song	137
The Crowned Beast	125
The Cursed Statue	129
The Desert Labyrinth	158
The Eye of the Sandstorm	152
The Gut Check Challenge	203
The Lost Pilgrimage	196
The Perfect Drink	161
The Serpent's Jaws	145
The Seven Heroines	160
The Silent Swordswomen	155
The Skull's Eye	212
The Spring of Power	211
The Spring of Wisdom	127
The Stolen Heirloom	122
The Test of Wood	198
The Three Giant Brothers	142
The Two Rings	178
The Undefeated Champ	156
Trial of Second Sight	197
Trial of the Labyrinth	213
Trial of Thunder	175
Trial on the Cliff	186
Under a Red Moon	176
Watch Out for the Flowers	119

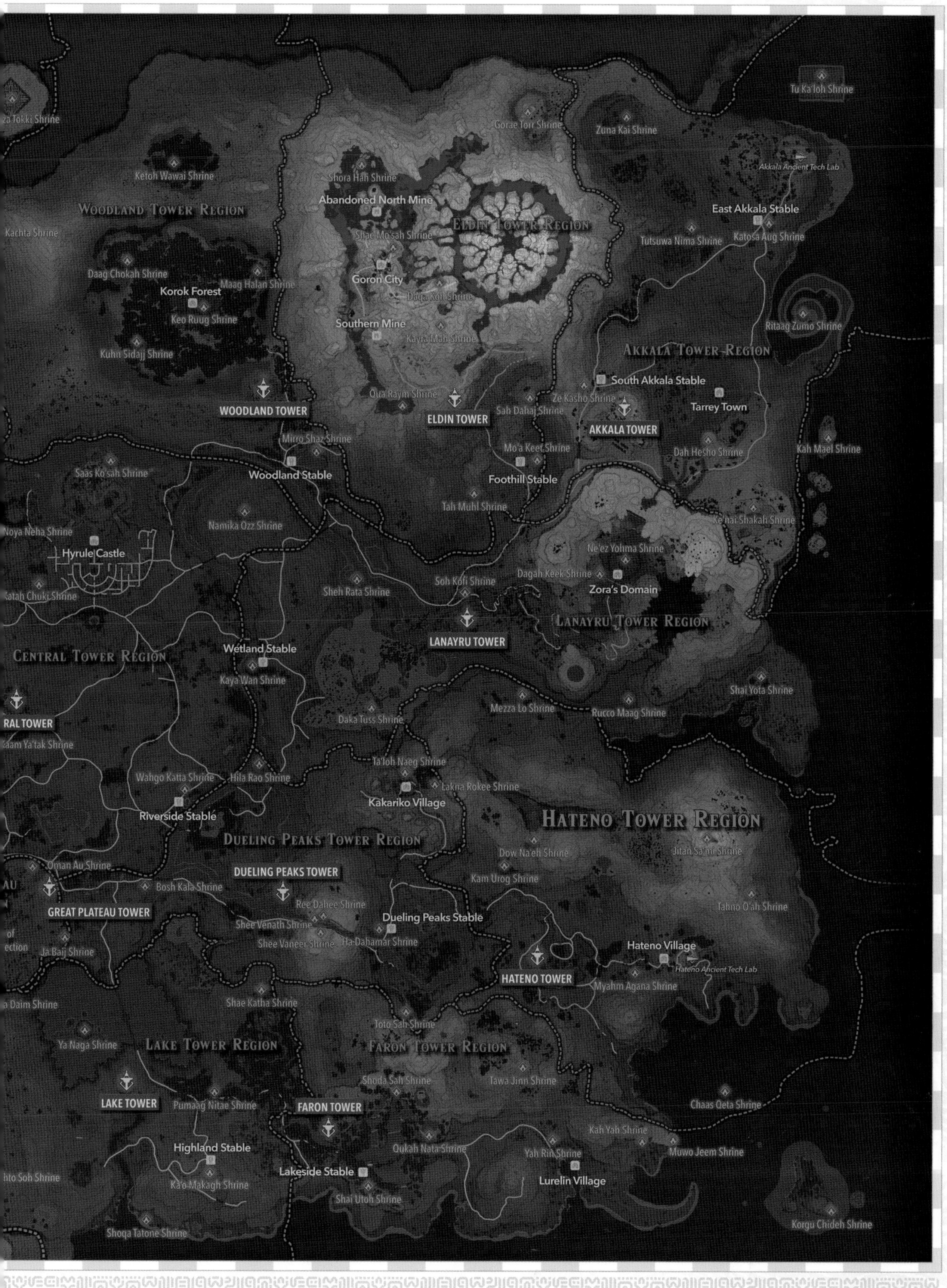

Tu Ka'loh Shrine
Zuna Kai Shrine
Gorae Torr Shrine
Akkala Ancient Tech Lab
Ketoh Wawai Shrine
Shora Hah Shrine
Abandoned North Mine
East Akkala Stable
Woodland Tower Region
Eldin Tower Region
Kachta Shrine
Shae Mo'sah Shrine
Tutsuwa Nima Shrine
Katosa Aug Shrine
Daag Chokah Shrine
Goron City
Korok Forest
Maag Halan Shrine
Daqa Koh Shrine
Keo Ruug Shrine
Southern Mine
Ritaag Zumo Shrine
Kayra Mah Shrine
Kuhn Sidajj Shrine
Akkala Tower Region
South Akkala Stable
Qua Raym Shrine
Ze Kasho Shrine
Tarrey Town
Woodland Tower
Eldin Tower
Sah Dahaj Shrine
Akkala Tower
Mirro Shaz Shrine
Mo'a Keet Shrine
Dah Hesho Shrine
Kah Mael Shrine
Saas Ko'sah Shrine
Woodland Stable
Foothill Stable
Tah Muhl Shrine
Namika Ozz Shrine
Ke'nai Shakah Shrine
Noya Neha Shrine
Hyrule Castle
Ne'ez Yohma Shrine
Sheh Rata Shrine
Soh Kofi Shrine
Dagah Keek Shrine
Zora's Domain
Katah Chuki Shrine
Lanayru Tower Region
Lanayru Tower
Central Tower Region
Wetland Stable
Kaya Wan Shrine
Shai Yota Shrine
Mezza Lo Shrine
Rucco Maag Shrine
Daka Tuss Shrine
Central Tower
Kaam Ya'tak Shrine
Ta'loh Naeg Shrine
Wahgo Katta Shrine
Hila Rao Shrine
Lakna Rokee Shrine
Kakariko Village
Riverside Stable
Hateno Tower Region
Dueling Peaks Tower Region
Dow Na'eh Shrine
Jitan Sa'mi Shrine
Oman Au Shrine
Dueling Peaks Tower
Kam Urog Shrine
Bosh Kala Shrine
Ree Dahee Shrine
Tahno O'ah Shrine
Great Plateau Tower
Dueling Peaks Stable
Shee Venath Shrine
Shee Vaneer Shrine
Ha Dahamar Shrine
Ja Baij Shrine
Hateno Village
Hateno Ancient Tech Lab
Hateno Tower
Myahm Agana Shrine
Daim Shrine
Shae Katha Shrine
Toto Sah Shrine
Ya Naga Shrine
Lake Tower Region
Faron Tower Region
Shoda Sah Shrine
Tawa Jinn Shrine
Lake Tower
Pumaag Nitae Shrine
Faron Tower
Chaas Qeta Shrine
Kah Yah Shrine
Highland Stable
Qukah Nata Shrine
Yah Rin Shrine
Muwo Jeem Shrine
Lakeside Stable
Lurelin Village
Ishto Soh Shrine
Ka'o Makagh Shrine
Shai Utoh Shrine
Shoqa Tatone Shrine
Korgu Chideh Shrine

DUELING PEAKS TOWER SHRINES

BOSH KALA SHRINE

This shrine is located to the east of the Great Plateau Tower, a few steps to the south of the road that leads to the Dueling Peaks, just before the Hylia River.

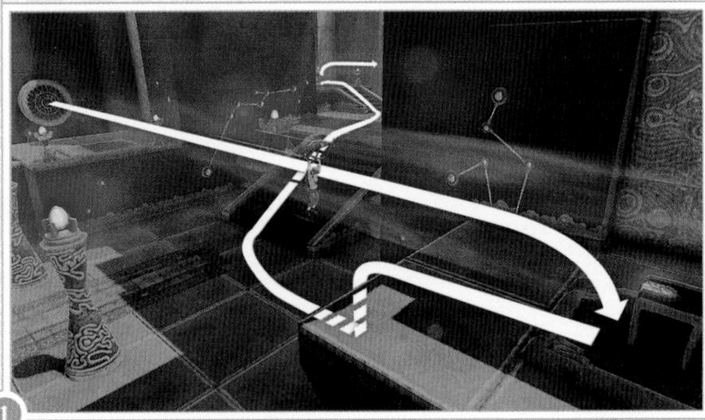

1

This easy shrine acts as an introduction to the effects of wind on your paraglider. Head up the stairs to your left, then glide all the way across the room to the first treasure chest. The wind at your back makes this child's play. Proceed to the next room when you're ready and use the wind from the fan to your left to cross the room in the same manner.

2

The final fan makes it easy to glide to the altar. Don't forget to put the paraglider away with Ⓑ when you reach the platform, though, as your speed can easily take you too far, above the abyss. Before you do so, consider making a small detour to your right to open the second treasure chest on the far ledge: this is best attempted directly from the fan, opening the paraglider at the peak of your jump, and curving toward the treasure chest just as you reach the altar's platform.

HA DAHAMAR SHRINE

This shrine lies in the small pond just west of the Dueling Peaks Stable. It is surrounded by spikes that you can glide above from the small plateau directly southwest of the shrine.

1

Cross the first two gaps by using blocks of ice generated with Cryonis as stepping stones. After the second one, turn around and use the same method to reach the treasure chest on the elevated platform.

2

In the main room, you need to summon three blocks of ice in the positions shown on the picture above to guide the orb to its concave slot.

HILA RAO SHRINE

SHRINE QUEST: WATCH OUT FOR THE FLOWERS

This shrine lies on the small Floret Sandbar island, to the north of the Dueling Peaks Tower.

1 To reach this shrine, you must first carefully navigate your way through Magda's maze of flowers without touching any of them. Follow the path shown above, walking slowly to avoid taking any chances. If you struggle, note that you can create a fire-induced updraft to glide directly to the entrance.

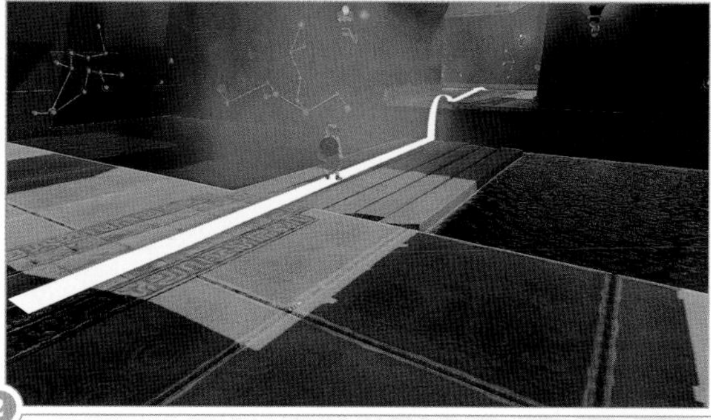

2 Once inside the shrine, step on the wooden raft to cross the first stream. Note that you can stop it with Stasis if you wish.

3 Proceed in the same manner to cross the second stream, but consider pausing briefly on the way to lift the treasure chest at the bottom using Magnesis.

4 In the final room, raise the second treasure chest out of the water with Cryonis so that you can open it. Summon a second block of ice close to the destructible rocks, then climb on top of it. Throw a bomb to blast your way through the rocks before you make your way to the altar.

SHEE VENATH SHRINE

This shrine is built just beneath the summit of the northern Dueling Peak.

1 This puzzle might seem very obscure, until you realize that there is a "twin" version of it in the Shee Vaneer Shrine. All you need to do is rearrange the orbs so that they reproduce their starting configuration in that shrine, as shown on the above picture.

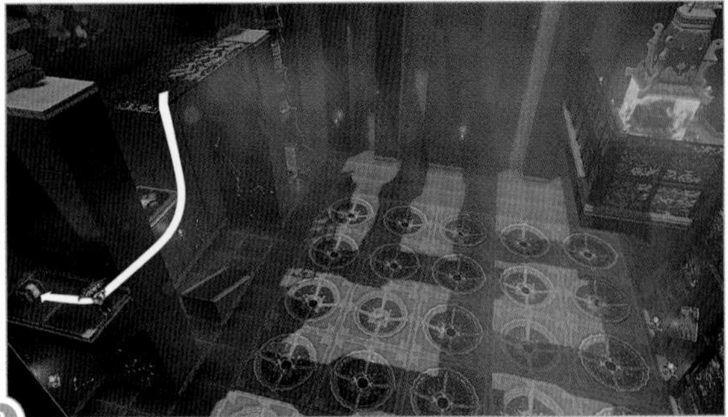

2 Before you examine the altar, let the elevator take you to the "observation deck". From here, you can glide to the treasure chest behind the wall adjacent to the elevator.

SHEE VANEER SHRINE

This shrine lies at the top of the southern Dueling Peak.

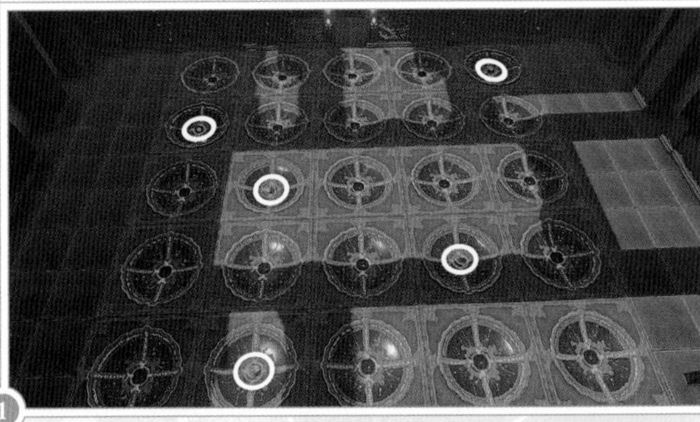

1 This is the "twin" version of the Shee Venath Shrine. All you need to do is rearrange the orbs so that they reproduce their starting configuration in that shrine, as shown on the above picture. This opens the door leading to the altar.

2 Before you examine the altar, let the elevator take you to the "observation deck". From here, you can glide to the treasure chest behind the wall adjacent to the elevator.

REE DAHEE SHRINE

This shrine is found between the Dueling Peaks, on the cliff road that overlooks the river's north shore.

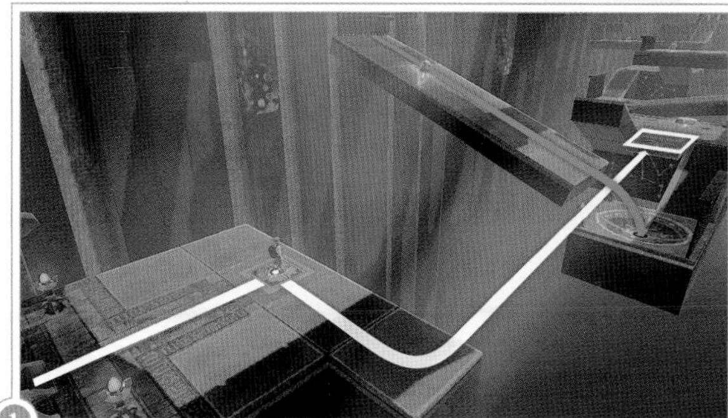

1 Step on the floor switch to make an orb fall in the concave slot. This activates a moving platform that takes you to the next step.

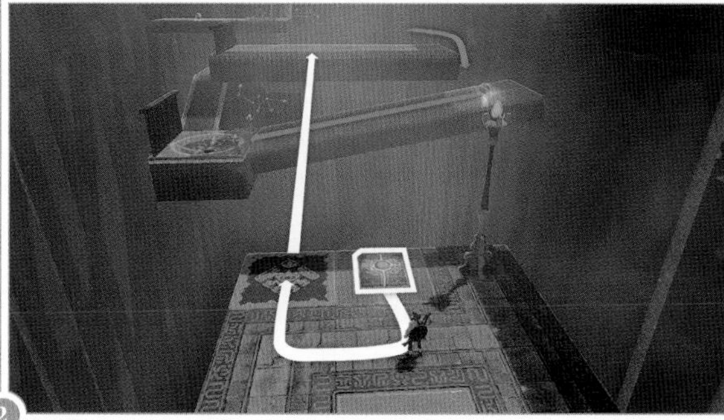

2 As previously, step on the floor switch to release an orb. This time, move away from the switch just before the orb reaches the end of the first platform, so that the slope of the second platform slows it down just enough for it to not fall. It will then gently roll down to the concave slot. You can now take the moving platform to the final section of the shrine.

3 Stand on the floor switch again to release an orb. This time step away just before the orb reaches the end of the platform: the idea is that the platform will move up and act as a "springboard", enabling the orb to make it to the concave slot. Once you succeed, a moving platform takes you to the platform you just used.

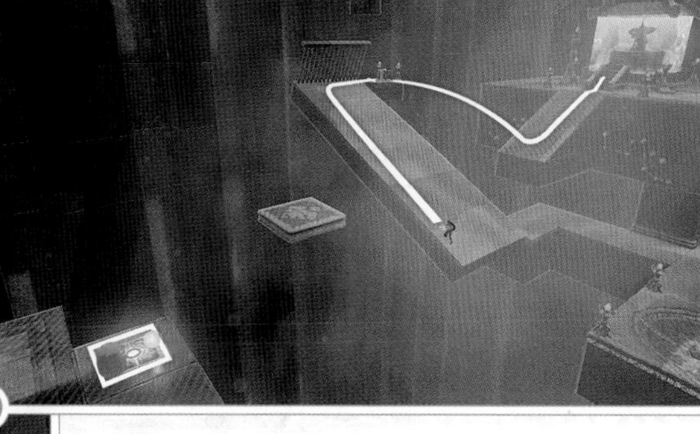

4 Before you head to the altar, grab a metal barrel with Magnesis and drop it on the floor switch you activated in step 3. This will raise the platform, giving you access to the treasure chest.

TA'LOH NAEG SHRINE

This shrine is found on the hill to the northeast of Kakariko Village.

1

This shrine acts as an introduction to some of the key combat features. Follow the on-screen instructions to complete it. Two treasure chests are available in the first room, and a third one on the way to the altar.

LAKNA ROKEE SHRINE

SHRINE QUEST: THE STOLEN HEIRLOOM

This shrine is located to the east of Kakariko Village, in the woods south of the nearby Great Fairy Fountain.

1

You can reveal this shrine by dropping an orb in the pedestal to the east of Kakariko Village, close to the local Great Fairy Fountain. The orb in question lies right by Impa, inside her house at Kakariko Village. However, you can only obtain it if you have completed three local quests (Flown the Coop, By Firefly's Light, Find the Fairy Fountain). If so, visit Impa's house to trigger a cutscene and the The Stolen Heirloom shrine quest. Now sit by a fire and wait for night to come. At around 10:00 PM, you will notice that Dorian, one of the soldiers guarding Impa's house, leaves his post.

2

Follow Dorian from a safe distance, remaining stealthy at all times, until he reaches the pedestal to the east of Kakariko Village (a short distance to the south of the Great Fairy Fountain). When he stops moving and asks someone to show themselves, move closer to trigger a cutscene. Defeat the Yiga Blademaster to receive the orb. Once inside the shrine, head to the altar, collecting the contents of the treasure chest on the way.

TOTO SAH SHRINE

You will find this shrine to the southeast of the Dueling Peaks, along the small stream that branches off from the main river.

1

This shrine is actually hidden behind destructible rocks. You can easily blow these up from the opposite shore using a bomb arrow. Alternatively, you can throw a bomb in the river upstream, and wait until the current takes it to the destructible rocks, at which point you can detonate the explosive.

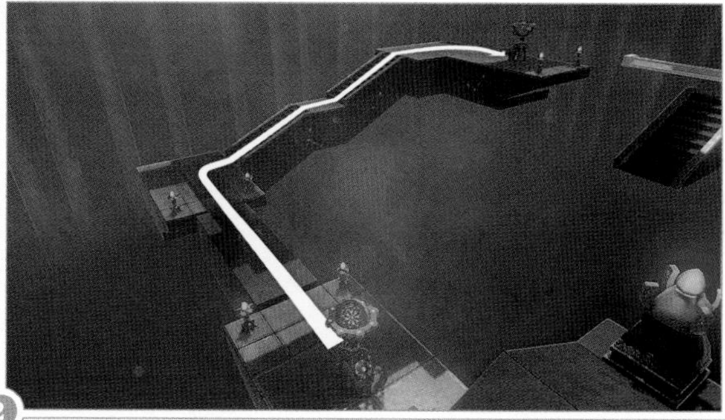

2

Inside the shrine, interact with the first terminal to trigger a puzzle based on the gyroscopic features of your controller. You need to align the pillar horizontally so as to create a bridge leading to the next platform. However, if you turn your controller upside down, you will reveal the opposite side of the pillar, where a treasure chest is hidden.

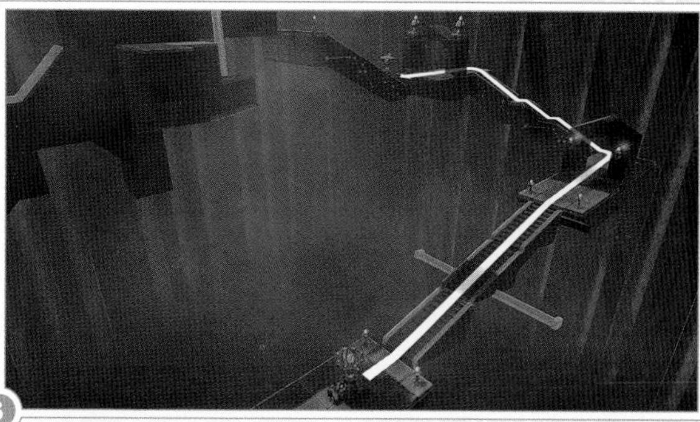

3

For the second puzzle, you must first align all three sets of stairs, then angle them so that they create a bridge with the next platform, as illustrated above. As usual with these puzzles, start from the default, flat position and angle your controller very gently: this will make it easier to adjust the rotating device in all three dimensions.

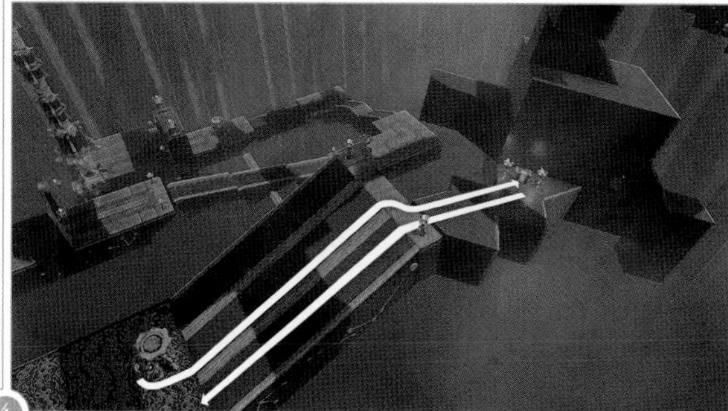

4

The third puzzle is a little harder than the others. You must first reach the treasure chest on the opposite side of the structure. Flip your controller upside down, then make the necessary adjustments to have both access to the chest and the possibility of jumping back to the terminal. Opening the chest is indispensable as it contains a small key required to unlock the final door.

5

Angle the rotating device so that the stairs slide down from their initial position. Next, slightly adjust the device's orientation to create a bridge leading to the locked door, as shown above. The altar awaits on the other side of the locked door.

Hateno Tower Shrines

MYAHM AGANA SHRINE

This shrine lies just south of Hateno Village, on a small plateau overlooking the general store.

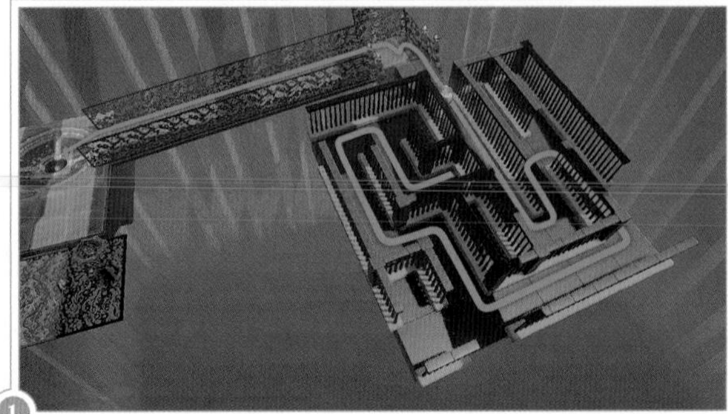

1 Interact with the terminal at the top of the steps. This enables you to maneuver the platform with the orb thanks to the gyroscopic functions of your controller. Your goal is to get the orb through the maze to the final straight line, then give it momentum and raise the platform at the last second for the orb to jump above the gap and land on the fenced ledge. It will then automatically roll down the slope to the concave slot, and open the door leading to the altar.

2 If you struggle with the maze, one tip can make things much easier: just turn your controller upside down. The platform's rear side is actually free of any walls – making it substantially easier to adjust the orb's course to the fenced section.

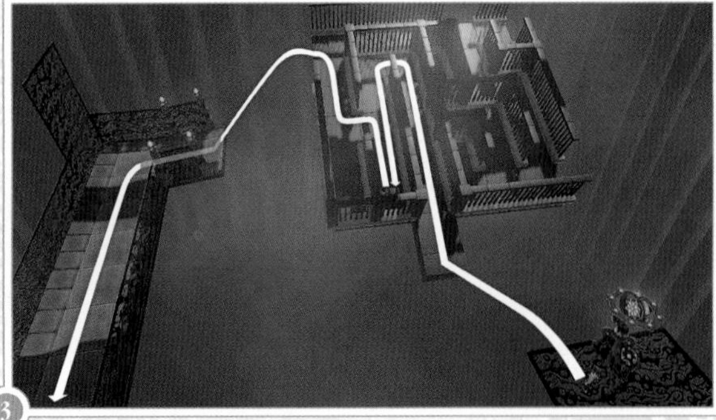

3 Before you head from the terminal to the altar, consider opening the chest hidden in the maze. The easiest way to reach it is to angle the platform toward your position near the terminal: if you lower it sufficiently, you can easily glide to it. Take the contents of the chest and head to the altar via the fenced section.

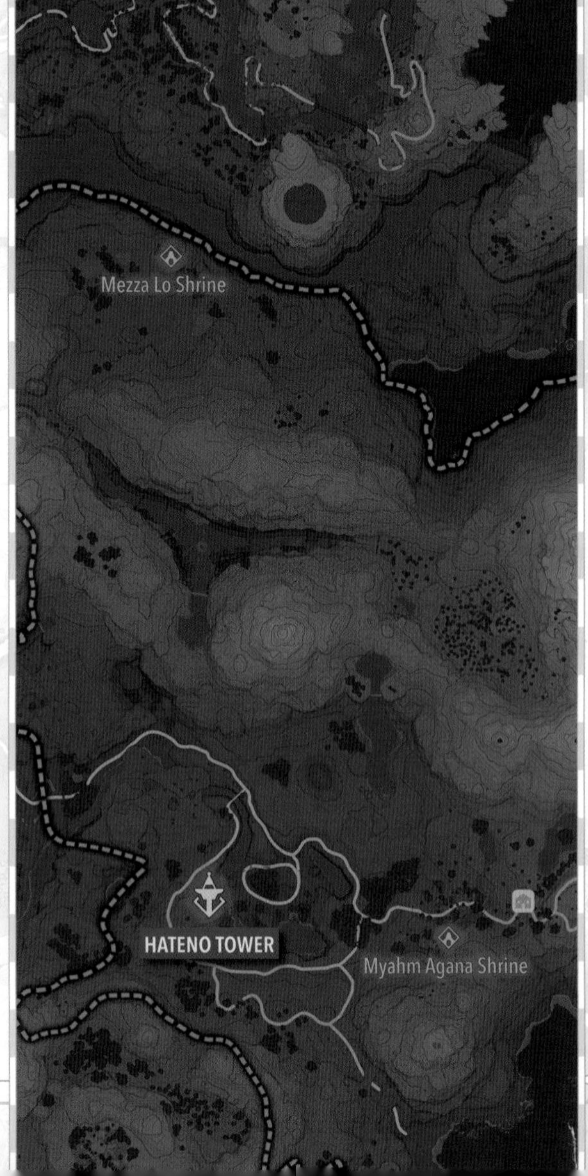

MEZZA LO SHRINE

SHRINE QUEST: THE CROWNED BEAST

This shrine is located to the southeast of Lanayru Tower, in the north section of Rabia Plain, though revealing it requires you to complete a local quest.

1. Speak to Kass, who is standing on a rock right by the shrine's activation pedestal, to start the quest.

2. You must now quietly approach one of the mountain buck deers in the area and mount it. To achieve this, it is highly recommended that you wear the full stealth armor set (from Kakariko Village's armor shop), as deer are extremely wary and skittish. Alternatively, a Level-2 stealth elixir can also work. If you have none of these at hand, try gliding from an elevated position to take the animal by surprise. Once in close proximity, press Ⓐ to mount it, then repeatedly press L to calm it down. From this point forward, it will behave like a horse: ride the deer to the pedestal to reveal the Mezza Lo Shrine.

3. Once inside the shrine, head to the crystal and hit it three times to align the rotating block with your platform. Drop a bomb next to the crystal, then move to the rotating block. Detonate the bomb and you will be taken to the shrine's only treasure chest.

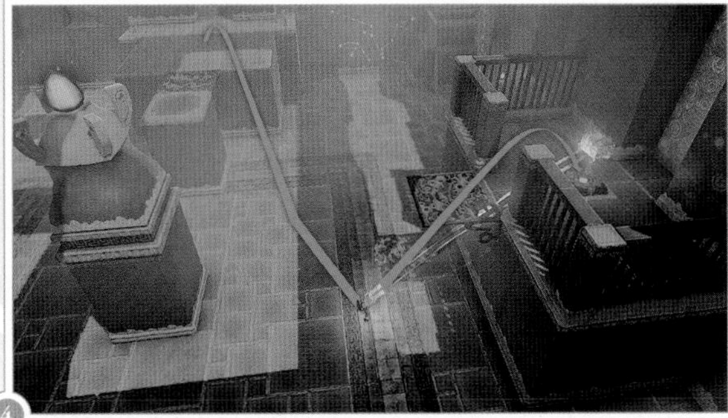

4. Lift the chest with Magnesis and drop down with it to the ground floor. Lift the chest again and move it on top of the floor switch in the fenced area, 90 degrees clockwise compared to the initial position of the chest. This raises the door leading to the altar.

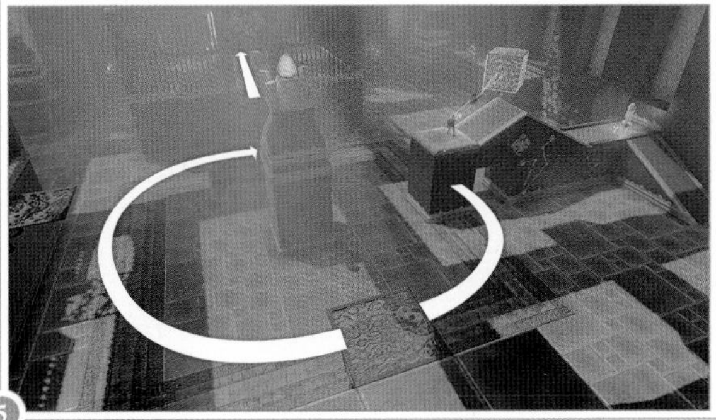

5. Return to the crystal and hit it three times to move the rotating block close to you. You must now activate the crystal three more times, but this time while standing on the rotating block. To achieve this, first drop a bomb next to the crystal. Next, cast Stasis on the laser beam emitter, and immediately use Magnesis to move the metal cube out of the way (anywhere on the ground floor will do) while you position Link on the rotating platform. When Stasis ends, the laser will activate the crystal once. Fire an arrow at the crystal to activate it a second time. Finally, detonate the bomb to activate the crystal one last time, and thus reach the altar.

TAHNO O'AH SHRINE

SHRINE QUEST: SECRET OF THE CEDARS

This shrine is located to the northeast of the Hateno Research Lab, inside a small cave in the snow mountains.

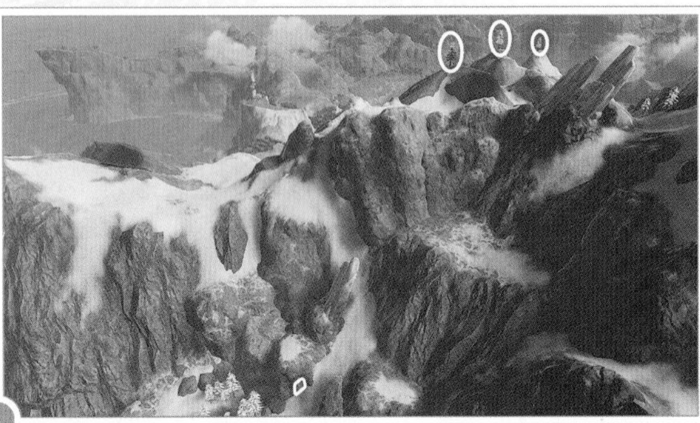

1 The challenge with this shrine is to find it. The clues given by Clavia should help: look at the line formed by the three summit trees, and follow it toward the east. You will find destructible rocks on a small plateau on the east side of the mountains. Blow it up with a bomb to reveal the Tahno O'ah Shrine. Note that you will need Level 2 cold resistance (❄) in order to not take damage in this region. Once inside the shrine, head to the altar, collecting the contents of the treasure chest on the way.

CHAAS QETA SHRINE

This shrine is located on the small Tenoko Island. You can reach it by gliding from the nearby Cape Cales, to the southwest.

1 This shrine pits you against a Guardian Scout IV. You can find detailed analysis and combat strategy for this creature on page 312.

Jitan Sa'mi Shrine

Tahno O'ah Shrine

HATENO TOWER

Chaas Qeta Shrine

JITAN SA'MI SHRINE

SHRINE QUEST: THE SPRING OF WISDOM

This shrine is hidden inside a cave at the summit of Mount Lanayru.

1

Clearing this shrine poses no problem whatsoever. The real difficulty here is to reveal it. Medda, a man located behind the buildings across the street from the dye shop in Hateno, will put you on the right track by triggering a shrine quest if you speak to him. After speaking to him, head to the top of Mount Lanayru, where you will encounter a giant dragon. Your goal is to free it from Malice goo by hitting corruption points all over its body (these take the form of an orange-glowing eyeball). Start by firing an arrow on the corruption point on its head. This will cause the dragon to fly away.

2

Now head to the mountain's peak via the path to the right of the Spring of Wisdom. You must rid the creature of all of its corruption points with arrows. The easiest way to achieve this is to follow it while gliding: aiming while in midair will give you the benefit of the slow-motion effect, making it easier to align your shots.

3

Once all corruption points are destroyed, you will be returned to the Spring of Wisdom. Fire one more arrow at the dragon to receive one of its scales. Pick it up and drop it in the spring to reveal the shrine. Once inside, head to the altar and collect the contents of the treasure chest on the way.

DOW NA'EH SHRINE

This shrine can be found to the north of Hateno Tower, behind the waterfall at the southern end of the Lanayru Promenade. A tunnel to the right of the waterfall will lead you to it.

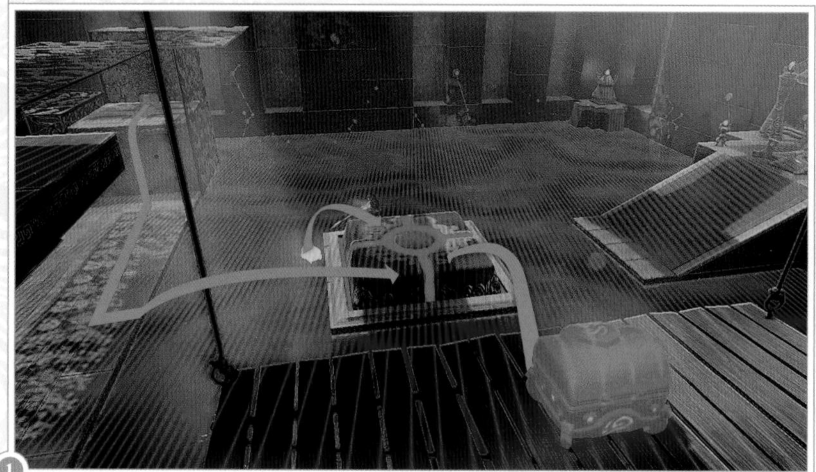

Your first task is to place all three treasure chests in the area on the central floor switch using Magnesis. One is immediately available in the water. A second one lies on a wooden ledge: make it fall either by burning the ledge with a fire arrow, or by cutting the two ropes holding it with standard arrows. The third one rests on the elevator platform. Once you have opened all three and they are in position, a metal cube will be revealed.

Move the metal cube to the elevator with Magnesis. Ride the elevator to the ledge above, then look down to the cube as the elevator takes it back to the lower level. Use this opportunity to drop down to the top of the cube, from which you can leap to the platform with the altar.

KAM UROG SHRINE

SHRINE QUEST: THE CURSED STATUE

When you complete the corresponding shrine quest, this shrine will appear at the end of the canyon littered with small statues, to the north of the Cliffs of Quince.

1

Calip, a character from Fort Hateno, will trigger this quest for you, though you can actually complete it irrespective of whether you spoke to him or not. Head to the end of the canyon littered with small statues, to the north of the Cliffs of Quince (themselves to the north of the Hateno Tower). If you are in this position at 09:00 PM, you will see a statue whose eyes are glowing purple. Hit this statue's face with an arrow to reveal the Kam Urog Shrine.

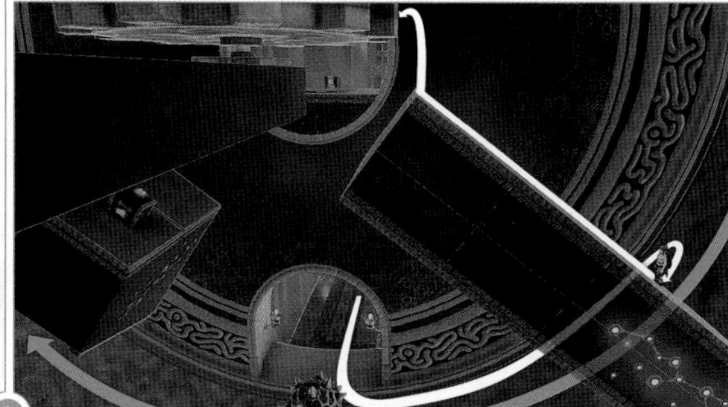

2

Inside the shrine, proceed down the ramp and into the chamber with rotating blocks. Walk to the base of one of the long ramps and the vertical rotation of the structure will soon put you on top of that same ramp, from which you can reach the central cogwheel. From here, you can glide to two treasure chests: one in a fixed alcove opposite the cogwheel, and the other on one of the smaller rotating blocks. You can reach the latter by gliding from the central cogwheel when the platform in question passes beneath the cogwheel.

3

Once you have opened both chests, return to the central cogwheel and wait for one of the smaller, triangular rotating blocks to be within reach. Jump to its side, then calmly walk over its edge when the rotation puts it in an almost vertical position. This will enable you to reach the steps on its upper side.

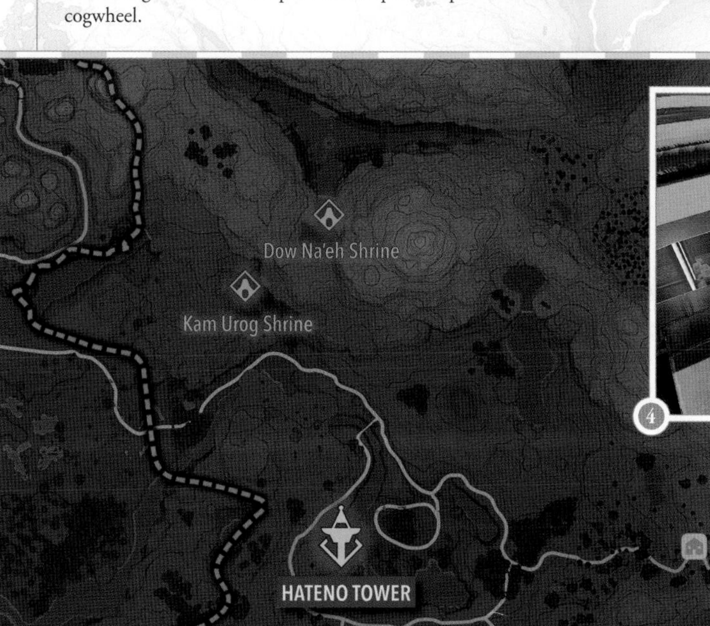

4

From the stairs, leap to the chamber's exit. The altar is then only a few feet away.

Lanayru Tower Shrines

NE'EZ YOHMA SHRINE

This shrine lies in plain sight at the heart of Zora's Domain.

1

This shrine relies on your mastery of the Cryonis rune. First, go halfway up the slope, dodging any boulders that roll down in your direction, and block the laser beam with Cryonis. Position a block of ice so that its top side is inches below the tip of the triangular platform just beyond the laser beam: this will both give you access to the treasure chest and act as a makeshift barrier for the orb that you will soon send rolling down. Once you are ready, head to the orb at the top of the slope.

2

Materialize a block of ice behind the orb to make it fall. Once it stops in front of the concave platform below, summon another ice block, this time beneath the orb, to make it roll down that platform, then all the way down to the next concave platform (this is where your ice block from step 1 comes into play).

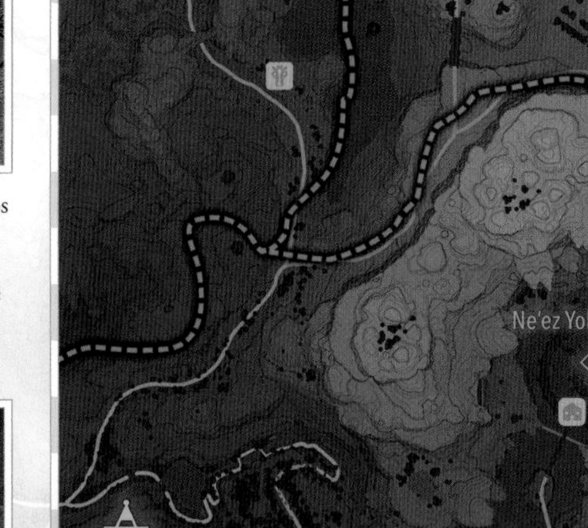

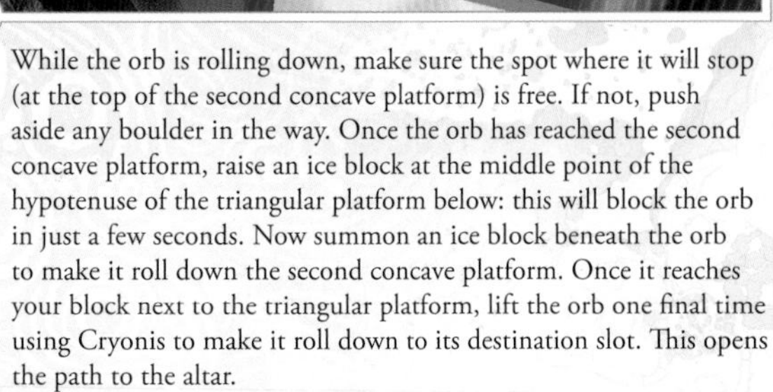

3

While the orb is rolling down, make sure the spot where it will stop (at the top of the second concave platform) is free. If not, push aside any boulder in the way. Once the orb has reached the second concave platform, raise an ice block at the middle point of the hypotenuse of the triangular platform below: this will block the orb in just a few seconds. Now summon an ice block beneath the orb to make it roll down the second concave platform. Once it reaches your block next to the triangular platform, lift the orb one final time using Cryonis to make it roll down to its destination slot. This opens the path to the altar.

RUCCO MAAG SHRINE

This shrine is found to the south of Zora's Domain, across the Rutala River.

1 This shrine is surrounded by barbs. You can either navigate the maze these form, or bypass it entirely by gliding over it, either from the nearby high cliff, or after creating a fire-induced updraft.

2 The shrine's puzzle requires you to have the five torches jutting from the central cube all lit simultaneously. You can rotate the cube by hitting the nearby crystals: it will move in the direction in which the affected crystal points to. The key to success is avoiding any torch coming into contact with water, either from the pool or from the fountain. The easiest way to achieve this is with fire arrows. If you do not have any, create a campfire by dropping a bundle of wood which you can ignite with a flint or red Chuchu jelly. Move a standard arrow close to the flames and it will then act as a fire arrow.

3 To solve the puzzle from its default position, you only need to complete a few simple steps. First, light up the two adjacent torches (to your right) with a fire arrow. Next, hit the only horizontal crystal to make the cube rotate horizontally: the fountain should now be pointing toward the crystals.

4 Finally, light up the torch to the left of the cube with a fire arrow. With all five of them set ablaze, the way to the altar will open up.

5 Before you leave, consider opening the two treasure chests that lie on elevated platforms on the far wall. The easiest way to achieve this is to set on fire the wooden ledges they rest on using fire arrows.

SOH KOFI SHRINE

This shrine is just north of the Lanayru Tower, overlooking the Zora River.

1 This shrine pits you against a Guardian Scout II. You can find detailed analysis and combat strategy for this creature on page 312.

KAH MAEL SHRINE

This shrine is found on Tingel island, off the coast to the east of Akkala Tower.

1 To access this shrine, you must first remove the large slab that blocks the way. You could try to stop it in time with Stasis and build up energy to move it aside, but there is a much easier way: drop an octo balloon on it. This will lift the slab, enabling you to glide to the entrance. You can obtain octo balloons by defeating Octoroks, two of which are found in the area.

2 Inside the shrine, step on the left pan of the balance scale, leaving the barrel alone. Look up and cut the two ropes holding the wooden ledge: this causes the metal cube to fall on the opposite pan, propelling Link high in the air. Draw the paraglider at the peak of his course and glide to the treasure chest in the far corner.

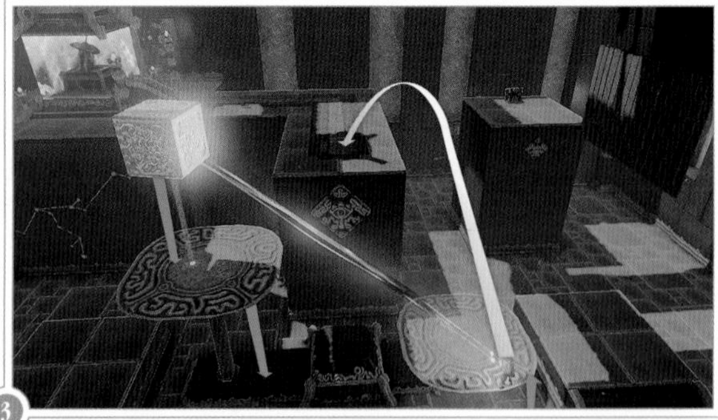

3 From the platform with the treasure chest, you can jump directly to the platform with the altar if you sprint, jump, and glide to it with flawless execution. If you struggle to achieve this, head back to the lowered pan of the balance scale, grab the metal cube with Magnesis, and drop it on the opposite pan from the maximum possible height: when it falls, it propels Link high in the air again, enabling you to glide to the altar.

Kah Mael Shrine
Soh Kofi Shrine
LANAYRU TOWER
Kaya Wan Shrine

KAYA WAN SHRINE

This shrine lies at the west edge of the Lanayru Wetlands, a few steps to the west of the Wetland Stable.

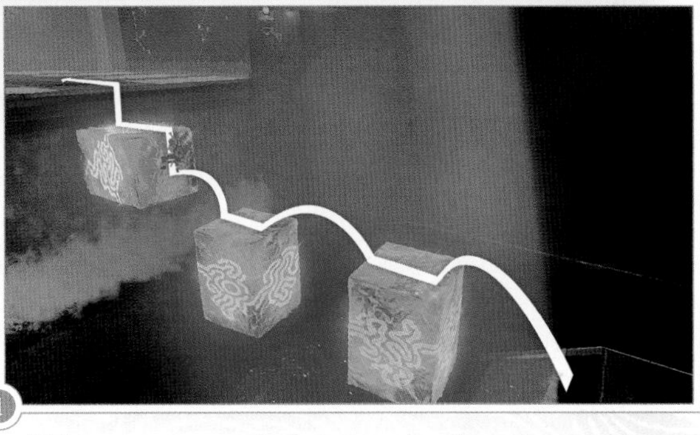

1

Make your way across the first room using Cryonis to create stepping stones.

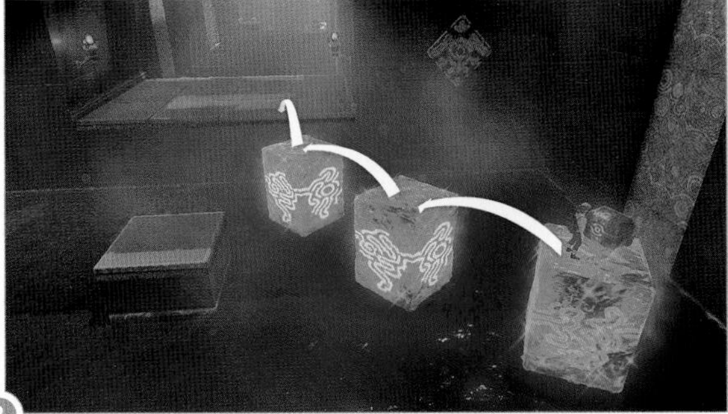

2

In the second room, eliminate the Guardian Scout with arrows or by sending its laser beam back to it with a perfect guard. You can now lift the treasure chest on the right with an ice block, then proceed to the third section of the shrine with more ice blocks positioned as stepping stones.

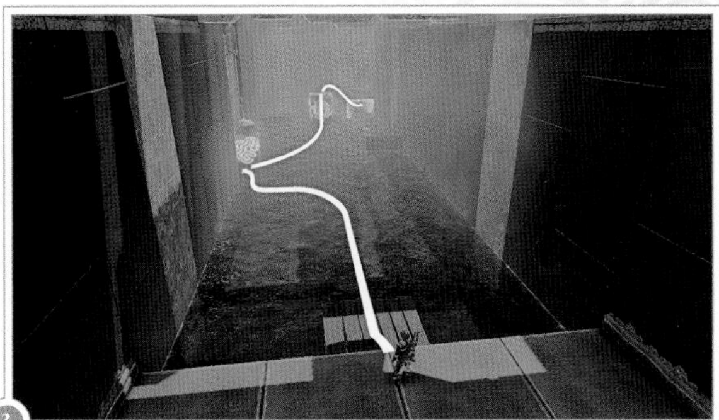

3

In the final section of this shrine, eliminate the two Guardian Scouts with arrows (or whatever other method you prefer). Drop down to the raft when it passes beneath Link and look to your left as you drift down the stream: summon a block of ice beneath the gate to lift it; this gives you access to a second treasure chest. If you struggle, note that you can stop the raft's movement with a pillar of ice, giving you ample time to plan your next move. You can now position a block of ice just before the waterfall and glide to the altar.

SHEH RATA SHRINE

This shrine is located to the west of the Lanayru Tower, on a small island just southwest of Zelo Pond. To access it, you must burn down the bramble surrounding it, with a fire arrow, for example.

1

Before you do anything else in this shrine, drop to the ledge to the right of your starting position to find a treasure chest. You must now activate the crystal: you can do this either with an arrow, or by pushing the rotating lever to the left of your starting position (which makes the laser beam rotate, hitting the crystal after several seconds). This raises the level of the water, enabling you to swim across the room.

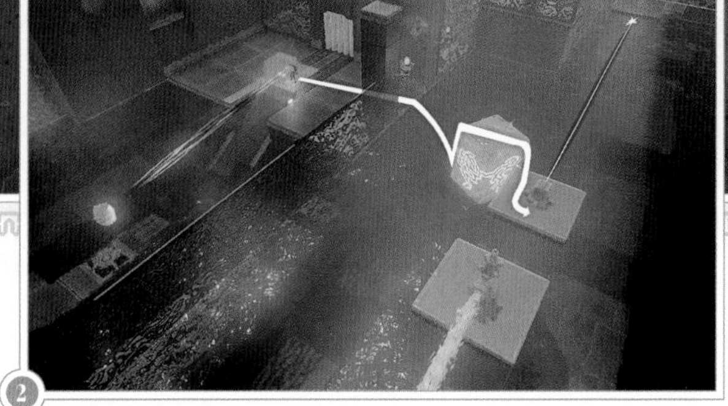

2

Pick up the barrel with Magnesis, and position it above the floor switch that can be seen at the bottom of the pool. You can test this by raising the barrel high in the air and dropping it: it should sink until it touches the floor switch, then return to the surface. Note that you can create ice blocks with Cryonis to adjust the barrel more accurately if required. Once you're ready, create a block of ice in the main room so that you can jump to the pillar where the laser-emitting device rests. From here, fire an arrow at the crystal: this will lower the water level again, causing the barrel to press the floor switch, and thus opening the door.

3

If you are not interested in the second treasure chest, you can glide to the platform where you found the barrel. If the barrel is not in the correct position, pick it up and drop it on the switch, then head through the door to the altar. If, on the other hand, you do want to open the second chest, ignore this step and move on to the next one.

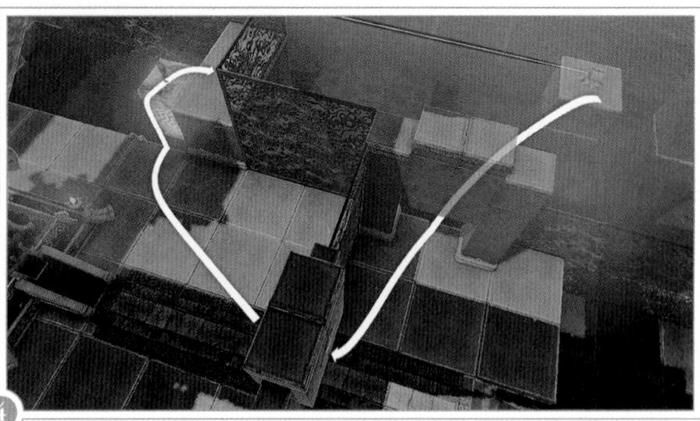

4

To access the second treasure chest, you will need to be swift (and your positioning of the barrel above the floor switch must have been perfect). Fire an arrow at the crystal one more time to cause the water level to rise again. As soon as you let the arrow fly, glide to the platform and sprint through the door before it closes. If you fail, simply repeat the maneuver. If you made it past the door, summon a block of ice with Cryonis in the pool to the right of the altar and use this as a stepping stone to reach the second treasure chest.

DAKA TUSS SHRINE

You will find this shrine on Shrine Island, one of the many islands in the archipelago to the southwest of the Lanayru Tower.

1

In the first room, your task is to grab the scoop at the bottom of the water with Magnesis, and maneuver it so that you can lift an orb with it. Slowly move the scoop above the fenced area, and drop the orb inside by pressing the scoop against a wall. The orb will fall into the concave slot, which opens the nearby gate.

2

Head to the second room, keeping the scoop with you. This time, you need to lift an orb with the scoop, and gently drop the orb on the top of the cage. As long as the orb remains on the cage, even if it's on the very edge, you are fine. Once this is achieved, position the scoop above the floor switch at the bottom of the pool: the scoop will sink and press the switch. This causes the cage's ceiling to open, enabling the ball to fall in the concave slot. This rids the room of the water.

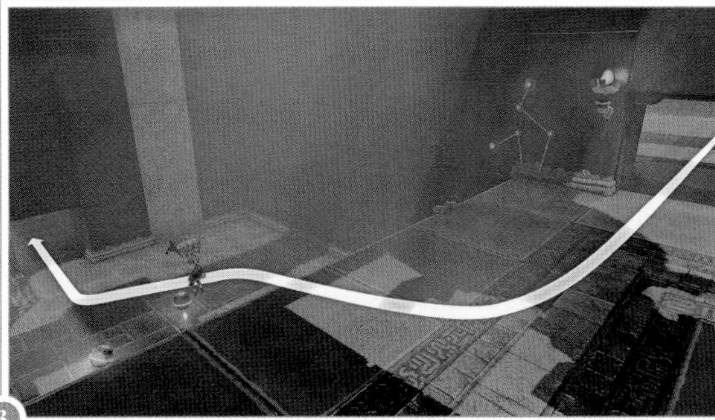

3

Take the time to visit the first room again. With the water gone, a door now gives you access to a treasure chest.

4

Finally return to the second room and go through the door at the bottom of the now-empty pool to find the altar.

SHAI YOTA SHRINE

SHRINE QUEST: MASTER OF THE WIND

This shrine is located in Horon Lagoon, to the southeast of Zora's Domain.

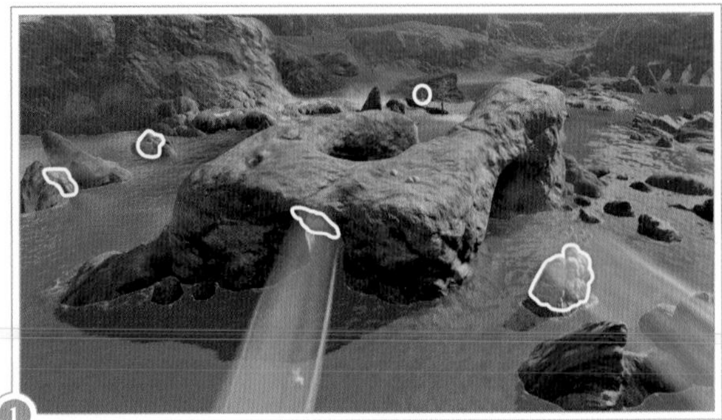

1

Speak to Kass, on the west shore of Horon Lagoon, to activate this quest. To reveal the shrine, you must first annihilate four blocks of destructible rocks scattered in the area. The gusts of wind and updrafts enable you to get close to each one of them. Bombs work well to destroy the rocks, though you should take into account the strength of the wind when you throw them.

2

The most difficult block to destroy is the one fixed to one of the central structure's archways. One solution is to climb to the top of the archway in question and drop a bomb at your feet so that it rolls down: the wind will blow the bomb back in the block's direction, at which point you can detonate it. An easier alternative is to fire a bomb arrow at the block. In fact, if you have spare bomb arrows, you can get rid of all the blocks with no hassle. Note that bomb arrows are ineffective when it's raining, though.

3

Once all four blocks are destroyed, head to the top of the central structure, and glide in the direction of the glowing dais. With the wind at your back, reaching it should be no problem. Make sure you land on the dais with the paraglider still out, though: adjust your trajectory and speed with ● to achieve this. If you fold it back prior to landing, the dais will not activate. When you succeed, the Shai Yota Shrine emerges from the ground. Once inside, head to the altar, collecting the contents of the treasure chest on the way.

DAGAH KEEK SHRINE

SHRINE QUEST: THE CEREMONIAL SONG

This shrine can be found to the southwest of Zora's Domain, though it is initially buried in the ground.

1

Once you have completed the Divine Beast Vah Ruta dungeon (see page 56), speak to Laruta at Zora's Domain to trigger this shrine quest.

2

Your first objective is retrieve the Ceremonial Trident that fell under Zora's Domain west bridge, close to the cliff. Create a block of ice with Cryonis in the middle of the river, then stand on it and use Magnesis to retrieve the weapon.

3

Now head to the pedestal submerged at the base of the Veiled Falls. Swim up the waterfall using the Zora armor, then glide back down toward the center of the pedestal. When you are a few yards above it, press the attack button to thrust either the ceremonial trident or the lightscale trident into it. This will reveal the shrine, which you can clear instantly after opening the chest on the way.

Faron Tower Shrines

YAH RIN SHRINE

This shrine overlooks Lurelin Village, to the far southeast of the Faron region.

1

Step on the lowered weighing pan of the balance scale and take control of the cube with Magnesis. Transfer the cube on the other weighing pan to reach the platform above. A small guardian awaits at the bottom of the steps. Stun it with a shock arrow if you wish, then eliminate it, ideally with an ancient weapon, if you have one.

2

Grab the treasure chest beyond the fence with Magnesis, and drop it on the nearby floor panel to open the door. You can open the chest either beforehand or afterwards.

3

In the next room, lower the two weighing pans on the left-hand side with the treasure chest that you previously dropped on the floor panel. Position Link on the farther pan, near the wall.

4

Now move the treasure chest to the other weighing pan adjacent to the wall. With the pan raised, you can open the second treasure chest. Once its contents are yours, hop to the weighing pan that you just lowered.

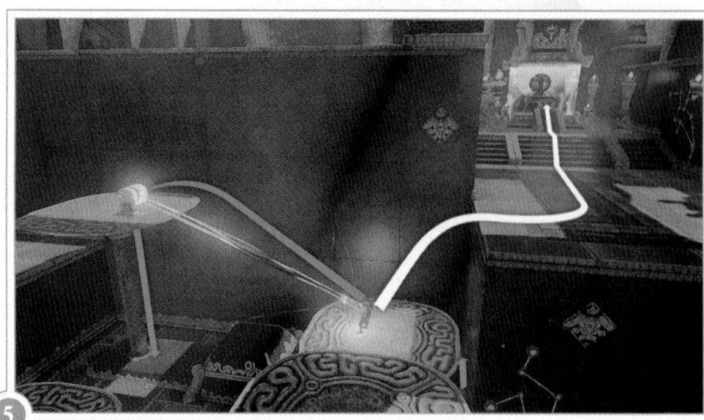

5

Finally, transfer the original chest to the weighing pan you raised a minute ago (the one adjacent to the wall). This will raise Link high enough for him to easily reach the final platform. Head to the altar to complete the shrine.

QUKAH NATA SHRINE

SHRINE QUEST: A SONG OF STORMS

This shrine lies to the east of Faron Tower, on the south shore of Calora Lake. It is initially concealed, until you complete the corresponding shrine quest.

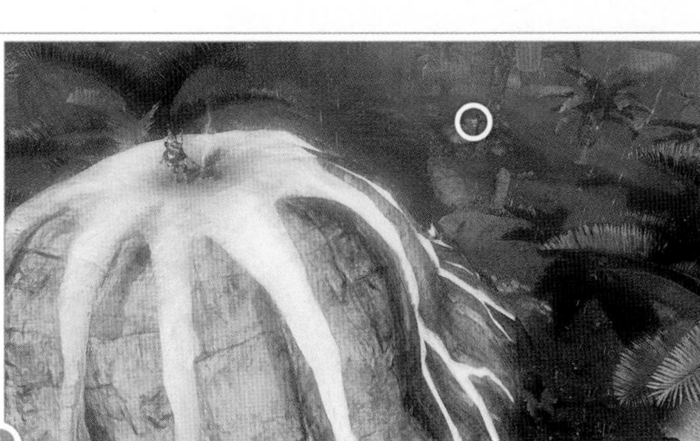

1. Kass, the traveling singer, will give you clues to locate this shrine when you talk to him, in the forest to the east of Calora Lake. To reveal the secret, you must stand at the top of the mound shown here, and have Link draw a lightning bolt to his position by wearing metallic equipment. You will take some damage in the process, and need to pick up your lost gear afterwards, but this is the most reliable way to succeed. Alternatively, you could try dropping a metallic item on the mound to draw lightning, but be aware that the item needs to be carefully positioned in the very center of the mound's top.

2. Once inside the Qukah Nata Shrine, open the treasure chest inside and head to the altar.

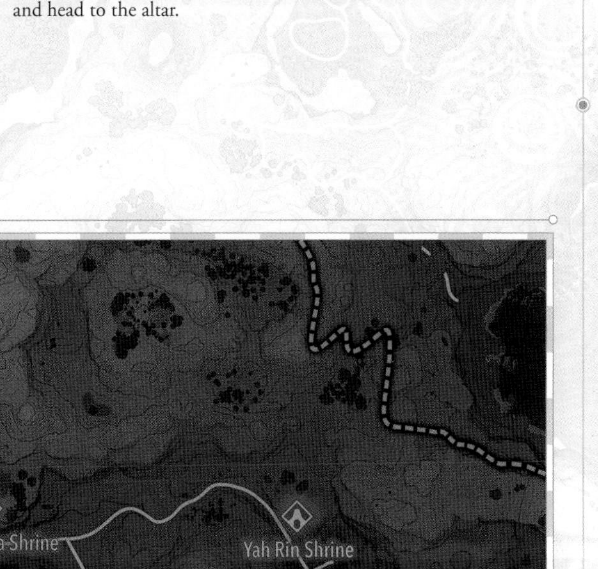

SHODA SAH SHRINE

This shrine is hidden behind the waterfall just south of Riola Spring. You can reach it via a small path to the right of the waterfall.

1 Your primary objective is to propel a metal orb onto each of the concave platforms. There are two main methods to achieve this. The first one consists of dropping an orb onto one of the launchers and activating it by hitting the nearby crystal with a remote bomb, for example. We suggest you begin with the one on your right from your starting position. The only difficulty is timing the propelling of the orb so that it lands on the moving platform. You must activate the switch roughly two seconds before the moving platform reaches the middle point of its course. Proceed in a similar fashion for the second platform, timing the crystal activation so that the orb passes beneath the right-hand moving panel (note that you must drop the orb near the launcher's edge closest to the crystal). Both of these steps are illustrated in our screenshot, although there is actually a much easier way to achieve the same result...

2 A painless solution to placing both orbs in their respective concave platforms is to drop them in the water (do so on the ramp leading into the water to avoid potential interferences with moving platforms). You can then materialize a Cryonis block underneath them, then climb onto the block and toss the orbs onto the platforms. Once both are in place, open the treasure chests that were propelled from the upper platforms and landed close to the launchers. One of them contains a small key, which you can use to open the locked gate and reach the altar.

KAH YAH SHRINE

SHRINE QUEST: A FRAGMENTED MONUMENT

This shrine is concealed in the Palmorae Ruins and appears after you complete the corresponding quest.

1

Speak to Garini to initiate this quest. Your goal is to find three fragments of a stone monument and show a picture of each to Garini. Note that they glow brighter at night, making it a little easier to locate them. Once Garini has seen all three, stand on one of the two nearby pedestals and crouch: Garini will do the same, causing the Kah Yah Shrine to appear. The first monument shard lies a short distance to the east of Garini, along the cliff that leads to the beach.

2

The second monument shard can be found southwest of Garini. It is submerged in shallow waters, close to some boxes and barrels.

3

The third monument shard lies at the very tip of Soka Point, the curved peninsula south of Palmorae Beach.

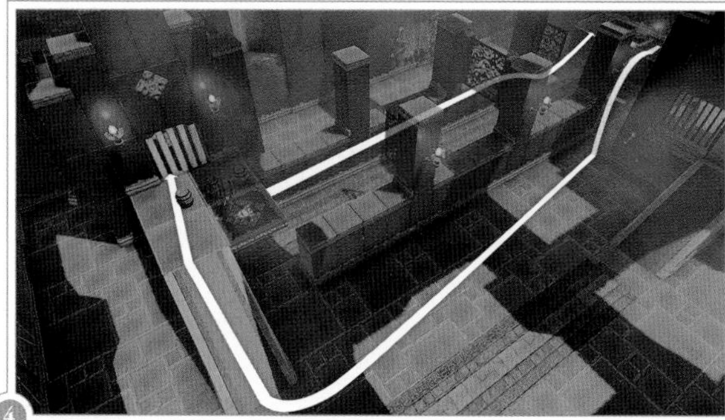

4

Once inside the shrine, go up the ramp to your left and pick up one of the wooden barrels. Walk to the moving platform when it arrives. After passing the first lateral grate, drop the barrel on the platform's right-hand side, then crouch to pass beneath the next grate. Stay on the right to avoid the final lateral grate, then pick up the barrel again and drop it on the floor switch at the end of the passage. This gives you access to the first treasure chest, which contains a small key. You can use this to open the locked door in the center of the shrine and activate the altar. Before you do so, though, you might want to take the time to obtain the second treasure chest.

5

To get the second chest, head up the ramp on the other side of the room and grab another barrel. Step on the moving platform as soon as it arrives and drop the barrel on it, then draw your bow and aim at the crystal that appears on your right. Hit the crystal just before you reach the closed gate, then immediately turn to your right and hit the crystal again right after you pass that same gate. Hit the crystal too early or too late and the path will be blocked by a gate, forcing you to start over. At the other end of the passage, drop the barrel on the floor switch to raise the door leading to the second treasure chest.

TAWA JINN SHRINE

SHRINE QUEST: THE THREE GIANT BROTHERS

This shrine is located to the south of the Hateno Tower.

1. To activate this quest, interact with the stone tablet found on Mount Taran, just west of Taran Pass. Your objective is to drop three orbs in three corresponding pedestals. The difficulty is that all three orbs are each found on the body of strong versions of the Hinox enemy type. Each of these foes has its own entry in the album, so make sure you take a picture of them all. If you struggle against any of them, climb to the top of one of the giant bones scattered around the arena: you can fire arrows at the Hinox's eye from here with total impunity.

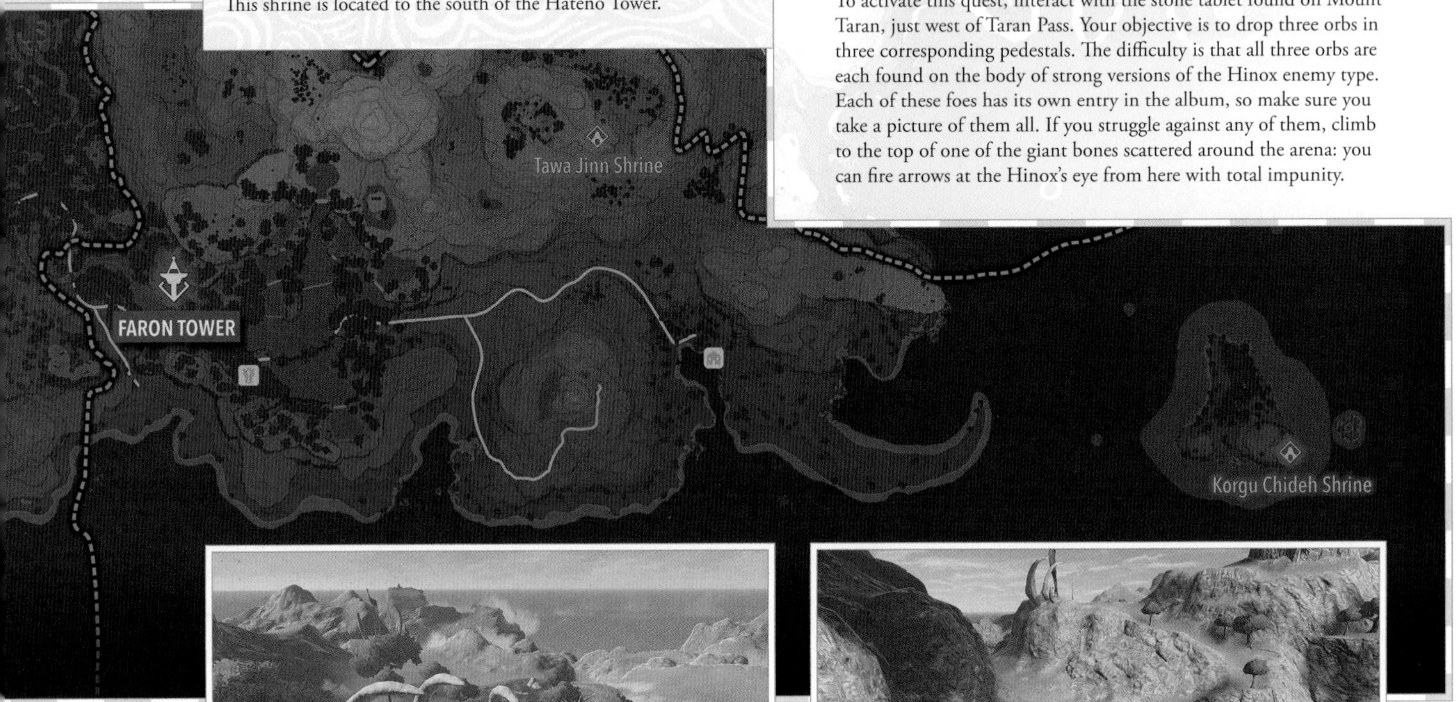

Tawa Jinn Shrine

Korgu Chideh Shrine

2. The Hinox (oldest kin) awaits in the Rabella Wetlands.

3. The Hinox (youngest kin) lurks in Hanu Pond.

4. The Hinox (middle kin) is found in Uten Marsh.

5. Once you have retrieved all three orbs from the Hinox monsters and dropped them in the pedestal slots, you will reveal the Tawa Jinn Shrine. Inside the shrine, head to the altar, collecting the contents of the treasure chest on the way.

KORGU CHIDEH SHRINE

SHRINE QUEST: STRANDED ON EVENTIDE

This shrine is located on Eventide Island, in the southeast corner of the world map. You can reach it by gliding from the tip of Cape Cales (if you have a well-developed stamina wheel) or by steering a raft to the island with a Korok leaf.

1

This quest begins automatically when you set foot on Eventide Island. It offers a unique challenge, depriving you of all your equipment and resources. You must gather materials on site to succeed. Your goal is to drop three orbs (indicated by grey circles in the above screenshot) in three corresponding concave slots located at the three apexes of the triangle that forms the island.

2

Collectibles of interest include mighty bananas (to replenish hearts), bows (from defeated archers), arrows (from archers and wooden crates), the soldier's claymore (found in a chest that you can lift from the mud pond with Magnesis), and another sword (from a treasure chest close to the southeast pedestal). Make sure you keep your most powerful weapons for the battle against the Hinox. When facing weak creatures, such as Chuchus and Bokoblins, keep in mind that your bombs are free and very effective. This will save your precious resources.

3

To reach the north pedestal, throw an orb in the water and summon an ice block beneath it with Cryonis. You can then climb on top of the block, and throw the orb to the concave slot from there.

4

The pedestal to the southeast is covered by a large slab. Your best option is to lift it with an octo balloon. You can obtain octo balloons by defeating an Octorok in the island's central forest. Once the slab is out of the way, drop the nearby orb in its slot.

5

The pedestal to the southwest is guarded by several enemies and partly covered by a metal cube that you can remove with Magnesis. The real challenge, however, is to defeat the Hinox who is wearing the third orb around its neck. Stun it by shooting arrows at its open eye, then follow up with sword combos for a swift victory. If you wasted your powerful blades on other targets, things will prove more challenging. As a worst-case scenario, turn to your bombs, which can actually deal reasonable damage when they detonate on the monster's eye. After your victory, take the orb to the pedestal to reveal the Korgu Chideh Shrine and claim your hard-earned spirit orb. As a last resort, note that you can sever the monster's necklace with an arrow, then pick up the orb and flee toward the pedestal if you do not wish to take down the Hinox.

SHAI UTOH SHRINE

This shrine can be found just south of the Lakeside Stable, hidden in a natural rock cave. Destroy the rock blocking the entrance with a remote bomb to access it.

1

Cast Stasis on the seesaw platform and use it to reach the floor above, then repeat this with the next platform. You can open the first treasure chest at the top.

2

Jump back on the second seesaw platform to raise its opposite end, and freeze it with Stasis. You can now make your way to the third seesaw platform. Lower its far end then turn around and fix it with Stasis: now sprint up the ramp and jump to the final, horizontal seesaw platform as quickly as possible to reach the altar. If you're not fast enough and fall, simply repeat the maneuver.

3

Reaching the second, elevated treasure chest is entirely optional and may seem like an impossible task at first. The solution is to stand on the far end of the seesaw platform closest to the chest in question and use Magnesis to drop the first chest so that it acts as a lever and catapults you high in the air: draw your paraglider at the apex of Link's course to gain access to the platform where the treasure lies. Pre-aligning Link in the direction of the chest greatly helps here.

MUWO JEEM SHRINE

This shrine rests atop Cape Cales, in the southeast corner of the world map.

1 This shrine pits you against a Guardian Scout III. You can find detailed analysis and combat strategy for this creature on page 312.

LAKE TOWER SHRINES

SHAE KATHA SHRINE

SHRINE QUEST: THE SERPENT'S JAWS

You will find this shrine at the Spring of Courage, to the southwest of the Dueling Peaks.

1 Kass will put you on the track of this shrine by initiating a shrine quest if you speak to him. He awaits in Pagos Woods, to the west of the bridge that crosses the Floria River.

2 The Spring of Courage is located to the southwest of the Dueling Peaks, to the north of the Dracozu Lake. Pray on the small altar in front of the goddess statue and she will ask you to bring her one of Farosh's scales.

3 Farosh is a flying thunder dragon that regularly roams in the three following areas: the Gerudo Highlands, the region with many waterfalls to the east of Faron Tower, and above Lake Hylia (where she dives in and out of the water before crossing over the Bridge of Hylia). When you manage to get within bow range, hit any part of her body with an arrow: she will drop a scale in the corresponding location. Take this back to the Spring of Courage and put it in the water to complete the quest and reveal the Shae Katha Shrine. Head inside and open the treasure chest on your way to the altar.

LAKE TOWER SHRINES

KA'O MAKAGH SHRINE

This shrine overlooks the Highland Stable, a short climb to the south.

1

Thanks to the power of Magnesis, you can easily open the two sets of large metallic doors. The first one gives you access to the main room, and the second one to a treasure chest. Preemptively eliminate the two Guardian Scouts that roam in the area before you proceed.

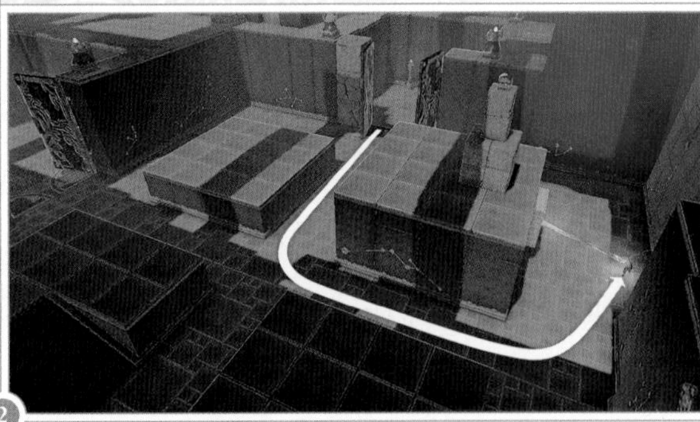

2

A second, hidden treasure chest is within immediate reach: head to the back of the structure with the pile of rock cubes on it. Magnesis will enable you to remove a steel cube inside the structure, behind which the chest awaits.

3

Clearing this shrine might seem impossible to you at this point, until you realize that one of the doors leading to the first treasure chest is fixed to destructible rocks. Destroy these with bombs to free the door.

4

Now grab the metal door that you freed and position it as a bridge between the platform with the stairs and the one closest to the altar. Cross this makeshift bridge and you will be one step away from completing the shrine.

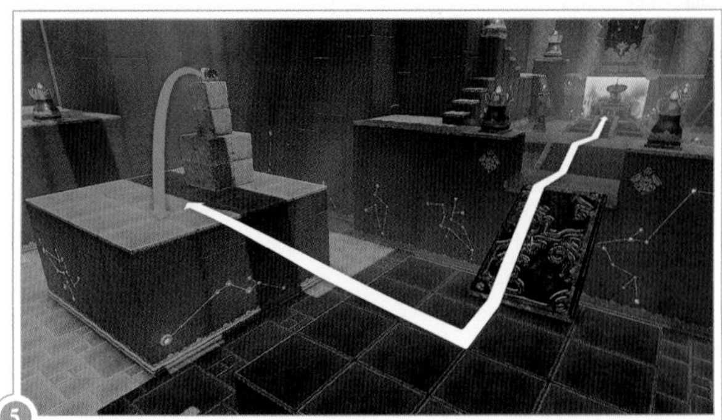

5

Take control of the metal door again, this time to connect your current platform with the platform with the chest at the top of the piles of rocks. Grab the chest with Magnesis, then move the door again so that it acts as a bridge leading to the altar. If you struggle to adjust the door's position with Magnesis, feel free to place the steel cube so that it forms an extension of your current platform.

SHOQA TATONE SHRINE

SHRINE QUEST: GUARDIAN SLIDESHOW

This shrine is hidden on Puffer Beach, to the south of Lake Tower. You need to complete the corresponding quest to reveal it.

1 Speak to Loone on Puffer Beach. She will ask you to show her three specific types of Guardians, which you can achieve by taking pictures of them. Guardian Scouts are plentiful in shrines (for example, in the Oman Au Shrine on the Great Plateau). Guardian Skywatchers can be encountered in various places, such as Hyrule Castle or at the base of Akkala Tower. Guardian Stalkers are relatively common; you can easily photograph one from the top of Central Tower, for example.

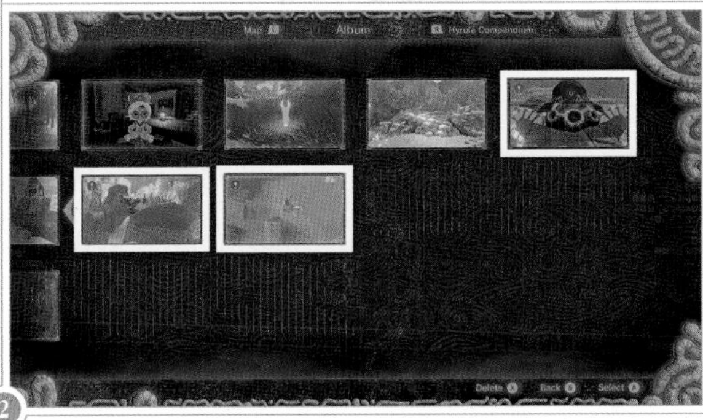

2 Once you have all three pictures saved in your album (denoted by a red exclamation mark icon), return to Loone. She will let you pick up the orb, which you can drop on the nearby dais to reveal the Shoqa Tatone Shrine. This shrine pits you against a Guardian Scout II. You can find detailed analysis and combat strategy for this creature on page 312.

PUMAAG NITAE SHRINE

This shrine lies in the woods between Finra Woods and Pagos Woods.

1 This shrine pits you against a Guardian Scout II. You can find detailed analysis and combat strategy for this creature on page 312.

ISHTO SOH SHRINE

This shrine is located atop a small plateau just east of Daval Peak. You can identify it by the plume of smoke originating from a campfire in the immediate vicinity.

1 This puzzle may seem impossible to solve, until you realize that you can pick up the small block emitting a laser beam. Stop it briefly with Stasis to avoid taking any risk (and open the nearby chest in the process), then pick it up. Now drop it on the moving platform, facing the crystal in the center.

2 With the first step achieved, you can now reap your rewards. Glide from your starting position to the pillars at the back. After a couple of switch activations, you can open the second treasure chest. Then go up the steps that lead to the altar to receive your spirit orb.

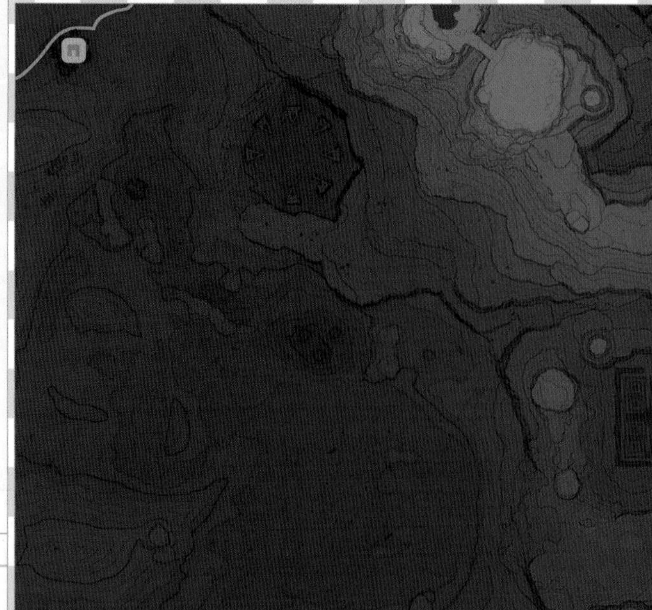

YA NAGA SHRINE

This shrine is concealed on Hylia Island, to the west of the Bridge of Hylia. The rocks surrounding it make it hard to see but it is freely accessible at any time.

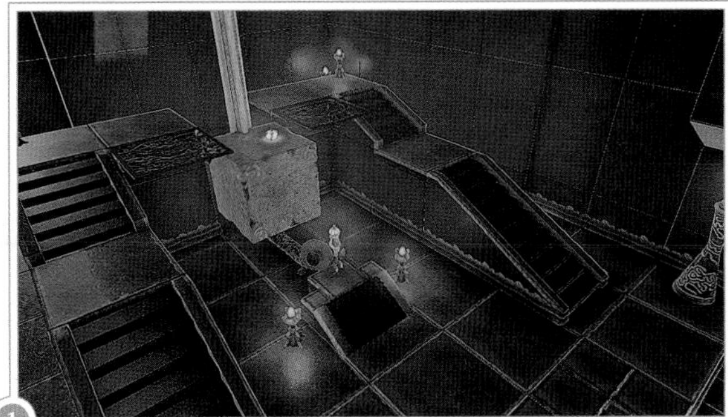

1. Make your way up to the cube and drop a cube bomb on it. Next, walk to the stairs at the base of the cube and drop a round bomb in the tubular structure.

2. Now take a few steps back and look up in the direction of the destructible blocks in the ceiling. With the round bombs selected, press L to detonate the one you put in the tubular structure: this will propel the cube all the way to the ceiling. During its ascent, switch to the cube bombs and press L again right as the cube nears the destructible blocks: the detonation will clear the path.

3. Finally, drop another round bomb in the tubular structure and make your way to the top of the cube, ideally facing to the right from the entrance to make it easier to reach the next chest. Detonate the bomb and this time it will be Link who is sent high in the air. Draw your paraglider at the peak of his course and glide to the treasure chest at the top of a pillar. You can then walk casually to the altar.

JEE NOH SHRINE

This shrine stands directly to the east of Wasteland Tower.

1

In the first room, move close to the platform's edge so that Link and the concave platform are aligned perpendicularly with the conveyor belt, as shown in this picture. When the orb passes between Link and the concave platform, immobilize it with Stasis. Now hit it with an arrow while it is frozen in time: this will give it momentum, making it fall in the concave platform once the Stasis effect ends. (Note that you can alternatively cast Stasis on the conveyor belt to immobilize the orb, if you prefer.) Repeat the exact same procedure in the second room, after first eliminating the two Guardian Scouts, either by reflecting their laser beams back at them with a perfect guard, or by shooting them with arrows.

2

In the next room, start by grabbing the treasure chest with Magnesis and bring it back to your position to open it. Next, pick up the nearby orb and make your way across the first conveyor belt, timing your progression so that a large rock shields you from the beam. Pause on the pillar to the left and drop the orb at your feet.

3

Now stop the nearby laser-emitting device with Stasis, immediately retrieve the orb, and walk across the next conveyer belt. Slow down as you come close to the third laser beam, then resume your march to the final platform as soon as a large rock shields you. Drop the orb in the concave platform before heading through the door to reach the altar on the other side.

KAY NOH SHRINE

This shrine is located close to the Gerudo Desert entrance, at the top of the cliff that overlooks the Gerudo Canyon Stable.

1

In the first room, pick up the electric orb right in front of your starting position and drop it on the empty pedestal to your right.

2

In the second room, head to the right-hand dead end and eliminate the Guardian Scout. Now sever the rope that an electric orb is hanging from (with an arrow, for example), and take the orb to the pedestal. This will enable you to reach the treasure chest further back. When you go through the door in the center of the room, be ready to face a Guardian Scout in the next corridor.

3

In the final room, use Magnesis to rearrange the two small cubes in the right-hand pool so that they conduct the electricity (see picture), which will open the gate leading to the altar. Don't forget to take down the treasure chest above the entrance door with Magnesis before you leave.

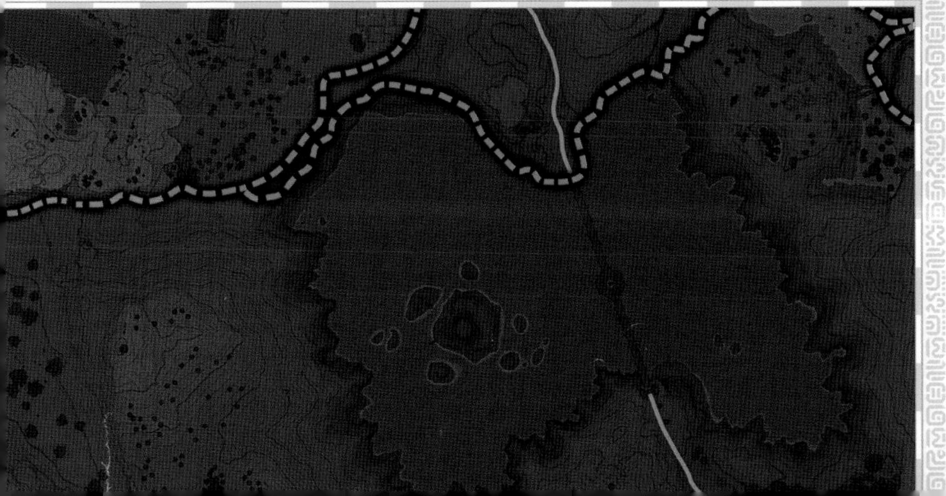

DAKO TAH SHRINE

SHRINE QUEST: THE EYE OF THE SANDSTORM

This shrine can be found on a small rock plateau to the north of the Gerudo Desert, a short distance to the southeast of Gerudo Tower. You can trigger the associated shrine quest by speaking to Nobiro, at Kara Kara Bazaar – he is found on the west side of the outpost, at an elevated lookout, looking in the direction of the shrine.

1

Follow the hallways until you reach the room with the electric cube, eliminating the Guardian Scout on your path. Step on the moving platform to reach it, then grab the electric cube with Magnesis. Still standing on the moving platform, keep the cube close to the electric cable until you reach the side from which you arrived. Now move onto the platform with the orange crystal and position the cube close to the crystal with Magnesis. You might find it easier to navigate this section by carrying the cube manually (rather than by controlling it with Magnesis). Pause briefly during your ascent (moving the cube away from the crystal) to open the treasure chest on the intermediate floor. Once you have it, reactivate the crystal with the cube and go all the way to the top.

2

Once on the upper platform, drop the cube on the metal slabs below: this will electrify them, eliminating the two Guardian Scouts instantly. Lift it again with Magnesis and put it down in a safe position. Now drop down yourself, open the treasure chest, and push the large metal cube away to open a passage. You can now pick up the electric cube and make your way to the moving platform at the far end.

3

This step is optional: instead of carrying the electric cube up the ramp, put it down and run down the slope to your right. Hit the crystal to activate a moving platform, which will take you to a secret treasure chest. Once you have opened it, return to the cube and go all the way up.

4

You can now take the electric cube to the top of the shrine via the elevator. Put it down on the pedestal to activate a final moving platform. Step on it and turn on Magnesis mode. Once you are within range of the large metal cube, push it backward to free the way to the altar. You can clear the shrine here, or complete a final step to find an additional chest.

5

After the right angle, stay on the moving platform and turn around, pulling the metal cube to your left. This will enable you to reach the fourth treasure chest as the moving platform returns to the electric cube. Once you have opened the chest, wait for the platform to come back and jump onto it to reach the altar.

SUMA SAHMA SHRINE

SHRINE QUEST: SECRET OF THE SNOWY PEAKS

This shrine is concealed near the top of Mount Granajh, to the southeast of Wasteland Tower. You have to complete a specific quest to unlock it.

1 To activate this quest, you must interact with the Mountain Peak Log inside a ruined shack toward the top of Mount Granajh.

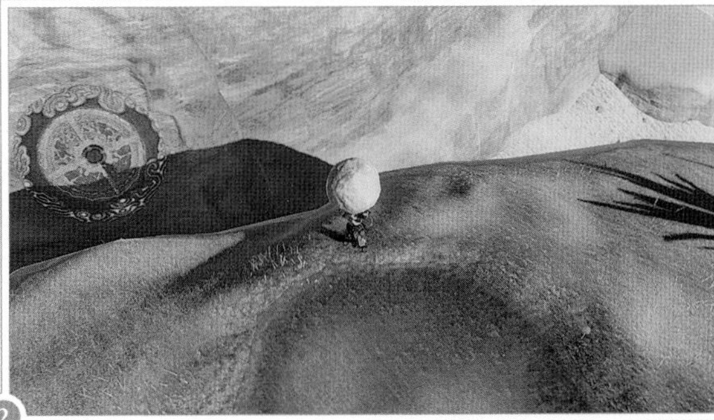

2 To solve this riddle you must cast a shadow on the center circle of the pedestal of the nearby cliff. To achieve this, the easiest option is to pick up any snowball and stand with it above your head at approximately 4:20 PM. The snowball's shadow must be perfectly aligned on the pedestal's core, as shown above. Alternatively, drop a snowball in the smaller of the two puddles of water close to the shack, then summon a block of ice directly beneath the snowball so that it rests at the top of the block. However, the former option will give you more flexibility to adjust the position of the shadow as required. When you succeed, you will reveal the Suma Sahma Shrine.

3 Once inside the shrine, head to the altar, collecting the contents of the treasure chest on the way.

DAQO CHISAY SHRINE

This shrine is clearly visible a few steps away from Gerudo Town's main entrance.

1 Start by focusing on the left-hand side of the room. Use Magnesis to position the barrel and the cube as shown here, which will reveal a second barrel.

2 Rearrange the two barrels and the cube as shown above: this opens the door behind which you can find a metal chest. Now take all four objects (the two barrels, the cube, and the chest) to the right-hand side of the room.

3 The configuration required to lift the gate behind which a second metal cube is hidden is shown in this picture.

4 Finally, take the two metal cubes and position one on each side of the stairs leading to the altar, which will now be within easy reach.

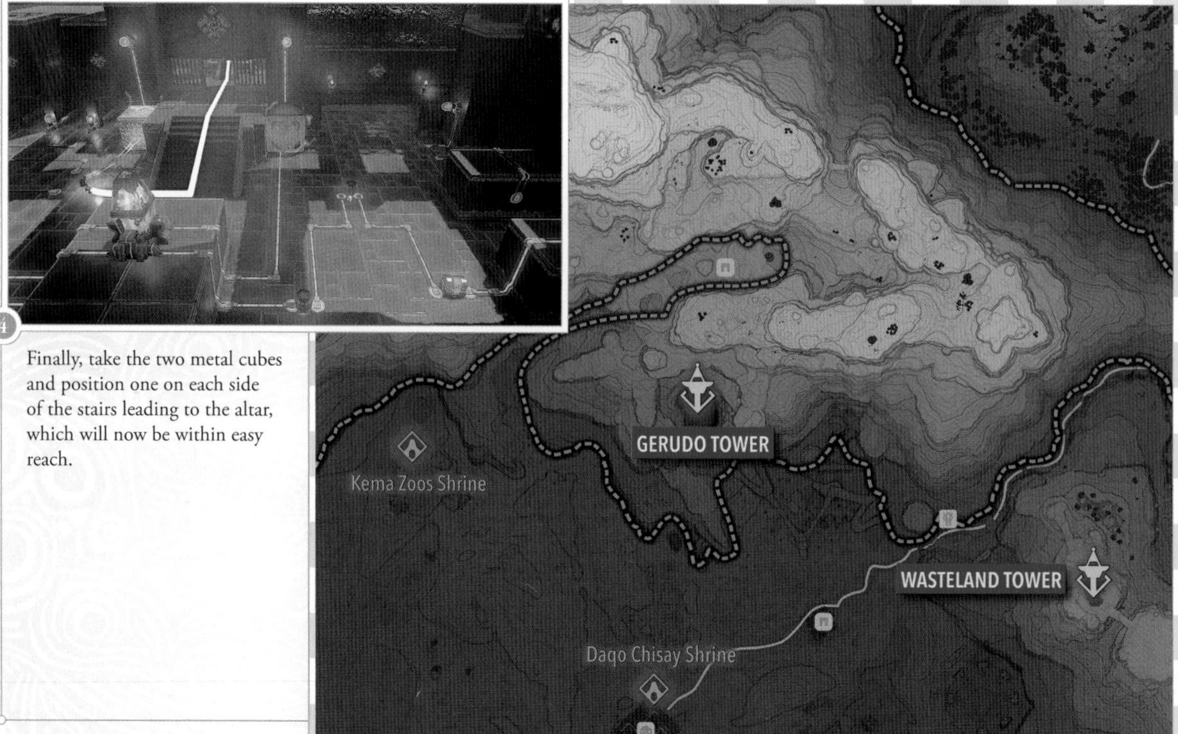

KEMA ZOOS SHRINE

SHRINE QUEST: THE SILENT SWORDSWOMEN

This shrine is located in the northwest corner of the Gerudo Desert, in the middle of the perpetual sandstorm.

1 Laine, who stands guard at the northwest exit of Gerudo Town, will put you on the track of this shrine by telling you to follow the guidance of the statues in the sandstorm. Run in the direction where each points: you will be directed from statue to statue until you reach the Kema Zoos Shrine.

2 Inside the shrine, step on either ramp and grab the electric orb with Magnesis when it is still in the launcher closest to your position.

3 Take the orb to the far left corner of the room and drop it on the electrode above the fence. This will raise the door, giving you access to the treasure chest inside.

4 Finally, lift the orb again with Magnesis and drop it near the electrode in the right corner of the room. This will open the path to the altar.

RAQA ZUNZO SHRINE

SHRINE QUEST: THE UNDEFEATED CHAMP

This shrine lies in the desert sand, a short distance from the south of Gerudo Town. You can reveal it by completing the corresponding quest.

1 After clearing the Divine Beast Vah Naboris dungeon, head to the sand-seal rally area to the south of Gerudo Town. Speak to Shabonne to take part in the race and agree to pay the 50-rupee fee. Make sure you have at least one shield available.

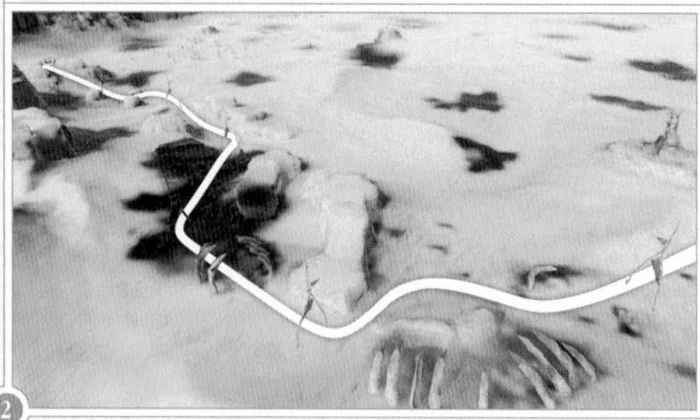

2 Your task in this race is to reach the goal line in under a minute and a half while still passing under every arch on the way. The path is relatively easy to follow, with occasional obstacles that you must zigzag through. Two key tactics will improve your chances of succeeding. Firstly, make sure you press Ⓐ to dash whenever your seal slows down: you should be at maximum speed at all times, except for very brief moments when you're realigning your seal to avoid an obstacle. Secondly, relax and try to steer gently through the curves: harsh turns will only slow you down. Victory rewards you with an orb, which you can drop in the nearby concave slot to reveal the Raqa Zunzo Shrine.

3 Once inside, head to the altar, collecting the contents of the treasure chest on the way.

HAWA KOTH SHRINE

This shrine can be found in the far southwest corner of the world map, underneath the Gerudo Great Skeleton located at Dragon's Exile.

1

Grab the two metal cubes and position them on both sides of the small pillars, as illustrated above. This will open the nearby door.

2

In the second room, pick up the treasure chest in the water with Magnesis and take it back to your position. You can then grab the electric orb with Magnesis, and drop it close to the crystal. The orb is tied by a short chain, so make sure no pillar stands in-between: you need the chain's full length to reach the crystal. When you succeed, a small elevator platform will be activated: ride it to the level above and eliminate the three Guardian Scouts a little farther down the room.

3

Seize the electric orb close to the elevator platform with Magnesis and pull it high in the air before you cross the bridge. You do not want to activate any of the crystals on the bridge with it. Once on the other side, drop the orb on the small ledge overlooking the bridge: this will create a path leading to a second treasure chest. Now take the orb one more time and drop it on the pedestal by the gate.

4

In the final room, cast Stasis on the rock cube closest to you in the middle lane. While it is frozen in time, step on the floor switch, then quickly move the metal slider toward the right with Magnesis: it should be positioned across the middle and right lanes, as shown above. Once this is achieved, you can step off the floor switch: with all crystals now aligned and connected, the gate behind you will open, giving you access to a chest and a cogwheel.

5

Using Magnesis, take the cogwheel back to the previous room and insert it in the mechanism above the gate to open it and reveal the path to the altar.

DILA MAAG SHRINE

SHRINE QUEST: THE DESERT LABYRINTH

This shrine is found at the heart of the South Lomei Labyrinth. To access it, you must complete the local shrine quest.

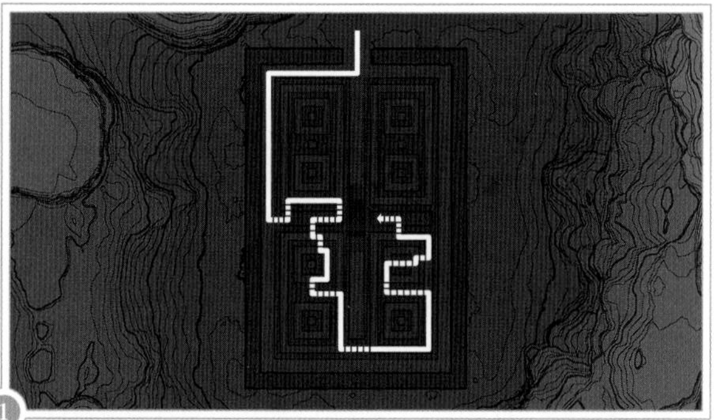

1 The South Lomei Labyrinth is found to the east of the Gerudo Desert. As intimidating as it may seem, clearing it is in fact relatively easy once you know how to proceed. If you plan to go through the maze in a traditional way, follow the path shown on the above map.

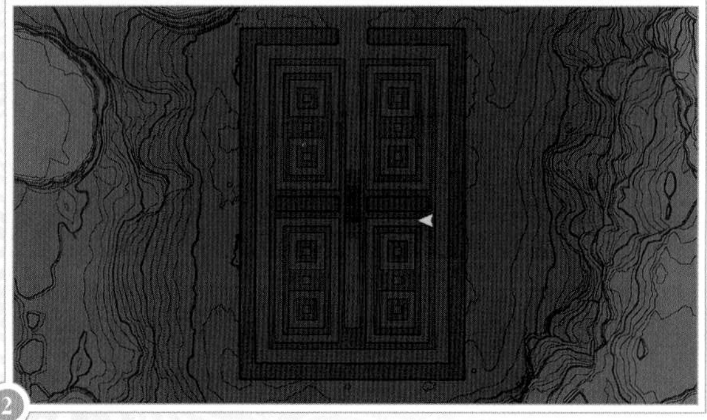

2 Alternatively, you can take a shortcut by climbing to the top of the structure and heading to the position shown on this picture, in the southeast quadrant of the maze.

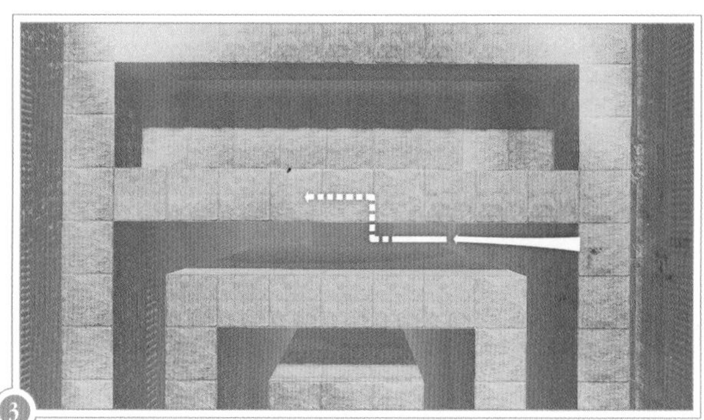

3 From this position, easily recognizable thanks to the presence of purple Malice goo, drop and take the corridor a few steps to the west. This leads directly to the Dila Maag Shrine. Once inside, head to the altar, collecting the contents of the treasure chest on the way.

THO KAYU SHRINE

This shrine is buried in the Toruma Dunes, to the west of Gerudo Town.

1

Head to the Toruma Dunes, to the west of Gerudo Town. Before you attempt anything, eliminate the Molduga sub-boss. This giant sandworm is a fearsome enemy that can deplete most, if not all, of your hearts in a single blow. The key to defeating it is to exploit the fact that it detects you through vibrations while submerged. Step on one of the rocks and throw a round bomb at the monster. It will mistake the bomb for you and swallow it: detonate the explosive while your foe is in the air; it will collapse on the sand, giving you a chance to inflict massive damage. Unleash your most powerful combos, for instance a charged, spinning attack with a two-handed blade. When the creature regains consciousness and dives beneath the sand again, head back to a rock or pillar and repeat the bomb trick until you prevail.

2

Once the Molduga has fallen, you can reveal this shrine by lighting the four torches in the area. Any fire-elemental weapon will do the trick here.

3

Inside the shrine, open the chest then head to the altar.

KORSH O'HU SHRINE

SHRINE QUEST: THE SEVEN HEROINES

This shrine is found to the east of Gerudo Town. You can hear about it from Rotana, a character reading books in the northwest part of Gerudo Town.

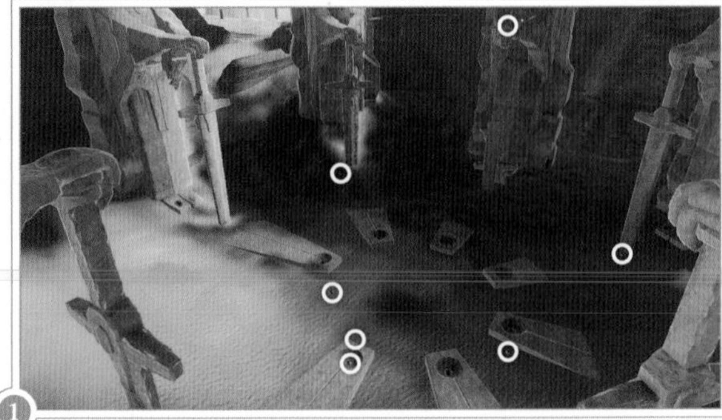

1

This shrine is initially buried beneath the sand, in the center of the circle formed by the large warrior statues. To reveal it, you must solve a puzzle involving seven metal orbs that each have to be placed in the right concave slot at the center using Magnesis. First, make sure you gather all the orbs in the area: one is already in position, three are in plain view; two are partly buried in the sand; one lies at the top of one of the statues' joined hands. Once you have all seven, you can proceed to the next step.

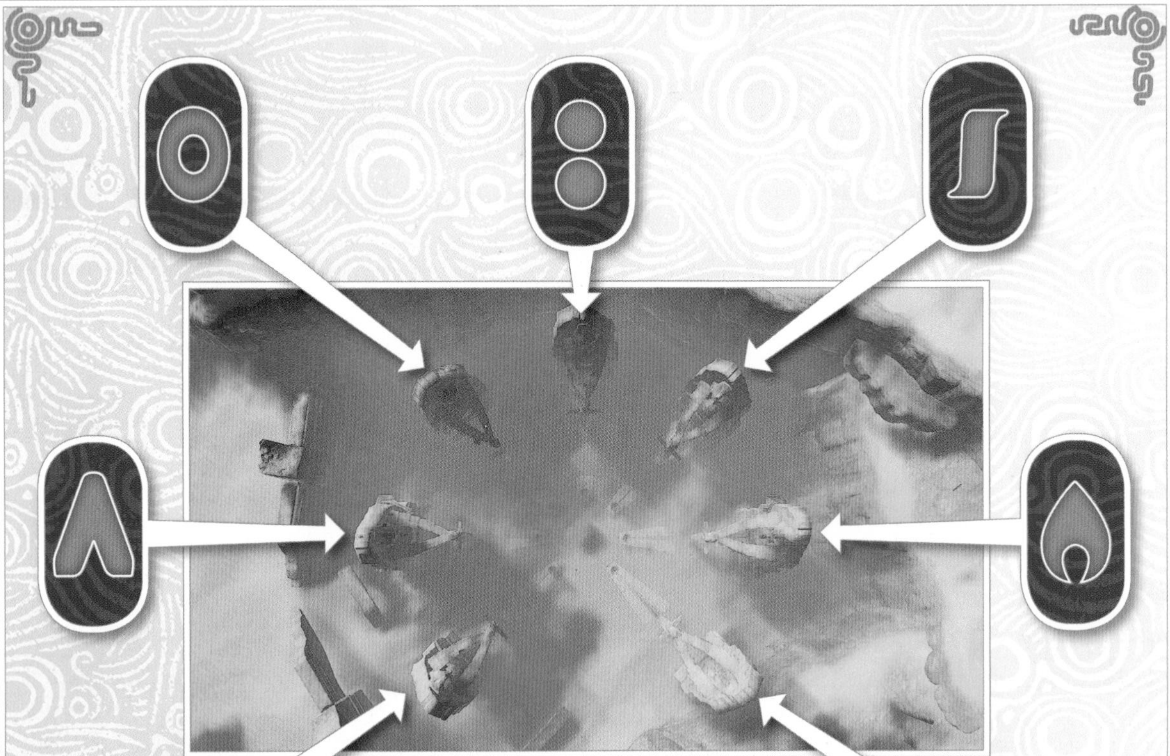

2

The key to solving the puzzle is to match each orb with its respective slot. This can be achieved by pairing them based on the symbol they bear. The symbol on each orb is immediately apparent. For statues, you must look a little harder, as each symbol appears in a different position: on a foot, on a head, on a sword, and so forth. If you struggle, the above picture shows the complete solution. When all orbs are in the correct position, the shrine will emerge from the sand. Once inside the Korsh O'hu Shrine, head to the altar, retrieving the contents of the treasure chest on the way.

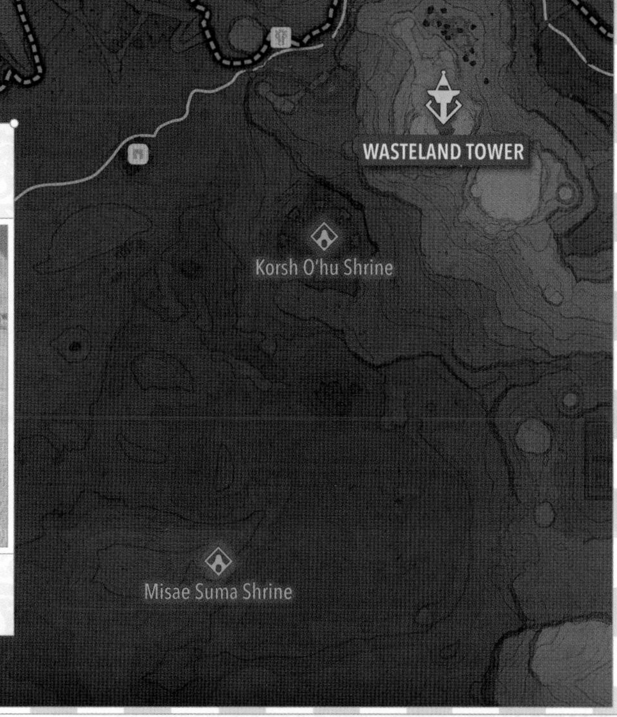

MISAE SUMA SHRINE

SHRINE QUEST: THE PERFECT DRINK

This shrine is located in the southeast corner of the Gerudo Desert, to the east of the Southern Oasis.

1 When you reach the shrine, you'll find that a Gerudo named Pokki has collapsed on its terminal, preventing you from accessing it. Your next task is to get her a Noble Pursuit drink.

2 Head back to Gerudo Town and speak to Furosa, the woman behind the counter in the bar behind the jewelry shop, in the north part of the town.

3 Now visit the ice house during the day. This is an underground room found directly to the north of Gerudo Town. You can enter it via a floor hatch beneath a very large flat rock. Speak to Anche inside to obtain a large ice cube.

4 You must now make your way across the ruins between the ice house and Gerudo Town, while carrying the ice cube above your head. Walking to the other end of the ruins is by no means difficult, but enemies on the way will slow you down. The best solution is to avoid them altogether, even if this means making a small detour. If combat is unavoidable, put the cube down and eliminate your enemies quickly, then resume your march toward Furosa at the south end of the ruins. To avoid any possible encounter, feel free to walk on the sand a few steps to the east of the ruins. Drop the ice cube in front of her to complete the challenge. You can now return to Pokki outside the Misae Suma Shrine. With her favorite drink awaiting at Gerudo Town, she frees the terminal, giving you access to the shrine – inside which you can open a treasure chest and walk straight to the altar.

Gerudo Tower Shrines

KUH TAKKAR SHRINE

This shrine lies in the eastern part of the Gerudo Highlands, at the foot of the Laparoh Mesa peak.

1 The shrine is initially concealed under a thick layer of ice. You must melt the ice, ideally with fire arrows (the most efficient and fastest option), or by any other means if you are patient (such as creating a campfire with a bundle of wood that you have set ablaze).

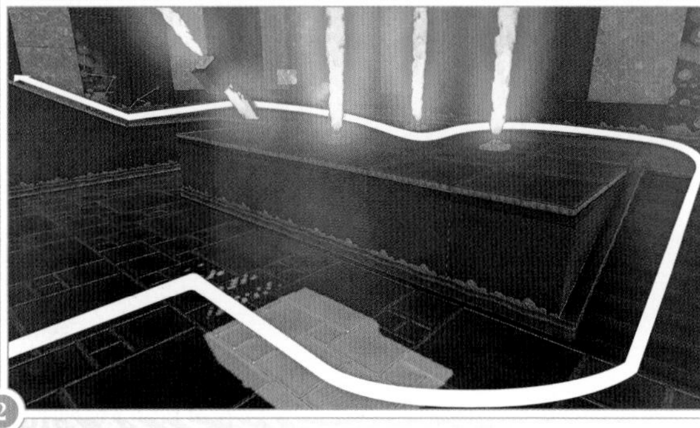

2 Inside the shrine, your goal is to make your way to the top of the structure while carrying an ice cube, avoiding flame hazards on the way. Make sure you remove any fire-elemental weapons or arrows from Link's current equipment to avoid melting it. When you're ready, pick up the ice cube and walk up the ramp. Zigzag between the vertical flames, then throw the cube to get it past the rotating flames without taking any chances. Drop the cube when you reach the horizontal flames.

3 With the cube safely on the floor, run underneath the flames to the small pool of lava. Grab the metal cube from the lava with Magnesis and drop it in front of the horizontal flames. If you angle it diagonally, it can block all three streams simultaneously. Pick up the ice cube and drop it in front of the lava pool.

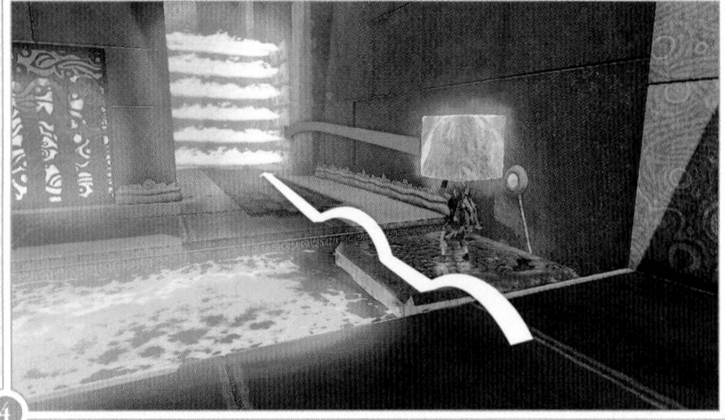

4 Retrieve the metal cube with Magnesis and drop it in the lava to create a bridge. Hop on it while carrying the ice cube, then grab the metal cube again and use it to block the wall of flames. Pick up the ice block and take it past the flames.

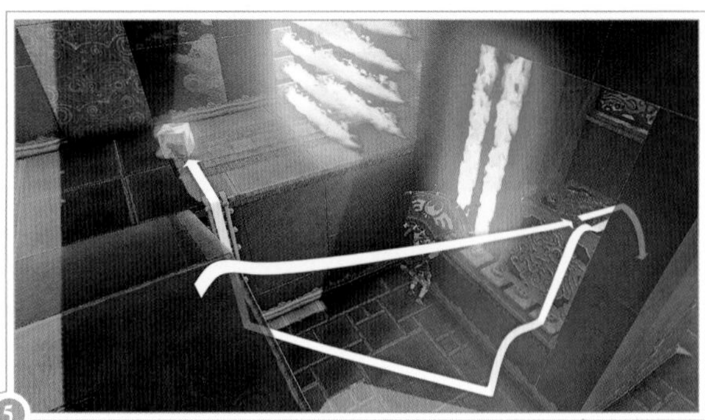

5 Once on the other side of the wall of flames, put the ice cube down and grab the metal cube with Magnesis again. Drop it on the wall of flames to your left, on the floor below. Now go up the ramp and glide from there to the metal cube. You will find a treasure chest next to it. Use the ladder to climb back to the ice cube and retrieve the metal cube.

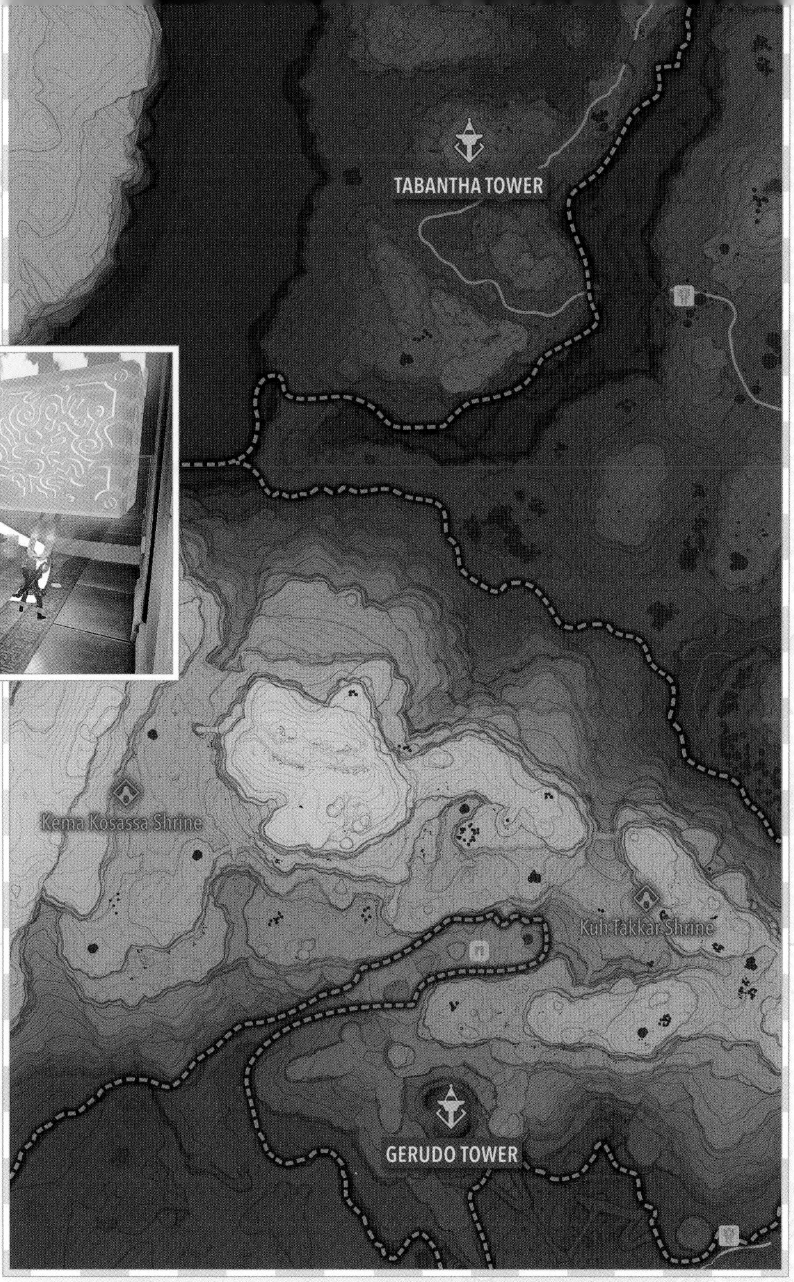

TABANTHA TOWER

Kema Kosassa Shrine

Kuh Takkar Shrine

GERUDO TOWER

6 When in front of the final wall of flames, throw your block of ice through it, making sure it lands well beyond it. Next, lift the metal cube with Magnesis and use it to shield yourself from the flames coming from above. Once on the other side, pick up the ice cube and walk to the altar: the gate will open automatically as you get close to it.

KEMA KOSASSA SHRINE

This shrine lies at the foot of Mount Agaat, near the western edge of the Gerudo Highlands.

1 This shrine pits you against a Guardian Scout IV. You can find detailed analysis and combat strategy for this creature on page 312. By default, you have no obstacle to hide behind when your opponent performs its spinning attack, but you can create your own by summoning ice pillars with Cryonis. If you are caught by surprise and cannot do this in time, consider stunning your enemy with a shock arrow to stop it in its tracks.

SHO DANTU SHRINE

This shrine is located to the northwest of Gerudo Tower, on one of the plateaus overlooking the canyon that leads to the Yiga Clan Hideout.

1

To make the shrine appear, you must first drop a luminous stone on the glowing pedestal. If you do not have any in your inventory, you can obtain luminous stones by destroying the mineral deposits surrounding the pedestal.

2

Inside the shrine, look to your left and destroy the wooden crates with a bomb. This gives you access to a room beyond.

3

Drop a cube bomb on the launcher and detonate it when it's at the peak of its course. This will trigger a crystal that opens the door to the right of your entrance point in the shrine. Collect the contents of the treasure hidden behind the pillar before you head to the newly opened room.

4

Your goal here is the same as in the previous room, however, you must activate the launcher yourself via the crystal hidden at the back of the pillar. Drop a spherical bomb next to the crystal and a cube bomb on the launcher. Now detonate the spherical bomb first, and quickly switch to the cube bomb rune. Blow the cube bomb at the top of its peak to trigger the opening of the door in the middle room.

5

In the final room, drop both a cube bomb and a round bomb in one of the two launchers. The cube bomb will end up on the central pillar where a crystal rests, while the round bomb will be propelled back and forth between the two launchers. Now step on either of the two pedestals by the entrance and look in the direction of the crystal. When the round bomb lands on one of the launchers, detonate the cube bomb: this will raise the pedestal you are standing on.

6 Finally, step off the pedestal and stand in front of the locked door. Look in the direction of the launchers and detonate the round bomb as it passes above the crystal. This will raise the gate, giving you access to the altar.

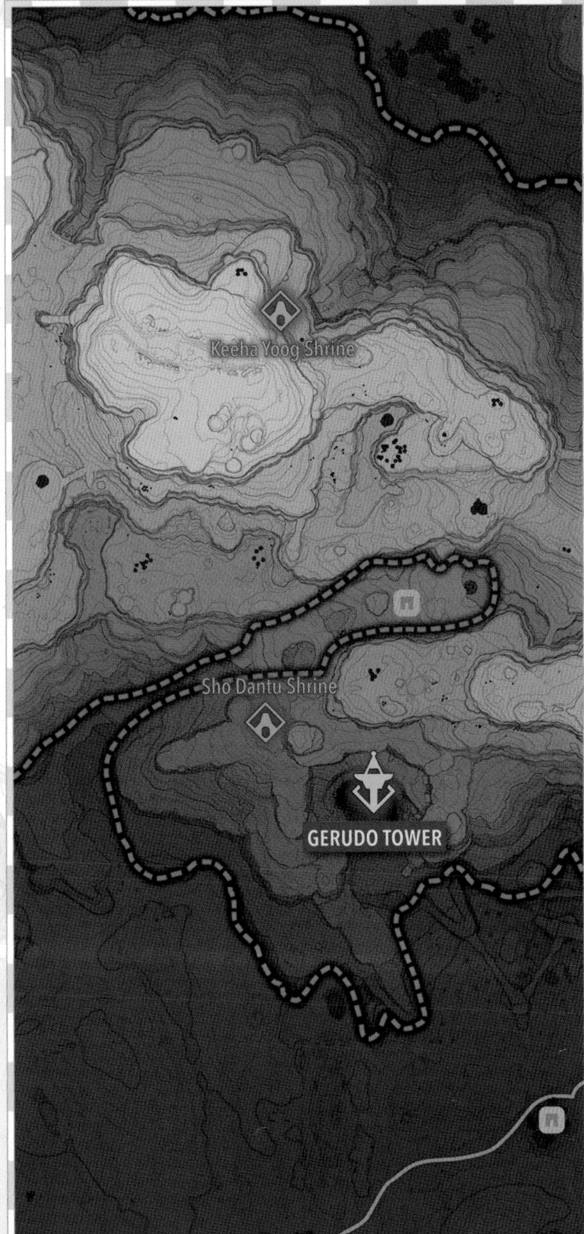

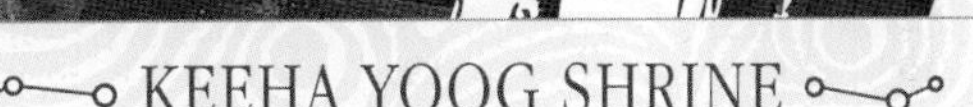

KEEHA YOOG SHRINE

SHRINE QUEST: CLIFFSIDE ETCHINGS

This shrine is located in the Gerudo Highlands, to the northeast of the Gerudo Summit. You can trigger the associated shrine quest by speaking to Geggle at the Tabantha Bridge Stable: he runs up to the cliff south of the stable during the daytime and peers southwest, directly toward the etching far off in the distance.

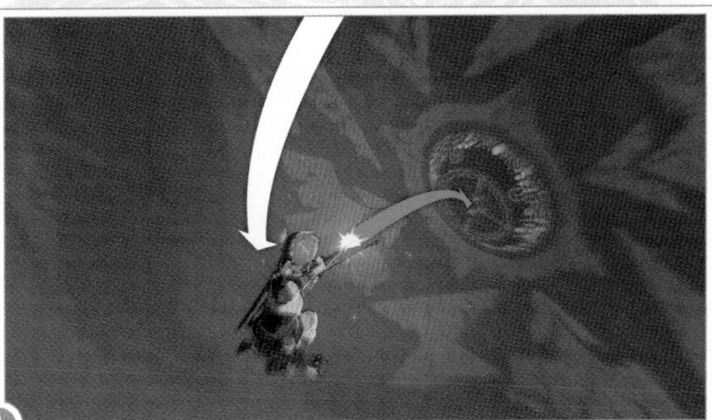

1 Head to the plateau to the northeast of Gerudo Summit and look in the direction of the large electricity symbol visible on the cliff. You must hit the dais at the center of it with an electrical charge. The easiest way to achieve this is to fire a shock arrow. This will cause the shrine to appear. If your bow does not have sufficient range to reach the dais from below, you can climb to a point above it, then glide back down, hitting the target during your descent. Once inside, open the treasure chest on your way to the altar.

JOLOO NAH SHRINE

SHRINE QUEST: TEST OF WILL

This shrine is located to the north of Wasteland Tower, on the east side of Koukot Plateau.

Speak to any of the three Gorons next to two platforms surrounded by braziers. Your goal is to complete two "endurance" trials. For the first test, you will need Level 2 heat resistance, induced either by armor or an elixir. For the second test, you need Level 2 flame guard, though pieces of armor providing this effect are forbidden: you must rely on a powerful elixir lasting for at least two minutes (for example, by combining multiple fireproof lizards or smotherwing butterflies with monster parts, all available in the vicinity). Thanks to these effects, you will take no damage whatsoever, enabling you to easily pass the test without flinching and thus reveal the Joloo Nah Shrine.

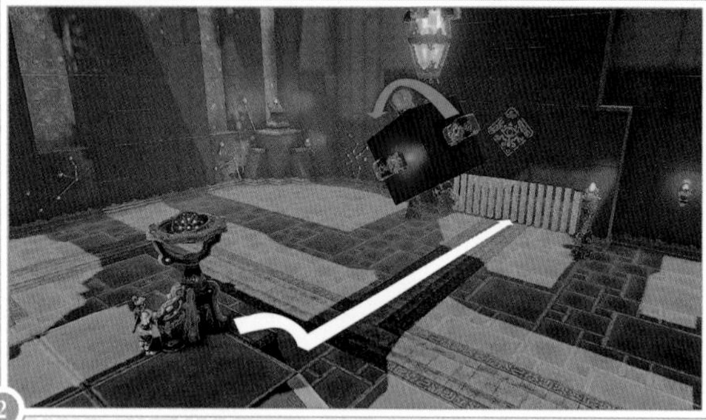

In the shrine's first room, interact with the terminal. You must rotate your gyroscopic controller in all directions to ensure that all of the electrodes on the cube (one per cube side) are activated by the crystal on the ceiling. The gate will open once you succeed.

In the second room, use the terminal to align the central cube with your controller in such a way that the four wind streams form an "X" on your screen. Three of the windmills will start spinning; only the one in the bottom-right corner will not. Once this is done, climb up the ramp to your left and glide to the treasure chest in the corner. Note that you must remain in the wind stream at all times as you cannot afford to lose any altitude to reach the chest. If you struggle, realign the cube so that the stream flows a little higher, making the gliding maneuver easier.

Grab the metal cube with Magnesis and move it on top of the right-hand floor switch. This will cause the windmill that wasn't spinning to rise and to start spinning. Now glide to the left-hand floor switch and step on it. Stop it in time with Stasis while it's activated, then sprint through the gate before the effect ends and the door closes.

In the final room, interact with the terminal to face a puzzle similar to the one in the first room. Your goal is to rotate the cube so that the torches on each of its sides light up by touching the torches hanging from the ceiling. The difficulty here is that there are water fountains that will extinguish the fire if you are not careful. To simplify the process, make the second treasure chest fall to your position by burning the wooden ledge it rests on. Now drop the chest on the switch at the foot of the left fountain: this lowers the pillar, removing the water stream from the equation and making the cube rotation much easier. Alternatively, you can light up a couple of the torches on the top faces of the cube with the hanging torches, and leave the cube oriented diagonally toward you (ensuring that no torch is in contact with water). Finish the job by setting ablaze the remaining torches with fire arrows, which will open the way to the altar.

SASA KAI SHRINE

SHRINE QUEST: SIGN OF THE SHADOW

This shrine lies a short distance to the southeast of Gerudo Tower. It is initially buried in the ground, and you can reveal it by completing the corresponding quest.

1 Speak to Kass at the top of Gerudo Tower. The riddle in his song refers to a dais to the southeast of the tower, which you can see from his position.

2 Stand on the dais between 3:00 PM and 4:00 PM (the dais will glow during this time window) and shoot an arrow at the top of Gerudo Tower, or even slightly above it. This will activate the dais, causing the Sasa Kai Shrine to appear.

3 This shrine pits you against a Guardian Scout III. You can find detailed analysis and combat strategy for this creature on page 312.

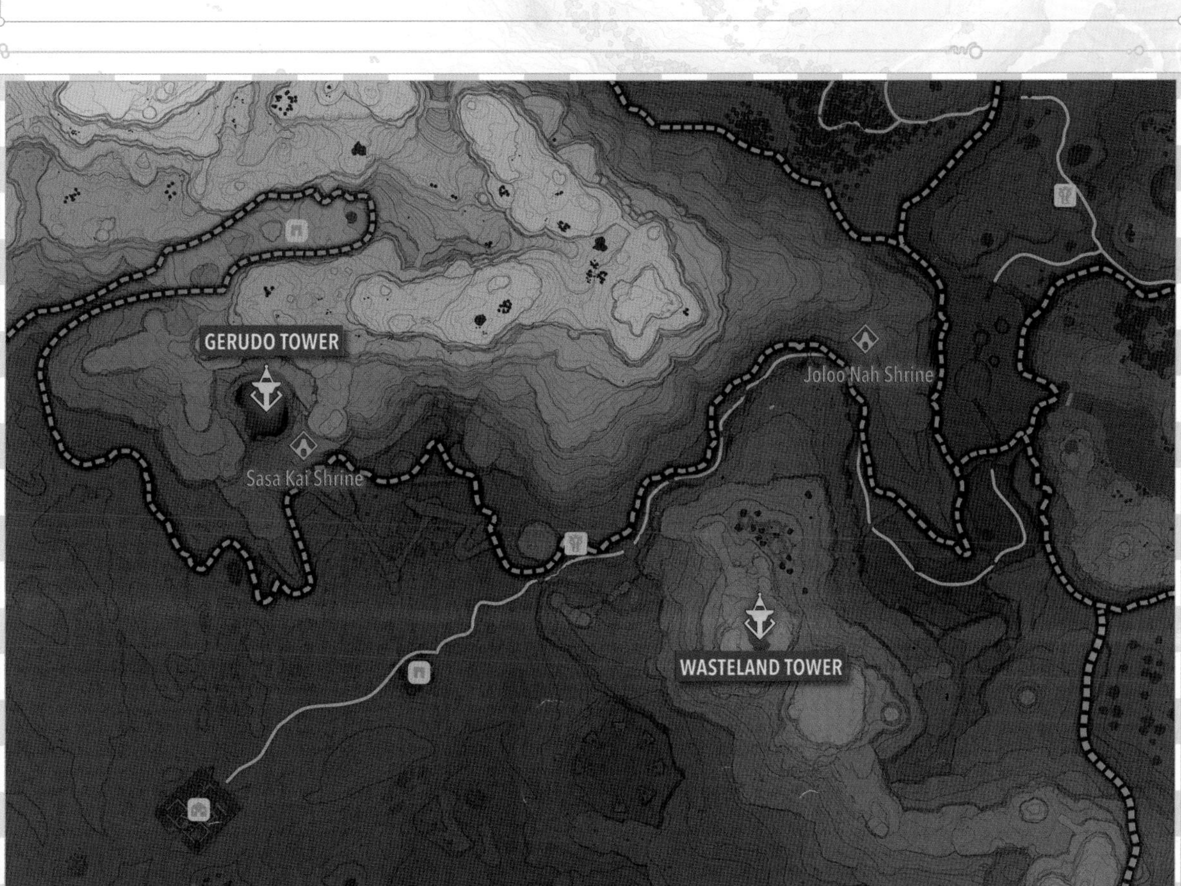

Central Tower Shrines

ROTA OOH SHRINE

This shrine is located on a small plateau overlooking the Outskirt Stable, a short distance to the southwest.

1 Start by hitting the crystal on your right to reveal an orb, as well as a path on your left leading to a treasure chest. Once the small key is yours, pick up the orb and drop it in front of the shrine's entrance. You can now hit the crystal again to return the rotating structure to its original position.

2 Open the locked door with the small key, then pick up the orb and throw it in the small enclosure to your right. Now activate the nearby crystal again (with an arrow or a bomb detonation, for example): the orb will thus reach its intended slot, triggering a launcher in the center.

3 Stand on the launcher to be propelled high in the air, and open the paraglider to reach the treasure chest on the small ledge.

4 Finally, return to the launcher to be propelled again, but this time draw your bow while Link is at the top of his course: the slow-motion effect gives you ample time to aim at the crystal, which will rotate the structure and cause a platform to appear beneath your feet. You can now walk straight to the altar.

KAAM YA'TAK SHRINE

This shrine lies to the southwest of the Central Tower.

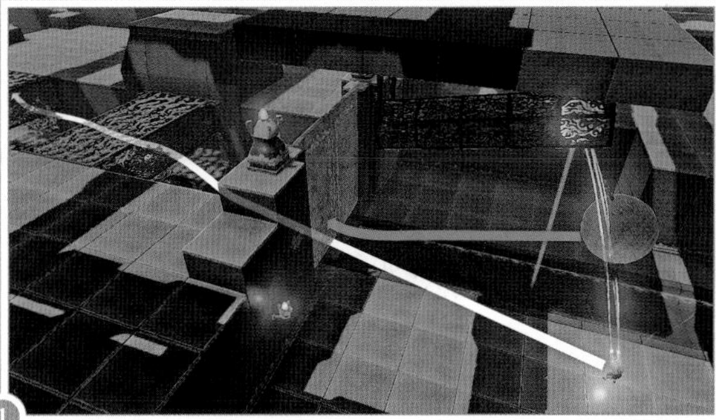

1 Use Magnesis to pull the ball from which a boulder is hanging all the way to the right. When it slides back down the slope, it will cause the boulder to slam into the doors, which will open them. In the next section, you must reach the other end of the corridor without getting crushed by the spiked boulders. Feel free to stop them with Stasis to take no chances.

2 Eliminate the Guardian Scouts, then set the red leaves on fire (either with a fire arrow or a standard arrow set ablaze with one of the torches): this will cause the boulder to fall and open the doors for you. Don't forget to open the treasure chest close to the boulder's original position. You will find a second one immediately to your left, beyond the newly opened doors.

3 Follow the corridors until you reach the position shown here (you will encounter two Guardian Scouts on the way). Immobilize the rotating platform on the floor with Stasis before you cross it. A little further you will find a terminal that gives you control of a hammer via the gyroscopic function of your controller: slam it into the metal ball to send a boulder along the ramp, and, ultimately, against the doors. Don't forget to open the treasure chest just to the left of the doors before you proceed.

4 In the next room, burn the leaves with a fire arrow as you did earlier. Cast Stasis on the rotating floor platform, then step on the nearby floor switch precisely as a boulder reaches the bottom of the slope (it needs to have enough speed to jump above the gap). This requires precise timing, so it might take you a few attempts before you make it. The trick is that the rotating floor platform must still be frozen in time when the boulder reaches it. Go through the doors once they are open.

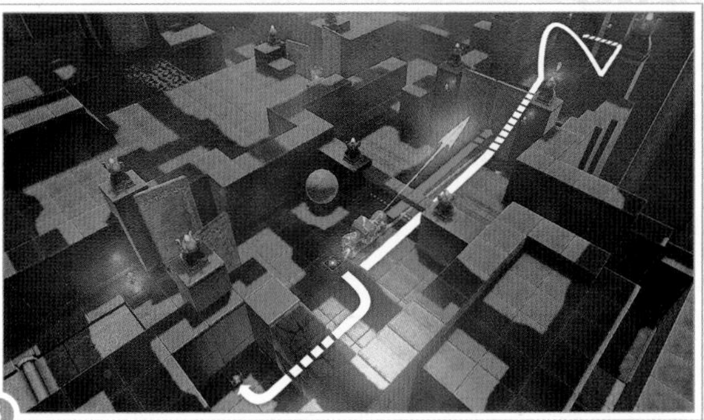

5 For the final section of this shrine, you must step on the floor switch to open the fence, then cast Stasis on the hammer on wheels, and hit it multiple times with a heavy weapon: it must gather enough momentum to blast open the doors at the opposite end. Before you head toward the altar, turn around and destroy the rock blocks with a bomb to reveal a passage leading to a fourth treasure chest. Now head through the doors and stand on the tile adjacent to the crystal. Hitting the crystal will propel you upward, all the way to the altar, which you can safely glide to. Note that a fifth chest awaits just above the crystal, behind a fence: you can reach it from the back via the ledge that runs below the altar.

NOYA NEHA SHRINE

This shrine is hidden inside a small cave on the island to the west of Hyrule Castle. You can get rid of the bramble surrounding it with a fire arrow. Once the path is clear, blow up the destructible rocks blocking the entrance with a bomb or bomb arrow.

1 This shrine pits you against a Guardian Scout II. You can find detailed analysis and combat strategy for this creature on page 312.

DAH KASO SHRINE

This shrine lies to the west of the Great Plateau, concealed underneath the Digdogg Suspension Bridge connecting Central Hyrule to the Wasteland region.

1 This shrine pits you against a Guardian Scout II. You can find detailed analysis and combat strategy for this creature on page 312.

WAHGO KATTA SHRINE

This shrine lies in plain sight a short walk to the north from the Riverside Stable.

1 Climb to the top of the stack of cubes and open the treasure chest.

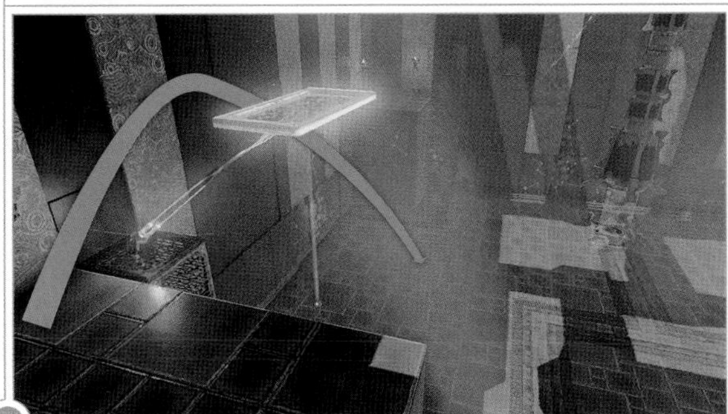

2 Thanks to Magnesis, you can now transfer all three cubes so that they form another pile close to the platform featuring a metal slab. From the top of the pile of cubes, grab the metal slab with Magnesis and drop it on the floor.

3 Finally, pile the three cubes on top of each other close to the platform with the altar. You might find it a little easier if you do so against a wall. Grab the metal slab with Magnesis and position it as a bridge connecting the pile of cubes to the altar. You may need to make minor adjustments, but the idea is really straightforward. Once everything is in place, walk to the altar.

KATAH CHUKI SHRINE

This shrine can be found to the west of Hyrule Castle Town Ruins, a few steps away from the fortification.

1 This shrine pits you against a Guardian Scout II. You can find detailed analysis and combat strategy for this creature on page 312.

NAMIKA OZZ SHRINE

This shrine lies to the east of Hyrule Castle, in Crenel Hills. It is concealed in the largest of the natural rock cirques.

1 In this shrine you must face a Guardian Scout III. You can find detailed analysis and combat strategy for this creature on page 312.

SAAS KO'SAH SHRINE

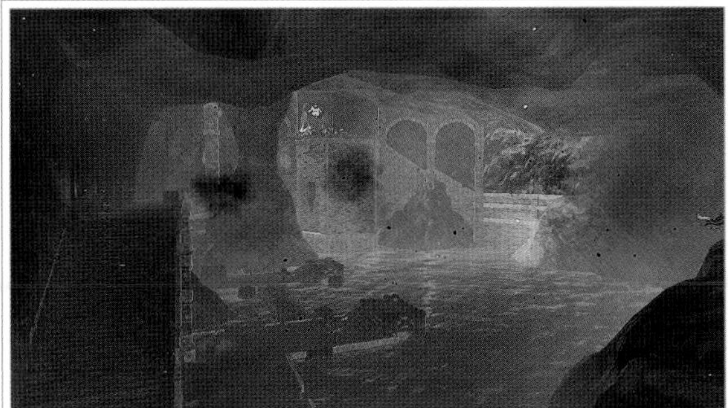

This shrine is hidden inside Hyrule Castle's Docks.

1 To reach the Docks, head to the northwest entrance of Hyrule Castle.

2 Once inside, climb up the stairs until you reach a large, unlit brazier. Set it ablaze using one of the nearby torches or a fire arrow: this will cause the shrine to appear.

3 Inside the shrine you must face a Guardian Scout IV. You can find detailed analysis and combat strategy for this creature on page 312. Note that you can lift metal blocks inserted in the floor with Magnesis to shield yourself from this foe's attacks.

RIDGELAND TOWER SHRINES

ZALTA WA SHRINE

This shrine is found southeast of the Ridgeland Tower, in plain sight in the Breach of Demise canyon.

1 Fire an arrow at the orb on your right to make it fall in the concave slot beneath. This will reveal a second orb.

2 Pick up the second orb and stand on the floor switch: this will raise a gate, through which you can throw the orb to a second concave slot. This will then trigger a platform in the center of the room to move back and forth.

3 Step on the floor tile by the crystal in the center of the room, and hit the crystal as the moving platform is coming in your direction: this will propel Link high in the air, enabling him to reach the moving platform. Feel free to glide briefly, if required.

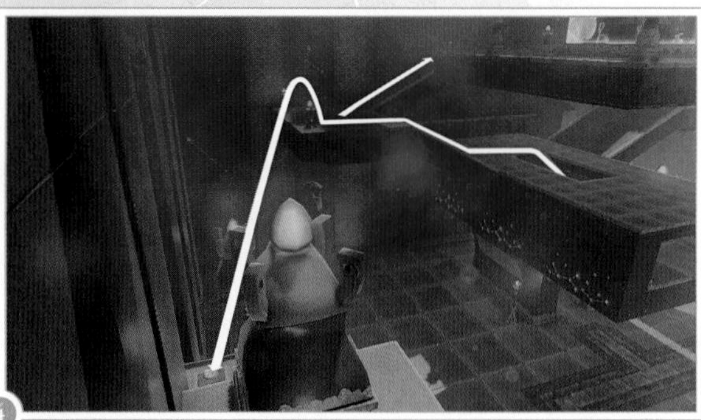

4 You can now walk up the slopes, all the way up to the altar. Consider making a brief detour when you reach the intermediate landing: there's a treasure chest that you can glide to on top of the structure where you threw the second orb.

TOH YAHSA SHRINE

SHRINE QUEST: TRIAL OF THUNDER

This shrine is hidden on the main island of the Thundra Plateau, to the west of Ridgeland Tower. You must first complete a shrine quest to reveal it.

1

This puzzle takes place on a plateau that features four pillars, each bearing a symbol and a slot. Your goal is to drop an orb with the corresponding symbol in each of the slots. Two of the orbs are on the plateau itself (one in plain sight, the other at the top of a pillar); the other two are at the top of statues located around the plateau. The plateau's height makes it impossible to take the latter two orbs to their destination by foot. You must somehow propel them there. All along, thunderstorm conditions complicate the situation. Make sure you unequip any gear made of metal to avoid being struck by lightning.

2

One way to get the two remote orbs to the plateau is to cast Stasis on them, then hit them repeatedly so as to give them enough speed to land on the plateau. You must move them a couple of steps forward from their starting position to have enough room to maneuver. To climb to them despite the rain, make three climbing moves then jump, and repeat this. Link will still slip, but you will get there eventually. Alternatively, activate Revali's Gale to create an updraft, which will only be possible after you have cleared the Divine Beast Vah Medoh dungeon (see page 80): you can then get to the top of the statue instantly.

3

To make the Stasis maneuver easier, make sure you hit the two remote orbs with a two-handed weapon, ideally an iron sledgehammer (which can be obtained from the Tanagar Canyon Course, just west of the Tabantha Bridge Stable). Seven blows will guarantee maximum momentum, sending the orb straight onto the plateau as long as you aim correctly. Pre-align Link in advance in such a way that his and the orb's center of gravity are on the same axis at the plateau. Once all four orbs are on the plateau, drop each one of them in its respective slot, matching them according to the symbols on the pillars. This will cause the Toh Yahsa shrine to appear.

4

Once inside the shrine, start by blowing up all of the destructible rocks with bombs. This will reveal three objects: a metal cube, a treasure chest underneath your starting position, and a giant floor switch underneath the platform with the altar. Take control of the metal cube with Magnesis and use it as a battering ram to push the second treasure chest off the tall pillar to your right.

5

After you secured the contents of both chests, lift the cube with Magnesis and position it at the base of the structure with the ladders leading to the altar. Use it as a stepping stone to reach the intermediate landing (at the top of the first ladder), then turn around and grab the cube again with Magnesis. Drop the cube on the giant floor switch to lift the gate and gain access to the altar.

MIJAH ROKEE SHRINE

SHRINE QUEST: UNDER A RED MOON

This shrine is located to the southwest of the Ridgeland Tower, on Washa's Bluff.

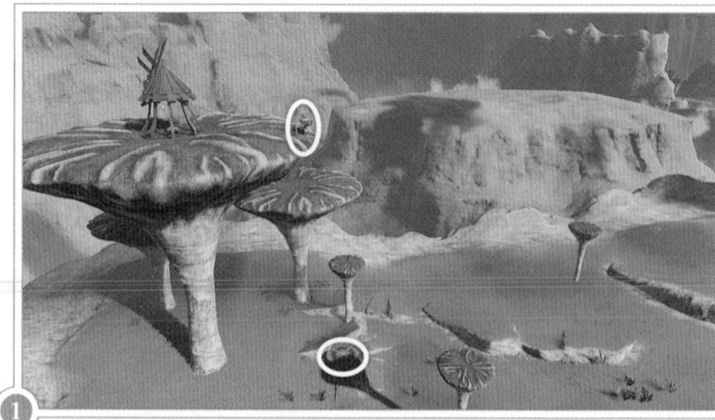

1 Speak to Kass at the top of the tallest mushroom-shaped spire at the south end of Washa's Bluff. The spire has a small canopy at its top, making it easy to identify from a distance. Kass's song refers to the blood moon, the dais below Kass's position, and something about having nothing between you and the night air.

2 To reveal the Mijah Rokee Shrine, stand on the dais wearing no equipment whatsoever (no armor, no weapon, no bow, no shield) during a blood moon. You can either manually trigger a blood moon by passing time at a campfire, or attend to other tasks and return to the dais when a blood moon naturally occurs in your playthrough. The time window during which a blood moon is active (and therefore when this quest can be completed) is from 9:00 PM until 1:00 AM.

3 Inside the shrine you have to face a Guardian Scout III. You can find detailed analysis and combat strategy for this creature on page 312.

SHAE LOYA SHRINE

This shrine is located to the southeast of Tabantha Tower, across Tanagar Canyon.

1

Stand on the floor tile facing the orb that is regularly sent high in the air. Stop the orb in time when it is at the apex of its course with Stasis, then hit it with a few arrows while it is frozen. This will cause it to deviate from its course, ending up in the concave slot at the bottom.

2

There are two chests that you can reach now: one by cutting the ropes that hold up the wooden ledge to your right, and one by being propelled by the launcher and gliding all the way to the orb's original position.

3

Finally, return to the launcher and this time look in the direction of the wall with a gate at its base. At the peak of your trajectory, fire an arrow at the crystal in the small alcove. This will lift the gate, giving you access to the altar.

MAAG NO'RAH SHRINE

This shrine is very well hidden inside a sealed cave midway between Hebra and Ridgeland Towers.

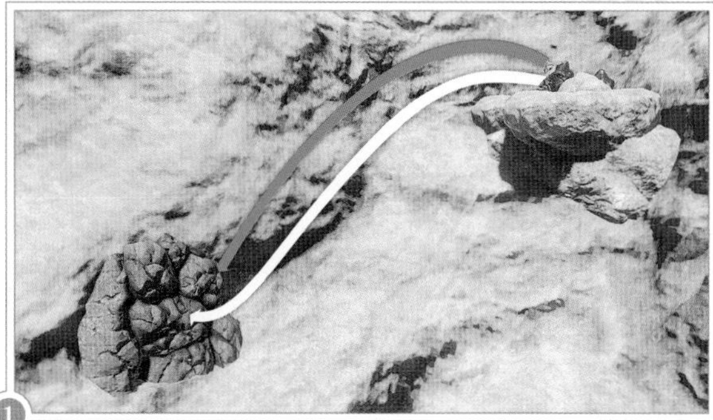

1

Finding this shrine can prove really tricky. It lies inside a tiny cave to the north of Linder's Brow. If you draw a line between Hebra and Ridgeland Towers, this shrine is almost exactly in the middle. To destroy the rocks blocking the entrance, either fire a bomb arrow, or climb to the small rock ledge overlooking the entrance and throw a normal bomb from here. You can then reach the shrine easily. Once inside, head to the altar, collecting the contents of the treasure chest on the way.

SHEEM DAGOZE SHRINE

SHRINE QUEST: THE TWO RINGS

THE POSITIONS OF THE SHRINES COVERED HERE ARE SHOWN ON PAGE 176.

This shrine will appear to the south of Ridgeland Tower after you have completed the corresponding quest.

1

To initiate the quest, you must speak to Kass, who stands at the top of a small rock structure, just north of the bridge that connects the West Hyrule Plains to the Nima Plain.

2

The solution to Kass's riddle is to fire a single arrow that goes through two rock holes. This is possible in the rock field to the west of the road, right in front of Kass. Head to the rock with a hole in the far northwest corner of the field, at the foot of a low cliff. Aim to the southeast and then fire an arrow right through the hole in front of you and the next one after that, as illustrated here. Aim above your target to factor in the arrow's drop. Once you make it, the Sheem Dagoze Shrine will appear. Don't forget to pick up any arrows from previously failed attempts.

3

Inside the shrine, step on the left-hand floor switch and wait until the orb reaches the concave slot below.

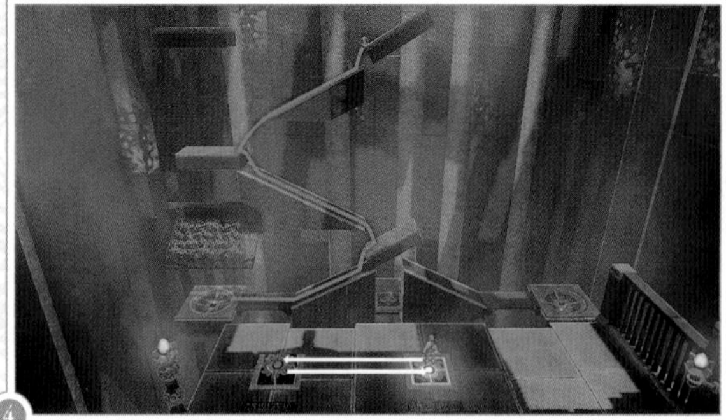

4

Now step on the right-hand floor switch to release a second orb. As soon as it leaves its original platform, sprint to the left-hand switch. The instant that the orb leaves the second platform, rush back to the right-hand switch. If all went according to plan, the second orb will reach its slot as well, which opens the nearby door leading to the altar. If you failed, you will need to start over.

5

Before you leave the shrine, glide to the small platform in the middle of the two concave slots. You will find a treasure chest there, as well as a floor switch activating the nearby platform, which will take you back to the altar.

MOGG LATAN SHRINE

This shrine is located to the southwest of the Ridgeland Tower, across the river, on the south side of Satori Mountain's peak.

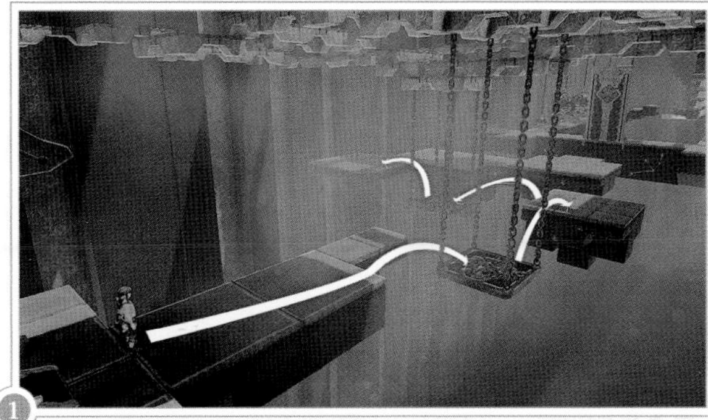

1

Jump on the swinging platform to cross the chasm, then make the next platform swing with Magnesis to achieve the same result.

2

When you reach the drawbridge, make it fall to your position by cutting the two ropes holding it with arrows. This will enable you to cross over and open the treasure chest on the other side.

3

You will find spiked boulders hanging from chains further along. Hold them one by one with Magnesis and put them aside to enable you to pass. Release them gently then move on to the next one. This will give you access to a second treasure chest.

4

For the next challenge, pull the nearby sliding platform to you with Magnesis, then step on it and let it take you closer to the other sliding platforms. Pull them one by one to form stairs. You can reach the final treasure chest by gliding to it from the penultimate sliding platform. Create stairs from the chest's platform to reach the ledge above.

5

In the final challenge, you must burn the ivy to be able to push the gates open with Magnesis – the altar can be found on the other side. You can hit the nearby crystal to reveal lanterns, but it's easier to just shoot a fire arrow or use any other means at your disposal to generate fire.

TABANTHA TOWER SHRINES

AKH VA'QUOT SHRINE

This shrine is located in Rito Village, on one of the higher landings.

First, climb the stairs to your right to reach a room with a pool of water and a crystal at the far end. There are actually three treasure chests in this room. The first one is behind the gate, which you can raise by hitting the crystal with an arrow. The other two are located in small alcoves on your right as you look toward the crystal. Summon Cryonis ice blocks in front of them and leap to the alcoves to open the chests.

To solve the puzzle in the main room, you must realign the fans as shown in the picture to the left. This implies hitting the bottom-left and top-left crystals three times each, and all the other crystals once. You can then make your way to the altar.

BAREEDA NAAG SHRINE

SHRINE QUEST: THE ANCIENT RITO SONG

This shrine is located directly to the south of Rito Village, though it is initially buried in the ground.

1. To initiate this quest, you must have completed the Divine Beast Vah Medoh dungeon (see page 80). If you meet this requirement, speak to Bedoli, who is standing on the same level as the Akh Va'quot Shrine in Rito Village. You can obtain additional hints by speaking to Bedoli's sister – Laissa – but this is entirely optional.

2. Your next objective is to head to the activation pedestal at the cliff's edge directly south of Rito Village. Stand on this pedestal at 12:40, and hit it with a fire-infused weapon or arrow when it starts glowing to reveal the Bareeda Naag Shrine. This corresponds to the moment when the sun shines through the hole in Rito Village's peak, illuminating the pedestal with a heart shape.

3. Inside the shrine, climb up the ladder and drop a round bomb in the cannon. Detonate it once it's in position. Repeat this to make the cannon fire an orb toward the far wall. Your goal is to reach the glowing target, with moving platforms acting as obstacles on the way. Repeat this until you hit the target, which will open the nearby door. Before you leave, don't forget to destroy the rocks close to your entrance point: you will find a chest behind them.

4. You can activate the altar immediately if you wish to clear the shrine, but there is another similar room a little farther. Use the exact same strategy to gain access to a second treasure chest.

SHA WARVO SHRINE

You will find this shrine on a small plateau overlooking the road leading to the Flight Range.

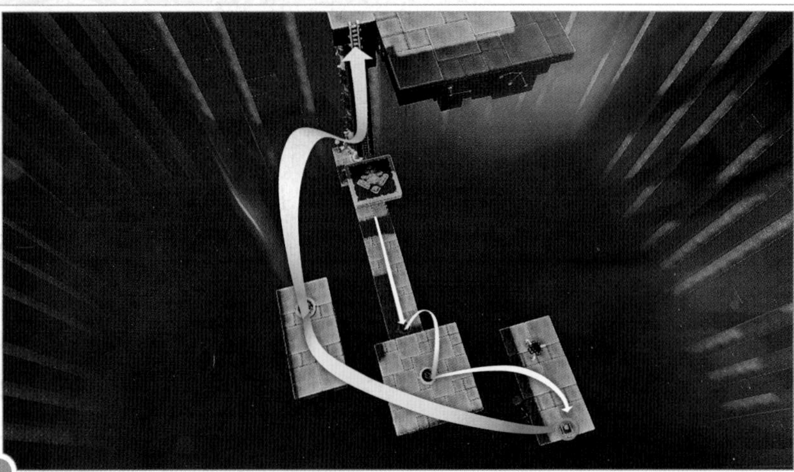

Draw your paraglider on the first two updrafts. Head left at the top of the second one: eliminate the Guardian Scout on the platform (with arrows or a slash attack), then retrieve the contents of the treasure chest. The third updraft on the opposite platform will take you to a moving platform, from which you can leap to a long ladder.

At the top of the ladder, take the updraft and glide to the far side of the nearby pillar, where you will find a small alcove. A final updraft is hidden inside, leading you to the very top of the shrine: from here, you can glide to a second chest on a distant platform, and to the altar.

VOO LOTA SHRINE

SHRINE QUEST: RECITAL AT WARBLER'S NEST

This shrine appears to the west of Rito Village once you complete a shrine quest, which is only possible after you have cleared the Divine Beast Vah Medoh dungeon (see page 80).

1

After clearing the Divine Beast Vah Medoh dungeon, speak to Amali, next to Rito Village's shrine. She will ask you to find Kheel, who is waiting for her sisters at Warbler's Nest, to the west of Rito Village. Once you have completed this first assignment, Kheel will ask you to bring her four sisters back to her: Cree is at the general store; Kotts is at the pond close to the village entrance; Notts is on the cliff directly above the armor shop. After speaking to all three, cook salmon meunière by combining hearty salmon, Tabantha wheat, and goat butter. Give this to Genli, who is waiting by the village cooking pot.

2

Once all sisters are together, take the Korok Leaf they give you, listen to their song, and step on the glowing structure in the center of the nearby sculptures. Your goal is to send a gust of wind at each sculpture in the correct order. Using the number of spikes at the top of each sculpture as a reference, the order is: IIII, IIIII, III, I, and II. This will cause the Voo Lota Shrine to appear nearby.

3

Once inside the shrine, climb up the long ladder to reach the main room and glide along the path shown on the above picture to reach the first treasure chest. The fans will give you enough momentum to travel long distances. The only difficulty resides in your ability to avoid the spike traps by putting away the paraglider just in time to fall on the landings without getting hurt.

4

Use the same procedure to reach the second treasure chest at the opposite end of the room, and then the altar in the center, which you can access with the small key found in the first chest.

KAH OKEO SHRINE

This shrine is located in the southwest corner of the Tabantha region, to the west of the Rayne Highlands.

1 To access this shrine, you must first remove the large rock slab that blocks the way. You could try to cast Stasis on it and build up energy to move it aside, but there is an easier way: drop an octo balloon on it: this will lift the rock slab, enabling you to glide to the entrance. You can obtain octo balloons by defeating Octoroks, which are relatively common in Hyrule.

2 Collect the Korok Leaf from the treasure chest and climb up the ramp. Standing in front of the gate, unleash a gust of wind on the nearby windmill, then rush through the gate before it closes again. Head to the next room (leaving the explosive barrel alone), where you will encounter three Guardian Scouts. Eliminate them before proceeding.

3 Return to the upper floor and swing the Korok Leaf at the windmill: a small platform carried by balloons will appear. Step on it and use the Korok Leaf to steer it. Stop in the corner behind you to retrieve a treasure chest, then head to the ledge on the opposite side of the room. Jump down and follow the linear path until you encounter a Guardian Scout. Throw a bomb at it to eliminate it while destroying the rock block simultaneously.

4

When you reach the very large room, step on the pedestal and activate the windmill with your Korok Leaf to be launched high in the air. Glide to the treasure chest on the left, then to the upper ladder. Detonate a bomb on the destructible rock to reveal an updraft that will take you to the top of the pillar.

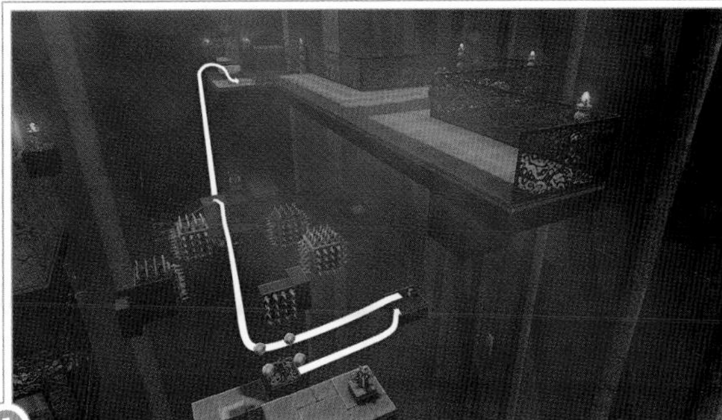

5

Once activated with the Korok Leaf, the windmill at the top will cause a new platform carried by balloons to appear. Make your way to the nearby chest, then carefully navigate between the spikes to reach the other side of the room. You will need to make regular course adjustments with the leaf to avoid these hazards. Activate the next windmill with the Korok Leaf to be propelled high in the air once again: glide to the floor level in front of you.

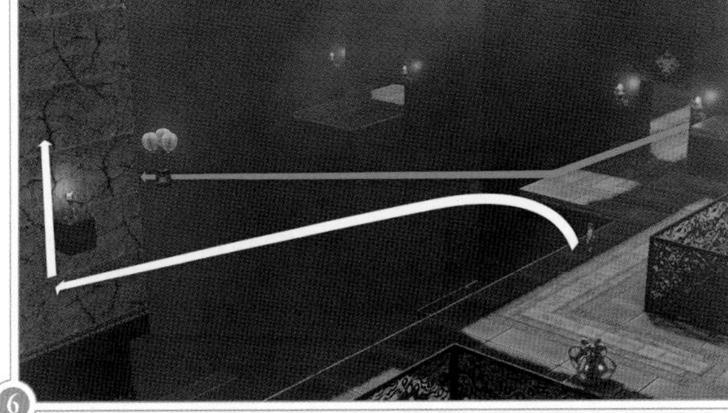

6

Your goal here is to blow up the large pillar of destructible rocks. The easiest way to do this is with a single bomb arrow. If you don't have any, you must trigger the windmill in the small room and push the floating barrel that this generates toward the blocks. Note that the barrel is slow to start but gathers momentum, so focus on its direction rather than its speed. Once it's close to the destructible blocks, hit it with a fire arrow (or let it detonate by itself if it's heading for a torch). The explosion will reveal a new updraft. Use this to reach the top of the shrine, where a chest with a small key awaits.

7

Glide to the ledge that connects the two rooms, as shown above. Make sure you open the final treasure chest as you go down the shaft leading to the locked door. Unlock it with the small key and interact with the altar to clear this shrine.

TENA KO'SAH SHRINE

This shrine can be found south of Tabantha Tower, at the east end of the Ancient Columns area.

1

This shrine pits you against a Guardian Scout IV. You can find detailed analysis and combat strategy for this creature on page 312.

HEBRA TOWER SHRINES

HIA MIU SHRINE

THE POSITIONS OF THE SHRINES COVERED HERE ARE SHOWN ON PAGES 188-189.

This shrine is located in the far northwest corner of the map, at the base of the Icefall Foothills.

1

This shrine pits you against a Guardian Scout IV. You can find detailed analysis and combat strategy for this creature on page 312. You have no obstacle to hide behind when your opponent performs its spinning attack, but you can raise blocks of metal with Magnesis to achieve the same result.

QAZA TOKKI SHRINE

SHRINE QUEST: TRIAL ON THE CLIFF

This shrine is found at the heart of the North Lomei Labyrinth, to the northeast of Tabantha Snowfield.

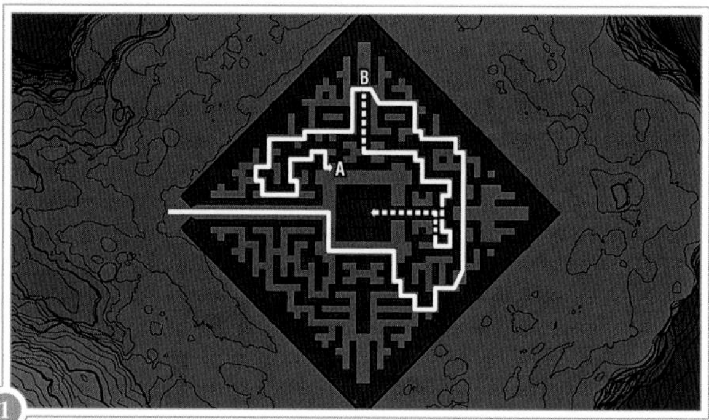

1

If you wish to go through the maze at ground level, follow the path until you reach position A and destroy the glowing eyeball to remove the malice goo. Backtrack to position B and enter the tunnel passage, which will now lead you to a ladder, and eventually to the center of the labyrinth.

2

Alternatively, you can take a shortcut by climbing to the top of the labyrinth's walls and dropping in the small section that looks like a "∏", just east of the maze's center. You can use the above picture as a reference.

3

Climb to the top of the low wall, as shown here, to find a set of stairs. A linear corridor will then take you to the center of the maze, where the Qaza Tokki Shrine awaits. Once inside, open the chest and head to the altar.

MOZO SHENNO SHRINE

SHRINE QUEST: THE BIRD IN THE MOUNTAIN

This shrine lies inside a small cave hidden at the top of Biron Snowshelf, right under the eastern edge of the plateau. Molli, a young Rito found close to Harth during the day at Rito Village, puts you on the right track if you speak to her.

1 This shrine pits you against a Guardian Scout IV. You can find detailed analysis and combat strategy for this creature on page 312. Note that you can raise blocks of metal with Magnesis and hide behind them when your opponent performs its spinning attack.

SHADA NAW SHRINE

This shrine is located a few steps north of Selmie's Spot.

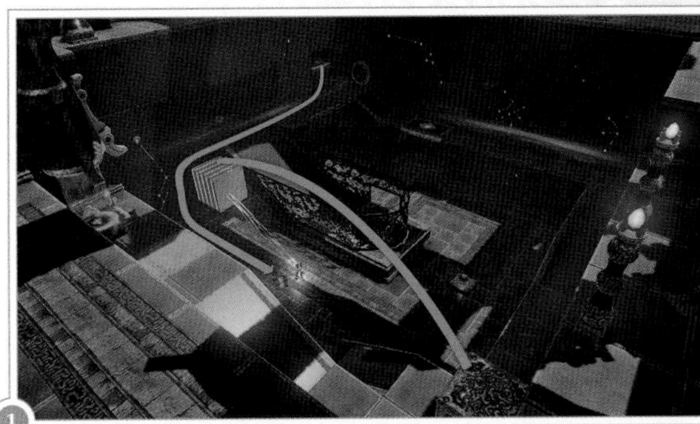

1 To get this shrine's only treasure chest out of the way, grab it with Magnesis and pull it back to you. While you're at it, pull out the block hidden in the wall right by the enclosure with the concave slot, and drop the metal cube on top of it, as illustrated above.

2 To reach the altar on the upper platform, you must stand on the two floor tiles with glowing squares on them, right in front of your starting position, when the orb reaches the concave slot. One solution is to drop the orb in front of the fan at the bottom of the nearby slope. The fans will push the orb all the way to the concave slot… assuming you time the maneuver so that the orb passes on the moving platform when it bridges the two ledges. This is eminently achievable, but there is another, potentially much easier, option.

3 The alternative option consists of manually walking with the orb inside the enclosure with the concave slot. Drop the orb on the flat surface, cast Stasis on it, then hit it three or four times with a swift weapon (a one-handed sword or a spear) so that the orb rolls up the slope once the Stasis effect ends. It will then roll back down, and ultimately enter the slot, but this should give you ample time to stand on the tiles with the glowing squares. Once at the top of the structure, you will only be a few steps away from the altar.

SHA GEHMA SHRINE

This shrine lies to the far north of Tabantha Snowfield.

1 Your priority is to retrieve the small key from the treasure chest with a metal cube on top of it. Grab the cube with Magnesis from the intermediate landing and lift it high in the air. Drop the cube on one of the moving platforms as it passes beneath, then freeze the cube with Stasis. You can now glide down to the chest and open it before the effect ends. The small key it contains opens the nearby door leading to the altar.

2 Before you examine the altar, make sure you open the second treasure chest on a pillar by gliding to it from above.

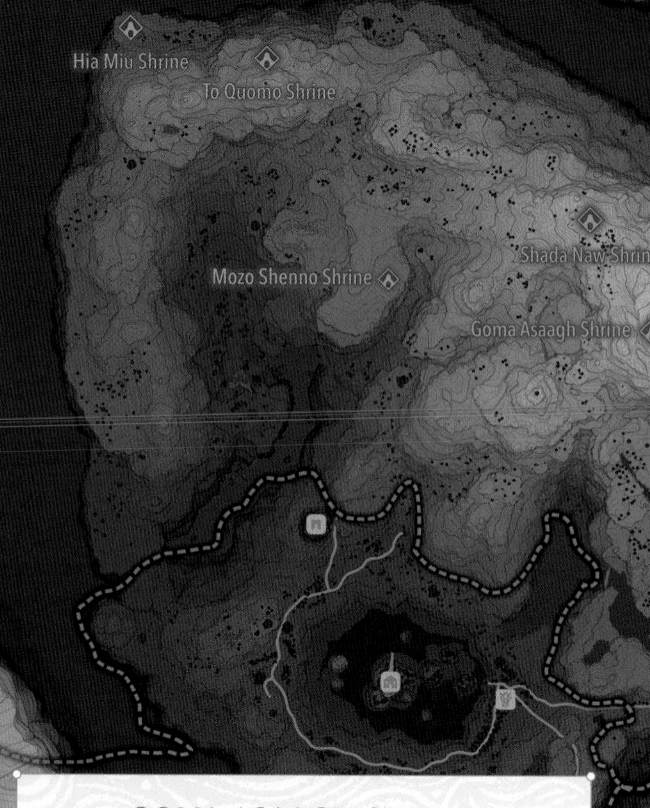

GOMA ASAAGH SHRINE

This shrine is hidden in a small cave at the foot of Hebra Peak, behind large blocks of ice.

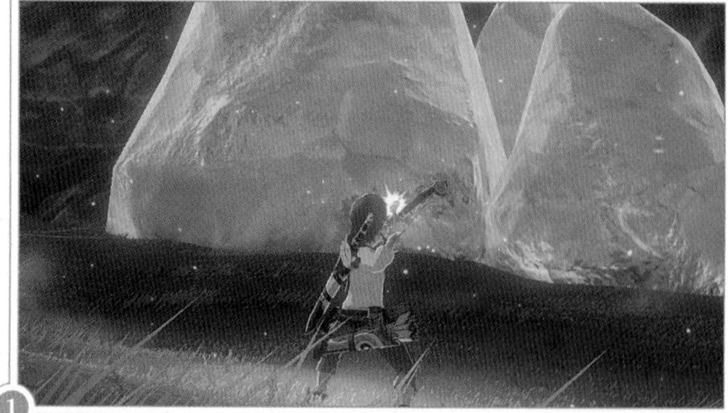

1 To access this shrine, you must first melt the ice blocks outside the entrance. You can achieve this with a few fire arrows. Alternatively, you can set up a campfire right next to the ice by dropping a bundle of wood and lighting it with a flint, red Chuchu jelly, or a fire-infused weapon. The process takes much longer with the latter option, though, whereas fire arrows work instantly. Inside the shrine you will face a Guardian Scout IV. You can find detailed analysis and combat strategy for this creature on page 312. Note that you can summon blocks of ice with Cryonis and hide behind them when your opponent performs its spinning attack.

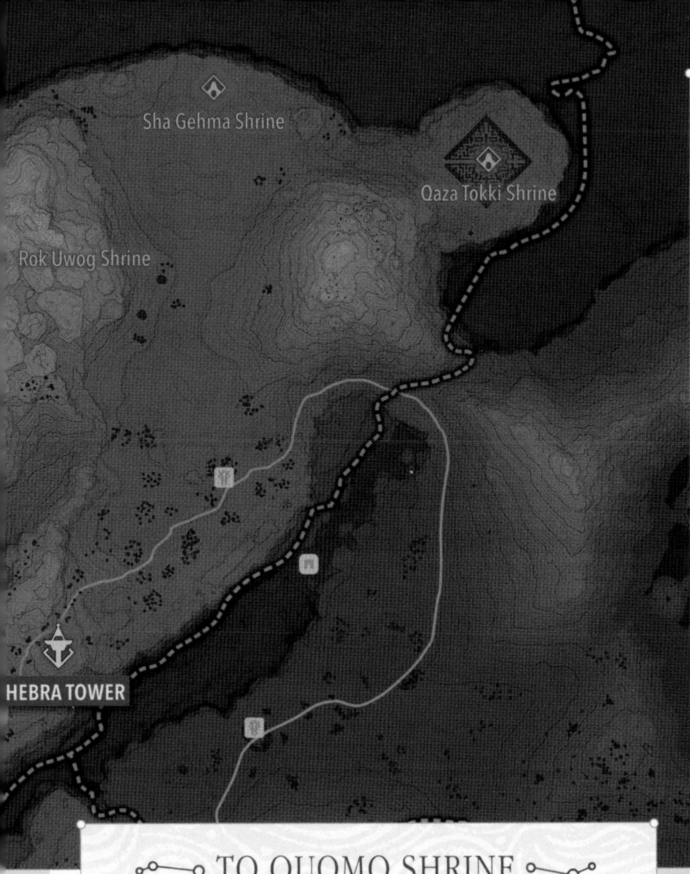

TO QUOMO SHRINE

This shrine is found inside a cave at the heart of Hebra North Summit.

1 To access this shrine you must first remove the door that is preventing you from entering. The door is easy to find: look for a small blue pond on your map, to the east of Hebra North Summit, and the door is a few steps to the west of it. The trick here is to summon two blocks of ice with Cryonis to "fill" the pond: this will ensure that a snowball rolling from the top of the hill will keep going until it smashes through the door rather than falling into the pond. Now climb to the top of the hill and pick up a snowball. Drop it on the ground and it will roll all the way down and across the pond and right through the door, thanks to your makeshift ice-block bridge. You can then head through the cave entrance, where the shrine awaits. Once inside the shrine, head to the altar, collecting the contents of the treasure chest on the way.

ROK UWOG SHRINE

This shrine can be found north of Hebra Tower, at the north end of Pikida Stonegrove.

1 From your initial position, you can grab the treasure chest in the wall in front of you with Magnesis, and reveal a hole in the wall to your left either by burning the ivy or by detonating a bomb. Head through the hole when you're ready.

2 Defeat the Guardian Scout, then blow up the wooden crate with a bomb. You can now climb up the ramp and eliminate a second Guardian Scout on the other side.

3 When you reach the floor switch behind a fence, you must destroy the barrels on top of the switch. You can do so either with a spear-type weapon, or a fire arrow. This will open the nearby door, enabling you to retrieve the small key from the chest. Climb the ladder to return to the entrance. You can now unlock the door with the small key to reach the altar.

MAKA RAH SHRINE

THE POSITIONS OF THE SHRINES COVERED HERE ARE SHOWN ON PAGES 192-193.

This shrine is hidden inside a cave, about halfway along the western side of Lake Kilsie, to the northwest of Rito Village.

1 It is possible to get a glimpse of the shrine from the lake's docks through a small crack in the cliff (as shown on the picture to the left), but the only way in is via an opening in the same cliff, a little further along to the northeast. Head inside this opening and follow the cave all the way to the end to reach the shrine.

2 Inside the shrine, head to the barred door and light up the torch to your left to open it. The rotating platform beyond is not as difficult to navigate as you might initially fear. Wait until a clear path between the spikes appears then make your way to the other side. Step on the floor switch to reveal the next room.

3 You must eliminate four Guardian Scouts in the next room. A single shock arrow aimed in the middle of them can take them out all at once, especially if you wield a bow that fires multiple arrows simultaneously. Once they're all down, create blocks of ice with Cryonis to reach the treasure chest and the floor switch on the ledges.

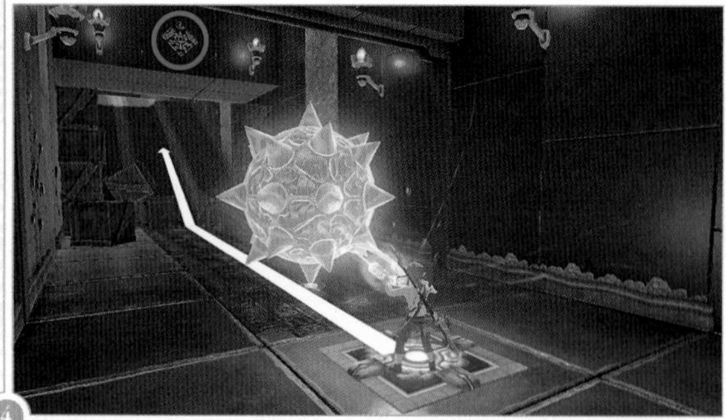

4 When you step on the next floor switch, a giant spiked boulder will start rolling in your direction. As soon as it smashes through the wooden crates, grab it with Magnesis. You can also sprint back to the previous room and hide around a corner if you prefer. Once you're ready, run up the ramp and turn around: you can blow up some destructible rocks with a bomb to reveal a treasure chest. Grab it with Magnesis and take it back to your position to open it.

5 Step on the final switch at the bottom of the slope. Be ready to stop an incoming spiked boulder with Magnesis, then leave it on the side, anywhere on the platform. Grab the treasure chest in the alcove with Magnesis before heading up the ramp to the altar.

RIN OYAA SHRINE

This shrine lies to the northeast of the Hebra Tower, a few steps away from the Snowfield Stable.

1 Grab one of the metal cubes with Magnesis and drop it in the middle of the alcove to your right (from your starting position). This will act as a stepping stone, enabling you to reach the treasure chest in a minute.

2 You must now stand on the tiles with the glowing squares (close to where you just dropped a metal cube) as the orb reaches the concave slot. There are many ways to solve this puzzle. You could, for example, use Stasis on the orb to freeze it while it is exposed to the penultimate fan, sprinting to the tiles before the effect ends. The easiest solution, though, is shown above: first drop the second metal cube in the middle of the flat platform just before the concave slot, then drop the orb just before the cube, walk to the tiles with the glowing squares, and from here lift the metal cube with Magnesis. The wind from the fan will push the orb into the slot, while you are already in position on the tiles.

3 From your elevated position, you can now hop to the treasure chest, and then to the altar.

LANNO KOOH SHRINE

This shrine is hidden in a cave directly west of Hebra Tower, just north of the eastern tip of Hebra Plunge.

1 The shrine is surrounded by ice-cold water. No matter how well protected you are, you will take damage from prolonged exposure. The easiest way to reach it is to enter the cave via the east side and make a dash for it. Heal as required and run as fast as you can to avoid taking too much damage. Alternatively, you could cut a tree upstream, push the trunk in the river, and stand on it, but this is hard to engineer, and will not necessarily protect you from the freezing cold water. Once inside the shrine, head to the altar, collecting the contents of the treasure chest on the way.

DUNBA TAAG SHRINE

This shrine is located to the southwest of the Hebra Tower, at the bottom of Tanagar Canyon, in the canyon's bend directly south of Tama Pond.

1

In the first room, cast Stasis on the cogwheel so that the platform fixed to it remains perfectly horizontal. This will ensure that the boulder rolling down from the ramp will hit the pressure switch on the left – thus opening the door. If the switch is only partly pressed into its slot, repeat until it is fully activated.

2

In the second room, take a left as you enter and move close to the abyss by the closed gate. From here, you can throw a few bombs toward the rock cubes to make them fall and reveal a pressure switch behind them. Next, pick up one of the nearby barrels and drop it on the floor by the abyss, facing the stack of rock cubes. Your goal is to cast Stasis on the barrel, then hit it multiple times (preferably with a two-handed weapon) so that it packs enough energy to press the switch into the wall and raise the nearby gate (giving you access to the treasure chest). Try to align Link exactly in the axis of the switch: you can use the vector arrow that appears during Stasis to identify the trajectory that the barrel will take, and adjust your position accordingly if required.

3

Staying on the same side of the large room, head to the next section beyond the fence and drop into the pit. Push the boulder to the bottom of the slope, then drop two bombs at its base (one of each type). Now cast Stasis on the boulder and detonate the two bombs to propel the boulder on the floor switch beyond. This will open the nearby gate, behind which a chest awaits.

4

Finally, go to the far end of the large room and repeat the trick with the barrels. Drop one close to the platform's edge, cast Stasis on it, then hit it repeatedly to build up momentum. The barrel needs to be projected at maximum speed against the large rock slab to make it fall: keep hitting the barrel until the vector arrow turns red. Two-handed weapons (particularly a sledgehammer) can really make a difference here. Once you succeed, the door leading to the altar will open.

GEE HA'RAH SHRINE

This shrine is hidden northwest of Hebra Tower, just south of Kopeeki Drifts.

1 To access this shrine you must first hit the gate leading to it with a large snowball. To achieve this, head to the top of the slope that overlooks the shrine, at the foot of Kopeeki Drifts' southernmost cliff. Pick up a snowball and roll it down the second "track" from the left. (If you want to take a shortcut, you can actually pick up a snowball at the bottom of the slope, by the gate, and drop it directly at the top of the final segment of the track.)

2 In the shrine's first room, sever the rope holding the large boulder with an arrow: the boulder will drop on the pressure switch below, opening the door in the process.

3 Take a left after the door. When you reach a boulder tied to two ropes, cut the left-hand one: this way, the boulder will press the switch. This opens the nearby door, behind which a treasure chest awaits. Once you have secured its contents, retrace your steps and go straight, leaving the shrine's entrance room on your right.

4 In the final room, cast Stasis on the boulder, then quickly cut both ropes while it is frozen in time. It will fall on the switch once the effect ends, giving you access to the altar.

WOODLAND TOWER SHRINES

MIRRO SHAZ SHRINE

THE POSITIONS OF THE SHRINES COVERED HERE ARE SHOWN ON PAGE 197.

This shrine lies in the open, a short distance northeast of the Woodland Stable.

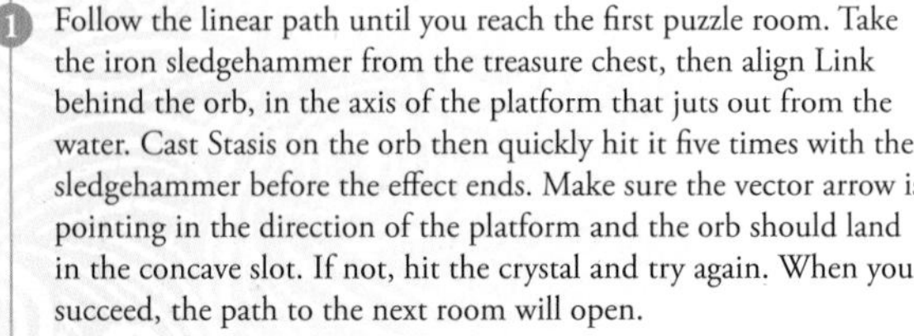

1 Follow the linear path until you reach the first puzzle room. Take the iron sledgehammer from the treasure chest, then align Link behind the orb, in the axis of the platform that juts out from the water. Cast Stasis on the orb then quickly hit it five times with the sledgehammer before the effect ends. Make sure the vector arrow is pointing in the direction of the platform and the orb should land in the concave slot. If not, hit the crystal and try again. When you succeed, the path to the next room will open.

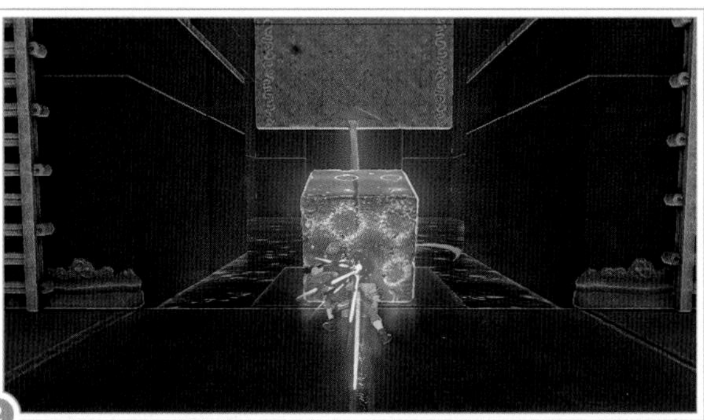

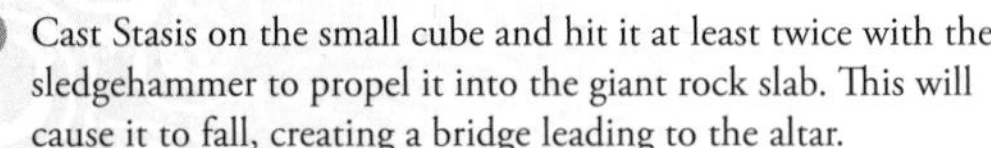

2 Cast Stasis on the small cube and hit it at least twice with the sledgehammer to propel it into the giant rock slab. This will cause it to fall, creating a bridge leading to the altar.

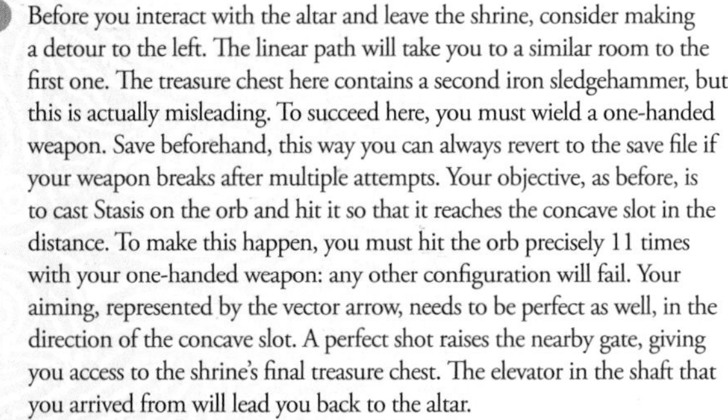

3 Before you interact with the altar and leave the shrine, consider making a detour to the left. The linear path will take you to a similar room to the first one. The treasure chest here contains a second iron sledgehammer, but this is actually misleading. To succeed here, you must wield a one-handed weapon. Save beforehand, this way you can always revert to the save file if your weapon breaks after multiple attempts. Your objective, as before, is to cast Stasis on the orb and hit it so that it reaches the concave slot in the distance. To make this happen, you must hit the orb precisely 11 times with your one-handed weapon: any other configuration will fail. Your aiming, represented by the vector arrow, needs to be perfect as well, in the direction of the concave slot. A perfect shot raises the nearby gate, giving you access to the shrine's final treasure chest. The elevator in the shaft that you arrived from will lead you back to the altar.

MONYA TOMA SHRINE

You will find this shrine northeast of Ridgeland Tower, close to the summit of Salari Hill.

1 Run past the first corner to your left and destroy the wooden crates above with bomb explosions. From here, hit the crystal on the nearby platform with an arrow to make that platform rotate, then repeat.

KETOH WAWAI SHRINE

SHRINE QUEST: SHROUDED SHRINE

This shrine is concealed at the heart of the Thyphlo Ruins, to the north of the Great Hyrule Forest. It is revealed by completing a shrine quest.

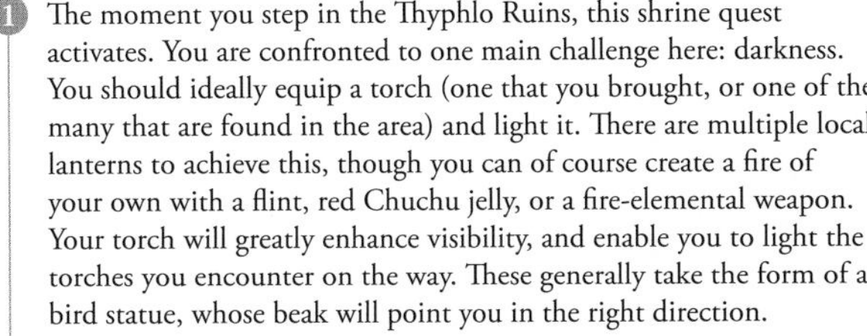

1 The moment you step in the Thyphlo Ruins, this shrine quest activates. You are confronted to one main challenge here: darkness. You should ideally equip a torch (one that you brought, or one of the many that are found in the area) and light it. There are multiple local lanterns to achieve this, though you can of course create a fire of your own with a flint, red Chuchu jelly, or a fire-elemental weapon. Your torch will greatly enhance visibility, and enable you to light the torches you encounter on the way. These generally take the form of a bird statue, whose beak will point you in the right direction.

2 If you have completed the Divine Beast Vah Rudania dungeon (see page 92), you can make navigation easier even without a torch by holding the block button (as long as you have at least one charge of Daruk's Protection available). The aura provided by this power lights up your surroundings a little. Other makeshift methods to get a sense of what surrounds you include aiming with a fire arrow, bomb explosions, as well as Urbosa's Fury, the power you obtain at the end of the Divine Beast Vah Naboris dungeon (see page 68). Keep in mind that cutting shrubs or small trees will often reward you with a tree branch, which can temporarily replace a torch.

3 When you reach the pedestal, you are only a few steps away from the forest's only real danger: a Hinox. You can find detailed coverage of this creature in our Bestiary (see page 316), though fighting in the dark makes this a somewhat different experience. Start by lighting as many torches as you can in the area to improve your chances. You should also note that the Hinox's eye is visible when it's open: this is your cue to hitting it with an arrow, then rushing to its position and unleashing a powerful combo. Repeat this until the creature falls. Pick up the orb that it releases and drop it into the pedestal to reveal the Ketoh Wawai Shrine. Once inside, open the treasure chest then head to the altar.

1

2

3

2

Now make your way to the launcher close to the shrine's entrance: it will propel you to a second launcher, which will then in turn propel you to the treasure chest at the top of the platform you rotated twice. Open the chest, then hit the crystal a third time (with a bomb, for example).

3

Finally, return to the entrance, pick up the orb and drop it on the first launcher. It should be propelled from one launcher to the next, all the way to the concave slot. This will lift the gate, giving you access to the altar.

RONA KACHTA SHRINE

This shrine is hidden at the northeast end of the Tanagar Canyon, inside the Forgotten Temple.

1 The real difficulty here is to reach the shrine. You will find it at the far end of the Forgotten Temple, and it is guarded by numerous Decayed Guardians. Unless you're willing to destroy them all by deflecting their laser beam back at them, the easiest solution is to speed through the entire location, using the updrafts to remain airborne most of the time. If you stay at maximum velocity all along, all enemy shots should miss. If required, adjust your trajectory slightly to be perpendicular to a beam when a laser comes from behind.

2 Once inside the shrine, head to the altar, collecting the contents of the treasure chest on the way.

DAAG CHOKAH SHRINE

SHRINE QUEST: THE LOST PILGRIMAGE

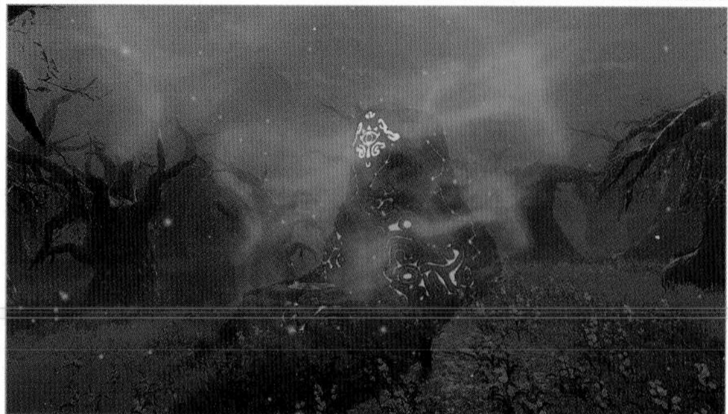

This shrine is hidden in the northwest corner of the Great Hyrule Forest.

1 Speak to Chio in the Korok Forest to begin the Korok trials. Now speak to Tasho at the northwest exit of the Korok Forest to initiate this quest. Your objective is to tail a small Korok called Oaki. Crouch-walk (◉) during the entire sequence: not only does this correspond to Oaki's walking pace, but it also makes you silent. Note that a stealth bonus from armor or an elixir will also help. Remain at a reasonable distance to avoid being seen, particularly after you pass a beehive on your right: Oaki will turn around shortly afterwards. Keep Oaki's figure and ears in sight, making slight camera adjustments if required to keep track of him. If you struggle, consider activating Magnesis mode: you will lose the ability to crouch-walk, so take it very slow, but the magenta "filter" should help you discern Oaki's figure more easily.

2 When Oaki walks through an uprooted, hollow tree trunk, follow him from a distance but wait at the end of the trunk, keeping Oaki in sight by rotating the camera sideways: he will soon backtrack a few yards and would spot you if you were in plain sight. A little later, he will call for help as a wolf passes by: do not move, this is a false alarm. Remain at a safe distance until he reaches the shrine and starts celebrating – at which point you can interact with the shrine's terminal. Once inside the Daag Chokah Shrine, open the treasure chest then head to the altar.

KUHN SIDAJJ SHRINE

SHRINE QUEST: TRIAL OF SECOND SIGHT

This shrine is concealed in the Great Hyrule Forest, on the shore of Lake Salia.

1 After initiating the Korok Trials by speaking to Chio in the Korok Forest, go through the southwestern exit of the Korok Forest. Speak to Zooki, who stands on a rock, approximately at mid-distance between the Korok Forest and Lake Salia.

2 You must now find your way in the fog, which might seem impossible until you realize that you can use Magnesis as a visual guide. Activate this rune with L, then walk toward the trees that have an iron boulder inside their "mouths." If you cannot spot the next one in line, walk around a little, rotating the camera: you will soon identify the characteristic magenta hue of a metal object.

3 When you reach a clearing with a rusty shield at its center, grab the shield with Magnesis and place it inside the mouth of the tree at the base of which lies a stone tablet. This will trigger the appearance of a treasure chest in the mouth of a nearby tree.

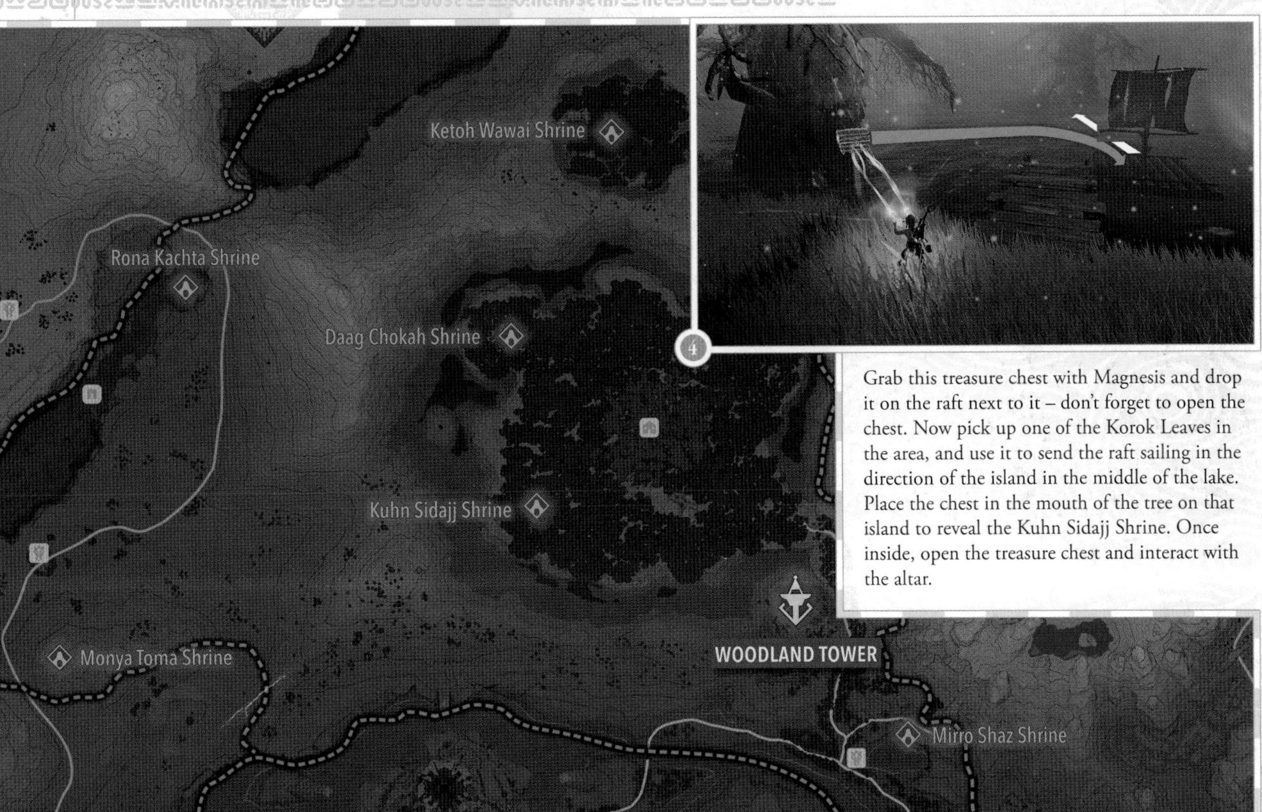

4 Grab this treasure chest with Magnesis and drop it on the raft next to it – don't forget to open the chest. Now pick up one of the Korok Leaves in the area, and use it to send the raft sailing in the direction of the island in the middle of the lake. Place the chest in the mouth of the tree on that island to reveal the Kuhn Sidajj Shrine. Once inside, open the treasure chest and interact with the altar.

MAAG HALAN SHRINE

SHRINE QUEST: THE TEST OF WOOD

This shrine lies in the Mido Swamp, in the northeast section of the Great Hyrule Forest.

1

Speak to Chio in the Korok Forest to begin the Korok trials. Now speak to Damia at the eastern exit of the Korok Forest to initiate this quest. Your objective is to reach the shrine at the back of the area without breaking a single piece of the equipment given to you by Damia.

2

To spare your equipment, make sure you eliminate all the weaker enemies such as Keeses, Chuchus, and even Stalkoblins, with bombs. When you reach a large stack of wooden crates blocking the way, destroy them with a bomb too. Stay away from the bogs in the area: falling in them would take you back to the beginning of the trial.

3

When you reach a large bog with Octorocks, make sure you eliminate the Stalkoblin archers with arrows, as their ice arrows can be really annoying. Deal with the Octoroks next as they could make you fall in the bog.

4

Summon blocks of ice with Cryonis to cross the large bog. Be very careful how you position them and jump cautiously: a single misstep and you'll have to start over.

5

Turn right after crossing the large bog and you will find a second one. Eliminate the archer that shoots fire arrows as a matter of priority. Note that you can actually use any updraft generated by fire (from arrows or Fire Chuchus) to cross the bog quickly if you wish. Otherwise, blocks of ice created by Cryonis and careful jumps are your best bet. The quest will be completed when you reach the Maag Halan Shrine. Once inside, open the treasure chest and interact with the altar.

KEO RUUG SHRINE

This shrine is found at the heart of Korok Forest.

1 In this puzzle, you must drop an orb in each "lane" of concave slots, each lane being associated with a specific constellation. Blue torches on both sides of the room enable you to number each slot in each lane: I, II, III, IIII, IIIII. Your goal is to associate a number to each lane with an orb using the information provided on the far wall of the shrine.

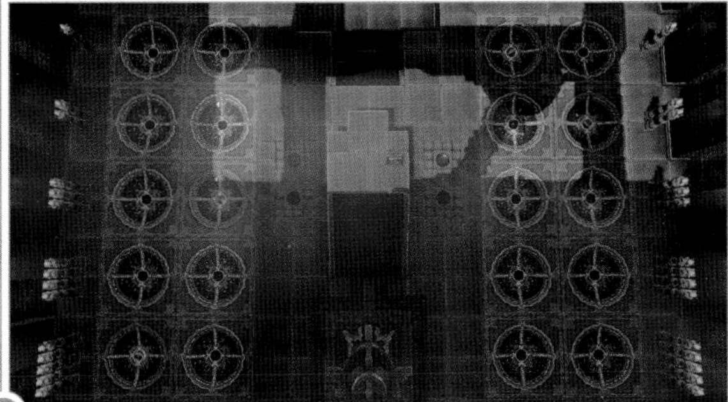

2 The solution to the puzzle is to count the amount of constellations that correspond to the one associated with each lane. The first lane, to your left as you begin, is a small constellation of three stars. There are five such constellations on the wall, so you must drop an orb in slot number five (IIIII) for that lane. Repeat this for all lanes to open the gate. If you would like to have the solution clearly spelled out for you, here it is: left lane = 5; center-left lane = 3; center-right lane = 1; right lane = 2.

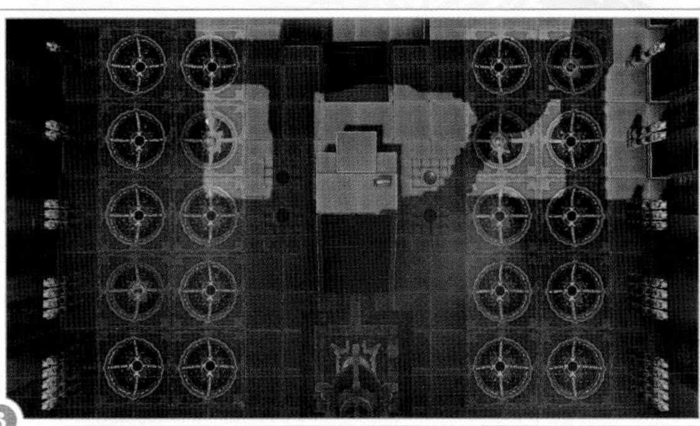

3 Before you interact with the altar in the second part of the shrine, turn around and you will find a second set of constellations. This constitutes a new, similar puzzle, which you can solve using the same method. Return to the orbs, and align them accordingly. The solution here is: left lane = 4; center-left lane = 2; center-right lane = 2; right lane = 1. This will give you access to a treasure chest just beneath the second wall of constellations.

Eldin Tower Shrines

Tah Muhl Shrine

SHRINE QUEST: A LANDSCAPE OF A STABLE

This shrine lies to the southwest of the Foothill Stable, directly to the south of Death Mountain.

1

You will receive this shrine quest by speaking to Mayro at the Foothill Stable. This challenges you to find a shrine based on what you see on a painting adorning the stable's wall. Head to the shrine's location, at the end of a small canyon to the southwest, as shown on the picture to the left.

2

Once inside the Tah Muhl Shrine, clear the ivy on the first room's wall to reveal an opening leading to the second room. You can use fire arrows to achieve this, standard arrows set ablaze with torches, or, even better, remote bombs to save your precious resources.

3

In the second room, start by burning the ivy to your left as you enter. The fire will spread all the way to the treasure chest on the wooden ledge beyond the fence: grab the small key that it yields with Magnesis, and make it fly above the fence, all the way back to Link. You can use this to open the locked door, behind which lies a second treasure chest.

4

You can now destroy all the wooden crates and ivy in the rest of the room using bombs. This will reveal a third treasure chest in the corner close to the fence, and a fourth one in an alcove that was hidden by ivy. Once you're ready, head up the ramp to the altar.

QUA RAYM SHRINE

This shrine awaits to the east of Woodland Tower, in the middle of Goronbi Lake.

1

This shrine revolves heavily around balance scales. First, focus on the balance scale in front of you. Burn the wooden crate on the left-hand pan using a fire arrow, or a standard arrow set ablaze with one of the torches. This will cause the other pan to move down: retrieve the small key from the treasure chest, then head to the locked door and open it. You now have access to three metal cubes.

2

If you want to access the second treasure chest, turn your attention to the other balance scale (to the left of your starting position). Drop a metal cube on the left-hand pan to lower it. Position a second metal cube at the foot of the nearby stairs, and use it as a stepping stone to reach that same left-hand pan. From here, grab the metal cube next to you (the one on the left-hand pan), and transfer it to the right-hand pan. This will raise your pan, giving you access to the second chest.

3

Finally, return to the balance scale in the center of the room. Step on the right-hand pan (the one with the first chest where you obtained the small key). From this position, throw a bomb to the destructible rocks that block the path to the altar. If you struggle, a bomb arrow will make this much easier. Still in the same position on the right-hand pan, place one metal cube next to you (on the right-hand pan), and two metal cubes on the left-hand pan. This will raise your pan, but the metal cube close to you will protect you from the spikes above. From here, you can walk straight to the altar.

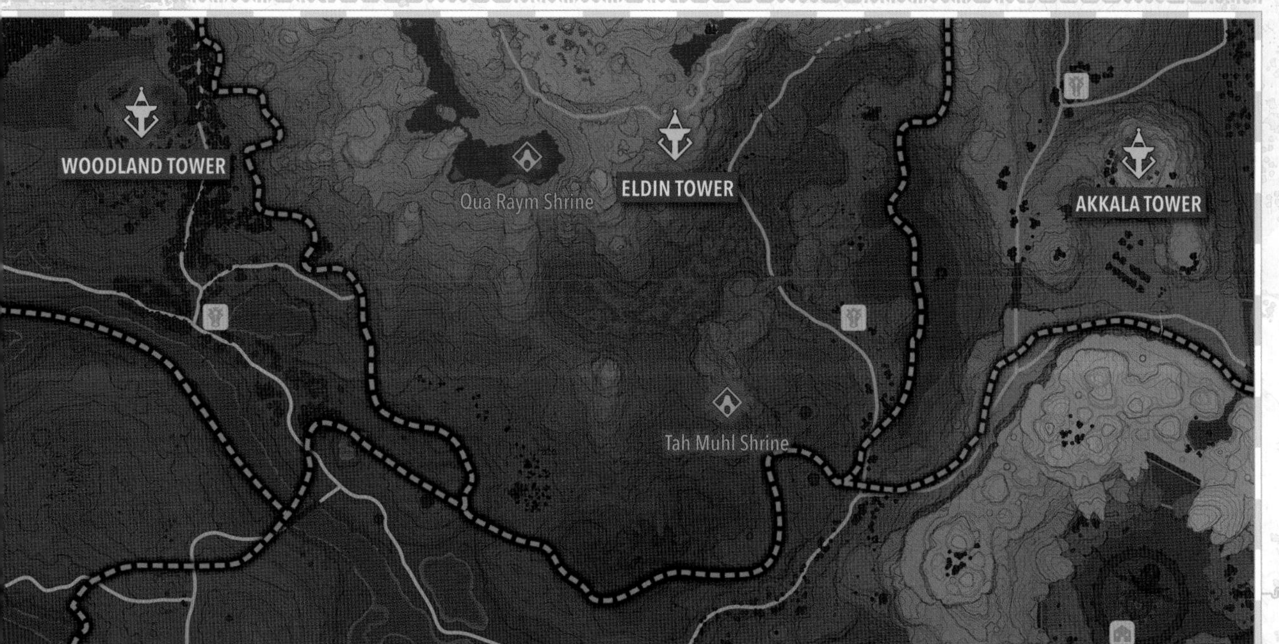

KAYRA MAH SHRINE

SHRINE QUEST: A BROTHER'S ROAST

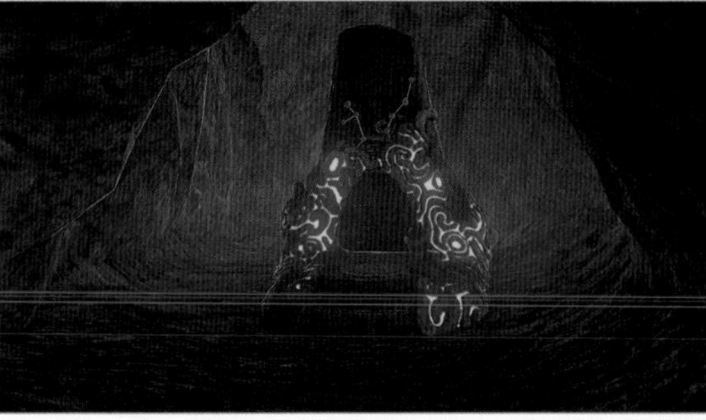

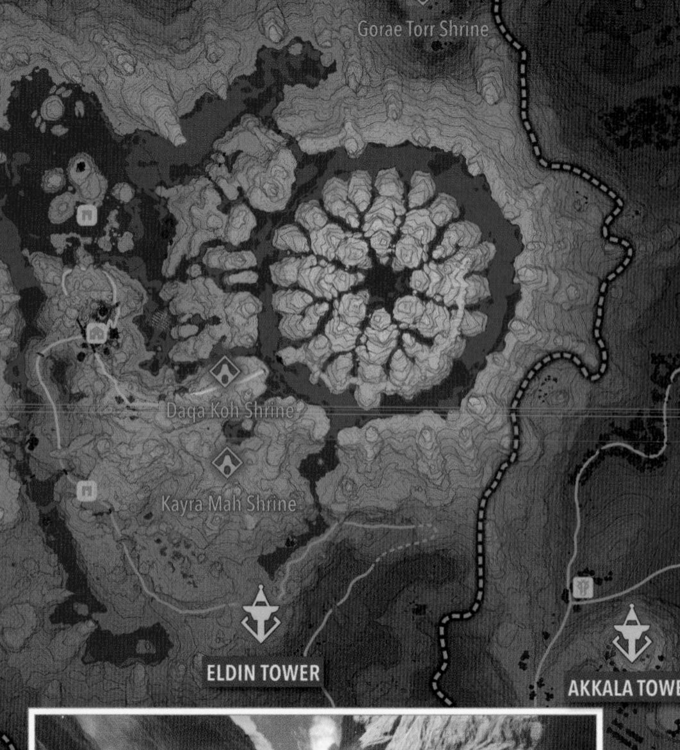

You will find this shrine to the southeast of the Goron Hot Springs, inside a cave known as Gorko Tunnel.

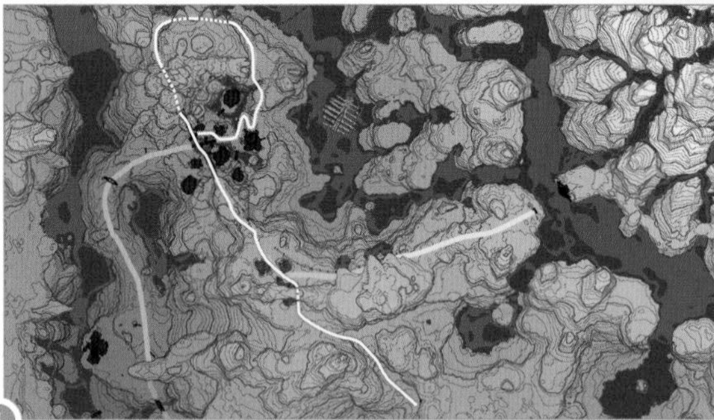

1

You first need to speak to Bladon in Goron City's northwest hut. Now head southeast, through the Goron Hot Springs, and follow the trail of torches to Gorko Tunnel, where you will receive this shrine quest. Your goal is to bring back a grilled rock roast from the bottom of Gortram Cliff, directly to your left as you exit the cave.

2

Once you have a grilled rock roast, you must carefully go back up the slope to Gorko Tunnel. The difficulty is that boulders unpredictably roll down the cliff, forcing you to zigzag and plan ahead. If you drop the item, it will usually slide all the way back down the slope, forcing you to start over. Once you have managed to take it to Gonguron, the Kayra Mah Shrine will be revealed.

3

Inside the shrine, you just need to go up the ramp. There are three lanes, separated by fences, and boulders are regularly released randomly on two of the lanes. These can cause a lot of damage, so you must either dodge them or stop them with Stasis or Magnesis. As a rule, one lane will remain hazard-free, so try to anticipate this and always be in the currently safe lane. You will notice that rupees are occasionally dropped among the boulders, and you can catch them by standing on their way. These streams of rupees are of little value at first, but the later ones, released near the top of the ramp, can be worth the trouble.

4

There are two treasure chests hidden in this shrine. The first one lies in a small alcove on your right-hand side as you run up the ramp. The second one rests on an elevated ledge on the left-hand side: you can easily glide to it from the top of the ramp. Once you have secured their contents, head to the altar.

GORAE TORR SHRINE

SHRINE QUEST: THE GUT CHECK CHALLENGE

This shrine is located to the north of Death Mountain, at the top of Gut Check Rock.

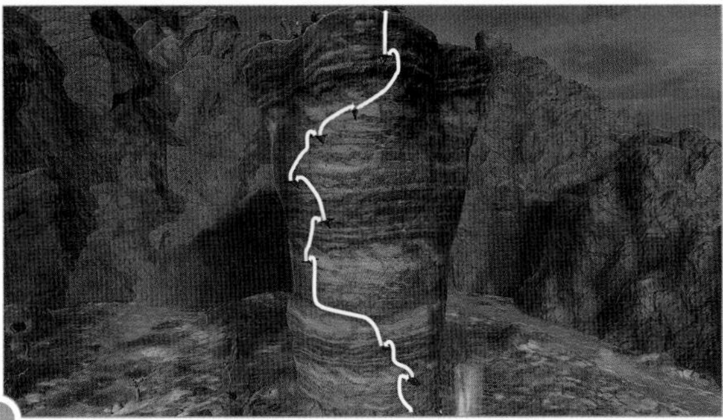

1

When you reach this shrine, you initially cannot enter it. You must first speak to Bayge and pass his Gut Check Challenge. This is a mini-game requiring you to climb to the top of the peak in limited time, while also collecting at least 100 rupees on your way. To make things easy, tackle this challenge with a very extended stamina wheel (which can be done by exchanging spirit orbs for stamina vessels when interacting with goddess statues). This will enable you to jump constantly between each protruding beam, making you much faster. In addition, equipping armor pieces with the climb speed bonus effect will greatly help as well. Generally speaking, pay little attention to green rupees unless they're directly in your way, and prioritize the ones with higher values instead. After you succeed, the Gorae Torr Shrine will be all yours. Once inside, head to the altar, making sure you open the treasure chest on the way.

DAQA KOH SHRINE

This shrine is located to the east of the Goron Hot Springs, just prior to reaching the Bridge of Eldin.

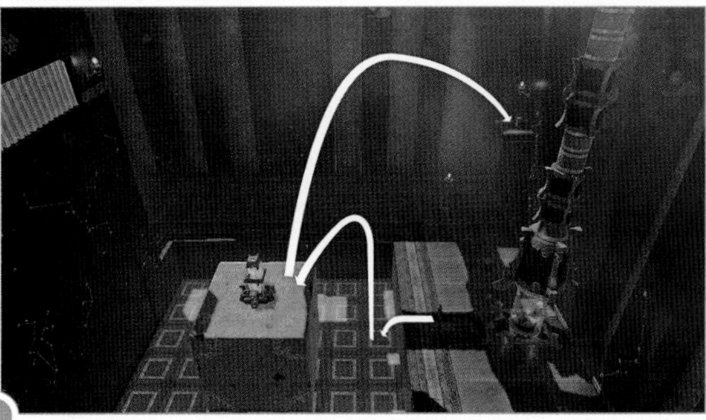

1

Drop into the central pit and wait until the platform's upward movement launches you in the air. Draw your paraglider when Link is at the top of his flight and you can easily land on the large rock cube in the center. Now turn around and look in the direction of your entrance point in the shrine: when both Link and the cube are propelled upward, you can glide to the treasure chest found on a small ledge to your left.

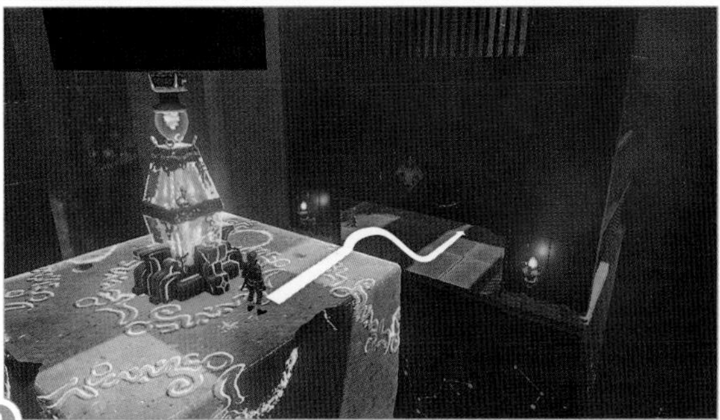

2

After you have opened the chest, head back to the top of the rock cube. When it is next launched in the air and reaches the apex of its course (the green crystal being in contact with the device on the ceiling), cast Stasis on the rock cube: this will keep the gate open for a few seconds, giving you plenty of time to glide to the exit without having to worry about the short timing window during which the gate is normally open.

Shora Hah Shrine

Shae Mo'sah Shrine

WOODLAND TOWER

ELDIN TOWER

AKKALA TOWER

Mo'a Keet Shrine

MO'A KEET SHRINE

This shrine overlooks the Foothill Stable, to the south of Death Moutain.

1 Cast Stasis on the boulder as it reaches the very bottom of its course. Run up the ramp while it is frozen in time.

2 Once on the intermediate landing, head to the right-hand ramp and grab the metal boulder with Magnesis as it rolls down toward you. Drop it on a flat surface close to you, then go up the ramp to open the treasure chest at the top.

3 You can now take control of the metal boulder again with Magnesis, and use it as a shield of sorts to force your way up the left-hand ramp. This will push the stone boulders that roll down the ramp all the way back up, enabling you to reach the altar at the top.

SHAE MO'SAH SHRINE

This shrine lies at the northern exit of Goron City, at the top of the hill leading to the Abandoned North Mine.

1

In the first room, use a bomb (or a fire arrow) to destroy the wooden ledge close to the door. Pick up the barrel that falls and drop it on the floor switch to open the door. You can find your first treasure chest a few steps to your left after the door. (Note that you can alternatively step on the floor switch and cast Stasis on it to keep the door temporarily open.)

2

In the next room, eliminate the three Guardian Scouts, then open the treasure chest close to the ramp. Once you're done, go up the ramp.

3

Before you head up the staircase, open the treasure chest on its opposite side, then step on the floor switch at the top of the stairs. This will reveal a hanging lantern, which you can swing with Magnesis to set the nearby leaves ablaze. Once the adjacent wooden ledge burns, the metal ball that was on it will fall and roll down until it's blocked by a closed gate. Go around the room until you find a second floor switch: when you step on it, the gate will open, and the metal ball will fall on the wheel below, causing the nearby door to open. Sprint through it before it closes to find a new treasure chest containing a small key, then walk up the nearby ramp and drop back down into the main room.

4

Open the locked door with your newly acquired small key. In the next room, either burn or destroy the wooden ledge, then drop the barrel that falls on the nearby floor switch. Alternatively, you could stand on that same switch and cast Stasis on it to keep the door open, giving you access to the altar.

SHORA HAH SHRINE

THE POSITION OF THE SHRINE COVERED HERE IS SHOWN ON PAGE 204.

This shrine lies in the northwest corner of Darunia Lake, to the north of Goron City.

1

To reach this shrine, you must use the mine cart on the edge of the lava lake, a short distance to the northeast of Goron City. Jump inside the cart and drop a round bomb in the receptacle at the back. When you detonate the bomb, the cart will be propelled along the rails. Repeat this whenever the cart comes to a near halt until you reach the shrine (but avoid causing too many explosions as this could send the cart in the lava).

2

Inside the shrine, raise the spiked metal block with Magnesis and walk underneath it. Once on the other side, take a left and align the two smaller metal blocks so that they form stepping stones leading to the treasure chest. Readjust them, this time to gain access to the nearby blue lantern. Pick up the torch (a critical item for this shrine) and set it ablaze with the blue flame.

3

Note that you cannot sprint while holding the blue flame: Link would put the torch away, thus extinguishing the flame. Jog back to the central lantern and light it with the blue flame. You must now light the lantern beyond the wall-mounted fountains to activate an elevator. This can be achieved easily by walking underneath the two fountains on your right: as long as you hold Ⓨ, Link will hold the torch in front of him in a low position, without any risk of extinguishing it.

4

Light an arrow with the blue flame and fire it in the direction of the lantern on the elevator. This will raise a platform close to the central lantern, giving you access to a floor switch.

5

Have Magnesis ready as you step on the floor switch: a spiked boulder will start rolling in your direction; grab it and drop it in the lava to clear the path. Head up the ramp and eliminate the Guardian Scouts on the next platform, where you will find two treasure chests. When you're ready, light your torch with the blue flame from the lantern on the elevator, then use it to set ablaze the lantern where you just fought the Guardian Scouts to raise the nearby gate.

6 In the next section, light the first lantern. You must now light the next two lanterns simultaneously, otherwise water fountains will instantly extinguish them. You can do so by lighting an arrow with the blue flame, and aligning a shot that goes through both lanterns simultaneously. Light your torch before you proceed to the next section.

7 Light the next lantern, then repeat the same maneuver as in the previous section: light an arrow with the blue flame and, when the two lanterns on the moving platforms are aligned at the middle point of their course, light them simultaneously with a single arrow. This will create an updraft that enables you to cross the gap. Make sure you stop on the second moving platform before you continue.

8 Use the lantern on the second moving platform to light the right-hand lantern on the next large platform with an arrow. Now glide to that platform and light the left-hand lantern with your torch.

9 Cast Stasis on the water fountain, then quickly switch to Magnesis and move the block with the lantern you just lit to the far side. The next updraft enables you to reach a treasure chest hidden behind a pillar on your right. The other chest, close to the lantern, can be grabbed with Magnesis.

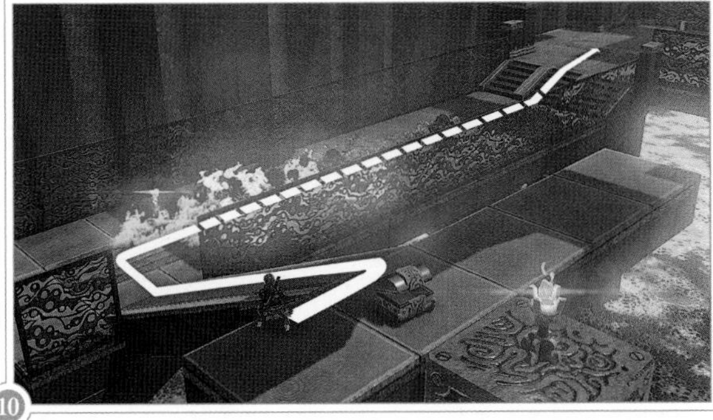

10 Light an arrow and fire it at the leaves on the next platform, down the ramp: this will cause the Guardian Scouts to burn to death without giving them a chance to fight back. Now light your torch and head to the final section with all the lanterns.

11 Light the lone lantern with your torch and open the nearby treasure chest. Finally, light your torch one last time and perform a circular charged attack while in the center of the circle formed by the lanterns. This will light them all simultaneously, opening the path to the altar. Note that it might take you a few attempts to light all of the lanterns at once: position Link centrally and make minor adjustments based on which lantern is not lit. Set your torch ablaze again via the nearby lantern whenever required and persevere. A few patient attempts is all it takes to succeed, there is no special trick that you can apply here.

SAH DAHAJ SHRINE

This shrine lies to the west of Akkala Tower, close to the northern tip of Cephla Lake.

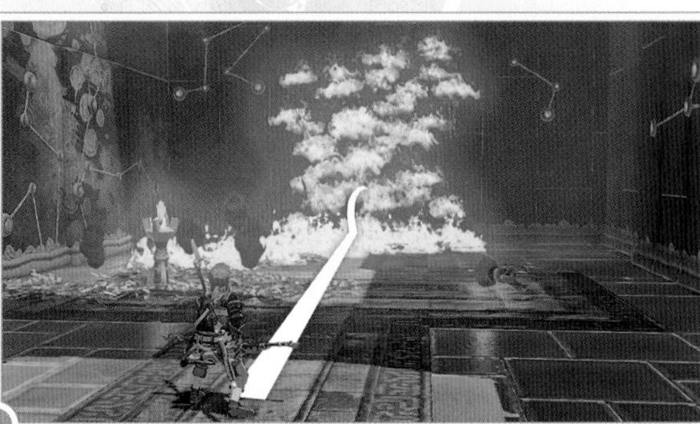

1. Remove the ivy with any form of fire or a bomb to reveal an opening in the wall in front of you. A Guardian Scout awaits beyond: eliminate it however you please – a guardian weapon can expedite the process.

2. Climb up the ladder and set the ivy on fire or get rid of it with a bomb.

3. In the next room, your primary goal is to destroy the two wooden crates in the fenced area, either with fire or bombs: once they disappear, the slab they held will fall on the floor switch, thus opening the locked door leading to the altar. You can also open the treasure chest on the wooden ledge after taking it down to your position with Magnesis.

Akkala Tower Shrines

DAH HESHO SHRINE

This shrine lies to the southeast of Akkala Tower, on the cliff overlooking Lake Akkala.

1 This shrine pits you against a Guardian Scout II. You can find detailed analysis and combat strategy for this creature on page 312.

KATOSA AUG SHRINE

You will find this shrine next to the East Akkala Stable, a little to the south of Bloodleaf Lake

1 Head to the terminal to your right to initiate a gyroscopic-based puzzle. In this game of "miniature golf," your objective is to putt the orb (the ball) into the concave slot (the hole). This requires you to angle your shot in a straight line, with just enough speed to reach the slot, but not so much that the orb would fall beyond the edge. If you fail, cancel and try again until you get the hang of it. Succeeding will unlock a moving platform that takes you across the room to the altar.

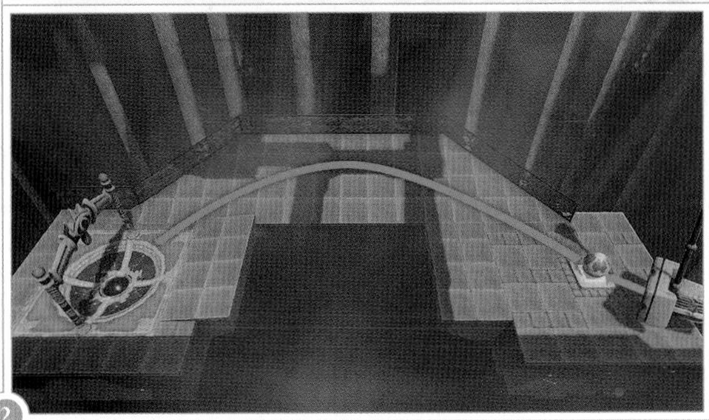

2 Before you interact with the altar, consider making a detour to the room further back. A terminal will invite you to play a second game of miniature golf. This time you must aim your putt diagonally toward the top so that the orb curves its way to the concave slot, as shown above. This will trigger a moving platform to your right, leading to the shrine's sole treasure chest.

ZE KASHO SHRINE

This shrine rests to the northwest of Akkala Tower. It overlooks the South Akkala Stable.

1

Interact with the terminal and use the gyroscopic functions of your controller to create a path to the door. As you tilt the platform in a direction, the spikes move along the lines visible on the platform. There are many possible configurations leading to the exit. You can find one in the above picture. Once the path is clear, jump to the platform, and then to the door.

2

In the second room, hit the crystal then make your way across the room as the blocks rotate, shielding you from the laser beams. Use bombs or arrows to hit the crystal again if you get stuck in the middle of the beams.

3

If you want to open the treasure chest, you must reach the top of the final rotating platform. This can only be achieved by hitting the crystal (either with an arrow or a bomb) while this block is in its bottom position. The rotation leads it back to its top position (from the left-hand side looking from the entrance): use this opportunity to drop to it during its ascent, and slowly walk toward the block's angle to step on its upper side as it rotates. Once it stops, you can glide to the nearby platform where the treasure chest lies.

4

In the final room, interact with the terminal to face another puzzle based on gyroscopic controls. Your goal here is simple: guiding one orb into each of the three slots with a floor switch. Starting from a flat position, gently angle your controller to the right so that all orbs move accordingly. Tilt the controller slightly toward you to pull the orbs toward their respective slots and you should succeed almost immediately. If you struggle, move all three orbs back to the top-left corner and try again. This really isn't as hard as it looks – the trick lies in your ability to angle the controller very slowly to keep control of each orb's momentum. Once you're done, head through the door and to the altar.

TUTSUWA NIMA SHRINE

SHRINE QUEST: THE SPRING OF POWER

You will find this shrine at the Spring of Power after completing the corresponding shrine quest.

1

The Spring of Power is located to the west of the East Akkala Stable. When you interact with the goddess statue, she will ask you to bring her one of Dinraal's scales.

2

Dinraal is a flying fire dragon that regularly roams around the northernmost section of the world map, to the north of Death Mountain and Eldin Mountains. The Eldin Great Skeleton, which you can easily reach from the nearby Gorae Torr Shrine, is a great place to hunt for the dragon. When you manage to get within bow range, hit any part of his body with an arrow: he will drop a scale nearby. Take this back to the Spring of Power and put it in the water. This will complete the quest and reveal the Tutsuwa Nima Shrine.

3

This shrine pits you against a Guardian Scout IV. You can find detailed analysis and combat strategy for this creature on page 312. You have no obstacle to hide behind when your opponent performs its spinning attack, but you can summon blocks of ice with Cryonis to achieve the same result.

KE'NAI SHAKAH SHRINE

This shrine is hidden inside Ulria Grotto, to the northeast of Zora's Domain.

1 Finding this shrine is actually the real challenge here. It is concealed behind a destructible rock wall, just beneath the top of the cliff. You must destroy that wall with a bomb arrow from the opposite cliff, as shown in the above picture (aim higher than your objective to take into account the arrow's drop). You can then use the nearby updraft to glide to the shrine itself.

2 Inside the shrine you will face a Guardian Scout III. You can find detailed analysis and combat strategy for this creature on page 312.

ZUNA KAI SHRINE

SHRINE QUEST: THE SKULL'S EYE

This shrine awaits to the northeast of Death Mountain, at the top of the peak that forms the right "eye" of Skull Lake

1 After proving your identity to Robbie during the "Robbie's Research" side quest (see page 229), speak to Jerrin at Akkala Ancient Tech Lab to activate this shrine quest. Your goal is to reach the top of the peak in the middle of Skull Lake (which looks like the skull's right "eye" on the map). The easiest way to do this is to glide from the highest point of the cliff to the north of Skull Lake. Once inside the Zuna Kai Shrine, head to the altar, making sure you open the treasure chest on the way.

TU KA'LOH SHRINE

SHRINE QUEST: TRIAL OF THE LABYRINTH

This shrine is found on Lomei Labyrinth Island.

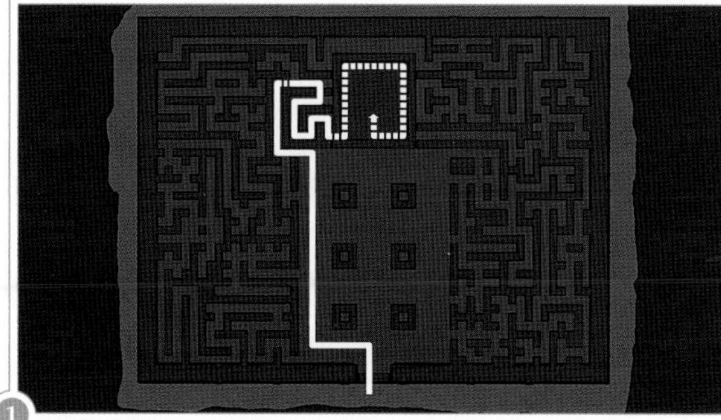

1 You can reach this labyrinth by gliding from the cliff at Akkala Ancient Tech Lab. As with the other mazes, you can choose to go through the maze in a traditional way: follow the path shown on the above map.

2 Alternatively, you can take a shortcut by climbing to the top of the structure and head to the position shown on this picture, to the southwest of the main building where the shrines rests. There are multiple Guardians in the area, but it is relatively easy to avoid them.

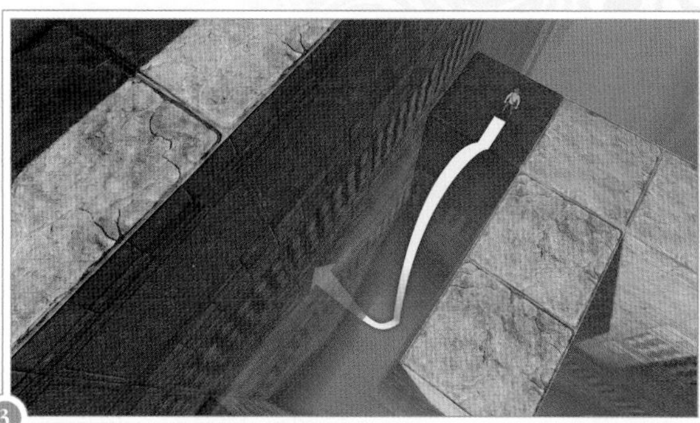

3 From this position, drop down and take the corridor to the east. Climb up the ladder and follow the way to the shrine. Note that you will encounter a vertical shaft with bramble: burn it down and follow the path: it leads to a fire-infused flameblade. Once inside the Tu Ka'loh Shrine, head to the altar, making sure you open the treasure chest on the way.

RITAAG ZUMO SHRINE

SHRINE QUEST: INTO THE VORTEX

This shrine is hidden in the center of the spiral peninsula located on the east coast of the Akkala region.

1 To reveal this shrine, you must pick up the orb at the start of the spiral, and take it to the pedestal in the center of the peninsula. There are multiple methods to achieve this: you can walk the whole way, which will require you to defeat many enemies on your path; you can take the raft at the south of the peninsula if you have a Korok Leaf to steer it; or you can throw the orb in the water and lift it with blocks of ice (generated by Cryonis), and repeat until you reach the pedestal. The shrine will appear once you drop the orb in its slot. There is no further challenge inside: head to the altar, collecting the contents of the treasure chest on the way.

Side Quests

This chapter offers easy-to-use solutions for all 76 side quests that you can encounter during your travels through Hyrule.

For ease of reference, we have sorted side quests by region. These are initially fogged over, their highways, contours, and major landmarks a mystery, but are revealed when you activate each local tower. The order we've chosen follows the same broad progression suggested by the Walkthrough chapter.

We begin with a map showing the positions of all towers, plus tips on how to scale them where appropriate, as activating these is an essential step to completing side quests in an optimal fashion.

Our coverage of each region starts with a large map where roman numerals are used to show the positions of quest vendors and, where applicable, associated objectives. The pages that follow each map offer traditional walkthroughs for the side quests that appear in the corresponding map portion.

Whenever you decide to undertake a side quest, don't forget to select it as your current mission in the Adventure Log menu: this will ensure that active waypoints on the map and mini-map point to relevant locations. In some instances, direct waypoints will lead you to your objective. In others, a waypoint will remain on the position of the quest vendor, making you solely responsible for figuring out what to do next. Certain NPCs (particularly those in villages) have daily routines that can occasionally make them elusive, so making use of the Adventure Log can sometimes help when you need to find a particular individual.

TOWERS

The local tower should be your first destination whenever you visit a new region, particularly if you plan on completing side quests or other optional challenges. Unlocking the regional map will not just reveal the topographical layout of the area, but also show the names of each landmark you visit, making navigation much easier. Furthermore, activated towers turn into fast travel spots, enabling you to warp to them whenever you please.

This map shows the position of each tower. We also offer advice on how to scale them whenever the ascent is a puzzle in its own right.

CENTRAL TOWER: This tower is surrounded by Guardians. The most dangerous of these is the Guardian Stalker to the south, but two Decayed Guardians to the east and west also complicate matters. Make your approach from the south and try to at least eliminate the Stalker with perfect guards. You can then start climbing, making regular jumps to speed up your ascent. Use the horizontal ledges to both catch your breath and shield yourself from incoming attacks. If you move at sufficient pace, the Decayed Guardians may not fire at all. This is a beneficial situation, as the explosions they cause can cause you to fall.

HEBRA TOWER: The base of this tower is surrounded by ice blocks. Move to the south side of the tower, where the terrain is flat, drop a bundle of wood, then light it to create a campfire. This will cause the blocks to melt after a few seconds, enabling you to climb to the top. Fire arrows will also work if you have a few to spare. If you obtain the Revali's Gale power in advance, you can even fly above the ice blocks and reach the top of the tower almost instantly.

TABANTHA TOWER: Malice goo prevents you from making a straightforward ascent with this tower. Instead, climb to the top of the pillar southwest of the tower and look to the northeast; from here, you can eliminate the glowing eyeball fixed to the pillar. This will cause the pillar to fall, creating a natural bridge leading to the tower – which you can now easily ascend.

RIDGELAND TOWER: This tower is surrounded by water and guarded by multiple Electric Wizzrobes and Electric Lizalfos. If you are spotted while swimming, this will make any resultant combat scenario extremely awkward, with every enemy assault likely to shock you (which, of course, will cause Link to drop equipped weapons or shields). The best approach is to clear an angle of approach from solid ground. Take out all enemies within reach using a bow, then swim straight to the tower and climb up; there is no need to worry about the enemies that do not notice you.

GERUDO TOWER: This tower is extremely tall, and only features horizontal ledges at its very top. You therefore need to glide to it from a very high point. The plateau to the northwest of the tower, which you can reach from the nearby Karusa Valley, is a good option. Glide from this plateau to the tower and you will end up well within range of the first ledge, where you can catch your breath. The top of the tower is then mere seconds away.

WASTELAND TOWER: This tower is surrounded by bog. Should you fall in, you will be instantly returned to your previous spot on dry land with one less heart. Gliding to reach the tower is not an option as strong winds seem to perpetually blow against you. The best solution, then, is to summon blocks of ice with Cryonis, creating stepping-stones to reach the tower. If your stamina wheel is limited, climb to the top of the rock pillar closest to the tower first. This will enable you to refill your entire gauge before you begin the main ascent.

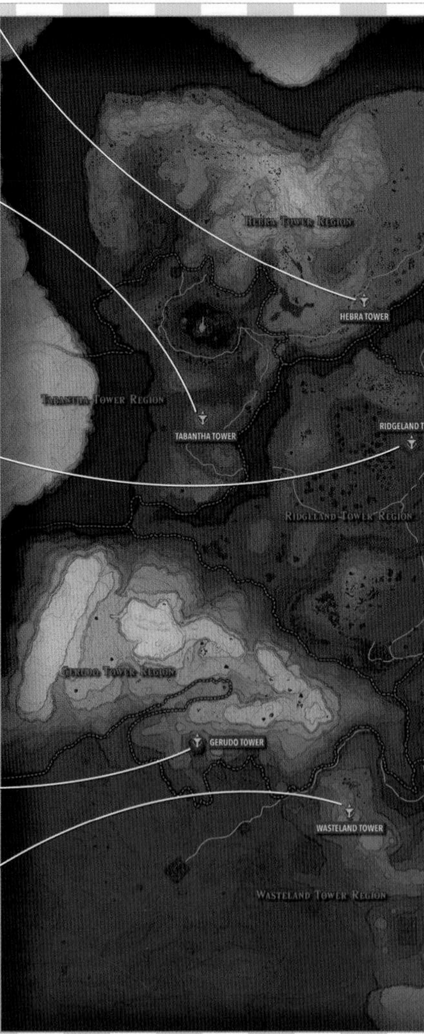

GREAT PLATEAU TOWER: You reach the top of this tower automatically during the game's prologue.

WOODLAND TOWER: This tower is surrounded by a large enemy outpost built on a bog. Eliminate any hostiles directly in your way, particularly Fire Wizzrobes who can really hinder your progression; don't forget that they can be taken down instantly with an ice arrow. To cross the bog, summon as many ice blocks as you need with Cryonis or glide over from a vantage point.

LANAYRU TOWER: An efficient way to climb Lanayru Tower is to make your approach from the northwest. Climb up the long ladder leading to the top of the lookout platform, then glide from there to the tower itself. The rest of the ascent is straightforward.

AKKALA TOWER: This is one of the harder towers to scale. Make your way up the Akkala Citadel Ruins however you see fit; the long stairs that run around the mountain is the most obvious route, though you will need to hide whenever a Guardian Skywatcher comes your way. You can also climb the cliffs if you prefer. Once at the base of the tower, begin your approach from the structure's north face. Shoot an arrow at the glowing eyeball through the partly destroyed gate. This will release a thin metal slab. Grab this with Magnesis and drop it on the floor above. You must now reach that very position. You can do so by moving to the tower's south side and gliding to a goo-free wall. Once you arrive at the slab, lift it with Magnesis and drop it so that it creates a makeshift bridge between the stairs and the tower itself, as illustrated above. You should then climb to the top of the tower without touching any Malice goo. If you have completed the Rito quest, you can naturally use Revali's Gale to fly above the goo instantly.

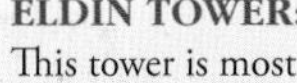

ELDIN TOWER: This tower is most easily accessed from the hot springs to the south. Walk up the bumpy slope made of igneous rock. The tower ascent itself poses no particular challenge.

HATENO TOWER: This tower is partly covered and surrounded by bramble, but navigating these hazards isn't difficult. Start your ascent from the southwest or southeast, stopping at each ledge on the way to refill your stamina bar.

FARON TOWER: The first horizontal ledges of this tower are fairly high above the ground, making a standard climb unlikely during your initial visit unless you have an unusually well-developed stamina wheel. You can, however, reveal two updrafts in the immediate vicinity: one to the south of the tower, and one to the north. Drop an octo balloon on the rock slabs on the ground to uncover them. Catching these updrafts will propel you high enough to make the rest of the ascent very manageable.

LAKE TOWER: This tower is guarded by a few enemies, including Lizalfos archers. Once you have eliminated them, the climb itself poses no specific problems.

DUELING PEAKS TOWER: This tower is very easy to climb. Start your ascent from the nearby shore.

DUELING PEAKS TOWER REGION

SIDE QUEST OVERVIEW (WALKTHROUGHS OVERLEAF)

ICON	NAME	PAGE
I	MISKO, THE GREAT BANDIT	220
II	THE PRICELESS MARACAS	220
III	WILD HORSES	220
IV	FLOWN THE COOP	221
V	ARROWS OF BURNING HEAT	221
VI – IX	KOKO'S KITCHEN	222
	COOKING WITH KOKO	222
	KOKO CUISINE	222
	KOKO'S SPECIALTY	223
X	PLAYTIME WITH COTTLA	223
XI	FIND THE FAIRY FOUNTAIN	223
XII	BY FIREFLY'S LIGHT	223

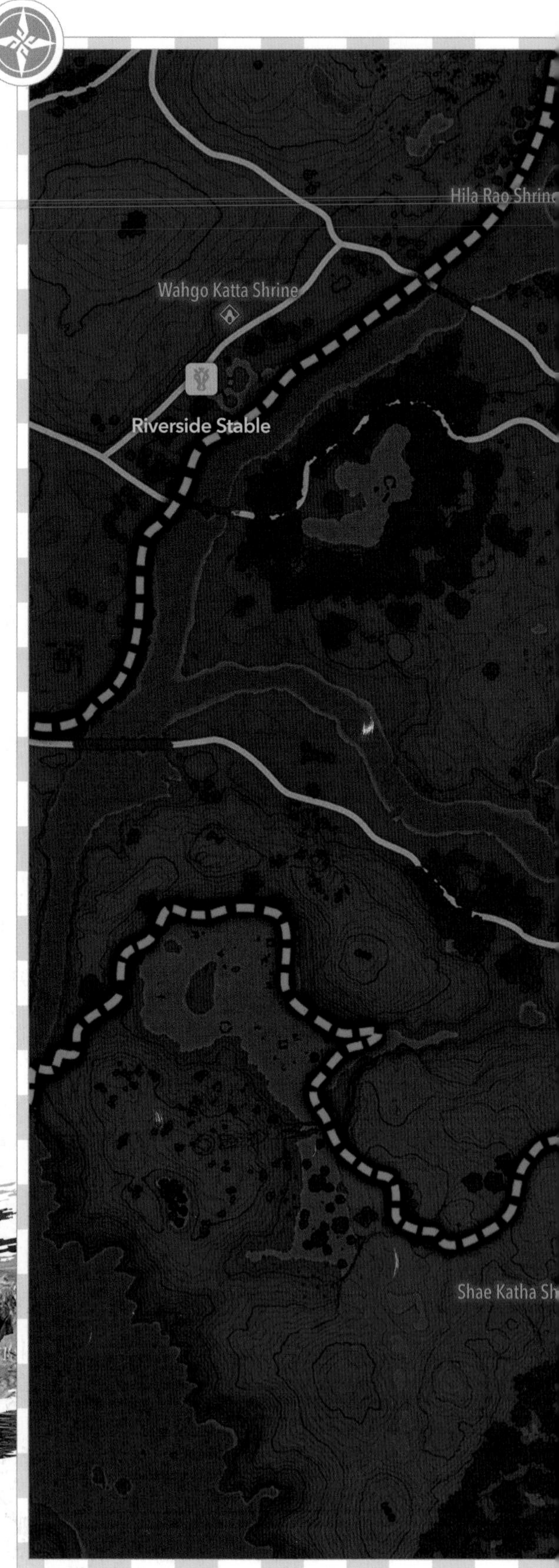

Ta'loh Naeg Shrine
Great Fairy Fountain
Lakna Rokee Shrine
XI
Kakariko Village
IV
X
XI
VI VII VIII IX
V
XII
Kakariko Village
II
Kam Urog Shrine
DUELING PEAKS TOWER
DUELING PEAKS TOWER REGION
Ree Dahee Shrine
Shee Venath Shrine
Fort Hateno
III
Ha Dahamar Shrine
Dueling Peaks Stable
I
Shee Vaneer Shrine
Toto Sah Shrine

I MISKO, THE GREAT BANDIT

1 Speak to Domidak and Prissen at the Dueling Peaks Stable. If you agree to pay 100 rupees, they will give you hints referring to a secret treasure cache and trigger this side quest.

2 The secret location in question is found to the southeast of the Dueling Peaks, at the end of the small stream that branches off from the main river. Climb to the destructible rocks on the cliff and blow them up with a bomb. You will find **multiple treasure chests** (including another behind yet more destructible rocks), and complete the quest in the process. Undertaking this mission early in the adventure can be an extremely effective way to gain an advantage over your enemies by acquiring advanced weapons.

II THE PRICELESS MARACAS

1 On your way to Kakariko Village to meet Impa for the first time, you can speak to a creature called Hestu to the northeast of Kakariko Bridge.

2 Head to the outpost a short distance to the east and eliminate all enemies, then take the maracas back to Hestu. As a reward, he will offer you a very useful service for the rest of the adventure: he will grant you **additional inventory slots** for your weapons, bows, or shields in exchange for Korok seeds that you deliver to him.

III WILD HORSES

1 Speak to Rensa, the man by the counter at the Dueling Peaks Stable. He will challenge you to mount a wild horse and take it back to him in under two minutes.

2 You can find many wild horses around the stable. Move close to one of these by carefully crouch-walking during an approach from behind, then press Ⓐ to mount it. Press L repeatedly to soothe the horse until it calms down. You can then ride it back to the stable, steering with Ⓛ and increasing your speed with Ⓐ. As long as you return within the time limit, Rensa will reward you with a **purple rupee**.

IV FLOWN THE COOP

1 To trigger this quest, speak to Cado while he watches his cuccos at noon, opposite the armor shop. This is only possible after interacting with the guards in front of Impa's house at least once.

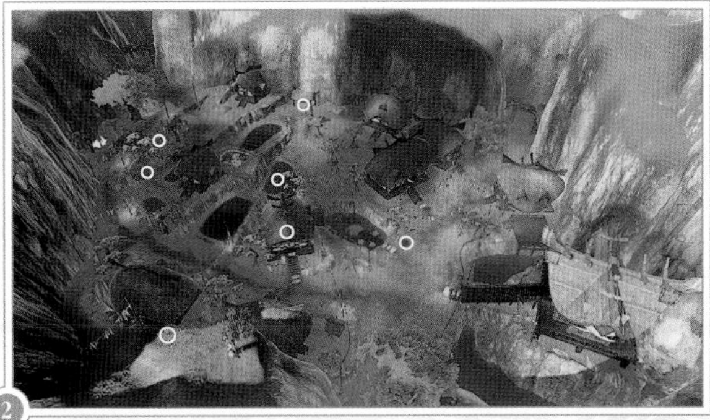

2 Your goal is to retrieve seven cuccos found milling around the village, including two that often stand on rooftops and another situated on the ledge overlooking the armor shop. Place them all inside the enclosure to complete the assignment. Cado will reward you with a **purple rupee**.

V ARROWS OF BURNING HEAT

1 After completing the "Seek Out Impa" main quest, speak to Rola, the owner of the general store that sells arrows in Kakariko Village. She needs you to light the four candles behind the village's goddess statue.

2 To light the candles, you can use fire arrows, standard arrows set ablaze at the nearby campfire, or even a fire-elemental melee weapon (leap to each candle and perform a jump slash). Once you're done, return to Rola to complete the mission and receive a **red rupee**.

KOKO'S KITCHEN

Speak to Koko, a child found by the cooking pot next to the general store in Kakariko Village. She will only be available during the early afternoon, from approximately noon to 7:00PM. Purchase a swift carrot from the nearby general store, then deliver it to the child to complete this short mission and receive your reward: a **hasty veggie cream soup**.

COOKING WITH KOKO

Speak to Koko again after completing her previous quest (Koko's Kitchen). This time she needs goat butter, which you can also purchase from the nearby general store. Once you have completed your delivery, she will reward you with a **hot buttered apple**.

KOKO CUISINE

Speak to Koko again after completing her previous quest (Cooking with Koko). Give her some raw meat to complete this mission. You will most likely already have some in your inventory at this point; if not, hunt a mammal found in the region, such as a fox or a boar, and collect the meat it yields. Koko will thank you with a **tough meat-stuffed pumpkin**.

IX KOKO'S SPECIALTY

1 Speak to Koko again after completing her previous quest (Koko Cuisine). You must secure Courser Bee honey for her. You can find a beehive in the forest to the northwest of Kakariko Village. Alternatively, you can warp to the Owa Daim Shrine on the Great Plateau and glide to the nearby enemy outpost, a short distance to the north: there is a beehive in the small rock alcove barred by planks. Shoot it with an arrow and collect the item that falls on the ground. Your reward for this quest is an **energizing honeyed apple**.

X PLAYTIME WITH COTTLA

1 Speak to Cottla during the day. You will encounter her most often between noon and 4:00 PM around the armor shop. Choose to play tag with her. Once the game begins, sprint after her and you should catch up in no time. She will offer her thanks for this entertaining diversion with **rock salt**. If you choose to play hide-and-seek with the child, you will find her hidden behind Impa's house.

XI FIND THE FAIRY FOUNTAIN

1 Speak to Pikango in Kakariko Village after you have obtained the camera rune in Hateno Village, then follow him.

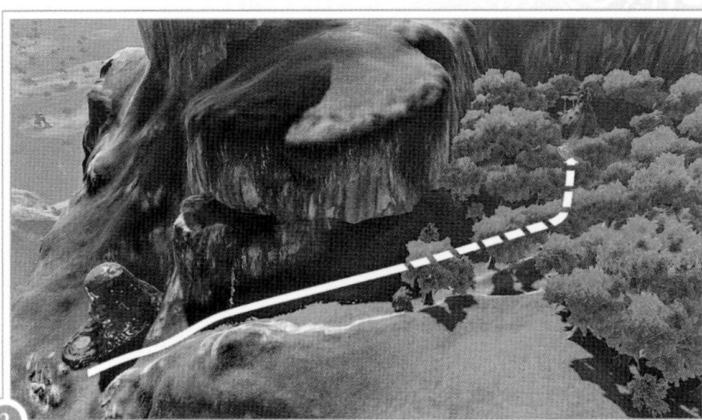

2 Activate the Great Fairy Fountain to the northeast of the village (this will cost you 100 rupees if this is the first fountain you unlock), then take a picture of it and report to Pikango. He will thank you by offering **hints** regarding the location of the captured memories stored in your Sheikah Slate's album. After completing this quest, Pikango can usually be found at various stables throughout Hyrule.

XII BY FIREFLY'S LIGHT

1 This becomes available after you complete the "Find the Fairy Fountain" and "Flown the Coop" quests. You will receive this assignment from Lasli, the woman who stands outside Kakariko's armor shop during the day, but then walks to her home in the southeast corner of the village at night. Speak to her from 10:00PM onwards to trigger this quest.

2 Your goal is to catch five sunset fireflies in the area. These are plentiful in Kakariko Village after dusk as long as it is not raining: crouch-walk toward them and collect them with Ⓐ. Once you have reached the quota, select all five of them in your inventory, hold them in your hands, and release them inside Lasli's house to secure your reward: a **purple rupee**.

Hateno Tower Region

SIDE QUEST OVERVIEW (WALKTHROUGHS OVERLEAF)

ICON	NAME	PAGE
I	THE STATUE'S BARGAIN	226
II	THE WEAPON CONNOISSEUR	226
III	A GIFT FOR MY BELOVED	228
IV	THE SHEEP RUSTLERS	228
V	ROBBIE'S RESEARCH	229
VI	SLATED FOR UPGRADES	229
VII	SUNSHROOM SENSING	230
VIII	THE HERO'S CACHE	230
IX	HYLIAN HOMEOWNER	231
X	FROM THE GROUND UP	232

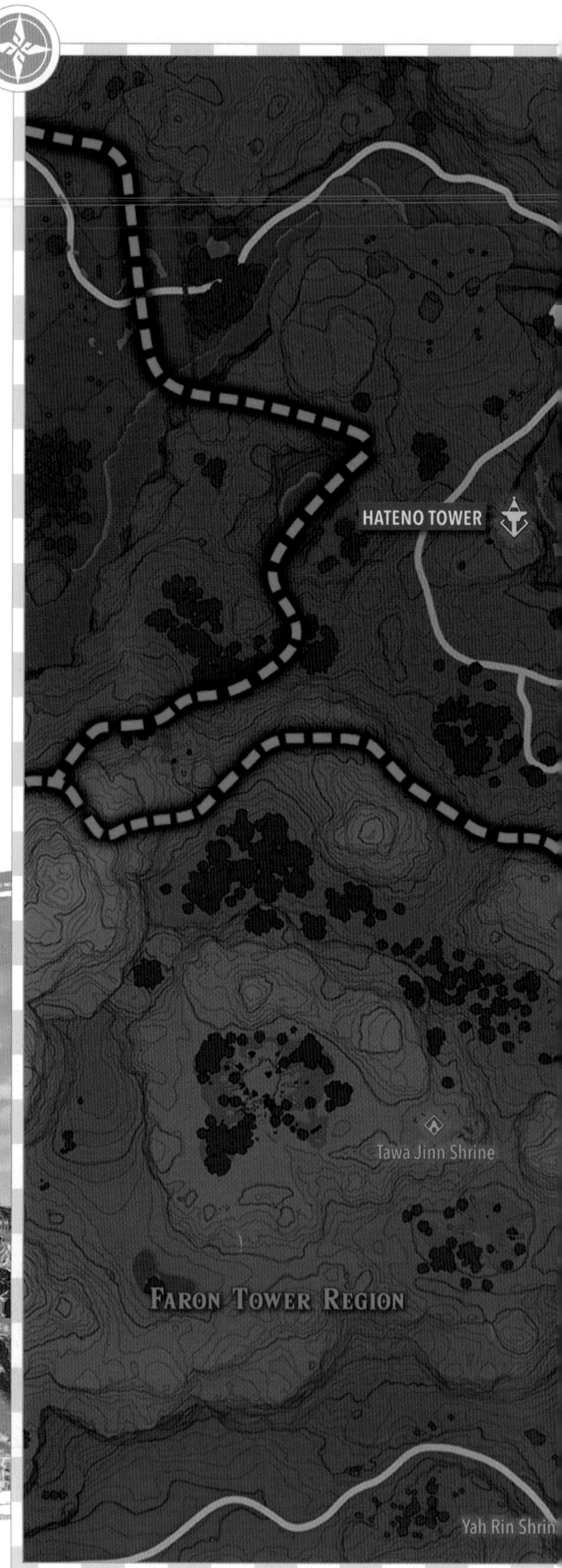

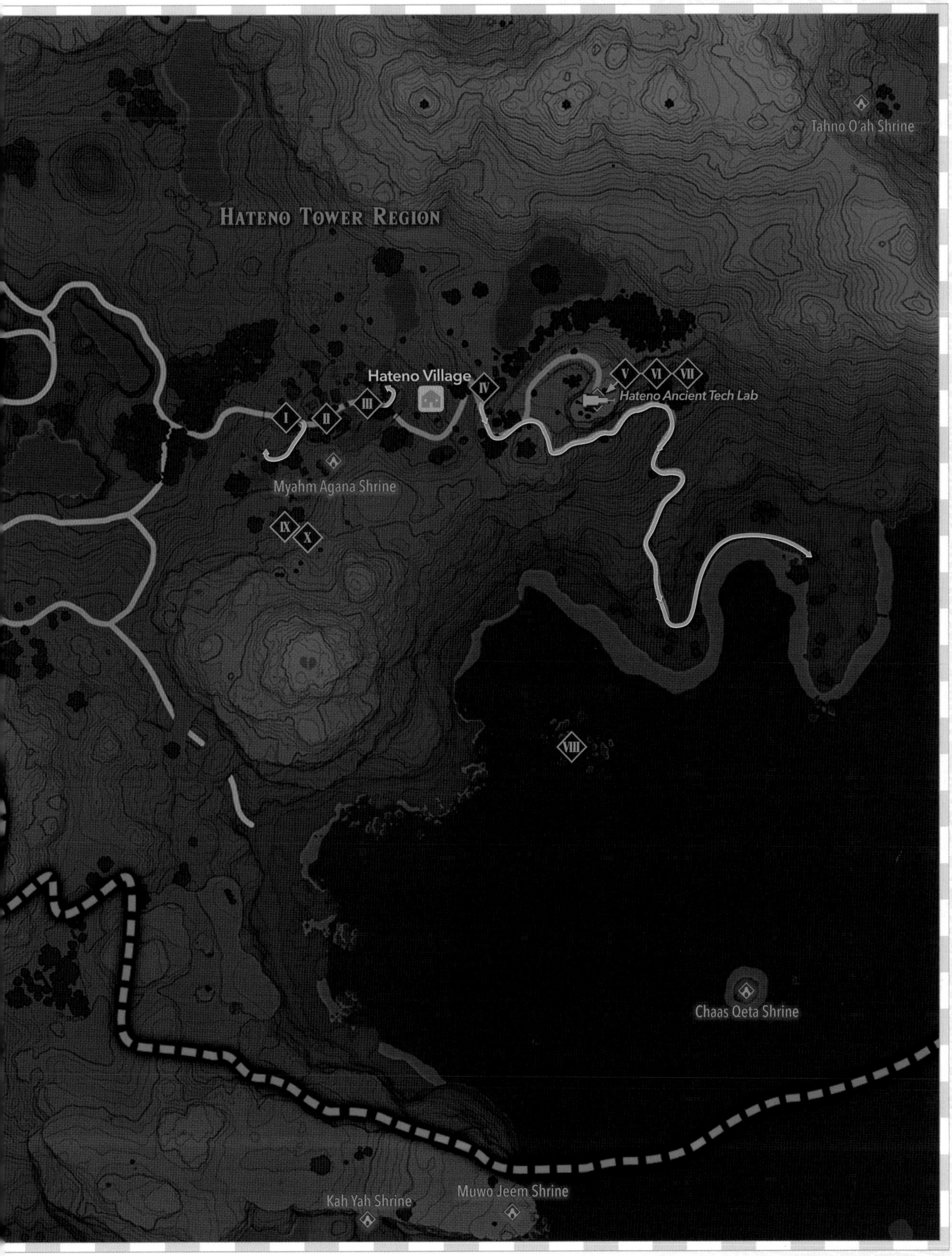

Tahno O'ah Shrine

HATENO TOWER REGION

Hateno Village

I II III IV V VI VII

Hateno Ancient Tech Lab

Myahm Agana Shrine

IX X

VIII

Chaas Qeta Shrine

Kah Yah Shrine

Muwo Jeem Shrine

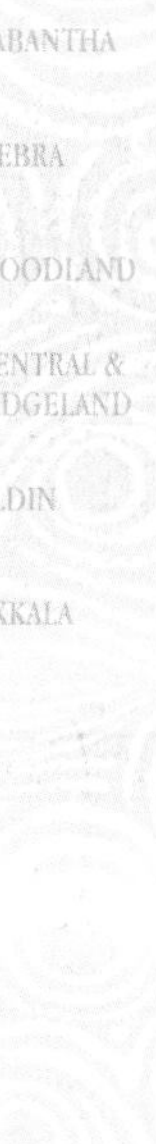

THE STATUE'S BARGAIN

If you speak to a child called Teebo in Hateno Village, he will take you to a strange statue by Firly Pond. Speak to the statue to trigger the quest, then speak to it again to regain the essence it took from you. This is a simple introduction to a feature that enables you to turn a heart container into a stamina vessel, or vice versa, for a mere 20 rupees. Should you ever change your mind about how you have invested your spirit orbs, this system offers you a chance to reallocate them as you see fit.

THE WEAPON CONNOISSEUR

Speak to Nebb, one of the children running around in the streets of Hateno Village during the day. This will trigger a long-term quest during which the child asks you to show him various weapons. Every time you take one back to him (it only needs to be in your inventory, not necessarily equipped), he will offer you a reward, then detail your next target. As his whims will take you all over Hyrule, including some highly dangerous locations, it makes sense to complete this quest gradually. Make a note of where his next weapon might be found, then make a detour to collect it when other objectives lead you to its general neighborhood.

First, Nebb wants you to show him a traveler's sword. You can find one of these in the valley that leads to Zora's Domain, just east of Inogo Bridge. The blade lies close to two abandoned wooden carts. Pick it up and take it back to Nebb: he will reward you with a **red rupee**.

Next, Nebb wants to see a fire rod. This is a weapon dropped by Fire Wizzrobes. You can find one of these creatures in the Military Training Camp, directly to the south of Woodland Tower. A single ice arrow will defeat it instantly. Show the weapon to Nebb and he will give you a **red rupee**.

4 Nebb now asks for a Moblin club. You can find Moblins that are highly likely to wield this weapon in various locations; a typical place to look would be Upland Zorana, to the north of Zora's Domain. Show the weapon to Nebb and he will thank you with a **purple rupee**.

5 Nebb's next request is a duplex bow. This is the signature weapon used by Yiga Footsoldiers. These tend to appear frequently near the entrance of the Yiga Clan Hideout, to the north of the Gerudo Desert. Retrieve one of their bows at the next opportunity and take it back to Nebb to obtain a **purple rupee**.

6 Nebb now needs you to acquire a windcleaver for him. This is a weapon wielded by Yiga Blademasters, who appear frequently on the road between the Lanayru Tower and the Foothill Stable after you have cleared the Yiga Clan Hideout (see page 66). Retrieve a windcleaver from one of these foes and show it to Nebb to obtain a **silver rupee**.

7 For his next task, Nebb asks you to show him an ancient battle axe+. You can acquire one by defeating a Guardian Scout III. These are found inside various shrines, such as Muwo Jeem, Sasa Kai, Namika Ozz, and Mijah Rokee. Take the weapon back to Nebb and he will reward you with a **silver rupee**.

8 Nebb's next assignment is to secure a frostspear. You can find one of these by defeating a Lizalfos in an outpost with a skull-shaped building in the Hebra region (climb up from the Mozo Shenno Shrine and head northwest across the Biron Snowshelf). Very late in the adventure, you can also acquire one by defeating a Lizalfos on one of the upper walkways of the Coliseum Ruins, in the south part of the Central Tower region. Show this to Nebb to obtain a **gold rupee**.

9 Nebb now asks you to collect an ancient short sword for him. You can purchase this from Cherry at the Akkala Ancient Tech Lab if you have completed the "Robbie's Research" side quest (covered overleaf). This will cost you 1,000 rupees, as well as 15 ancient springs, 5 ancient shafts, and 2 ancient cores. Show the weapon to Nebb to obtain a **diamond**.

A GIFT FOR MY BELOVED

1 Speak to Manny, who is usually found between Hateno Village's dye shop and the local inn.

2 Once the quest is active, walk behind the inn's counter and ask Prima what she likes. Return to Manny and he will give you a new objective: to find 10 restless crickets for him.

3 The easiest way to catch large numbers of restless crickets is to head to a field with tall grass, such as the one to the northwest of Hateno Village. Select a long two-handed sword and hold Ⓨ to initiate a charged attack. Tilt Ⓛ in any direction to begin cutting the grass rapidly. Cancel the attack with Ⓑ before you run out of stamina, or to avoid wasting the weapon's durability. Whenever you notice a restless cricket revealed by this "lawn-mowing" process, cancel the move and sprint over to retrieve it. With this technique, it is possible to gather many insects in next to no time. Return to Manny when you're done and he will reward you with a **silver rupee**.

THE SHEEP RUSTLERS

1 Speak to Koyin, who watches over her flock outside the farm located between Hateno Village and the Tech Lab. She needs you to slay a group of monsters.

2 Head to Hateno Beach, to the southeast of the village, and eliminate the group of creatures that congregate at the outpost, on the east side of the bay. After getting rid of all of them, report to Koyin. She will reward you with **10 bottles of fresh milk**.

V ROBBIE'S RESEARCH

1 After showing Purah a picture of herself during the main quest in the Hateno Ancient Tech Lab, speak to her again to trigger this mission.

2 You first need to find Robbie at the Akkala Ancient Tech Lab, in the northeast corner of Hyrule. Once inside, speak to Robbie. When he requires proof of your identity, remove all your armor pieces to show your scars, then speak to him again.

3 Pick up the torch leaning against the shelves in the Tech Lab, and head to Tumlea Heights, just west of the Tech Lab. Light your torch with the blue flame found there, then head back to the Tech Lab. Ideally, you should eliminate potential enemies beforehand to prevent them from harassing you on the return journey, as you cannot sprint while carrying the blue flame. Don't forget to regularly light lanterns as you pass them: these will enable you to retrieve the blue flame without having to go back to Tumlea Heights should your torch be extinguished for any reason.

4 After igniting the furnace outside the Tech Lab with the blue flame, speak to Robbie again to complete the assignment and receive **three ancient arrows**. This also unlocks a new shop, which you can access by speaking to Cherry. It specializes in equipment of the "ancient" variety – the sort that is effective against Guardians.

AKKALA ANCIENT TECH LAB SHOP

ITEM	PRICE (RUPEES)	MATERIALS REQUIRED
Ancient Arrow	90	Ancient Screw x2, Ancient Shaft x1, Arrow x1
Ancient Arrow x3	250	Ancient Screw x6, Ancient Shaft x3, Arrow x3
Ancient Arrow x5	400	Ancient Spring x5, Ancient Shaft x5, Arrow x5
Ancient Short Sword	1,000	Ancient Spring x15, Ancient Shaft x 5, Ancient Core x2
Ancient Shield	1,000	Ancient Gear x10, Ancient Spring x 15, Giant Ancient Core x1
Ancient Bladesaw	1,000	Ancient Screw x15, Ancient Shaft x5, Ancient Core x2
Ancient Spear	1,000	Ancient Gear x15, Ancient Shaft x5, Ancient Core x2
Ancient Bow	1,000	Ancient Gear x 10, Ancient Spring x15, Giant Ancient Core x1
Ancient Helm	2,000	Ancient Gear x20, Ancient Shaft x5, Ancient Core x3
Ancient Cuirass	2,000	Ancient Gear x20, Ancient Screw x5, Ancient Core x3
Ancient Greaves	2,000	Ancient Gear x20, Ancient Spring x5, Ancient Core x3

VI SLATED FOR UPGRADES

1 After acquiring the camera rune from Purah at the Hateno Ancient Tech Lab, speak to her again to initiate this quest. If you give her three ancient screws, three ancient shafts, and three ancient cores, she will **upgrade** your Sheikah Sensor, Remote Bomb, and Stasis runes respectively. The materials in question can be obtained by defeating Guardians, commonly encountered in shrines and around Hyrule Castle.

VII SUNSHROOM SENSING

1 Once you've acquired the Sheikah Sensor+ upgrade, speak to Symin inside the Hateno Ancient Tech Lab. Take a picture of the sunshroom at the back of the building, then show it to him.

2 Symin now requires three sunshrooms, which you can easily collect in Retsam Forest, just north of the Tech Lab. Take the items back to him to complete the assignment and receive **three hearty truffles** as a reward.

VIII THE HERO'S CACHE

1 Speak to Kass on the tall rock in the middle of Kitano Bay. He mentions a treasure "at 17 of 24," which is your only clue.

2 If you convert "17 of 24" to a clock position, where north corresponds to noon, the riddle means 5 o'clock. Looking at the group of rocks jutting out of the water as a clock, move to the ones in the bottom-right section, where a needle would point to show 5 o'clock. You will find a treasure chest hidden between the rocks. Grab it with Magnesis and open it to obtain a **gold rupee** and complete the assignment.

1 Speak to Bolson in Hateno Village. He and his men work around a house to the south of Firly Pond. He will sell you the house in exchange for 3,000 rupees and 30 bundles of wood. This is a long-term task, though you can actually fulfil both objectives rather quickly if you know where to look.

2 The best method to acquire rupees is by selling gemstones. Every time you destroy an ore deposit, you will find at least one gemstone, and often many more. The Talus sub-bosses are also a great source of precious stones. Gather these diligently and you should reach the 3,000 rupee milestone in no time.

3 Wood is a resource that you can retrieve every time you destroy a felled tree. You can knock down trees and shatter the tree trunks, transforming them into bundles of wood, with an axe or a bomb. Bombs are an excellent choice as they have no durability limit, and can hit multiple trees simultaneously. Recommended locations to farm wood include the area around the old man's hut on the Great Plateau, the Rito Stable (where many tree trunks are conveniently lined up and waiting to be turned into bundles of wood), and the valley leading to Zora's Domain, where suitable trees abound.

4 Once you've paid Bolson, you still need to furnish your home and decorate its exterior. To do so, you will need to make multiple payments to Bolson of 100 rupees each: weapon mounts (x2), bow mounts (x3), shield mounts (x3), bed (x1), lighting (x1), door (x1), sign (x1), flowers (x1), and trees (x1). Purchase all of these upgrades – for a combined cost of 1,400 rupees – and you will finally complete the quest.

HOMEOWNING

Owning your own house and upgrading it offers two tangible benefits:

- You can sleep in your bed at any time, enabling you to restore your entire health bar for free.
- You can use the mounts in the living room to store weapons, bows, and shields that you do not necessarily want to carry with you. Each mount can carry a single piece. This can be a great way to put precious items in safe keeping, for example, weapons that you need for specific uses (such as powerful ancient blades effective against Guardians, or weapons required to complete Nebb's side quest – The Weapon Connoisseur).

1 After you have purchased a house as part of the "Hylian Homeowner" side quest, speak to Bolson and Hudson. This mission officially begins when Hudson departs for the Akkala region. Meet Hudson on the small island in the middle of Lake Akkala. He requires your help to gather more wood and to recruit people for his new settlement: Tarrey Town. First, you must deliver 10 bundles of wood to him. See the box-out on the page to your right for wood gathering tips.

2 After you deliver the first 10 bundles of wood to Hudson, he will ask you to find a strong Goron. Warp to the Eldin region and speak to Greyson at the Southern Mine when he sits by the cooking pot at night. Once he's on his way to Tarrey Town, warp back there and speak to Hudson again. You now have access to a gemstone shop in the village.

3 After you give Hudson another 20 bundles of wood, he will ask you to find someone with a gift for tailoring. Head to Kara Kara Bazaar and talk to Rhondson (while not wearing the full Gerudo outfit) during the day – the Gerudo beneath the canopy outside the inn. Head back to Tarrey Town after she departs and speak to Hudson. You can now buy the desert voe line of clothes from Rhondson in the village.

4 Give Hudson the 30 bundles of wood he now needs to move on to his next request: a Rito merchant. Warp to Rito Village and speak to Fyson, who is found close to the goddess statue. Return to Tarrey Town and speak to Hudson once again. Fyson has opened a brand new general store in the meantime, where you can buy all sorts of arrows for competitive prices.

5 Give Hudson another 50 bundles of wood and he will ask you to find a person who can officiate. Warp to Zora's Domain and speak to Kapson, on the floor above the shrine. After he leaves for Tarrey Town, fast travel there and talk to Hudson, who can be found at Rhondson's clothes shop. He will then ask you to invite guests for him.

6 Warp to Hateno and invite Bolson and Karson to the wedding ceremony. Head to Hateno Village and you should find them close to Link's house. Once they're on their way, return to Tarrey Town and talk to Hudson to begin the wedding. Speak to Hudson one last time after the ceremony to obtain your final reward for completing this lengthy quest: **three diamonds**. Note that Kapson has opened an inn in the meantime, where you can rest whenever you please for no charge.

WOOD-FARMING TIPS

You must gather a lot of wood for this quest. The following locations offer great opportunities to acquire sizable quantities of this resource.

The best place to begin is undoubtedly the Rito Stable, where there are many tree trunks ready for a bomb explosion that will turn them into wood. Stop by this stable often and you will soon have very large stocks of this valuable resource.

Another location where you can farm wood, even at a very early stage in the adventure, is the old man's hut on the Great Plateau. Most of the trees in the area can be knocked down, then processed into wood with bombs or the axe available in front of the hut.

The valley leading to Zora's Domain is also packed with suitable trees. A single trek can reward you with dozens of bundles of wood, though you will need to eliminate a few Lizalfos during the process.

Finally, over a dozen bundles of wood can be picked up for free at the enemy outpost to the east of the Yiga Clan Hideout. If you ever pass through this area while going after shrines or side quests, be sure to claim these on the way.

LANAYRU TOWER REGION

SIDE QUEST OVERVIEW (WALKTHROUGHS OVERLEAF)

ICON	NAME	PAGE
I	SPECIAL DELIVERY	236
II	DIVING IS BEAUTY!	237
III	LYNEL SAFARI	237
IV	FROG CATCHING	237
V	THE GIANT OF RALIS POND	238
VI	LUMINOUS STONE GATHERING	238
VII	A WIFE WASHED AWAY	239
VIII	RIVERBED REWARD	239
IX	ZORA STONE MONUMENTS	240

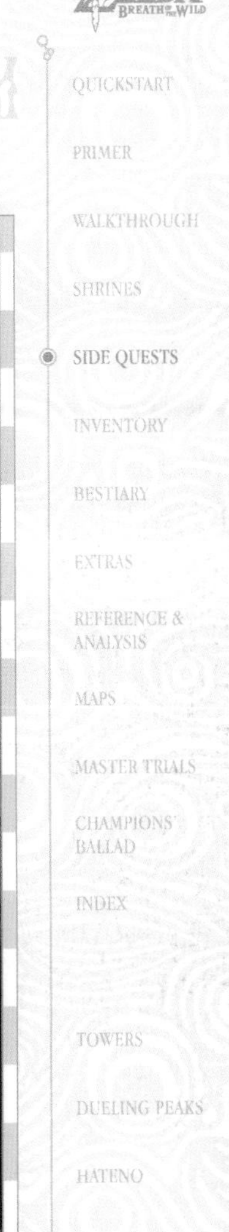

IX
V
II
III
IV
VII
VI
Zora's Domain

V
Ne'ez Yohma Shrine
IV
Dagah Keek Shrine
Zora's Domain
Soh Kofi Shrine
Ralis Pond
I
LANAYRU TOWER
LANAYRU TOWER REGION
Mezza Lo Shrine
Rucco Maag Shrine
Daka Tuss Shrine
Ta'loh Naeg Shrine
Lakna Rokee Shrine
Kakariko Village
HATENO TOWER REGION

SPECIAL DELIVERY

1 After completing the Divine Beast Vah Ruta main quest, speak to Finley on the Bank of Wishes, in the valley leading to Zora's Domain. She will throw a letter down the river and will ask you to follow the item without losing sight of it until you find out who picks it up. You additionally need to ensure the letter isn't destroyed by Octoroks on the way: try to eliminate these enemies quickly when you run into them, for example with arrows.

2 Dive in the water and swim until you run into a wooden barrier that blocks the letter. Stand on the nearby rock, pick up the letter and throw it to the other side; you can also destroy the barrier if you prefer.

3 Keep following the letter down the river, regularly catching your breath by standing on flat surfaces near the shore. After you pass Inogo Bridge, the letter will get stuck against wooden crates and debris under an enemy outpost suspended on piles: you must destroy these obstacles with a bomb or bomb arrow *before* the letter reaches them (otherwise the explosion will shatter the letter too). This can be achieved while standing on a small rock in the middle of the river, close to the bridge.

4 The letter will end up in a small inlet in Mercay Island, where a man called Sasan is making camp. Speak to him to trigger a cutscene.

5 Finally, warp to Zora's Domain and talk to Finley and Sasan, who can be found on one of the round platforms in the west half of the town. They will reward you with a **gold rupee**.

II DIVING IS BEAUTY!

1 After initiating the Divine Beast Vah Ruta main quest, speak to Gruve at the base of the stairs leading to the throne room in Zora's Domain, then dive (same command as jumping) from the edge of the platform next to him.

2 Swim back up the waterfall thanks to the special effect of your Zora Armor. Gruve will reward you with **five fleet-lotus seeds.**

III LYNEL SAFARI

1 After initiating the Divine Beast Vah Ruta main quest, speak to Laflat, who is standing a few steps to the east of the stairs leading to the throne room in Zora's Domain. She needs a picture of the Lynel that roams on Ploymus Mountain.

2 The main quest in this region takes you there, with the Zora Armor enabling you to swim up the waterfalls and reach your destination very quickly. Take a picture of the Lynel on your way to Divine Beast Vah Ruta (see page 52), and show it to Laflat later. She will reward you with the **Zora Greaves**, which enable you to swim faster.

IV FROG CATCHING

1 After clearing the Divine Beast Vah Ruta dungeon, speak to Tumbo during the day at Zora's Domain – a child that runs around the statue opposite the shrine. He will ask you to find five hot-footed frogs for him.

2 During rainy weather, these frogs are usually plentiful near bodies of water such as Ralis Pond or the small pool to the south of Luto's Crossing. Once you have at least five in your inventory, deliver them to Tumbo to obtain an **armoranth**.

V THE GIANT OF RALIS POND

1 After clearing the Divine Beast Vah Ruta dungeon, speak to Torfeau, on the plaza underneath the throne room in Zora's Domain.

2 Cross the nearby bridge and head to Ralis Pond, to the southwest. Apply the usual tactics to eliminate the Hinox, shooting arrows at its open eye and following up with melee combos while the beast is stunned. Return to Torfeau once the creature falls to receive a **silver rupee**.

VI LUMINOUS STONE GATHERING

1 After clearing the Divine Beast Vah Ruta dungeon speak to Ledo, who needs 10 luminous stones.

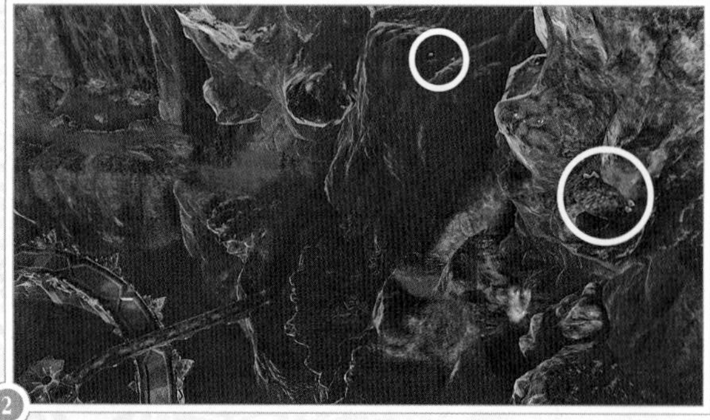

2 You can find multiple ore deposits that may contain these minerals on the plateaus overlooking the northwest bridge of Zora's Domain. The Upland Zorana area has multiple spots where you can gather luminous stones.

3 Alternatively, you can warp to the Sho Dantu Shrine near the entrance to the Yiga Clan Hideout, where four deposits await your attention. There are more right behind the Kuh Takkar Shrine, to the east of the Yiga Clan Hideout. Once you have 10 of the required gems, return to Ledo to receive **two diamonds**. After you complete the quest, Ledo will continue to trade in 10 luminous stones, but for one diamond instead of two.

VII A WIFE WASHED AWAY

After clearing the Divine Beast Vah Ruta dungeon, speak to Fronk. He can be found during the day on the round platform a few steps to the east of the general store in Zora's Domain.

His wife awaits in the Lake Tower region, on the small islet east of Hylia Island. She will give you **five staminoka basses** when you talk to her, which will complete the quest.

VIII RIVERBED REWARD

Speak to Izra, on the shore of the river right by the Wetland Stable. He needs your help to lift a treasure chest out of the water, which is easily achieved with Magnesis. Open the chest to either find a **royal broadsword** or a **knight's broadsword**, then speak to him again to complete this short assignment.

After clearing the Divine Beast Vah Ruta dungeon, speak to Jiahto at the far end of the plaza underneath the throne room in Zora's Domain. He will ask you to search for 10 stone monuments in the area surrounding Zora's Domain. They are all similar in appearance to the example in front of him.

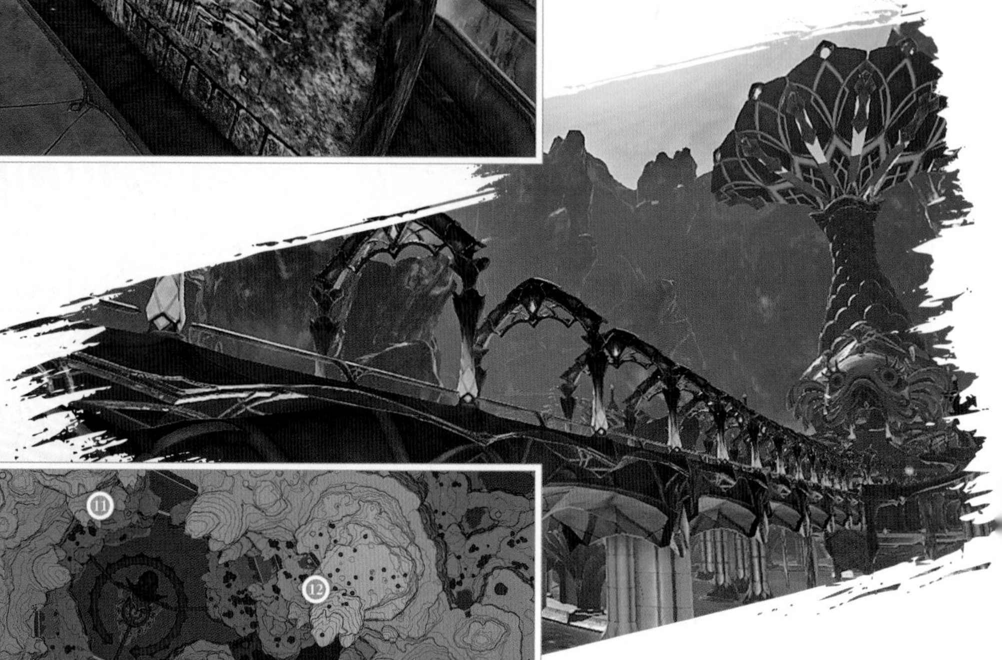

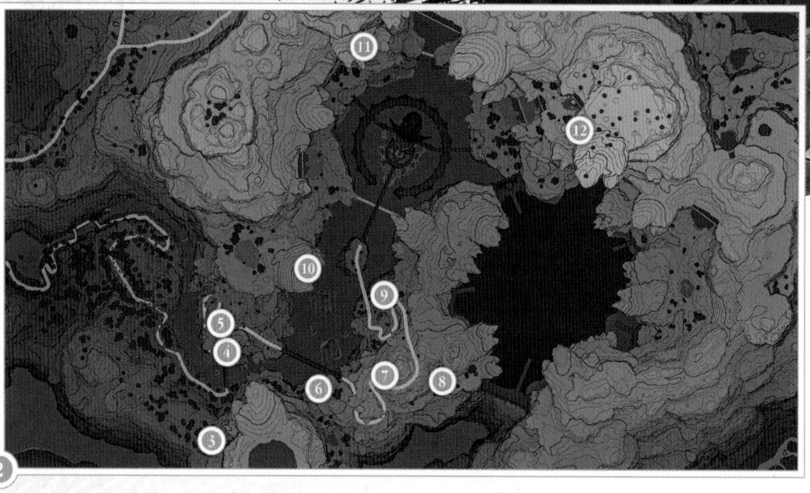

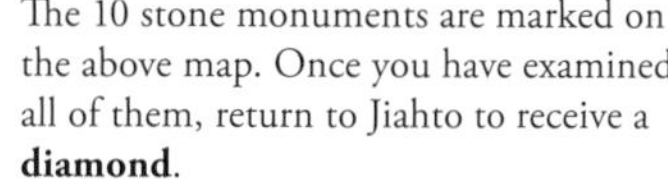

The 10 stone monuments are marked on the above map. Once you have examined all of them, return to Jiahto to receive a **diamond**.

This stone monument is found in the Zodobon Highlands, at the base of the mountain on which Divine Beast Vah Ruta stands after you have freed it from Ganon's blight.

This stone monument rests on a ledge high above the north end of Oren Bridge.

5 This stone monument lies directly on the path leading to Zora's Domain, approximately midway between Oren Bridge and Luto's Crossing.

6 This stone monument is located a short distance to the south of Luto's Crossing. You can glide to it directly from the bridge.

7 You will find this stone monument directly on the path leading to Zora's Domain during the ascent of Ruto Mountain.

8 When you reach the summit of Ruto Mountain, drop down the cliff on the south side to reach this stone monument.

9 This stone monument is on your right just before you step on the bridge leading to Zora's Domain.

10 From the bridge leading to Zora's Domain, look to the west: you will see this stone monument on the shore of Ruto Lake.

11 This stone monument stands on a ledge overlooking the northwest bridge of Zora's Domain.

12 This stone monument is found on the plateau at the base of the final waterfall leading to the summit of Ploymus Mountain – a few steps to the south of Lulu Lake.

FARON TOWER REGION

SIDE QUEST OVERVIEW

ICON	NAME	PAGE
I	WHAT'S FOR DINNER?	See overleaf
II	SUNKEN TREASURE	
III	TAKE BACK THE SEA	
IV	A GIFT OF NIGHTSHADE	
V	THUNDER MAGNET	

Hateno Tower Region

Hateno Village

HATENO TOWER

Hateno Ancient Tech Lab

Myahm Agana Shrine

Faron Tower Region

Tawa Jinn Shrine

Qukah Nata Shrine

Yah Rin Shrine

Kah Yah Shrine

Muwo Jeem Shrine

I

III

II

Lurelin Village

Yambi Lake

IV

WHAT'S FOR DINNER?

1 Speak to Kiana outside her house at Lurelin Village during the day.

2 To make seafood paella, she needs goat butter (which you can buy from a general store in Rito Village or Kakariko Village) and a hearty blueshell snail (which you can find on the village's beaches). If you struggle with the hearty blueshell snail, select it as the target of your Sheikah Sensor (Ⓨ while on the map screen) to make the process easier. You will get a **silver rupee** as a reward for your efforts.

II SUNKEN TREASURE

1 Speak to Rozel in Lurelin Village. He is often encountered on the pier or outside his home. The quest begins after you ask him "about the ocean."

2 To reach the desired location with Rozel's raft, you will need a Korok leaf. If you do not have one with you, consider warping back to the Great Plateau. You will find a Korok leaf on the northeast shore of the River of the Dead. If you have already been to the Korok Forest, you can also find multiple Korok leaves there.

3 Once you have a Korok leaf, step on Rozel's raft, sever the rope anchoring it to the pier, then start propelling air towards the sail. Your goal is to reach the three small rocks jutting out of the water to the south.

4 Stop the raft in the middle of the triangle formed by the three rocks and activate Magnesis. You will notice multiple submerged treasure chests: grab them with Magnesis and pull them back to your position. You will obtain, among other rewards, a **thunderblade** and multiple **gemstones**. Toss the chests back in the water once you're done and report to Rozel to complete the quest.

III TAKE BACK THE SEA

1 Speak to Sebasto, a fisherman found on the Lurelin Village beach during the day. He will ask you to defeat a group of monsters on Aris Beach to the west.

2 A waypoint will guide you to the correct location if you select this as your active quest. Try to eliminate at least some of the archers from a distance with arrows, then make your approach from the west, where you will find sea level access to the various wooden platforms. Take the remaining monsters down one by one. If one of them should fall into the water, you must finish it off: your objective is only complete once all hostiles have been dispatched. Once the task is done, report to Sebasto to receive a **silver rupee**.

IV A GIFT OF NIGHTSHADE

1 Speak to Wabbin at the south tip of the heart-shaped pond on Tuft Mountain. He requires a blue nightshade to declare his love to the nearby Gerudo lady. Note that there are multiple hearty radishes in the area, which can be a great way to fill your inventory with powerful restorative items if you cook them one by one.

2 You can find a blue nightshade very close to here: head west and glide across Yambi Lake. You will find two of these flowers on the west shore. There are several more at the south end of the lake. Give the flower to Wabbin, then agree to offer it to the woman for him. Once the two meet, you will be rewarded with a **red rupee** and a **silver rupee**.

V THUNDER MAGNET

1 Talk to Cima at the Lakeside Stable, a short distance to the southeast of Faron Tower. Your mission is to investigate why the stable is frequently struck by lightning.

2 Climb the long ladder to reach the lookout platform. From here, glide to the stable's rooftop, then climb either side of the horse head structure. Once at the top, you will notice an axe. Pick it up, then report to Cima to receive the **rubber helm**, a helmet with shock resistance properties.

LAKE TOWER REGION

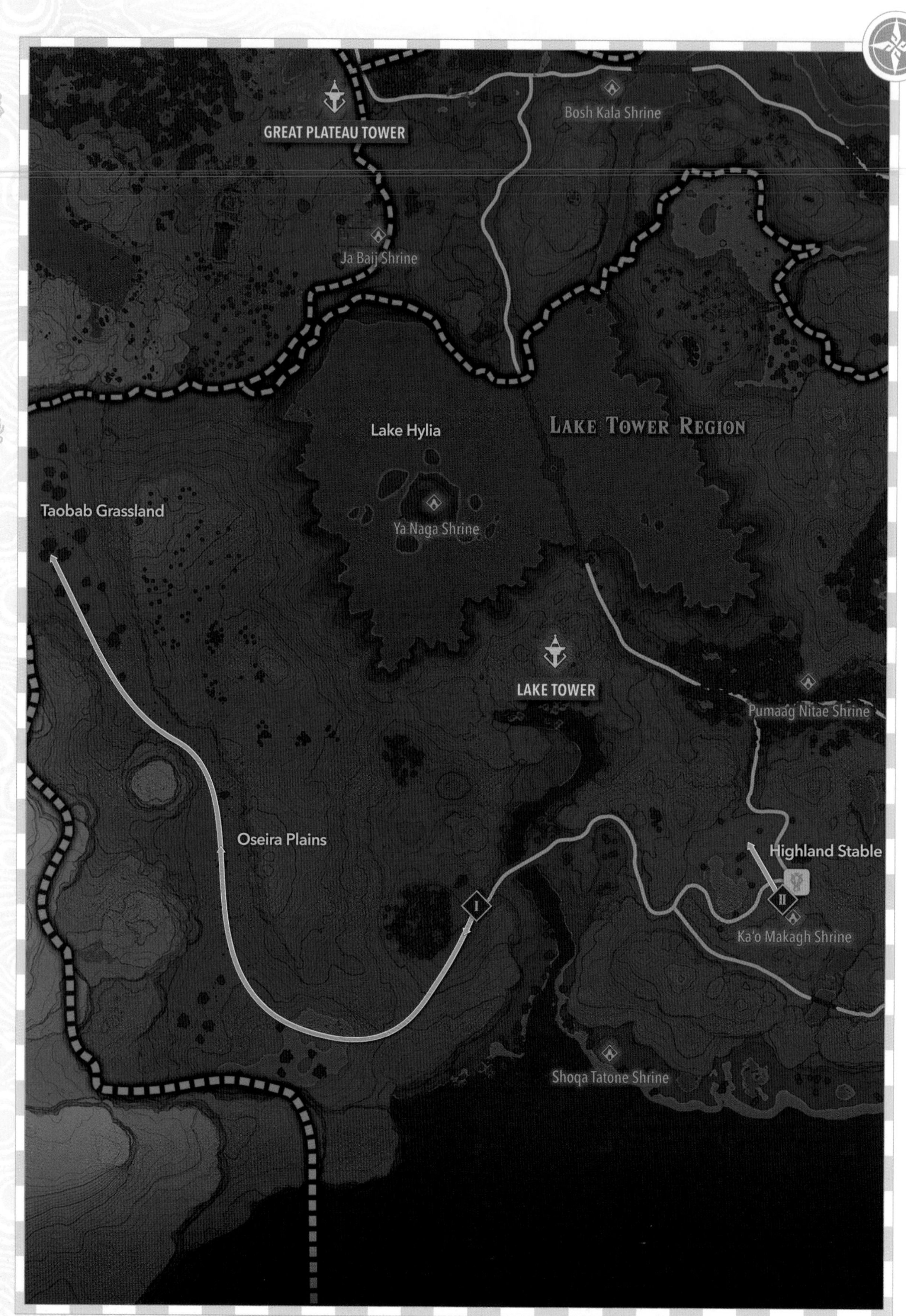

I HUNT FOR THE GIANT HORSE

1 Head to the Mounted Archery Camp, a short distance to the northwest of the mouth of the Menoat River. Speak to Straia, who will ask you to capture a giant horse.

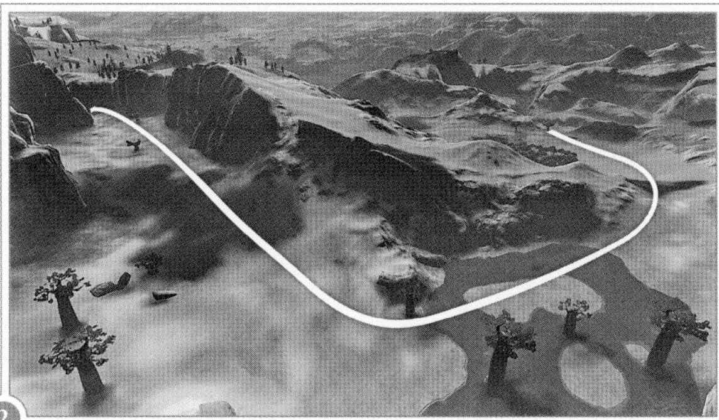

2 Now travel to Taobab Grassland, to the northwest of your current position and west of Lake Hylia. A waypoint will lead you there if you select this as your active quest. The easiest path is through the Oseira Plains to the west. As you proceed through this area you will encounter two high-level Lynels. If you are sufficiently strong and confident enough to defeat them, do so: not only will you obtain valuable item drops, you will also greatly simplify your return journey.

3 Once at Taobab Grassland, look for a very large horse. You can capture it in the standard fashion, though this one is warier and will require you to crouch-walk at the slowest possible speed over the final yards of your approach, tilting Ⓛ very gently. If you struggle, consider consuming food or equipping armor that provides a stealth effect. Once you mount the horse, press L repeatedly to soothe it. You may need more than two circles of a stamina wheel to prevent the animal from dislodging Link, so have food with stamina restoration properties at the ready. Once the horse is calm, retrace your steps and take the giant horse back to Straia. If you did not eliminate the two Lynels on your way here, you must move at full speed and do your utmost to avoid them. If you save beforehand, you can always retry should things go awry – but, ideally, defeating the Lynels in advance is the best option. When you show the animal to Straia (ZL + Ⓐ), he will reward you with a **silver rupee**. Note that you can register the giant horse if you wish to keep the mighty steed: it has a prodigious strength stat, at the expense of the ability to gallop.

II THE HORSEBACK HOODLUMS

1 Talk to Perosa at the Highland Stable, which is located to the southeast of Lake Tower. She will ask you to eliminate a gang of miscreants who have taken over the area.

2 The five Bokoblins in question are just outside the stable. As they are riding horses, you should ideally be on horseback too. Arrows work very well to take them down from a distance. If you opt for melee combat, wield a long spear to benefit from its superior range. Once all five are dead, return to Perosa to receive an **endura carrot**.

WASTELAND TOWER REGION

SIDE QUEST OVERVIEW (WALKTHROUGHS OVERLEAF)

ICON	NAME	PAGE
I	GOOD-SIZED HORSE	250
II	MISSING IN ACTION	250
III	RUSHROOM RUSH!	250
IV	AN ICE GUY	251
V	TOOLS OF THE TRADE	251
VI	THE SECRET CLUB'S SECRET	251
VII	MEDICINAL MOLDUGA	252
VIII	THE EIGHTH HEROINE	252
IX	THE FORGOTTEN SWORD	252
X	THE THUNDER HELM	253
XI	THE MYSTERY POLLUTER	253
XII	THE SEARCH FOR BARTA	253

INCLEMENT CONDITIONS

The Wasteland region features freezing nights (Level 1 cold resistance will suffice), and sweltering days. In the center of the desert (Gerudo Town and its general vicinity), Level 1 heat resistance is perfectly adequate. In the more remote areas (such as the far south, southwest, and west), Level 2 heat resistance is required to avoid deleterious effects.

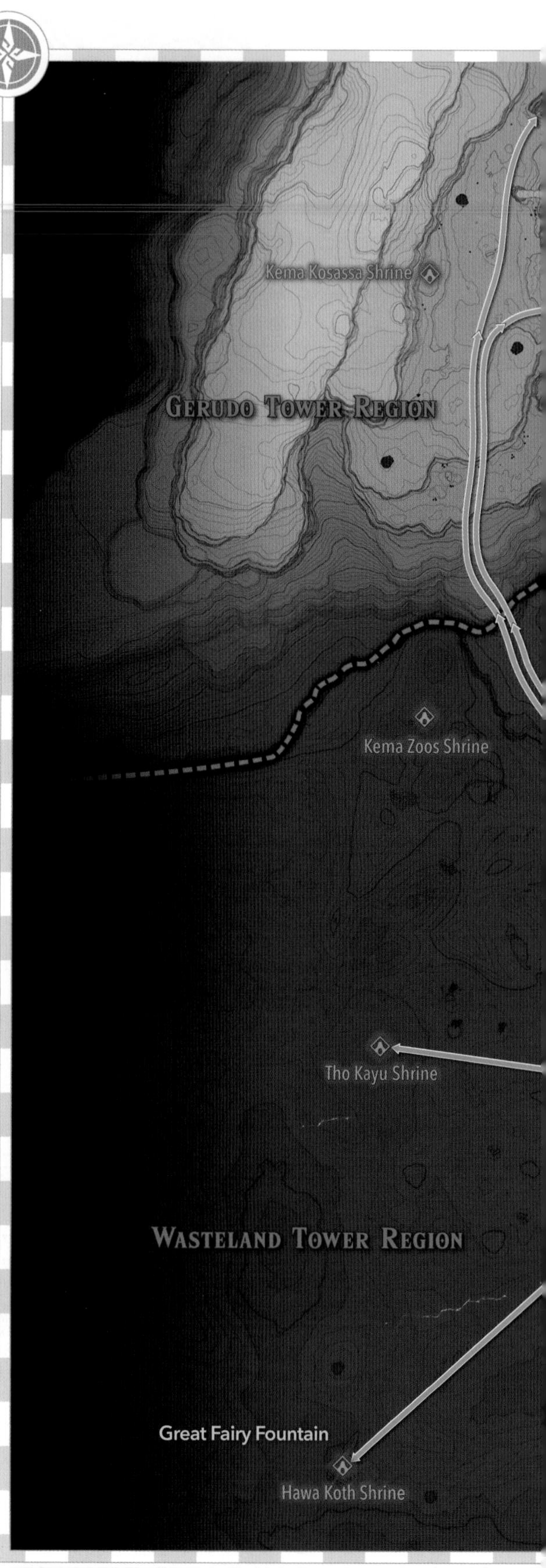

Mogg Latan Shrine
Keeha Yoog Shrine
Gerudo Summit
Kuh Takkar Shrine
Outskirt Stable
Rota Ooh Shrine
Yiga Clan Hideout
Sho Dantu Shrine
Joloo Nah Shrine
Dah Kaso Shrine
GERUDO TOWER
I
Keh Namut Shrine
Sasa Kai Shrine
Gerudo Canyon Stable
II
III
Dako Tah Shrine
Kay Noh Shrine
Jee Noh Shrine
Kara Kara Bazaar
WASTELAND TOWER
IV
Daqo Chisay Shrine
VIII
VII
IX
XII
XI
V
Gerudo Town
VII
XII
X
VI
Raqa Zunzo Shrine
Suma Sahma Shrine
Dila Maag Shrine
Gerudo Town
Misae Suma Shrine

I GOOD-SIZED HORSE

Speak to Zyle in the Gerudo Canyon, between Koukot Plateau and Mount Nabooru. He will ask you to bring him any horse that would be suitable for a man of his stature. If you have a spare registered horse of standard size, summon it from the Gerudo Canyon Stable and take it to Zyle; otherwise, warp to the Dueling Peaks Stable and capture any wild horse in the vicinity, then register it. Warp back to the Gerudo Canyon Stable and ride this new mount to Zyle's position. Should he approve, he will buy it from you for **300 rupees**.

II MISSING IN ACTION

Speak to Sesami at the Gerudo Canyon Stable. He will ask you to find four of his friends in the Koukot Plateau area: Oliff, Flaxel, Canolo, and Palme. All four can be found on the elevated ledges built on the cliffs of the canyon to the north of Koukot Plateau (north of Wasteland Tower).

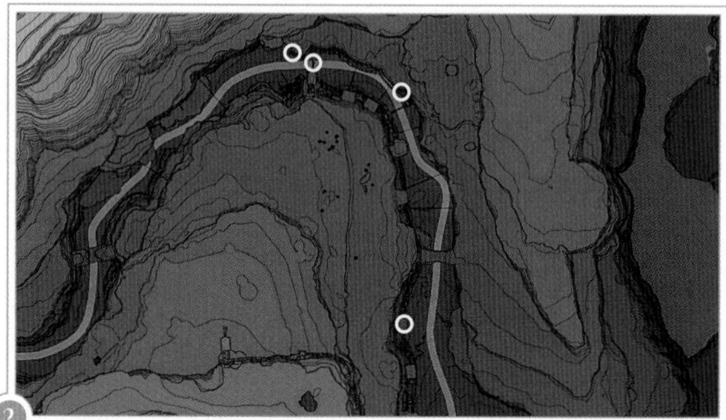

The positions of all four targets are shown on the above map. You will generally need to eliminate all enemies in the area before you can speak to the person that needs to be rescued.

Oliff, Flaxel, and Canolo are all on the wooden walkways close to the waypoint marker that appears on the in-game map if you select this as your active mission.

Palme is located on a wooden walkway a little further to the south. Once you have rescued all four, return to Sesami to receive a **gold rupee**.

III RUSHROOM RUSH!

Speak to Pirou at the Gerudo Canyon Stable between 8:00AM and 3:00AM. He will require 55 rushrooms, the purple fungi that grows on cliffs. This is a long-term quest that you can complete by gradually accumulating rushrooms during your travels. Once you make your way to the Korok Forest you can actually buy four rushrooms for 12 rupees apiece, which can save you a little time and effort. These are renewed as time goes by, so occasionally warping to the Korok Forest will enable you to increase your stocks at regular intervals in order to close this quest at a fairly early stage in the adventure. Your reward for delivering 55 of them to Pirou is a **diamond** found in a treasure chest at the back of the stable.

IV AN ICE GUY

1

Speak to Guy at Kara Kara Bazar. He needs a chilly elixir, which you can cook by combining a winterwing butterfly and a monster part (such as a Bokoblin horn). The insects are common in the Gerudo Canyon and on the high plateaus surrounding Wasteland Tower. Cook the elixir then give it to Guy and he will reward you with a **purple rupee**.

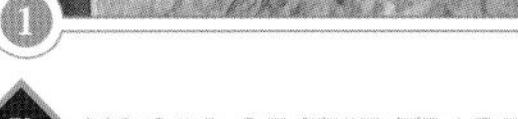

V TOOLS OF THE TRADE

1 Speak to Isha in Gerudo Town, outside the Jewelry shop. She requires 10 pieces of flint to reopen her shop.

2 Flint is a relatively common resource that you can obtain at random by destroying ore deposits in mountainous regions. As a rule, the Eldin region is a good place to farm these stones.

3

When you supply the requested pieces of flint to Isha, she will reopen her Jewelry shop, in which you can buy head accessories that offer special effects. To thank you, she will offer you a choice of the following three items:

- **Ruby circlet** (grants cold resistance: this can be useful when combined with the warm doublet for going through the Gerudo Highlands unharmed if you haven't yet purchased the snowquill set from Rito Village)
- **Sapphire circlet** (grants heat resistance: useful to survive in the desert until you acquire either of the Gerudo outfits)
- **Topaz earrings** (grants electric resistance: potentially useful against the Divine Beast Vah Naboris boss)

VI THE SECRET CLUB'S SECRET

1 If you examine the back door of Gerudo Town's armor shop, to the southeast of the premises, you will be asked for a password. Failing to provide the correct code will trigger this quest, and means that you must wait until the next day before you can make a new attempt.

2 To learn the password you must surreptitiously listen in on the conversation that the women are having at the bar in the north part of town. First, talk to these women to trigger the conversation, then head to the adjacent building (where Rotana is reading a book) and eavesdrop on them through the window. You will hear that the required code is: GSC◆ (which stands for "Gerudo Secret Club"). If a sufficient period of time since your original attempt has elapsed, you can now return to the secret door with the password to gain entry. This will give you access to a **new clothes shop** where you can purchase the radiant and desert voe outfits.

VII MEDICINAL MOLDUGA

1 Speak to Malena, who can usually be found in the courtyard where the soldiers train (in the west corner of Gerudo Town) or in front of Riju's mansion.

2 The Molduga guts she requires are dropped by the Molduga sub-boss type. The one closest to your position roams the Toruma Dunes, to the west of Gerudo Town. To defeat it, stand on a rock or ledge (in short: anything but sand), and throw a round bomb in its direction. When it emerges from the sand to swallow the explosive, detonate it. You can then follow up with extended combos, then sprint back to safety and repeat. Turn to page 318 for additional advice if required. Take the Molduga guts back to Malena to receive a **gold rupee**.

VIII THE EIGHTH HEROINE

1 Once you have bought the Gerudo outfit from Vilia during the main quest, equip it and speak to Bozai, a man who jogs around Gerudo Town. If you ask for his boots, you can trigger the quest and borrow his snow boots to help you to achieve the necessary goal.

2 The statue he sends you after can be found in the Gerudo Highlands, to the northwest of the Gerudo Summit. The statue is most easily reached from the snowfield above, though there are updrafts that will take you to it from below if you happen to fall or approach from the north. Stand on the statue's joined hands to photograph its torso (or take a picture of its entire body, if you prefer), then show the picture to Bozai to receive the **sand boots**, which enable you to maintain your normal movement speed on sand.

IX THE FORGOTTEN SWORD

1 After completing "The Eighth Heroine," equip the Gerudo outfit and speak to Bozai again, who can now be found under a canopy close to Gerudo Town's main entrance. This time he needs you to photograph the lost sword of the statue from his previous quest.

2 The sword lies at the top of the Gerudo Summit, at the heart of the Gerudo Highlands. Take a picture of it and show this to Bozai to obtain the **snow boots**, which enable you to maintain your normal movement speed on deep snow.

X THE THUNDER HELM

After clearing the Divine Beast Vah Naboris dungeon, interact with the **Thunder Helm** next to Riju inside her mansion. She will give it to you once you have completed the following side quests in Gerudo Town: Tools of the Trade, Medicinal Molduga, The Mystery Polluter, and The Search for Barta.

XI THE MYSTERY POLLUTER

After clearing the Divine Beast Vah Naboris dungeon and beginning Riju's quest ("The Thunder Helm"), speak to Dalia, who is found in the northern corner of Gerudo Town during the day. She will ask you to ascertain who is polluting her water source.

Head to the town's west corner and make your way to the rooftops. Talk to Calyban, a woman eating melons. She will stop polluting the water if you supply her with 10 wildberries.

The closest location where you can acquire wildberries is on the snowfields of the Gerudo Highlands. The plateau directly north of the Gerudo Tower, to the west of Sapphia's Table, features a few trees: you will find well over 10 wildberries at this site alone. There are also many wildberries around the Rito Stable, which is very convenient if you can warp to it. Take them back to Calyban, then report to Dalia to be rewarded with a **hydromelon**.

XII THE SEARCH FOR BARTA

After clearing the Divine Beast Vah Naboris dungeon and starting Riju's quest ("The Thunder Helm"), speak to Liana, the woman conducting a training session in the courtyard in the west corner of Gerudo Town. If you do not have a hearty durian in your inventory, purchase one before you set out.

Head to the Gerudo Great Skeleton, in the far southwest of the region, and you will find Barta under the fossil's head. You will need Level 2 heat resistance here, which you can trigger with food and/or clothes. Give her a hearty durian to save her, then return to Liana. She will thank you with a **silver rupee**.

TABANTHA TOWER REGION

SIDE QUEST OVERVIEW (WALKTHROUGHS OVERLEAF)

ICON	NAME	PAGE
I	CURRY FOR WHAT AILS YOU	See overleaf
II	THE APPLE OF MY EYE	
III	THE SPARK OF ROMANCE	
IV	FACE THE FROST TALUS	
V	FIND KHEEL	

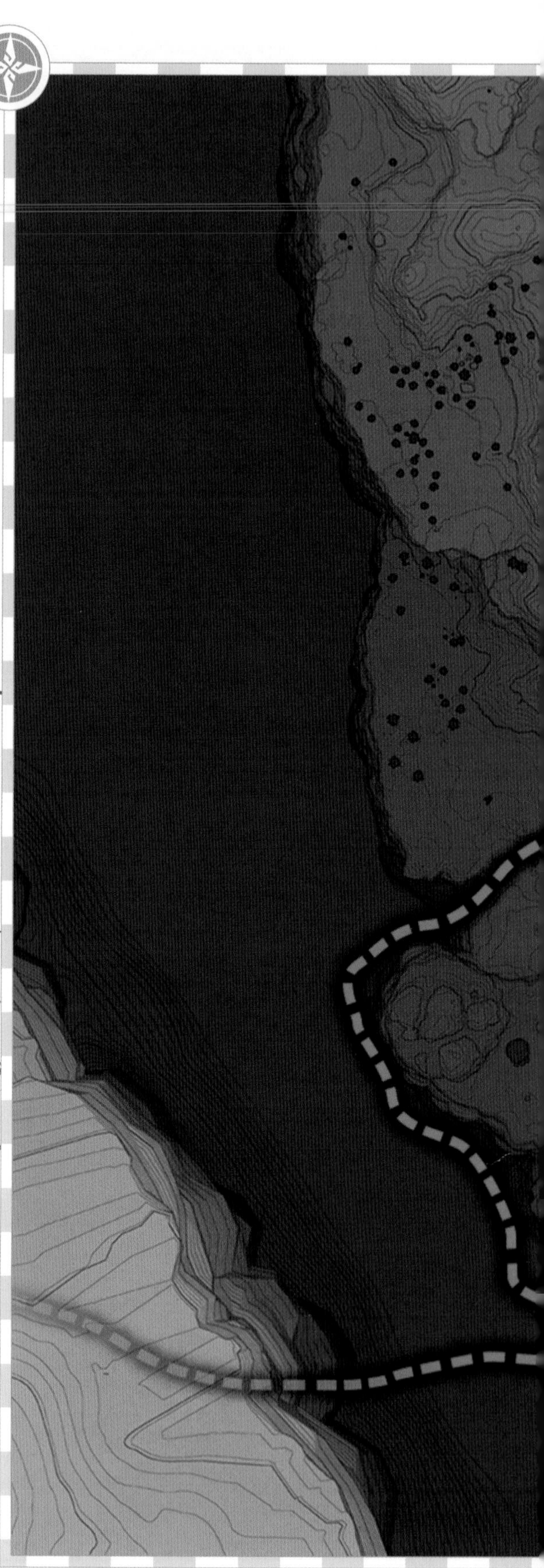

Mozo Shenno Shrine
Coldsnap Hollow
Hebra Tower Region
Maka Rah Shrine
Flight Range
Sha Warvo Shrine
III
II
IV
I
V
Rito Village
Rito Stable
Akh Va'quot Shrine
Voo Lota Shrine
Bareeda Naag Shrine
Tabantha Tower Region

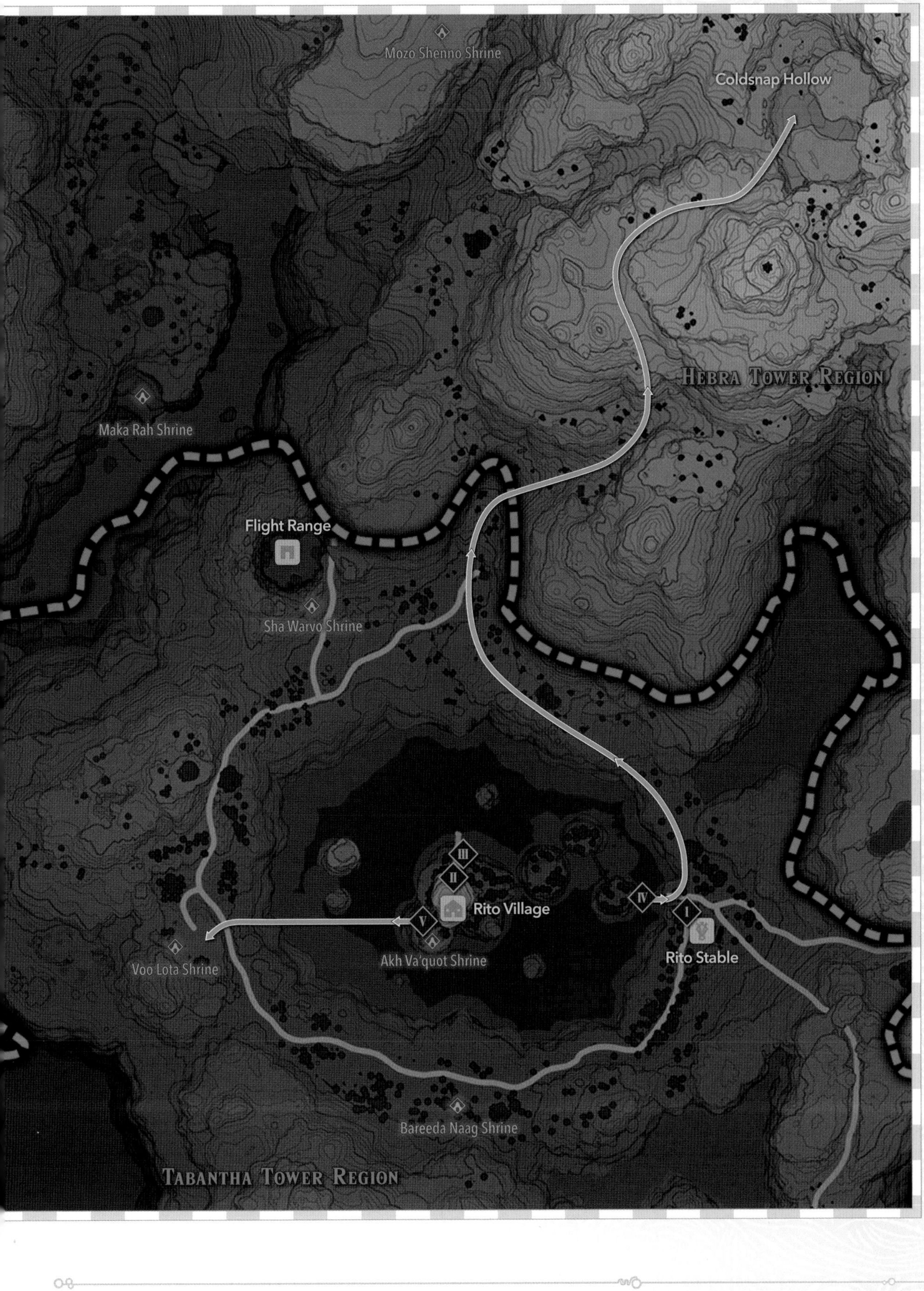

I CURRY FOR WHAT AILS YOU

1 Lester, a man found close to the cooking pot at the Rito Stable, will ask you to find Goron spice for him.

2 This ingredient can be purchased in Goron City's general store. Deliver it to Lester and he will reward you with a **purple rupee**. After you complete the quest, he will trade in Goron spice for Hylian rice.

II THE APPLE OF MY EYE

1 Speak to Juney, who is found next to Kaneli's hut in Rito Village during the day. She requires a baked apple – an item that you may well have in your inventory, enabling you to complete the quest instantly.

2 If you do not have any at hand, find a raw apple and drop it by a campfire: it will soon turn into a baked apple. Deliver it to Juney and she will reward you with a **silver rupee**. You can continue to turn in baked apples to Juney after completing this quest: her payments are initially small but they increase gradually.

III THE SPARK OF ROMANCE

1 Speak to Jogo during the day, inside Rito Village's inn. He needs some flint – an item that you are likely to have in your inventory.

2 If you have yet to acquire pieces of flint, note that they will appear randomly when you destroy ore deposits in mountainous regions. The Eldin region is a particularly good place to farm for it. Give a single piece to Jogo to obtain a **silver rupee**. You can continue to turn in flint to Jogo after completing this quest to receive small (but increasing) rupee payments.

IV FACE THE FROST TALUS

1 After completing the Divine Beast Vah Medoh dungeon, speak to Gesane, the Rito patrolling on the first wooden bridge leading to Rito Village. He will ask you to destroy a Frost Talus.

2 Head to Coldsnap Hollow, at the heart of the Hebra Mountains to the north. A waypoint will guide you there if you select this as your active quest. The Frost Talus will freeze you if you come into contact with it. You have two options to prevent this: you can use fire arrows or fire-infused weapons to heat the sub-boss up, before attacking it as usual and climbing on its back to strike its weak point, or you can equip a complete snowquill armor set upgraded at least twice via great fairies to trigger the unfreezable effect (which removes the need to heat up your enemy). Report to Gesane after you defeat the creature to receive a **silver rupee**.

V FIND KHEEL

1 After completing the Divine Beast Vah Medoh dungeon, speak to Amali, next to Rito Village's shrine. She will ask you to find Kheel.

2 Kheel is waiting for her sisters at Warbler's Nest, to the west of Rito Village. After speaking to her, report to Amali back in Rito Village and she will give you a **purple rupee**.

Hebra Tower Region

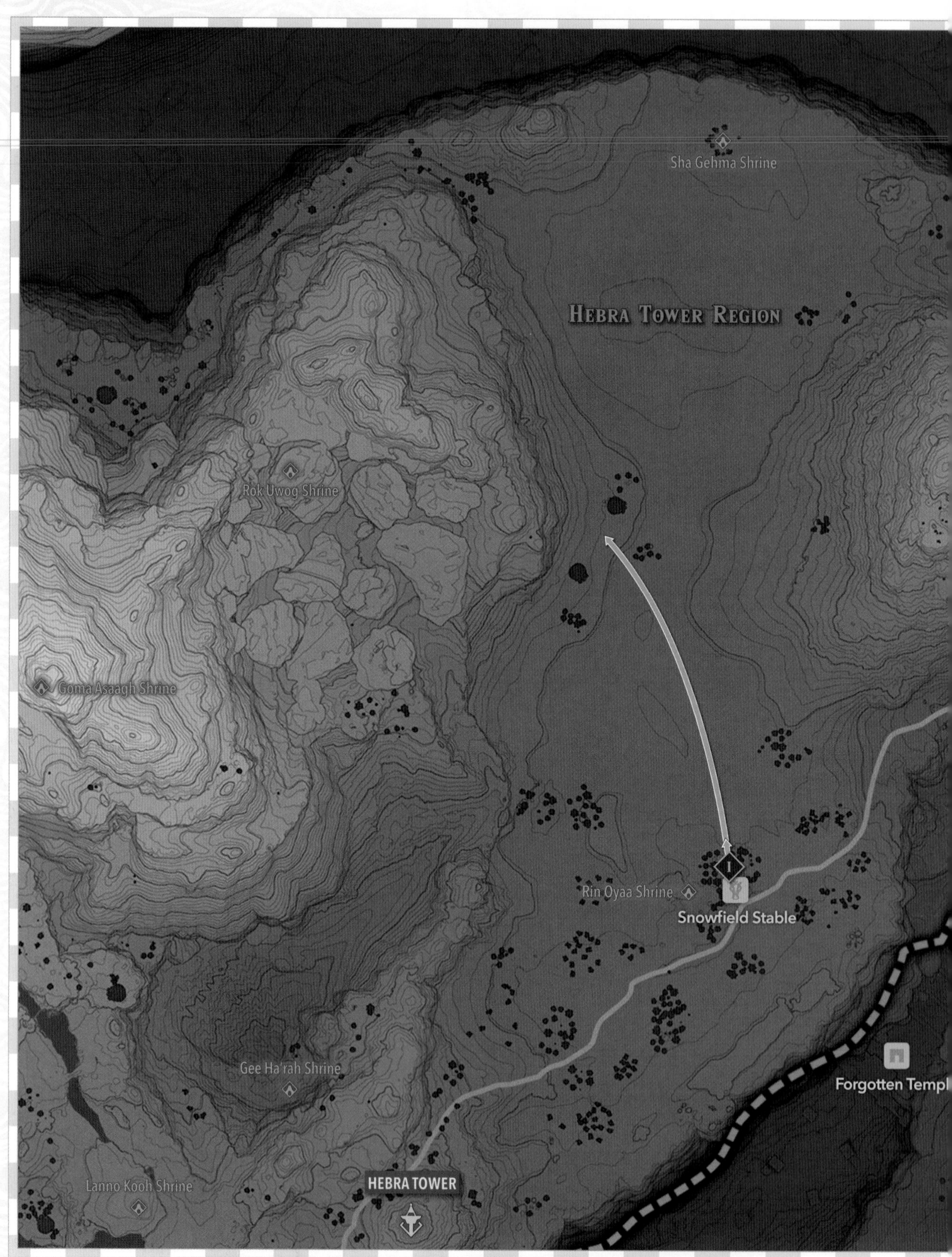

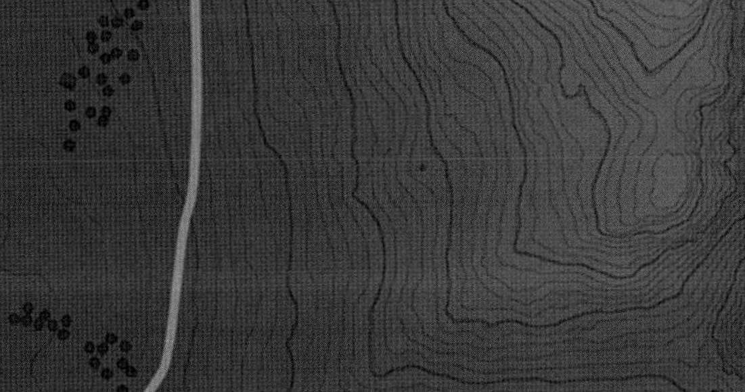

I STALHORSE: PICTURED!

1 Speak to Juannelle at the Snowfield Stable. She wants to see what a Stalhorse looks like.

2 Wait until evening (sitting by a fire to pass time, if required), then head to the north until you have an enemy outpost consisting of two skull-shaped huts in sight. You will soon see a Stalhorse ridden by a Stalkoblin. Take a picture of it with the camera, then show this to Juannelle to obtain a **silver rupee**. Note that the Stalhorse can actually be mounted, but can't be registered at a stable.

GLACIAL TEMPERATURES

The Hebra region is extremely chilly, so you will need Level 2 cold resistance to survive the punishing conditions. Furthermore, many enemies in this region have attacks that can freeze you. You can prevent this by wearing the complete snowquill armor set upgraded at least twice by great fairies: this will grant you the unfreezable effect.

Woodland Tower Region

SIDE QUEST OVERVIEW (WALKTHROUGHS OVERLEAF)

ICON	NAME	PAGE
I	BALLOON FLIGHT	262
II	A FREEZING ROD	262
III	THE KOROK TRIALS	263
IV	LEGENDARY RABBIT TRIAL	263
V	LEVIATHAN BONES	264
VI	A GIFT FROM THE MONKS	264
VII	RIDDLES OF HYRULE	265

Woodland Tower Region
Ketoh Wawai Shrine
VII
IV
III
II
Keo Ruug Shrine
Korok Forest
Shora Hah Shrine
Abandoned North Mine
Shae Mo'sah Shrine
Goron City
Daag Chokah Shrine
Maag Halan Shrine
Korok Forest
Keo Ruug Shrine
Southern Mine
Kuhn Sidajj Shrine
The Lost Woods
WOODLAND TOWER
Qua Raym Shrine
Mirro Shaz Shrine
Woodland Stable
I
Saas Ko'sah Shrine
Namika Ozz Shrine
Hyrule Castle

BALLOON FLIGHT

1 Speak to Shamae during the day at the Woodland Stable to trigger this quest.

2 Drop two octo balloons on one of the barrels in front of Shamae. You can obtain octo balloons by defeating any Octorok; you can find some in Pico Pond, right by the stable. It's possible to fix two balloons on a barrel simultaneously, but you can also drop them one after the other. The quest will be completed when the barrel flies high in the air. Shamae will reward you with a **star fragment**.

A FREEZING ROD

After initiating the The Hero's Sword main quest, speak to Kula in Korok Forest. He can usually be found walking in the area where the Master Sword initially rests. He requires an ice-infused rod.

1

2 You can obtain an Ice Rod from an Ice Wizzrobe. One of these creatures roams on the road between Lanayru Tower and the Foothill Stable; another convenient specimen can sometimes be found floating around the Kuh Takaar Shrine in the Gerudo Highlands. Delivering an Ice Rod to Kula leads to a **silver rupee** reward.

3 Alternatively, you can retrieve a Blizzard Rod from a Blizzrobe. The closest one to your current position is located in one in the round structures at Crenel Hills, to the east of Hyrule Castle. Securing this weapon for Kula will lead to the upgraded reward of a **gold rupee**.

III THE KOROK TRIALS

1 After initiating the The Hero's Sword main quest, speak to Chio in the Korok Forest, near the entrance leading to the local shops. He will challenge you to complete three trials. These are actually shrine quests, which we cover in the Shrines chapter. Return to Chio after you have cleared all three to obtain your reward: three **big hearty truffles**.

2 **The Lost Pilgrimage:** This is triggered by speaking to Tasho at the northwest exit of the Korok Forest. Your objective is to tail a small Korok called Oaki without being detected: see page 196 for guidance.

3 **Trial of Second Sight:** Go through the southwestern exit of the Korok Forest and speak to Zooki. Your task is to find your way through the fog by using Magnesis to intuit clues from the environment. See page 197 for details.

4 **The Test of Wood:** Speak to Damia at the eastern exit of the Korok Forest. Your goal is to reach the shrine at the back of the area without breaking a single piece of the equipment given to you by Damia. You can find a walkthrough for this challenge on page 198.

IV LEGENDARY RABBIT TRIAL

1 After initiating The Hero's Sword (main quest) and The Priceless Maracas (side quest), speak to Peeks in the Korok Forest. He can usually be found roaming outside or inside the Great Deku Tree.

2 Peeks requires a picture of a Blupee – a glowing rabbit-like creature occasionally encountered in forests at night. The best location to find one is at the top of Satori Mountain, in the south part of the Ridgeland Tower region. You will find a small pond there where Blupees often gather around the mysterious Lord of the Mountain; this only happens when a large glow visible from a great distance highlights this location, though. Take a photograph of one of them and show it to Peeks to receive a **silver rupee**.

V LEVIATHAN BONES

1 Speak to the researchers at the Serenne Stable, who will request that you supply them with photographs of Leviathan skulls.

2 One Leviathan is located close to the Great Fairy Fountain to the southwest of Gerudo Town.

3 You can find another at the northern edge of the Eldin region, in the East Deplian Badlands.

4 The final Leviathan is also the hardest. It is hidden inside the ice cave featuring the To Quomo Shrine in the Hebra North Summit region (see page 189). Once you have photographs of all three skulls, show them to the researchers to receive a **gold rupee**.

VI A GIFT FROM THE MONKS

1 When you complete the final, 120th shrine by interacting with its altar, you will trigger this quest. You will be told that a reward awaits you at the Forgotten Temple. This is a secret landmark found at the north end of the Tanagar Canyon.

2 The Forgotten Temple is guarded by numerous Decayed Guardians. Unless you're willing to destroy them all by redirecting their laser beams, the easiest solution is to speed through the entire location, using the updrafts to remain airborne most of the time. If you remain at maximum velocity throughout, all enemy shots should miss. When required, make small lateral adjustments to avoid shots fired from behind. Your reward is no less than the **"of the Wild" armor set** (Cap of the Wild, Tunic of the Wild, Trousers of the Wild). You will find it at the foot of the goddess statue at the back of the local shrine.

1 If you climb to the top of the Great Deku Tree in Korok Forest, Walton will challenge you to take the ultimate trial. This is actually a series of riddles that you must decipher. Whenever you have found the solution to a riddle, drop the corresponding item on the leaf in front of Walton to proceed to the next step. If you manage to solve all riddles, Walton will reward you with a **diamond**.

2 The "small, red, round, and sweet" item Walton refers to is, of course, an apple.

3 "Kakariko Village's specialty fruit," which grows under Olkin's watchful eyes, is the fortified pumpkin. You can buy one from the old man for 20 rupees.

4 A "sultry shroom that will warm your bones" alludes to a sunshroom. Sunshrooms abound in Retsam Forest, just north of the Hateno Ancient Tech Lab.

5 A fish whose "scales and tail will zap you" is the voltfin trout. You can find specimens of this species in Lake Totori, which surrounds Rito Village, and Strock Lake. They are rather rare, though, so be patient in your search and regularly refresh your stamina by catching your breath on dry land.

6 The final item "starts with an H and ends with an oof": a Lynel hoof. This item is dropped by the fearsome Lynels. See page 328 for their locations, and page 314 for advice on how to defeat them.

Central & Ridgeland Tower Regions

SIDE QUEST OVERVIEW (WALKTHROUGHS OVERLEAF)

ICON	NAME	PAGE
I	A GIFT FOR THE GREAT FAIRY	See overleaf
II	THE ROYAL GUARD'S GEAR	
III	A RARE FIND	
IV	MY HERO	
V	A ROYAL RECIPE	
VI	THE ROYAL WHITE STALLION	

Serenne Stable
Monya Toma Shrine
WOODLAND TOWER
Mirro Shaz Shrine
Saas Ko'sah Shrine
Woodland Stable
RIDGELAND TOWER
Namika Ozz Shrine
Hyrule Castle
Zalta Wa Shrine
Noya Neha Shrine
Hyrule Castle Town Ruins
Katah Chuki Shrine
Wetland Stable
Central Tower Region
Kaya Wan Shrine
CENTRAL TOWER
Hyrule Field
Kaam Ya'tak Shrine
Safula Hill
Hila Rao Shrine
Wahgo Katta Shrine
II
III
V
Riverside Stable
Rota Ooh Shrine
VI
IV
Outskirt Stable
Dueling Peaks Tower Region
Oman Au Shrine
DUELING PEAKS TOWER
Great Plateau Tower Region
Bosh Kala Shrine
Dah Kaso Shrine
GREAT PLATEAU TOWER
Ree Dahee Shrine
Shee Venath Shrine
Shrine of Resurrection
Shee Vaneer Shrine
Keh Namut Shrine
Ja Baij Shrine

I A GIFT FOR THE GREAT FAIRY

1 Speak to Toren at the Tabantha Bridge Stable, at the west edge of the Ridgeland region. He will give you **500 rupees** and ask you to find a Great Fairy Fountain for him by climbing the Tabantha Tower and locating the fountain by using the tower's afternoon shadow.

2 The fountain is located to the south of Tabantha Tower, at the base of Piper Ridge. It is in the small pond that is visible on your map. Report back to Toren when you're done to complete the assignment.

II THE ROYAL GUARD'S GEAR

1 Speak to Parcy at the Riverside Stable. She will ask you to find an item of the royal guard series.

2 This requires a visit to Hyrule Castle. You can find a royal guard's sword behind a doorway blocked by destructible rocks, in the corridor to the left when you reach the top of the stairs after visiting the armory (see step 9 on page 106 for details). After completing the quest, you can keep trading in items of this series for gems by speaking to Parcy, if you wish.

III A RARE FIND

1 Speak to Trott at the Outskirt Stable. He needs raw gourmet meat to feel more energized. This is an ingredient that you can obtain from various large mammals, including wolves, bears, buffalos, and rhinos. A single piece is enough to sate Trott's appetite, who will reward you with a **silver rupee**. Note that Trott will continue to buy raw gourmet meat for 100 rupees after you have completed this quest.

IV MY HERO

1 Speak to Aliza, under one of the trees surrounding the Outskirt Stable. All you need to complete this quest is to show her the Master Sword (see page 100). She will then recognize you as the hero and reward you with a **star fragment**.

V A ROYAL RECIPE

1 Speak to Gotter at the Riverside Stable, in the southeast of Hyrule Field. He needs you to retrieve something from Hyrule Castle.

2 You can find two recipes in Hyrule Castle's library: one on a large wooden table on the ground floor, and another on a small bookstand on one of the upper walkways.

3 The two recipes are as follows:

- **Fruitcake:** two or three pieces of fruit of different varieties (for example, an apple, a mighty banana, and a wildberry), tabantha wheat, and cane sugar.
- **Monster cake:** monster extract (available from Kilton, or as a gift from a traveler assailed by monsters in Hyrule Field), tabantha wheat, goat butter, and cane sugar.

Cook either of them for Gotter and he will reward you with a **silver rupee.** Prepare and deliver the other cake to obtain another silver rupee if you wish. Note that Tabantha wheat, goat butter, and cane sugar can all be purchased at Rito Village.

VI THE ROYAL WHITE STALLION

1 Speak to Toffa at the Outskirt Stable, in the far southwest of the Central Tower region. He asks you to find a specific white horse.

2 Head to Safula Hill, across the river to the northwest, where the horse in question roams.

3 You can tame it in the same way as any other horse, though it is extremely vigilant: you will need to crouch-walk at the slowest possible speed over the final yards of your approach. If you struggle, consider consuming food or equipping armor that confers a stealth effect. Once you mount the horse, press L repeatedly to soothe it. You might need over two circle's worth of stamina wheel to prevent the animal from throwing you aside; use food that restores stamina if required. Once it is calm, take it back to the stable to register it – and, incidentally, gaze in awe at its stats. You can now speak to Toffa again while riding the horse to receive your reward: the **royal saddle** and **royal bridle**.

Eldin Tower Region

SIDE QUEST OVERVIEW

ICON	NAME	PAGE
I	FIREPROOF LIZARD ROUNDUP	See overleaf
II	THE ROAD TO RESPECT	
III	DEATH MOUNTAIN'S SECRET	
IV	THE JEWEL TRADE	

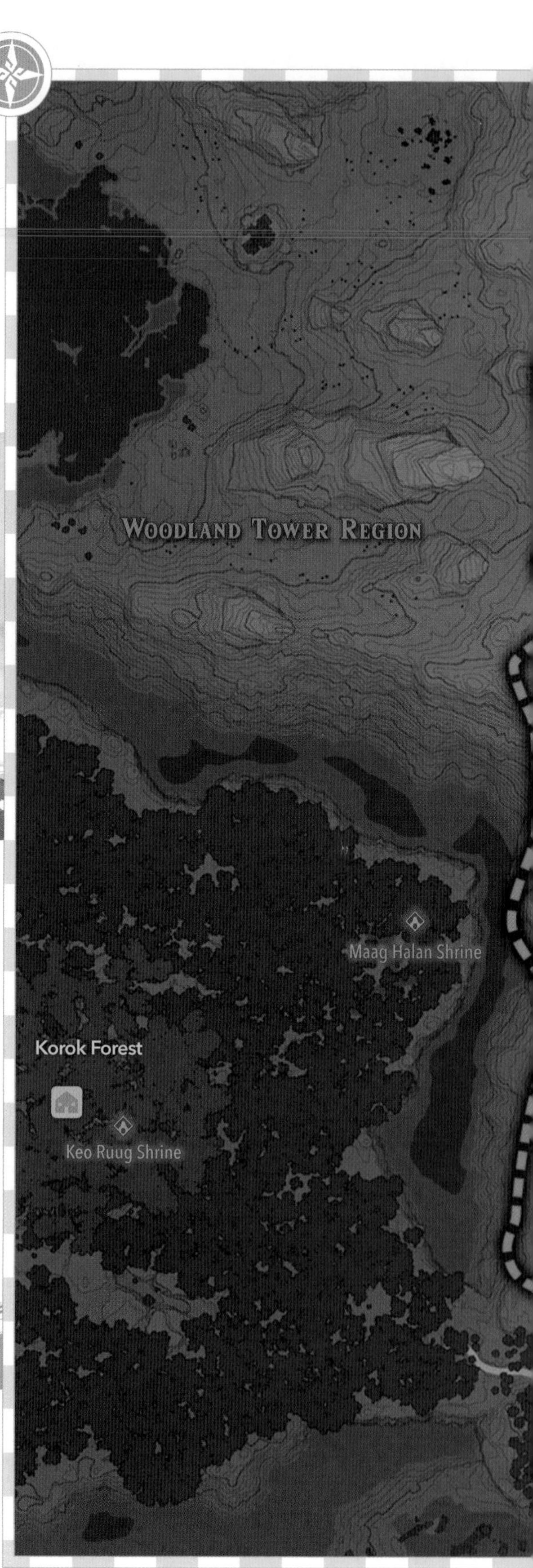

Scorching Temperatures

Link must have the flame guard effect active to survive in the harsh and unforgiving Eldin region. Level 1 is sufficient on the road leading to Goron City, but you will need Level 2 flame guard when you venture further into the territory. To enjoy complete protection against fire, you will need to wear the complete flamebreaker armor set, upgraded at least twice by great fairies: this will grant the fireproof effect.

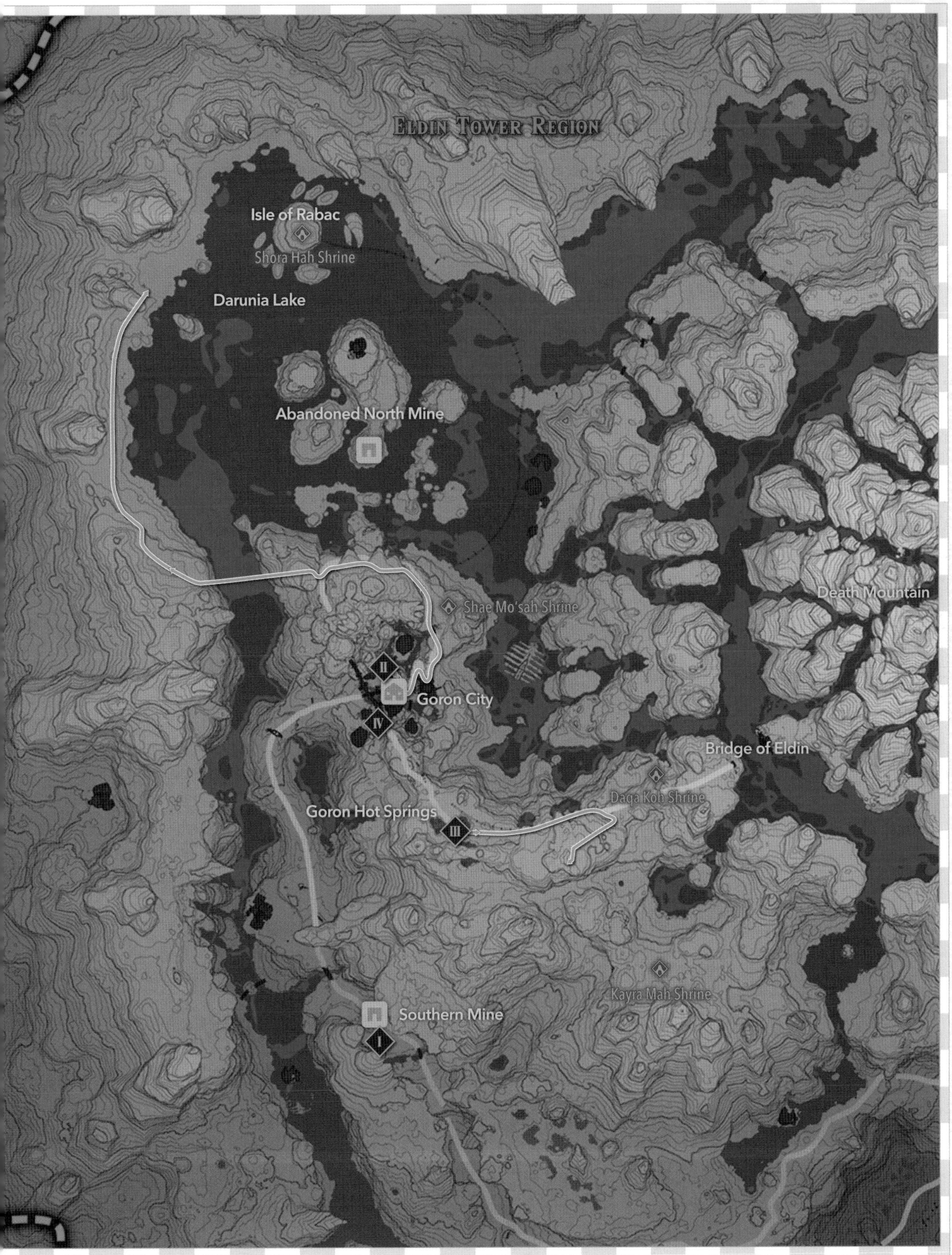

Eldin Tower Region
Isle of Rabac
Shora Hah Shrine
Darunia Lake
Abandoned North Mine
Shae Mo'sah Shrine
Death Mountain
II
Goron City
IV
Bridge of Eldin
Daqa Koh Shrine
Goron Hot Springs
III
Kayra Mah Shrine
Southern Mine
I

I FIREPROOF LIZARD ROUNDUP

1 Speak to Kima at the Southern Mine. He needs you to catch 10 fireproof lizards.

2 Fireproof lizards are relatively common in the Southern Mine area: look for them in rocky locations, such as the cliffs and ledges above the positions where the miners dig during the day. When you spot a lizard, make your approach while crouch-walking to avoid startling it. Once you meet the specified quota, Kima will reward you with the **flamebreaker armor** – a piece of chest armor that grants the flame guard effect. After you complete the quest, Kima will buy every three fireproof lizards that you bring to him for 20 rupees, though we suggest you keep them for other purposes, particularly armor upgrades.

II THE ROAD TO RESPECT

1 Speak to Fugo in Goron City. He needs you to defeat the Igneo Talus at Darunia Lake, to the northwest of the settlement.

2 Head to the northwest shore of Darunia Lake, directly west of the Isle of Rabac. During the battle, freeze the monster with any ice-infused weapon or arrow to cool it down, force a collapse with a bomb, then clamber onto its back to attack its weak point. Repeat this strategy until the creature has been defeated, then report to Fugo to obtain a **silver rupee**.

III DEATH MOUNTAIN'S SECRET

Speak to Dugby, a young Goron soaking in the Goron Hot Springs during the day, a short distance to the southeast of Goron City. Understanding his awkwardly-pronounced words isn't easy, but you should catch enough to interpret that a treasure is hidden somewhere between the Goron Hot Springs and the Bridge of Eldin. If you speak to him while is sleeping, he will give you an additional clue.

Head to the top of the middle lava waterfall, on the way to the Bridge of Eldin. You will find destructible rocks at the base of the small rock peak there. Shatter these with a bomb to find a **drillshaft** in a hiding spot. Report to Dugby to complete the mission.

IV THE JEWEL TRADE

After completing the Divine Beast Vah Rudania dungeon, speak to Ramella, a Gerudo found in Goron City. She needs 10 pieces of amber, which you will likely have in stock at this stage. If not, destroy ore deposits – which are plentiful in the region – until you meet the quota. She will pay you **500 rupees** in exchange. After you complete this quest, Ramella will continue to buy your gems, 10 at a time. The gems she asks for will vary but she will always give you more rupees than you would get by selling them at a store.

Akkala Tower Region

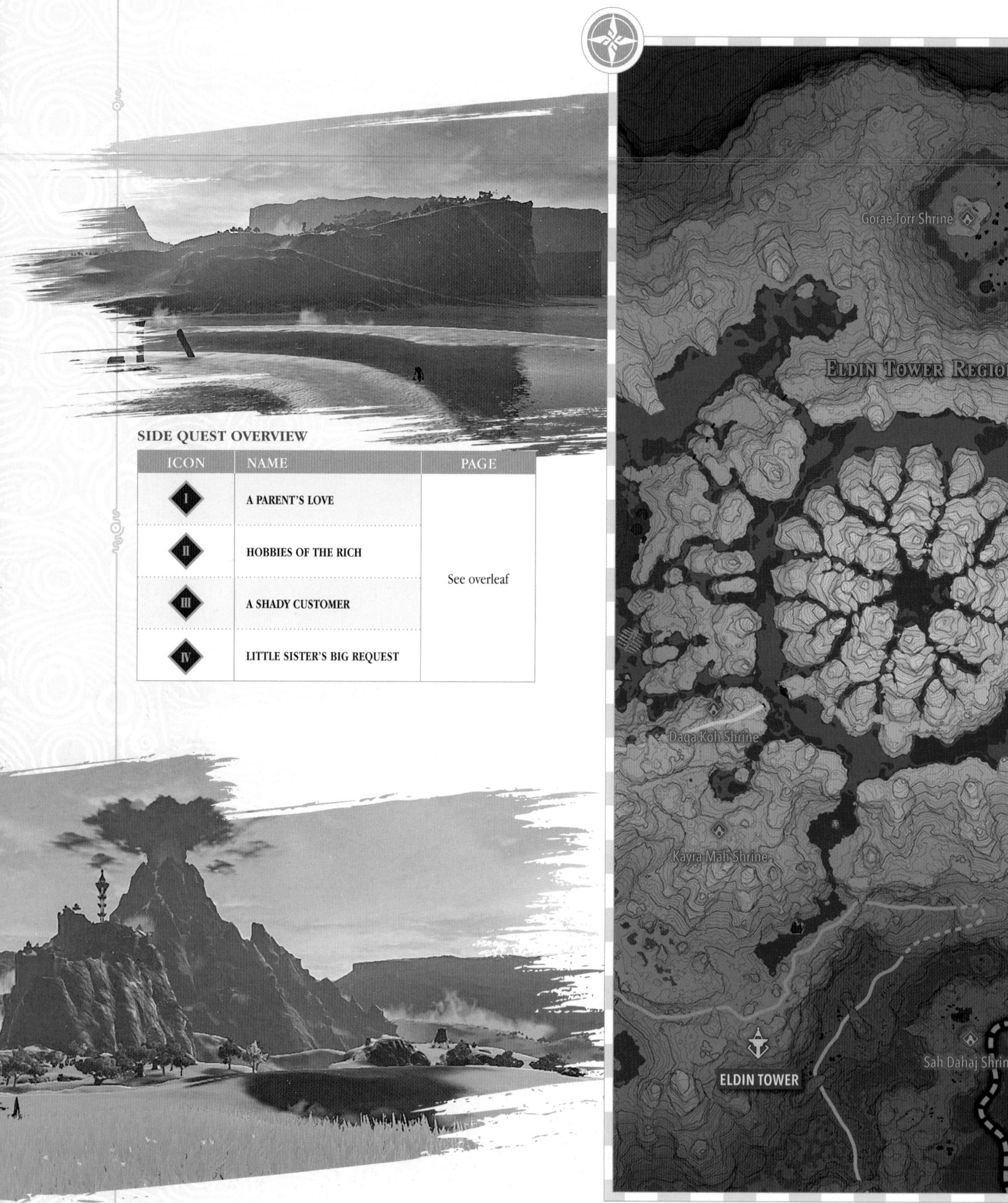

SIDE QUEST OVERVIEW

ICON	NAME	PAGE
I	A PARENT'S LOVE	See overleaf
II	HOBBIES OF THE RICH	
III	A SHADY CUSTOMER	
IV	LITTLE SISTER'S BIG REQUEST	

Tu Ka'loh Shrine

Skull Lake

Zuna Kai Shrine

Akkala Ancient Tech Lab

East Akkala Stable

III

Katosa Aug Shrine

Tutsuwa Nima Shrine

AKKALA TOWER REGION

Ritaag Zumo Shrine

South Akkala Stable

IV

Ze Kasho Shrine

Torin Wetland

Tarrey Town

II

I

AKKALA TOWER

Great Fairy Fountain

Dah Hesho Shrine

Kah Mael Shrine

1

After Hudson has founded Tarrey Town (see page 232), head to the settlement's southernmost house. Standing by the open window outside at night, from 10:00PM onwards, listen to the conversation between Ruli and her husband Hagie. This will officially trigger the quest.

2

If you have yet to meet Kilton, head to the small island that corresponds to the left "eye" of Skull Lake, in the north of the Akkala region, in the evening. Once you have introduced yourself, this unusual vendor will sell you monster parts. His shop will subsequently appear on the outskirts of all main villages and towns, but only at night (see page 342).

3

Warp to a settlement at night; we'll choose Kakariko Village in this instance, where you can find Kilton on the south shore of Lantern Lake, above the village. Sell a few monster parts to earn at least nine "mon," the shop's currency, then purchase some monster extract.

4

Using any cooking pot, prepare a dish comprising monster extract (purchased from Kilton), tabantha wheat, goat butter, and cane sugar (all sold at Rito Village's general store). This will lead to the creation of a monster cake. Give this to Ruli back in Tarrey Town, and speak to her one more time to complete the mission and receive a **gold rupee**.

II HOBBIES OF THE RICH

1 After Hudson has founded Tarrey Town (see page 232), head to the village's west side and speak to Hagie. He will give you a **silver rupee** in advance, and expect you to eliminate two Guardians in the Torin Wetland, directly to the west of Tarrey Town. You can actually glide directly there from Hagie's position.

2 Both specimens are Guardian Stalkers, which can be hard to manage simultaneously. Choose one and attack it when it is far from the other, ideally by perfect-guarding to destroy it with its own laser beams. There are also a few Decayed Guardians that may activate as you pass nearby: stay well clear of these to avoid any additional complications. Report to Hagie to receive the second part of your payment: a **red rupee**.

III A SHADY CUSTOMER

1 Speak to Hoz at the East Akkala Stable. He would like you to investigate the owner of the Fang and Bone shop.

2 If you have not introduced yourself to Kilton yet, wait until the evening then head to the small island that corresponds to the left "eye" of Skull Lake in the north of the Akkala region. After Link has met him, Kilton will sell monster parts from stores situated on the outskirts of all main villages and towns – but only at night (see page 342). Take a picture of him with the camera from up close, then show this to Hoz to receive a **silver rupee**.

IV LITTLE SISTER'S BIG REQUEST

1 Speak to Jana at the South Akkala Stable during the day and give her an armoranth – a plant that grows in the Akkala Highlands. The nearby Torin Wetland is a good place to search. When she asks you why you came here, answer either "I'm a traveler" or "I'm just wandering."

2 Speak to Gleema, Jana's little sister, who can also be found in the South Akkala Stable during the day. Once you have discovered her secret, speak to Jana again. Your mission is now to retrieve three types of insect. Note that these can occasionally be sold by Beedle, the wandering merchant found at stables.

- **Cold darners** are relatively common in the Tabantha Frontier and Hyrule Ridge regions.
- **Warm darners** are found in the Akkala Highlands and Hyrule Field regions.
- **Electric darners** are usually encountered during rainy weather in the Gerudo Desert (look on the hills at the base of the Wasteland Tower) or on Thundra Plateau.

Once you have all three specimens, speak to Jana, then Gleema, then Jana again to obtain a **silver rupee** as a reward.

INVENTORY

This chapter provides complete inventory lists and statistics, including parameters that are hidden in the game but can be of crucial importance. By learning how to make more informed selections, you can opt for the best possible equipment in any given situation.

Added Effects

A number of items in your inventory can provide added effects when equipped or consumed. The accompanying table lists all possible buffs and describes the nature of their effects.

Note that food-induced buffs that only last for a set duration do not stack. You can only have one such buff at a time and any new one will overwrite the last one, even if it's weaker (for example Level 1 attack boost replacing a Level 2).

ADDED EFFECT OVERVIEW

ICON	EFFECT	DESCRIPTION
	Extra Hearts	Temporary yellow hearts that cannot be refilled
	Stamina Restoration	Restoration of a depleted stamina wheel
	Extra Stamina	Temporary yellow extension of the stamina wheel that cannot be refilled
	Flame Guard	Prevents damage from lava-induced extreme temperatures
	Heat Resistance	Prevents damage from scorching temperatures
	Cold Resistance	Prevents damage from freezing temperatures
	Shock Resistance	Prevents electric damage
	Movement Speed Up	Increases your movement speed
	Night Speed Up	Increases your movement speed at night
	Attack Up	Increases your weapon attack damage by 20% (Level 1), 30% (Level 2), or 50% (Level 3)
	Defense Up	Increases your defense by 4 (Level 1), 12 (Level 2), or 24 (Level 3), reducing damage from enemies
	Climb Speed Up	Increases your movement speed while climbing
	Stealth Up	Increases your stealth capabilities
	Sand Travel	Maintains your normal movement speed on sand
	Snow Travel	Maintains your normal movement speed on deep snow

ICON	EFFECT	DESCRIPTION
	Swim Speed Up	Increases your movement speed while swimming
	Swim Up Waterfalls	Enables you to swim up waterfalls
	Spin Attack	Enables you to perform a spin attack while swimming
	Swim Dash Stamina Up	Reduces stamina consumption when swim-dashing
	Guardian Resist	Reduces damage received from Guardians
	Ancient Proficiency	Increases damage inflicted with weapons of the Ancient/Guardian type
	Stal Lure	Increases the spawn rate of Stal monsters
	Charge Atk. Stamina Up	Reduces stamina consumption when performing charged attacks
	Climb Stamina Up	Reduces stamina consumption when climbing
	Fireproof	Makes you immune to the burnt effect
	Unfreezable	Makes you immune to the frozen effect
	Unshockable	Makes you immune to the shock effect
	Lightning Proof	Makes you immune to lightning
	Master Sword Beam Up	Increases the damage inflicted by the Master Sword's beam attack
	Bone Atk. Up	Increases damage inflicted with bone weapons
–	Disguise	Enables you to walk incognito among monsters of the corresponding type

Armor

Link's armor determines how well he resists damage. It can also provide added effects. In this section, we reveal all the details for all armor parts. Each piece is covered in a dedicated data sheet, which offers the following information:

- **Defense:** The numerical defense value of a garment ( ). The higher Link's armor-induced defense stat is, the less damage he will take from enemy attacks.
- **Sell price:** How many rupees you can get by selling each item.
- **Body part:** Whether the piece in question is designed to protect Link's head, chest, or legs.
- **Added effect:** Any special effect triggered while the armor part is equipped.
- **Set bonus:** When you upgrade the three pieces of a set to Level 2 (★★), wearing the full outfit provides an additional secret special effect.
- **Availability:** How/where the item can be obtained.
- **Upgrades:** This reveals the materials you need to invest to upgrade an armor piece via a great fairy, and the defense value obtained as a result. The more fountains you have visited, the greater potential you have for upgrading your outfits. Turn to page 326 for details.

INDIVIDUAL PIECES

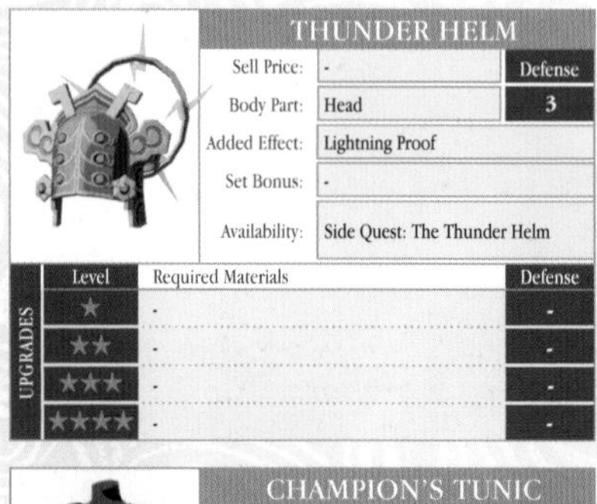

THUNDER HELM

		Defense
Sell Price:	-	
Body Part:	Head	3
Added Effect:	Lightning Proof	
Set Bonus:	-	
Availability:	Side Quest: The Thunder Helm	

UPGRADES Level	Required Materials	Defense
★	-	-
★★	-	-
★★★	-	-
★★★★	-	-

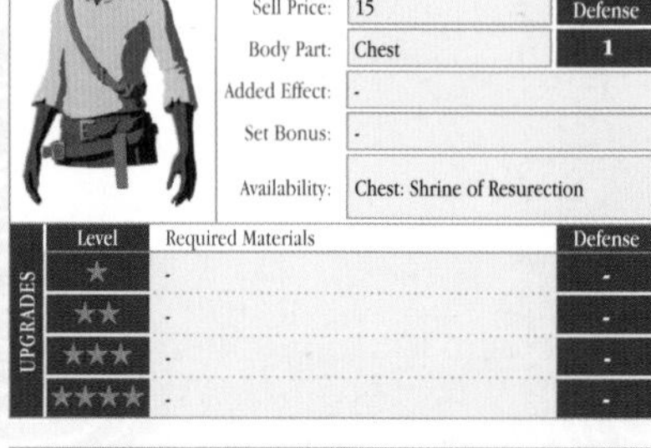

OLD SHIRT

		Defense
Sell Price:	15	
Body Part:	Chest	1
Added Effect:	-	
Set Bonus:	-	
Availability:	Chest: Shrine of Resurection	

UPGRADES Level	Required Materials	Defense
★	-	-
★★	-	-
★★★	-	-
★★★★	-	-

WARM DOUBLET

		Defense
Sell Price:	20	
Body Part:	Chest	1
Added Effect:	Cold Resistance	
Set Bonus:	-	
Availability:	Gift from the old man during the prologue; Shop: Hateno Village	

UPGRADES Level	Required Materials	Defense
★	-	-
★★	-	-
★★★	-	-
★★★★	-	-

CHAMPION'S TUNIC

		Defense
Sell Price:	-	
Body Part:	Chest	5
Added Effect:	See Enemy HP	
Set Bonus:	-	
Availability:	Main Quest: Captured Memories	

UPGRADES Level	Required Materials	Defense
★	Silent Princess x 3	8
★★	Silent Princess x 3, Shard of Farosh's Horn x 2	14
★★★	Silent Princess x 3, Shard of Naydra's Horn x 2	22
★★★★	Silent Princess x 10, Shard of Dinraal's Horn x 2	32

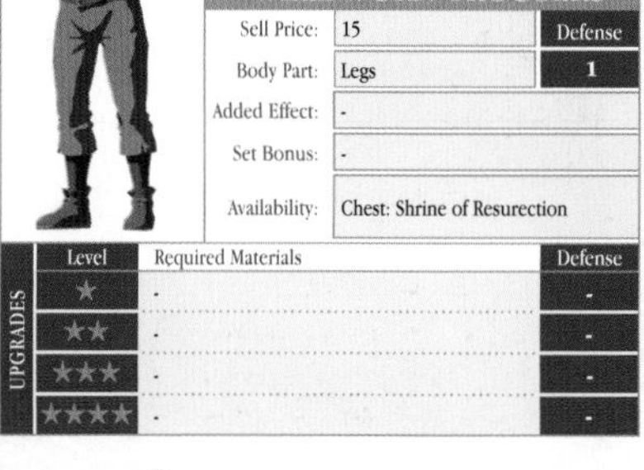

WELL-WORN TROUSERS

		Defense
Sell Price:	15	
Body Part:	Legs	1
Added Effect:	-	
Set Bonus:	-	
Availability:	Chest: Shrine of Resurection	

UPGRADES Level	Required Materials	Defense
★	-	-
★★	-	-
★★★	-	-
★★★★	-	-

SAND BOOTS

		Defense
Sell Price:	200	
Body Part:	Legs	3
Added Effect:	Sand Travel	
Set Bonus:	-	
Availability:	Side Quest: The Eighth Heroine	

UPGRADES Level	Required Materials	Defense
★	Molduga Fin x 5, Hightail Lizard x 10	5
★★	Molduga Fin x 10, Swift Carrot x 10	8
★★★	Molduga Guts x 2, Rushroom x 15	12
★★★★	Molduga Guts x 4, Swift Violet x 15	20

SNOW BOOTS

		Defense
Sell Price:	200	
Body Part:	Legs	3
Added Effect:	Snow Travel	
Set Bonus:	-	
Availability:	Side Quest: The Forgotten Sword	

UPGRADES Level	Required Materials	Defense
★	Octorok Tentacle x 5, Hightail Lizard x 10	5
★★	Octo Balloon x 5, Swift Carrot x 10	8
★★★	Octorok Eyeball x 5, Rushroom x 15	12
★★★★	Naydra's Scale x 2, Swift Violet x 15	20

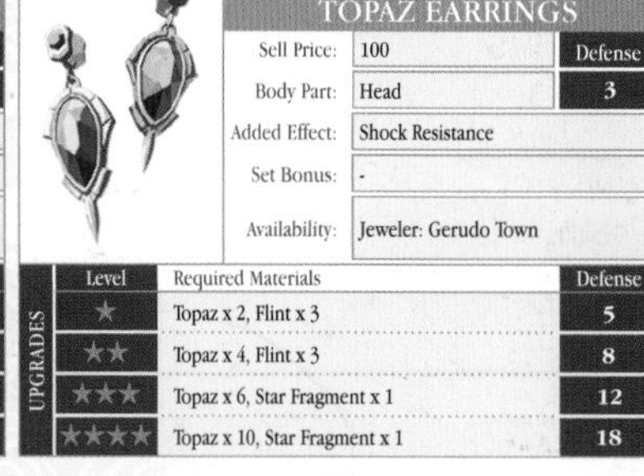

TOPAZ EARRINGS

		Defense
Sell Price:	100	
Body Part:	Head	3
Added Effect:	Shock Resistance	
Set Bonus:	-	
Availability:	Jeweler: Gerudo Town	

UPGRADES Level	Required Materials	Defense
★	Topaz x 2, Flint x 3	5
★★	Topaz x 4, Flint x 3	8
★★★	Topaz x 6, Star Fragment x 1	12
★★★★	Topaz x 10, Star Fragment x 1	18

OPAL EARRINGS

		Defense
Sell Price:	40	
Body Part:	Head	3
Added Effect:	Swim Speed Up	
Set Bonus:	-	
Availability:	Jeweler: Gerudo Town	

UPGRADES Level	Required Materials	Defense
★	Opal x 5, Flint x 3	5
★★	Opal x 8, Flint x 3	8
★★★	Opal x 16, Flint x 3	12
★★★★	Opal x 20, Flint x 3	20

INDIVIDUAL PIECES (CONTINUED)

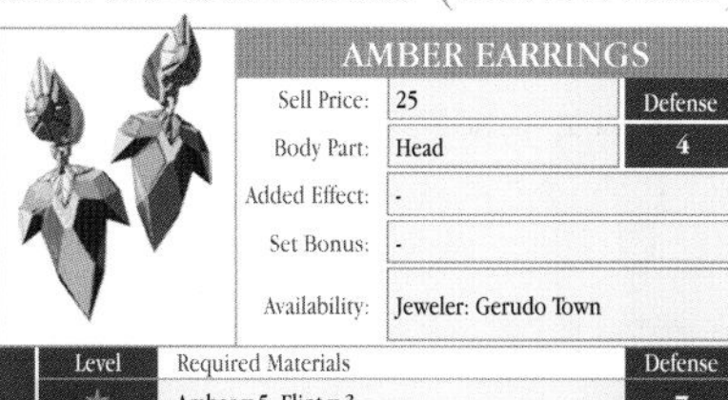

AMBER EARRINGS

		Defense
Sell Price:	25	4
Body Part:	Head	
Added Effect:	-	
Set Bonus:	-	
Availability:	Jeweler: Gerudo Town	

Upgrades Level	Required Materials	Defense
★	Amber x 5, Flint x 3	7
★★	Amber x 10, Flint x 3	12
★★★	Amber x 20, Flint x 3	18
★★★★	Amber x 30, Flint x 3	28

DIAMOND CIRCLET

		Defense
Sell Price:	375	4
Body Part:	Head	
Added Effect:	Guardian Resist	
Set Bonus:	-	
Availability:	Jeweler: Gerudo Town; Chest: Under Tu Ka'loh Shrine	

Upgrades Level	Required Materials	Defense
★	Diamond x 2, Flint x 3	7
★★	Diamond x 4, Flint x 3	12
★★★	Diamond x 6, Star Fragment x 1	18
★★★★	Diamond x 10, Star Fragment x 1	28

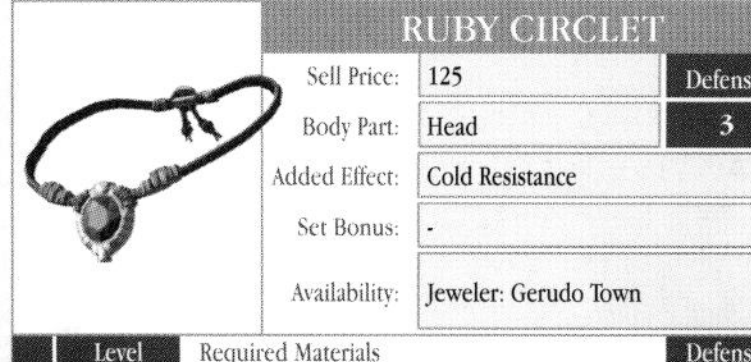

RUBY CIRCLET

		Defense
Sell Price:	125	3
Body Part:	Head	
Added Effect:	Cold Resistance	
Set Bonus:	-	
Availability:	Jeweler: Gerudo Town	

Upgrades Level	Required Materials	Defense
★	Ruby x 2, Flint x 3	5
★★	Ruby x 4, Flint x 3	8
★★★	Ruby x 6, Star Fragment x 1	12
★★★★	Ruby x 10, Star Fragment x 1	20

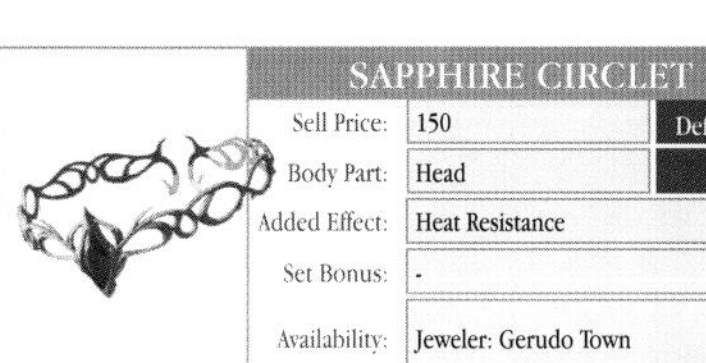

SAPPHIRE CIRCLET

		Defense
Sell Price:	150	3
Body Part:	Head	
Added Effect:	Heat Resistance	
Set Bonus:	-	
Availability:	Jeweler: Gerudo Town	

Upgrades Level	Required Materials	Defense
★	Sapphire x 2, Flint x 3	5
★★	Sapphire x 4, Flint x 3	8
★★★	Sapphire x 6, Star Fragment x 1	12
★★★★	Sapphire x 10, Star Fragment x 1	20

SHEIK'S MASK

		Defense
Sell Price:	125	2
Body Part:	Head	
Added Effect:	Stealth Up	
Set Bonus:	-	
Availability:	Unlocked by corresponding amiibo	

Upgrades Level	Required Materials	Defense
★	Silent Princess x 1, Star Fragment x 1	4
★★	Silent Princess x 2, Star Fragment x 2	6
★★★	Silent Princess x 3, Star Fragment x 3	9
★★★★	Silent Princess x 4, Star Fragment x 4	16

BOKOBLIN MASK

		Defense
Sell Price:	9	3
Body Part:	Head	
Added Effect:	Bokoblin Disguise	
Set Bonus:	-	
Availability:	Kilton's Monster Shop	

Upgrades Level	Required Materials	Defense
★	-	-
★★	-	-
★★★	-	-
★★★★	-	-

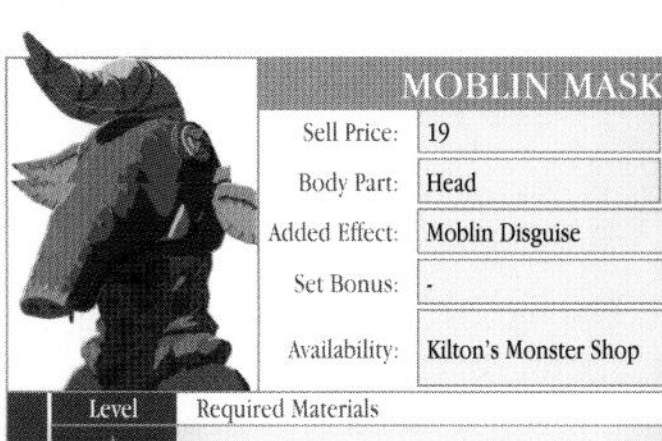

MOBLIN MASK

		Defense
Sell Price:	19	3
Body Part:	Head	
Added Effect:	Moblin Disguise	
Set Bonus:	-	
Availability:	Kilton's Monster Shop	

Upgrades Level	Required Materials	Defense
★	-	-
★★	-	-
★★★	-	-
★★★★	-	-

LIZALFOS MASK

		Defense
Sell Price:	29	3
Body Part:	Head	
Added Effect:	Lizalfos Disguise	
Set Bonus:	-	
Availability:	Kilton's Monster Shop	

Upgrades Level	Required Materials	Defense
★	-	-
★★	-	-
★★★	-	-
★★★★	-	-

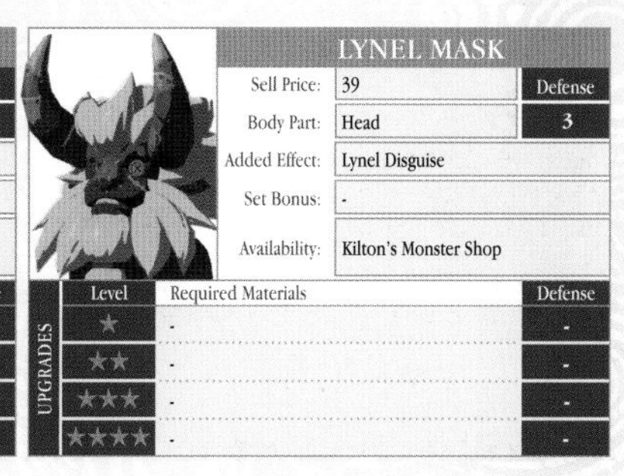

LYNEL MASK

		Defense
Sell Price:	39	3
Body Part:	Head	
Added Effect:	Lynel Disguise	
Set Bonus:	-	
Availability:	Kilton's Monster Shop	

Upgrades Level	Required Materials	Defense
★	-	-
★★	-	-
★★★	-	-
★★★★	-	-

ARMOR SETS

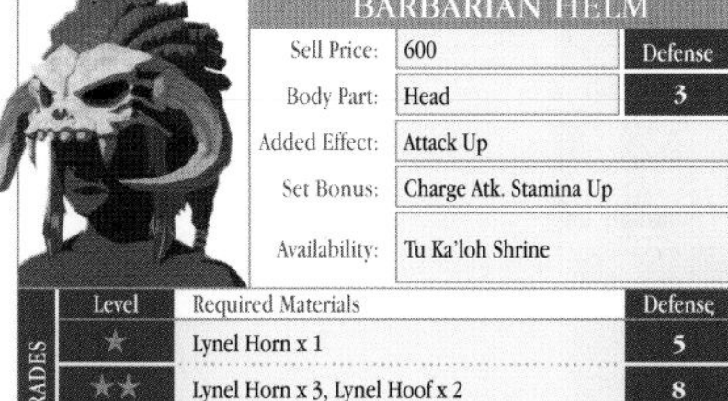

BARBARIAN HELM

		Defense
Sell Price:	600	3
Body Part:	Head	
Added Effect:	Attack Up	
Set Bonus:	Charge Atk. Stamina Up	
Availability:	Tu Ka'loh Shrine	

Upgrades Level	Required Materials	Defense
★	Lynel Horn x 1	5
★★	Lynel Horn x 3, Lynel Hoof x 2	8
★★★	Lynel Hoof x 4, Lynel Guts x 1	12
★★★★	Lynel Guts x 2, Shard of Dinraal's Horn x 1	20

BARBARIAN ARMOR

		Defense
Sell Price:	600	3
Body Part:	Chest	
Added Effect:	Attack Up	
Set Bonus:	Charge Atk. Stamina Up	
Availability:	Dila Maag Shrine	

Upgrades Level	Required Materials	Defense
★	Lynel Horn x 1	5
★★	Lynel Horn x 3, Lynel Hoof x 2	8
★★★	Lynel Hoof x 4, Lynel Guts x 1	12
★★★★	Lynel Guts x 2, Shard of Farosh's Horn x 1	20

BARBARIAN LEG WRAPS

		Defense
Sell Price:	600	3
Body Part:	Legs	
Added Effect:	Attack Up	
Set Bonus:	Charge Atk. Stamina Up	
Availability:	Qaza Tokki Shrine	

Upgrades Level	Required Materials	Defense
★	Lynel Horn x 1	5
★★	Lynel Horn x 3, Lynel Hoof x 2	8
★★★	Lynel Hoof x 4, Lynel Guts x 1	12
★★★★	Lynel Guts x 2, Shard of Naydra's Horn x 1	20

CLIMBER'S BANDANNA

		Defense
Sell Price:	600	3
Body Part:	Head	
Added Effect:	Climb Speed Up	
Set Bonus:	Climb Stamina Up	
Availability:	Ree Dahee Shrine	

Upgrades Level	Required Materials	Defense
★	Keese Wing x 3, Rushroom x 3	5
★★	Electric Keese Wing x 5, Hightail Lizard x 5	8
★★★	Ice Keese Wing x 5, Hot-Footed Frog x 10	12
★★★★	Fire Keese Wing x 5, Swift Violet x 15	20

CLIMBING GEAR

		Defense
Sell Price:	600	3
Body Part:	Chest	
Added Effect:	Climb Speed Up	
Set Bonus:	Climb Stamina Up	
Availability:	Chaas Qeta Shrine	

Upgrades Level	Required Materials	Defense
★	Keese Wing x 3, Rushroom x 3	5
★★	Electric Keese Wing x 5, Hightail Lizard x 5	8
★★★	Ice Keese Wing x 5, Hot-Footed Frog x 10	12
★★★★	Fire Keese Wing x 5, Swift Violet x 15	20

CLIMBING BOOTS

		Defense
Sell Price:	600	3
Body Part:	Legs	
Added Effect:	Climb Speed Up	
Set Bonus:	Climb Stamina Up	
Availability:	Tahno O'ah Shrine	

Upgrades Level	Required Materials	Defense
★	Keese Wing x 3, Rushroom x 3	5
★★	Electric Keese Wing x 5, Hightail Lizard x 5	8
★★★	Ice Keese Wing x 5, Hot-Footed Frog x 10	12
★★★★	Fire Keese Wing x 5, Swift Violet x 15	20

DARK HOOD

		Defense
Sell Price:	9	3
Body Part:	Head	
Added Effect:	-	
Set Bonus:	Night Speed Up	
Availability:	Kilton's Monster Shop	

Upgrades Level	Required Materials	Defense
★	-	-
★★	-	-
★★★	-	-
★★★★	-	-

DARK TUNIC

		Defense
Sell Price:	9	3
Body Part:	Chest	
Added Effect:	-	
Set Bonus:	Night Speed Up	
Availability:	Kilton's Monster Shop	

Upgrades Level	Required Materials	Defense
★	-	-
★★	-	-
★★★	-	-
★★★★	-	-

DARK TROUSERS

		Defense
Sell Price:	9	3
Body Part:	Legs	
Added Effect:	-	
Set Bonus:	Night Speed Up	
Availability:	Kilton's Monster Shop	

Upgrades Level	Required Materials	Defense
★	-	-
★★	-	-
★★★	-	-
★★★★	-	-

DESERT VOE HEADBAND

Sell Price:	115	Defense
Body Part:	Head	3
Added Effect:	Heat Resistance	
Set Bonus:	Shock Resistance	
Availability:	Shop: Gerudo Secret Club; Rhondson's Shop: Tarrey Town	

UPGRADES Level	Required Materials	Defense
★	White Chuchu Jelly x 3	5
★★	White Chuchu Jelly x 5, Ice Keese Wing x 3	8
★★★	Ice Keese Wing x 8, Icy Lizalfos Tail x 3	12
★★★★	Icy Lizalfos Tail x 10, Sapphire x 5	20

DESERT VOE SPAULDER

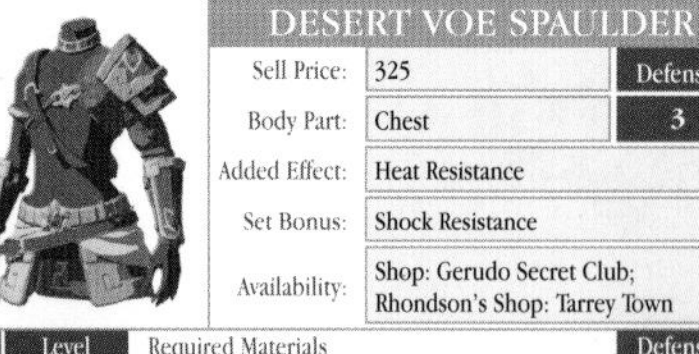

Sell Price:	325	Defense
Body Part:	Chest	3
Added Effect:	Heat Resistance	
Set Bonus:	Shock Resistance	
Availability:	Shop: Gerudo Secret Club; Rhondson's Shop: Tarrey Town	

UPGRADES Level	Required Materials	Defense
★	White Chuchu Jelly x 3	5
★★	White Chuchu Jelly x 5, Ice Keese Wing x 3	8
★★★	Ice Keese Wing x 8, Icy Lizalfos Tail x 3	12
★★★★	Icy Lizalfos Tail x 10, Sapphire x 5	20

DESERT VOE TROUSERS

Sell Price:	165	Defense
Body Part:	Legs	3
Added Effect:	Heat Resistance	
Set Bonus:	Shock Resistance	
Availability:	Shop: Gerudo Secret Club; Rhondson's Shop: Tarrey Town	

UPGRADES Level	Required Materials	Defense
★	White Chuchu Jelly x 3	5
★★	White Chuchu Jelly x 5, Ice Keese Wing x 3	8
★★★	Ice Keese Wing x 8, Icy Lizalfos Tail x 3	12
★★★★	Icy Lizalfos Tail x 10, Sapphire x 5	20

FIERCE DEITY MASK

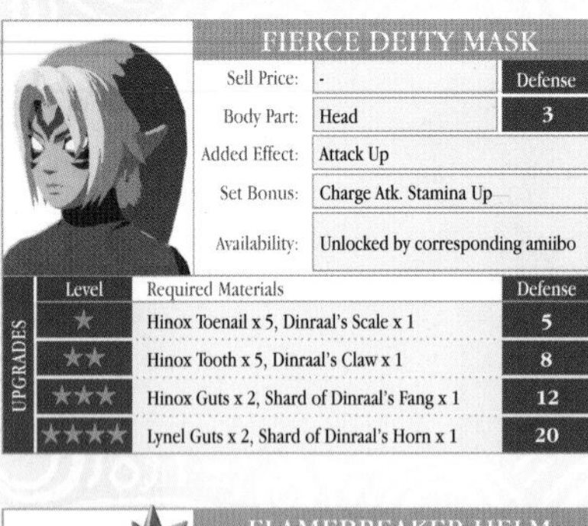

Sell Price:	-	Defense
Body Part:	Head	3
Added Effect:	Attack Up	
Set Bonus:	Charge Atk. Stamina Up	
Availability:	Unlocked by corresponding amiibo	

UPGRADES Level	Required Materials	Defense
★	Hinox Toenail x 5, Dinraal's Scale x 1	5
★★	Hinox Tooth x 5, Dinraal's Claw x 1	8
★★★	Hinox Guts x 2, Shard of Dinraal's Fang x 1	12
★★★★	Lynel Guts x 2, Shard of Dinraal's Horn x 1	20

FIERCE DEITY ARMOR

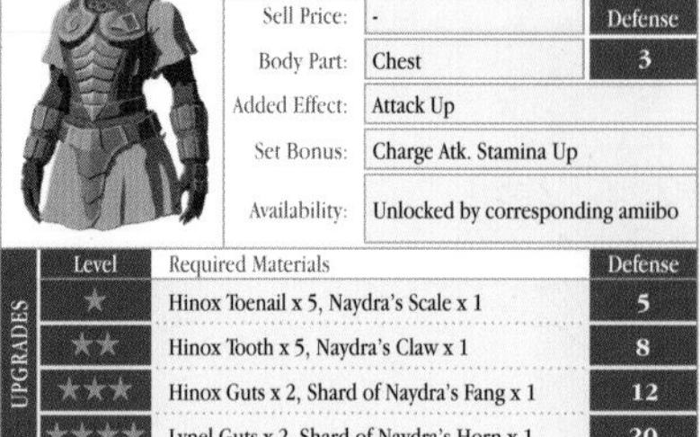

Sell Price:	-	Defense
Body Part:	Chest	3
Added Effect:	Attack Up	
Set Bonus:	Charge Atk. Stamina Up	
Availability:	Unlocked by corresponding amiibo	

UPGRADES Level	Required Materials	Defense
★	Hinox Toenail x 5, Naydra's Scale x 1	5
★★	Hinox Tooth x 5, Naydra's Claw x 1	8
★★★	Hinox Guts x 2, Shard of Naydra's Fang x 1	12
★★★★	Lynel Guts x 2, Shard of Naydra's Horn x 1	20

FIERCE DEITY BOOTS

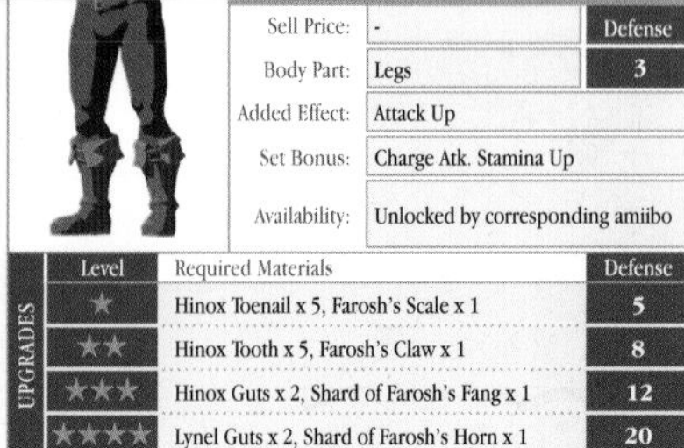

Sell Price:	-	Defense
Body Part:	Legs	3
Added Effect:	Attack Up	
Set Bonus:	Charge Atk. Stamina Up	
Availability:	Unlocked by corresponding amiibo	

UPGRADES Level	Required Materials	Defense
★	Hinox Toenail x 5, Farosh's Scale x 1	5
★★	Hinox Tooth x 5, Farosh's Claw x 1	8
★★★	Hinox Guts x 2, Shard of Farosh's Fang x 1	12
★★★★	Lynel Guts x 2, Shard of Farosh's Horn x 1	20

FLAMEBREAKER HELM

Sell Price:	500	Defense
Body Part:	Head	3
Added Effect:	Flame Guard	
Set Bonus:	Fireproof	
Availability:	Shop: Goron City	

UPGRADES Level	Required Materials	Defense
★	Fireproof Lizard x 1, Moblin Horn x 2	5
★★	Fireproof Lizard x 3, Moblin Fang x 4	8
★★★	Smotherwing Butterfly x 3, Moblin Guts x 3	12
★★★★	Smotherwing Butterfly x 5, Hinox Guts x 2	20

FLAMEBREAKER ARMOR

Sell Price:	150	Defense
Body Part:	Chest	3
Added Effect:	Flame Guard	
Set Bonus:	Fireproof	
Availability:	Shop: Goron City	

UPGRADES Level	Required Materials	Defense
★	Fireproof Lizard x 1, Moblin Horn x 2	5
★★	Fireproof Lizard x 3, Moblin Fang x 4	8
★★★	Smotherwing Butterfly x 3, Moblin Guts x 3	12
★★★★	Smotherwing Butterfly x 5, Hinox Guts x 2	20

FLAMEBREAKER BOOTS

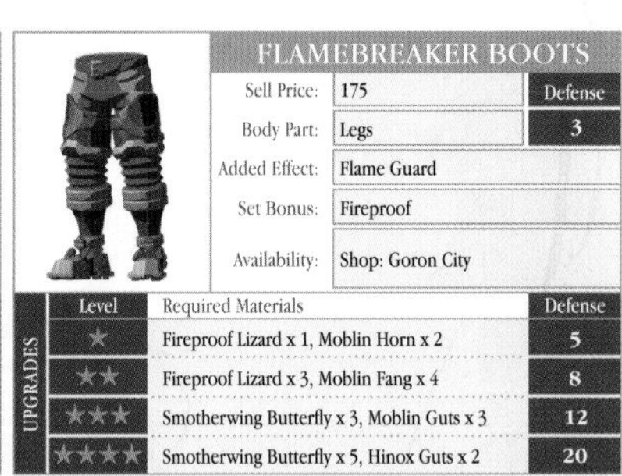

Sell Price:	175	Defense
Body Part:	Legs	3
Added Effect:	Flame Guard	
Set Bonus:	Fireproof	
Availability:	Shop: Goron City	

UPGRADES Level	Required Materials	Defense
★	Fireproof Lizard x 1, Moblin Horn x 2	5
★★	Fireproof Lizard x 3, Moblin Fang x 4	8
★★★	Smotherwing Butterfly x 3, Moblin Guts x 3	12
★★★★	Smotherwing Butterfly x 5, Hinox Guts x 2	20

GERUDO VEIL*

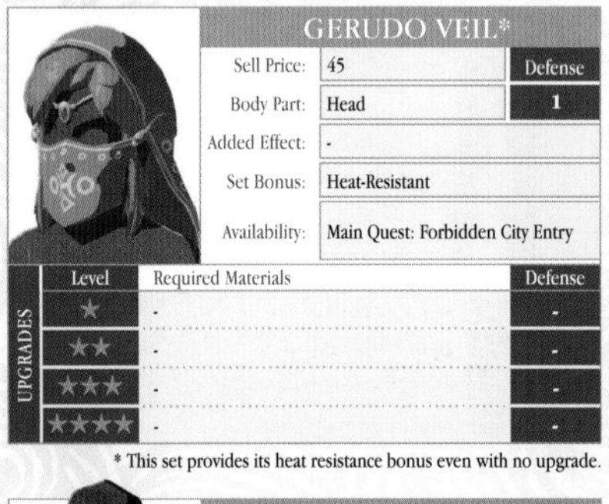

Sell Price:	45	Defense
Body Part:	Head	1
Added Effect:	-	
Set Bonus:	Heat-Resistant	
Availability:	Main Quest: Forbidden City Entry	

UPGRADES Level	Required Materials	Defense
★	-	-
★★	-	-
★★★	-	-
★★★★	-	-

* This set provides its heat resistance bonus even with no upgrade.

GERUDO TOP*

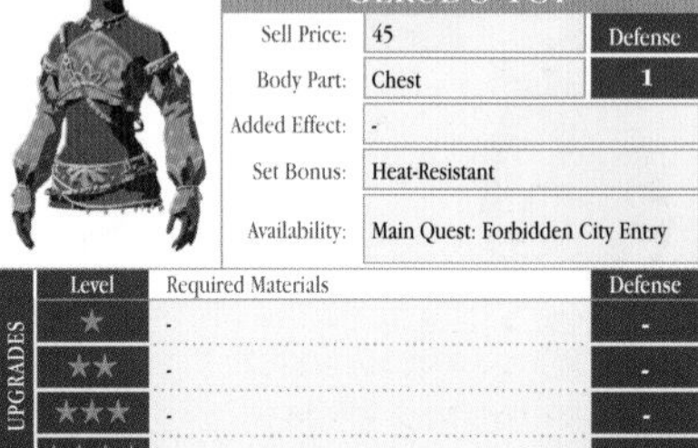

Sell Price:	45	Defense
Body Part:	Chest	1
Added Effect:	-	
Set Bonus:	Heat-Resistant	
Availability:	Main Quest: Forbidden City Entry	

UPGRADES Level	Required Materials	Defense
★	-	-
★★	-	-
★★★	-	-
★★★★	-	-

* This set provides its heat resistance bonus even with no upgrade.

GERUDO SIRWAL*

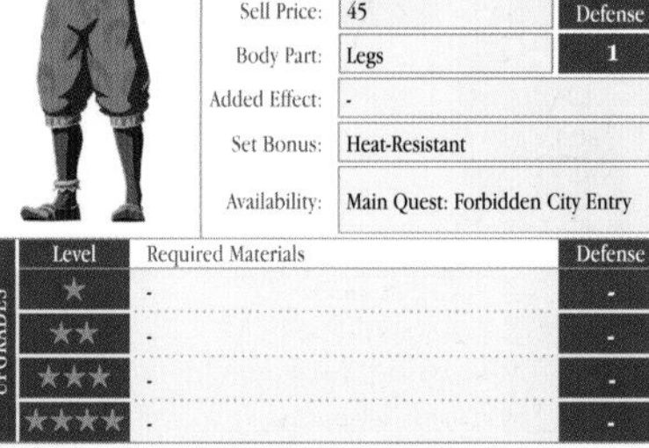

Sell Price:	45	Defense
Body Part:	Legs	1
Added Effect:	-	
Set Bonus:	Heat-Resistant	
Availability:	Main Quest: Forbidden City Entry	

UPGRADES Level	Required Materials	Defense
★	-	-
★★	-	-
★★★	-	-
★★★★	-	-

* This set provides its heat resistance bonus even with no upgrade.

ANCIENT HELM

Sell Price:	125	Defense
Body Part:	Head	4
Added Effect:	Guardian Resist	
Set Bonus:	Ancient Proficiency	
Availability:	Shop: Akkala Ancient Tech Lab	

UPGRADES Level	Required Materials	Defense
★	Ancient Screw x 5, Ancient Spring x 5	7
★★	Ancient Spring x 15, Ancient Gear x 10	12
★★★	Ancient Shaft x 15, Ancient Core x 5	18
★★★★	Star Fragment x 1, Giant Ancient Core x 2	28

ANCIENT CUIRASS

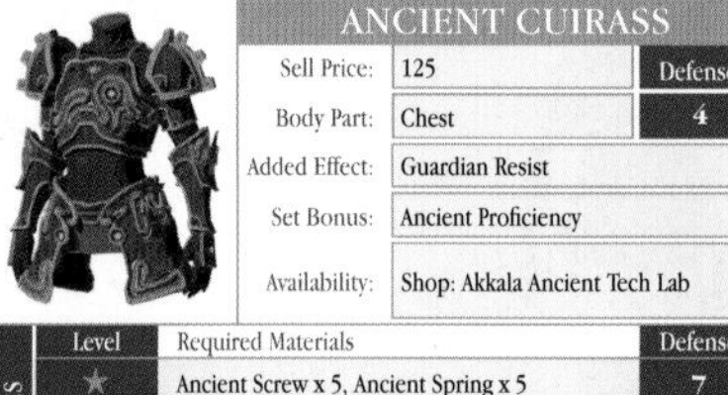

Sell Price:	125	Defense
Body Part:	Chest	4
Added Effect:	Guardian Resist	
Set Bonus:	Ancient Proficiency	
Availability:	Shop: Akkala Ancient Tech Lab	

UPGRADES Level	Required Materials	Defense
★	Ancient Screw x 5, Ancient Spring x 5	7
★★	Ancient Spring x 15, Ancient Gear x 10	12
★★★	Ancient Shaft x 15, Ancient Core x 5	18
★★★★	Star Fragment x 1, Giant Ancient Core x 2	28

ANCIENT GREAVES

Sell Price:	125	Defense
Body Part:	Legs	4
Added Effect:	Guardian Resist	
Set Bonus:	Ancient Proficiency	
Availability:	Shop: Akkala Ancient Tech Lab	

UPGRADES Level	Required Materials	Defense
★	Ancient Screw x 5, Ancient Spring x 5	7
★★	Ancient Spring x 15, Ancient Gear x 10	12
★★★	Ancient Shaft x 15, Ancient Core x 5	18
★★★★	Star Fragment x 1, Giant Ancient Core x 2	28

CAP OF THE SKY

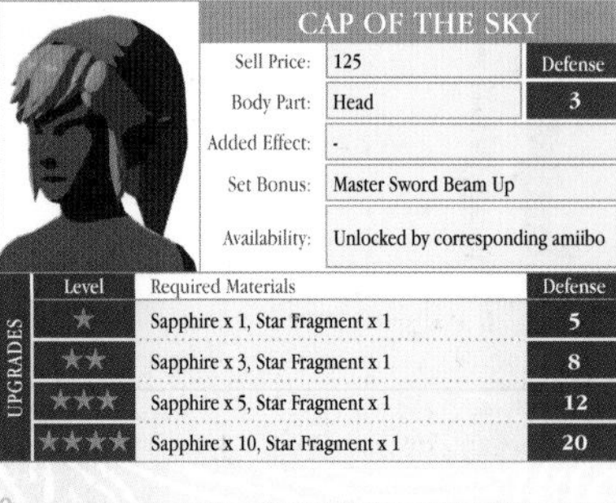

Sell Price:	125	Defense
Body Part:	Head	3
Added Effect:	-	
Set Bonus:	Master Sword Beam Up	
Availability:	Unlocked by corresponding amiibo	

UPGRADES Level	Required Materials	Defense
★	Sapphire x 1, Star Fragment x 1	5
★★	Sapphire x 3, Star Fragment x 1	8
★★★	Sapphire x 5, Star Fragment x 1	12
★★★★	Sapphire x 10, Star Fragment x 1	20

TUNIC OF THE SKY

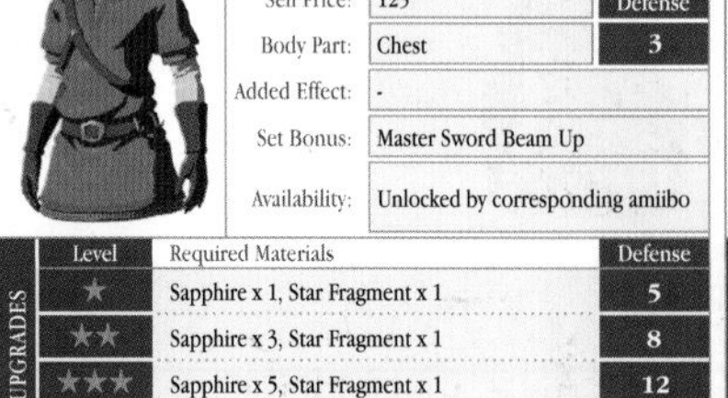

Sell Price:	125	Defense
Body Part:	Chest	3
Added Effect:	-	
Set Bonus:	Master Sword Beam Up	
Availability:	Unlocked by corresponding amiibo	

UPGRADES Level	Required Materials	Defense
★	Sapphire x 1, Star Fragment x 1	5
★★	Sapphire x 3, Star Fragment x 1	8
★★★	Sapphire x 5, Star Fragment x 1	12
★★★★	Sapphire x 10, Star Fragment x 1	20

TROUSERS OF THE SKY

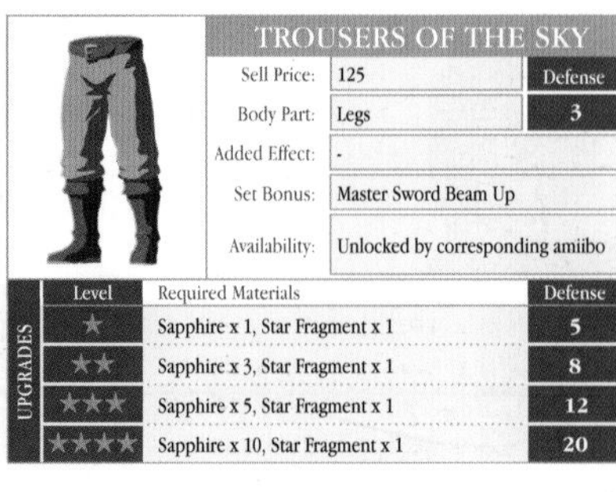

Sell Price:	125	Defense
Body Part:	Legs	3
Added Effect:	-	
Set Bonus:	Master Sword Beam Up	
Availability:	Unlocked by corresponding amiibo	

UPGRADES Level	Required Materials	Defense
★	Sapphire x 1, Star Fragment x 1	5
★★	Sapphire x 3, Star Fragment x 1	8
★★★	Sapphire x 5, Star Fragment x 1	12
★★★★	Sapphire x 10, Star Fragment x 1	20

CAP OF TIME

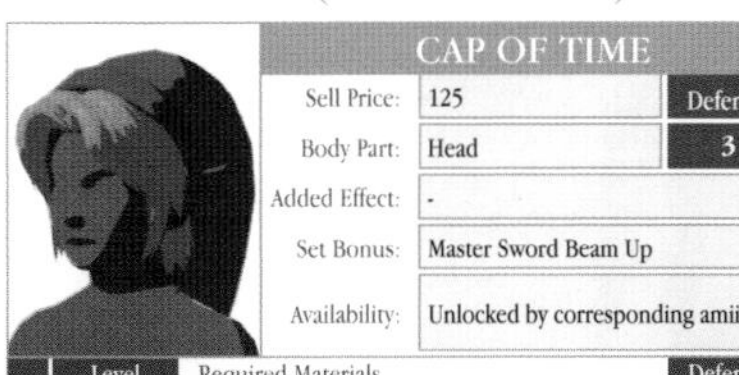

		Defense
Sell Price:	125	3
Body Part:	Head	
Added Effect:	-	
Set Bonus:	Master Sword Beam Up	
Availability:	Unlocked by corresponding amiibo	

UPGRADES

Level	Required Materials	Defense
★	Amber x 3, Star Fragment x 1	5
★★	Amber x 5, Star Fragment x 1	8
★★★	Amber x 15, Star Fragment x 1	12
★★★★	Amber x 30, Star Fragment x 1	20

TUNIC OF TIME

		Defense
Sell Price:	125	3
Body Part:	Chest	
Added Effect:	-	
Set Bonus:	Master Sword Beam Up	
Availability:	Unlocked by corresponding amiibo	

UPGRADES

Level	Required Materials	Defense
★	Amber x 3, Star Fragment x 1	5
★★	Amber x 5, Star Fragment x 1	8
★★★	Amber x 15, Star Fragment x 1	12
★★★★	Amber x 30, Star Fragment x 1	20

TROUSERS OF TIME

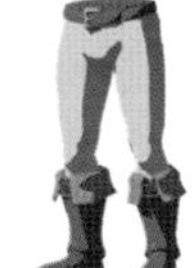

		Defense
Sell Price:	125	3
Body Part:	Legs	
Added Effect:	-	
Set Bonus:	Master Sword Beam Up	
Availability:	Unlocked by corresponding amiibo	

UPGRADES

Level	Required Materials	Defense
★	Amber x 3, Star Fragment x 1	5
★★	Amber x 5, Star Fragment x 1	8
★★★	Amber x 15, Star Fragment x 1	12
★★★★	Amber x 30, Star Fragment x 1	20

CAP OF TWILIGHT

		Defense
Sell Price:	125	3
Body Part:	Head	
Added Effect:	-	
Set Bonus:	Master Sword Beam Up	
Availability:	Unlocked by corresponding amiibo	

UPGRADES

Level	Required Materials	Defense
★	Topaz x 1, Star Fragment x 1	5
★★	Topaz x 3, Star Fragment x 1	8
★★★	Topaz x 5, Star Fragment x 1	12
★★★★	Topaz x 10, Star Fragment x 1	20

TUNIC OF TWILIGHT

		Defense
Sell Price:	125	3
Body Part:	Chest	
Added Effect:	-	
Set Bonus:	Master Sword Beam Up	
Availability:	Unlocked by corresponding amiibo	

UPGRADES

Level	Required Materials	Defense
★	Topaz x 1, Star Fragment x 1	5
★★	Topaz x 3, Star Fragment x 1	8
★★★	Topaz x 5, Star Fragment x 1	12
★★★★	Topaz x 10, Star Fragment x 1	20

TROUSERS OF TWILIGHT

		Defense
Sell Price:	125	3
Body Part:	Legs	
Added Effect:	-	
Set Bonus:	Master Sword Beam Up	
Availability:	Unlocked by corresponding amiibo	

UPGRADES

Level	Required Materials	Defense
★	Topaz x 1, Star Fragment x 1	5
★★	Topaz x 3, Star Fragment x 1	8
★★★	Topaz x 5, Star Fragment x 1	12
★★★★	Topaz x 10, Star Fragment x 1	20

CAP OF THE WILD

		Defense
Sell Price:	-	4
Body Part:	Head	
Added Effect:	-	
Set Bonus:	Master Sword Beam Up	
Availability:	Side Quest: A Gift from the Monks	

UPGRADES

Level	Required Materials	Defense
★	Acorn x 10, Farosh's Scale x 2	7
★★	Courser Bee Honey x 5, Farosh's Claw x 2	12
★★★	Energetic Rhino Beetle x 5, Shard of Farosh's Fang x 2	18
★★★★	Star Fragment x 1, Shard of Farosh's Horn x 2	28

TUNIC OF THE WILD

		Defense
Sell Price:	-	4
Body Part:	Chest	
Added Effect:	-	
Set Bonus:	Master Sword Beam Up	
Availability:	Side Quest: A Gift from the Monks	

UPGRADES

Level	Required Materials	Defense
★	Acorn x 10, Naydra's Scale x 2	7
★★	Courser Bee Honey x 5, Naydra's Claw x 2	12
★★★	Energetic Rhino Beetle x 5, Shard of Naydra's Fang x 2	18
★★★★	Star Fragment x 1, Shard of Naydra's Horn x 2	28

TROUSERS OF THE WILD

		Defense
Sell Price:	-	4
Body Part:	Legs	
Added Effect:	-	
Set Bonus:	Master Sword Beam Up	
Availability:	Side Quest: A Gift from the Monks	

UPGRADES

Level	Required Materials	Defense
★	Acorn x 10, Dinraal's Scale x 2	7
★★	Courser Bee Honey x 5, Dinraal's Claw x 2	12
★★★	Energetic Rhino Beetle x 5, Shard of Dinraal's Fang x 2	18
★★★★	Star Fragment x 1, Shard of Dinraal's Horn x 2	28

CAP OF THE WIND

		Defense
Sell Price:	125	3
Body Part:	Head	
Added Effect:	-	
Set Bonus:	Master Sword Beam Up	
Availability:	Unlocked by corresponding amiibo	

UPGRADES

Level	Required Materials	Defense
★	Opal x 3, Star Fragment x 1	5
★★	Opal x 5, Star Fragment x 1	8
★★★	Opal x 10, Star Fragment x 1	12
★★★★	Opal x 20, Star Fragment x 1	20

TUNIC OF THE WIND

		Defense
Sell Price:	125	3
Body Part:	Chest	
Added Effect:	-	
Set Bonus:	Master Sword Beam Up	
Availability:	Unlocked by corresponding amiibo	

UPGRADES

Level	Required Materials	Defense
★	Opal x 3, Star Fragment x 1	5
★★	Opal x 5, Star Fragment x 1	8
★★★	Opal x 10, Star Fragment x 1	12
★★★★	Opal x 20, Star Fragment x 1	20

TROUSERS OF THE WIND

		Defense
Sell Price:	125	3
Body Part:	Legs	
Added Effect:	-	
Set Bonus:	Master Sword Beam Up	
Availability:	Unlocked by corresponding amiibo	

UPGRADES

Level	Required Materials	Defense
★	Opal x 3, Star Fragment x 1	5
★★	Opal x 5, Star Fragment x 1	8
★★★	Opal x 10, Star Fragment x 1	12
★★★★	Opal x 20, Star Fragment x 1	20

CAP OF THE HERO

		Defense
Sell Price:	125	3
Body Part:	Head	
Added Effect:	-	
Set Bonus:	Master Sword Beam Up	
Availability:	Unlocked by corresponding amiibo	

UPGRADES

Level	Required Materials	Defense
★	Ruby x 1, Star Fragment x 1	5
★★	Ruby x 3, Star Fragment x 1	8
★★★	Ruby x 5, Star Fragment x 1	12
★★★★	Ruby x 10, Star Fragment x 1	20

TUNIC OF THE HERO

		Defense
Sell Price:	125	3
Body Part:	Chest	
Added Effect:	-	
Set Bonus:	Master Sword Beam Up	
Availability:	Unlocked by corresponding amiibo	

UPGRADES

Level	Required Materials	Defense
★	Ruby x 1, Star Fragment x 1	5
★★	Ruby x 3, Star Fragment x 1	8
★★★	Ruby x 5, Star Fragment x 1	12
★★★★	Ruby x 10, Star Fragment x 1	20

TROUSERS OF THE HERO

		Defense
Sell Price:	125	3
Body Part:	Legs	
Added Effect:	-	
Set Bonus:	Master Sword Beam Up	
Availability:	Unlocked by corresponding amiibo	

UPGRADES

Level	Required Materials	Defense
★	Ruby x 1, Star Fragment x 1	5
★★	Ruby x 3, Star Fragment x 1	8
★★★	Ruby x 5, Star Fragment x 1	12
★★★★	Ruby x 10, Star Fragment x 1	20

HYLIAN HOOD

		Defense
Sell Price:	15	3
Body Part:	Head	
Added Effect:	-	
Set Bonus:	-	
Availability:	Shop: Hateno Village	

UPGRADES

Level	Required Materials	Defense
★	Bokoblin Horn x 5	5
★★	Bokoblin Horn x 8, Bokoblin Fang x 5	8
★★★	Bokoblin Fang x 10, Bokoblin Guts x 5	12
★★★★	Bokoblin Guts x 15, Amber x 15	20

HYLIAN TUNIC

		Defense
Sell Price:	30	3
Body Part:	Chest	
Added Effect:	-	
Set Bonus:	-	
Availability:	Shop: Hateno Village	

UPGRADES

Level	Required Materials	Defense
★	Bokoblin Horn x 5	5
★★	Bokoblin Horn x 8, Bokoblin Fang x 5	8
★★★	Bokoblin Fang x 10, Bokoblin Guts x 5	12
★★★★	Bokoblin Guts x 15, Amber x 15	20

HYLIAN TROUSERS

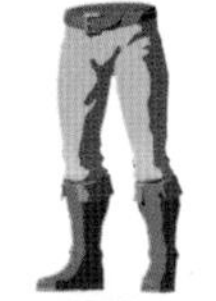

		Defense
Sell Price:	25	3
Body Part:	Legs	
Added Effect:	-	
Set Bonus:	-	
Availability:	Shop: Hateno Village	

UPGRADES

Level	Required Materials	Defense
★	Bokoblin Horn x 5	5
★★	Bokoblin Horn x 8, Bokoblin Fang x 5	8
★★★	Bokoblin Fang x 10, Bokoblin Guts x 5	12
★★★★	Bokoblin Guts x 15, Amber x 15	20

RADIANT MASK

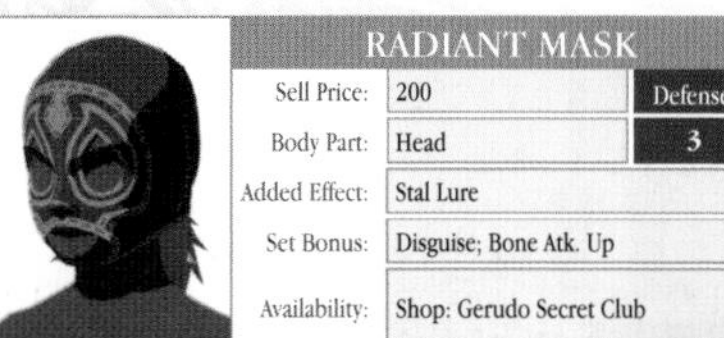

Sell Price:	200
Body Part:	Head
Defense	3
Added Effect:	Stal Lure
Set Bonus:	Disguise; Bone Atk. Up
Availability:	Shop: Gerudo Secret Club

Level	Required Materials	Defense
★	Luminous Stone x 5, Bokoblin Guts x 3	5
★★	Luminous Stone x 8, Moblin Guts x 3	8
★★★	Luminous Stone x 10, Molduga Guts x 2	12
★★★★	Luminous Stone x 20, Lynel Guts x 1	20

RADIANT SHIRT

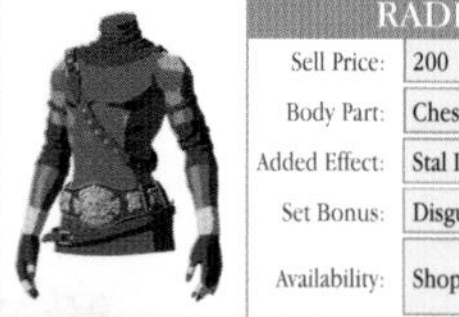

Sell Price:	200
Body Part:	Chest
Defense	3
Added Effect:	Stal Lure
Set Bonus:	Disguise; Bone Atk. Up
Availability:	Shop: Gerudo Secret Club

Level	Required Materials	Defense
★	Luminous Stone x 5, Bokoblin Guts x 3	5
★★	Luminous Stone x 8, Moblin Guts x 3	8
★★★	Luminous Stone x 10, Molduga Guts x 2	12
★★★★	Luminous Stone x 20, Lynel Guts x 1	20

RADIANT TIGHTS

Sell Price:	200
Body Part:	Legs
Defense	3
Added Effect:	Stal Lure
Set Bonus:	Disguise; Bone Atk. Up
Availability:	Shop: Gerudo Secret Club

Level	Required Materials	Defense
★	Luminous Stone x 5, Bokoblin Guts x 3	5
★★	Luminous Stone x 8, Moblin Guts x 3	8
★★★	Luminous Stone x 10, Molduga Guts x 2	12
★★★★	Luminous Stone x 20, Lynel Guts x 1	20

RUBBER HELM

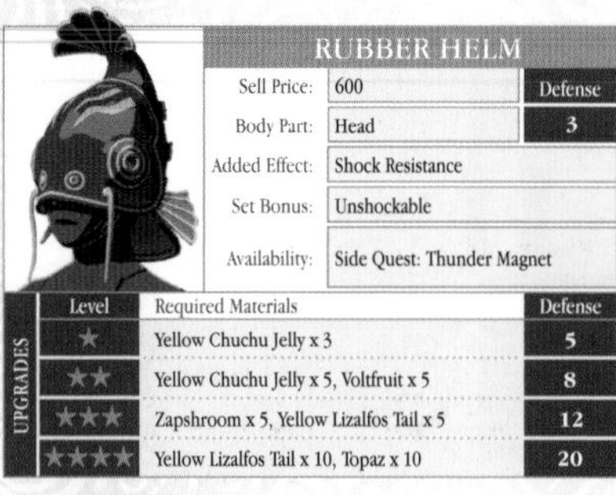

Sell Price:	600
Body Part:	Head
Defense	3
Added Effect:	Shock Resistance
Set Bonus:	Unshockable
Availability:	Side Quest: Thunder Magnet

Level	Required Materials	Defense
★	Yellow Chuchu Jelly x 3	5
★★	Yellow Chuchu Jelly x 5, Voltfruit x 5	8
★★★	Zapshroom x 5, Yellow Lizalfos Tail x 5	12
★★★★	Yellow Lizalfos Tail x 10, Topaz x 10	20

RUBBER ARMOR

Sell Price:	600
Body Part:	Chest
Defense	3
Added Effect:	Shock Resistance
Set Bonus:	Unshockable
Availability:	Toh Yahsa Shrine

Level	Required Materials	Defense
★	Yellow Chuchu Jelly x 3	5
★★	Yellow Chuchu Jelly x 5, Voltfruit x 5	8
★★★	Zapshroom x 5, Yellow Lizalfos Tail x 5	12
★★★★	Yellow Lizalfos Tail x 10, Topaz x 10	20

RUBBER TIGHTS

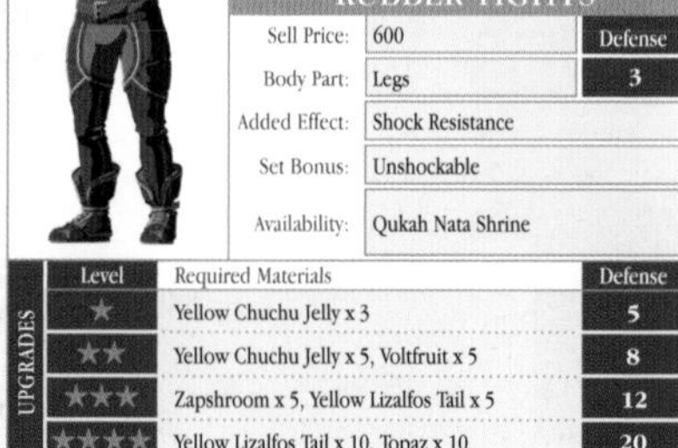

Sell Price:	600
Body Part:	Legs
Defense	3
Added Effect:	Shock Resistance
Set Bonus:	Unshockable
Availability:	Qukah Nata Shrine

Level	Required Materials	Defense
★	Yellow Chuchu Jelly x 3	5
★★	Yellow Chuchu Jelly x 5, Voltfruit x 5	8
★★★	Zapshroom x 5, Yellow Lizalfos Tail x 5	12
★★★★	Yellow Lizalfos Tail x 10, Topaz x 10	20

SNOWQUILL HEADDRESS

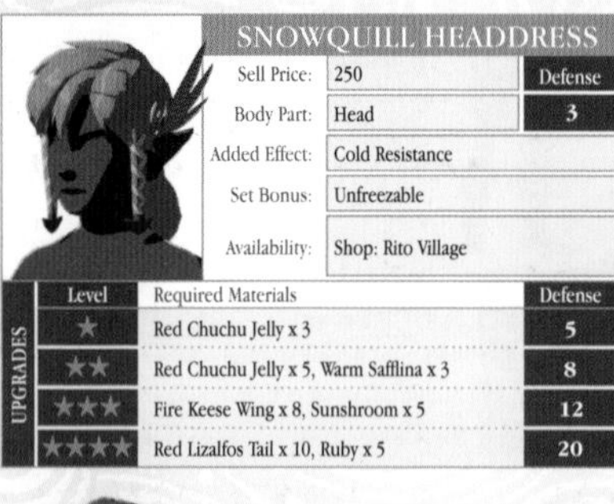

Sell Price:	250
Body Part:	Head
Defense	3
Added Effect:	Cold Resistance
Set Bonus:	Unfreezable
Availability:	Shop: Rito Village

Level	Required Materials	Defense
★	Red Chuchu Jelly x 3	5
★★	Red Chuchu Jelly x 5, Warm Safflina x 3	8
★★★	Fire Keese Wing x 8, Sunshroom x 5	12
★★★★	Red Lizalfos Tail x 10, Ruby x 5	20

SNOWQUILL TUNIC

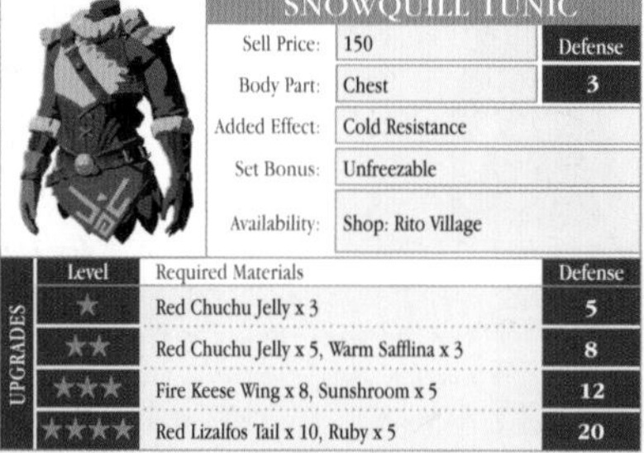

Sell Price:	150
Body Part:	Chest
Defense	3
Added Effect:	Cold Resistance
Set Bonus:	Unfreezable
Availability:	Shop: Rito Village

Level	Required Materials	Defense
★	Red Chuchu Jelly x 3	5
★★	Red Chuchu Jelly x 5, Warm Safflina x 3	8
★★★	Fire Keese Wing x 8, Sunshroom x 5	12
★★★★	Red Lizalfos Tail x 10, Ruby x 5	20

SNOWQUILL TROUSERS

Sell Price:	140
Body Part:	Legs
Defense	3
Added Effect:	Cold Resistance
Set Bonus:	Unfreezable
Availability:	Shop: Rito Village

Level	Required Materials	Defense
★	Red Chuchu Jelly x 3	5
★★	Red Chuchu Jelly x 5, Warm Safflina x 3	8
★★★	Fire Keese Wing x 8, Sunshroom x 5	12
★★★★	Red Lizalfos Tail x 10, Ruby x 5	20

SOLDIER'S HELM

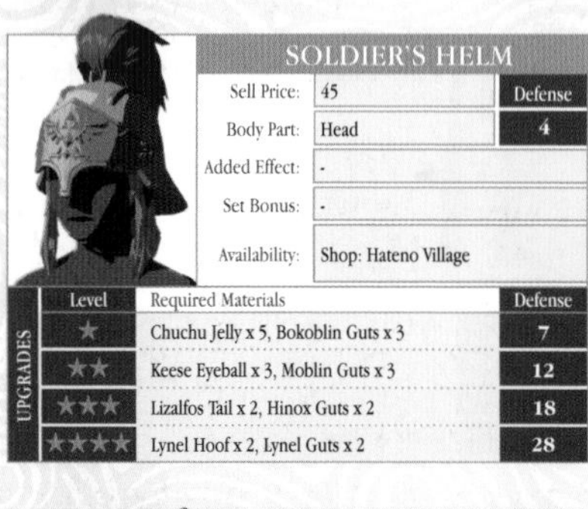

Sell Price:	45
Body Part:	Head
Defense	4
Added Effect:	-
Set Bonus:	-
Availability:	Shop: Hateno Village

Level	Required Materials	Defense
★	Chuchu Jelly x 5, Bokoblin Guts x 3	7
★★	Keese Eyeball x 3, Moblin Guts x 3	12
★★★	Lizalfos Tail x 2, Hinox Guts x 2	18
★★★★	Lynel Hoof x 2, Lynel Guts x 2	28

SOLDIER'S ARMOR

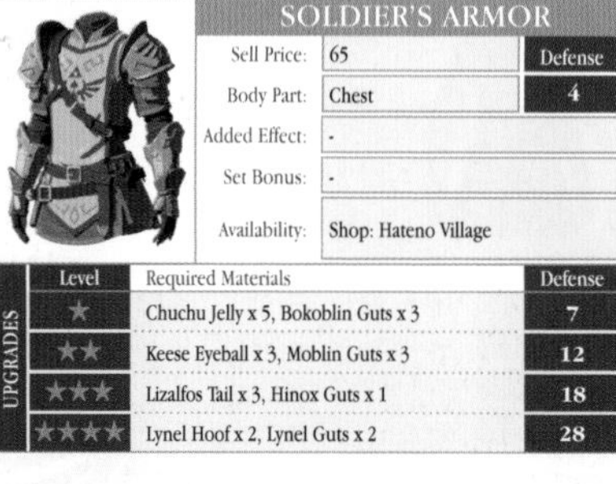

Sell Price:	65
Body Part:	Chest
Defense	4
Added Effect:	-
Set Bonus:	-
Availability:	Shop: Hateno Village

Level	Required Materials	Defense
★	Chuchu Jelly x 5, Bokoblin Guts x 3	7
★★	Keese Eyeball x 3, Moblin Guts x 3	12
★★★	Lizalfos Tail x 3, Hinox Guts x 1	18
★★★★	Lynel Hoof x 2, Lynel Guts x 2	28

SOLDIER'S GREAVES

Sell Price:	50
Body Part:	Legs
Defense	4
Added Effect:	-
Set Bonus:	-
Availability:	Shop: Hateno Village

Level	Required Materials	Defense
★	Chuchu Jelly x 5, Bokoblin Guts x 3	7
★★	Keese Eyeball x 3, Moblin Guts x 3	12
★★★	Lizalfos Tail x 3, Hinox Guts x 1	18
★★★★	Lynel Hoof x 2, Lynel Guts x 2	28

STEALTH MASK

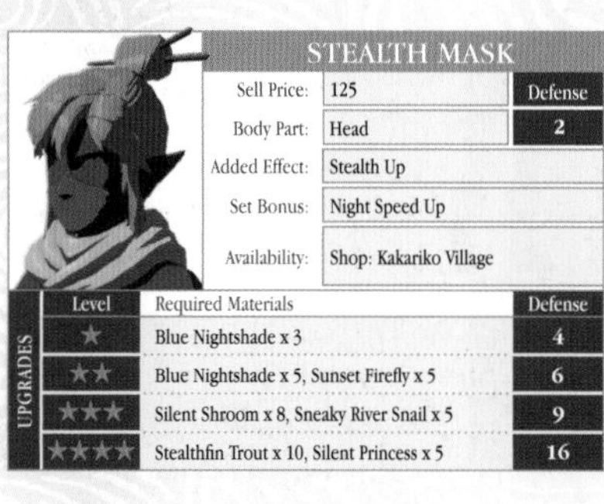

Sell Price:	125
Body Part:	Head
Defense	2
Added Effect:	Stealth Up
Set Bonus:	Night Speed Up
Availability:	Shop: Kakariko Village

Level	Required Materials	Defense
★	Blue Nightshade x 3	4
★★	Blue Nightshade x 5, Sunset Firefly x 5	6
★★★	Silent Shroom x 8, Sneaky River Snail x 5	9
★★★★	Stealthfin Trout x 10, Silent Princess x 5	16

STEALTH CHEST GUARD

Sell Price:	175
Body Part:	Chest
Defense	2
Added Effect:	Stealth Up
Set Bonus:	Night Speed Up
Availability:	Shop: Kakariko Village

Level	Required Materials	Defense
★	Blue Nightshade x 3	4
★★	Blue Nightshade x 5, Sunset Firefly x 5	6
★★★	Silent Shroom x 8, Sneaky River Snail x 5	9
★★★★	Stealthfin Trout x 10, Silent Princess x 5	16

STEALTH TIGHTS

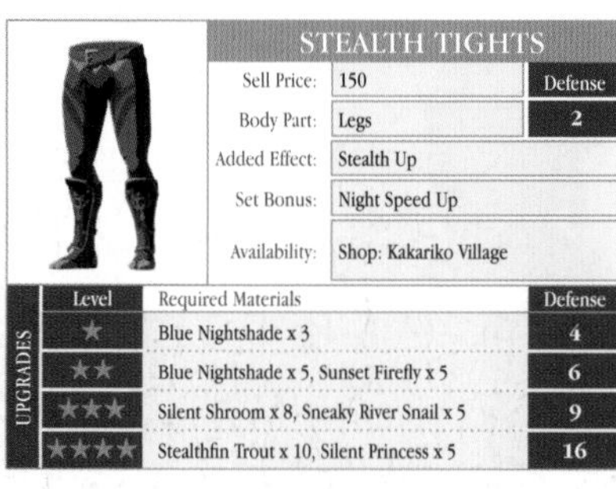

Sell Price:	150
Body Part:	Legs
Defense	2
Added Effect:	Stealth Up
Set Bonus:	Night Speed Up
Availability:	Shop: Kakariko Village

Level	Required Materials	Defense
★	Blue Nightshade x 3	4
★★	Blue Nightshade x 5, Sunset Firefly x 5	6
★★★	Silent Shroom x 8, Sneaky River Snail x 5	9
★★★★	Stealthfin Trout x 10, Silent Princess x 5	16

ZORA HELM

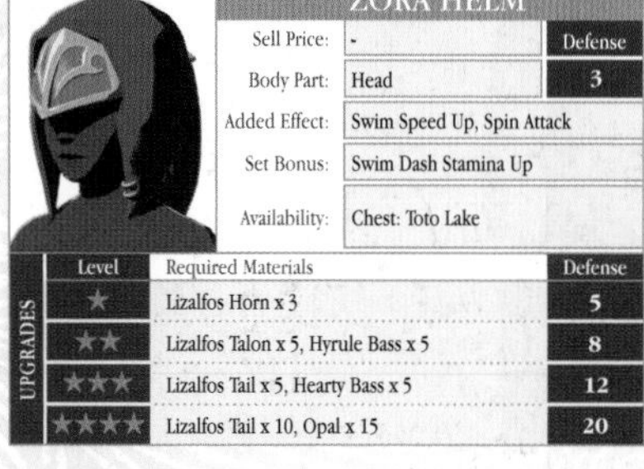

Sell Price:	-
Body Part:	Head
Defense	3
Added Effect:	Swim Speed Up, Spin Attack
Set Bonus:	Swim Dash Stamina Up
Availability:	Chest: Toto Lake

Level	Required Materials	Defense
★	Lizalfos Horn x 3	5
★★	Lizalfos Talon x 5, Hyrule Bass x 5	8
★★★	Lizalfos Tail x 5, Hearty Bass x 5	12
★★★★	Lizalfos Tail x 10, Opal x 15	20

ZORA ARMOR

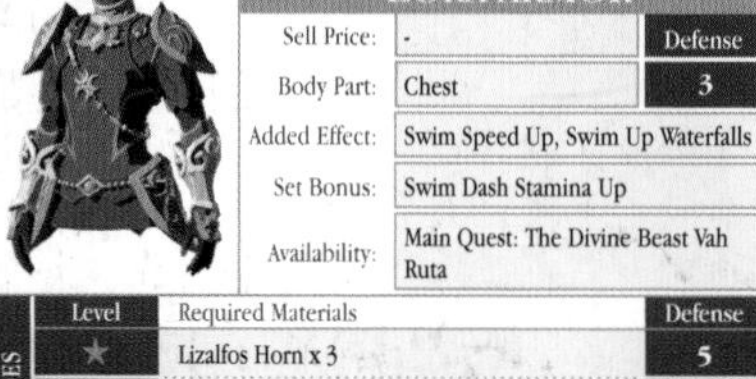

Sell Price:	-
Body Part:	Chest
Defense	3
Added Effect:	Swim Speed Up, Swim Up Waterfalls
Set Bonus:	Swim Dash Stamina Up
Availability:	Main Quest: The Divine Beast Vah Ruta

Level	Required Materials	Defense
★	Lizalfos Horn x 3	5
★★	Lizalfos Talon x 5, Hyrule Bass x 5	8
★★★	Lizalfos Tail x 5, Hearty Bass x 5	12
★★★★	Lizalfos Tail x 10, Opal x 15	20

ZORA GREAVES

Sell Price:	-
Body Part:	Legs
Defense	3
Added Effect:	Swim Speed Up
Set Bonus:	Swim Dash Stamina Up
Availability:	Side Quest: Lynel Safari

Level	Required Materials	Defense
★	Lizalfos Horn x 3	5
★★	Lizalfos Talon x 5, Hyrule Bass x 5	8
★★★	Lizalfos Tail x 5, Hearty Bass x 5	12
★★★★	Lizalfos Tail x 10, Opal x 15	20

WEAPONS

WEAPON CATEGORIES

There are three categories of weapons in *Breath of the Wild*, each with distinct strengths and weaknesses.

ONE-HANDED WEAPONS

One-handed weapons are excellent all-round tools. Though not particularly impressive in terms of raw power, they enable you to wield your shield simultaneously, making it easy to switch to a defensive stance on the fly. This is truly pivotal: in many battles, particularly when you fight an enemy that you are not perfectly familiar with, being able to draw your shield instantly often proves invaluable.

TWO-HANDED WEAPONS

The polar opposite of one-handed blades, two-handed weapons are slower and incompatible with shield usage: you must sheathe your blade with Ⓑ before you can block, which requires practice and sharp reflexes to achieve in the midst of intense battles. However, they are unparalleled in terms of brute force, and give you access to devastating, multi-hit charged attacks. With a robust two-handed weapon, you can make short work of practically all creatures in the game – including the fiercest sub-bosses.

SPEARS

Spears combine some of the traits of the other two categories. As with one-handed weapons, they offer relatively low raw power but a rather high attack rate; like two-handed weapons, they are incompatible with shield usage and must therefore be sheathed before you can parry. Their signature feature, though, is notably long reach. They excel when employed against elemental creatures where you have a pressing need to avoid physical contact, elevated adversaries such as Wizzrobes, or to hit targets that might otherwise be out of reach – such as the crystal on the back of a Talus. They can also be a very effective way to keep more agile or aggressive opponents at bay.

ELEMENTAL WEAPONS

Though not blessed with remarkable hitting power or durability, elemental weapons cause effects that are potent enough to warrant that you carry at least one of each type in your inventory at all times.

- **Flame weapons** set their target ablaze, causing panic. They are instantly lethal against ice-imbued creatures such as the Ice-Breath Lizalfos.
- **Frost weapons** freeze their victim, completely neutralizing them for a short spell, and leading to a 3x damage modifier for your next blow while they are still immobilized. These weapons are deadly against fire-imbued creatures such as Fire Wizzrobes.
- **Lightning weapons** electrocute the opponents they hit, stunning them for a brief time and causing them to drop equipped weapons or shields.

Spears are potentially the most valuable of all elemental weapons, as their long reach enables you to strike and inflict their effects from a safe distance. Frostspears are particularly useful: freezing susceptible targets will naturally halt their assault. A highly efficient strategy is to tap an adversary with a frostspear to apply its effect, then switch to your most powerful weapon to shatter the ice. This is enough to deny many enemies the ability to go on the offensive, while simultaneously reducing overall weapon durability loss – the combination has very low overheads.

DAMAGE CALCULATION

By default, your attacks deplete a target's HP by an amount that corresponds to your weapon's power value. A sword with a power of 10 will remove 10 HP from your opponent's health bar. The champion's tunic reveals the total hit points for each enemy you fight.

With Link, his armor-induced defense stat is subtracted from the total attack value. Each of his hearts is equivalent to 4 HP. If Link has five hearts (5 x 4 = 20 HP), a defense value of 2, and he sustains a blow with a value of 12 damage, he ends up with two-and-a-half hearts: 20 - (12 - 2) = 10 HP = 2.5 hearts. Certain attacks inflict extra damage, as listed here:

- **Critical hits:** damage x2.
- **Thrown weapons:** damage x2
- **Sneakstrikes:** damage x8.
- **Shock attacks:** damage +20.
- **Freezing attacks:** damage +10 (instant death on fire-imbued creatures).
- **Ice-shattering attacks:** damage x3.
- **Fire attacks:** damage +10 (instant death on ice-imbued creatures).
- **Upgraded bombs:** damage x2 (24 instead of 12 per explosion).

WEAPON BONUSES & DATA SHEETS

As you progress in the adventure and cause enemies to "rank up" (leading to the appearance of archetype variations identified by their different colors), you will start to regularly obtain better weapons and weapons with unique bonuses. This applies to both enemy drops and weapons found in treasure chests.

The data sheets on the following pages reveal not only the base stats for all weapons, but also the nature of their possible perks.

ATTACK POWER

- **Base:** The base damage you inflict with a weapon.
- **Bonus** (rank I: ; rank II:): A flat value added to the weapon's base attack power. Each bonus is randomly determined in a minimum-maximum range. For example, a royal broadsword (base power 36) with a rank-I bonus (6 ▸ 12) will have an attack value anywhere between 42 (36 + 6) and 48 (36 + 12).

DURABILITY

- **Base:** The base durability of a weapon. Every hit against a target or solid object lowers this value. When it reaches 0, the weapon will break.
- **Bonus** (rank I: ; rank II:): A flat value added to the weapon's base durability. As with attack power, each bonus is randomly determined in a minimum-maximum range.

THROW DISTANCE

- **Base:** The distance in meters over which a weapon can be thrown.
- **Bonus** ( ) : A multiplier randomly determined in a minimum-maximum range that increases the distance over which the weapon can be hurled. For the few weapons that cannot be thrown (such as the Master Sword), our data sheets reveal which alternative effect they offer instead.

AVAILABILITY

A list of locations where each weapon is most commonly encountered. Keep in mind that these are not exhaustive: you may also find them in other locales.

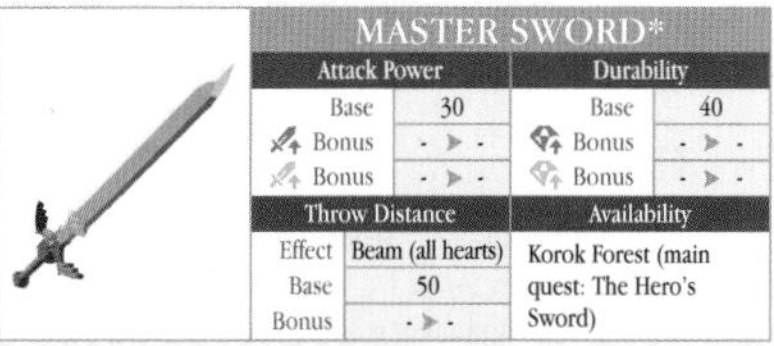

MASTER SWORD*

Attack Power		Durability	
Base	30	Base	40
Bonus	- ▶ -	Bonus	- ▶ -
Bonus	- ▶ -	Bonus	- ▶ -
Throw Distance		**Availability**	
Effect	Beam (all hearts)	Korok Forest (main quest: The Hero's Sword)	
Base	50		
Bonus	- ▶ -		

TREE BRANCH

Attack Power		Durability	
Base	2	Base	4
Bonus	2 ▶ 2	Bonus	1 ▶ 1
Bonus	3 ▶ 4	Bonus	2 ▶ 2
Throw Distance		**Availability**	
Effect	Weapon thrown	Hyrule Field, West Necluda (cut small trees/shrubs)	
Base	5		
Bonus	x1.5 ▶ x2		

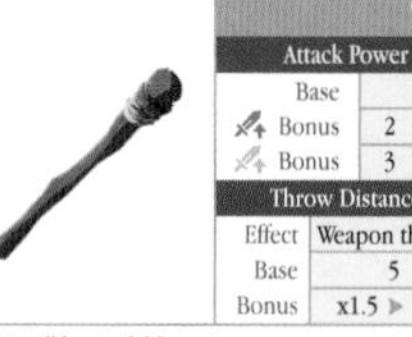

TORCH

Attack Power		Durability	
Base	2	Base	8
Bonus	2 ▶ 2	Bonus	1 ▶ 2
Bonus	3 ▶ 4	Bonus	3 ▶ 4
Throw Distance		**Availability**	
Effect	Weapon thrown	Great Hyrule Forest, Hyrule Field, inside the Tech Labs	
Base	5		
Bonus	x1.5 ▶ x2		

* Deals double damage when fighting Ganon and his minions. Has infinite durability: once its energy has been depleted, there is a cooldown period of a few minutes before it will be available again.

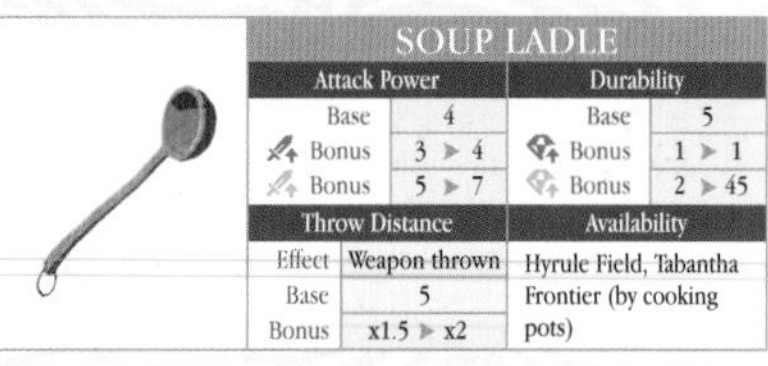

SOUP LADLE

Attack Power		Durability	
Base	4	Base	5
Bonus	3 ▶ 4	Bonus	1 ▶ 1
Bonus	5 ▶ 7	Bonus	2 ▶ 45
Throw Distance		**Availability**	
Effect	Weapon thrown	Hyrule Field, Tabantha Frontier (by cooking pots)	
Base	5		
Bonus	x1.5 ▶ x2		

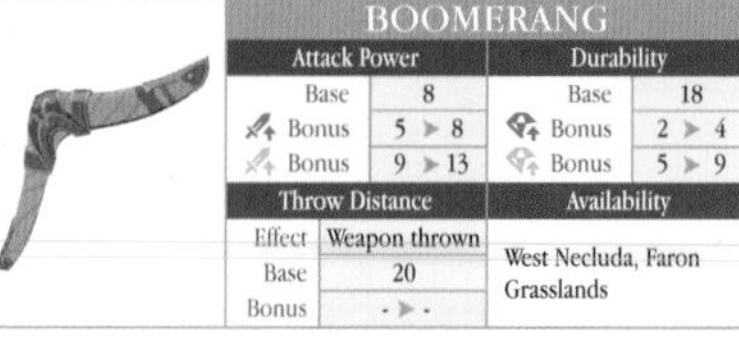

BOOMERANG

Attack Power		Durability	
Base	8	Base	18
Bonus	5 ▶ 8	Bonus	2 ▶ 4
Bonus	9 ▶ 13	Bonus	5 ▶ 9
Throw Distance		**Availability**	
Effect	Weapon thrown	West Necluda, Faron Grasslands	
Base	20		
Bonus	- ▶ -		

SPRING-LOADED HAMMER

Attack Power		Durability	
Base	1	Base	80
Bonus	1 ▶ 1	Bonus	9 ▶ 17
Bonus	2 ▶ 2	Bonus	18 ▶ 41
Throw Distance		**Availability**	
Effect	Weapon thrown	Kiltonís shop	
Base	5		
Bonus	x1.5 ▶ x2		

TRAVELER'S SWORD

Attack Power		Durability	
Base	5	Base	20
Bonus	3 ▶ 5	Bonus	1 ▶ 2
Bonus	6 ▶ 8	Bonus	3 ▶ 3
Throw Distance		**Availability**	
Effect	Weapon thrown	Hyrule Field, West Necluda	
Base	5		
Bonus	x1.5 ▶ x2		

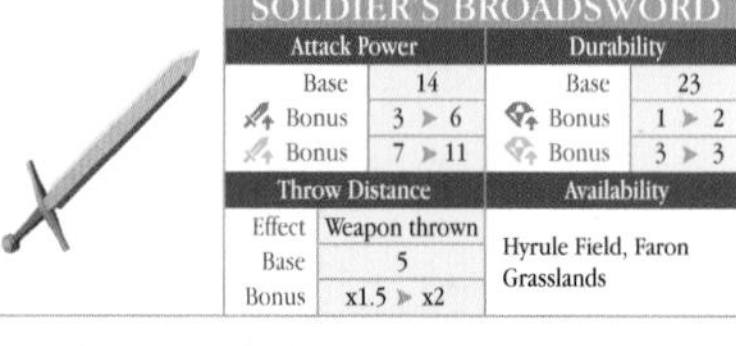

SOLDIER'S BROADSWORD

Attack Power		Durability	
Base	14	Base	23
Bonus	3 ▶ 6	Bonus	1 ▶ 2
Bonus	7 ▶ 11	Bonus	3 ▶ 3
Throw Distance		**Availability**	
Effect	Weapon thrown	Hyrule Field, Faron Grasslands	
Base	5		
Bonus	x1.5 ▶ x2		

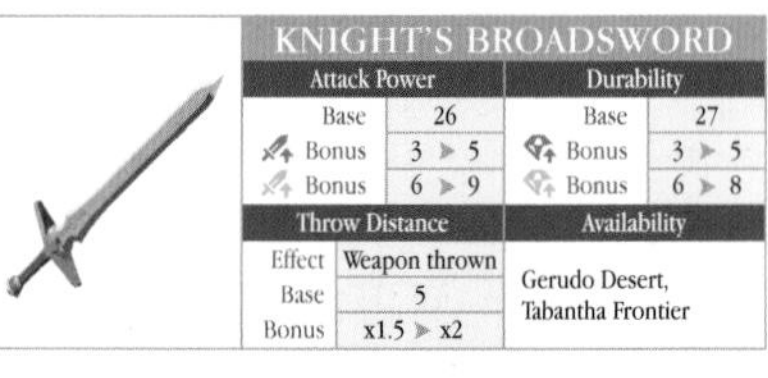

KNIGHT'S BROADSWORD

Attack Power		Durability	
Base	26	Base	27
Bonus	3 ▶ 5	Bonus	3 ▶ 5
Bonus	6 ▶ 9	Bonus	6 ▶ 8
Throw Distance		**Availability**	
Effect	Weapon thrown	Gerudo Desert, Tabantha Frontier	
Base	5		
Bonus	x1.5 ▶ x2		

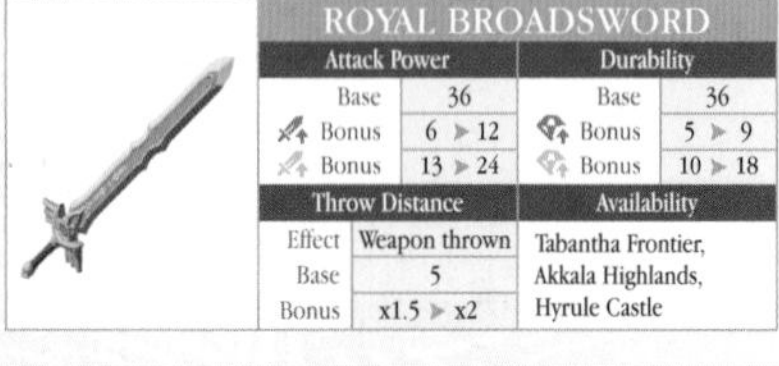

ROYAL BROADSWORD

Attack Power		Durability	
Base	36	Base	36
Bonus	6 ▶ 12	Bonus	5 ▶ 9
Bonus	13 ▶ 24	Bonus	10 ▶ 18
Throw Distance		**Availability**	
Effect	Weapon thrown	Tabantha Frontier, Akkala Highlands, Hyrule Castle	
Base	5		
Bonus	x1.5 ▶ x2		

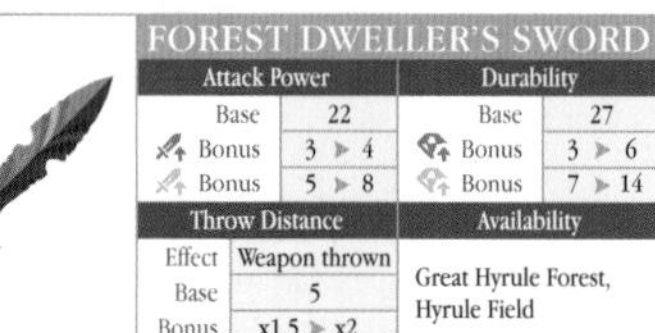

FOREST DWELLER'S SWORD

Attack Power		Durability	
Base	22	Base	27
Bonus	3 ▶ 4	Bonus	3 ▶ 6
Bonus	5 ▶ 8	Bonus	7 ▶ 14
Throw Distance		**Availability**	
Effect	Weapon thrown	Great Hyrule Forest, Hyrule Field	
Base	5		
Bonus	x1.5 ▶ x2		

ZORA SWORD

Attack Power		Durability	
Base	15	Base	27
Bonus	4 ▶ 6	Bonus	3 ▶ 6
Bonus	7 ▶ 12	Bonus	7 ▶ 14
Throw Distance		**Availability**	
Effect	Weapon thrown	Lanayru Great Spring, East Necluda	
Base	5		
Bonus	x1.5 ▶ x2		

FEATHERED EDGE

Attack Power		Durability	
Base	15	Base	27
Bonus	4 ▶ 6	Bonus	3 ▶ 6
Bonus	7 ▶ 12	Bonus	7 ▶ 14
Throw Distance		**Availability**	
Effect	Weapon thrown	Tabantha Frontier, Hyrule Field	
Base	5		
Bonus	x1.5 ▶ x2		

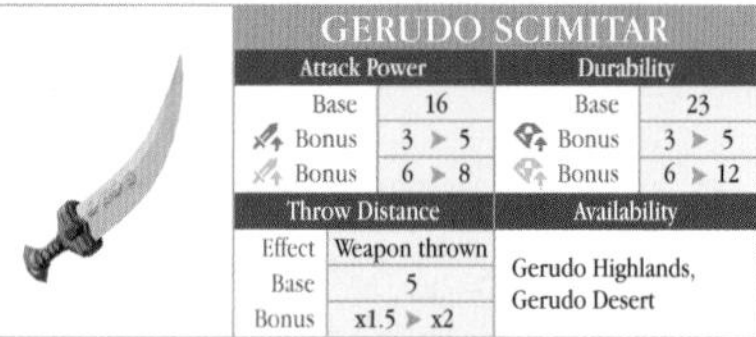

GERUDO SCIMITAR

Attack Power		Durability	
Base	16	Base	23
Bonus	3 ▶ 5	Bonus	3 ▶ 5
Bonus	6 ▶ 8	Bonus	6 ▶ 12
Throw Distance		**Availability**	
Effect	Weapon thrown	Gerudo Highlands, Gerudo Desert	
Base	5		
Bonus	x1.5 ▶ x2		

MOONLIGHT SCIMITAR

Attack Power		Durability	
Base	25	Base	32
Bonus	2 ▶ 4	Bonus	4 ▶ 7
Bonus	5 ▶ 6	Bonus	8 ▶ 16
Throw Distance		**Availability**	
Effect	Weapon thrown	Gerudo Highlands, Gerudo Desert	
Base	5		
Bonus	x1.5 ▶ x2		

SCIMITAR OF THE SEVEN*

Attack Power		Durability	
Base	32	Base	60
Bonus	3 ▶ 5	Bonus	6 ▶ 12
Bonus	6 ▶ 10	Bonus	13 ▶ 30
Throw Distance		**Availability**	
Effect	Weapon thrown	Reward for clearing Divine Beast Vah Naboris dungeon	
Base	5		
Bonus	x1.5 ▶ x2		

EIGHTFOLD BLADE

Attack Power		Durability	
Base	15	Base	26
Bonus	4 ▶ 6	Bonus	3 ▶ 6
Bonus	7 ▶ 12	Bonus	7 ▶ 13
Throw Distance		**Availability**	
Effect	Weapon thrown	West Necluda, Lake Hylia	
Base	5		
Bonus	x1.5 ▶ x2		

ANCIENT SHORT SWORD

Attack Power		Durability	
Base	40	Base	54
Bonus	7 ▶ 14	Bonus	6 ▶ 11
Bonus	15 ▶ 27	Bonus	12 ▶ 27
Throw Distance		**Availability**	
Effect	Weapon thrown	Akkala Ancient Tech Lab	
Base	5		
Bonus	x1.5 ▶ x2		

* After obtaining this weapon as a reward and destroying it in battle, it can be re-forged by Buliara in Gerudo Town.

RUSTY BROADSWORD

Attack Power		Durability	
Base	6	Base	8
Bonus	4 ▶ 6	Bonus	1 ▶ 2
Bonus	7 ▶ 10	Bonus	3 ▶ 4
Throw Distance		**Availability**	
Effect	Weapon thrown	Hyrule Field, Eldin Canyon, Hyrule Castle	
Base	5		
Bonus	x1.5 ▶ x2		

ROYAL GUARD'S SWORD

Attack Power		Durability	
Base	48	Base	14
Bonus	9 ▶ 16	Bonus	2 ▶ 3
Bonus	17 ▶ 33	Bonus	4 ▶ 7
Throw Distance		**Availability**	
Effect	Weapon thrown	Hyrule Castle	
Base	5		
Bonus	x1.5 ▶ x2		

FLAMEBLADE

Attack Power		Durability	
Base	24	Base	36
Bonus	6 ▶ 9	Bonus	4 ▶ 8
Bonus	10 ▶ 19	Bonus	9 ▶ 18
Throw Distance		**Availability**	
Effect	Weapon thrown	Coliseum Ruins, East Necluda	
Base	5		
Bonus	x1.5 ▶ x2		

FROSTBLADE

Attack Power		Durability	
Base	20	Base	30
Bonus	5 ▶ 8	Bonus	4 ▶ 8
Bonus	9 ▶ 16	Bonus	9 ▶ 18
Throw Distance		**Availability**	
Effect	Weapon thrown	Gerudo Highlands, Coliseum Ruins	
Base	5		
Bonus	x1.5 ▶ x2		

THUNDERBLADE

Attack Power		Durability	
Base	22	Base	36
Bonus	5 ▶ 8	Bonus	4 ▶ 8
Bonus	9 ▶ 18	Bonus	9 ▶ 18
Throw Distance		**Availability**	
Effect	Weapon thrown	Coliseum Ruins, West Necluda	
Base	5		
Bonus	x1.5 ▶ x2		

GODDESS SWORD

Attack Power		Durability	
Base	28	Base	45
Bonus	6 ▶ 10	Bonus	5 ▶ 9
Bonus	11 ▶ 17	Bonus	10 ▶ 23
Throw Distance		**Availability**	
Effect	Weapon thrown	Unlocked by corresponding amiibo	
Base	5		
Bonus	x1.5 ▶ x2		

SWORD

Attack Power		Durability	
Base	22	Base	27
Bonus	5 ▶ 8	Bonus	3 ▶ 6
Bonus	9 ▶ 14	Bonus	7 ▶ 14
Throw Distance		**Availability**	
Effect	Weapon thrown	Unlocked by corresponding amiibo	
Base	5		
Bonus	x1.5 ▶ x2		

SEA-BREEZE BOOMERANG

Attack Power		Durability	
Base	20	Base	20
Bonus	4 ▶ 7	Bonus	2 ▶ 4
Bonus	8 ▶ 12	Bonus	5 ▶ 10
Throw Distance		**Availability**	
Effect	Weapon thrown	Unlocked by corresponding amiibo	
Base	20		
Bonus	- ▶ -		

BOKO CLUB

Attack Power		Durability	
Base	4	Base	12
Bonus	2 ▶ 4	Bonus	2 ▶ 3
Bonus	5 ▶ 7	Bonus	4 ▶ 6
Throw Distance		**Availability**	
Effect	Weapon thrown	Hyrule Field, West Necluda	
Base	5		
Bonus	x1.5 ▶ x2		

SPIKED BOKO CLUB

Attack Power		Durability	
Base	12	Base	14
Bonus	3 ▶ 6	Bonus	2 ▶ 3
Bonus	7 ▶ 11	Bonus	4 ▶ 7
Throw Distance		**Availability**	
Effect	Weapon thrown	Faron Grasslands, East Necluda	
Base	5		
Bonus	x1.5 ▶ x2		

DRAGONBONE BOKO CLUB

Attack Power		Durability	
Base	24	Base	18
Bonus	7 ▶ 13	Bonus	2 ▶ 4
Bonus	14 ▶ 26	Bonus	5 ▶ 9
Throw Distance		**Availability**	
Effect	Weapon thrown	Hyrule Ridge, Necluda Sea	
Base	5		
Bonus	x1.5 ▶ x2		

LIZAL BOOMERANG

Attack Power		Durability	
Base	14	Base	17
Bonus	3 ▶ 5	Bonus	2 ▶ 4
Bonus	6 ▶ 9	Bonus	5 ▶ 9
Throw Distance		**Availability**	
Effect	Weapon thrown	Lake Hylia, Lanayru Wetlands	
Base	5		
Bonus	- ▶ -		

ONE-HANDED WEAPONS (CONTINUED)

LIZAL FORKED BOOMERANG

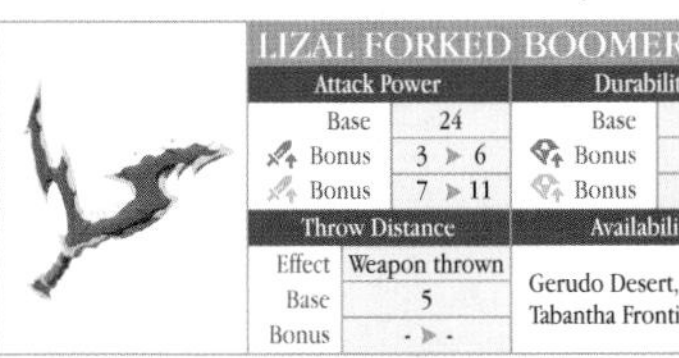

Attack Power		Durability	
Base	24	Base	23
Bonus	3 ▶ 6	Bonus	3 ▶ 5
Bonus	7 ▶ 11	Bonus	6 ▶ 12
Throw Distance		**Availability**	
Effect	Weapon thrown	Gerudo Desert, Tabantha Frontier	
Base	5		
Bonus	- ▶ -		

LIZAL TRI-BOOMERANG

Attack Power		Durability	
Base	36	Base	27
Bonus	6 ▶ 12	Bonus	3 ▶ 6
Bonus	13 ▶ 24	Bonus	7 ▶ 14
Throw Distance		**Availability**	
Effect	Weapon thrown	Hebra Mountains, Akkala Highlands	
Base	5		
Bonus	- ▶ -		

GUARDIAN SWORD

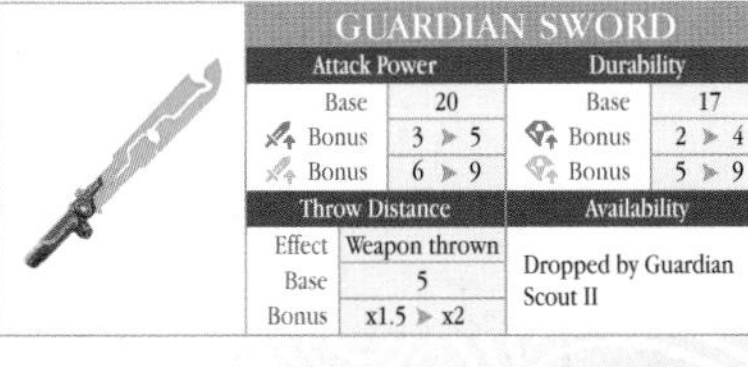

Attack Power		Durability	
Base	20	Base	17
Bonus	3 ▶ 5	Bonus	2 ▶ 4
Bonus	6 ▶ 9	Bonus	5 ▶ 9
Throw Distance		**Availability**	
Effect	Weapon thrown	Dropped by Guardian Scout II	
Base	5		
Bonus	x1.5 ▶ x2		

GUARDIAN SWORD+

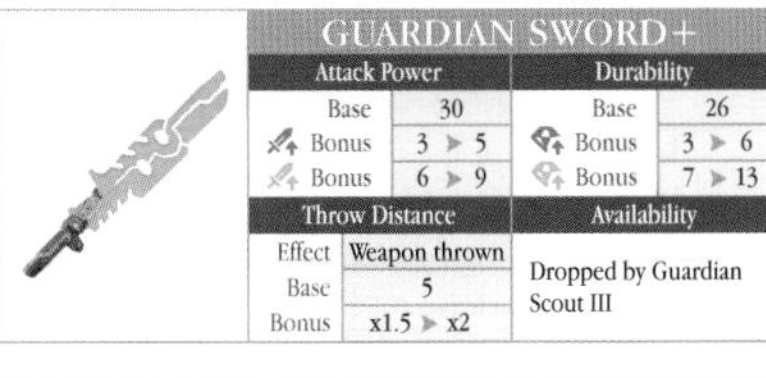

Attack Power		Durability	
Base	30	Base	26
Bonus	3 ▶ 5	Bonus	3 ▶ 6
Bonus	6 ▶ 9	Bonus	7 ▶ 13
Throw Distance		**Availability**	
Effect	Weapon thrown	Dropped by Guardian Scout III	
Base	5		
Bonus	x1.5 ▶ x2		

GUARDIAN SWORD++

Attack Power		Durability	
Base	40	Base	32
Bonus	5 ▶ 10	Bonus	4 ▶ 7
Bonus	11 ▶ 20	Bonus	8 ▶ 16
Throw Distance		**Availability**	
Effect	Weapon thrown	Dropped by Guardian Scout IV	
Base	5		
Bonus	x1.5 ▶ x2		

LYNEL SWORD

Attack Power		Durability	
Base	24	Base	26
Bonus	3 ▶ 6	Bonus	3 ▶ 6
Bonus	7 ▶ 11	Bonus	7 ▶ 13
Throw Distance		**Availability**	
Effect	Weapon thrown	Dropped by Lynels	
Base	5		
Bonus	x1.5 ▶ x2		

MIGHTY LYNEL SWORD

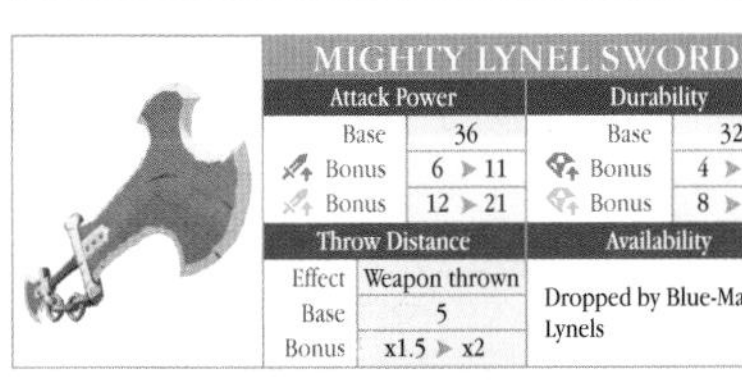

Attack Power		Durability	
Base	36	Base	32
Bonus	6 ▶ 11	Bonus	4 ▶ 7
Bonus	12 ▶ 21	Bonus	8 ▶ 16
Throw Distance		**Availability**	
Effect	Weapon thrown	Dropped by Blue-Maned Lynels	
Base	5		
Bonus	x1.5 ▶ x2		

SAVAGE LYNEL SWORD

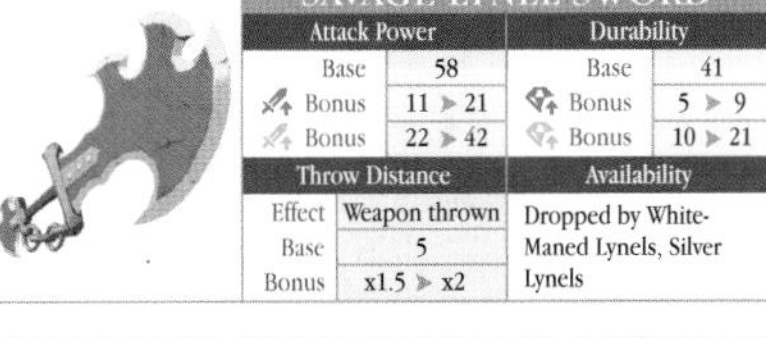

Attack Power		Durability	
Base	58	Base	41
Bonus	11 ▶ 21	Bonus	5 ▶ 9
Bonus	22 ▶ 42	Bonus	10 ▶ 21
Throw Distance		**Availability**	
Effect	Weapon thrown	Dropped by White-Maned Lynels, Silver Lynels	
Base	5		
Bonus	x1.5 ▶ x2		

FIRE ROD

Attack Power		Durability	
Base	5	Base	14
Bonus	3 ▶ 3	Bonus	2 ▶ 3
Bonus	4 ▶ 8	Bonus	4 ▶ 7
Throw Distance		**Availability**	
Effect	1 fire ball	Gerudo Highlands, Great Hyrule Forest	
Base	30		
Bonus	- ▶ -		

METEOR ROD

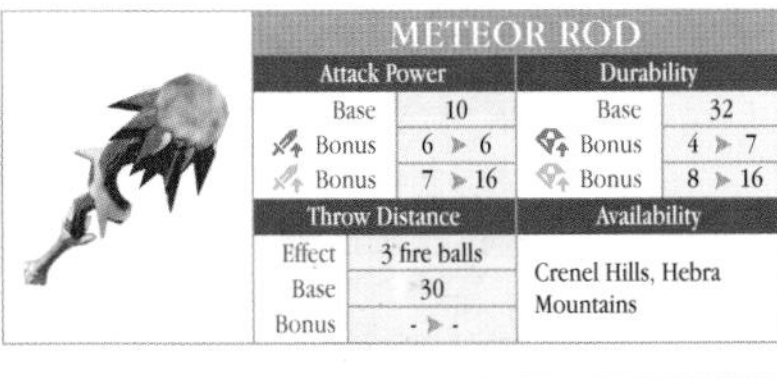

Attack Power		Durability	
Base	10	Base	32
Bonus	6 ▶ 6	Bonus	4 ▶ 7
Bonus	7 ▶ 16	Bonus	8 ▶ 16
Throw Distance		**Availability**	
Effect	3 fire balls	Crenel Hills, Hebra Mountains	
Base	30		
Bonus	- ▶ -		

ICE ROD

Attack Power		Durability	
Base	5	Base	14
Bonus	3 ▶ 3	Bonus	2 ▶ 3
Bonus	4 ▶ 8	Bonus	4 ▶ 7
Throw Distance		**Availability**	
Effect	1 ice ball	Gerudo Highlands, Eldin Canyon	
Base	30		
Bonus	- ▶ -		

BLIZZARD ROD

Attack Power		Durability	
Base	10	Base	32
Bonus	5 ▶ 6	Bonus	4 ▶ 7
Bonus	7 ▶ 16	Bonus	8 ▶ 16
Throw Distance		**Availability**	
Effect	3 ice balls	Gerudo Highlands, Hebra Mountains, Crenel Hills	
Base	30		
Bonus	- ▶ -		

LIGHTNING ROD

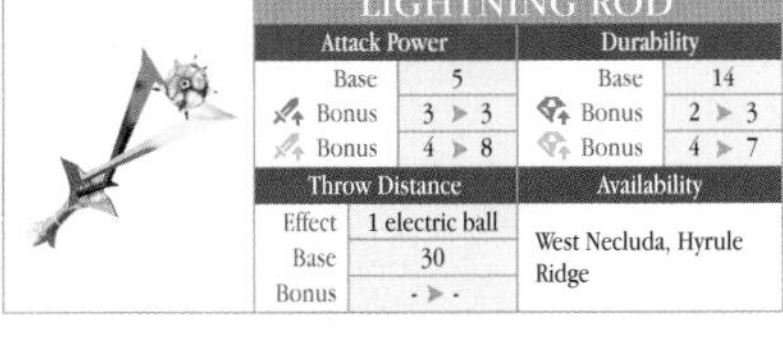

Attack Power		Durability	
Base	5	Base	14
Bonus	3 ▶ 3	Bonus	2 ▶ 3
Bonus	4 ▶ 8	Bonus	4 ▶ 7
Throw Distance		**Availability**	
Effect	1 electric ball	West Necluda, Hyrule Ridge	
Base	30		
Bonus	- ▶ -		

THUNDERSTORM ROD

Attack Power		Durability	
Base	10	Base	32
Bonus	5 ▶ 6	Bonus	4 ▶ 7
Bonus	7 ▶ 16	Bonus	8 ▶ 16
Throw Distance		**Availability**	
Effect	3 electric balls	Crenel Hills, Hyrule Ridge	
Base	30		
Bonus	- ▶ -		

VICIOUS SICKLE

Attack Power		Durability	
Base	16	Base	14
Bonus	4 ▶ 6	Bonus	2 ▶ 3
Bonus	7 ▶ 13	Bonus	4 ▶ 7
Throw Distance		**Availability**	
Effect	Weapon thrown	Dropped by Yiga Footsoldiers	
Base	5		
Bonus	x1.5 ▶ x2		

DEMON CARVER

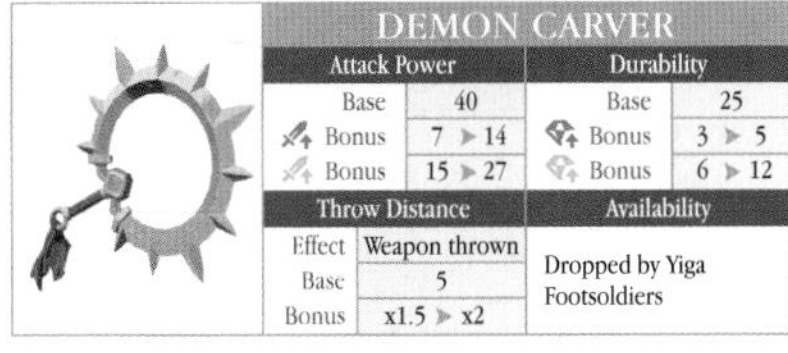

Attack Power		Durability	
Base	40	Base	25
Bonus	7 ▶ 14	Bonus	3 ▶ 5
Bonus	15 ▶ 27	Bonus	6 ▶ 12
Throw Distance		**Availability**	
Effect	Weapon thrown	Dropped by Yiga Footsoldiers	
Base	5		
Bonus	x1.5 ▶ x2		

BOKOBLIN ARM

Attack Power		Durability	
Base	5	Base	5
Bonus	1 ▶ 2	Bonus	1 ▶ 3
Bonus	3 ▶ 5	Bonus	4 ▶ 5
Throw Distance		**Availability**	
Effect	Weapon thrown	Dropped by Stalkoblins	
Base	5		
Bonus	x1.5 ▶ x2		

LIZALFOS ARM

Attack Power		Durability	
Base	12	Base	8
Bonus	1 ▶ 5	Bonus	2 ▶ 5
Bonus	6 ▶ 8	Bonus	6 ▶ 8
Throw Distance		**Availability**	
Effect	Weapon thrown	Dropped by Stalizalfos	
Base	5		
Bonus	- ▶ -		

TWO-HANDED WEAPONS

KOROK LEAF

Attack Power		Durability	
Base	1	Base	25
Bonus	- ▶ -	Bonus	2 ▶ 2
Bonus	- ▶ -	Bonus	6 ▶ 12
Throw Distance		**Availability**	
Effect	Wind gust	Hyrule Field, West Necluda	
Base	5		
Bonus	- ▶ -		

FARMING HOE

Attack Power		Durability	
Base	16	Base	6
Bonus	8 ▶ 14	Bonus	1 ▶ 2
Bonus	15 ▶ 20	Bonus	3 ▶ 3
Throw Distance		**Availability**	
Effect	Weapon thrown	Hyrule Field, West Necluda	
Base	5		
Bonus	x1.5 ▶ x2		

BOAT OAR

Attack Power		Durability	
Base	14	Base	8
Bonus	7 ▶ 13	Bonus	1 ▶ 2
Bonus	14 ▶ 26	Bonus	3 ▶ 4
Throw Distance		**Availability**	
Effect	Weapon thrown	East Necluda, Necluda Sea	
Base	5		
Bonus	x1.5 ▶ x2		

WOODCUTTER'S AXE

Attack Power		Durability	
Base	3	Base	47
Bonus	2 ▶ 3	Bonus	4 ▶ 8
Bonus	4 ▶ 6	Bonus	9 ▶ 18
Throw Distance		**Availability**	
Effect	Weapon thrown	At various stables	
Base	5		
Bonus	x1.5 ▶ x2		

DOUBLE AXE

Attack Power		Durability	
Base	18	Base	52
Bonus	9 ▶ 16	Bonus	5 ▶ 9
Bonus	17 ▶ 22	Bonus	10 ▶ 21
Throw Distance		**Availability**	
Effect	Weapon thrown	At various stables	
Base	5		
Bonus	x1.5 ▶ x2		

IRON SLEDGEHAMMER

Attack Power		Durability	
Base	12	Base	40
Bonus	6 ▶ 11	Bonus	4 ▶ 8
Bonus	12 ▶ 22	Bonus	9 ▶ 18
Throw Distance		**Availability**	
Effect	Weapon thrown	Eldin Canyon, Akkala Highlands, Tanagar Canyon Course	
Base	5		
Bonus	x1.5 ▶ x2		

GIANT BOOMERANG

Attack Power		Durability	
Base	25	Base	40
Bonus	6 ▶ 11	Bonus	4 ▶ 8
Bonus	12 ▶ 22	Bonus	9 ▶ 18
Throw Distance		**Availability**	
Effect	Weapon thrown	West Necluda, Hebra Mountains	
Base	5		
Bonus	- ▶ -		

TRAVELER'S CLAYMORE

Attack Power		Durability	
Base	10	Base	20
Bonus	3 ▶ 5	Bonus	2 ▶ 3
Bonus	6 ▶ 9	Bonus	4 ▶ 4
Throw Distance		**Availability**	
Effect	Weapon thrown	Hyrule Field, West Necluda	
Base	5		
Bonus	x1.5 ▶ x2		

SOLDIER'S CLAYMORE

Attack Power		Durability	
Base	20	Base	25
Bonus	5 ▶ 9	Bonus	1 ▶ 2
Bonus	10 ▶ 17	Bonus	3 ▶ 3
Throw Distance		**Availability**	
Effect	Weapon thrown	Hyrule Field, Faron Grasslands	
Base	5		
Bonus	x1.5 ▶ x2		

KNIGHT'S CLAYMORE

Attack Power		Durability	
Base	38	Base	30
Bonus	4 ▶ 7	Bonus	3 ▶ 5
Bonus	8 ▶ 13	Bonus	6 ▶ 8
Throw Distance		**Availability**	
Effect	Weapon thrown	Gerudo Desert, Tabantha Frontier	
Base	5		
Bonus	x1.5 ▶ x2		

ROYAL CLAYMORE

Attack Power		Durability	
Base	52	Base	40
Bonus	5 ▶ 10	Bonus	5 ▶ 9
Bonus	11 ▶ 20	Bonus	10 ▶ 18
Throw Distance		**Availability**	
Effect	Weapon thrown	Gerudo Desert, Tabantha Frontier, Hyrule Castle	
Base	5		
Bonus	x1.5 ▶ x2		

SILVER LONGSWORD

Attack Power		Durability	
Base	22	Base	30
Bonus	6 ▶ 8	Bonus	3 ▶ 6
Bonus	9 ▶ 19	Bonus	7 ▶ 14
Throw Distance		**Availability**	
Effect	Weapon thrown	Lanayru Great Spring, Lanayru Wetlands	
Base	5		
Bonus	x1.5 ▶ x2		

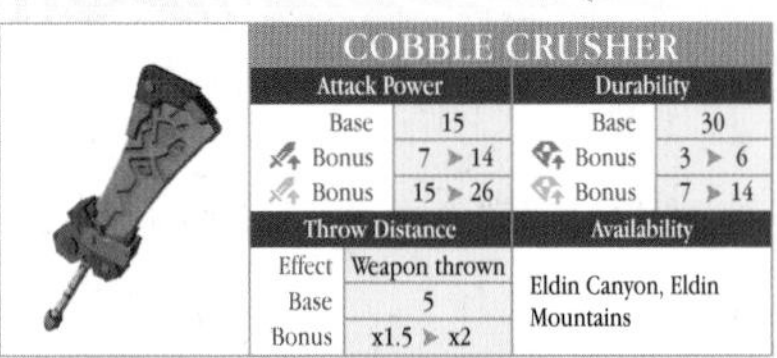

COBBLE CRUSHER

Attack Power		Durability	
Base	15	Base	30
Bonus	7 ▶ 14	Bonus	3 ▶ 6
Bonus	15 ▶ 26	Bonus	7 ▶ 14
Throw Distance		**Availability**	
Effect	Weapon thrown	Eldin Canyon, Eldin Mountains	
Base	5		
Bonus	x1.5 ▶ x2		

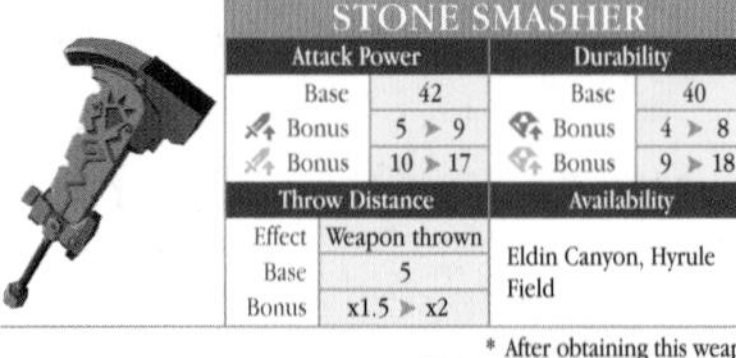

STONE SMASHER

Attack Power		Durability	
Base	42	Base	40
Bonus	5 ▶ 9	Bonus	4 ▶ 8
Bonus	10 ▶ 17	Bonus	9 ▶ 18
Throw Distance		**Availability**	
Effect	Weapon thrown	Eldin Canyon, Hyrule Field	
Base	5		
Bonus	x1.5 ▶ x2		

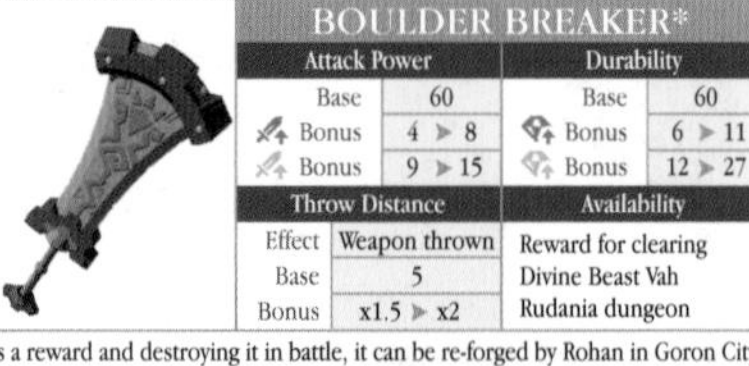

BOULDER BREAKER*

Attack Power		Durability	
Base	60	Base	60
Bonus	4 ▶ 8	Bonus	6 ▶ 11
Bonus	9 ▶ 15	Bonus	12 ▶ 27
Throw Distance		**Availability**	
Effect	Weapon thrown	Reward for clearing Divine Beast Vah Rudania dungeon	
Base	5		
Bonus	x1.5 ▶ x2		

* After obtaining this weapon as a reward and destroying it in battle, it can be re-forged by Rohan in Goron City.

GOLDEN CLAYMORE

Attack Power		Durability	
Base	28	Base	30
Bonus	4 ▶ 8	Bonus	6 ▶ 11
Bonus	9 ▶ 15	Bonus	12 ▶ 27
Throw Distance		**Availability**	
Effect	Weapon thrown	Gerudo Highlands, Hyrule Ridge	
Base	5		
Bonus	x1.5 ▶ x2		

EIGHTFOLD LONGBLADE

Attack Power		Durability	
Base	32	Base	25
Bonus	4 ▶ 6	Bonus	3 ▶ 5
Bonus	7 ▶ 11	Bonus	6 ▶ 12
Throw Distance		**Availability**	
Effect	Weapon thrown	West Necluda, Lanayru Great Spring	
Base	5		
Bonus	x1.5 ▶ x2		

EDGE OF DUALITY

Attack Power		Durability	
Base	50	Base	35
Bonus	5 ▶ 10	Bonus	4 ▶ 7
Bonus	11 ▶ 19	Bonus	8 ▶ 16
Throw Distance		**Availability**	
Effect	Weapon thrown	Hyrule Field, West Necluda	
Base	5		
Bonus	x1.5 ▶ x2		

ANCIENT BLADESAW

Attack Power		Durability	
Base	55	Base	50
Bonus	11 ▶ 20	Bonus	5 ▶ 9
Bonus	21 ▶ 33	Bonus	10 ▶ 23
Throw Distance		**Availability**	
Effect	Weapon thrown	Akkala Ancient Tech Lab	
Base	5		
Bonus	x1.5 ▶ x2		

RUSTY CLAYMORE

Attack Power		Durability	
Base	12	Base	10
Bonus	6 ▶ 11	Bonus	1 ▶ 2
Bonus	12 ▶ 22	Bonus	3 ▶ 5
Throw Distance		**Availability**	
Effect	Weapon thrown	Hyrule Field, Eldin Canyon, Hyrule Castle	
Base	5		
Bonus	x1.5 ▶ x2		

ROYAL GUARD'S CLAYMORE

Attack Power		Durability	
Base	72	Base	15
Bonus	14 ▶ 26	Bonus	3 ▶ 8
Bonus	27 ▶ 44	Bonus	9 ▶ 35
Throw Distance		**Availability**	
Effect	Weapon thrown	Hyrule Castle	
Base	5		
Bonus	x1.5 ▶ x2		

GREAT FLAMEBLADE

Attack Power		Durability	
Base	34	Base	50
Bonus	7 ▶ 12	Bonus	5 ▶ 15
Bonus	13 ▶ 21	Bonus	16 ▶ 30
Throw Distance		**Availability**	
Effect	Weapon thrown	Coliseum Ruins, Eldin Canyon	
Base	5		
Bonus	x1.5 ▶ x2		

GREAT FROSTBLADE

Attack Power		Durability	
Base	30	Base	40
Bonus	6 ▶ 11	Bonus	5 ▶ 15
Bonus	12 ▶ 18	Bonus	16 ▶ 30
Throw Distance		**Availability**	
Effect	Weapon thrown	Coliseum Ruins, Hebra Mountains	
Base	5		
Bonus	x1.5 ▶ x2		

GREAT THUNDERBLADE

Attack Power		Durability	
Base	32	Base	50
Bonus	7 ▶ 12	Bonus	5 ▶ 15
Bonus	13 ▶ 20	Bonus	16 ▶ 30
Throw Distance		**Availability**	
Effect	Weapon thrown	Coliseum Ruins, Tabantha Frontier	
Base	5		
Bonus	x1.5 ▶ x2		

SWORD OF THE SIX SAGES

Attack Power		Durability	
Base	48	Base	50
Bonus	5 ▶ 10	Bonus	8 ▶ 25
Bonus	11 ▶ 19	Bonus	26 ▶ 43
Throw Distance		**Availability**	
Effect	Weapon thrown	Unlocked by corresponding amiibo	
Base	5		
Bonus	x1.5 ▶ x2		

BIGGORON'S SWORD

Attack Power		Durability	
Base	50	Base	60
Bonus	5 ▶ 10	Bonus	9 ▶ 30
Bonus	11 ▶ 19	Bonus	31 ▶ 51
Throw Distance		**Availability**	
Effect	Weapon thrown	Unlocked by corresponding amiibo	
Base	5		
Bonus	x1.5 ▶ x2		

FIERCE DEITY SWORD

Attack Power		Durability	
Base	60	Base	35
Bonus	6 ▶ 12	Bonus	6 ▶ 18
Bonus	13 ▶ 23	Bonus	19 ▶ 30
Throw Distance		**Availability**	
Effect	Weapon thrown	Unlocked by corresponding amiibo	
Base	5		
Bonus	x1.5 ▶ x2		

BOKO BAT

Attack Power		Durability	
Base	6	Base	8
Bonus	3 ▶ 6	Bonus	1 ▶ 2
Bonus	7 ▶ 11	Bonus	3 ▶ 4
Throw Distance		**Availability**	
Effect	Weapon thrown	Hyrule Field, West Necluda	
Base	5		
Bonus	x1.5 ▶ x2		

SPIKED BOKO BAT

Attack Power		Durability	
Base	18	Base	12
Bonus	5 ▶ 9	Bonus	2 ▶ 3
Bonus	10 ▶ 17	Bonus	4 ▶ 6
Throw Distance		**Availability**	
Effect	Weapon thrown	Faron Grasslands, East Necluda	
Base	5		
Bonus	x1.5 ▶ x2		

DRAGONBONE BOKO BAT

Attack Power		Durability	
Base	36	Base	16
Bonus	6 ▶ 12	Bonus	2 ▶ 3
Bonus	13 ▶ 24	Bonus	4 ▶ 8
Throw Distance		**Availability**	
Effect	Weapon thrown	Hyrule Ridge, Necluda Sea	
Base	5		
Bonus	x1.5 ▶ x2		

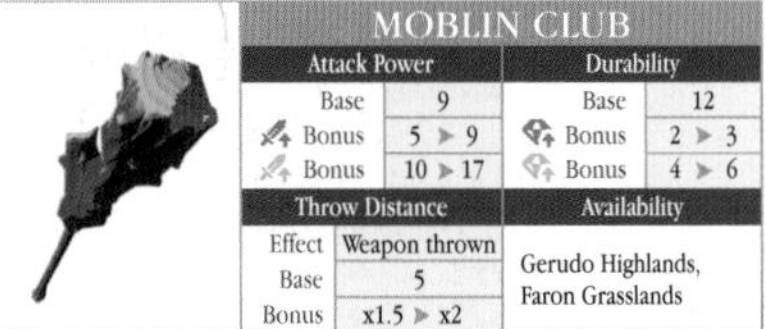

MOBLIN CLUB

Attack Power		Durability	
Base	9	Base	12
Bonus	5 ▶ 9	Bonus	2 ▶ 3
Bonus	10 ▶ 17	Bonus	4 ▶ 6
Throw Distance		**Availability**	
Effect	Weapon thrown	Gerudo Highlands, Faron Grasslands	
Base	5		
Bonus	x1.5 ▶ x2		

SPIKED MOBLIN CLUB

Attack Power		Durability	
Base	27	Base	18
Bonus	5 ▶ 9	Bonus	2 ▶ 4
Bonus	10 ▶ 17	Bonus	5 ▶ 9
Throw Distance		**Availability**	
Effect	Weapon thrown	Hyrule Field, Akkala Highlands	
Base	5		
Bonus	x1.5 ▶ x2		

DRAGONBONE MOBLIN CLUB

Attack Power		Durability	
Base	45	Base	24
Bonus	5 ▶ 10	Bonus	3 ▶ 5
Bonus	11 ▶ 20	Bonus	6 ▶ 11
Throw Distance		**Availability**	
Effect	Weapon thrown	Hebra Mountains, Eldin Mountains	
Base	5		
Bonus	x1.5 ▶ x2		

ANCIENT BATTLE AXE

Attack Power		Durability	
Base	30	Base	15
Bonus	4 ▶ 8	Bonus	2 ▶ 3
Bonus	9 ▶ 14	Bonus	4 ▶ 7
Throw Distance		**Availability**	
Effect	Weapon thrown	Dropped by Guardian Scout II	
Base	5		
Bonus	x1.5 ▶ x2		

ANCIENT BATTLE AXE+

Attack Power		Durability	
Base	45	Base	20
Bonus	4 ▶ 8	Bonus	2 ▶ 4
Bonus	9 ▶ 14	Bonus	5 ▶ 9
Throw Distance		**Availability**	
Effect	Weapon thrown	Dropped by Guardian Scout III	
Base	5		
Bonus	x1.5 ▶ x2		

ANCIENT BATTLE AXE++

Attack Power		Durability	
Base	60	Base	25
Bonus	4 ▶ 8	Bonus	3 ▶ 5
Bonus	9 ▶ 15	Bonus	6 ▶ 12
Throw Distance		**Availability**	
Effect	Weapon thrown	Dropped by Guardian Scout IV	
Base	5		
Bonus	x1.5 ▶ x2		

LYNEL CRUSHER

Attack Power		Durability	
Base	36	Base	20
Bonus	5 ▶ 9	Bonus	2 ▶ 4
Bonus	10 ▶ 17	Bonus	5 ▶ 9
Throw Distance		**Availability**	
Effect	Weapon thrown	Dropped by Lynels	
Base	5		
Bonus	x1.5 ▶ x2		

MIGHTY LYNEL CRUSHER

Attack Power		Durability	
Base	54	Base	25
Bonus	6 ▶ 12	Bonus	3 ▶ 5
Bonus	13 ▶ 23	Bonus	6 ▶ 12
Throw Distance		**Availability**	
Effect	Weapon thrown	Dropped by Blue-Maned Lynels	
Base	5		
Bonus	x1.5 ▶ x2		

SAVAGE LYNEL CRUSHER

Attack Power		Durability	
Base	78	Base	35
Bonus	8 ▶ 15	Bonus	4 ▶ 7
Bonus	16 ▶ 30	Bonus	8 ▶ 16
Throw Distance		**Availability**	
Effect	Weapon thrown	Dropped by White-Maned Lynels, Silver Lynels	
Base	5		
Bonus	x1.5 ▶ x2		

WINDCLEAVER

Attack Power		Durability	
Base	40	Base	25
Bonus	5 ▶ 8	Bonus	6 ▶ 15
Bonus	9 ▶ 14	Bonus	16 ▶ 24
Throw Distance		**Availability**	
Effect	Weapon thrown	Dropped by Yiga Blademasters	
Base	20		
Bonus	x1 ▶ x2		

MOBLIN ARM

Attack Power		Durability	
Base	15	Base	5
Bonus	4 ▶ 6	Bonus	1 ▶ 3
Bonus	7 ▶ 13	Bonus	4 ▶ 20
Throw Distance		**Availability**	
Effect	Weapon thrown	Dropped by Stalmoblins	
Base	5		
Bonus	x1.5 ▶ x2		

WOODEN MOP

Attack Power		Durability	
Base	5	Base	8
Bonus	2 ▶ 4	Bonus	1 ▶ 2
Bonus	5 ▶ 5	Bonus	3 ▶ 4
Throw Distance		Availability	
Effect	Weapon thrown	East Necluda, Hyrule Field	
Base	5		
Bonus	x1.5 ▶ x2		

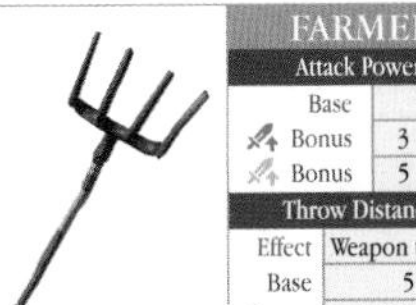

FARMER'S PITCHFORK

Attack Power		Durability	
Base	7	Base	12
Bonus	3 ▶ 4	Bonus	2 ▶ 3
Bonus	5 ▶ 6	Bonus	4 ▶ 6
Throw Distance		Availability	
Effect	Weapon thrown	East Necluda, West Necluda	
Base	5		
Bonus	x1.5 ▶ x2		

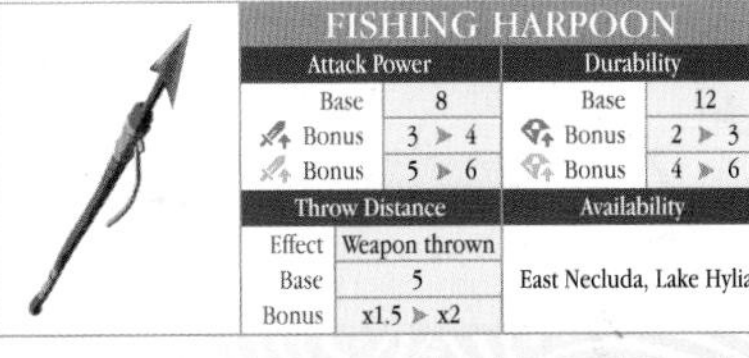

FISHING HARPOON

Attack Power		Durability	
Base	8	Base	12
Bonus	3 ▶ 4	Bonus	2 ▶ 3
Bonus	5 ▶ 6	Bonus	4 ▶ 6
Throw Distance		Availability	
Effect	Weapon thrown	East Necluda, Lake Hylia	
Base	5		
Bonus	x1.5 ▶ x2		

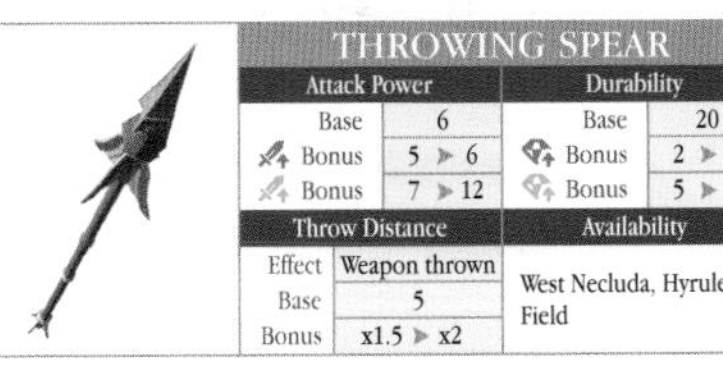

THROWING SPEAR

Attack Power		Durability	
Base	6	Base	20
Bonus	5 ▶ 6	Bonus	2 ▶ 4
Bonus	7 ▶ 12	Bonus	5 ▶ 9
Throw Distance		Availability	
Effect	Weapon thrown	West Necluda, Hyrule Field	
Base	5		
Bonus	x1.5 ▶ x2		

TRAVELER'S SPEAR

Attack Power		Durability	
Base	3	Base	30
Bonus	1 ▶ 2	Bonus	2 ▶ 3
Bonus	3 ▶ 3	Bonus	4 ▶ 4
Throw Distance		Availability	
Effect	Weapon thrown	West Necluda, Hyrule Field	
Base	5		
Bonus	x1.5 ▶ x2		

SOLDIER'S SPEAR

Attack Power		Durability	
Base	7	Base	35
Bonus	2 ▶ 3	Bonus	1 ▶ 2
Bonus	4 ▶ 5	Bonus	3 ▶ 3
Throw Distance		Availability	
Effect	Weapon thrown	Hyrule Field, Faron Grasslands	
Base	5		
Bonus	x1.5 ▶ x2		

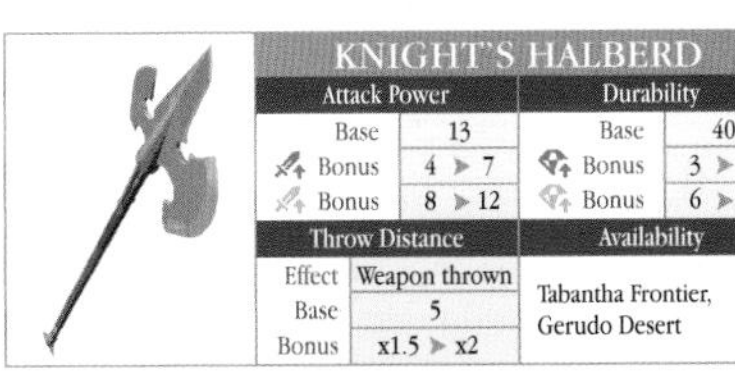

KNIGHT'S HALBERD

Attack Power		Durability	
Base	13	Base	40
Bonus	4 ▶ 7	Bonus	3 ▶ 5
Bonus	8 ▶ 12	Bonus	6 ▶ 8
Throw Distance		Availability	
Effect	Weapon thrown	Tabantha Frontier, Gerudo Desert	
Base	5		
Bonus	x1.5 ▶ x2		

ROYAL HALBERD

Attack Power		Durability	
Base	26	Base	50
Bonus	5 ▶ 10	Bonus	4 ▶ 8
Bonus	11 ▶ 20	Bonus	9 ▶ 15
Throw Distance		Availability	
Effect	Weapon thrown	Gerudo Highlands, Tabantha Frontier	
Base	5		
Bonus	x1.5 ▶ x2		

FOREST DWELLER'S SPEAR

Attack Power		Durability	
Base	11	Base	35
Bonus	4 ▶ 6	Bonus	4 ▶ 7
Bonus	7 ▶ 11	Bonus	8 ▶ 16
Throw Distance		Availability	
Effect	Weapon thrown	Great Hyrule Forest, Hyrule Ridge	
Base	5		
Bonus	x1.5 ▶ x2		

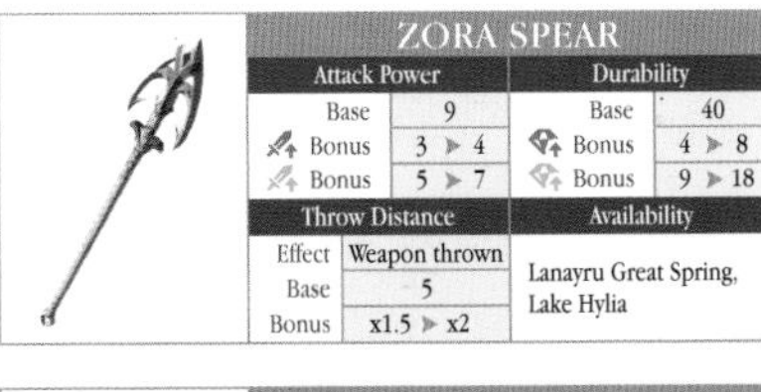

ZORA SPEAR

Attack Power		Durability	
Base	9	Base	40
Bonus	3 ▶ 4	Bonus	4 ▶ 8
Bonus	5 ▶ 7	Bonus	9 ▶ 18
Throw Distance		Availability	
Effect	Weapon thrown	Lanayru Great Spring, Lake Hylia	
Base	5		
Bonus	x1.5 ▶ x2		

SILVERSCALE SPEAR

Attack Power		Durability	
Base	12	Base	40
Bonus	4 ▶ 7	Bonus	4 ▶ 8
Bonus	8 ▶ 12	Bonus	9 ▶ 18
Throw Distance		Availability	
Effect	Weapon thrown	Akkala Highlands, Lanayru Great Spring	
Base	5		
Bonus	x1.5 ▶ x2		

CEREMONIAL TRIDENT*

Attack Power		Durability	
Base	14	Base	40
Bonus	5 ▶ 8	Bonus	3 ▶ 6
Bonus	9 ▶ 13	Bonus	7 ▶ 14
Throw Distance		Availability	
Effect	Weapon thrown	Zora's Domain	
Base	5		
Bonus	x1.5 ▶ x2		

* Can be forged again by the blacksmith at Zora's Domain when it breaks.

LIGHTSCALE TRIDENT*

Attack Power		Durability	
Base	22	Base	70
Bonus	5 ▶ 9	Bonus	7 ▶ 13
Bonus	10 ▶ 18	Bonus	14 ▶ 32
Throw Distance		Availability	
Effect	Weapon thrown	Reward for clearing the Divine Beast Vah Ruta dungeon	
Base	5		
Bonus	x1.5 ▶ x2		

* Can be forged again by the blacksmith at Zora's Domain when it breaks

DRILLSHAFT

Attack Power		Durability	
Base	14	Base	50
Bonus	5 ▶ 8	Bonus	5 ▶ 9
Bonus	9 ▶ 13	Bonus	10 ▶ 23
Throw Distance		Availability	
Effect	Weapon thrown	Eldin Canyon, Hebra Mountains	
Base	5		
Bonus	x1.5 ▶ x2		

FEATHERED SPEAR

Attack Power		Durability	
Base	10	Base	35
Bonus	3 ▶ 5	Bonus	4 ▶ 7
Bonus	6 ▶ 8	Bonus	8 ▶ 16
Throw Distance		Availability	
Effect	Weapon thrown	Tabantha Frontier, Hyrule Field	
Base	5		
Bonus	x1.5 ▶ x2		

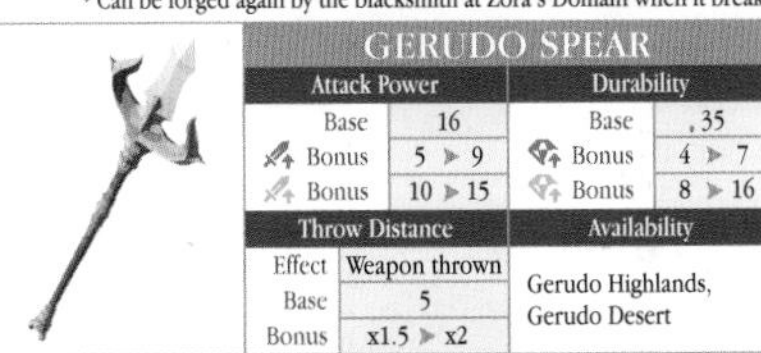

GERUDO SPEAR

Attack Power		Durability	
Base	16	Base	35
Bonus	5 ▶ 9	Bonus	4 ▶ 7
Bonus	10 ▶ 15	Bonus	8 ▶ 16
Throw Distance		Availability	
Effect	Weapon thrown	Gerudo Highlands, Gerudo Desert	
Base	5		
Bonus	x1.5 ▶ x2		

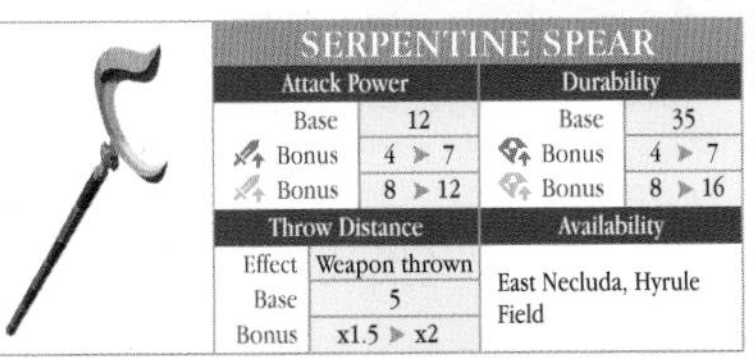

SERPENTINE SPEAR

Attack Power		Durability	
Base	12	Base	35
Bonus	4 ▶ 7	Bonus	4 ▶ 7
Bonus	8 ▶ 12	Bonus	8 ▶ 16
Throw Distance		Availability	
Effect	Weapon thrown	East Necluda, Hyrule Field	
Base	5		
Bonus	x1.5 ▶ x2		

ANCIENT SPEAR

Attack Power		Durability	
Base	30	Base	50
Bonus	6 ▶ 12	Bonus	5 ▶ 9
Bonus	13 ▶ 24	Bonus	10 ▶ 23
Throw Distance		Availability	
Effect	Weapon thrown	Akkala Ancient Tech Lab	
Base	5		
Bonus	x1.5 ▶ x2		

RUSTY HALBERD

Attack Power		Durability	
Base	5	Base	15
Bonus	4 ▶ 5	Bonus	2 ▶ 3
Bonus	6 ▶ 10	Bonus	4 ▶ 7
Throw Distance		Availability	
Effect	Weapon thrown	Hyrule Field, Great Hyrule Forest	
Base	5		
Bonus	x1.5 ▶ x2		

ROYAL GUARD'S SPEAR

Attack Power		Durability	
Base	32	Base	15
Bonus	7 ▶ 13	Bonus	2 ▶ 3
Bonus	14 ▶ 25	Bonus	4 ▶ 7
Throw Distance		Availability	
Effect	Weapon thrown	Hyrule Castle	
Base	5		
Bonus	x1.5 ▶ x2		

FLAMESPEAR

Attack Power		Durability	
Base	24	Base	50
Bonus	5 ▶ 10	Bonus	5 ▶ 9
Bonus	11 ▶ 19	Bonus	10 ▶ 23
Throw Distance		Availability	
Effect	Weapon thrown	Coliseum Ruins, Hebra Mountains	
Base	5		
Bonus	x1.5 ▶ x2		

FROSTSPEAR

Attack Power		Durability	
Base	20	Base	40
Bonus	4 ▶ 8	Bonus	5 ▶ 9
Bonus	9 ▶ 16	Bonus	10 ▶ 23
Throw Distance		Availability	
Effect	Weapon thrown	Coliseum Ruins, Hebra Mountains	
Base	5		
Bonus	x1.5 ▶ x2		

THUNDERSPEAR

Attack Power		Durability	
Base	22	Base	50
Bonus	5 ▶ 9	Bonus	5 ▶ 9
Bonus	10 ▶ 18	Bonus	10 ▶ 23
Throw Distance		Availability	
Effect	Weapon thrown	Coliseum Ruins, Hyrule Ridge	
Base	5		
Bonus	x1.5 ▶ x2		

BOKO SPEAR

Attack Power		Durability	
Base	2	Base	12
Bonus	1 ▶ 2	Bonus	2 ▶ 3
Bonus	3 ▶ 3	Bonus	4 ▶ 6
Throw Distance		Availability	
Effect	Weapon thrown	West Necluda, Hyrule Field	
Base	5		
Bonus	x1.5 ▶ x2		

SPIKED BOKO SPEAR

Attack Power		Durability	
Base	6	Base	15
Bonus	2 ▶ 3	Bonus	2 ▶ 3
Bonus	4 ▶ 5	Bonus	4 ▶ 7
Throw Distance		Availability	
Effect	Weapon thrown	Faron Grasslands, East Necluda	
Base	5		
Bonus	x1.5 ▶ x2		

DRAGONBONE BOKO SPEAR

Attack Power		Durability	
Base	12	Base	20
Bonus	2 ▶ 4	Bonus	2 ▶ 4
Bonus	5 ▶ 7	Bonus	5 ▶ 9
Throw Distance		Availability	
Effect	Weapon thrown	Necluda Sea, Hyrule Ridge	
Base	5		
Bonus	x1.5 ▶ x2		

MOBLIN SPEAR

Attack Power		Durability	
Base	4	Base	15
Bonus	2 ▶ 3	Bonus	2 ▶ 3
Bonus	4 ▶ 4	Bonus	4 ▶ 7
Throw Distance		Availability	
Effect	Weapon thrown	Faron Grasslands, Gerudo Highlands	
Base	5		
Bonus	x1.5 ▶ x2		

SPIKED MOBLIN SPEAR

Attack Power		Durability	
Base	9	Base	20
Bonus	2 ▶ 3	Bonus	2 ▶ 4
Bonus	4 ▶ 5	Bonus	5 ▶ 9
Throw Distance		Availability	
Effect	Weapon thrown	Gerudo Highlands, Akkala Highlands	
Base	5		
Bonus	x1.5 ▶ x2		

DRAGONBONE MOBLIN SPEAR

Attack Power		Durability	
Base	15	Base	25
Bonus	2 ▶ 4	Bonus	3 ▶ 5
Bonus	5 ▶ 7	Bonus	6 ▶ 12
Throw Distance		Availability	
Effect	Weapon thrown	Hebra Mountains, Eldin Mountains	
Base	5		
Bonus	x1.5 ▶ x2		

LIZAL SPEAR

Attack Power		Durability	
Base	7	Base	18
Bonus	2 ▶ 3	Bonus	2 ▶ 4
Bonus	4 ▶ 4	Bonus	5 ▶ 9
Throw Distance		Availability	
Effect	Weapon thrown	Lanayru Wetlands, East Necluda	
Base	5		
Bonus	x1.5 ▶ x2		

SPEARS (CONTINUED)

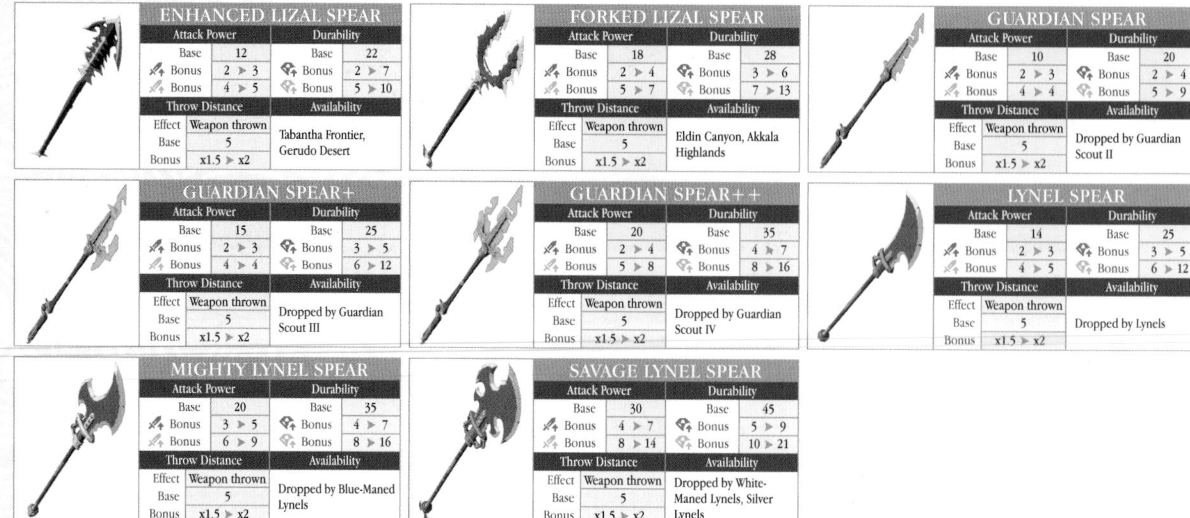

ENHANCED LIZAL SPEAR

Attack Power		Durability	
Base	12	Base	22
Bonus	2 ▶ 3	Bonus	2 ▶ 7
Bonus	4 ▶ 5	Bonus	5 ▶ 10
Throw Distance		**Availability**	
Effect	Weapon thrown	Tabantha Frontier, Gerudo Desert	
Base	5		
Bonus	x1.5 ▶ x2		

FORKED LIZAL SPEAR

Attack Power		Durability	
Base	18	Base	28
Bonus	2 ▶ 4	Bonus	3 ▶ 6
Bonus	5 ▶ 7	Bonus	7 ▶ 13
Throw Distance		**Availability**	
Effect	Weapon thrown	Eldin Canyon, Akkala Highlands	
Base	5		
Bonus	x1.5 ▶ x2		

GUARDIAN SPEAR

Attack Power		Durability	
Base	10	Base	20
Bonus	2 ▶ 3	Bonus	2 ▶ 4
Bonus	4 ▶ 4	Bonus	5 ▶ 9
Throw Distance		**Availability**	
Effect	Weapon thrown	Dropped by Guardian Scout II	
Base	5		
Bonus	x1.5 ▶ x2		

GUARDIAN SPEAR+

Attack Power		Durability	
Base	15	Base	25
Bonus	2 ▶ 3	Bonus	3 ▶ 5
Bonus	4 ▶ 4	Bonus	6 ▶ 12
Throw Distance		**Availability**	
Effect	Weapon thrown	Dropped by Guardian Scout III	
Base	5		
Bonus	x1.5 ▶ x2		

GUARDIAN SPEAR++

Attack Power		Durability	
Base	20	Base	35
Bonus	2 ▶ 4	Bonus	4 ▶ 7
Bonus	5 ▶ 8	Bonus	8 ▶ 16
Throw Distance		**Availability**	
Effect	Weapon thrown	Dropped by Guardian Scout IV	
Base	5		
Bonus	x1.5 ▶ x2		

LYNEL SPEAR

Attack Power		Durability	
Base	14	Base	25
Bonus	2 ▶ 3	Bonus	3 ▶ 5
Bonus	4 ▶ 5	Bonus	6 ▶ 12
Throw Distance		**Availability**	
Effect	Weapon thrown	Dropped by Lynels	
Base	5		
Bonus	x1.5 ▶ x2		

MIGHTY LYNEL SPEAR

Attack Power		Durability	
Base	20	Base	35
Bonus	3 ▶ 5	Bonus	4 ▶ 7
Bonus	6 ▶ 9	Bonus	8 ▶ 16
Throw Distance		**Availability**	
Effect	Weapon thrown	Dropped by Blue-Maned Lynels	
Base	5		
Bonus	x1.5 ▶ x2		

SAVAGE LYNEL SPEAR

Attack Power		Durability	
Base	30	Base	45
Bonus	4 ▶ 7	Bonus	5 ▶ 9
Bonus	8 ▶ 14	Bonus	10 ▶ 21
Throw Distance		**Availability**	
Effect	Weapon thrown	Dropped by White-Maned Lynels, Silver Lynels	
Base	5		
Bonus	x1.5 ▶ x2		

SHIELDS

In this section, we offer the following information for all shields:

- **Durability:** Every hit that you block with a shield lowers its durability. When it reaches 0, the shield will break. Note that the focused laser beams fired by Guardians can destroy almost any shield with a single hit. If you are not confident in your ability to perfect guard, you should equip your least-valuable shield in such situations. Note that just like for weapons, the durability of shields can be improved through bonuses.
- **Availability:** A list of locations where each shield is most commonly encountered.
- **Parry Power:** The attack power of the shield with the parry command (ZL + A). This has nothing to do with the efficiency of perfect guards. It is a simple measure of the offensive power of a shield when used as a weapon with the parry move – a feature you should generally avoid as it has very short reach, a very low attack rate, and it leaves Link exposed for a long time.

SHIELDS

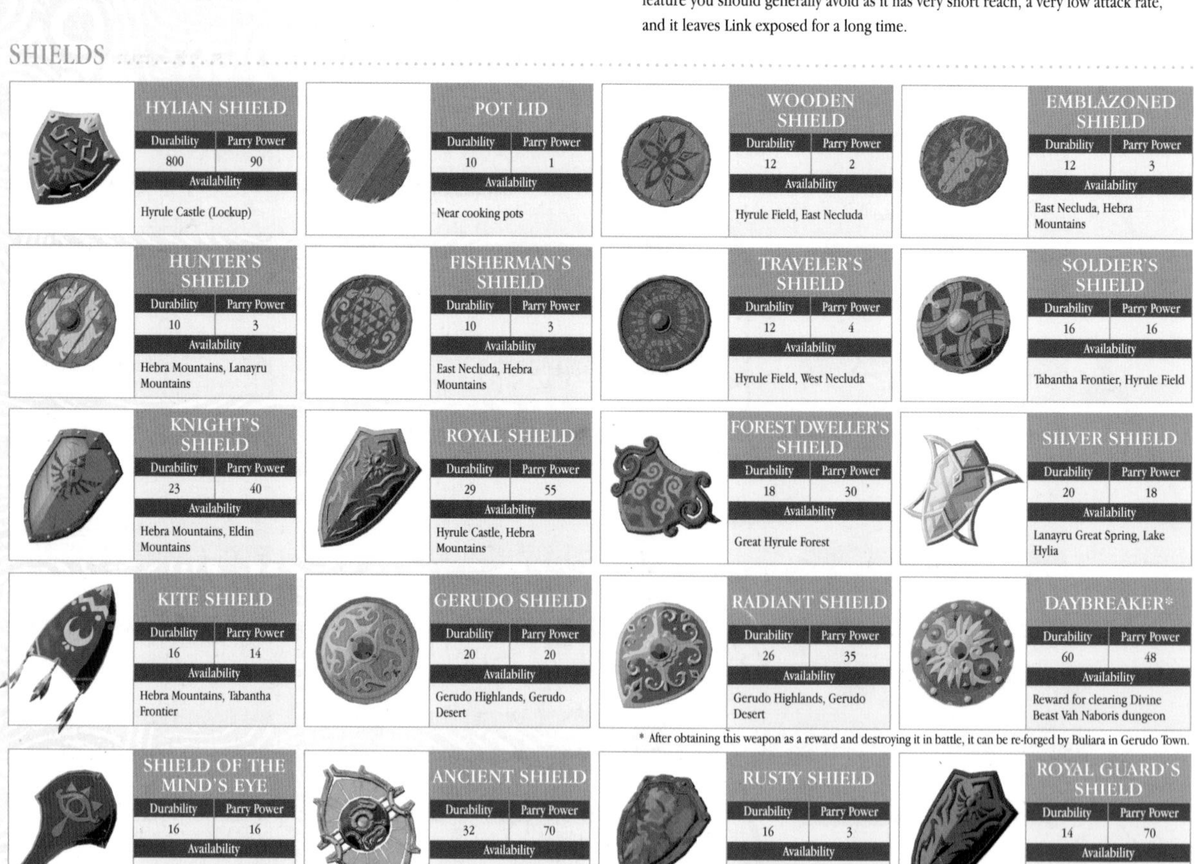

Shield	Durability	Parry Power	Availability
HYLIAN SHIELD	800	90	Hyrule Castle (Lockup)
POT LID	10	1	Near cooking pots
WOODEN SHIELD	12	2	Hyrule Field, East Necluda
EMBLAZONED SHIELD	12	3	East Necluda, Hebra Mountains
HUNTER'S SHIELD	10	3	Hebra Mountains, Lanayru Mountains
FISHERMAN'S SHIELD	10	3	East Necluda, Hebra Mountains
TRAVELER'S SHIELD	12	4	Hyrule Field, West Necluda
SOLDIER'S SHIELD	16	16	Tabantha Frontier, Hyrule Field
KNIGHT'S SHIELD	23	40	Hebra Mountains, Eldin Mountains
ROYAL SHIELD	29	55	Hyrule Castle, Hebra Mountains
FOREST DWELLER'S SHIELD	18	30	Great Hyrule Forest
SILVER SHIELD	20	18	Lanayru Great Spring, Lake Hylia
KITE SHIELD	16	14	Hebra Mountains, Tabantha Frontier
GERUDO SHIELD	20	20	Gerudo Highlands, Gerudo Desert
RADIANT SHIELD	26	35	Gerudo Highlands, Gerudo Desert
DAYBREAKER*	60	48	Reward for clearing Divine Beast Vah Naboris dungeon
SHIELD OF THE MIND'S EYE	16	16	West Necluda, East Necluda
ANCIENT SHIELD	32	70	Akkala Ancient Tech Lab
RUSTY SHIELD	16	3	Hyrule Castle, Hyrule Field, East Necluda
ROYAL GUARD'S SHIELD	14	70	Hyrule Castle
HERO'S SHIELD	90	65	Unlocked by corresponding amiibo
BOKO SHIELD	5	3	Hyrule Field, West Necluda
SPIKED BOKO SHIELD	7	10	Faron Grasslands, East Necluda
DRAGONBONE BOKO SHIELD	8	25	Hyrule Ridge, Necluda Sea

* After obtaining this weapon as a reward and destroying it in battle, it can be re-forged by Buliara in Gerudo Town.

SHIELDS (CONTINUED)

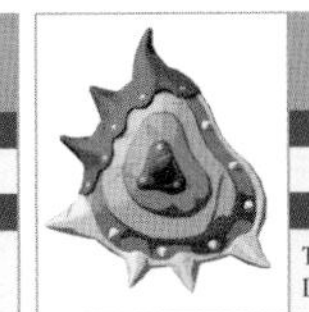
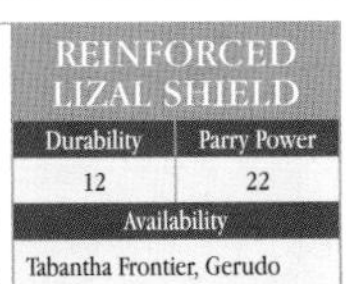

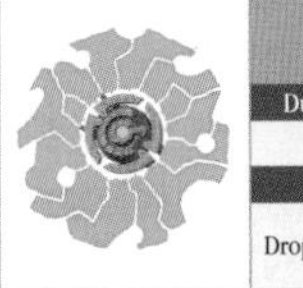
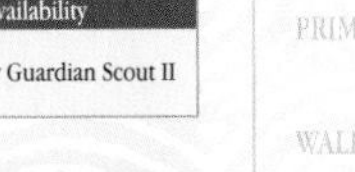
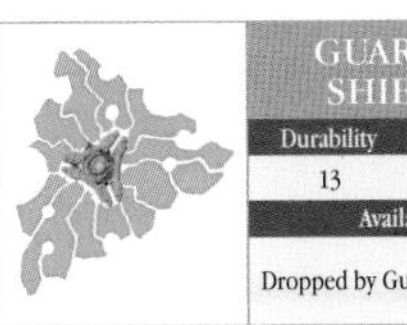
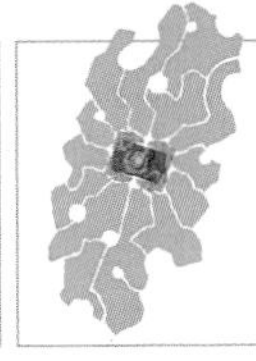
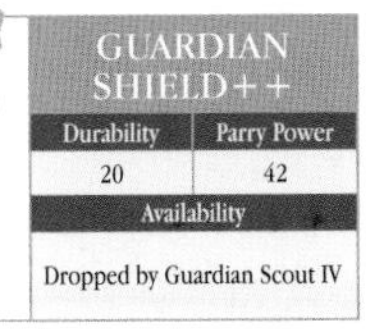
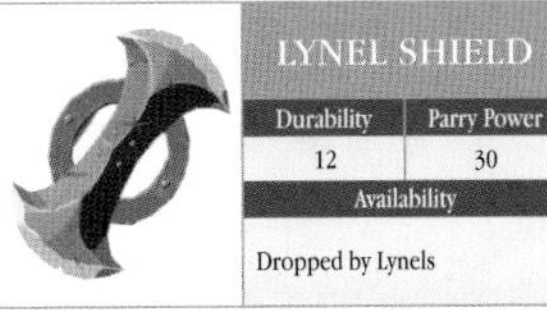
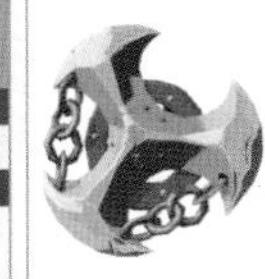
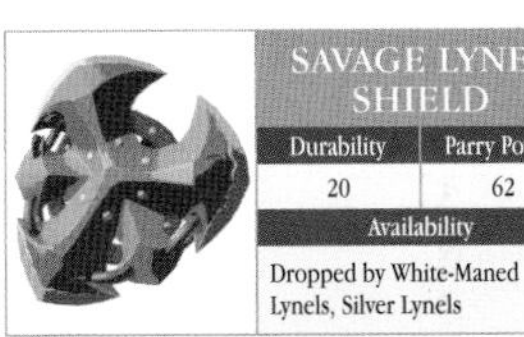

Shield	Durability	Parry Power	Availability
LIZAL SHIELD	8	15	Lake Hylia, East Necluda
REINFORCED LIZAL SHIELD	12	22	Tabantha Frontier, Gerudo Desert
STEEL LIZAL SHIELD	15	35	Hebra Mountains, Akkala Highlands
GUARDIAN SHIELD	10	18	Dropped by Guardian Scout II
GUARDIAN SHIELD+	13	30	Dropped by Guardian Scout III
GUARDIAN SHIELD++	20	42	Dropped by Guardian Scout IV
LYNEL SHIELD	12	30	Dropped by Lynels
MIGHTY LYNEL SHIELD	15	44	Dropped by Blue-Maned Lynels
SAVAGE LYNEL SHIELD	20	62	Dropped by White-Maned Lynels, Silver Lynels

Bows

The table here lists all bows in the game with the following information:

- **Attack Power:** The base attack power of the bow when you shoot an arrow. If the arrow has its own power or if the bow has a power bonus, it is added to this value.
- **Durability:** Every arrow that you fire with a bow lowers its durability. When this value reaches 0, the bow will break. The base durability of bows can be increased by bonuses.
- **Range:** The distance covered by arrows fired by this bow before they start dropping under the effect of gravity. This is a vital parameter when aiming at distant targets, most notably when taking part in mini-games such as horseback archery.
- **Multiple Arrows:** The quantity of arrows fired simultaneously by multiple-shot bows. You only consume one arrow per use no matter how many are actually fired. Based on your progression, certain bows (particularly the multiple-shot ones) can be enhanced by the Five-Shot Burst bonus, enabling them to fire five arrows at a time.
- **Quick Shot:** Certain bows can enjoy this bonus, enabling them to fire arrows in rapid succession.
- **Availability:** A list of locations where each bow is most likely to be found.

BOWS

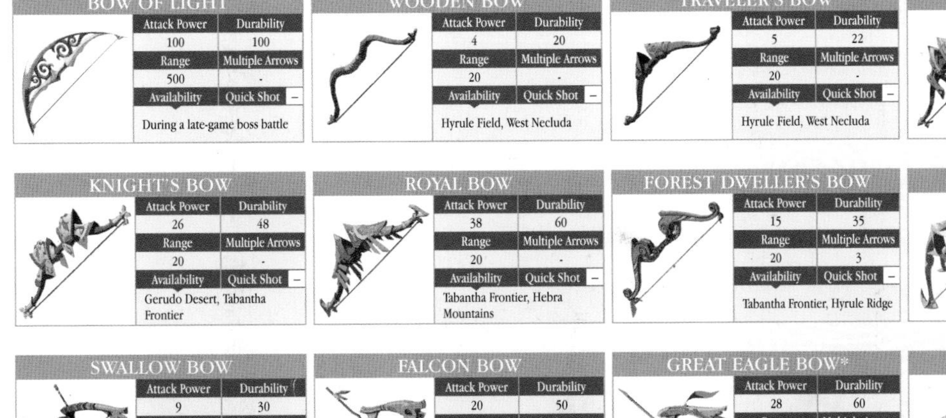

Bow	Attack Power	Durability	Range	Multiple Arrows	Quick Shot	Availability
BOW OF LIGHT	100	100	500	-	-	During a late-game boss battle
WOODEN BOW	4	20	20	-	-	Hyrule Field, West Necluda
TRAVELER'S BOW	5	22	20	-	-	Hyrule Field, West Necluda
SOLDIER'S BOW	14	36	20	-	-	Hyrule Field, Faron Grasslands
KNIGHT'S BOW	26	48	20	-	-	Gerudo Desert, Tabantha Frontier
ROYAL BOW	38	60	20	-	-	Tabantha Frontier, Hebra Mountains
FOREST DWELLER'S BOW	15	35	20	3	-	Tabantha Frontier, Hyrule Ridge
SILVER BOW	15	40	20	-	-	Lanayru Great Spring, Akkala Highlands
SWALLOW BOW	9	30	40	-	-	Tabantha Frontier, Hebra Mountains
FALCON BOW	20	50	40	-	-	Tabantha Frontier, Hebra Mountains
GREAT EAGLE BOW*	28	60	40	3	-	Reward for clearing Divine Beast Vah Medoh dungeon
GOLDEN BOW	14	60	20	-	-	Gerudo Highlands, Gerudo Desert
PHRENIC BOW	10	45	40	-	-	West Necluda, East Necluda
ANCIENT BOW	44	120	40	-	-	Akkala Ancient Tech Lab
ROYAL GUARD'S BOW	50	20	30	-	-	Hyrule Castle
TWILIGHT BOW	30	100	8,000	-	-	Unlocked by corresponding amiibo
BOKO BOW	4	16	20	-	-	Hyrule Field, West Necluda
SPIKED BOKO BOW	12	20	20	-	✔	Faron Grasslands, East Necluda
DRAGON BONE BOKO BOW	24	30	20	-	✔	Hyrule Field, Hyrule Ridge
LIZAL BOW	14	25	20	-	-	Lanayru Great Spring, Lanayru Wetlands

* Can be forged again by Harth at Rito Village when it breaks.

BOWS (CONTINUED)

REINFORCED LIZAL BOW

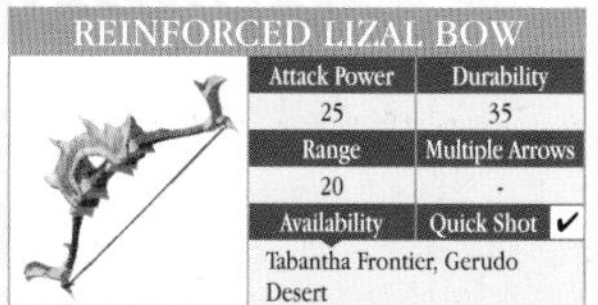

Attack Power	Durability
25	35
Range	**Multiple Arrows**
20	-
Availability	**Quick Shot** ✔
Tabantha Frontier, Gerudo Desert	

STEEL LIZAL BOW

Attack Power	Durability
36	50
Range	**Multiple Arrows**
20	-
Availability	**Quick Shot** ✔
Hebra Mountains, Akkala Highlands	

LYNEL BOW

Attack Power	Durability
10	30
Range	**Multiple Arrows**
20	3
Availability	**Quick Shot** –
Dropped by Lynels	

MIGHTY LYNEL BOW

Attack Power	Durability
20	35
Range	**Multiple Arrows**
20	3
Availability	**Quick Shot** –
Dropped by Blue-Maned Lynels	

SAVAGE LYNEL BOW

Attack Power	Durability
32	45
Range	**Multiple Arrows**
20	3
Availability	**Quick Shot** ✔
Dropped by White-Maned Lynels, Silver Lynels	

DUPLEX BOW

Attack Power	Durability
14	18
Range	**Multiple Arrows**
40	2
Availability	**Quick Shot** ✔
Yiga Clan hideout, dropped by Yiga Footsoldiers	

ARROWS

Arrows have countless applications: not merely a great way to dispatch or stun opponents from a safe distance, they are also used to solve many puzzles. It therefore makes sense to maintain a large stock of these projectiles at all times. Whenever you have an opportunity to purchase some, particularly in bundles, be sure to do so: the nominal rupee investment is well worth it. Blowing up wooden crates with bombs is also an effective way to regularly top up your ammo.

Arrows with elemental or special effects are even more valuable than their standard counterparts. Their magical properties make them both deadly in battle and extremely useful in solving puzzles or interacting with the environment. These arrows can prove particularly potent when fired with multiple-shot bows.

ARROWS

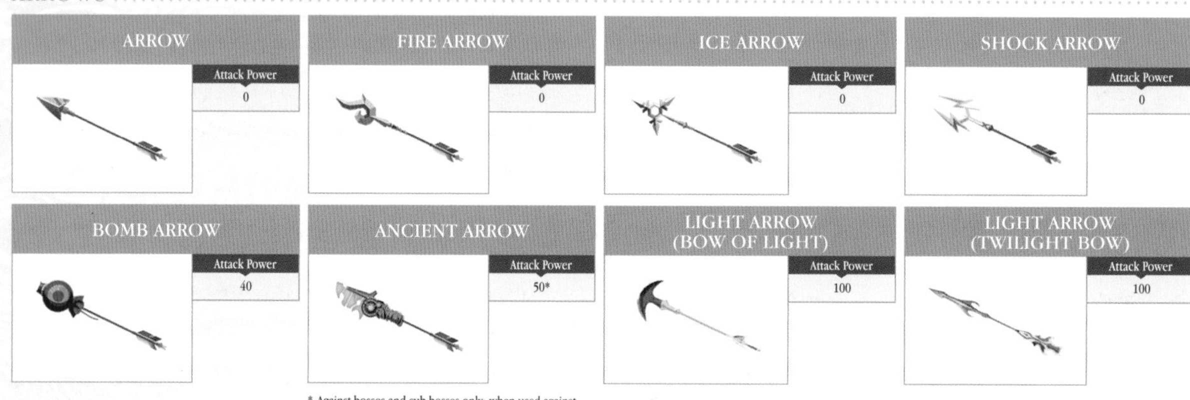

Arrow	Attack Power
ARROW	0
FIRE ARROW	0
ICE ARROW	0
SHOCK ARROW	0
BOMB ARROW	40
ANCIENT ARROW	50*
LIGHT ARROW (BOW OF LIGHT)	100
LIGHT ARROW (TWILIGHT BOW)	100

* Against bosses and sub-bosses only; when used against Guardians, ancient arrows deplete 1/3 of their HP; standard enemies vanish instantly when hit.

MATERIALS

Materials include important resources (such as armor upgrade parts) and all of the items that can be prepared into other forms with cooking pots, either by themselves or when combined with other items. For each object, we provide the following important parameters:

- **Sell price:** The standard price that merchants will pay.
- **HP recovery:** How much HP an ingredient will restore if consumed raw. The healing properties of roasted items and cooked items are increased by 50% and 100% respectively. Don't forget that 4 HP corresponds to a single heart.
- **Category (see table to the right):** This determines the nature of the added effect that each material confers if cooked (as well as the prefix added to the corresponding dishes). See the Cooked Food section for more details.
- **Potency Grade:** A measure of the material's potency in terms of added effect inducement, ranging from E (weakest effect) to A (strongest effect). See the Cooked Food section for more details.
- **Duration factor:** The time in seconds that this material contributes to any added effect in a cooking recipe.
- **Availability:** A non-exhaustive list of locations where each item is commonly found.

CATEGORY OVERVIEW

NAME	ADDED EFFECT
Hearty	Extra Hearts
Energizing	Stamina Restoration
Enduring	Extra Stamina
Fireproof	Flame Guard
Chilly	Heat Resistance
Spicy	Cold Resistance
Electro	Shock Resistance
Hasty	Movement Speed Up
Sneaky	Stealth Up
Mighty	Attack Up
Tough	Defense Up

MATERIALS

ICON	NAME	SELL PRICE	HP RECOVERY	CATEGORY	POTENCY GRADE	DURATION FACTOR	AVAILABILITY
	Acorn	2	1	-	-	50**	Dropped by squirrels
	Amber	30	-	-	-	-	Ore deposits; all Talus types; all Silver enemies
	Ancient Core	80	-	-	-	190	Dropped by Guardians
	Ancient Gear	30	-	-	-	110	Dropped by Guardians
	Ancient Screw	12	-	-	-	70	Dropped by Guardians
	Ancient Shaft	40	-	-	-	110	Dropped by Guardians
	Ancient Spring	15	-	-	-	70	Dropped by Guardians
	Apple	3	2	-	-	30	Great Plateau, Hyrule Field, East Necluda
	Armoranth	5	-	Tough	E	50	Akkala Highlands, Hyrule Ridge
	Armored Carp	10	4	Tough	B	50	Lanayru Great Spring, East Necluda
	Armored Porgy	10	4	Tough	A	50	Necluda Sea, Lanayru Sea
	Big Hearty Radish	15	16	Hearty	A	-	Hebra Mountains, Gerudo Highlands
	Big Hearty Truffle	15	12	Hearty	B	-	Hebra Mountains, Mount Lanayru
	Bird Egg	3	4	-	-	90**	Found in certain tall trees and cliffside bird's nests; dropped by cuccos; sold in Kakariko Village's and Hateno Village's general stores
	Bladed Rhino Beetle	4	-	Mighty	E	50	West Necluda, East Necluda
	Blue Nightshade	4	-	Sneaky	E	120	West Necluda, Lanayru Great Spring
	Bokoblin Fang	8	-	-	-	110	Dropped by Bokoblins
	Bokoblin Guts	20	-	-	-	190	Dropped by Bokoblins
	Bokoblin Horn	3	-	-	-	70	Dropped by Bokoblins
	Bright-Eyed Crab	10	4	Energizing	B	-	Lanayru Great Spring, Eldin Canyon
	Cane Sugar	3	-	-	-	80**	Sold in Rito Village's general store
	Chickaloo Tree Nut	3	1	-	-	40**	Dropped by small birds
	Chillfin Trout	6	4	Chilly	C	150	Hebra Mountains, Tabantha Frontier
	Chillshroom	4	2	Chilly	C	150	Eldin Canyon, Gerudo Highlands
	Chuchu Jelly	5	-	-	-	70	Dropped by Chuchus
	Cold Darner	2	-	Chilly	C	150	Tabantha Frontier, Hyrule Ridge
	Cool Safflina	3	-	Chilly	E	150	Gerudo Desert, Hyrule Ridge
	Courser Bee Honey	10	8	Energizing	B	-	Hit a bee hive
	Diamond	500	-	-	-	-	Rare ore deposits; all Talus except default type; all Silver enemies
	Dinraal's Claw	180	-	-	-	210**	Fire an arrow at Dinraal's feet
	Dinraal's Scale	150	-	-	-	90**	Fire an arrow at Dinraal's body
	Electric Darner	2	-	Electro	A	150	Hyrule Ridge, Gerudo Desert
	Electric Keese Wing	6	-	-	-	110	Dropped by Electric Keese
	Electric Safflina	3	-	Electro	D	150	Gerudo Desert, Hyrule Ridge
	Endura Carrot	30	8	Enduring	A	-	Kakariko Village
	Endura Shroom	6	4	Enduring	C	-	Hyrule Ridge, Hyrule Field
	Energetic Rhino Beetle	30	-	Energizing	A	-	Akkala Highlands, West Necluda
	Fairy	2	20	-	-	30	Around Great Fairy Fountains
	Farosh's Claw	180	-	-	-	210**	Fire an arrow at Farosh's feet
	Farosh's Scale	150	-	-	-	90**	Fire an arrow at Farosh's body
	Fire Keese Wing	6	-	-	-	110	Dropped by Fire Keese
	Fireproof Lizard	5	-	Fireproof	E	150	Eldin Canyon, Death Mountain
	Fleet-Lotus Seeds	5	2	Hasty	B	60	Lanayru Wetlands, Lanayru Great Spring
	Flint	5	-	-	-	-	Ore deposits; all Talus types
	Fortified Pumpkin	5	2	Tough	B	50	Hyrule Field, West Necluda
	Fresh Milk	3	2	-	-	80**	Sold in Hateno Village's general store
	Giant Ancient Core	200	-	-	-	190	Dropped by Guardians
	Goat Butter	3	-	-	-	80**	Sold in Rito Village's and Kakariko Village's general stores
	Goron Spice	4	-	-	-	90**	Sold in Goron City's general store
	Hearty Bass	18	8	Hearty	D	-	West Necluda, Akkala Highlands
	Hearty Blueshell Snail	15	12	Hearty	C	-	Necluda Sea, Lanayru Sea
	Hearty Durian	15	12	Hearty	B	-	West Necluda, Faron Grasslands
	Hearty Lizard	20	-	Hearty	B	-	Gerudo Desert, Necluda Sea
	Hearty Radish	8	10	Hearty	C	-	Akkala Highlands, Lanayru Great Spring
	Hearty Salmon	10	16	Hearty	B	-	Hebra Mountains, Tabantha Frontier
	Hearty Truffle	6	8	Hearty	E	-	Hebra Mountains, Great Hyrule Forest
	Hightail Lizard	2	-	Hasty	E	60	West Necluda, East Necluda
	Hinox Guts	80	-	-	-	190	Dropped by Hinox
	Hinox Toenail	20	-	-	-	70	Dropped by Hinox
	Hinox Tooth	35	-	-	-	110	Dropped by Hinox
	Hot-Footed Frog	2	-	Hasty	B	60	Lanayru Great Spring, Hyrule Ridge
	Hydromelon	4	2	Chilly	E	150	Gerudo Desert, Faron Grasslands

* Only when cooked.
** Reduced to 30 for all subsequent additions in the same recipe.
*** Random: Can randomly affect recipe parameters positively or negatively.

MATERIALS (CONTINUED)

Icon	Name	Sell Price	HP Recovery	Category	Potency Grade	Duration Factor	Availability
	Hylian Rice	3	4	-	-	60**	Cut tall grass in Hyrule Field; sold in Hateno Village's and Zora's Domain's general stores
	Hylian Shroom	3	2	-	-	30	Hyrule Ridge, Hyrule Field
	Hyrule Bass	6	4	-	-	30	Hyrule Field, West Necluda
	Hyrule Herb	3	4	-	-	30	Hyrule Ridge, East Necluda
	Ice Keese Wing	6	-	-	-	110	Dropped by Ice Keese
	Icy Lizalfos Tail	35	-	-	-	190	Dropped by Ice-Breath Lizalfos
	Ironshell Crab	8	4	Tough	B	50	Necluda Sea, East Necluda
	Ironshroom	5	2	Tough	B	50	Lanayru Great Spring, West Necluda
	Keese Eyeball	20	-	-	-	190	Dropped by Keese
	Keese Wing	2	-	-	-	70	Dropped by Keese
	Lizalfos Horn	10	-	-	-	70	Dropped by Lizalfos
	Lizalfos Tail	28	-	-	-	190	Dropped by Lizalfos
	Lizalfos Talon	15	-	-	-	110	Dropped by Lizalfos
	Luminous Stone	70	-	-	-	-	Luminous stone deposit; Stone Talus (Luminous)
	Lynel Guts	200	-	-	-	190	Dropped by Lynels
	Lynel Hoof	50	-	-	-	110	Dropped by Lynels
	Lynel Horn	40	-	-	-	70	Dropped by Lynels
	Mighty Bananas	5	2	Mighty	B	50	Faron
	Mighty Carp	10	4	Mighty	B	50	Akkala Highlands, Lanayru Great Spring
	Mighty Porgy	10	4	Mighty	A	50	Necluda Sea, Lanayru Sea
	Mighty Thistle	5	-	Mighty	E	50	West Necluda, Faron Grasslands
	Moblin Fang	12	-	-	-	110	Dropped by Moblins
	Moblin Guts	25	-	-	-	190	Dropped by Moblins
	Moblin Horn	5	-	-	-	70	Dropped by Moblins
	Molduga Fin	30	-	-	-	110	Dropped by Moldugas
	Molduga Guts	110	-	-	-	190	Dropped by Moldugas
	Monster Extract	3	***	-	***	***	Kilton's monster shop
	Naydra's Claw	180	-	-	-	210**	Fire an arrow at Naydra's feet
	Naydra's Scale	150	-	-	-	90**	Fire an arrow at Naydra's body
	Octo Balloon	5	-	-	-	70	Dropped by Octoroks
	Octorok Eyeball	25	-	-	-	110	Dropped by Octoroks
	Octorok Tentacle	10	-	-	-	70	Dropped by Octoroks
	Opal	60	-	-	-	-	Ore deposits; all Talus types; all Silver enemies
	Palm Fruit	4	4	-	-	30	East Necluda, Gerudo Desert
	Raw Bird Drumstick	8	4	-	-	30	Dropped by small birds
	Raw Bird Thigh	15	6	-	-	30	Dropped by small birds
	Raw Gourmet Meat	35	12	-	-	30	Dropped by the biggest, most dangerous mammals
	Raw Meat	8	4	-	-	30	Dropped by small, harmless mammals
	Raw Prime Meat	15	6	-	-	30	Dropped by bigger, more dangerous mammals
	Raw Whole Bird	35	12	-	-	30	Dropped by white pigeons and Eldin ostriches
	Razorclaw Crab	8	4	Mighty	B	50	Necluda Sea, East Necluda
	Razorshroom	5	2	Mighty	B	50	West Necluda, East Necluda
	Red Chuchu Jelly	10	-	-	-	110	Dropped by Fire Chuchus
	Red Lizalfos Tail	35	-	-	-	190	Dropped by Fire-Breath Lizalfos
	Restless Cricket	2	-	Energizing	D	-	Hyrule Field, East Necluda
	Rock Salt	2	-	-	-	60**	Ore deposits
	Ruby	210	-	-	-	-	Ore deposits; Talus (standard, Luminous and Igneo types); all Silver enemies
	Rugged Rhino Beetle	4	-	Tough	E	50	Hyrule Field, Faron Grasslands
	Rushroom	3	2	Hasty	E	60	Great Hyrule Forest, Tabantha Frontier
	Sanke Carp	20	4	-	-	30	West Necluda
	Sapphire	260	-	-	-	-	Ore deposits; Talus (Frost and Rare types); all Silver enemies
	Shard of Dinraal's Fang	250	-	-	-	630**	Fire an arrow at Dinraal's mouth
	Shard of Dinraal's Horn	300	-	-	-	1800	Fire an arrow at Dinraal's horn
	Shard of Farosh's Fang	250	-	-	-	630**	Fire an arrow at Farosh's mouth
	Shard of Farosh's Horn	300	-	-	-	1800	Fire an arrow at Farosh's horn
	Shard of Naydra's Fang	250	-	-	-	630**	Fire an arrow at Naydra's mouth
	Shard of Naydra's Horn	300	-	-	-	1800	Fire an arrow at Naydra's horn
	Silent Princess	10	8*	Sneaky	A	120	Hyrule Ridge, West Necluda,
	Silent Shroom	3	2	Sneaky	C	120	Hyrule Field, Akkala Highlands
	Sizzlefin Trout	6	4	Spicy	C	150	Eldin Canyon, Eldin Mountains
	Smotherwing Butterfly	2	-	Fireproof	D	150	Eldin Canyon, Death Mountain
	Sneaky River Snail	6	4	Sneaky	E	120	West Necluda, Lanayru Great Spring
	Spicy Pepper	3	2	Spicy	E	150	Gerudo Desert, Tabantha Frontier
	Stamella Shroom	5	2	Energizing	C	-	Great Hyrule Forest, Hyrule Field
	Staminoka Bass	18	4	Energizing	A	-	Hyrule Field, West Necluda
	Star Fragment	300	-	-	-	30	Shooting stars
	Stealthfin Trout	10	4	Sneaky	C	120	Great Hyrule Forest, Eldin Mountains
	Summerwing Butterfly	2	-	Spicy	E	150	Great Hyrule Forest, Eldin Mountains
	Sunset Firefly	2	-	Sneaky	E	120	West Necluda, Korok Forest
	Sunshroom	4	2	Spicy	C	150	Deep Akkala, Gerudo Highlands
	Swift Carrot	4	2	Hasty	E	60	Hyrule Ridge, Faron Grasslands
	Swift Violet	10	-	Hasty	A	60	Hebra Mountains, Gerudo Highlands
	Tabantha Wheat	3	4	-	-	60**	Cut tall grass in the Tabantha region; sold in Rito Village's general store and in Gerudo Town's southernmost food shop and in Gerudo Town's southernmost food shop
	Thunderwing Butterfly	2	-	Electro	D	150	Hyrule Ridge, Gerudo Highlands
	Tireless Frog	20	16*	Enduring	B	-	Lanayru Great Spring, Hyrule Ridge
	Topaz	180	-	-	-	-	Ore deposits; Talus (Luminous and Rare types); all Silver enemies
	Voltfin Trout	6	4	Electro	A	150	Tabantha Frontier, Hyrule Ridge
	Voltfruit	4	2	Electro	D	150	Gerudo Desert, Gerudo Highlands
	Warm Darner	2	-	Spicy	C	150	Akkala Highlands, Hyrule Field
	Warm Safflina	3	-	Spicy	E	150	Gerudo Desert, Hyrule Ridge
	White Chuchu Jelly	10	-	-	-	110	Dropped by Ice Chuchus
	Wildberry	3	2	-	-	30	Hebra Mountains, Gerudo Highlands
	Winterwing Butterfly	2	-	Chilly	E	150	Hyrule Field, Tabantha Frontier
	Wood	2	-	-	-	-	Obtained by cutting trees
	Yellow Chuchu Jelly	10	-	-	-	110	Dropped by Electric Chuchus
	Yellow Lizalfos Tail	35	-	-	-	190	Dropped by Electric Lizalfos
	Zapshroom	4	2	Electro	A	150	Gerudo Highlands, Hyrule Ridge

* Only when cooked. ** Reduced to 30 for all subsequent additions in the same recipe.

Roasted and Frozen Food

Roasted food is obtained by exposing appropriate items to flames, such as dropping them close to a campfire. Roasting food increases the hearts recovered by an item by 50%, but removes any potential added effect.

Frozen food is obtained by exposing corresponding items to freezing temperatures. Frozen food restores the same amount of health as usual, but also provides heat resistance for one minute.

Unlike cooked dishes, items in this category can stack within the inventory, occupying a single slot even when you have multiple copies of them. Once roasted or frozen, an item can no longer be thrown or cooked.

ROASTED AND FROZEN FOOD

ICON	NAME	SELL PRICE	HP RECOVERY
	Baked Apple	3	3
	Baked Fortified Pumpkin	8	3
	Baked Palm Fruit	6	6
	Blackened Crab	12	6
	Blueshell Escargot	15	18
	Campfire Egg	5	6
	Charred Pepper	5	3
	Frozen Bass	14	8
	Frozen Bird Drumstick	15	4
	Frozen Bird Thigh	28	6
	Frozen Carp	18	4
	Frozen Crab	14	8
	Frozen Hearty Bass	14	8
	Frozen Hearty Salmon	18	16
	Frozen Porgy	18	4
	Frozen River Snail	10	4
	Frozen Trout	10	4
	Frozen Whole Bird	40	12
	Hard-Boiled Egg*	5	6
	Icy Gourmet Meat	40	12
	Icy Hearty Blueshell Snail	18	12
	Icy Meat	15	4
	Icy Prime Meat	28	6
	Roasted Acorn	2	2
	Roasted Armoranth	8	2
	Roasted Bass	9	6
	Roasted Big Radish	24	24
	Roasted Bird Drumstick	12	6
	Roasted Bird Thigh	24	9
	Roasted Carp	15	6
	Roasted Endura Carrot	38	12
	Roasted Hearty Bass	12	12
	Roasted Hearty Durian	12	18
	Roasted Hearty Salmon	15	18
	Roasted Hydromelon	8	3
	Roasted Lotus Seeds	8	3
	Roasted Mighty Bananas	8	3
	Roasted Mighty Thistle	8	2
	Roasted Porgy	15	6
	Roasted Radish	12	15
	Roasted Swift Carrot	6	3
	Roasted Tree Nut	2	2
	Roasted Trout	9	6
	Roasted Voltfruit	8	3
	Roasted Whole Bird	35	18
	Roasted Wildberry	5	3
	Seared Gourmet Steak	35	18
	Seared Prime Steak	24	9
	Seared Steak	12	6
	Sneaky River Escargot	9	6
	Toasted Big Hearty Truffle	24	18
	Toasted Hearty Truffle	8	12
	Toasty Chillshroom	6	3
	Toasty Endura Shroom	5	6
	Toasty Hylian Shroom	3	3
	Toasty Ironshroom	5	3
	Toasty Razorshroom	5	3
	Toasty Rushroom	5	3
	Toasty Silent Shroom	3	3
	Toasty Stamella Shroom	5	3
	Toasty Sunshroom	6	3
	Toasty Zapshroom	6	3

* Obtained by dropping a Bird Egg in boiling water, such as hot springs.

Cooked Food

Cooking is achieved by throwing anything from one to five materials into a cooking pot. As a rule, the process doubles the amount of health recovered by each ingredient. Certain items can also provide an added effect when cooked, such as cold resistance. Each cooked dish occupies its own slot in your inventory; you can hold up to 60 meals or elixirs at once.

Ingredients are sorted into categories based on the added effect they grant. When you use an ingredient that confers a bonus, the final dish is given a corresponding prefix. For example, the "spicy meat & seafood fry" is a variation of the base "meat & seafood fry" recipe, where the addition of a spicy pepper leads to the cold resistance added effect, as indicated by the "spicy" prefix.

Only one added effect (and, therefore, prefix) is possible for any meal; multiple added effects will cancel each other out when you cook the materials. However, ingredients with the same added effect (in other words, belonging to the same category) can stack to produce more potent buffs, depending on material potency grades – as explained in the following table.

ADDED EFFECT POTENCY

MATERIAL CATEGORY	ADDED EFFECT	POTENCY GRADES
Hearty	Full Recovery* + Extra Hearts	From 1 yellow heart (grade E) to 5 (grade A); effects stack additively
Energizing	Stamina Restoration	Potency varies per grade; effects stack additively
Enduring	Extra Stamina	
Fireproof	Flame Guard	May be stacked within the same category to achieve a higher-level effect (from Level 1 to Level 2 or 3). Higher-grade materials are better at increasing the effect level. Generally, you'll need grade A or grade B materials to produce a Level 3 effect.
Chilly	Heat Resistance	
Spicy	Cold Resistance	
Electro	Shock Resistance	
Hasty	Movement Speed Up	
Sneaky	Stealth Up	
Mighty	Attack Up	
Tough	Defense Up	

* Materials of the "hearty" category are worth a special mention: cooking a single one of them will refill all of your hearts, irrespective of the size of your health gauge. This makes these items really precious in the late game, when you can have up to 30 hearts in total.

You will occasionally hear a special sound effect while cooking. This indicates a critical success and, with the precise outcome depending on the recipe, the resultant dish will offer one of the following bonuses at random:

- Three extra hearts
- An extra yellow heart
- An extra two-fifths of a stamina wheel (green or yellow)
- Effect duration increased by five minutes
- The tier of an added effect is raised (for example, you obtain Level 2 cold resistance instead of Level 1).

Critical successes can be guaranteed by cooking during a Blood Moon, or by using either a star fragment or a dragon body part in a recipe.

All the base foods (without prefix) that you can cook are listed here. Aesthetic considerations aside, the visual appearance of a meal is generally of no meaningful consequence; prefixes and actual parameters are all determined by the individual materials you use to prepare them. When you select a combination of materials that satisfies multiple recipes, the game will prioritize the one that comes first in our list (this secret hierarchy explains why a handful of recipes appear multiple times).

COOKED FOOD

FRUITCAKE

Ingredients: Apple or Wildberry + Any fruit + Tabantha Wheat + Cane Sugar

SEAFOOD PAELLA

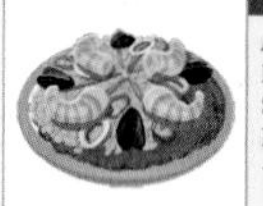

Ingredients: Any porgy + Hearty Blueshell Snail + Hylian Rice + Goat Butter + Rock Salt

MONSTER CURRY

Ingredients: Hylian Rice + Goron Spice + Monster Extract

MONSTER RICE BALLS

Ingredients: Hylian Rice + Rock Salt + Monster Extract

MONSTER CAKE

Ingredients: Tabantha Wheat + Cane Sugar + Goat Butter + Monster Extract

MONSTER SOUP

Ingredients: Fresh Milk + Tabantha Wheat + Goat Butter + Monster Extract

MONSTER STEW

Ingredients: Any meat + Any seafood + Monster Extract

CREAMY HEART SOUP

Ingredients: Any radish + Hydromelon + Voltfruit + Fresh Milk

CLAM CHOWDER

Ingredients: Fresh Milk + Tabantha Wheat + Goat Butter + Hearty Blueshell Snail

PUMPKIN STEW

Ingredients: Fresh Milk + Tabantha Wheat + Goat Butter + Fortified Pumpkin

GOURMET MEAT STEW

Ingredients: Fresh Milk + Tabantha Wheat + Goat Butter + Raw Gourmet Meat or Raw Bird Thigh

PRIME MEAT STEW

Ingredients: Fresh Milk + Tabantha Wheat + Goat Butter + Raw Prime Meat or Raw Bird Thigh

MEAT STEW

Ingredients: Fresh Milk + Tabantha Wheat + Goat Butter + Raw Meat or Raw Bird Drumstick

GOURMET MEAT CURRY

Ingredients: Raw Gourmet Meat + Hylian Rice + Goron Spice

GOURMET POULTRY CURRY

Ingredients: Raw Whole Bird + Hylian Rice + Goron Spice

PRIME MEAT CURRY

Ingredients: Raw Prime Meat + Hylian Rice + Goron Spice

PRIME POULTRY CURRY

Ingredients: Raw Bird Thigh + Hylian Rice + Goron Spice

MEAT CURRY

Ingredients: Raw Meat + Hylian Rice + Goron Spice

POULTRY CURRY

Ingredients: Raw Bird Drumstick + Hylian Rice + Goron Spice

SEAFOOD CURRY

Ingredients: Hearty Blueshell Snail or Any porgy + Hylian Rice + Goron Spice

VEGETABLE CURRY

Ingredients: Any carrot or pumpkin + Hylian Rice + Goron Spice

PUMPKIN PIE

Ingredients: Fortified Pumpkin + Tabantha Wheat + Cane Sugar + Goat Butter

CARROT CAKE

Ingredients: Any carrot + Tabantha Wheat + Cane Sugar + Goat Butter

WILDBERRY CREPE

Ingredients: Fresh Milk + Bird Egg + Tabantha Wheat + Cane Sugar + Wildberry

HONEY CREPE

Ingredients: Fresh Milk + Bird Egg + Tabantha Wheat + Cane Sugar + Courser Bee Honey

COOKED FOOD (CONTINUED)

PLAIN CREPE

Ingredients
Fresh Milk + Bird Egg + Tabantha Wheat + Cane Sugar

APPLE PIE

Ingredients
Apple + Tabantha Wheat + Cane Sugar + Goat Butter

NUTCAKE

Ingredients
Any nut + Tabantha Wheat + Cane Sugar + Goat Butter

EGG TART

Ingredients
Bird Egg + Tabantha Wheat + Cane Sugar + Goat Butter

EGG PUDDING

Ingredients
Fresh Milk + Bird Egg + Cane Sugar

FRIED BANANAS

Ingredients
Mighty Bananas + Tabantha Wheat + Cane Sugar

FRUIT PIE

Ingredients
Any fruit + Tabantha Wheat + Cane Sugar + Goat Butter

MEAT PIE

Ingredients
Tabantha Wheat + Goat Butter + Rock Salt + Any meat

FISH PIE

Ingredients
Tabantha Wheat + Goat Butter + Rock Salt + Any seafood

SALMON MEUNIÈRE
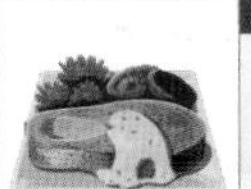
Ingredients
Tabantha Wheat + Goat Butter + Hearty Salmon

SALMON RISOTTO

Ingredients
Hylian Rice + Goat Butter + Rock Salt + Hearty Salmon

CRAB RISOTTO

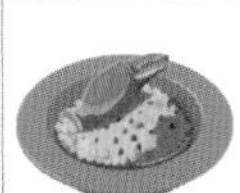
Ingredients
Hylian Rice + Goat Butter + Rock Salt + Any crab

VEGETABLE RISOTTO

Ingredients
Hylian Rice + Goat Butter + Rock Salt + Any carrot or pumpkin

MUSHROOM RISOTTO

Ingredients
Hylian Rice + Goat Butter + Rock Salt + Any mushroom

CREAM OF MUSHROOM SOUP

Ingredients
Fresh Milk + Rock Salt + Any mushroom + Any vegetable, herb or flower

VEGGIE CREAM SOUP

Ingredients
Fresh Milk + Rock Salt + Any carrot or pumpkin

CREAMY MEAT SOUP
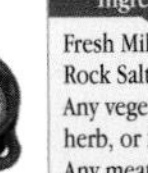
Ingredients
Fresh Milk + Rock Salt + Any vegetable, herb, or flower + Any meat

CREAMY SEAFOOD SOUP

Ingredients
Fresh Milk + Rock Salt + Any vegetable, herb, or flower + Any seafood

CREAM OF VEGETABLE SOUP

Ingredients
Fresh Milk + Rock Salt + Any vegetable, herb, or flower

CARROT STEW

Ingredients
Fresh Milk + Tabantha Wheat + Goat Butter + Any carrot

MUSHROOM OMELET

Ingredients
Any mushroom + Bird Egg + Goat Butter + Rock Salt

CRAB OMELET WITH RICE

Ingredients
Hylian Rice + Bird Egg + Rock Salt + Any crab

GOURMET POULTRY PILAF
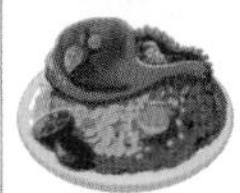
Ingredients
Raw Whole Bird + Hylian Rice + Bird Egg + Goat Butter

PRIME POULTRY PILAF
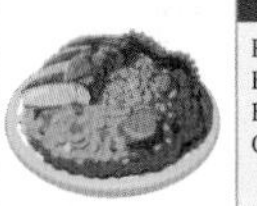
Ingredients
Raw Bird Thigh + Hylian Rice + Bird Egg + Goat Butter

POULTRY PILAF
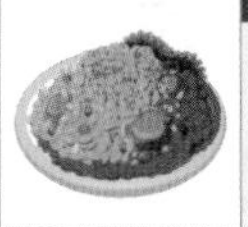
Ingredients
Raw Bird Drumstick + Hylian Rice + Bird Egg + Goat Butter

VEGETABLE OMELET

Ingredients
Any vegetable, herb or flower + Bird Egg + Goat Butter + Rock Salt

PORGY MEUNIÈRE

Ingredients
Tabantha Wheat + Goat Butter + Any porgy

SEAFOOD MEUNIÈRE

Ingredients
Tabantha Wheat + Goat Butter + Any seafood

SEAFOOD FRIED RICE

Ingredients
Hylian Rice + Rock Salt + Hearty Blueshell Snail or any porgy

CURRY PILAF

Ingredients
Hylian Rice + Goron Spice + Goat Butter

GOURMET MEAT AND RICE BOWL

Ingredients
Raw Gourmet Meat or Raw Whole Bird + Hylian Rice + Rock Salt

PRIME MEAT AND RICE BOWL

Ingredients
Raw Prime Meat or Raw Bird Thigh + Hylian Rice + Rock Salt

MEAT AND RICE BOWL

Ingredients
Raw Meat or Raw Bird Drumstick + Hylian Rice + Rock Salt

FRIED EGG AND RICE
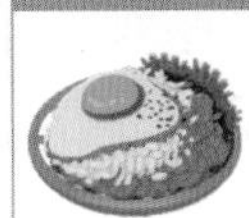
Ingredients
Hylian Rice + Bird Egg

MEATY RICE BALLS

Ingredients
Hylian Rice + Any meat

SEAFOOD RICE BALLS

Ingredients
Hylian Rice + Any fish

MUSHROOM RICE BALLS

Ingredients
Hylian Rice + Any mushroom

VEGGIE RICE BALLS

Ingredients
Hylian Rice + Any vegetable, herb or flower

HOT BUTTERED APPLE

Ingredients
Apple + Goat Butter

MEAT-STUFFED PUMPKIN

Ingredients
Fortified Pumpkin + Any meat

GLAZED MEAT

Ingredients
Any meat + Courser Bee Honey

GLAZED SEAFOOD

Ingredients
Any seafood + Courser Bee Honey

GLAZED MUSHROOMS

Ingredients
Any mushroom + Courser Bee Honey

GLAZED VEGGIES

Ingredients
Any vegetable + Courser Bee Honey

CURRY RICE

Ingredients
Hylian Rice + Goron Spice

HONEYED APPLE

Ingredients
Apple + Courser Bee Honey

HONEYED FRUITS

Ingredients
Any fruit + Courser Bee Honey

GOURMET SPICED MEAT SKEWER

Ingredients
Raw Gourmet Meat + Goron Spice

PRIME SPICED MEAT SKEWER

Ingredients
Raw Prime Meat + Goron Spice

SPICED MEAT SKEWER

Ingredients
Raw Meat + Goron Spice

QUICKSTART
PRIMER
WALKTHROUGH
SHRINES
SIDE QUESTS
INVENTORY
BESTIARY
EXTRAS
REFERENCE & ANALYSIS
MAPS
MASTER TRIALS
CHAMPIONS' BALLAD
INDEX
ADDED EFFECTS
ARMOR
WEAPONS
SHIELDS
BOWS
ARROWS
MATERIALS
ROASTED/FROZEN FOOD
COOKED FOOD
ELIXIRS
IMPORTANT ITEMS

FRAGRANT MUSHROOM SAUTÉ

Ingredients
Any mushroom + Goron Spice

HERB SAUTÉ

Ingredients
Any vegetable, herb or flower + Goron Spice

SALT-GRILLED GOURMET MEAT

Ingredients
Raw Gourmet Meat or Raw Whole Bird + Rock Salt

SALT-GRILLED PRIME MEAT

Ingredients
Raw Prime Meat or Raw Bird Thigh + Rock Salt

SALT-GRILLED MEAT

Ingredients
Raw Meat or Raw Bird Drumstick + Rock Salt

CRAB STIR-FRY

Ingredients
Any crab + Goron Spice

SALT-GRILLED CRAB

Ingredients
Any crab + Rock Salt

SALT-GRILLED FISH

Ingredients
Any fish + Rock Salt

WHEAT BREAD

Ingredients
Tabantha Wheat + Rock Salt

SALT-GRILLED GREENS

Ingredients
Any vegetable, herb or flower + Rock Salt

SALT-GRILLED MUSHROOMS

Ingredients
Any mushroom + Rock Salt

COPIOUS MEAT SKEWERS

Ingredients
Any variety of four different meats

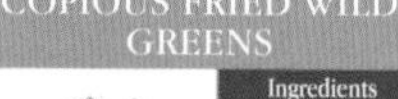

COPIOUS FRIED WILD GREENS

Ingredients
Any variety of four different vegetables, herbs or flowers

COPIOUS SIMMERED FRUIT

Ingredients
Any variety of four different fruits

COPIOUS MUSHROOM SKEWERS

Ingredients
Any variety of four different mushrooms

COPIOUS FISH SKEWERS

Ingredients
Any variety of four different fishes

FRIED WILD GREENS

Ingredients
Any vegetable, herb or flower + Any vegetable, herb or flower

GOURMET MEAT AND SEAFOOD FRY

Ingredients
Raw Gourmet Meat or Raw Whole Bird + Any seafood

PRIME MEAT AND SEAFOOD FRY

Ingredients
Raw Prime Meat or Raw Bird Thigh + Any seafood

MEAT AND SEAFOOD FRY

Ingredients
Raw Meat or Raw Bird Drumstick + Any seafood

PEPPER STEAK

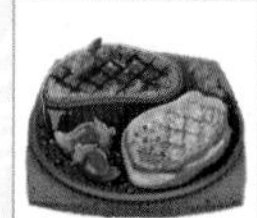

Ingredients
Any meat + Spicy Pepper

PEPPER SEAFOOD

Ingredients
Any seafood + Spicy Pepper

STEAMED MEAT

Ingredients
Any vegetable, herb or flower + Any meat

STEAMED FISH

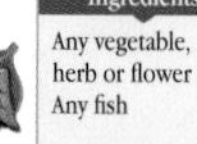

Ingredients
Any vegetable, herb or flower + Any fish

STEAMED MUSHROOMS

Ingredients
Any vegetable, herb or flower + Any mushroom

STEAMED FRUIT

Ingredients
Any vegetable, herb or flower + Any fruit

FISH AND MUSHROOM SKEWER

Ingredients
Any fish + Any mushroom

MEAT AND MUSHROOM SKEWER

Ingredients
Any meat + Any mushroom

FRUIT AND MUSHROOM MIX

Ingredients
Any fruit + Any mushroom

MEAT SKEWER

Ingredients
Any meat

SEAFOOD SKEWER

Ingredients
Any crab or snail

FISH SKEWER

Ingredients
Any fish

OMELET

Ingredients
Bird Egg

WARM MILK

Ingredients
Fresh Milk

MUSHROOM SKEWER

Ingredients
Any mushroom

FRIED WILD GREENS

Ingredients
Any vegetable, herb or flower

SIMMERED FRUIT

Ingredients
Any fruit

SAUTÉED NUTS

Ingredients
Any nut

FAIRY TONIC

Ingredients
Fairy

FAIRY TONIC

Ingredients
Fairy + Any gemstone + Any monster part + Any small animal

FAIRY TONIC

Ingredients
Fairy + Any monster part + Any small animal

FAIRY TONIC

Ingredients
Fairy + Any gemstone, any monster part or any small animal

SAUTÉED PEPPERS

Ingredients
Spicy Pepper

HONEY CANDY

Ingredients
Courser Bee Honey

ROCK-HARD FOOD

Ingredients
Wood or any gemstone

ELIXIR

Ingredients
Any monster part + Any small animal (see overleaf for details)

DUBIOUS FOOD

Ingredients
Any monster part or any small animal + Any other ingredient (or any unspecified combination)

Elixirs

You can create elixirs by cooking resources harvested from small animals (which offer added effects) and monster parts (which extend the duration of these buffs). The same rules that govern the nomenclature and parameters of cooked food apply to elixirs.

ELIXIRS

ICON	NAME	RECIPE	EFFECT
	Hearty Elixir	Monster part + hearty animal	Extra Hearts
	Energizing Elixir	Monster part + energizing animal	Stamina Restoration
	Enduring Elixir	Monster part + enduring animal	Extra Stamina
	Fireproof Elixir	Monster part + fireproof animal	Flame Guard
	Chilly Elixir	Monster part + chilly animal	Heat Resistance
	Spicy Elixir	Monster part + spicy animal	Cold Resistance
	Electro Elixir	Monster part + electro animal	Electric Resistance
	Hasty Elixir	Monster part + hasty animal	Movement Speed Up
	Sneaky Elixir	Monster part + sneaky animal	Stealth Up
	Mighty Elixir	Monster part + mighty animal	Attack Up
	Tough Elixir	Monster part + tough animal	Defense Up

Important Items

Items in this category are linked to quests or other similar objectives.

IMPORTANT ITEMS

ICON	NAME	AVAILABILITY
	Sheikah Slate	Prologue
	Mipha's Grace	Clear the Divine Vah Ruta dungeon
	Revali's Gale	Clear the Divine Vah Medoh dungeon
	Daruk's Protection	Clear the Divine Vah Rudania dungeon
	Urbosa's Fury	Clear the Divine Vah Naboris dungeon
	Stamina Vessel	Trade in four spirit orbs
	Heart Container	Trade in four spirit orbs; complete any dungeon
	Small Key	In certain shrines
	Spirit Orb	One per completed shrine
	Korok Seed	One per Korok found
	Hestu's Maracas	Side quest: The Priceless Maracas
	Thunder Helm	Side quest: The Thunder Helm
	Classified Envelope	Main quest: Captured Memories
	Hestu's Gift	Find all 900 Korok Seeds
	Medal of Honor: Talus	Defeat all 40 Talus and speak to Kilton
	Medal of Honor: Hinox	Defeat all 40 Hinox and speak to Kilton
	Medal of Honor: Molduga	Defeat all 4 Moldugas and speak to Kilton
	Paraglider	Complete the prologue
	Stable Bridle	Default
	Traveler's Bridle	Unlocked by corresponding amiibo
	Knight's Bridle	Mini-game: Horseback Archery
	Royal Bridle	Side quest: The Royal White Stallion
	Extravagant Bridle	Mini-game: Obstacle Course
	Monster Bridle	Kilton's shop
	Stable Saddle	Default
	Traveler's Saddle	Unlocked by corresponding amiibo
	Knight's Saddle	Mini-game: Horseback Archery
	Royal Saddle	Side quest: The Royal White Stallion
	Extravagant Saddle	Mini-game: Obstacle Course
	Monster Saddle	Kilton's shop

BESTIARY

This chapter analyzes the many assailants you will encounter during your travels through Hyrule. For each type of creature, we offer a list of key attributes and essential combat strategies that will help you make the right decisions in the midst of each battle.

Almost every enemy species in the game exists in multiple variants:

- **Elemental variants** are infused with fire, ice, or electricity. Making contact with them or being struck by an attack usually inflicts a corresponding status effect: fire burns Link, ice freezes him (waggle Ⓛ in all directions to recover), while electricity deals shock damage (and causes him to drop any weapon or shield he has in his hands). Fire and ice are considered as opposing elements: hitting a fire-imbued creature with ice will cause instant death, and vice versa.

- **Color variants** are stronger versions of the base enemy. When you begin the adventure, you will almost invariably encounter the default incarnation of each species. As you eliminate successive foes, however, a hidden counter keeps a secret tally of your combat triumphs. When the total hits specific milestones, some of the foes you run into will "rank up." Suddenly, for example, Blue Bokoblins and Blue Moblins will begin to appear. Higher-rank versions of each species are stronger: they have greater health pools and inflict more damage. They can even have new and improved attack patterns. This is not all bad news, however, as superior enemies carry improved loot, including better equipment. Learning to gauge the strength of large groups of opponents based on the color variations featured within their ranks is an important skill that you will need to develop over the course of your adventure.

In the tables listing key attributes for each enemy type, we reveal two important stats.

- **HP:** The enemy's starting health, as represented by the red gauge above its head. If you reduce this gauge to 0, the monster will die and yield items. By equipping the champion's tunic (offered by Impa when you unlock the first Captured Memory – see page 50), you can see an exact numerical HP value for most opponents.

- **Rank:** A general evaluation of each creature's overall dangerousness. In traditional video game parlance, this could be described as a monster's "level."

For each creature, you will also find a list of locations where they are commonly encountered (though these are not exhaustive: they may crop up in other locales), and which items they can drop. As a rule, the higher the rank of an opponent, the better the potential drops in their expanded loot tables will be.

Chuchus

KEY ATTRIBUTES

	NAME	HP (SMALL)	HP (MEDIUM)	HP (LARGE)	RANK	COMMON LOCATIONS	ITEM DROPS
	CHUCHU	3	20	48	1	Hyrule Field, West Necluda	Chuchu Jelly
	FIRE CHUCHU	12	20	48	1	Eldin Canyon, Eldin Mountains	Red Chuchu Jelly
	ICE CHUCHU	12	20	48	1	Hebra Mountains, Gerudo Highlands	White Chuchu Jelly
	ELECTRIC CHUCHU	12	20	48	1	Gerudo Highlands, East Necluda	Yellow Chuchu Jelly

STRATEGY

Chuchus exist in three sizes (small, medium, large), though they all pose very little challenge; these enemies are nuisances first and foremost. They are weak and slow, and will usually fall to a single hit. However, the elemental ones are marginally more dangerous: they will affect you with the element they are infused with if you touch them, and they will detonate and cause area-of-effect damage after sustaining a fatal blow. To avoid the blast, eliminate them from distance with an arrow or a melee weapon with sufficient reach, such as a spear. Remote bombs also work brilliantly.

When killed, Chuchus yield jelly of the element they are imbued with. This is a potentially very useful item, as jelly can be later employed to reproduce the explosion caused by Chuchus when they die. You can exploit this feature to generate fires with red jelly, extinguish flames with neutral jelly, freeze targets with white jelly, or to electrocute targets with yellow jelly. Note that neutral jelly can be turned into a colored variety by exposing it to the corresponding element: fire, snow, or lightning.

KEESE

KEY ATTRIBUTES

NAME	HP	RANK	COMMON LOCATIONS	ITEM DROPS
KEESE	1	2	Hyrule Field, East Necluda	Keese Wing, Keese Eyeball
FIRE KEESE	1	2	Eldin Canyon, Eldin Mountains	Fire Keese Wing, Keese Eyeball
ICE KEESE	1	2	Hebra Mountains, Gerudo Highlands	Ice Keese Wing, Keese Eyeball
ELECTRIC KEESE	1	2	Lanayru Great Spring, East Necluda	Electric Keese Wing, Keese Eyeball

STRATEGY

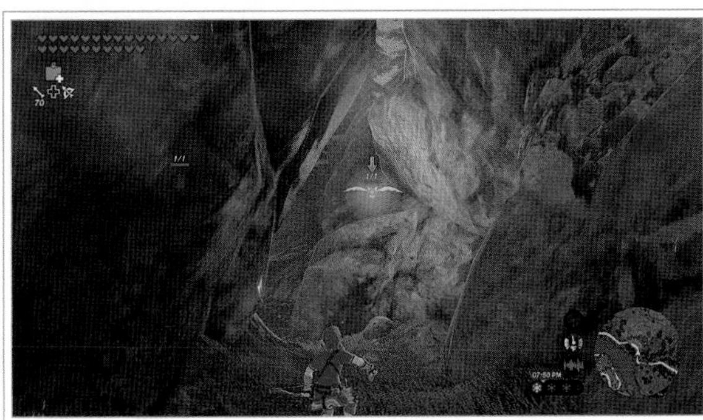

Though the two species are very different to look at, Keese are effectively flying Chuchus. They pose very little threat on their own; however, their mobility makes them slightly more dangerous. The easiest way to eliminate them is to lock on and attack with a weapon. Against the elemental versions, which can burn, freeze, or shock you, a weapon with reach can help to ensure you remain unharmed.

During your travels, you will occasionally run into Keese swarms. Despite their large numbers, these are far from threatening. In fact, they offer you a great opportunity to amass item drops in significant quantities. Have a bomb at the ready when they fly in your direction, then aim to detonate it at the heart of the swarm: it will rain wings and eyeballs, which you can put to profit in recipes or by selling them to Kilton.

Octoroks

KEY ATTRIBUTES

	NAME	HP	RANK	COMMON LOCATIONS	ITEM DROPS
	WATER OCTOROK	8	5	West Necluda, Hyrule Field	Octorok Tentacle, Octo Balloon, Octorok Eyeball
	FOREST OCTOROK	8	5	Hyrule Ridge, Deep Akkala	Octorok Tentacle, Octo Balloon, Octorok Eyeball
	ROCK OCTOROK	8	5	Eldin Canyon, Gerudo Highlands	Octorok Tentacle, Octo Balloon, Octorok Eyeball
	SNOW OCTOROK	8	5	Gerudo Highlands, Tabantha Frontier	Octorok Tentacle, Octo Balloon, Octorok Eyeball
	TREASURE OCTOROK	8	5	Gerudo Highlands, Gerudo Desert	Octorok Tentacle, Octo Balloon, Octorok Eyeball, Rupees (green to silver)

STRATEGY

Octoroks are octopus-like creatures that briefly jump out of the water or ground to spit a rock at you, then plunge back out of sight. Very weak, they will fall to virtually any attack instantly. However, hitting them can prove a little awkward. Arrows and bombs work well when they are visible; melee weapons can also be employed at close range. The most stylish way to defeat them, though, is to redirect their projectiles back at them by blocking with a shield. As long as you hold your shield aloft to deflect it, the rock will home in on its sender. You can even perfect guard to propel the rock at greater speed.

Treasure Octoroks behave a little differently: they attempt to lure their prey into range with an illusion designed to evoke avarice, and will emerge from the ground to attack when you move sufficiently close. You can easily see through this subterfuge with Magnesis, as the rune will reveal that they are not metallic. All Octoroks have one thing in common: they often yield Octo balloons. These thoroughly useful items can be dropped on heavy objects to lift them. It's always worthwhile to keep a stock of Octo balloons, as they can be employed to simplify certain puzzles and move obstructions that cannot be manipulated with Magnesis.

WIZZROBES

KEY ATTRIBUTES

NAME	HP	RANK	COMMON LOCATIONS	ITEM DROPS
 FIRE WIZZROBE*	150	10	Hyrule Field, Great Hyrule Forest	Fire Rod
 ICE WIZZROBE**	150	10	Gerudo Highlands, Hyrule Field	Ice Rod
 ELECTRIC WIZZROBE	150	10	Hyrule Ridge, West Necluda	Lightning Rod
 METEO WIZZROBE*	300	18	Hyrule Field, Eldin Canyon	Meteor Rod
 BLIZZROBE**	300	18	Hyrule Field, Hebra Mountains	Blizzard Rod
 THUNDER WIZZROBE	300	18	Hyrule Field, Tabantha Frontier	Thunderstorm Rod

* Weak to ice ** Weak to fire

STRATEGY

Wizzrobes are potentially very dangerous opponents. They walk on thin air, a few yards above the ground, and become temporarily invisible once they spot you, making them elusive targets. They can assail you with a rain of projectiles, and summon elemental Keese or Chuchus to assist them in battle. Ideally, you should always aspire to eliminate them before they notice Link. When this is not possible, speed is key: look to engineer a very swift conclusion to these fights. Fire and Meteo Wizzrobes can be defeated instantly with a solitary ice arrow, while Ice Wizzrobes and Blizzrobes will fall to a single fire arrow. Electric and Thunder Wizzrobes are rather more troublesome as they lack an elemental vulnerability, so your best option is to target them with your most powerful bow.

If you stand below a Wizzrobe, a powerful spear can give you just enough reach to strike your opponent with great force, enabling you to annihilate it very quickly. These weapons are also effective against elemental Keese or Chuchus, which makes them a consistently good choice in these confrontations. Alternatively, you can knock down Wizzrobes by shooting them in the head with any type of bow, before finishing them off with melee attacks.

BOKOBLINS

KEY ATTRIBUTES

NAME	HP	RANK	COMMON LOCATIONS	ITEM DROPS
BOKOBLIN	13	6	Great Plateau, Hyrule Field	Bokoblin Horn, Bokoblin Fang
BLUE BOKOBLIN	72	12	Gerudo Highlands, Gerudo Desert	Bokoblin Horn, Bokoblin Fang, Bokoblin Guts
BLACK BOKOBLIN	240	20	Hyrule Field, Gerudo Highlands	Bokoblin Horn, Bokoblin Fang, Bokoblin Guts
STALKOBLIN	1	12	Hyrule Field, Great Hyrule Forest	Bokoblin Horn, Bokoblin Fang
SILVER BOKOBLIN	720	30	Greater Hyrule	Bokoblin Horn, Bokoblin Fang, Bokoblin Guts, Amber, Opal, Topaz, Ruby, Sapphire, Diamond

STRATEGY

Bokoblins are very straightforward enemies. When alerted they will attempt to pick up whichever weapon is closest to them, and then mostly adopt simple attack patterns at close range. This makes them ideal sparring partners should you have a need to practice *Breath of the Wild*'s two most essential combat moves: perfect dodge and perfect guard. Hold your shield aloft and either jump backwards or press Ⓐ just before one of their attacks connects. If your timing is off, you will still generally block the strike, taking no damage. If you aim to defeat most Bokoblins in this manner, you will refine your counterattacking instincts in a way that will serve you well later in the adventure.

The most dangerous move employed by Bokoblins is their charged attack, which works in the same way as Link's multi-hit spinning assault when he is equipped with a two-handed blade. This is especially dangerous when they wield spears. Blocking with a shield is enough to interrupt their assault, though, so remain on the defensive and seize the first counter opportunity.

MOBLINS

KEY ATTRIBUTES

NAME	HP	RANK	COMMON LOCATIONS	ITEM DROPS
MOBLIN	56	12	Hyrule Field, East Necluda	Moblin Horn, Moblin Fang
BLUE MOBLIN	144	24	Hyrule Field, Deep Akkala	Moblin Horn, Moblin Fang, Moblin Guts
BLACK MOBLIN	360	28	Hyrule Field, Eldin Canyon	Moblin Horn, Moblin Fang, Moblin Guts
STALMOBLIN	2	24	Great Hyrule Forest, Gerudo Highlands	Moblin Horn, Moblin Fang
SILVER MOBLIN	1,080	34	Greater Hyrule	Moblin Horn, Moblin Fang, Moblin Guts, Amber, Opal, Topaz, Ruby, Sapphire, Diamond

STRATEGY

Moblins are similar to Bokoblins, though they enjoy greater reach and power due to their more imposing stature. They are, nevertheless, fairly ponderous enemies that favor basic melee tactics. Aim to perfect dodge their lateral blows with back flips and their overhead strikes with side hops to set up decisive counter opportunities.

The relatively slow nature of Moblins makes them highly susceptible to charged attacks. Wielding a two-handed weapon, you can potentially decimate entire groups of these creatures while spinning. Your weapon's durability will obviously suffer as a consequence, but this can be a quick and efficient way to take down multiple foes simultaneously.

LIZALFOS

KEY ATTRIBUTES

NAME	HP	RANK	COMMON LOCATIONS	ITEM DROPS
LIZALFOS	50	10	Lanayru Great Spring, Gerudo Desert	Lizalfos Horn, Lizalfos Talon
BLUE LIZALFOS	120	22	Tabantha Frontier, Gerudo Desert	Lizalfos Horn, Lizalfos Talon, Lizalfos Tail
BLACK LIZALFOS	288	26	Hyrule Field, Hebra Mountains	Lizalfos Horn, Lizalfos Talon, Lizalfos Tail
STALIZALFOS	1	22	Gerudo Desert, Hyrule Ridge	Lizalfos Horn, Lizalfos Talon
FIRE-BREATH LIZALFOS*	160	26	Eldin Canyon, Gerudo Desert	Lizalfos Horn, Lizalfos Talon, Red Lizalfos Tail
ICE-BREATH LIZALFOS**	288	26	Gerudo Highlands, Hebra Mountains	Lizalfos Horn, Lizalfos Talon, Icy Lizalfos Tail
ELECTRIC LIZALFOS	288	26	Gerudo Desert, Hyrule Ridge	Lizalfos Horn, Lizalfos Talon, Yellow Lizalfos Tail
SILVER LIZALFOS	864	32	Greater Hyrule	Lizalfos Horn, Lizalfos Talon, Lizalfos Tail, Amber, Opal, Topaz, Ruby, Sapphire, Diamond

* Weak to ice ** Weak to fire

STRATEGY

The Lizalfos is a very nimble opponent. They dash to your position to attack, then quickly withdraw, making it awkward to strike them with standard melee blows. The aerial assaults where they dive in your direction are best countered with a perfect dodge side hop. Generally speaking, given their rapid reactions and propensity for hit-and-run tactics, a reliable approach is to allow a Lizalfos to move towards you and attack first, then punish their aggression with a counter.

The Lizalfos has a prominent weakness: its horn. If you hit a horn with an arrow, you will cause critical damage and topple your target. With the Electric Lizalfos, this will also generate a spherical blast. In close proximity, a bow that fires multiple arrows can make it relatively easy to score such "horn shots" without aiming. You can then follow up with a melee combo.

YIGA CLAN

KEY ATTRIBUTES

NAME	HP	RANK	COMMON LOCATIONS	ITEM DROPS
YIGA FOOTSOLDIER	64*	12	Karusa Valley, surprise attacks in various locations	Rupees (Green, Blue, Red, Purple), Mighty Bananas
YIGA BLADEMASTER	400	22	Surprise attacks in various locations	Amber, Opal, Topaz, Ruby, Sapphire, Mighty Bananas

* The melee variant of Yiga Footsoldiers has 72 HP.

STRATEGY

Most Yiga Footsoldiers are fairly predictable as they only have one attack: they warp high in the air and fire an arrow at you. They can be a little hard to follow, though there are clear audio cues that betray their general whereabouts. You should note that they always fall directly to the ground after their signature assault. An effective way to eliminate them is therefore to sprint to that position while they are still airborne, then assail them with due vigor when they fall in front of you. You will occasionally run into a Footsoldier variant that can use melee attacks. These are usually disguised as travelers on the road who will attack Link after he starts a conversation with them.

Blademasters are significantly more dangerous, as they can both tank your hits and deal more damage. They regularly unleash a swift beam that can hit you from afar; when they raise their weapons high above their head, be prepared to side hop. Their most annoying attack, though, takes the form of a small crater that appears below Link's feet and tracks his movements. After a few seconds, a rock spike is thrust forth from the ground, knocking Link over if he is within the area of effect. The best way to avoid this is to leap vertically and open your paraglider: the steam released from the crater will work as an updraft, taking you out of range of the rock spike, and enabling you to glide to your target to launch your own attack.

Cursed Monsters

KEY ATTRIBUTES

NAME	HP	RANK	COMMON LOCATIONS	ITEM DROPS
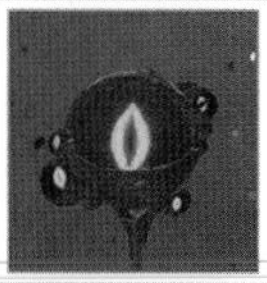 GLOWING EYEBALL	1	1	Close to Malice goo; common in dungeons	–
 CURSED BOKOBLIN	1	1	Spawned from mouths connected to glowing eyeballs	–
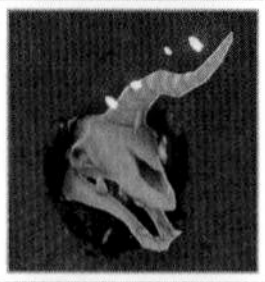 CURSED MOBLIN	30	1		–
 CURSED LIZALFOS	1	1		–

STRATEGY

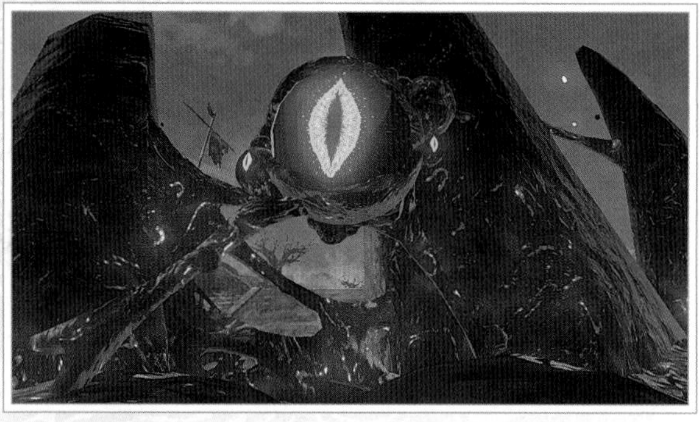

Glowing eyeballs are a recurring feature in dungeons and wherever large pockets of Malice goo appear, such as in Hyrule Castle. Hitting them with any weapon will kill them instantly, though arrows are usually the tool of choice. Eliminating a glowing eyeball will always remove the area of Malice linked to it. If this includes a mouth that generates cursed monsters, the monster-spawning maw will disappear as well. Make these targets a priority whenever you encounter them, both to clear the path and to avoid unnecessary encounters with cursed pests.

Cursed creatures emerge from "mouths" that appear on certain patches of Malice goo. They typically fly around, slowly homing in on your position. As a rule, a single hit with any weapon is sufficient to take them down. With their excellent reach, spears are a great way to get rid of these enemies quickly.

Guardian Vehicles

KEY ATTRIBUTES

NAME	HP	RANK	COMMON LOCATIONS	ITEM DROPS
GUARDIAN STALKER	1,500	15	Hyrule Field	Ancient Screw, Ancient Spring, Ancient Gear, Ancient Shaft, Ancient Core, Giant Ancient Core
GUARDIAN SKYWATCHER	1,500	15	Hyrule Field, Akkala Highlands	
GUARDIAN TURRET	1,500	10	Hyrule Castle	
DECAYED GUARDIAN	500	5	Hyrule Field, Hyrule Castle	Ancient Screw, Ancient Spring, Ancient Gear, Ancient Shaft
SENTRY	1,000	0	Death Mountain	Ancient Screw, Ancient Spring, Ancient Gear, Ancient Shaft, Ancient Core

STRATEGY

Guardian vehicles are primarily detection devices. The moment you enter their field of vision, they start focusing a red aiming laser at you. After a few seconds, they will emit a powerful blue beam in your direction. If this hits you, you will suffer significant damage, though you can easily escape a beam by sprinting perpendicularly. If you block it with a shield, you will take no damage but the shield will be destroyed. Though it takes time to master, by far the most efficient way to defeat these opponents is to employ the perfect guard technique. Holding a shield aloft, press Ⓐ just before the beam hits you to deflect it back to the Guardian. This is definitely a talent that you should refine as early as possible in the adventure, as it will prove useful on countless occasions – and especially so during boss encounters and other major battles. The ideal time to make the button press varies in accordance with the distance between Link and his assailant. Over reasonable distances, you can obviously track the movement of the beam and react accordingly. In close proximity, however, you must press the button just before the beam actually appears; the best time is usually when blue energy accumulates close to the machine's eye.

Technically, you can damage a Guardian with standard weapons, but this will take a devastating toll on their durability. Ancient weapons (obtained from other Guardians or from Robbie at the Akkala Ancient Tech Lab) are more efficient, but will also break fairly rapidly when employed to chip away at these resilient opponents. This is why perfect-guarding laser beams is so essential: as long as you have a good command of the required timing, it costs you nothing. If you struggle with the perfect guard command, there are a few tricks you can use to prevent the laser beam. The easiest is to fire an arrow at the machine's blue eye. Shock arrows make the process even easier as they will electrocute the device, canceling the attack and neutralizing it for several seconds. Ancient arrows (found as a collectible in Hyrule Castle and available for purchase from Robbie) are also an option, inflicting devastating damage to Guardians. Finally, note that you can immobilize Stalkers by cutting their legs, and Skywatchers by destroying their propellers.

Guardian Scouts

KEY ATTRIBUTES

NAME	HP	RANK	COMMON LOCATIONS	ITEM DROPS	NOTES
GUARDIAN SCOUT I	13	4	Various shrines	Ancient Screw, Ancient Spring	Wields no melee weapon
GUARDIAN SCOUT II	375	14	Various shrines	Ancient Screw, Ancient Spring, Ancient Gear, Ancient Shaft	Wields one standard melee weapon
GUARDIAN SCOUT III	1,500	24	Various shrines	Ancient Screw, Ancient Spring, Ancient Gear, Ancient Shaft, Ancient Core	Wields two "+" melee weapons
GUARDIAN SCOUT IV	3,000	34	Various shrines	Ancient Screw, Ancient Spring, Ancient Gear, Ancient Shaft, Ancient Core	Wields three "++" melee weapons

STRATEGY

QUICK SHOTS: Guardian Scouts often unleash a quick volley of gun shots as they move toward you. These are usually of no consequence. Ignore them completely, focusing on the strategy you have chosen to eliminate your target.

STANDARD ATTACKS: The primary method of attack for Guardian Scouts is to deal melee blows with the weapon(s) they are wielding. These are all fairly predictable, and you should have no problem identifying the best perfect dodge window with a little practice. Follow up with flurry rushes and standard combos, ideally with an ancient weapon if you have one to hand.

SPINNING BLADE ATTACK: You will regularly see a Scout leap backward and focus briefly with its weapons at the ready. This will be followed seconds later by a swirling attack where the machine closes in on your position. This is very difficult to dodge, so the best course of action is to hide behind a suitable obstruction, such as a pillar. The Scout will crash into it, damaging itself in the process and suffering a short stun effect: use this opportunity to unleash your best combos. Certain shrines do not feature natural cover points. In these instances, you must create them yourself. If there is water at your feet, summon a pillar of ice with Cryonis; if you spot blocks of metal in the ground, raise them with Magnesis. These two scenarios are illustrated in the above pictures. If you do not have enough time to complete these maneuvers, a shock or ice arrow can also halt their advance.

SPINNING LASER ATTACK: With this attack, a Scout first puts its weapons away, then its head will start spinning moments later, unleashing a laser beam that hits everything within a relatively small radius. If you do not have the time to sprint away, draw your paraglider: the updraft generated by the laser should enable you to float until it is safe to land. Alternatively, a shock or ice arrow will interrupt the assault.

FOCUSED LASER ATTACK: Once you have depleted most of your opponent's health, it will put all of its weapons away and start charging a powerful laser beam – the exact same attack as the one employed by Guardian Vehicles. You have two options at this stage: either rush to your target and attack relentlessly until it falls (which only makes sense if you are powerful enough to deliver the coup de grâce within a few seconds), or step back, draw your shield, and perfect guard the beam. If you are fighting at close quarters, don't forget that you must execute the parry command just *before* the beam is emitted.

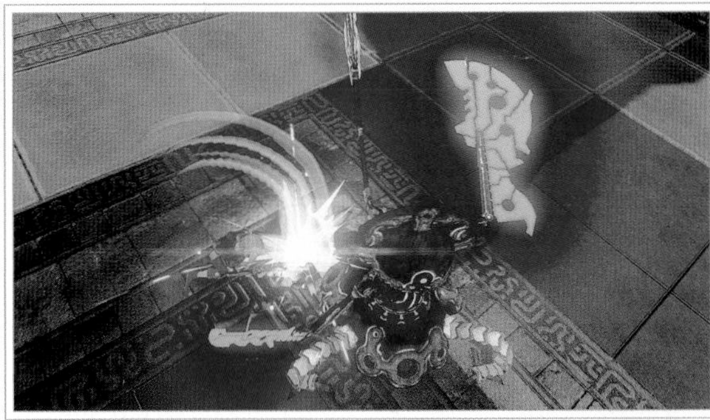

BRUTE-FORCE STRATEGY: One of the most effective options against Guardian Scouts, irrespective of their rank, is to attack them with charged attacks while wielding a two-handed weapon, ideally an ancient battle axe. Rotate around them throughout the assault, positioning Link on the side opposite to where the Scout is currently facing. The direction where a Scout is about to attack can be inferred from the weapon it is currently using. The moment you spot one being pulled backwards, move to the other side to avoid the imminent blow. If you remain locked on, this is very easy to engineer: spin continuously by holding Ⓨ and adjust your direction with Ⓛ. With a little practice and a well-developed stamina wheel, it is possible to eliminate any Scout very quickly and painlessly with this method.

ELEMENTAL STRATEGY: Another safe approach against Scouts, particularly the stronger models, is to deploy elemental weapons. Hit them with any ice-infused sword or arrow to freeze them, then switch to the most powerful item in your inventory: it will deal triple damage by shattering the ice. Switch back to your ice weapon and continue the process until your foe falls. Alternatively, you can use lightning-imbued weapons to shock a Scout for a few seconds, then unleash a combo with a stronger weapon. Shock damage is enhanced if your opponent is standing on surface water.

TALUS

KEY ATTRIBUTES

NAME	HP	RANK	COMMON LOCATIONS	ITEM DROPS
STONE TALUS	300	16	See map on page 328	Flint, Amber, Opal, Ruby
STONE TALUS (LUMINOUS)	600	20	See map on page 328	Flint, Amber, Opal, Luminous Stone, Topaz, Diamond
STONE TALUS (RARE)	900	24	See map on page 328	Flint, Amber, Opal, Topaz, Ruby, Sapphire, Diamond
IGNEO TALUS	800	24	See map on page 328	Flint, Opal, Ruby, Diamond
FROST TALUS	800	24	See map on page 328	Flint, Opal, Sapphire, Diamond
STONE PEBBLIT	20	5	Greater Hyrule	Flint, Amber, Opal
IGNEO PEBBLIT	20	5	Eldin Canyon, Eldin Mountains	Flint, Amber, Ruby
FROST PEBBLIT	20	5	Hebra Mountains, Gerudo Highlands	Flint, Amber, Ruby

STRATEGY

All Talus enemies rely on a primary attack strategy: though they may occasionally use their rock "arms" to swipe at Link, they will usually just hurl them at speed in his direction. These are difficult to dodge given their size, and are replaced afterwards, so it's in your best interests to act decisively to defeat these foes.

The most straightforward strategy against a Talus is to blow up its arms with bombs. Every time you are successful, the creature will collapse: use this opportunity to climb onto their backs and attack their crystal weak point. Locking on to this specific vulnerability immediately may help you land a few extra blows.

Weapons of choice to attack the crystal on a Talus's back include all those that are designed to break stone: iron sledgehammers, cobble crushers, stone smashers, and boulder breakers – all of which are found in the Eldin region. Not only do these weapons suffer lower durability reductions when hitting crystals, but they also inflict enhanced damage against them.

When a Talus has its crystal on its side, you can actually reach it from the ground without having to climb on the creature's back. This is most easily achieved with weapons with long reach, such as spears. Lock on to the crystal and attack repeatedly to end these battles quickly. This works very well against the Talus in Hyrule Castle's East Passage, for example.

The Igneo Talus is a variant encountered in the Eldin region. Any contact with one of these will burn Link unless he is equipped with a complete flamebreaker armor set, upgraded to level 2 (★★) by a great fairy to imbue it with the fireproof effect. An alternative solution is to attack the monster with any ice-infused weapon or arrow to cool it down, knock it down with a bomb, then climb on its back to attack its weak point as usual. Repeat this strategy until the creature falls.

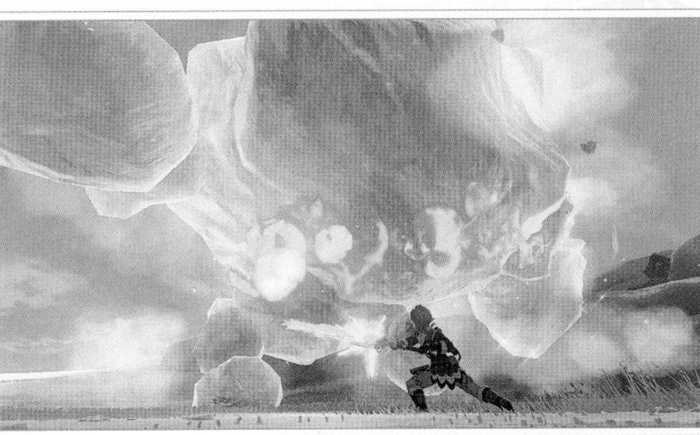

The Frost Talus is the ice equivalent of the Igneo Talus. They will freeze Link on contact unless you wear a full snowquill armor set, upgraded to Level 2 (★★) by a great fairy to unlock the unfreezable effect. If you don't have this enhanced outfit, you should use fire arrows to melt the ice on the monster's body, then proceed as usual.

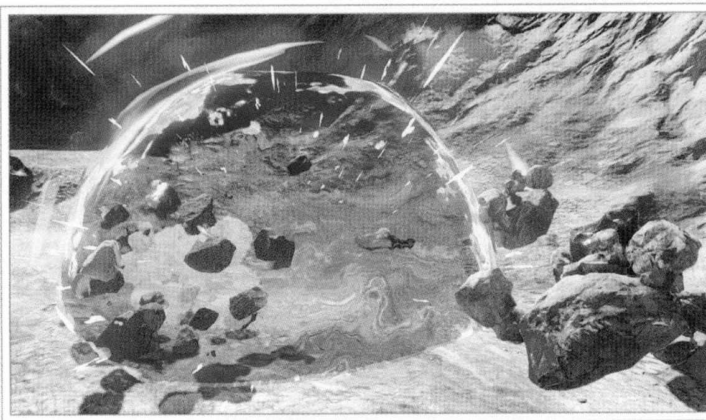

Pebblits are miniature versions of the Talus. They are far less dangerous, but can be troublesome when encountered in groups. Easy ways to get rid of them include bombs, which can take out several at a time, and all weapons effective against rocks, such as iron sledgehammers.

Each Talus will usually drop large quantities of gemstones when you defeat it. Once you are fully familiar with their attack patterns and can defeat them rapidly, farming these creatures can be an excellent way to gather significant quantities of high-value resources to sell.

Hinox

KEY ATTRIBUTES

NAME	HP	RANK	COMMON LOCATIONS	ITEM DROPS
HINOX	600	16	See map on page 328	Hinox Toenail, Hinox Tooth, Hinox Guts, Apple, Wildberry, Palm Fruit, Voltfruit, Mighty Bananas, Fortified Pumpkin, Hearty Durian
BLUE HINOX	800	20		Hinox Toenail, Hinox Tooth, Hinox Guts, Roasted Bass, Roasted Hearty Bass, Roasted Hearty Salmon, Roasted Trout, Roasted Carp, Roasted Porgy, Sneaky River Escargot, Blueshell Escargot, Blackened Crab
BLACK HINOX	1,000	24		Hinox Toenail, Hinox Tooth, Hinox Guts, Seared Steak, Seared Prime Steak, Seared Gourmet Steak, Roasted Bird Drumstick, Roasted Bird Thigh, Roasted Whole Bird
STALNOX	1,000	20		Hinox Tooth

STRATEGY

As a rule, a Hinox will be asleep when you arrive in its habitat. If you move quietly in its vicinity, it will not wake up unless you attack it. Exploit this weakness by opening hostilities with a charged attack while wielding a two-handed sword. You actually have enough time to deal multiple blows before the beast can ready itself, causing severe damage. The best strategy, if you have the right kind of equipment, is to position yourself close to the creature's head while it's still sleeping, then align a clean arrow shot at its eye – optimally with a multiple-shot bow, and with bomb arrows selected for maximum effect. As this will inflict significant damage, the sub-boss will rear up only to fall directly back down on its behind, giving you plenty of time to set about it with a barrage of blows or charged attacks.

As long as a Hinox is still asleep, you can climb onto its body if you have a stealth effect active. From here, you are free to steal its equipment, or even pilfer the orb hanging from the monster's necklace where applicable.

Once a Hinox is awake, it will only perform melee attacks. If it wrenches a tree out of the ground, this improvised weapon can have a *lot* of reach – so be prepared to backflip or block accordingly.

A Hinox's eye is its principal vulnerability. Hitting it with an arrow inflicts critical damage, temporarily incapacitating the beast. Rush to close range and attack, then retreat and repeat.

The most effective way to deplete a Hinox's health is to knock it down with an arrow, then stand between its legs and execute a charged attack with a powerful two-handed sword. You will inflict many hits in a very short time. Be ready to cancel the assault with Ⓑ and back flip the moment your opponent gets back to its feet. If you dodge the next blow, you should have an opportunity to resume your offensive for a quick finish.

If a Hinox begins to protect its eye after a few direct hits, it becomes harder to neutralize the creature. Either walk backwards while aiming, patiently waiting for an opening to present itself, or move within melee range and focus on counterattacking.

When you encounter a Hinox wearing leg armor, do not attempt to assail it from below with melee attacks: this will rapidly deplete your weapon's durability. The best solution in these instances is to exploit the vulnerability that its protective garb introduces. If the leg armor is made of wood, set it ablaze with a fire arrow; if it's made of metal, fry it with a shock arrow.

The Stalnox is a unique variant of this sub-boss. It is functionally equivalent to the others, and can be fought with the same strategies, but with one caveat: when its health bar is almost completely depleted, you must hit the creature's eye to bring the battle to a close. The monster will otherwise keep resurrecting until you deal this very specific finishing blow.

MOLDUGA

KEY ATTRIBUTES

	NAME	HP	RANK	COMMON LOCATIONS	ITEM DROPS
	MOLDUGA	1,500	20	Gerudo Desert, see map on page 328	Molduga Fin, Molduga Guts, Treasure Chests

STRATEGY

Moldugas are giant worms that "swim" beneath the sands and detect vibrations on the surface above to locate their prey. If you run on patches of sand within their territories, they will close in on you and emerge rapidly to cause significant damage. To avoid this, position Link on a rock or another suitably solid elevated surface as soon as the battle begins. Anything where you are not standing directly on sand will work.

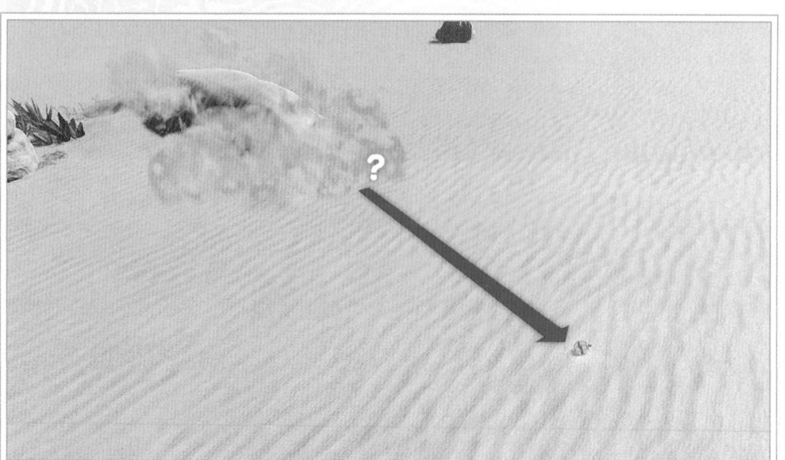

Once you have found an appropriate vantage point, throw a round bomb onto the sand. If the Molduga detects it, a question mark will appear to indicate that fact. It will then head towards the bomb and emerge to swallow it.

Once the bomb is in the Molduga's mouth or belly, detonate it. The blast will incapacitate the beast for a fairly long time.

Sprint or glide to the Molduga and attack while it is stunned. A charged attack with a two-handed sword can deal enormous amounts of damage here.

Once the Molduga recovers, you have two options. The safe option is simply to head back to an elevated position, then repeat the routine until you defeat it.

The second option is a little more risky, and requires a multi-hit bow to really shine, but can lead to shorter battle times. When your enemy recovers, move towards a safe position, but remain on the sand and walk around until the Molduga identifies you: it will approach, its body partly emerging from the sand, in search of an opportunity to lunge at Link. If you quickly move to safety just before it arrives, though, you have nothing to fear. The Molduga will then remain exposed as it searches for Link. Select your multiple-hit bow and fire a bomb arrow at the creature: the explosion will inflict massive damage and incapacitate it. You can then follow up with a melee combo to finish it off.

Lynels

KEY ATTRIBUTES

NAME	HP	RANK	COMMON LOCATIONS	ITEM DROPS
 LYNEL	2,000	30	See map on page 328	Lynel Horn, Lynel Hoof, Lynel Guts
 BLUE-MANED LYNEL	3,000	34		Lynel Horn, Lynel Hoof, Lynel Guts
 WHITE-MANED LYNEL	4,000	38		Lynel Horn, Lynel Hoof, Lynel Guts
 SILVER LYNEL	6,000	42		Lynel Horn, Lynel Hoof, Lynel Guts, Amber, Opal, Topaz, Ruby, Sapphire, Diamond

STRATEGY

Lynels are possibly the fiercest creatures in the entire game, with the strongest varieties being arguably more redoubtable and deadly than *Breath of the Wild*'s main bosses. The White-Maned Lynel and Silver Lynel will seriously put your strategic and defensive prowess to the test.

MELEE ASSAULTS: The standard (and most regular) attacks employed by Lynels are melee-based: lateral sweeps, overhead strikes and spinning attacks are common gambits. They also regularly execute "bull charges" where they run at full speed towards Link to propel him from his feet. An important fact to remember is that *all* of these assaults can be perfect guarded – and most, but not all, can also be perfect dodged. The precise timing required for successful counters varies in accordance with the weapon that each specimen wields, which means that lots of practice is required. We strongly suggest that you create a manual save before an encounter against a low-rank Lynel and practice perfect guards until you feel totally comfortable, reloading to repeat as many times as required. This might be a little overwhelming at first, but you will soon improve, and this will greatly improve your level of performance against these mighty creatures in future encounters.

ARROWS: Over long distances, or should you climb to an elevated vantage point, Lynels will fire elemental arrows at you. Their level of accuracy is impressive: they can shoot straight at you with great precision, or employ curved trick-shot trajectories, and they have unlimited ammo. In short: long-range duels are highly unlikely to work in your favor.

FIREBALLS: The three more advanced Lynel varieties can hurl fireballs. These are large and fast. If you plan to dodge, sprint perpendicularly to them and you should be safe. If you're close enough, a better alternative is to sprint diagonally to the Lynel's side: you need just enough lateral motion to avoid the first fireball, but not so much that you move away from your target. Once you move within range of your foe, unleash a charged attack with a two-handed sword while the creature is busy hurling its remaining projectiles. Stay on the move while spinning, circling around behind the Lynel to remain out of reach of its attacks for as long as possible.

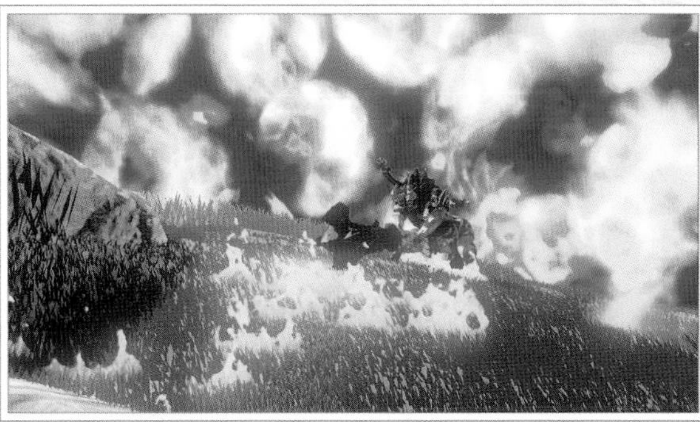

FIRE EXPLOSIONS: High-rank Lynels regularly roar, emitting a large soundwave, and follow up by slamming their weapon to the ground. This causes a fiery explosion with a very large blast radius. Either sprint away to escape the area of effect, or block it with your shield. This attack has a long preparation time, so you can actually use this opportunity to land a few blows while your enemy is not focusing on you. (You can even exploit this time window to shoot an arrow at the monster's face to stun it – we describe this tactic in greater detail further down on this page.)

STALWART DEFENSE: If you are confident in your defensive capabilities, a counter-oriented strategy is a very viable approach against a Lynel. Perform perfect guards against all physical assaults and follow up with standard combos. Taking down the strongest Lynel varieties with this method can take a while depending on the strength of your weapons – but with the right timing and a lot of practice, it works very consistently. In a pinch, if you are not ready for an incoming assault, note that you can cast Stasis+ on your opponent to freeze it in time, though this offers no more than a second or two of respite.

FACE SHOTS: For expert players, the ultimate strategy involves precision marksmanship. Every time you hit a Lynel's face with an arrow, it will be stunned. This can seem hard to achieve at first, as you are aiming for a small hitbox on an agile, fast-moving target. With a little experience and the right equipment, though, this becomes less challenging than you might fear. At very close range while wielding a multiple-shot bow, pre-align the camera toward the Lynel's face and then shoot "from the hip," without wasting time with direct aiming; the gyroscope-based motion controls can enable you to make subtle, last-second adjustments. This maneuver is best performed in two specific scenarios: when your opponent prepares slow, strong attacks such as fire explosions; and after perfect guarding a physical blow. After every successful "face shot," you can follow up with a couple of blows, then mount the creature (press Ⓐ while close to its rear) for a few additional bonus strikes that will not reduce your weapon's durability. Once you have been dislodged, you can quickly draw the paraglider and align another arrow to the face with the assistance of the slow-motion effect.

URBOSA'S FURY: If you struggle to finish off a Lynel, Urbosa's Fury (which you acquire by completing the Divine Beast Vah Naboris dungeon) can make a real difference. Unleash the finishing hit of a charged attack (after triggering a perfect guard, for example) and this will cause lightning to rain down in the area, stunning your opponent and dealing massive damage. This offers an opportunity to deal a few more blows and mount your foe. Having the full three charges of this special power available when the battle begins will make every encounter against a Lynel much easier.

DROPS: Lynels wield some of the best equipment in the game – and these pieces are yours to collect when they topple for the last time. If you learn to defeat them efficiently, they offer one of the best farming opportunities for late-game combat items. There are locations with multiple Lynels in a relatively small zone (such as Hyrule Castle) where you can take down two or three in succession, filling your inventory with powerful weapons, shields, and bows.

STAL MONSTERS

Stal monsters tend to appear only at night. These skeletal adversaries always correspond to a standard enemy archetype. A Stalkoblin, for instance, is the skeletal variety of a Bokoblin. Stal creatures are defined by their fragility: a single blow will often scatter their bones. However, unless you strike their heads to eliminate them for good, they will magically reform and resume their attack. With the Stalnox (the skeleton variant of a Hinox), it's actually the eye that you must hit in order to finish off the creature. Also note that each Stalnox drops a rare elemental weapon upon defeat.

BOSSES

We cover all boss battles in greater detail in the Walkthrough chapter. The page references in the accompanying table will lead you to the relevant pages should you need further guidance. Bosses do not have a rank stat as their level of dangerousness varies from one playthrough to another depending on the order in which you defeat them.

KEY ATTRIBUTES

NAME	HP	COMMON LOCATIONS	ITEM DROPS	PAGE
MASTER KOHGA	300	Yiga Clan Hideout	–	67
THUNDERBLIGHT GANON	800	Divine Beast Vah Naboris	–	74
FIREBLIGHT GANON	800	Divine Beast Vah Rudania	–	95
WATERBLIGHT GANON	800	Divine Beast Vah Ruta	–	60
WINDBLIGHT GANON	800	Divine Beast Vah Medoh	–	84
CALAMITY GANON	8,000	Hyrule Castle	–	108
DARK BEAST GANON	–	Hyrule Castle	–	111

STRATEGY

MASTER KOHGA: This opponent summons large boulders and hurls them at you. The most effective strategy is to hit Master Kohga with an arrow when he has one held aloft above his head. This will cause it to fall on him, causing very significant damage.

THUNDERBLIGHT GANON: This opponent's most dangerous attack occurs when he warps multiple times in your direction, quickly zigzagging to your left and right before dealing a powerful blow. As the monster warps to your right and readies its attack, poised to strike, perform a perfect dodge backflip: if successful, this will grant you an opportunity to unleash a full flurry rush combo, and follow up with a second combo. When your opponent summons small metal pillars around your position in an attempt to electrocute you, sprint away from the pillars and head to the upper walkways. You can then grab one of the pillars with Magnesis and position it close to the boss. The next lightning bolt that strikes the area will electrocute your enemy.

FIREBLIGHT GANON: The most effective way to defeat this boss is to focus on melee combat. Perfect dodge its assaults and follow up with flurry rushes. The rest of the time, circle around your enemy and maintain a steady barrage of melee strikes. You can often flank it and deal large amounts of damage while the creature is busy performing wayward forward blows. When your opponent summons an impenetrable aura around its body, throw a bomb, which will pass through the force field, then detonate it. This will stun your target, enabling you to run in and attack.

WATERBLIGHT GANON: This boss will often perform melee attacks with its spear. The best counter against this is to perfect dodge each blow and follow up with a flurry rush. Waterblight Ganon's signature move is to throw blocks of ice at you: have Cryonis ready when this happens, and sweep the screen with your reticle, destroying all projectiles as they move within range.

WINDBLIGHT GANON: This opponent will throw all sorts of projectiles in your direction. To eliminate it, you can fire arrows at its eye (ideally while riding updrafts to enjoy the slow-motion effect that makes aiming much easier). Alternatively, you can rush to the monster whenever it materializes at ground level and assault it with your most powerful combos for a swift finish.

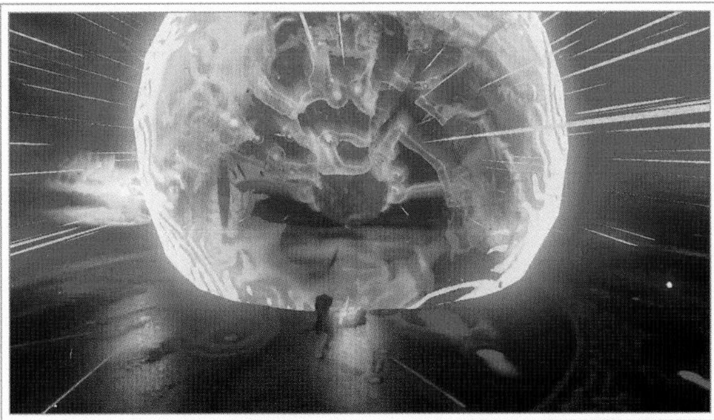

CALAMITY GANON: Ganon, in his true form, can use techniques employed by all four of his elemental variants. Arrows can be used to slowly chip away at his health, but the best way to cause large amounts of damage is via perfect dodges followed up by flurry rushes. If you are wielding the Master Sword (see page 103) and have a shield at the ready, you can inflict massive HP loss by perfect guarding your enemy's laser beam attacks. When Ganon summons a field of fire energy that initially makes him seem invincible, just defend calmly and consistently until you manage to create an opening, either by perfect guarding its beams or by using the perfect dodge/flurry rush combination against the monster's melee assaults.

DARK BEAST GANON: As soon as the final battle begins, collect the nearby Bow of Light. This offers unparalleled power and infinite ammo. With the Bow of Light drawn, fire arrows at the glyphs that appear on the creature's body. You must pierce three glyphs on each side, then one on the creature's belly. Your final target is the large eyeball, which you can only strike while riding an updraft.

EXTRAS

This chapter covers activities and challenges that are not listed in your Adventure Log, many of which contribute to your overall completion rate. We also document and discuss a variety of optional objectives, ranging from mini-games to secret missions and features.

Completion Rate

Your completion rate is a measure of how much you have accomplished in the game. Once you have defeated Ganon, it appears as a percentage in the lower-left corner of the map screen

Every relevant objective that you fulfill will contribute approximately 0.08% to your overall completion rate. This applies to the following actions:

- Every **shrine** that you discover: see the Shrines chapter on page 112.
- Every **boss** that you defeat: see the Walkthrough chapter on page 32.
- Every **Korok seed** that you obtain: see our dedicated section on page 330.
- Every **location** that you discover (with its name appearing on your screen and on the in-game map). Refer to our map poster for a complete overview.

Even though there is no reward for reaching the maximum 100% value, completionists will regard this as an achievement to aspire to.

Great Fairy Fountains

Great Fairy Fountains are unique landmarks that enable you to upgrade your clothes and pieces of armor. The map shown here illustrates the positions of all four fountains.

Once you have discovered a fountain, you must unlock it. This is achieved by paying a set sum of rupees. This total will increase with each successive Great Fairy Fountain that you activate. Note that you must unlock each fountain to make it appear on the map and add it to your overall completion rate.

The first fountain you unlock offers Level 1 outfit upgrades (★). Each subsequent fountain increases the available star level for garb enhancements until you gain access to the maximum Level 4 upgrades (★★★★). The first three Great Fairy Fountains require investments that are easy to afford at a relatively early stage of the adventure; the fourth is perhaps more of a long-term goal.

Upgrading pieces of armor improves their defense value – and therefore your resistance to damage. However, each enhancement requires a payment in materials. Initial upgrades for simple clothes can be bought for small quantities of basic resources – common monster parts such as Lizalfos horns, for instance. More advanced upgrades, on the other hand, can only be purchased with rare and precious goods such as dragon shards. You can find the complete list of all armor upgrades in our Inventory chapter (see page 280).

It's worth noting that certain armor sets can provide special effects when equipped if all three pieces have been upgraded to at least Level 2 (★★).

OVERVIEW

FOUNTAIN	FEE (RUPEES)	POSSIBLE UPGRADES
#1	100	★
#2	500	★★
#3	1,000	★★★
#4	10,000	★★★★

KAYSA'S GREAT FAIRY FOUNTAIN: A short distance to the south of the Tabantha Tower, at the base of Piper Ridge.

MIJA'S GREAT FAIRY FOUNTAIN: Within walking distance to the south of Tarrey Town, on the east shore of Lake Akkala.

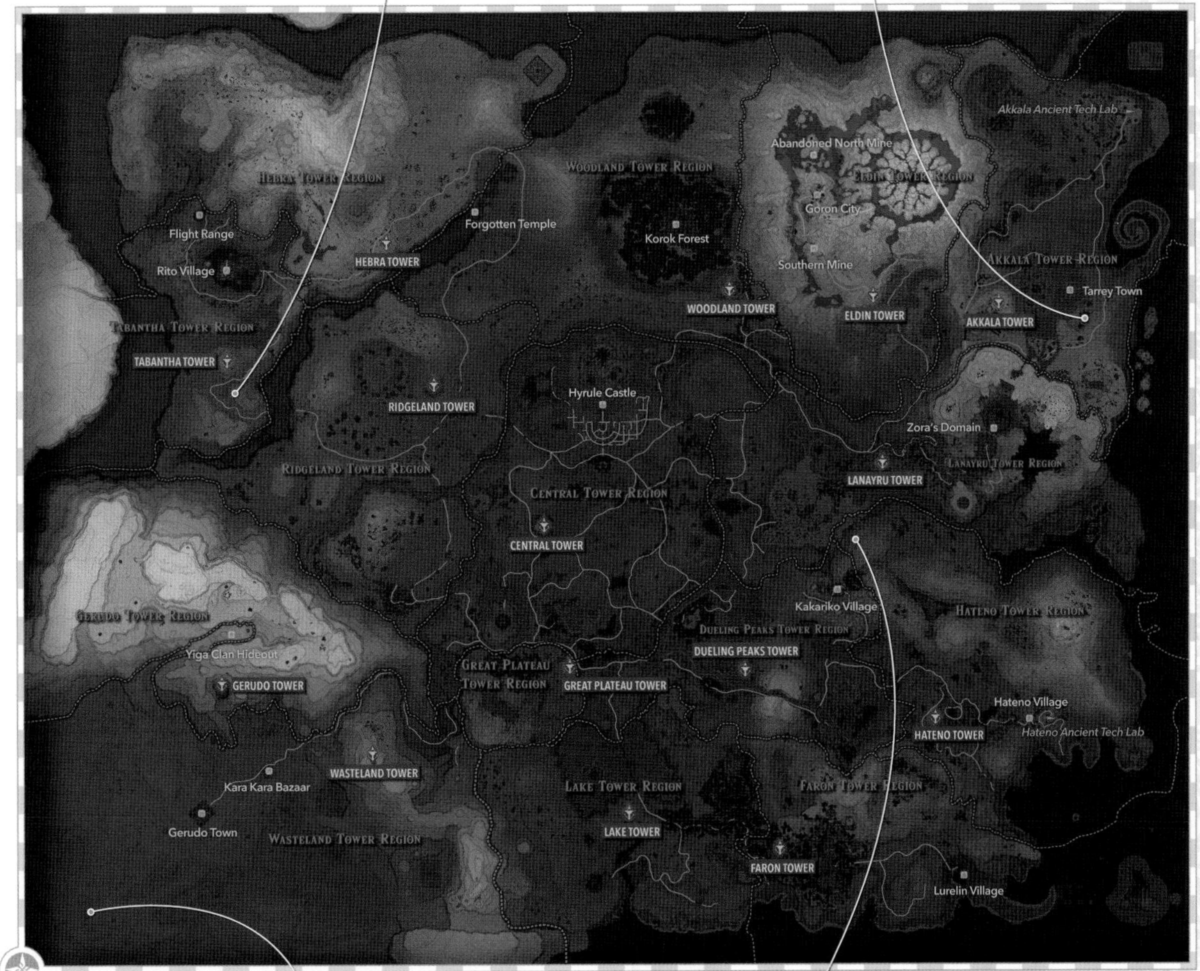

TERA'S GREAT FAIRY FOUNTAIN: Easy to find in the southwest corner of the Gerudo Desert, under the Gerudo Great Skeleton.

COTERA'S GREAT FAIRY FOUNTAIN: Likely the first fountain you will encounter, it lies to the northeast of Kakariko Village.

SUB-BOSSES

Sub-bosses are larger-than-usual enemies that can be encountered in specific locations. There are four primary archetypes – Talus, Hinox, Molduga, and Lynel – and multiple variants of each species. These include elemental versions that can prove deadly unless you have the right equipment to counter and survive their natural aptitudes.

The variant found at each spawn point is fixed for the Talus, Hinox, and Molduga archetypes: they remain the same no matter how far you are in the adventure. Most Lynels, on the other hand, "rank up" based on your progression. This map shows the default types that you will encounter at each spot early on in the game, but these will gradually be replaced by more dangerous variants, and, ultimately, by fearsome Silver Lynels. Even in the late-game, though, you can find a standard Lynel atop Ploymus Mountains, and Blue-Maned and White-Maned specimens inside Hyrule Castle's Gatehouses. Note that you can track down the location of sub-bosses by using the Sheikah Sensor+ and a corresponding picture of the specimen.

The following map shows the position of all sub-bosses in the game. You can find advice on how to defeat them in our Bestiary chapter (see page 314).

LEGEND

ARCHETYPE	ICON	VARIANT
Talus		Stone Talus
		Stone Talus (Luminous)
		Stone Talus (Rare)
		Igneo Talus
		Frost Talus
Hinox		Hinox
		Blue Hinox
		Black Hinox
		Stalnox*
Molduga		Molduga
Lynel		Lynel
		Blue-Maned Lynel
		White-Maned Lynel

* The Stalnox that spawn outdoors usually only come to life at night.

Abandoned North Mine
Akkala Ancient Tech Lab
Woodland Tower Region
Eldin Tower Region
rgotten Temple
Korok Forest
Goron City
Southern Mine
Akkala Tower Region
Akkala Tower
Tarrey Town
Woodland Tower
Eldin Tower
Hyrule Castle
Zora's Domain
Lanayru Tower Region
Lanayru Tower
Central Tower Region
Central Tower
Kakariko Village
Great Plateau Tower
Dueling Peaks Tower
Hateno Tower Region
reat Plateau Tower Region
Dueling Peaks Tower Region
Hateno Village
Hateno Ancient Tech Lab
Hateno Tower
Lake Tower Region
Lake Tower
Faron Tower
Faron Tower Region
Lurelin Village

Korok Seeds

You will receive a seed for every Korok that you find in the wild. The locations of all 900 Korok seeds are shown on the map poster supplied with this guide, and in the Maps chapter that begins on page 374.

There are various types of mini-challenges that you must discover and solve to reveal each Korok. These are all introduced here, and associated with an icon. You will find the exact same icons used on our maps, enabling you to identify which type of challenge awaits at each position. If you happen to do something that makes a puzzle impossible to complete, such as misplacing a vital object, worry not: the setup will be restored if you leave and return later.

Korok seeds are used to unlock additional inventory slots for your weapons, bows, and shields. You can acquire these extra slots by speaking to **Hestu**, a character that you will first encounter on your way from the Dueling Peaks Stable to Kakariko. After you retrieve his maracas for him (see page 220), you can randomly encounter him again at one of three stables along the Hylia River (Woodland Stable, Riverside Stable, or Wetland Stable). He then takes up permanent residence at Korok Forest. The cost of each additional slot in a category is exponential: the first slot costs a single seed, the second one costs two, and the expense rises rapidly thereafter. You need 441 seeds to unlock all inventory slots, but all 900 of them if you aspire to reach 100% game completion. If you do find every last Korok seed, you will receive a unique item known as Hestu's Gift, enabling you to trigger the creature's signature dance at will.

ROCK PATTERN: Small rocks are configured in a geometrical pattern, such as a circle, a spiral, or a cross. At least one rock is missing, and you need to place it in the correct position to complete the arrangement. As a rule, the loose rock can be found in the direction of the gap in the pattern: for example, if you see a gap on the south tip of a circle of rocks, it's likely that you will find the missing rock a few steps to the south. Consider using Stasis to locate missing rocks.

CUBE PATTERN: Small metal cubes are configured in symmetrical arrangements, with one anomaly – a cube is missing, or needs to be transferred from one structure to the other, and so forth. Fix the error with Magnesis and the seed is yours. The missing cube (or, for that matter, the "reference" twin structure) is sometimes not immediately apparent: activate Stasis or Magnesis and observe your surroundings (including underwater, behind waterfalls…) until you find all elements of the puzzle.

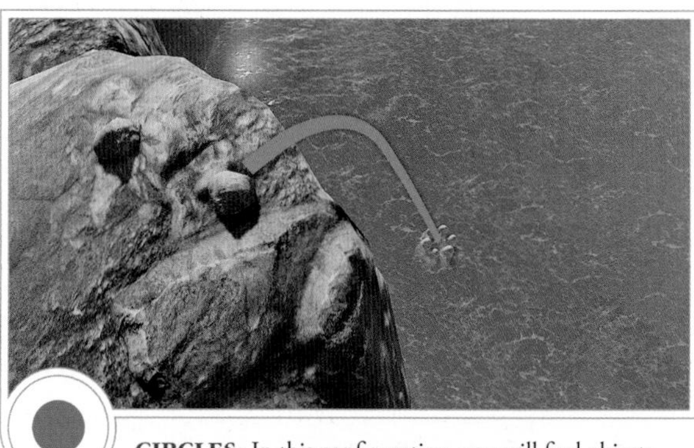

CIRCLES: In this configuration, you will find objects (often rocks jutting out from water) arranged in a circle, and multiple small rocks in a nearby location. Your goal is to throw one of the rocks into the circle. There are instances where you can use a Cryonis pillar to extend the potential range of the rock. Similarly, you will notice circles made of natural objects, such as water lilies: dive or simply fall through these after gliding to their position to reveal the hidden Korok; if this doesn't appear to work, try to begin your descent from a greater height.

NATURAL HIDING SPOT: Many Koroks are hidden under natural objects, particularly small rocks. These are most commonly found at elevated positions (such as mountain peaks, tall pillars, or atop large trees), or in other unusual locations: pick them up to reveal a Korok. Likewise, certain Koroks may be hidden in an ice block that you must melt, below a rock slab that can be lifted with an Octo balloon, behind destructible rocks that you need to blow up, under a large boulder that you need to propel away with Stasis or beneath layers of leaves that you can burn or remove with a bomb. Stasis can prove helpful with identifying such points of interactivity.

LEAVES WITH FAIRY DUST: When you notice a small trail of leaves with a fairy dust effect moving along a set course, intercept and examine it to reveal a Korok. There's no need to chase: you can wait in a location that it has traveled past and await its return. You will sometimes find a similar fairy dust effect in a fixed position – for example high in a tree, at the top of a spire, or on a rooftop.

RACE: Every time you encounter a tree stump with a leaf symbol, get ready for a race. The moment you step on the stump, a timer begins: you must go through the ring that appears before the countdown ends. These challenges can involve sprinting, climbing, gliding, shield-surfing, and swimming. Very occasionally, you will come across a series of fences conveniently aligned. If you jump over them while riding a horse, you will reveal a Korok.

FLOWER TRAILS: A daffodil growing alone in the middle of a path usually betrays the presence of a Korok. Approach it and it will disappear, reappearing a little further away (with a characteristic popping effect that may help you to locate it). Follow this trail until the Korok surrenders its prize. You will also encounter a variation where you interact with groups of flowers in a specific order: a single flower, then a pair of flowers, then a trio, and so forth.

FOOD OFFERING: You will regularly run into groups of aligned statues that have small trays in front of them. If you drop the right type of food on all trays, a Korok will be revealed. Most of the time, apples are the gift of choice. For statues honored by the Yiga clan, however, you must drop mighty bananas. There are instances where the "food" in question is less common, but the game will show you which ingredient is required in at least one of the trays – for example, an egg, or even a rusty shield. Occasionally you will face a single, empty tray: you can infer the correct offering by observing your immediate surroundings (for example, a hearty durian in a forest where these fruits are abundant).

ARCHERY: Whenever you spot a balloon, pop it with an arrow to reveal a Korok. Balloons will sometimes only appear when you stand next to a colored pinwheel: look around until you see them, then shoot them with an arrow (a feat made easier by wielding a long-range bow when facing distant targets). This will become more challenging when the balloons move, and especially so when their motions are quick and erratic. There are also frequent instances where your targets are acorns. These can be thrown in the air, hidden in a tree log, or hanging in an easy-to-miss location: beneath a bridge, inside a tree, or from a ceiling. Unlike balloons, acorns can be located with relative ease by activating Stasis. Very occasionally, you will encounter more unusual archery targets. These include Triforce emblems, pieces of fruit oddly positioned among other fruit types, or eye symbols.

BOULDERS: Here, one or more large boulders must be moved to nearby holes. If a boulder is on a slope, you can push it to make it roll down to the hole. If not, cast Stasis on it and strike it with a weapon in order to confer just the right amount of momentum to reach its destination. A variation of this puzzle will require you to use Magnesis to move chained metallic boulders to specific positions (a hollow tree stump, a well) or to form patterns.

TREE PATTERNS: If you see a pattern in the fruit growing on adjacent trees, there's probably a Korok behind it. For example: if three trees are aligned and two of them have a single apple, remove all the extraneous fruit from the third tree. Once all three look identical, you will receive your seed.

MINI-GAMES

Mini-games in *Breath of the Wild* generally require the payment of a nominal entry fee to secure your participation – usually 20 rupees, but occasionally 50 or even 100. Once you master them, however, you can receive rewards that will more than compensate for the initial expenditure.

The map shown here illustrates the locations of all mini-games. You can find more information about each mini-game over the pages that follow.

MINI-GAME OVERVIEW

(Walkthroughs Overleaf)

NAME	PAGE
Bird-Man Research Study	339
Boom Bam Golf	341
Carry the Ice!	334
Deer Hunting	339
Flight Range	336
Footrace	337
Gambling	336
Horseback Archery	341
Obstacle Course	338
Paraglider Course	340
Restoring the Blue Flame	340
Sand-Seal Racing	335
Shield-Surfing	335
Snowball Bowling	337
Super Gut Check Challenge	334
The Test of Wood – Revisited	338

Super Gut Check Challenge
Akkala Ancient Tech Lab
Abandoned North Mine
Woodland Tower Region
Eldin Tower Region
Goron City
Forgotten Temple
Korok Forest
Restoring the Blue Flame
Southern Mine
Akkala Tower Region
The Test of Wood – Revisited
Tarrey Town
Woodland Tower
Eldin Tower
Akkala Tower
Hyrule Castle
Zora's Domain
Lanayru Tower Region
Lanayru Tower
Central Tower Region
Central Tower
Kakariko Village
Hateno Tower Region
Dueling Peaks Tower Region
Dueling Peaks Tower
Deer Hunting
at Plateau
ower Region
Great Plateau Tower
Hateno Ancient Tech Lab
Hateno Tower
Hateno Village
Lake Tower Region
Faron Tower Region
Gambling
Lake Tower
Faron Tower
Paraglider Course
Lurelin Village
Horseback Archery
Obstacle Course

CARRY THE ICE!

1

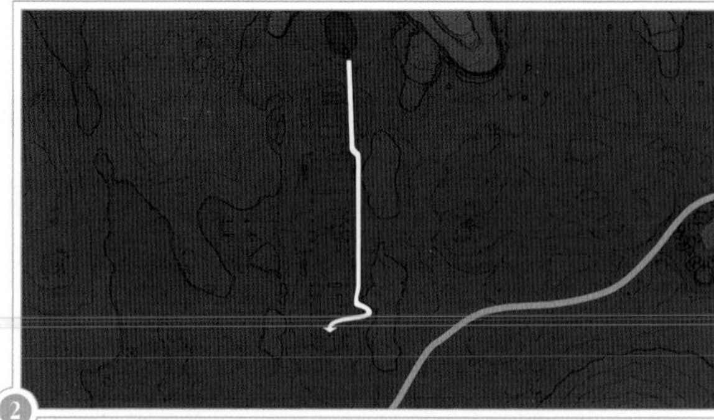

2

This mini-game will become available once you have completed the "The Perfect Drink" shrine quest (see page 161 for details). Visit the ice house during the day. This is an underground room found directly to the north of Gerudo Town. You can enter it via a floor hatch beneath a very large flat rock. Speak to Anche inside to begin the challenge. The entry fee is 50 rupees.

You must now make your way across the ruins between the ice house and Gerudo Town while carrying the ice cube above your head. The fastest way to reach your destination is to equip the sand boots (obtained from Bozai by completing the "The Eighth Heroine" side quest – see page 252). Stay on the sand on the east side of the ruins without ever stepping directly inside. The monsters in the area should not spot you, enabling you to reach Furosa at the south end of the ruins. Drop the ice cube in front of her in under two minutes to complete the challenge and she will reward you with a **gold rupee**. This can be repeated endlessly, and is actually a very efficient way to raise funds.

SUPER GUT CHECK CHALLENGE

1

This mini-game becomes available after you complete the "Gut Check Challenge" shrine quest (see page 203 for details). Warp to Gorae Torr Shrine, to the north of Death Mountain, then speak to Bayge to begin. Each attempt to win the Super Gut Check Challenge will cost you 100 rupees. Much like the original test of endurance, alacrity and avarice, your goal is to climb to the top of the peak in a limited time while also collecting at least **300 rupees** before you reach the finish. To make things much easier, we advise that you tackle this challenge once you have a fully maxed-out stamina wheel. This will enable you to jump regularly, shaving valuable seconds from your time. Furthermore, equipping armor pieces with the climb speed up bonus effect (see page 281) will also be beneficial. Generally speaking, ignore green rupees unless they're directly in your path, and prioritize those with higher values – particularly red and silver rupees. As long as you reach the top of the cliff in under three minutes and pick up the required **300 rupees**, you win the challenge and can keep the money. Bayge will even throw in an **endura shroom** as an additional reward.

2

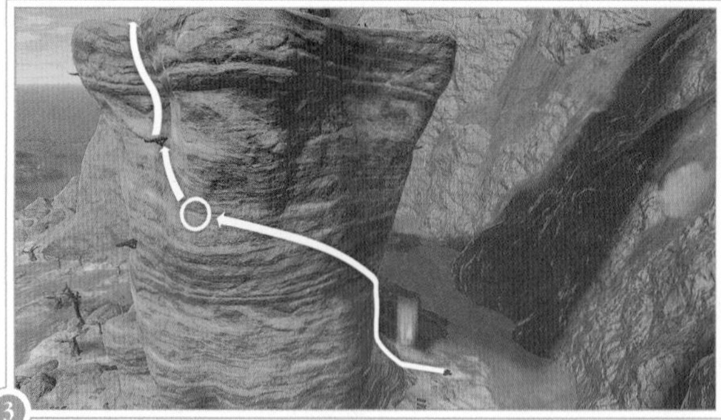

3

The most obvious way to complete this challenge is to climb the southwest cliff, right in front of you as you begin. Scale it as illustrated above, taking a left at the first branching path between two blue rupees. Follow the vertical trail to collect two silver rupees directly on your way. After the second, head to your right instead of going up: you will soon find a third silver rupee, guaranteeing that your total exceeds the required 300. You can then make your way to the finish line.

An alternative option is to climb diagonally to your left, following the trail of green rupees until you find a gold rupee hidden on the north face of the cliff. With a fully maxed-out stamina wheel, you can reach it as long as you do not jump on the way. Armor pieces with the climb speed up bonus will make this even easier. Once the gold rupee is yours, catch your breath on the protruding beam (a little further up on your left) before you push on to the top.

SHIELD-SURFING

1

Speak to Selmie in her wooden cabin (known as "Selmie's Spot") at the top of the Hebra Mountains. She will offer you the opportunity to take part in a shield-surfing challenge if you are prepared to pay a fee of 20 rupees.

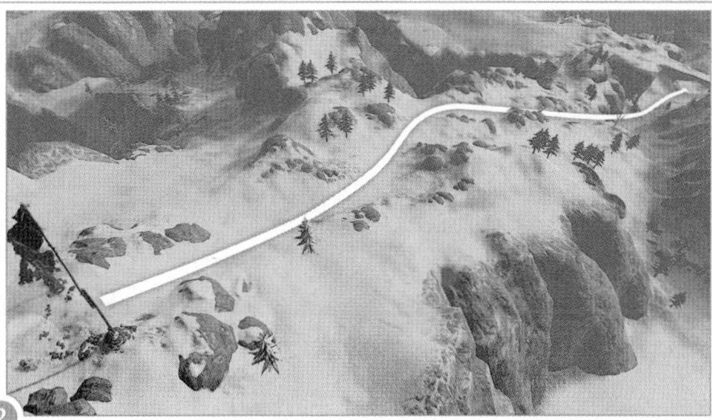

2

BEGINNER COURSE: Your objective is to shield-surf down the hill following the path illustrated above until you pass beneath a stone bridge at the bottom of the slope. To initiate shield-surfing, hold your shield aloft (ZL), jump (X), then tap A while airborne. You can then steer with L. Tilt L forward at all times to move at maximum speed, avoiding natural hazards and animals on the way. Your time on the beginner course needs to be under one minute in order to unlock the advanced course. When Selmie enquires as to what shield-surfing means to you, be sure to shrug rather than sounding too excited – otherwise, she will ask you to go through the initial course again.

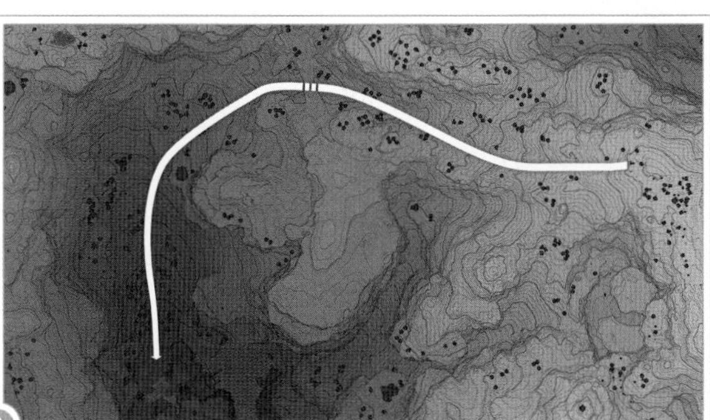

3

ADVANCED COURSE – FAIR PLAY: Once you've completed the beginner course in less than a minute and shrugged to answer Selmie's question, you can proceed to the advanced course. The rules here are exactly the same, but the track is longer: you must take a long, slow left turn after the stone bridge before going down a long straight, all the way to Sturnida Basin. The finish line is marked by large flags that are visible from a distance.

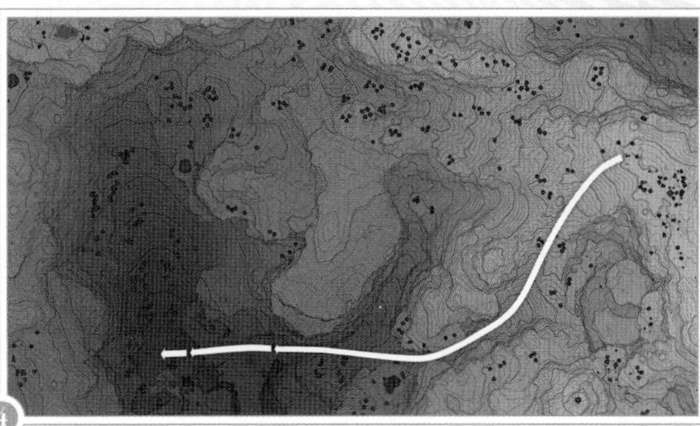

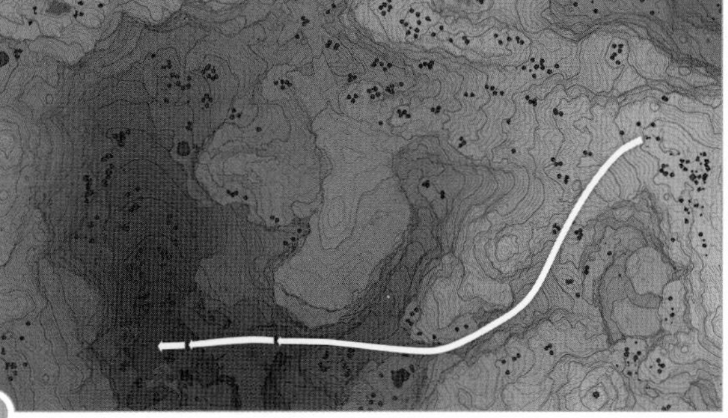

4

ADVANCED COURSE – PARAGLIDER TRICK: The idea here is to take a shortcut, surfing down the slope to the west of Coldsnap Hollow and ultimately to the south of Biron Snowshelf. When you reach the cliff overlooking Lake Kilsie, glide across to the finish line at Sturnida Basin. You might need to make the final few yards on foot but this is not a problem: you can cross the line in any fashion without consequence. Shield-surfing is always faster than sprinting, though, so try to remain on your shield whenever possible. This trick will enable you to complete the course in record time, and thus obtain a **royal shield**.

SAND-SEAL RACING

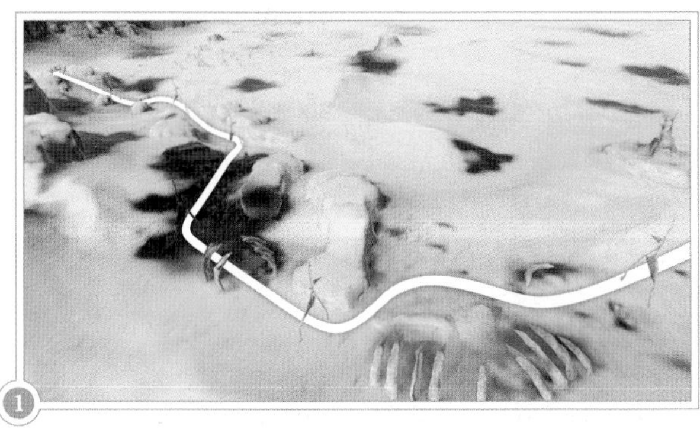

1

This mini-game becomes available after you have completed the "The Undefeated Champ" shrine quest (see page 156 for details). Speak to Shabonne at the sand-seal rally area, to the south of Gerudo Town. A race will begin if you agree to pay an entry fee of 100 rupees. This plays out in the same way as the shrine quest: you must reach the finish line in under a minute and a half while passing under every arch on the way. The course is identical, so you should have a working knowledge of how to move efficiently. Just make sure you press A to dash whenever your seal slows down, and make smooth turns to reach each arch; abrupt changes in direction will impede your progress. You will receive a **gold rupee** every time you complete the race under the 01:30 time requirement.

1 After completing the Divine Beast Vah Medoh dungeon, speak to Teba and his wife Saki in the hut next door to the village elder. Once he recovers from his wounds, Teba departs for the Flight Range. Meet him there and speak to his son, Tulin, to trigger this mini-game.

2 The challenge is similar to the one you faced here during the main story, though you must now eliminate as many targets as possible within a very short time. Hitting all 20 targets will reward you with a **gold rupee**.

FLIGHT RANGE TIPS

Hitting all targets in the Flight Range can prove extremely difficult. The following advice should help you to improve your performance.

- Be sure to activate slow-motion by aiming with your bow as often as possible: this slows the timer to a crawl, effectively extending the duration of each session. You should aspire to be in slow-motion at practically all times, except when you need to move to a different location or altitude, and when you run out of stamina.
- Be methodical and clean up each area of all targets before you move on; there are often targets above, below, or behind you. As long as slow-motion is active, you can check your surroundings without wasting too much time.
- When shooting at distant targets, don't forget to aim above them to take the arrow drop factor into account.
- Last but not least, try to equip a bow with extended range and the quick shot perk to increase your fire rate. The great eagle bow, the swallow bow (available for free inside Harth's hut, near the top of Rito Village), and the falcon bow (found in certain shrines) are all strong candidates for this challenge.

GAMBLING

1

The house in the northeast corner of Lurelin Village is home to a gambling mini-game. Speak to Cloyne inside to get started. The principle is simple: you place a stake of up to 100 rupees on one of three treasure chests, but only a single chest contains a reward in excess of your wager. If you select the correct container, which is purely a matter of luck, you will receive a modest return; if not, you will lose most of your investment. Statistically, you have very little chance of making a sustained profit with this mini-game, especially as the maximum return is a mere 300 rupees with a 100 rupee stake, so it's best to consider it as no more than a curiosity.

SNOWBALL BOWLING

You can play this mini-game at Pondo's Lodge, a short distance to the northeast of the Hebra Tower. Speak to Pondo to get an explanation of the rules and, once you're prepared, to begin. In this variant of bowling, your goal is to knock over the 10 pins at the foot of the hill with the snowball at the top. If you displace all pins on your first try, you will score a strike. If it takes you two tries to finish the job, you will score a spare. Each game will cost you 20 rupees.

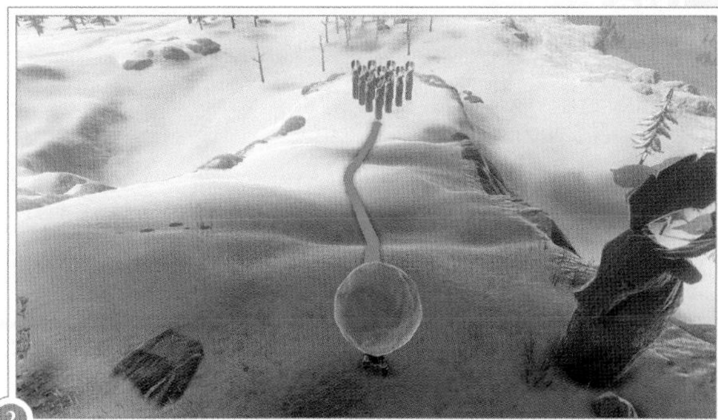

THE THROWING TECHNIQUE: The most straightforward way to score a strike is by picking up the snowball and throwing it with R. The complication here is that the hill is very bumpy, so you cannot aim directly at the upfront pin: you must take the uneven terrain into account. Our favorite approach is to position Link at mid-distance between the flat rock at the center of the lane, and the wooden pillar on the right side. Link should be oriented precisely towards the front pin. Once you throw the ball, it will inch a little to the left then to the right as it passes the two bumps on its course, but ultimately it should head straight into the lead pin at full speed and maximum size. By paying close attention to Link's direction and perfecting the approach detailed here, it is possible to score a strike with near-perfect consistency, making this a potentially very lucrative mini-game.

THE STASIS TECHNIQUE: If you have difficulties with the throwing technique, an alternative approach is to make use of Stasis. Move behind the ball's starting position and align Link so that he, the center of the ball, and the upfront pin are all aligned on the exact same axis. You must then hit the snowball five times with a one-handed weapon, turning the Stasis vector arrow orange. The projectile will then have just the right amount of speed to land precisely in front of the front pin. If your aim was true, this will lead to a guaranteed strike.

SNOWBALL BOWLING REWARDS

SCORE	REWARD
Strike (1st time)	Blizzard Rod
Strike (subsequent tries or if inventory full)	Gold Rupee
Spare	Silver Rupee
9 pins	Purple Rupee
8 pins	Red Rupee

FOOTRACE

Speak to Konba at the Footrace Check-In, to the north of the Tabantha Bridge Stable. You can identify it from a distance when it's not raining by looking for the plume of smoke that rises from his campfire. Your goal is to reach the finish line marked by flags at the top of the mountain. The first individual to reach it is the winner, and the path you take is entirely your choice. The only rule is that you cannot call your horse.

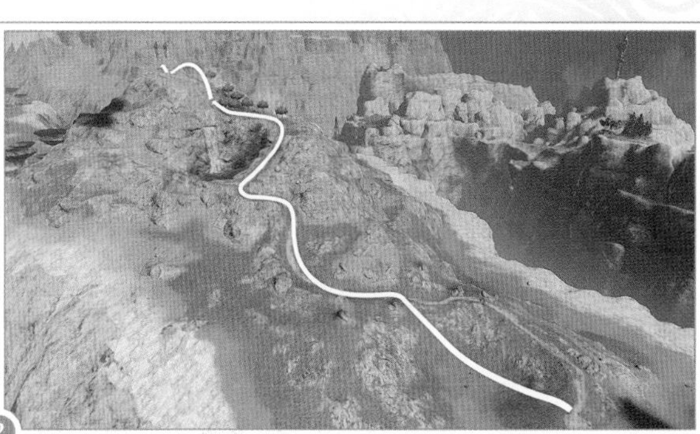

Beating Konba should not pose any problems, especially as you can employ many tricks to improve your performance: taking shortcuts while he remains on the main path, inducing a movement speed bonus with appropriate food, or even employing Revali's Gale to fly high in the air and glide over obstacles. An efficient course is illustrated on the above picture. If you take a right at the fork, and catch the updraft near the end of the race, you should easily win no matter what. The best reward you can get in this mini-game is a **silver rupee**.

1

Speak to Blynne while riding a horse at the Highland Stable. A horse with strong speed and stamina stats will make this challenge a little easier. The white horse obtained during another side quest ("The Royal White Stallion" – see page 269) is a very good choice here.

OBSTACLE COURSE TIPS

- Whenever you head towards an obstacle, always aim for the center of the horizontal bar and avoid last-second adjustments. Attempting to jump too close to the supporting posts will usually lead to a refusal, adding a significant (and, for the rewards, decisive) number of seconds to your time. Perfecting your riding style in order to make a clean approach to each jump is essential.
- Switch to maximum gallop speed in straight lines or when you have plenty of space, but remain at a canter for any demanding maneuver, such as a sharp turn before or after an obstacle.
- Try to plan ahead. Your approach to each obstacle should also take the next one into account. If a subsequent jump is to the left, for instance, make your approach to the intervening obstacle diagonally from the right to the left, therefore aligning yourself for the next hurdle.

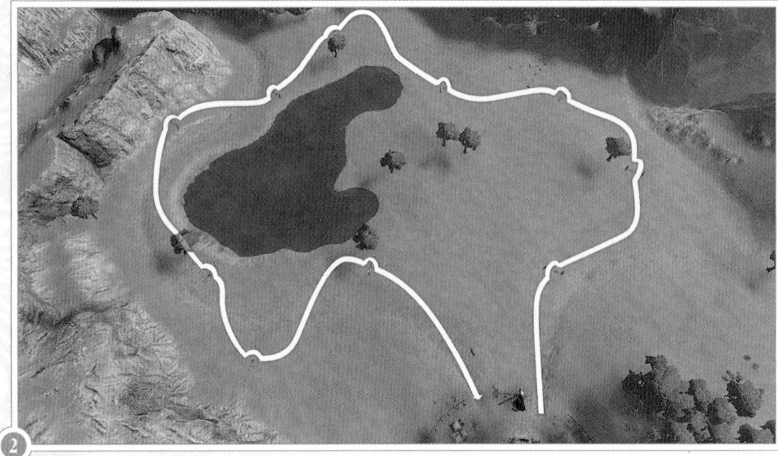

2

Your top priority for this challenge should be to pay special attention to your trajectory at all times. The picture to the left illustrates a perfect run in this obstacle course. It will likely take practice before you beat Blynne's personal record, but this map (and the nearby tips) should help you achieve this much more quickly. You will receive the **extravagant bridle** and **extravagant saddle** by completing the course in under 01:30 and 01:15 respectively.

THE TEST OF WOOD – REVISITED

1

This mini-game becomes available after you have completed the "Test of Wood" shrine quest (see page 198 for details). Speak to Damia again, still at the eastern exit of the Korok Forest. He will challenge you to go through the exact same Test of Wood, but this time within five minutes. If you achieve this, you will receive a **silver rupee** as a reward.

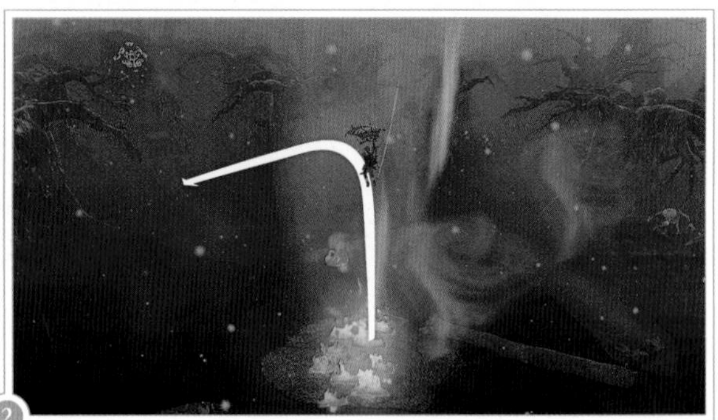

2

There are many ways to shave seconds off your time. The most important one is to use any fire-induced updraft to fly high in the air and bypass entire sections of the trial; the final bog can be skipped fairly consistently thanks to the presence of Fire Chuchus. You should also use powerful arrows to rapidly eliminate any archers or Octoroks that pose a threat to your progress. Bomb arrows can prove especially effective here.

DEER HUNTING

1

Speak to Dantz, the man taking care of his flock on the farm located between Hateno Village and the Tech Lab. He will invite you to take part in a hunting challenge where your objective is to eliminate as many deer as you can within a minute. Each successful kill will increase the total **rupees** he will reward you with. This is not a very lucrative mini-game, though, so you should regard it more as an opportunity for archery training.

2

The following tips will help you to attain high scores:

- Use a bow that is both powerful enough to take deer down with a single shot, and with a high rate of fire. The great eagle bow, the swallow bow, and the falcon bow are all excellent for this challenge.
- Have plenty of arrows in your inventory. If you struggle to aim with precision, consider firing bomb arrows to increase your chances of taking down targets even when your aim is a little off. Combining this approach with bows that fire multiple arrows at once can be a crude, unsportsmanlike, but *entirely effective* technique.
- Consider eating food that boosts your movement speed, which will improve your ability to locate new targets.
- Though this is not easy to engineer, you can consider jumping from a high point on the slope. If you quickly draw your paraglider and aim with your bow, you can briefly enjoy the slow-motion effect, making it easier to align clean shots on multiple targets. As a not inconsiderable fringe benefit, this will also slow the timer to a crawl.

BIRD-MAN RESEARCH STUDY

1

PREPARATIONS: Speak to Branli at the top of the Ridgeland Tower, and he will invite you to take part in a contest. Your objective is to glide as far as you can from the top of the tower. To maximize your potential range, you should ideally leave this mini-game until you have a mostly complete stamina wheel – two-and-a-half circles at very least. Consuming food or elixirs that restore depleted stamina or provide yellow temporary stamina bonuses can also work. Last, but not least, one special power can make a very significant difference here: Revali's Gale, which you obtain by completing the Rito quest line (see page 85). By activating this power (hold Ⓧ, then release), you will gain a substantial altitude boost at your starting point, increasing your potential range.

2

EXECUTION: Your priority in this mini-game is to land as far as you can from the tower. How much time you spend in the air is irrelevant; detours are to be avoided wherever possible, as your direct-line distance from the start point is all that matters. As long as your stamina wheel is sufficiently developed and you have Revali's Gale at hand, there are only three complications to take into account:

- Wind direction: adverse winds will slow you down, but a favorable prevailing breeze will be a boon.
- Your choice of landing site: the lowest possible altitude is water, so you should aim to land in a lake or river.
- Trajectory: your course should be as straight as possible.

Based on the above criteria, the most manageable destination is the Hyrule Castle Moat. Use Revali's Gale to fly high from your starting point next to Branli, then glide in a straight line towards Hyrule Castle. If the wind is not blowing against you, you can glide a few feet above the lowest point on the cliff, and therefore end up above the moat. With this method, you can easily pass the 800-meter milestone to earn a **silver rupee**.

RESTORING THE BLUE FLAME

This mini-game will become available once you have completed the "Robbie's Research" side quest (see page 229 for details). Speak to Aya at the East Akkala Stable and she will ask you to light the lantern next to her with the blue flame in less than three minutes. To complete this quest easily, take the time to prepare in advance. Make sure you have a torch in your inventory; if not, get the one inside the nearby Akkala Ancient Tech Lab. Light the lantern immediately to the north of the stable. Finally, summon your fastest horse from the stable. Optimally, this will be the white horse obtained from a side quest ("The Royal White Stallion" – see page 269).

When you're ready, climb on your horse and speak to Aya. As soon as the challenge begins, gallop to the blue flame opposite the stable, light your torch, then jog back to the lantern next to Aya. The first challenge of under three minutes is very easy. Blow out the lantern (for example, by dropping neutral Chuchu jelly next to it and shooting it with an arrow), then speak to Aya again to trigger the next difficulty level. When you reach the ultimate challenge, you must take an additional step: eat food that will give you a Level 3 movement speed bonus. This can be induced by cooking four fleet-lotus seeds together. With the effect active, you can gallop to the lantern to the north and then return to the lantern next to Aya *just* in time.

BLUE FLAME REWARDS

TIME	REWARD
Under 00:20	Gold Rupee
Under 01:00	Silver Rupee
Under 03:00	Purple Rupee

PARAGLIDER COURSE

This mini-game will become available once you have completed the Korgu Chideh Shrine (see page 143), which is found on Eventide Island in the southeast corner of the world map. Speak to Mimo outside the shrine's entrance to begin.

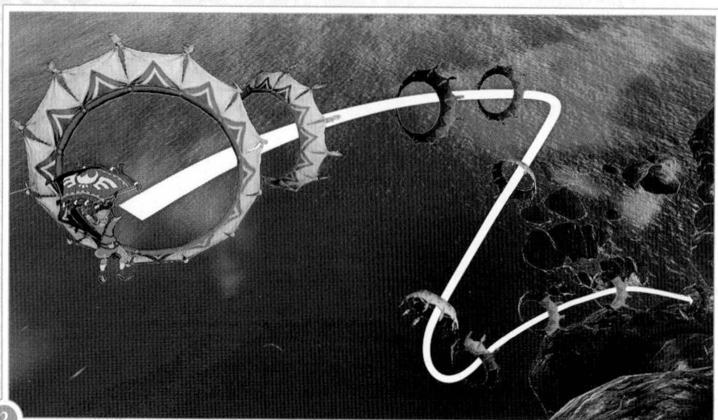

This mini-game challenges you to pass through courses of rings while gliding. The rings are displayed in lines that make the path to follow very clear, with occasional updrafts that will propel you high in the air. However, the game will end should you touch the ground. The most important requirement for attaining high scores is to have a fully maxed-out stamina wheel. Three circles will enable you to last long enough to beat even the Rito at their own game. For optimal results, plan your trajectory in advance to take smooth turns, and briefly put away the paraglider when you need to drop to pass through a ring beneath, or to quickly reach the lower reaches of an updraft.

Once you feel comfortable with the controls and layout of this mini-game, we suggest that you start each run by tackling the course on your right: this will take you very high in the air, enabling you to easily transfer to the second course when you reach the end of the first. You can clear over 40 rings with this strategy and obtain a **silver rupee** as a reward.

1

Speak to Modar at the south end of Tanagar Canyon to the southeast of the Tabantha Tower. He will offer you the opportunity to play a game of golf, where you use Stasis to propel the ball. As with the real-life sport, the objective is to reach the hole with as few strikes as possible (for the avoidance of all doubt, this refers to instances where the ball moves, not individual blows made to confer momentum). There are two iron sledgehammers next to Modar. Be sure to collect them, as they are the best tools to get the ball moving without inflicting needless wear-and-tear on your more valuable personal equipment.

2

One important point to note is that the ball doesn't roll much – it stops very quickly after hitting the ground, even when propelled at full speed. This means that you should imbue it with maximum momentum (represented by a red vector arrow) until you are close to the hole. Naturally, it's important to align Link so that the ball will travel directly towards the hole. One very effective approach is to hit the ball seven times with a sledgehammer from the tee shot. Repeat this power a second time to move the ball within reach of the hole. Finally, hit the ball four times to putt it. This "7-hit + 7-hit + 4-hit" strategy works consistently as long as your aim is true. With a little practice, scoring with three strokes becomes relatively easy, leading to a **silver rupee** reward.

HORSEBACK ARCHERY

1

Head to the Mounted Archery Camp while riding a horse, a short distance to the northwest of the mouth of the Menoat River in the Lake Tower region. Speak to Jini from the saddle: he will ask you if you want to take part in a drill. To do so, you will need at least one bow and dozens of arrows (which you can conveniently buy from this location). Your goal is to ride your horse while simultaneously shooting arrows to pop the balloons. Each drill will cost you 20 rupees.

2

The drill course in itself poses no problem whatsoever. The difficulty arises from the coordination required to both steer your horse and aim at the targets. If you succeed, you will receive the **knight's bridle** and **knight's saddle**.

HORSEBACK ARCHERY TIPS

Hitting 20 balloons in under one minute is a very demanding feat, but there are various tips that you can employ to increase your odds of success:

- Try to ride in a very steady fashion. Abrupt changes of direction will make it more difficult to aim.
- As a general rule, try to stay on the main path: it is much easier to rotate the camera than it is to steer the horse in the corresponding directions. Try to ride in straight lines, shooting during these sections, then concentrate on turning when required.
- Motion controls can be employed to make minor aiming adjustments.
- Try to equip a bow with the quick shot perk to increase your fire rate. The falcon bow and great eagle bow are great choices here, combining this useful enhancement with remarkably long range.
- You can slow down to a trot when you have multiple balloons in close proximity, but you really must spend most of the minute at a canter in order to make it to the end of the course, where multiple targets await.

KILTON

AVAILABILITY

Kilton can be met for the first time on the small island corresponding to the left eye of Skull Lake, in the north of the Akkala region. He is only present at night.

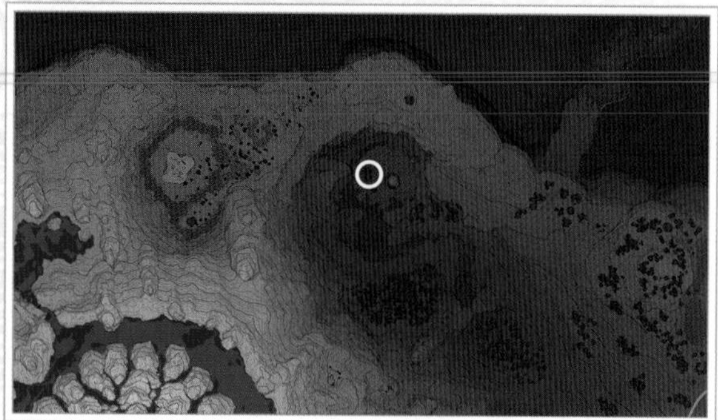

KILTON'S MONSTER SHOP

After you have spoken to him once at Skull Lake, this unusual wandering merchant will begin to tour the entire land. His shop can be found on the outskirts of all main villages and towns from 08:00PM to 04:00AM. It looks a little like a colorful hot-air balloon from a distance, which makes it relatively easy to identify.

Kilton specializes in monster parts. He will buy any such item that you are willing to part with, and will give you "mon" (💀) in exchange – a special currency that you use to purchase items from him.

KILTON'S MEDALS OF HONOR

If you speak to Kilton after completing the main storyline, he will be happy to talk about monsters with you. The three dialogue options available lead to conversations about specific sub-bosses.

In essence, Kilton will ask you to defeat every single specimen of three of the four sub-boss types that are found in Hyrule. Each time you achieve this for a particular species, he will reward you with a key item called a a Medal of Honor. You can track your current progress by talking to Kilton at any time. In addition, defeated specimens are marked with a star icon next to their health bar on subsequent encounters.

You can find a map showing the positions of all sub-bosses in a dedicated section of this chapter (see page 328), and advice on how to defeat them in our Bestiary (see page 314).

OVERVIEW

SUB-BOSS TYPE	SPECIMENS TO DEFEAT	REWARD
Talus	x40	Medal of Honor: Talus
Hinox	x40	Medal of Honor: Hinox
Molduga	x4	Medal of Honor: Molduga

KILTON'S SHOP LIST

IMAGE	ITEM	PRICE (💀)	NOTES
	Monster Extract	9	An ingredient for various recipes.
	Wooden Mop	19	A low-level spear weapon.
	Spring-Loaded Hammer	199	A weak weapon, but a novel one: the fourth swing in a combo will send the victim flying.
	Bokoblin Mask	99	Equip it to blend in with Bokoblins.
	Moblin Mask	199	Equip it to blend in with Moblins.
	Lizalfos Mask	299	Equip it to blend in with Lizalfos.
	Lynel Mask	999	Equip it to blend in temporarily with Lynels.
	Monster Bridle	399	A cosmetic accessory for your horse.
	Monster Saddle	299	A cosmetic accessory for your horse.
	Dark Hood	1,999	If you upgrade all three of these armor pieces to at least Level 2, wearing the full set will grant the Night Speed Up bonus, increasing your movement speed until dawn.
	Dark Tunic	999	
	Dark Trousers	999	

Dragons

Dragons are ancient spirits that you will encounter during your travels. Interacting with them is required to complete specific shrine quests. Note that they tend to appear more frequently during the day, particularly at sunrise.

AVAILABILITY

DINRAAL

- **Shrine Quest:** The Spring of Power (see page 211)
- **Habitat:** Appears in the northernmost section of the world map, to the north of Eldin Mountains, then travels through Tanagar Canyon.

NAYDRA

- **Shrine Quest:** The Spring of Wisdom (see page 127)
- **Habitat:** Lanayru region; easy to hit while on the Lanayru Promenade, but can also appear at the top of Mount Lanayru and in Lanayru Bay.

FAROSH

- **Shrine Quest:** The Serpent's Jaws (see page 145)
- **Habitat:** In the region with many waterfalls to the east of the Faron Tower; above Lake Hylia (where she dives in and out of the water before crossing over the Bridge of Hylia); above the Gerudo Highlands.

ITEM DROPS

Once you have completed the relevant shrine quest, head to the corresponding dragon's habitat, preferably around sunrise – and wait. When a dragon spawns, you will see her fly very high in the air first, before moving closer to the ground: this is your cue to move. Your goal is to hit the dragon with any type of arrow, making the most of the updrafts caused by the divinity to get within firing range. The body part you hit will determine the item the dragon will drop. The object in question glows during its fall and maintains its aura even while on the ground, but it's easy to lose track of it when the dragon emits elemental projectiles to deter you. Note that you can only obtain one item at a time: to acquire additional drops, you must tackle the divinity at a later date.

Dragon drops can be sold to merchants or to Kilton. Despite the relatively high prices they fetch, they have a secret and more valuable application: they can be used as powerful cooking ingredients to dramatically extend the duration of special effects, such as increased movement speed or enhanced defense. Consuming elixirs with such long-lasting properties can prove extremely helpful when you need to raid a dangerous area or confront extremely strong opponents (such as a Silver Lynel).

DRAGON PARTS

ITEM	BODY PART HIT	EFFECT DURATION BONUS
Horn Shard	Horn/crest	Max
Fang Shard	Fang/mouth	High
Claw	Leg/claw	Medium
Scale	Rest of the body	Low

DRAGON HABITATS

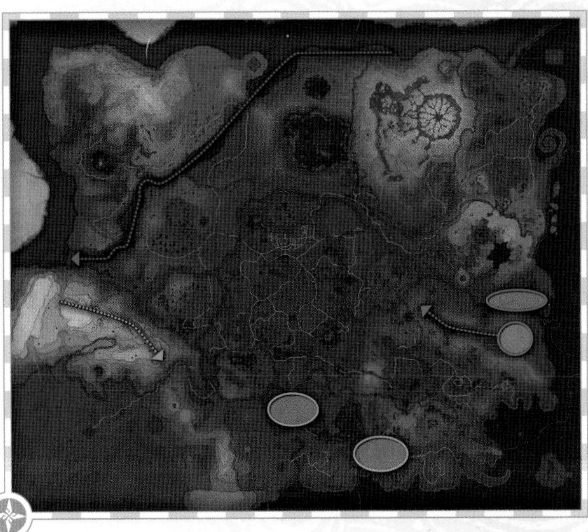

■ Dinraal ■ Naydra ■ Farosh

HYRULE COMPENDIUM

When you receive the camera rune during your visit to the Hateno Ancient Tech Lab, the Hyrule compendium is unlocked with it. Access this by displaying your map, then press R or ZR twice.

The compendium is a collection of 394* entries that you need to fill by taking pictures of the corresponding targets: animals, enemies, plants, and so forth. Every time you run into an item or creature that you have yet to encounter, make it a habit to photograph it immediately. Objects that you have not added to your compendium will appear in orange characters when you look at them through the camera: therefore, if you see a name in orange, take a picture and save it. You can later open the compendium to find a dedicated sheet offering details on the object in question. Note that you can buy missing pictures from Symin in Hateno Ancient Tech Lab. Once the compendium has been completely filled, speak to Symin to receive your reward: the Classified Envelope.

COMPENDIUM: CREATURES

#	NAME	NOTES
001	**Horse**	Near stables
002	**Giant Horse**	Side Quest: Hunt for the Giant Horse
003	**White Horse**	Side Quest: The Royal White Stallion
004	**Lord of the Mountain**	Satori Mountain
005	**Stalhorse**	Side Quest: Stalhorse: Pictured!
006	**Donkey**	In various stables and villages
007	**Sand Seal**	Gerudo Desert
008	**Patricia**	During the Approach to Divine Beast Vah Naboris
009	**Bushy-Tailed Squirrel**	Central Hyrule, Ridgeland
010	**Woodland Boar**	In many forests
011	**Red-Tusked Boar**	In many forests in the Akkala region
012	**Mountain Goat**	Ridgeland, Great Hyrule Forest
013	**White Goat**	West Necluda, Eldin Canyon
014	**Mountain Buck**	Hyrule Field, Lanayru Great Spring
015	**Mountain Doe**	Hyrule Field, Lanayru Great Spring
016	**Water Buffalo**	Lanayru Wetlands, Akkala Highlands
017	**Hateno Cow**	Hateno Village
018	**Highland Sheep**	East Necluda, Akkala Highlands
019	**Grassland Fox**	Hyrule Field, Lanayru Great Spring
020	**Snowcoat Fox**	Hebra Mountains, Tabantha Frontier
021	**Maraudo Wolf**	Tabantha Frontier, Great Hyrule Forest
022	**Wasteland Coyote**	Gerudo Desert, Gerudo Highlands
023	**Cold-Footed Wolf**	Hebra Mountains, Gerudo Highlands
024	**Tabantha Moose**	Hebra Mountains, Gerudo Highlands
025	**Great-Horned Rhinoceros**	Hebra Mountains, Gerudo Highlands
026	**Honeyvore Bear**	Tabantha Frontier, Akkala Highlands
027	**Grizzlemaw Bear**	Hebra Mountains, Gerudo Highlands
028	**Hylian Retriever**	Hebra Mountains, Akkala Highlands
029	**Blupee**	Satori Mountain
030	**Common Sparrow**	Hyrule Field, Hyrule Ridge
031	**Red Sparrow**	Hebra Mountains, Tabantha Frontier
032	**Blue Sparrow**	Great Hyrule Forest, Lanayru Great Spring
033	**Rainbow Sparrow**	Faron Grasslands, West Necluda
034	**Sand Sparrow**	Gerudo Desert
035	**Golden Sparrow**	Great Hyrule Forest, Eldin Canyon
036	**Wood Pigeon**	Great Hyrule Forest, Hyrule Ridge
037	**Rainbow Pigeon**	Great Hyrule Forest, Hyrule Ridge
038	**Hotfeather Pigeon**	Eldin Canyon, Eldin Mountains
039	**White Pigeon**	Hebra Mountains, Gerudo Highlands
040	**Mountain Crow**	Great Hyrule Forest, Hyrule Ridge
041	**Bright-Chested Duck**	Hyrule Field, Hyrule Ridge
042	**Blue-Winged Heron**	Hyrule Ridge, Faron Grasslands
043	**Pink Heron**	Hyrule Field, Hyrule Ridge
044	**Islander Hawk**	Hyrule Field, Hyrule Ridge
045	**Seagull**	Necluda Sea, Akkala Sea
046	**Eldin Ostrich**	Eldin Canyon, Eldin Mountains
047	**Cucco**	Kakariko Village
048	**Hyrule Bass**	Hyrule Field, West Necluda
049	**Hearty Bass**	West Necluda, Akkala Highlands
050	**Staminoka Bass**	Hyrule Field, West Necluda

COMPENDIUM: CREATURES (CONTINUED)

#	NAME	NOTES
051	**Hearty Salmon**	Hebra Mountains, Tabantha Frontier
052	**Chillfin Trout**	Hebra Mountains, Tabantha Frontier
053	**Sizzlefin Trout**	Eldin Canyon, Eldin Mountains
054	**Voltfin Trout**	Tabantha Frontier, Hyrule Ridge
055	**Stealthfin Trout**	Great Hyrule Forest, Eldin Mountains
056	**Mighty Carp**	Akkala Highlands, Lanayru Great Spring
057	**Armored Carp**	Lanayru Great Spring, East Necluda
058	**Sanke Carp**	West Necluda
059	**Mighty Porgy**	Necluda Sea, Lanayru Sea
060	**Armored Porgy**	Necluda Sea, Lanayru Sea
061	**Sneaky River Snail**	West Necluda, Lanayru Great Spring
062	**Hearty Blueshell Snail**	Necluda Sea, Lanayru Sea
063	**Razorclaw Crab**	Necluda Sea, East Necluda
064	**Ironshell Crab**	Necluda Sea, East Necluda
065	**Bright-Eyed Crab**	Lanayru Great Spring, Eldin Canyon
066	**Fairy**	Around Great Fairy Fountains
067	**Winterwing Butterfly**	Hyrule Field, Tabantha Frontier
068	**Summerwing Butterfly**	Great Hyrule Forest, Eldin Mountains
069	**Thunderwing Butterfly**	Hyrule Ridge, Gerudo Highlands
070	**Smotherwing Butterfly**	Eldin Canyon, Death Mountain
071	**Cold Darner**	Tabantha Frontier, Hyrule Ridge
072	**Warm Darner**	Akkala Highlands, Hyrule Field
073	**Electric Darner**	Hyrule Ridge, Gerudo Desert
074	**Restless Cricket**	Hyrule Field, East Necluda
075	**Bladed Rhino Beetle**	West Necluda, East Necluda
076	**Rugged Rhino Beetle**	Hyrule Field, Faron Grasslands
077	**Energetic Rhino Beetle**	Akkala Highlands, West Necluda
078	**Sunset Firefly**	Kakariko Village, Korok Forest
079	**Hot-Footed Frog**	Lanayru Great Spring, Hyrule Ridge
080	**Tireless Frog**	Lanayru Great Spring, Hyrule Ridge
081	**Hightail Lizard**	West Necluda, East Necluda
082	**Hearty Lizard**	Gerudo Desert, Necluda Sea
083	**Fireproof Lizard**	Eldin Canyon, Death Mountain

COMPENDIUM: MONSTERS

#	NAME	NOTES
084	**Chuchu**	Hyrule Field, West Necluda
085	**Fire Chuchu**	Eldin Canyon, Eldin Mountains
086	**Ice Chuchu**	Hebra Mountains, Gerudo Highlands
087	**Electric Chuchu**	Gerudo Highlands, East Necluda
088	**Keese**	Hyrule Field, East Necluda
089	**Fire Keese**	Eldin Canyon, Eldin Mountains
090	**Ice Keese**	Hebra Mountains, Gerudo Highlands
091	**Electric Keese**	Lanayru Great Spring, East Necluda
092	**Water Octorok**	West Necluda, Hyrule Field
093	**Forest Octorok**	Hyrule Ridge, Deep Akkala
094	**Rock Octorok**	Eldin Canyon, Gerudo Highlands
095	**Snow Octorok**	Gerudo Highlands, Tabantha Frontier
096	**Treasure Octorok**	Gerudo Highlands, Gerudo Desert

* By default, the total number of entries in the compendium is 385. If you purchase *Breath of the Wild*'s expansion pass, you can unlock an additional nine: four in The Champions' Ballad, and five exclusive to Master Mode. The tables on these pages feature the full 394 entries. Depending on the configuration of your playthrough, your version of the compendium might differ slightly in terms of entry order and numbering.

COMPENDIUM: MONSTERS (CONTINUED)

#	NAME	NOTES
097	**Sky Octorok**	The Master Trials DLC: Master Mode
098	**Fire Wizzrobe**	Hyrule Field, Great Hyrule Forest
099	**Ice Wizzrobe**	Gerudo Highlands, Hyrule Field
100	**Electric Wizzrobe**	Hyrule Ridge, West Necluda
101	**Meteo Wizzrobe**	Hyrule Field, Eldin Canyon
102	**Blizzrobe**	Hyrule Field, Hebra Mountains
103	**Thunder Wizzrobe**	Hyrule Field, Tabantha Frontier
104	**Bokoblin**	Great Plateau, Hyrule Field
105	**Blue Bokoblin**	Gerudo Highlands, Gerudo Desert
106	**Black Bokoblin**	Hyrule Field, Gerudo Highlands
107	**Stalkoblin**	Hyrule Field, Great Hyrule Forest
108	**Silver Bokoblin**	Greater Hyrule
109	**Golden Bokoblin**	The Master Trials DLC: Master Mode
110	**Moblin**	Hyrule Field, East Necluda
111	**Blue Moblin**	Hyrule Field, Deep Akkala
112	**Black Moblin**	Hyrule Field, Eldin Canyon
113	**Stalmoblin**	Great Hyrule Forest, Gerudo Highlands
114	**Silver Moblin**	Greater Hyrule
115	**Golden Moblin**	The Master Trials DLC: Master Mode
116	**Lizalfos**	Lanayru Great Spring, Gerudo Desert
117	**Blue Lizalfos**	Tabantha Frontier, Gerudo Desert
118	**Black Lizalfos**	Hyrule Field, Hebra Mountains
119	**Stalizalfos**	Gerudo Desert, Hyrule Ridge
120	**Fire-Breath Lizalfos**	Eldin Canyon, Gerudo Desert
121	**Ice-Breath Lizalfos**	Gerudo Highlands, Hebra Mountains
122	**Electric Lizalfos**	Gerudo Desert, Hyrule Ridge
123	**Silver Lizalfos**	Greater Hyrule
124	**Golden Lizalfos**	The Master Trials DLC: Master Mode
125	**Lynel**	See map on page 328
126	**Blue-Maned Lynel**	
127	**White-Maned Lynel**	
128	**Silver Lynel**	
129	**Golden Lynel**	The Master Trials DLC: Master Mode
130	**Guardian Stalker**	Hyrule Field
131	**Guardian Skywatcher**	Hyrule Field, Akkala Highlands
132	**Guardian Turret**	Hyrule Castle
133	**Decayed Guardian**	Great Plateau, Death Mountain
134	**Sentry**	Hyrule Field, Hyrule Castle
135	**Guardian Scout I**	Various shrines
136	**Guardian Scout II**	Various shrines
137	**Guardian Scout III**	Various shrines
138	**Guardian Scout IV**	Various shrines
139	**Yiga Footsoldier**	Karusa Valley, surprise attacks in various locations
140	**Yiga Blademaster**	Surprise attacks in various locations
141	**Master Kohga**	Yiga Clan Hideout
142	**Monk Maz Koshia**	The Champions' Ballad DLC: Main Quest
143	**Stone Talus**	See map on page 328
144	**Stone Talus (Luminous)**	
145	**Stone Talus (Rare)**	
146	**Igneo Talus**	
147	**Frost Talus**	
148	**Stone Pebblit**	Greater Hyrule
149	**Igneo Pebblit**	Eldin Canyon, Eldin Mountains
150	**Frost Pebblit**	Hebra Mountains, Gerudo Highlands
151	**Igneo Talus Titan**	The Champions' Ballad DLC: Lake Darman (Eldin)
152	**Hinox**	See map on page 328
153	**Blue Hinox**	
154	**Black Hinox**	

COMPENDIUM: MONSTERS (CONTINUED)

#	NAME	NOTES
155	**Stalnox**	See map on page 328
156	**Molduga**	
157	**Molduking**	The Champions' Ballad DLC: East Barrens (Gerudo Desert)
158	**Dinraal**	North of Eldin Mountains
159	**Naydra**	Lanayru Promenade
160	**Farosh**	East of the Faron Tower; above Lake Hylia; or above the Gerudo Highlands
161	**Cursed Bokoblin**	Dungeons, Hyrule Castle
162	**Cursed Moblin**	Dungeons, Hyrule Castle
163	**Cursed Lizalfos**	Dungeons, Hyrule Castle
164	**Thunderblight Ganon**	Divine Beast Vah Naboris
165	**Fireblight Ganon**	Divine Beast Vah Rudania
166	**Waterblight Ganon**	Divine Beast Vah Ruta
167	**Windblight Ganon**	Divine Beast Vah Medoh
168	**Calamity Ganon**	Hyrule Castle
169	**Dark Beast Ganon**	Hyrule Castle

COMPENDIUM: MATERIALS

#	NAME	NOTES
170	**Apple**	Great Plateau, Hyrule Field, East Necluda
171	**Palm Fruit**	East Necluda, Gerudo Desert
172	**Wildberry**	Hebra Mountains, Gerudo Highlands
173	**Hearty Durian**	West Necluda, Faron Grasslands
174	**Hydromelon**	Gerudo Desert, Faron Grasslands
175	**Spicy Pepper**	Gerudo Desert, Tabantha Frontier
176	**Voltfruit**	Gerudo Desert, Gerudo Highlands
177	**Fleet-Lotus Seeds**	Lanayru Wetlands, Lanayru Great Spring
178	**Mighty Bananas**	Faron
179	**Hylian Shroom**	Hyrule Field, West Necluda
180	**Endura Shroom**	Hyrule Ridge, Hyrule Field
181	**Stamella Shroom**	Hyrule Ridge, Hyrule Field
182	**Hearty Truffle**	Great Hyrule Forest, Hyrule Field
183	**Big Hearty Truffle**	Hebra Mountains, Great Hyrule Forest
184	**Chillshroom**	Hebra Mountains, Mount Lanayru
185	**Sunshroom**	Eldin Canyon, Gerudo Highlands
186	**Zapshroom**	Deep Akkala, Gerudo Highlands
187	**Rushroom**	Gerudo Highlands, Hyrule Ridge
188	**Razorshroom**	Great Hyrule Forest, Tabantha Frontier
189	**Ironshroom**	West Necluda, East Necluda
190	**Silent Shroom**	Lanayru Great Spring, West Necluda
191	**Hyrule Herb**	Hyrule Field, Akkala Highlands
192	**Hearty Radish**	Hyrule Ridge, East Necluda
193	**Big Hearty Radish**	Akkala Highlands, Lanayru Great Spring
194	**Cool Safflina**	Hebra Mountains, Gerudo Highlands
195	**Warm Safflina**	Gerudo Desert, Hyrule Ridge
196	**Electric Safflina**	Gerudo Desert, Hyrule Ridge
197	**Swift Carrot**	Kakariko Village
198	**Endura Carrot**	Hyrule Ridge, Faron Grasslands
199	**Fortified Pumpkin**	Kakariko Village
200	**Swift Violet**	Hebra Mountains, Gerudo Highlands
201	**Mighty Thistle**	West Necluda, Faron Grasslands
202	**Armoranth**	Akkala Highlands, Hyrule Ridge
203	**Blue Nightshade**	West Necluda, Lanayru Great Spring
204	**Silent Princess**	Hyrule Ridge, West Necluda,
205	**Courser Bee Honey**	Hyrule Field, Tabantha Frontier

HYRULE COMPENDIUM
(CONTINUED)

COMPENDIUM: WEAPONS

#	NAME	NOTES
206	**Master Sword**	Korok Forest
207	**Tree Branch**	Hyrule Field, West Necluda
208	**Torch**	Great Hyrule Forest, Hyrule Field
209	**Soup Ladle**	Hyrule Field, Tabantha Frontier
210	**Boomerang**	West Necluda, Faron Grasslands
211	**Spring-Loaded Hammer**	Kilton's shop
212	**Traveler's Sword**	Hyrule Field, West Necluda
213	**Soldier's Broadsword**	Hyrule Field, Faron Grasslands
214	**Knight's Broadsword**	Gerudo Desert, Tabantha Frontier
215	**Royal Broadsword**	Tabantha Frontier, Akkala Highlands
216	**Forest Dweller's Sword**	Great Hyrule Forest, Hyrule Field
217	**Zora Sword**	Lanayru Great Spring, East Necluda
218	**Feathered Edge**	Tabantha Frontier, Hyrule Field
219	**Gerudo Scimitar**	Gerudo Highlands, Gerudo Desert
220	**Moonlight Scimitar**	Gerudo Highlands, Gerudo Desert
221	**Scimitar of the Seven**	Reward for clearing Divine Beast Vah Naboris dungeon
222	**Eightfold Blade**	West Necluda, Lake Hylia
223	**Ancient Short Sword**	Akkala Ancient Tech Lab
224	**Rusty Broadsword**	Hyrule Field, Eldin Canyon, Hyrule Castle
225	**Royal Guard's Sword**	Hyrule Castle
226	**Flameblade**	Coliseum Ruins, East Necluda
227	**Frostblade**	Gerudo Highlands, Coliseum Ruins
228	**Thunderblade**	Coliseum Ruins, West Necluda
229	**Boko Club**	Hyrule Field, West Necluda
230	**Spiked Boko Club**	Faron Grasslands, East Necluda
231	**Dragonbone Boko Club**	Hyrule Ridge, Necluda Sea
232	**Lizal Boomerang**	Lake Hylia, Lanayru Wetlands
233	**Lizal Forked Boomerang**	Gerudo Desert, Tabantha Frontier
234	**Lizal Tri-Boomerang**	Hebra Mountains, Akkala Highlands
235	**Guardian Sword**	Dropped by Guardian Scouts II
236	**Guardian Sword+**	Dropped by Guardian Scouts III
237	**Guardian Sword++**	Dropped by Guardian Scouts IV
238	**Lynel Sword**	Dropped by Lynels
239	**Mighty Lynel Sword**	Dropped by Blue-Maned Lynels
240	**Savage Lynel Sword**	Dropped by White-Maned Lynels, Silver Lynels
241	**Fire Rod**	Gerudo Highlands, Great Hyrule Forest
242	**Meteor Rod**	Crenel Hills, Hebra Mountains
243	**Ice Rod**	Gerudo Highlands, Eldin Canyon
244	**Blizzard Rod**	Crenel Hills, Gerudo Highlands, Hebra Mountains
245	**Lightning Rod**	West Necluda, Hyrule Ridge
246	**Thunderstorm Rod**	Crenel Hills, Hyrule Ridge
247	**Vicious Sickle**	Dropped by Yiga Footsoldiers
248	**Demon Carver**	Dropped by Yiga Footsoldiers
249	**One-Hit Obliterator**	The Champions' Ballad DLC: Main Quest
250	**Bokoblin Arm**	Dropped by Stalkoblins
251	**Lizalfos Arm**	Dropped by Stalizalfos
252	**Korok Leaf**	Hyrule Field, West Necluda
253	**Farming Hoe**	Hyrule Field, West Necluda
254	**Boat Oar**	East Necluda, Necluda Sea

COMPENDIUM: WEAPONS (CONTINUED)

#	NAME	NOTES
255	**Woodcutter's Axe**	At various stables
256	**Double Axe**	At various stables
257	**Iron Sledgehammer**	Eldin Canyon, Akkala Highlands
258	**Giant Boomerang**	West Necluda, Hebra Mountains
259	**Traveler's Claymore**	Hyrule Field, West Necluda
260	**Soldier's Claymore**	Hyrule Field, Faron Grasslands
261	**Knight's Claymore**	Gerudo Desert, Tabantha Frontier
262	**Royal Claymore**	Gerudo Desert, Tabantha Frontier, Hyrule Castle
263	**Silver Longsword**	Lanayru Great Spring, Lanayru Wetlands
264	**Cobble Crusher**	Eldin Canyon, Eldin Mountains
265	**Stone Smasher**	Eldin Canyon, Hyrule Field
266	**Boulder Breaker**	Eldin Canyon; Divine Beast Vah Rudania dungeon reward
267	**Golden Claymore**	Gerudo Highlands, Hyrule Ridge
268	**Eightfold Longblade**	West Necluda, Lanayru Great Spring
269	**Edge of Duality**	Hyrule Field, West Necluda
270	**Ancient Bladesaw**	Akkala Ancient Tech Lab
271	**Rusty Claymore**	Hyrule Field, Eldin Canyon, Hyrule Castle
272	**Royal Guard's Claymore**	Hyrule Castle
273	**Great Flameblade**	Coliseum Ruins, Eldin Canyon
274	**Great Frostblade**	Coliseum Ruins, Hebra Mountains
275	**Great Thunderblade**	Coliseum Ruins, Tabantha Frontier
276	**Boko Bat**	Hyrule Field, West Necluda
277	**Spiked Boko Bat**	Faron Grasslands, East Necluda
278	**Dragonbone Boko Bat**	Hyrule Ridge, Necluda Sea
279	**Moblin Club**	Gerudo Highlands, Faron Grasslands
280	**Spiked Moblin Club**	Hyrule Field, Akkala Highlands
281	**Dragonbone Moblin Club**	Hebra Mountains, Eldin Mountains
282	**Ancient Battle Axe**	Dropped by Guardian Scout II
283	**Ancient Battle Axe+**	Dropped by Guardian Scout III
284	**Ancient Battle Axe++**	Dropped by Guardian Scout IV
285	**Lynel Crusher**	Dropped by Lynels
286	**Mighty Lynel Crusher**	Dropped by Blue-Maned Lynels
287	**Savage Lynel Crusher**	Dropped by White-Maned Lynels, Silver Lynels
288	**Windcleaver**	Dropped by Yiga Blademasters
289	**Moblin Arm**	Dropped by Stalmoblins
290	**Wooden Mop**	East Necluda, Hyrule Field
291	**Farmer's Pitchfork**	East Necluda, West Necluda
292	**Fishing Harpoon**	East Necluda, Lake Hylia
293	**Throwing Spear**	West Necluda, Hyrule Field
294	**Traveler's Spear**	West Necluda, Hyrule Field
295	**Soldier's Spear**	Hyrule Field, Faron Grasslands
296	**Knight's Halberd**	Tabantha Frontier, Gerudo Desert
297	**Royal Halberd**	Gerudo Highlands, Tabantha Frontier
298	**Forest Dweller's Spear**	Great Hyrule Forest, Hyrule Ridge
299	**Zora Spear**	Lanayru Great Spring, Lake Hylia
300	**Silverscale Spear**	Akkala Highlands, Lanayru Great Spring
301	**Ceremonial Trident**	The Ceremonial Song shrine quest
302	**Lightscale Trident**	Clear the Divine Beast Vah Ruta dungeon
303	**Drillshaft**	Eldin Canyon, Hebra Mountains

COMPENDIUM: WEAPONS (CONTINUED)

#	NAME	NOTES
304	**Feathered Spear**	Tabantha Frontier, Hyrule Field
305	**Gerudo Spear**	Gerudo Highlands, Gerudo Desert
306	**Serpentine Spear**	East Necluda, Hyrule Field
307	**Ancient Spear**	Akkala Ancient Tech Lab
308	**Rusty Halberd**	Hyrule Field, Great Hyrule Forest
309	**Royal Guard's Spear**	Hyrule Castle
310	**Flamespear**	Coliseum Ruins, Hebra Mountains
311	**Frostspear**	Coliseum Ruins, Hebra Mountains
312	**Thunderspear**	Coliseum Ruins, Hyrule Ridge
313	**Boko Spear**	West Necluda, Hyrule Field
314	**Spiked Boko Spear**	Faron Grasslands, East Necluda
315	**Dragonbone Boko Spear**	Necluda Sea, Hyrule Ridge
316	**Moblin Spear**	Faron Grasslands, Gerudo Highlands
317	**Spiked Moblin Spear**	Gerudo Highlands, Akkala Highlands
318	**Dragonbone Moblin Spear**	Hebra Mountains, Eldin Mountains
319	**Lizal Spear**	Lanayru Wetlands, East Necluda
320	**Enhanced Lizal Spear**	Tabantha Frontier, Gerudo Desert
321	**Forked Lizal Spear**	Eldin Canyon, Akkala Highlands
322	**Guardian Spear**	Dropped by Guardian Scouts II
323	**Guardian Spear+**	Dropped by Guardian Scouts III
324	**Guardian Spear++**	Dropped by Guardian Scouts IV
325	**Lynel Spear**	Dropped by Lynels
326	**Mighty Lynel Spear**	Dropped by Blue-Maned Lynels
327	**Savage Lynel Spear**	Dropped by White-Maned Lynels, Silver Lynels
328	**Bow of Light**	Available in a boss battle
329	**Wooden Bow**	Hyrule Field, West Necluda
330	**Traveler's Bow**	Hyrule Field, West Necluda
331	**Soldier's Bow**	Hyrule Field, Faron Grasslands
332	**Knight's Bow**	Gerudo Desert, Tabantha Frontier
333	**Royal Bow**	Tabantha Frontier, Hebra Mountains
334	**Forest Dweller's Bow**	Tabantha Frontier, Hyrule Ridge
335	**Silver Bow**	Lanayru Great Spring, Akkala Highlands
336	**Swallow Bow**	Rito Village, Hebra Mountains
337	**Falcon Bow**	Tabantha Frontier, Hebra Mountains
338	**Great Eagle Bow**	Reward for clearing Divine Beast Vah Medoh dungeon
339	**Golden Bow**	Gerudo Highlands, Gerudo Desert
340	**Phrenic Bow**	West Necluda, East Necluda
341	**Ancient Bow**	Akkala Ancient Tech Lab
342	**Royal Guard's Bow**	Hyrule Castle
343	**Boko Bow**	Hyrule Field, West Necluda
344	**Spiked Boko Bow**	Faron Grasslands, East Necluda
345	**Dragon Bone Boko Bow**	Hyrule Field, Hyrule Ridge
346	**Lizal Bow**	Lanayru Great Spring, Lanayru Wetlands
347	**Strengthened Lizal Bow**	Tabantha Frontier, Gerudo Desert
348	**Steel Lizal Bow**	Hebra Mountains, Akkala Highlands
349	**Lynel Bow**	Dropped by Lynels
350	**Mighty Lynel Bow**	Dropped by Blue-Maned Lynels
351	**Savage Lynel Bow**	Dropped by White-Maned Lynels, Silver Lynels
352	**Duplex Bow**	Gerudo Highlands

COMPENDIUM: WEAPONS (CONTINUED)

#	NAME	NOTES
353	**Arrow**	Dropped by Lizalfos, available in certain shops
354	**Fire Arrow**	Dropped by Lizalfos, available in certain shops
355	**Ice Arrow**	Dropped by Lizalfos, available in certain shops
356	**Shock Arrow**	Dropped by Lizalfos, available in certain shops
357	**Bomb Arrow**	Dropped by Lizalfos, available in certain shops
358	**Ancient Arrow**	Hyrule Castle, Akkala Ancient Tech Lab
359	**Hylian Shield**	Hyrule Castle's Lockup
360	**Pot Lid**	Near cooking pots
361	**Wooden Shield**	Hyrule Field, East Necluda
362	**Emblazoned Shield**	East Necluda, Hebra Mountains
363	**Hunter's Shield**	Hebra Mountains, Lanayru Mountains
364	**Fisherman's Shield**	East Necluda, Hebra Mountains
365	**Traveler's Shield**	Hyrule Field, West Necluda
366	**Soldier's Shield**	Tabantha Frontier, Hyrule Field
367	**Knight's Shield**	Hebra Mountains, Eldin Mountains
368	**Royal Shield**	Hyrule Castle, Hebra Mountains
369	**Forest Dweller's Shield**	Great Hyrule Forest
370	**Silver Shield**	Lanayru Great Spring, Lake Hylia
371	**Kite Shield**	Hebra Mountains, Tabantha Frontier
372	**Gerudo Shield**	Gerudo Highlands, Gerudo Desert
373	**Radiant Shield**	Gerudo Highlands, Gerudo Desert
374	**Daybreaker**	Reward for clearing Divine Beast Vah Naboris dungeon
375	**Shield of the Mind's Eye**	West Necluda, East Necluda
376	**Ancient Shield**	Akkala Ancient Tech Lab
377	**Rusty Shield**	Hyrule Castle
378	**Royal Guard's Shield**	Hyrule Castle
379	**Boko Shield**	Hyrule Field, West Necluda
380	**Spiked Boko Shield**	Faron Grasslands, East Necluda
381	**Dragonbone Boko Shield**	Hyrule Ridge, Necluda Sea
382	**Lizal Shield**	Lake Hylia, East Necluda
383	**Reinforced Lizal Shield**	Tabantha Frontier, Gerudo Desert
384	**Steel Lizal Shield**	Hebra Mountains, Akkala Highlands
385	**Guardian Shield**	Guardian Scout II
386	**Guardian Shield+**	Guardian Scout III
387	**Guardian Shield++**	Guardian Scout IV
388	**Lynel Shield**	Dropped by Lynels
389	**Mighty Lynel Shield**	Dropped by Blue-Maned Lynels
390	**Savage Lynel Shield**	Dropped by White-Maned Lynels, Silver Lynels

COMPENDIUM: TREASURE

#	NAME	NOTES
391	**Treasure Chest**	All over Hyrule
392	**Ore Deposit**	All over Hyrule
393	**Rare Ore Deposit**	All over Hyrule
394	**Luminous Stone Deposit**	All over Hyrule

GRANTÉ: If you have completed the "From the Ground Up" side quest (see page 232), you will find this character in Tarrey Town, on the terrace of the building to your right when you enter the settlement. Granté, who is actually the son of Robbie, sells a select number of high-value articles that you can acquire only once by traditional means. This includes the Hylian shield (from Hyrule Castle's Lockup), and the unique armor pieces that you can retrieve from various shrines. These articles become available in Granté's selection as and when you obtain them in the game. Should you break your Hylian shield or sell certain pieces of armor, this shop enables you to buy them back.

SHOOTING STARS: Whenever you notice a shooting star in the night sky, look where it lands. If you head to that destination, you will find a star fragment – a mysterious stone that is required in certain cooking recipes or to upgrade specific pieces of equipment via great fairies.

CUCCOS: When you hit a cucco with any weapon, it may lay an egg. Cuccos can be found in Kakariko Village, among many other places. Take care not to overdo it, though: if you strike a cucco too many times, you will be attacked by a horde of hens seeking revenge!

RIDING WILD ANIMALS: With stealth bonuses and a very careful approach, it is possible to take deer and bears by surprise and ride them as you would a horse. Wild animals are less compliant and cannot be registered, but this can nonetheless be a fun challenge.

FIRE IMMUNITY: Until you can afford a complete flamebreaker armor set upgraded to Level 2, note that there is a way to make Link temporarily immune to fire: submerge him in water. Once fully soaked, he can stand in flames without harm for a short period of time.

REFRESHING RUSTED WEAPONS: Instead of tossing a bomb at a Rock Octorok while it is inhaling, try throwing a rusty weapon or shield. The creature will return the item to you in brand-new condition!

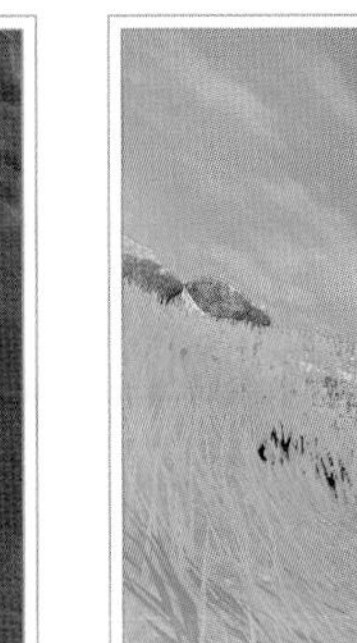

TOSS A BONE: If you throw the arm of a Stalizalfos, it will return to you like a boomerang.

SHIELD-SURFING: Shield-surfing works not only on snow, but also on grassy areas. Avoid rocky terrain at all costs, on the other hand, as this depletes shield durability very quickly. As a rule, only the sturdiest shields will enable you to shield-surf over long distances. Press Ⓨ to perform a 1080 spin while shield-surfing (a possible reference to a classic snowboarding Nintendo game), and simultaneously press Ⓧ and tilt Ⓛ sideways to execute tricks.

SWIMMING FASTER: You can swim faster without armor.

DOG TREASURE: If you offer four pieces of fruit and/or meat to a dog, it may lead you to a treasure chest in the area. The location of the dogs that might do this are listed in the table below.

DOG TREASURE LOCATIONS

LOCATION	TREASURE	LOCATION	TREASURE
Hateno Village	Silver Rupee	**Lurelin Village**	Star Fragment
Tarrey Town*	Bomb Arrow x5	**Highland Stable**	Silver Rupee
East Akkala Stable	Shock Arrow x10	**Lakeside Stable**	Forest Dweller's Spear
South Akkala Stable	Knight's Claymore	**Outskirt Stable**	Silver Rupee
Woodland Stable	Ice Arrow x10	**Gerudo Canyon Stable**	Ice Arrow x10
Snowfield Stable	Star Fragment	**Serenne Stable**	Gold Rupee
	Feathered Spear	**Wetland Stable**	Opal
Kara Kara Bazaar	Knight's Bow	**Dueling Peaks Stable**	Silver Rupee

* Only after Tarrey Town is fully developed by completing the "From the Ground Up" side quest.

BARE FOOT: Try to open a treasure chest while wearing no leg armor. Link will go through a special pain animation.

LAST DITCH EFFORT: When climbing, if you perform a jump while your stamina wheel is in its final red section, you will cover twice the usual distance.

SECRETS AND EASTER EGGS
(CONTINUED)

EVERY LITTLE HELPS: You can retrieve arrows stuck in a wooden shield after defeating the opponent who fired them at you. Similarly, if you dodge arrows from an enemy archer, you can collect them afterwards. You can also retrieve your own arrows when they miss their target.

AERIAL RECOVERY: Whenever you are sent flying, such as when caught in the radius of an explosion, you can draw your paraglider while airborne to cut short the animation sequence.

SELFIES: Link can take selfies with his camera. With the rune activated, press Ⓧ, then take a picture as usual. You can make him adopt one of eight different poses: four with Ⓛ, and another four with ZL + Ⓛ.

LORD OF THE MOUNTAIN: This unique creature can be found at the top of Satori Mountain, to the south of the Ridgeland Tower. Its availability is clearly signposted by the presence of a large blue glow that can be seen from a long distance. When you move within range, cautiously make your final approach from behind the horse, ideally with a maximum stealth bonus and by crouch-walking at all times. When you are only a few steps away, sprint and quickly press Ⓐ to mount the creature, then tap L rapidly to prevent it from dislodging you. If you soothe it efficiently, you should need approximately two full circles of stamina to fully subdue it. The Lord of the Mountain cannot be registered in stables, but it offers fully maxed-out attributes – making it incredibly fast. It's also an entry in your compendium, so be sure to take a picture of it before you let it go.

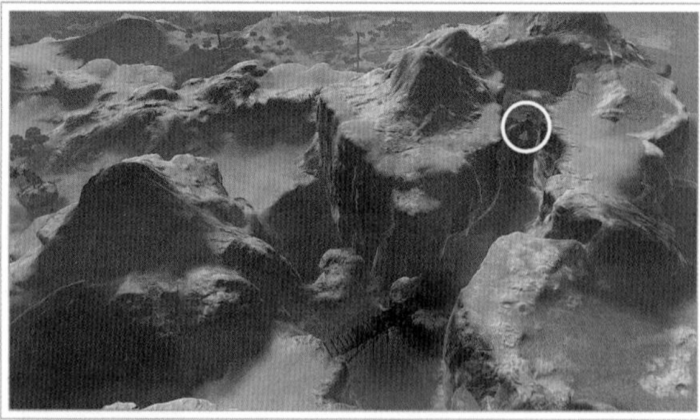

THE HORSE FAIRY: If you head to the Malanya Spring in the Lake Tower region, to the southeast of the Highland Stable, you will come across what looks exactly like a Great Fairy Fountain… but is not. Examine the fountain and pay a flat fee of 1,000 rupees to make Malanya appear. This unsettling character is none other than the horse fairy, and offers the unique service of reviving horses that have perished. This can be a welcome feature if you happen to lose your favorite steed, such as the remarkably fast white horse obtained during the "Royal White Stallion" side quest.

COLISEUM RUINS: The Coliseum is a dangerous landmark teeming with enemies. It is located to the north of the Great Plateau. As you progress in the adventure and cause monsters to rank up (see page 300), the Coliseum will eventually host many high-level opponents. These include a Silver Lynel – potentially the hardest creature to defeat in the game – as well as various foes equipped with elemental weapons. This means that a single successful late-game raid here will enable you to fill your inventory with an arsenal of blades infused with fire, lightning, and ice. You can also find two treasure chests at the very top of the ruins.

EASTER EGGS

The world of *Breath of the Wild* is full of subtle references to previous instalments in the series.

LOCATION	REFERENCE
Arbiter's Grounds	The fourth dungeon in *Twilight Princess*, located in the Gerudo Desert
Bannan Island	An island in the northwest of the World of the Ocean King in *Phantom Hourglass*
Bonooru's Stand, Pierre Plateau	Bonooru and Pierre are scarecrows that Link can play a melody for in *Ocarina of Time* and *Majora's Mask*
Bridge of Hylia	A great bridge that spans Lake Hylia in *Twilight Princess*
Crenel Hills, Crenel Peak	Mount Crenel is a mountainous region in *The Minish Cap*
Death Mountain	A recurring tall mountain in the series, usually home to dangerous monsters and hazards
Eagus Bridge	Eagus is an instructor who runs the Sparring Hall in *Skyward Sword*
Eldin	A divinity that gave its name to a province in both *Twilight Princess* and *Skyward Sword*
Faron Woods	A location that appears in both *Twilight Princess* and *Skyward Sword*
Forest of Time	The region where Link begins his quest in *Oracle of Ages*
Gerudo Desert	A region of Hyrule in *Twilight Princess*
Gleeok Bridge	Gleeok is a recurring dragon-like boss in the series
Goponga Island	Goponga Swamp is a region found in the northwest section of Koholint Island in *Link's Awakening*
Goron City	A town from *Ocarina of Time*
Goron Hot Springs	Locations in *Majora's Mask* and *Twilight Princess* where Link can recover his hearts
Gortram Cliff	Gortram is a Goron who runs a mini-game in *Skyward Sword*
Horon Lagoon	Horon Village is the central town in *Oracle of Seasons*
Horwell Bridge	Horwell is one of the Knight Academy instructors in *Skyward Sword*
Hyrule Castle	A staple of the series: the seat of Hyrule's royal family
Hyrule Field	A large, grassy region at the heart of Hyrule in many instalments in the series
Irch Plain	Irch is the name of a Korok in *The Wind Waker*
Kaepora Pass	Kaepora Gaebora is a recurring character in the series, who offers information and advice to Link
Kakariko Village	A recurring town in the series
Kanalet Ridge	Kanalet Castle is a mini-dungeon in *Link's Awakening*
Lake Hylia	A recurring lake in the series
Lanayru	A divinity and province name appearing in both *Twilight Princess* and *Skyward Sword*
Linebeck Island	Linebeck is the captain of the steamboat that Link uses to travel in *Phantom Hourglass*
Lost Woods	A recurring maze-like forest that must be navigated by following a specific route
Lulu Lake	Lulu is the singer of a popular Zora band in *Majora's Mask*
Mabe Village	A small village on Koholint Island in *Link's Awakening*
Martha's Landing	Martha is a mermaid encountered in *Link's Awakening*
Mercay Island	The island on which Link wakes up early on in the *Phantom Hourglass* adventure
Mido Swamp	Mido is the leader of the Kokiri in *Ocarina of Time*
Mikau Lake	Mikau is the guitarist of a popular Zora band in *Majora's Mask*
Molida Island	A fishing island in *Phantom Hourglass*
Mount Daphnes	Daphnes Nohansen Hyrule is an ancient king of Hyrule in *The Wind Waker*
Mount Floria, Lake Floria, Floria River	Floria Waterfall and Lake Floria are locations from *Twilight Princess* and *Skyward Sword*
Mount Gustaf	Gustaf was an ancient king of Hyrule in *The Minish Cap*
Mount Nabooru	Nabooru is the second-in-command of the Gerudo in *Ocarina of Time*
Nabi Lake	Nabi is the Japanese spelling of Navi, the fairy who accompanies Link during his adventure in *Ocarina of Time*
Oren Bridge	Oren is the queen of the Zora in *A Link Between Worlds*
Owlan Bridge	Owlan is one of the Knight Academy instructors in *Skyward Sword*
Piper Ridge	Piper is a resident of Skyloft in *Skyward Sword*
Ralis Pond	Ralis is the prince of the Zora in *Twilight Princess*
Rauru Settlement Ruins, Rauru Hillside	Rauru is a recurring figure in the series – an ancient Hylian and the Sage of Light in *Ocarina of Time*, memorialized in one of the stained glass windows in Hyrule Castle's basement in *The Wind Waker*
Romani Plains	Romani is the younger of two sisters who take care of Romani Ranch in *Majora's Mask*
Seres Scablands	Seres is the caretaker of the Sanctuary in *A Link Between Worlds*
Spectacle Rock	A recurring rock formation in the series
Spring of Power/Courage/Wisdom	Power, Courage, and Wisdom are the names of the three triangular pieces that form the Triforce
Stinger Cliffs	Stingers are manta-ray-like creatures in *Ocarina of Time*
Tabahl Woods	Tabahl Wasteland is an area on Koholint Island in *Link's Awakening*
Tal Tal Peak	Tal Tal Mountain Range and Tal Tal Heights are mountainous regions located on Koholint Island in *Link's Awakening*
Temple of Time	A recurring temple in the series
Tingel Island	Alludes to Tingle, a recurring character who first appeared in *Majora's Mask*
Toronbo Beach	A beach located in the southwest of Koholint Island in *Link's Awakening* called Toronbo Shores
Toto Lake	Toto is the manager of a popular Zora band in *Majora's Mask*
Trilby Plain	Trilby Highlands, a location from *The Minish Cap*
Tuft Mountain	Tuft is the king of Hytopia in *Tri Force Heroes*
Ukuku Plains	Ukuku Prairie is a large field in the center of Koholint Island in *Link's Awakening*
Zauz Island	Zauz is the blacksmith who forges the Phantom Sword for Link in *Phantom Hourglass*
Zora's Domain	A town from *Ocarina of Time*

Reference & Analysis

For players starting a new playthrough, especially on Master Mode, this chapter is packed with information on how to acquire the most useful weapons, upgrade every armor set with a minimum of effort, and cook the most efficient recipes. We also cover the inventories of every merchant in Hyrule, and useful miscellany such as where to find the best horses.

FARMING

Gathering resources (especially crafting materials for armor upgrades) is one of the biggest potential time-sinks in *Breath of the Wild*. Over the pages that follow, we'll show you where to find all of the items of prime interest, with a focus on very specific (and therefore entirely convenient) locales that yield items in noteworthy quantities.

This map illustrates fertile farming locations for some of the most important collectible items covered in this section.

LEGEND

	ICON	COLLECTIBLE
1		Acorn
2		Blue Nightshade
3		Chillshroom
4		Chuchu Jelly
5		Courser Bee Honey
6		Electric Keese Wing
7		Endura Carrot
8		Endura Shroom
9		Energetic Rhino Beetle
10		Fire Keese Wing
11		Fireproof Lizard
12		Fleet-Lotus Seeds
13		Hearty Bass & Hyrule Bass
14		Hearty Durian
15		Hightail Lizard
16		Hot-Footed Frog
17		Hyrule Bass
18		Ice Keese Wing
19		Ironshroom
20		Keese Wing & Keese Eyeball
21		Mighty Bananas
22		Octo Balloon
23		Octorok Eyeball
24		Octorok Tentacle
25		Razorshroom
26		Red Chuchu Jelly
27		Rushroom
28		Silent Princess
29		Silent Shroom
30		Smotherwing Butterfly
31		Sneaky River Snail
32		Stealthfin Trout
33		Sunset Firefly
34		Sunshroom
35		Swift Carrot
36		Swift Violet
37		Voltfruit
38		Warm Safflina
39		White Chuchu Jelly
40		Yellow Chuchu Jelly
41		Zapshroom

Woodland Tower Region
Eldin Tower Region
Akkala Ancient Tech Lab
Abandoned North Mine
Goron City
Forgotten Temple
Korok Forest
Southern Mine
Akkala Tower Region
ELDIN TOWER
WOODLAND TOWER
Tarrey Town
AKKALA TOWER
Hyrule Castle
Zora's Domain
Lanayru Tower Region
LANAYRU TOWER
Central Tower Region
CENTRAL TOWER
Kakariko Village
Hateno Tower Region
Dueling Peaks Tower Region
DUELING PEAKS TOWER
Great Plateau Tower Region
GREAT PLATEAU TOWER
Hateno Village
Hateno Ancient Tech Lab
HATENO TOWER
Faron Tower Region
Lake Tower Region
LAKE TOWER
FARON TOWER
Lurelin Village

INTRODUCTION

There are three essential tips that make item farming much easier:

- The more fast travel locations you have at your disposal, the easier it is to collect the items you need. Towers are a priority in order to reveal the map, and having a good coverage of unlocked shrines will significantly reduce time spent on journeys. Remember that you only need to interact with the front panel at a shrine to unlock it as a fast travel position.
- Get the Sheikah Sensor+ upgrade at Hateno Ancient Tech Lab as soon as it becomes available (see page 229). You can then take photographs of the few genuinely hard-to-find materials (such as Stealthfin Trout) and set the sensor to locate specimens in your vicinity.
- If you would like to maximize the damage that Link can inflict, work on accumulating the ancient materials and 6,000 rupees required to purchase the Ancient set from Akkala Ancient Tech Lab. With a little preparation, this will make things much easier when the time comes to hunt major monsters (especially Lynels). See page 360 for further details.

COOKING

While Link can cook and concoct a huge variety of meals and elixirs, we focus here on a select range of effects that can be gained from ingredients that are simple to farm in bulk when you know where to look.

We suspect that many *Breath of the Wild* players make limited use of food buffs. Once you learn where to harvest the necessary items quickly, though, you gain much more flexibility in terms of how you equip Link. You no longer need to rely on specialist armor sets that offer resistance from hot, cold or fiery conditions whenever you venture into Gerudo, Hebra and Eldin, for example. Once you have access to upgraded armor sets that augment damage, this makes a big difference.

For buffs that have a limited duration, you can (and should) top up the cooking pot with items that extend the timer: see the "Duration-Extending Ingredients" table for details. As we primarily focus on cooked meals over elixirs (gathering for the latter is much more demanding), we suggest that you make shopping trips to pick up the Goron spice, fresh milk, cane sugar, and goat butter that you can't collect in the wild – they extend the duration of temporary added effects by a fair amount and are much easier to acquire than dragon parts (which are best saved for the most essential recipes, given their potency and rarity).

If you gather ingredients and wait for a Blood Moon, you can cook up multiple meals between 11:30 PM and 12:10 AM to enjoy critical success bonuses in everything you prepare (see page 296). With the recipes detailed in the table to the right, this is only really appropriate when you might hope for a time limit to be extended – other potential cooking perks are nice, but far from essential.

There are two particular areas of Hyrule that offer abundant quantities of useful cooking items: Satori Mountain and the Faron region. We advise that you unlock all relevant shrines early in the adventure to facilitate fast and regular gathering trips.

EFFECT INGREDIENTS

ICON	EFFECT	OPTIMAL RECIPE	FARMING NOTES
	Chilly (Heat Resistance)	Chillshroom ( ) x3 + duration extender x2	Once you unlock the Jitan Sa'mi Shrine atop Mount Lanayru, you gain easy access to the Naydra Snowfield to the west, where you can gather approximately 80 chillshrooms.
	Electro (Shock Resistance)	Zapshroom ( ) x3 + duration extender x2	There are over 30 zapshrooms in Rok Woods to the south of Skull Lake in Akkala, with other valuable resources to farm while you're in the area. You can also find 15 at the south edge of Dalite Forest, to the south of Satori Mountain; glide there from the Mogg Latan Shrine to the north.
	Enduring (Full Stamina Recovery & Overfill)	Endura Shroom ( ) x1 (for full stamina recovery + small bonus overfill) Endura Carrot ( ) x5 (full recovery + two bonus wheels)	Energizing recipes aren't worth the trouble – an Enduring meal or elixir will restore Link's stamina *and* provide bonus wheel segments. The best material for easy refills is the endura shroom. You can find 10 in the band of trees next to the Gerudo Highlands cliffs southwest of Rutile Lake, then a further five in Dalite Forest to the east; both are easily accessed via the Mogg Latan Shrine on Satori Mountain. There are eight in the woods just south of Wetland Stable, and at least 10 in the Seres Scablands east of Tabantha Bridge Stable – though the latter are rather more spread out, making the Sheikah Sensor+ a must. Endura carrots are found at Great Fairy Fountains, but you can also obtain four to the north of the Mogg Latan Shrine, by the tree close to the pool on top of Satori Mountain, four directly south (in the band of trees just down from the shrine), and three on the east side of Rutile Lake (look close to the giant tree).
	Fireproof (Flame Guard)	Smotherwing Butterfly ( ) x4 + monster material x1	Fireproof lizards are easy to find at the Southern Mine en route to Goron City, but lack the potency to create full flame guard potions on their own, while Smotherwing Butterflies (which reach the threshold with four units) are ridiculously time-consuming to catch. You can purchase six of the latter in total for 60 rupees from Beedle at the Wetland Stable and East Akkala Stable. If you then fast travel to a distant location (such as Link's house in Hateno Village) and sleep until the next morning, Beedle should restock by the time you return.
	Hasty (Movement Speed Up)	Fleet-Lotus Seeds ( ) x4 + duration extender x1	Four grow in the water surrounding the Ne'ez Yohma Shrine at the heart of Zora's Domain, so make a habit of collecting these whenever you visit. There are 16 in the two pools east of the Monya Toma Shrine, just south of Serenne Stable. Another effortless farming spot is the Rabella Wetlands, where there are 15 to gather a short walk west of the the Tawa Jinn Shrine in the Faron region. You can also warp to the Daka Tuss Shrine, north of Kakariko Village, and head east until you reach the shore just below the lone giant tree on the cliffs leading to Quatta's Shelf (where a Guardian Stalker roams). If you trace a line from here to Moor Garrison Ruins in the northwest, you can find almost 40 plants within a few minutes.
	Hearty (Full HP Recovery & Extra Hearts)	Any Hearty ingredient ( ) x1	The hearty durian is the best ingredient to use due to the sheer ease of gathering it – and a single piece will grant four bonus hearts when cooked. There are 18 on the shelf directly north of Faron Tower, with six more on the plateau further north. Satori Mountain has 10 in a small wooded area with a pond a short walk east of the Mogg Latan Shrine, and a further six in the Rutile Lake forest to the southwest. Damel Forest, to the northwest of Faron Tower (just south of the Spring of Courage) has at least a few dozen hearty durians and many other valuable resources – but it's also home to quite a few enemies, particularly Lizalfos.
	Mighty (Attack Up)	Mighty Bananas ( ) or Razorshroom ( ) x4 + duration extender x1	Though you can easily collect 12 by the second pool northwest of Faron Tower, and 15 on Gogobi Shores southeast of Lurelin Village, there are dozens to be found on the Ubota Point mountain range south of the Lakeside Stable. Razorshrooms are equally valid. With these, there are two simple farming runs: in one, you start at the Monya Toma Shrine (close to the Serenne Stable) and gather those found on Elma Knolls to the east, then check the trees between there and Rauru Hillside further east (south of the Lost Woods) to amass approximately 30. The other is to start at the Woodland Stable and search the trees that line the road to the Lost Woods, which should net you a similar quantity. Note that this buff can be profitably carried forward into the Eventide Island shrine quest and the Trial of the Sword (see page 424), so enterprising players may opt to prepare a meal with a dragon's horn shard for max duration prior to tackling either.
	Sneaky (Stealth Up)	Silent Shroom ( ) x5 or Silent Princess ( ) x3 + duration extender x2	Silent princess, most commonly found close to Great Fairy Fountains, is the most powerful ingredient in this category, but you may prefer to save those for crafting. Silent shrooms are much easier to harvest. You can find 20 around Batrea Lake (plus ironshrooms), close to Riverside Stable, but there are also over 30 on the east bank of the river by the Toto Sah Shrine (south of Dueling Peaks Stable) and the cliffs by the waterfall to the south, not to mention countless specimens on the road to Zora's Domain from the Wetland Tower – especially on the west side of the U-shaped road section by Ruto Mountain.
	Spicy (Cold Resistance)	Sunshroom ( ) x3 + duration extender x2	There are two easy-to-reach locations where sunshrooms can be gathered quickly and in useful quantities: 12 in Retsam Forest, north of the Hateno Tech Lab, and over 20 just east of Gut Check Rock that you can harvest at regular intervals after unlocking the Gorae Torr shrine.
	Tough (Defense Up)	Ironshroom ( ) x4 + duration extender x1	A fairly casual search of the forest surrounding Batrea Lake, southeast of Riverside Stable, should net you 20 or 30 ironshrooms. You can also find at least 15 close to trees in the north of Rabia Plain, northeast of Kakariko Village's Great Fairy Fountain.

DURATION-EXTENDING INGREDIENTS

TYPE	DURATION	NOTES
Dragon Horn	30:00 (meals & elixirs)	See page 363 for farming advice. A single horn shard offers the maximum possible effect duration of 30 minutes, which makes it most appropriate with Mighty meals prior to extended sub-boss farming sessions.
Dragon Fang	10:30 (meals & elixirs)	
Dragon Claw	03:30 (meals & elixirs)	
Prime Monster Materials (all Guts, Lizalfos Tail, Keese Eyeball)	03:10 (elixirs only)	Applicable for the sole elixir of our recommended recipe list – the Flame Guard concoction. If you don't need the extended duration of a dragon part, we recommend the Keese eyeball – you'll accumulate these gradually during your travels, and they're not especially useful for anything else.
Goron Spice & Bird Egg	01:30 (meals only)	Goron spice is sold at Tanko's store in Goron City, where you can pick up three units (16 rupees each) per visit. Bird eggs can be gathered, with a modest amount of effort, from giant trees and cliffside nests. There are over 40 to collect in the Forest of Spirits on the Great Plateau, and they're also extremely common on the cliffs around the Muwo Jeem Shrine at the tip of Cape Cales, to the east of Lurelin Village. You can also pick up sizable quantities while collecting other ingredients from Rutile Lake and Dalite Forest south of Satori Mountain.
Cane Sugar, Fresh Milk & Goat Butter	01:20 (meals only)	Purchased from shopkeepers – see page 367.
Hylian Rice, Tabantha Wheat, Rock Salt	01:00 (meals only)	Hylian rice and Tabantha wheat can be collected by cutting tall grass in specific areas: the Necluda and Faron regions for rice, Hyrule Ridge and Tabantha Frontier for wheat. Rock salt is a common drop from ore deposits. Alternatively, you can buy all three from merchants.
Apple, Hyrule Herb, Hylian Shroom, Palm Fruit, Wildberry, all meat & fish without specific effects	00:30 (meals only)	If you have nothing else to hand, these common ingredients can be thrown into the pot for a little extra duration.

WEAPONS

This section focuses on high-value weapons that can be found in specific locations and that respawn with the passing of every Blood Moon.

Most of the best respawning weapons are found within Hyrule Castle (see page 106 for our tour in the Walkthrough chapter), which you can technically raid within minutes of leaving the Great Plateau if you have plenty of prior experience. Once you unlock the Saas Ko'sah shrine in the Docks as a fast travel position, you can then make regular returns to obtain valuable equipment and comestibles (including generous amounts of both standard and magic arrows). Navigation becomes instinctive after a few visits.

Two Expansion Pass items included in the first DLC package greatly simplify the process of looting Hyrule Castle. The Travel Medallion (see page 418) can be placed in a convenient position for accessing the interior areas on the south and west sides of the castle, for example. Even better, Majora's Mask (see page 414) prevents most enemies (with the exception of Guardians and the gatehouse Lynels) from identifying Link as a foe, which greatly simplifies each trip.

RESPAWNING WEAPONS

There are many weapons available in the open that respawn every Blood Moon, but only a relative handful that are of great value no matter what stage you have reached in the adventure.

NOTEWORTHY RESPAWNING WEAPONS

WEAPON	NOTES
Blizzard Rod	Found in Hyrule Castle's Lockup.
Edge of Duality	Examine the lower southeast part of the rock outcrop, midway between the Gerudo Tower and the Sho Dantu Shrine, to find rocks blocking a cave entrance. Move these aside with Stasis to find the Edge of Duality inside, along with other treasures.
Falcon Bow	Found in Hyrule Castle Guards' Chamber.
Frostspear	An exception to other weapons detailed here, as you need to fight the current owner (an Ice-Breath Lizalfos) to claim it. From the Mozo Shenno Shrine on the Biron Snowshelf in Hebra, zoom the map all the way in and look to the northwest to find a skull-shaped enemy camp. Your target (and two other Lizalfos) can be found inside. The easiest way to collect it is to hit the Lizalfos in question with a fire arrow from outside the closest eye socket, then drop in, grab your prize and fast travel elsewhere.
Great Flameblade	1: Inside the Ancient Tree Stump, directly west of Central Tower. 2: Hyrule Castle, just inside the entrance to the Docks. 3: Beneath the ribcage of the Eldin Great Skeleton.
Great Frostblade	In the room just beyond the upper south Library exit in Hyrule Castle.
Great Thunderblade	At the center of the three peaks of Cuho Mountain, northwest of Tabantha Tower.
Royal Bow	All in Hyrule Castle: 1: In the Armory. 2: On the balcony at the Observation Room. 3: Inside a cell at the Lockup.
Royal Claymore	1: On top of Tabantha Tower, turn and face northeast; there's a fallen stone pillar below. Glide down to the cliff just above it. 2: In Hyrule Castle's Armory. 3: Inside the Guards' Chamber in Hyrule Castle.
Royal Broadsword	Beneath the spiral staircase on the level below Zelda's room.
Royal Guard's Bow	Inside Zelda's bedroom in Hyrule Castle.
Royal Guard's Claymore	In a cell in Hyrule Castle's Lockup.
Stone Smasher	Move the metal shelf on the west side of the Library at Hyrule Castle and follow the passage behind it.
Thunderblade	In the Observation Room at Hyrule Castle.

ANCIENT WEAPONS

Though you will have noticed that all Guardians respawn at every Blood Moon, it's easy to overlook the fact that the same rule applies to all Guardian Scouts found inside shrines. While the lower models are of no real consequence, the more advanced Guardian Scouts found in Test of Strength shrines are a reliable, regularly replenished source of basic ancient materials and weapons. When combined with the upgraded Ancient armor set, the "++" grade axes and swords that you can acquire rival (and, with an additional Attack Up buff active, exceed) the best Lynel gear in terms of raw damage output.

TEST OF STRENGTH SHRINE FARMING

SHRINE (REGION)	TYPE	EQUIPMENT
Chaas Qeta (Necluda Sea)	Major	Ancient Battle Axe++, Guardian Sword++, Guardian Spear++
Dah Hesho (Akkala)	Minor	Ancient Battle Axe
Dah Kaso (Central Hyrule)	Minor	Guardian Spear
Goma Asaagh (Hebra)	Major	Ancient Battle Axe++, Guardian Sword++, Guardian Spear++
Hia Miu (Hebra)	Major	Ancient Battle Axe++, Guardian Sword++, Guardian Spear++
Katah Chuki (Central Hyrule)	Minor	Guardian Spear
Ke'nai Shakah (Akkala)	Modest	Ancient Battle Axe+, Guardian Sword+
Kema Kosassa (Gerudo Highlands)	Major	Ancient Battle Axe++, Guardian Spear++, Guardian Shield++
Mijah Rokee (Hyrule Ridge)	Modest	Guardian Sword+, Guardian Shield+
Mozo Shenno (Hebra)	Major	Ancient Battle Axe++, Guardian Sword++, Guardian Spear++
Muwo Jeem (Faron)	Modest	Ancient Battle Axe+, Guardian Shield+
Namika Ozz (Central Hyrule)	Modest	Ancient Battle Axe+, Guardian Spear+
Noya Neha (Central Hyrule)	Minor	Ancient Battle Axe
Pumaag Nitae (Faron)	Minor	Guardian Sword, Guardian Shield
Saas Ko'sah (Hyrule Castle)	Major	Ancient Battle Axe++, Guardian Sword++, Guardian Spear++
Sasa Kai (Gerudo)	Modest	Guardian Sword+, Guardian Shield+
Shoqa Tatone (Faron)	Modest	Guardian Spear+, Guardian Shield+
Soh Kofi (Lanayru)	Minor	Guardian Sword, Guardian Shield
Tena Ko'sah (Tabantha Frontier)	Major	Ancient Battle Axe++, Guardian Sword++, Guardian Spear++
Tutsuwa Nima (Akkala)	Major	Guardian Sword++, Guardian Spear++, Guardian Shield++

CHAMPION WEAPONS

Though not the most powerful in Hyrule, the four unique weapons acquired on completion of each Divine Beast dungeon are still interesting and fun to use. Should you misplace or break them, you can obtain replacements by delivering the necessary materials to specific individuals:

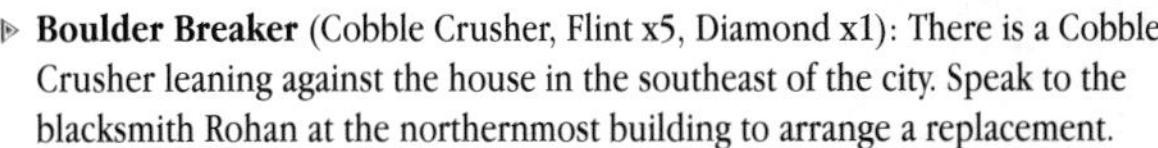

- **Boulder Breaker** (Cobble Crusher, Flint x5, Diamond x1): There is a Cobble Crusher leaning against the house in the southeast of the city. Speak to the blacksmith Rohan at the northernmost building to arrange a replacement.
- **Great Eagle Bow** (Swallow Bow, Wood x5, Diamond x1): Visit Harth in Rito Village; from the Akh Va'quot Shrine, his is the second building to the right when you reach the inner walkway. A Swallow Bow is found on the table to your left as you enter.
- **Lightscale Trident** (Zora Spear, Flint x5, Diamond x1): You can find a respawning Zora Spear in the pool directly behind the grand staircase that leads to King Dorephan. Deliver the required materials to Dento in the room just beyond the Coral Reef store.
- **Scimitar of the Seven** (Gerudo Scimitar, Flint x5, Diamond x1): From just inside the main Gerudo Town entrance, turn left and climb the short set of steps; a Gerudo Scimitar will spawn on a box inside the alcove. Buliara in the throne room will attend to the reconstruction of the blade. Though technically not a weapon, she will also craft a fresh Daybreaker for you if you give her the right ingredients (Gerudo Shield, Flint x5, Diamond x1).

ARMOR CRAFTING

While every armor set has its place and purpose, three (and, with The Master Trials DLC, four) armor sets offer noteworthy buffs when it matters most: in combat.

- **Ancient Set:** There is one configuration that is unparalleled in terms of its potential raw damage output. Purchased for 6,000 rupees (and a not insignificant quantity of spare parts) at the Akkala Ancient Tech Lab (see page 229), the Ancient set grants Link the Ancient Proficiency buff when all three parts are upgraded by two levels. This boosts Link's damage output while wielding Guardian/Ancient weaponry by a massive 80%. The best thing about this set is that the Ancient Proficiency buff stacks with the Attack Up status effect (+50% damage at Level 3), which you can bestow upon Link with a meal containing readily available ingredients. This makes it easy to farm Test of Strength shrines to obtain Guardian weaponry, particularly the Ancient Sword++ (40 base damage) and Ancient Axe++ (60 base damage), which can be employed to annihilate any enemy.
- **Radiant Set:** The Radiant set purchased from the Gerudo Secret Club (see page 251) works in a similar manner to the Ancient set, but its damage bonus is applied whenever Link wields Dragonbone weapons; again, your damage output can be further boosted with a food-induced Attack Up buff. The benefit of using it is that these weapons are encountered regularly throughout your travels, so it's a low-maintenance way to enjoy higher power with common, entirely disposal equipment. Moreover, as a fringe benefit, Stal monsters will no longer attack Link.
- **Barbarian Set:** Many *Breath of the Wild* players swear by the Barbarian garb, and the permanent 50% Attack Up buff and stamina cost reduction for charged attacks is certainly impressive.
- **Phantom Set:** If you have the Master Trials DLC, the Phantom set (see page 415) is an easily obtainable way to increase damage output if you compensate for its low armor rating with meals or elixirs that provide the full Defense Up buff. This is only a viable option early on in the adventure, though.

MATERIALS & MINOR MONSTER PARTS

If you aspire to upgrade each and every armor piece, these are all items that you should seek out from an early stage in the storyline.

COLLECTIBLE & MINOR MONSTER PART REQUIREMENTS

ICON	TYPE	REQUIRED FOR	FARMING NOTES
	Acorn	"of the Wild" set (x30)	A semi-regular drop whenever you knock down trees. You can acquire them in bulk (18, if you're thorough) at the Sage Temple Ruins on the west side of Hyrule Field. The Central Tower to the southeast is the closest fast travel point.
	Blue Nightshade	Stealth set (x24)	These surround the Great Fairy Fountain close to Kakariko Village; explore further east to find a few more, and scale the rock spire to the northwest to find an additional dozen or so.
	Chuchu Jelly	Soldier's set (x15)	You should easily accumulate the required total during your travels, but you will find several Chuchus in the Forest of Time if you need more: glide down from the Great Plateau Tower to the west.
	Courser Bee Honey	"of the Wild" set (x15)	A motherlode of six nests can be found in Uten Marsh, south of the Tawa Jinn Shrine in the Faron region. There are five in the wooded area surrounding Rutile Lake (southwest of the Mogg Latan Shrine on Satori Mountain), and three in the trees close to the cabin at Fort Hateno.
	Electric Keese Wing	Climbing set (x15)	There are seven on the path leading to Zora's Domain, right next to the Bank of Wishes; start at the Lanayru Tower and glide east. A further six can be found in a cave (with entrances to the north and south) directly north of the Shoda Sah Shrine (itself northeast of the Faron Tower).
	Energetic Rhino Beetle	"of the Wild" set (x15)	These can technically be found all over Hyrule, always on trees and at night, but are rather uncommon. There are two places where they are guaranteed to spawn. They are abundant in the Rok Woods, just south of Skull Lake. You can also collect five just south and southeast of the pool at Bronas Forest, a short glide to the east from Faron Tower. As a rule, they are very elusive. To avoid scaring them away, equip the complete Stealth armor set and minimize the noise you make during your approach.
	Fire Keese Wing	Climbing set (x15), Snowquill set (x24)	There are at least 12 Fire Keese that appear where the road from Foothill Stable to Goron City curves abruptly to the west. If you wait until night, though, there is an easier hunting ground where you can also acquire countless pieces of Red Chuchu Jelly. When you reach the Maw of Death Mountain north of Foothill Stable, scour the slope leading northwest to Eldin Tower; there are at least 20 in this vicinity. You do not need Flame Guard garb for this area, and it's a convenient way to reach the tower at a low level.
	Fireproof Lizard	Flamebreaker set (x12)	You can find all the fireproof lizards you'll ever need at the Southern Mine en route to Goron City; note that you'll need Level 1 Flame Guard protection in this area. In addition to those found in the open, you can find many more hiding beneath rocks.
	Hearty Bass	Zora set (x15)	Start at the Lakeside Stable. There are at least 10 by the trees that support Floria Bridge (use Cryonis pillars for easy fishing), and a further five to the northeast, at the base of the Calora Lake waterfall. You can also collect Hyrule Bass at the same time.
	Hightail Lizard	Climbing set (x15), Sand Boots (x10), Snow Boots (x10)	As well as those found at random in the open, these critters can be revealed in many areas of Hyrule by slashing tall grass; charged one-handed sword swings are effective. Be quick to collect them before they scuttle away. The grasslands just east of the Great Plateau are a good place to search.
	Hot-Footed Frog	Climbing set (x30)	You can find 20 in Rutile Lake southwest of the Mogg Latan shrine, 10 in the pool south of Ralis Pond en route to Zora's Domain, and a further 10 in the waters surrounding Malanya Spring where the Horse God resides (southeast of Highland Stable).
	Hyrule Bass	Zora set (x15)	A common fish found in many bodies of water. You can collect the required number for the Zora set in the areas we specify for the rare Hearty Bass.
	Ice Keese Wing	Climbing set (x15), Desert Voe set (x33)	Ice Keese spawn at night in most cold areas, but trekking frozen expanses to find the totals required can take an age. You should supplement those gathered in ambient encounters by visiting the following guaranteed locations: ▸ Five Ice Keese in the southernmost of two skull-shaped camps north of the Snowfield Stable. ▸ Five in a skull-shaped camp on Sapphia's Table, directly south of the Kuh Takkar Shrine in the Gerudo Highlands. ▸ Six on Zirco Mesa, a peak southeast of the Kuh Takkar Shrine. ▸ You should also find a few spawns on the south bank of the River of the Dead on the Great Plateau at night.

COLLECTIBLE & MINOR MONSTER PART REQUIREMENTS (CONTINUED)

ICON	TYPE	REQUIRED FOR	FARMING NOTES
	Keese Wing, Keese Eyeball	Climbing set (x9), Soldier's set (x9)	There are eight that always appear in the hollowed giant tree trunk just west of the Namika Ozz Shrine on Crenel Hills (east of Hyrule Castle). The Royal Ancient Lab Ruins and Irch Plain (west of Hyrule Castle) are a good hunting ground for swarms; the Monya Toma Shrine on Salari Hill to the northwest is the closest fast travel position.
	Octo Balloon	Snow Boots (x5)	You should routinely acquire sufficient balloons and tentacles, but the Octorok eyeball is a very rare drop. There are a few places where these creatures can be found in unusual concentrations: 17 in an approximate ring surrounding Thundra Plateau (where you find the Toh Yahsa Shrine), 16 in Rok Woods south of Skull Lake, and a further 16 on and around Guchini Plain west of Faron Tower.
	Octorok Eyeball	Snow Boots (x5)	
	Octorok Tentacle	Snow Boots (x5)	
	Red Chuchu Jelly	Snowquill set (x24)	See "Fire Keese Wings" – you can accumulate ridiculous quantities of the jelly on the slopes south of Eldin Tower.
	Rushroom	Climbing set (x9), Sand Boots (x15), Snow Boots (x15)	A commonplace sight on cliffs in Necluda, Tabantha Frontier and Hyrule Ridge, but especially abundant on the mountains that frame the Gerudo Desert, rushrooms can be time-consuming to collect. If you need to acquire them in bulk, try the following convenient farming spots: ▶ Warp to the Mogg Latan Shrine on Satori Mountain and head almost directly south to the small pool. From there, the cliff to the southeast has at least 10 in close proximity. ▶ You can find another 10 on the tall rock spire and northern cliff face at the Gerudo Canyon Stable. ▶ There are at least eight in close proximity on the cliff at the foot of the southeast side of Lake Tower, though you should deal with the two Lizalfos archers before you begin gathering. ▶ Warp to the Pumaag Nitae Shrine in Faron Woods and make the short journey to the bog north of Finra Woods. There are four rushrooms on the cliff to your right, and a further seven practically at ground level once you reach the bog.
	Silent Princess	Champion's Tunic (x19), Stealth set (x15), Sheik's Mask (x10)	As you can always find at least two silent princess flowers at Great Fairy Fountains, diligent collection on all visits should meet your needs. There are four at Cotera's fountain close to Kakariko Village, with an additional three on a rock spire to the northwest. You can also find two at the base of a tree located a short stroll to the southwest of the Mogg Latan Shrine on Satori Mountain.
	Silent Shroom	Stealth set (x24)	There are a dozen silent shrooms on the west side of Hickaly Woods, just over the river from the Toto Sah Shrine (south of Dueling Peaks Stable). A little further south, you can amass over 20 from the area below the waterfall and the cliff face itself.
	Smotherwing Butterfly	Flamebreaker set (x24)	Arguably the most difficult crafting material to find. Available in the area surrounding Death Mountain during daylight hours, they are most likely to appear close to surface lava – but are still unusually rare. Given the sheer time it takes to find the required quantity, it's better to gradually purchase them from Beedle. He has three in stock at both the Wetland Stable and East Akkala Stable for a modest 10 rupees apiece; fast travel to a distant location (such as Link's house in Hateno Village) and sleep until the next morning to refresh his inventory.
	Sneaky River Snail	Stealth set (x15)	There are six that you can collect in Zora's Domain (look by the pools on the floor level above the Ne'ez Yohma Shrine), and a dozen in the pools atop Farosh Hills (directly north of the Pumaag Nitae Shrine).
	Stealthfin Trout	Stealth set (x30)	Though you have a chance to find them in other bodies of water, these appear most regularly on the south and west of Lake Mekar. The best place to start is Mekar Island, west of the Lost Woods, though be wary of the Stal ambush that awaits first-time visitors. From there, use Cryonis pillars to search the surrounding waters. Stealthfin trout glow at night, so that's the best time to fish.
	Sunshroom	Snowquill set (x15)	There are 12 in Retsam Forest, a short glide north of the Hateno Tech Lab. You can also find over 20 just east of Gut Check Rock in the far north of the Akkala district.
	Sunset Firefly	Stealth set (x15)	These only appear at night. Kakariko Village is an obvious candidate, with over a dozen within easy reach. However, you can potentially catch over 30 at Rutile Lake southwest of the Mogg Latan Shrine on Satori Mountain – plus other valuable materials. You could also top up your stocks while collecting sneaky river snails in Farosh Hills.
	Swift Carrot	Sand Boots (x10), Snow Boots (x10)	Given the scarcity of this vegetable in the wild, the most practical solution is to buy them in Kakariko Village. However, there is one place where you can acquire five at no expense: the final woodlet on the eastern slope of Mount Satori, easily accessed by gliding down from the Mogg Latan Shrine.
	Swift Violet	Climbing set (x45), Sand Boots (x15), Snow Boots (x15)	There are three consistent farming spots. One is the waterfall behind the Ha Dahamar Shrine at the Dueling Peaks Stable. The second is just off the road to Kakariko Village, most easily reached via the spot where you retrieve Hestu's priceless maracas. If you look at the waterfall that feeds into Lake Siela, you'll see the plants (10 in total) to either side of it. Set a Travel Medallion position (if possible) to simplify collection. The highest concentration of Swift Violets, though, can be found on the mushroom trees in Ludfo's Bog, southwest of Ridgeland Tower. They only appear on specific trees, which you can see from below, so the gathering will take less time than you might fear. There are over 30 to collect if you're thorough.
	Voltfruit	Rubber set (x15)	The cactus-like plants that bear these fruits are clearly visible as you explore the Gerudo Desert. If you head directly north from the Great Fairy Fountain, you should find all 15 needed for the Rubber set before you draw level with Gerudo Town. Lorn, directly to your right as you enter Gerudo Town via the main gate, sells three at a time for 16 rupees apiece.
	Warm Saffina	Snowquill set (x9)	Most commonly found in the northern half of the Gerudo Desert, though there are always five plants close to the Great Fairy Fountain in the southeast. If you need more, there are at least seven that grow around the giant bones outside the Kema Zoos Shrine.
	White Chuchu Jelly	Desert Voe set (x24)	You can encounter almost a dozen smaller Ice Chuchus on the north and south banks of the River of the Dead on the Great Plateau, but the most profitable hunting ground is north of the Kema Kosassa Shrine on the Gerudo Highlands, with four large Ice Chuchus in the skull-shaped camp and more to the east as you approach the rock peninsula that looms above.
	Yellow Chuchu Jelly	Rubber set (x24)	Easy to farm on the slopes northwest of the Wasteland Tower, but there's an even better place to collect them. If you start at Lakeside Stable and climb the cliffs south of the Shai Utoh Shrine, you will soon reach a broad, sloped plateau above the beach. As you approach a conspicuous collection of four ore deposits on a rock outcrop, you will be ambushed by a ring of nine Yellow Chuchus.
	Zapshroom	Rubber set (x15)	There are twice as many as you need for crafting purposes in Rok Woods, south of Skull Lake. If you travel directly south from Mogg Latan Shrine on Satori Mountain, you can amass 15 at the base of the cliffs at the easternmost extent of the Gerudo Highlands.

MAJOR MONSTER PARTS

There is a hierarchy for monster part drops: the guts (Bokoblin, Moblin, Hinox, and Lynel) and tails (Lizalfos only) are the least common standard rewards. You don't get them at all for the lowest-rank enemies, and they're not absolutely guaranteed unless you defeat the third tier opponents (Black Bokoblin, Black Moblin, Black Lizalfos, Black Hinox, White-Maned Lynel). The exceptions are the elemental Lizalfos varieties (which should always drop their tails), the Molduga (which all offer the same item yield probabilities) and the Stalnox (as befits a giant skeleton, it only offers tooth drops).

Your regular nocturnal encounters with Stal enemies means that there's little purpose in attacking base-level Bokoblins, Moblins and Lizalfos for talons, horns and fangs: their skeletal equivalents will yield more than you'll ever need over time.

Silver (and, in Master Mode, gold) enemy varieties have a chance of dropping additional items when they die. These are usually gemstones, but there's a very small chance that you can also get a star fragment from Lynels. Only Bokoblins, Moblins, Lizalfos and Lynels have a gold tier.

MAJOR MONSTER PART REQUIREMENTS

ICON	TYPE	REQUIRED FOR
	Bokoblin Horn	Hylian set (x39)
	Bokoblin Fang	Hylian set (x45)
	Bokoblin Guts	Hylian set (x60), Radiant set (x9), Soldier's set (x9)
	Hinox Toenail	Fierce Deity set (x15)
	Hinox Tooth	Fierce Deity set (x15)
	Hinox Guts	Soldier's set (x4), Fierce Deity set (x6), Flamebreaker set (x6)
	Icy Lizalfos Tail	Desert Voe set (x39)
	Lizalfos Horn	Zora set (x9)
	Lizalfos Tail	Soldier's set (x8), Zora set (x45)
	Lizalfos Talon	Zora set (x15)
	Lynel Guts	Soldier's set (x6), Barbarian set (x9), Radiant set (x3), Fierce Deity set (x6)
	Lynel Hoof	Soldier's set (x6), Barbarian set (x18)
	Lynel Horn	Barbarian set (x12)
	Moblin Fang	Flamebreaker set (x12)
	Moblin Guts	Soldier's set (x9), Flamebreaker set (x9), Radiant set (x9)
	Moblin Horn	Flamebreaker set (x6)
	Molduga Fin	Sand Boots (x15)
	Molduga Guts	Radiant set (x6), Sand Boots (x6)
	Red Lizalfos Tail	Snowquill set (x30)
	Yellow Lizalfos Tail	Rubber set (x45)

- **Bokoblins** are the most common of the weapon-bearing monsters, so you shouldn't have trouble finding them. If you need the quantities of drops required to fully upgrade the Hylian set to scratch a completionist itch late in a playthrough, the entire Great Plateau, Blatchery Plain east of the Dueling Peaks Stable, and the woods just west of Hateno Village should be a good source of mid-level specimens that can drop Bokoblin Guts.
- The best place to hunt **Lizalfos** is the Lanayru Wetlands and, naturally, the road leading to Zora's Domain. They're also pretty common in the north of the Gerudo Desert.
- **Ice-Breath Lizalfos** are found in cold regions, and fall instantly to any fire weapon. Start at the Kuh Takkar Shrine in the Gerudo Highlands and head south to find five; if you then continue to Sapphia's Table to the south, you can locate a further five. Goflam's Secret Hot Spring northwest of the Shada Naw Shrine in Hebra also has five that are sufficiently spaced apart to beat individually without effort.
- **Electric Lizalfos** do not have an elemental weakness, but you can at least negate their signature area-of-effect attack by wearing the upgraded Rubber set. Starting at Faron Tower, you can find six Electric Lizalfos at the heart of Damel Forest to the northwest. There are two in the watery area north of Wasteland Tower, and another pair in the waters beneath Ridgeland Tower. Lure them to dry land before you start a fight!
- Look in the Gerudo Desert and the environs around Death Mountain for **Fire-Breath Lizalfos**, which fall to instakill attacks from ice weapons. There are four in the ruins that lie between Gerudo Town and the Northern Icehouse; just start at the Daqo Chisay Shrine and head north. There's always one below Eldin Tower, and two just outside the Qua Raym Shrine to the west. If you're game for a tougher fight, the Abandoned North Mine (start at the Shae Mo'sah Shrine just outside Goron City) is home to over 10.
- There are two prime locations for hunting **Moblins**: the area surrounding Hateno Tower, and Tumlea Heights close to the Akkala Ancient Tech Lab. Later in the story, investigate the Forest of Time and East Post Ruins – both are easy to reach from the Great Plateau Tower, and the Moblins there should mostly still be at relatively low levels.
- You can find precise locations for all **sub-bosses** (Talus, Molduga, Hinox, Stalnox, Lynel) on page 328.

ANCIENT MATERIALS

Required for the powerful Ancient set and for special items sold by Cherry at the Akkala Ancient Tech Lab, these collectibles are acquired by defeating Guardians.

Ancient Cores and Ancient Giant Cores are a bottleneck, as these are rare drops for high-level Guardians only. The best strategy is to farm Guardian Stalkers on Hyrule Field, which is more practical once you acquire the Master Sword, or upgrade the Ancient set to obtain the Ancient Proficiency bonus and farm Test of Strength shrines for their weapons beforehand (see page 358).

Whenever you encounter ruined Guardian Stalkers, check to see if they are firmly stuck to the ground. There are quite a few that can be overturned with a heavy metal object directed with Magnesis, revealing hidden materials beneath.

ANCIENT MATERIAL REQUIREMENTS

ICON	TYPE	REQUIRED FOR	FARMING NOTES
	Ancient Core	Ancient set (x9 for initial purchase, x15 for upgrades); Divine Helms (x20)	Occasionally dropped by Guardian Scouts III and IV, Stalkers, Skywatchers and Turrets; rare loot from shrine chests; can be bought from Teli (a wandering merchant in Necluda, see page 371).
	Ancient Gear	Ancient set (x60 for initial purchase, x30 for upgrades); Divine Helms (x40)	Moderately common drop from all Guardian varieties; more likely with major models.
	Ancient Screw	Ancient set (x5 for initial purchase, x15 for upgrades); Divine Helms (x20)	Common drop from all Guardians.
	Ancient Shaft	Ancient set (x5 for initial purchase, x45 for upgrades); Divine Helms (x60)	Moderately common drop from all Guardian varieties; more likely with major models.
	Ancient Spring	Ancient set (x5 for initial purchase, x60 for upgrades); Divine Helms (x80)	Common drop from all Guardians.
	Giant Ancient Core	Ancient set (x6); Divine Helms (x8)	Infrequently dropped by Stalkers, Skywatchers and Turrets; rare loot from shrine chests.

EXOTIC MATERIALS

If your only concern is to upgrade armor found in the base game, the required dragon parts and star fragments can easily be gradually acquired during the course of a standard playthrough. Completing amiibo sets, however, will take rather more effort – as a glance at the following table will confirm.

EXOTIC MATERIAL REQUIREMENTS

TYPE	REQUIRED FOR
Dinraal's Claw	"of the Wild" set (x2), Fierce Deity set (x1)
Dinraal's Fang	"of the Wild" set (x2), Fierce Deity set (x1)
Dinraal's Horn	Champion's Tunic (x2), "of the Wild" set (x2), Fierce Deity set (x1), Barbarian set (x1)
Dinraal's Scale	"of the Wild" set (x2), Fierce Deity set (x1)
Farosh's Claw	"of the Wild" set (x2), Fierce Deity set (x1)
Farosh's Fang	"of the Wild" set (x2), Fierce Deity set (x1)
Farosh's Horn	Champion's Tunic (x2), "of the Wild" set (x2), Fierce Deity set (x1), Barbarian set (x1)
Farosh's Scale	"of the Wild" set (x2), Fierce Deity set (x1)
Naydra's Claw	"of the Wild" set (x2), Fierce Deity set (x1)
Naydra's Fang	"of the Wild" set (x2), Fierce Deity set (x1)
Naydra's Horn	Champion's Tunic (x2), "of the Wild" set (x2), Fierce Deity set (x1), Barbarian set (x1)
Naydra's Scale	"of the Wild" set (x2), Fierce Deity set (x1), Snow Boots (x2)
Star Fragment	Diamond Circlet (x2), Ruby Circlet (x2), Sapphire Circlet (x2), Topaz Earrings (x2), Ancient set (x3), "of the Wild" set (x3), Sheik's Mask (x10), "of the Hero" set (x12), "of Time" set (x12), "of the Sky" set (x12), "of Twilight" set (x12), "of the Wind" set (x12), Divine Helms (x4)

The rules concerning dragon appearances (see page 343) have been adjusted since *Breath of the Wild's* launch. They are now harder to farm, so we present three reliable positions that guarantee encounters at specific times. We suggest that you visit and initiate the shrine quests at the Spring of Courage in the north of the Faron region (see page 145) and the Spring of Power in Akkala (see page 211) to "normalize" the routines of Farosh and Dinraal beforehand; a trip to the Spring of Wisdom on Mount Lanayru is, of course, mandatory to free Naydra of Malice (see page 127).

- **Farosh** is by far the easiest of the three dragons to farm, and the best choice if you are seeking to accumulate horn shards for long-lasting buffs in meals and elixirs. Warp to the Shai Utoh Shrine at the Lakeside Stable, use the cooking pot to wait until morning, then run out onto the Floria Bridge; you will see Farosh begin its descent over Floria Falls in the distance.

- **Naydra** will appear consistently if you wait at the east end of the Lanayru Promenade, ideally on the slopes north of the East Gate and at night.

- **Dinraal** can be the most capricious of the three dragons, but there's one position that offers both a reliable spawn time and a perfect elevation for easy shots. Fast travel to the Maag No'rah Shrine (northwest of Ridgeland Tower) at night and glide down to the edge of Tanagar Canyon. Dinraal arrives from the northeast.

STAR FRAGMENTS

The rarest of all crafting resources, a star fragment can potentially fall from the sky on any night between 09:00 PM and 3:30 AM, but the probability is far higher during full moons (and, anecdotally, the evenings to either side of them). Manual farming can be arduous and time-consuming, so we strongly advise that you make it a habit to look out for the vertical shafts of light that mark their landing positions whenever you are exploring at night. If you have the Expansion Pass, a trip to the far north of Akkala to collect the Travel Medallion (see page 418) will enable you to "bookmark" your position whenever you make a star fragment detour.

If you intend to manually farm star fragments there is a slow but simple strategy that you can employ. The shooting stars that mark the arrival of a fragment will always occur in the direction that the camera is facing. The trick to dedicated farming, then, is to equip Link with plenty of bundles of wood and a flame weapon for lighting campfires, then set up at a suitably high vantage point. You use the campfire to advance time to night – and then you wait.

Three vantage points that work well are the Great Plateau Tower looking over Hyrule Field, the southern Dueling Peak above the Shee Vaneer Shrine looking towards Hateno Tower, and the Lake Tower looking west towards Gerudo.

NOTES:

- Star fragments will immediately be lost if they should fall in certain locations, particularly deep water. If the distinctive vertical spire of light does not appear after the trail fizzles out, it's a dud.

- Unclaimed star fragments disappear at 05:00 AM sharp. If it seems unlikely that you'll reach one before the dawn deadline, create a campfire and choose to wait until the following night.

- Speak to Hino at the Dueling Peaks Stable for information on the phases of the moon, including imminent Blood Moons.

- Star fragments are rare drops from silver (and, in Master Mode, gold) Lynels.

- You can collect six star fragments from treasure chests around Hyrule: consult the Maps chapter (see page 374) to find them.

ORE PROSPECTING

We've prepared a shortlist of locations where you can reach valuable deposits within seconds of arriving at a local fast travel position. You can also consult three maps that document mining spots in locations with an unusually high quantity of nodes in a relatively small area. Once you know where to look, mining ore deposits is by far the most lucrative source of rupees in Hyrule, as most tend to respawn in a matter of days.

Before we continue, it would be remiss not to offer a few useful tips and insights to aid you in opportunistic prospecting while exploring Hyrule.

- There are three types of deposit: **standard ore deposits** (silver spots), **rare ore deposits** (gold spots) and **luminous stone deposits** (spots that are black at daytime and glow at night). Standard ore offers Amber, Rock Salt and Flint as common drops, with a small chance of Opal, Ruby, Sapphire and Topaz each time; you usually get one item, but occasionally two. Rare ore deposits have a high chance of yielding Opal, Ruby, Sapphire and Topaz, and a small possibility of a Diamond; Amber and Flint are still possible as booby prizes, but rare ore usually yields at least a few items. At night, luminous deposits emit a distinctive glow that you can see from long distances. They are your primary source of luminous stones, usually one unit (or two as a semi-common occurrence), though they also drop flint.
- As with many other objects, you can photograph ore deposits and set your Sheikah Slate to search for them as you travel. We would suggest that you favor rare ore deposits if you do this, as they are far more likely to yield valuable gemstones. They are also usually accompanied by two or three standard deposits.
- The contents of a deposit are only determined when Link strikes them. If you are keen for a rare ore node to give you a very specific gemstone, it's possible to save beforehand and reload if you don't get the desired outcome.
- Mining equipment (from the iron sledgehammer to the mighty boulder breaker) sustains a far lower durability cost when used to smash deposits.
- Talus sub-bosses also offer substantial amounts of ore when you defeat them. You can find their precise locations on page 328. Regularly farming the two rare ones within gliding distance from the Tabantha Tower (with another pair not too far) can provide a steady stream of high-value gemstones.

ORE REQUIREMENTS

ICON	TYPE	REQUIRED FOR
	Amber	Amber Earrings (x65), Hylian set (x45), "of Time" set (x159)
	Diamond	Diamond Circlet (x22)
	Flint	Amber Earrings (x12), Diamond Circlet (x6), Opal Earrings (x12), Ruby Circlet (x6), Sapphire Circlet (x6), Topaz Earrings (x6)
	Luminous Stone	Radiant set (x129, plus x9 for original purchase)
	Opal	Opal Earrings (x49), Zora set (x45), "of the Wind" set (x114)
	Ruby	Ruby Circlet (x22), Snowquill set (x15), "of the Hero" set (x57)
	Sapphire	Sapphire Circlet (x22), Desert Voe set (x15), "of the Sky" set (x57)
	Topaz	Topaz Earrings (x22), Rubber set (x30), "of Twilight" set (x57)

QUICK ORE COLLECTION SPOTS

FAST TRAVEL POINT	DIRECTIONS
Akkala Tower	There are two deposits including rare nodes within easy gliding range of the tower. Look for the long slope that leads down to Torin Wetland, to the east of the tower: one lies by the giant rock at the top of the slope, and the other is in an alcove at the base of the slope.
Dah Hesho Shrine (Akkala)	There are five deposits on the rocky outcrop to the southeast at Kaepora Pass, and four deposits directly north on the shore of Lake Akkala far below (plus two luminous nodes in plain sight further along).
Dako Tah Shrine (Gerudo Desert)	There are five deposits (one rare) on the southwest side of the rock outcrop here. If you then turn and head directly north, you'll find a further six at the base of the cliffs, and another three on the small plateau just above.
Dow Na'eh Shrine (Lanayru Promenade)	There are five deposits in the cave where the shrine is found.
Eldin Tower (East)	Glide east from the tower, then turn north to look at the narrow ledges on the cliff that leads down to the road below. There are five deposits in clear sight, including three rare. We suggest you try this first at night, when they are much easier to see.
Eldin Tower & Southern Mine	Starting at the tower, glide northwest to the area pockmarked by hot springs. There are several individual deposits in this area (though watch out for Lizalfos) which you can collect en route to the Southern Mine – one of the easiest and most profitable mining spots in Hyrule.
Eldin Tower (South)	If you face south on top of the tower at night, you should clearly see 11 luminous deposits in the areas below. If you glide further south, there are six regular deposits (one rare) to your left south of Lake Ferona.
Gorae Torr Shrine (Gut Check Rock)	There are three nodes (one rare) that you can see to the northwest from the rock spire, especially at night. Continue in the same direction to find four luminous deposits. If you then press west, following the road at the base of the cliff toward the Eldin Great Skeleton, there are many more deposits, including rare ones. It's a quick and very profitable run.
Hateno Tower	Face east on the tower, then glide down and scour the cliffs for deposits. There are more on the ground below, close to the river (including one rare).
Ishto Soh Shrine (Lake Tower Region)	Visit the pool southwest of the shrine to find five luminous deposits.
Joloo Nah Shrine (Gerudo Canyon)	Run south to find four deposits at the base of the east cliff. Continue further south and peer over the ledge just before the broken bridge to locate two more (one rare) just below.
Kah Mael Shrine (Akkala)	Three deposits (one rare) await on the east side of the rock outcrop south of the shrine.
Kah Okeo Shrine (Tabantha)	You can find three luminous deposits a short walk north of the grotto where the shrine is hidden, and six normal nodes (one rare) to the southeast; stay close to the cliffs on the east side to spot them.
Kam Urog Shrine (Hateno)	The cliff walls surrounding the shrine are dotted with ore, including two rare deposits. It's much easier to mine them if you have bomb arrows to spare; you could also use the Travel Medallion to create a useful warp position above.
Ke'nai Shakah Shrine (Akkala)	You can find half a dozen deposits (including a rare one) outside the shrine, on the cliffs across the chasm.
Kuh Takkar Shrine (Gerudo Highlands)	Five luminous deposits are found directly behind the shrine.
Monya Toma Shrine (Ridgeland)	Six luminous deposits are scattered on the rocks behind the shrine.
Shee Vaneer Shrine (Dueling Peaks)	Glide down to the lower area just east of the shrine to find five deposits (one rare). From here, you can explore the ledges below that run parallel to the road and river to find many more.
Sho Dantu Shrine (Gerudo)	There are four luminous deposits just outside the shrine.
Tabantha Tower	There are five luminous deposits on the north side of Nero Hill, and five standard nodes a little further to the east – but you'll need to evade (or disguise yourself from) numerous enemies to mine the latter. Keep pressing east and you will find six more deposits hidden behind destructible rocks just before you reach Tanagar Canyon.

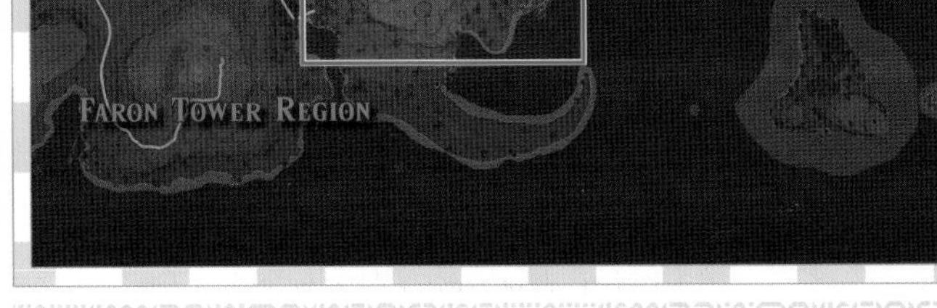

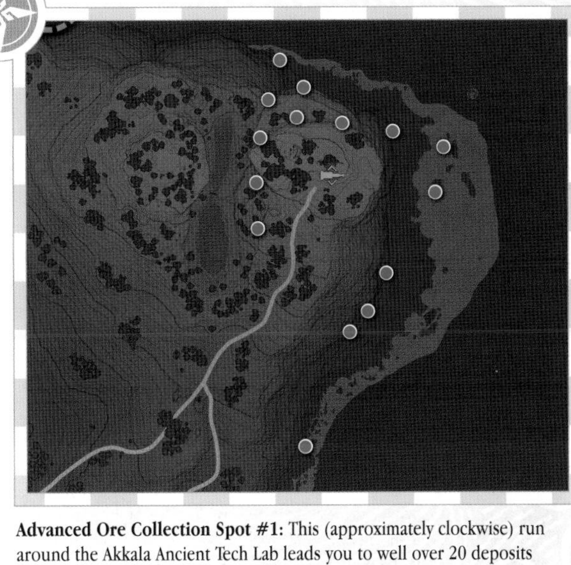
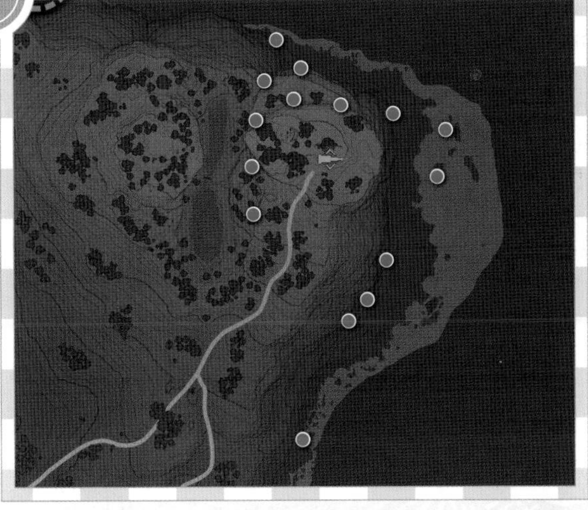

Advanced Ore Collection Spot #1: This (approximately clockwise) run around the Akkala Ancient Tech Lab leads you to well over 20 deposits (including four rare) in a few minutes. If you don't actively relish fighting Guardian Stalkers, avoid the deposits at the south of North Akkala Beach – there are two that wander the sands there.

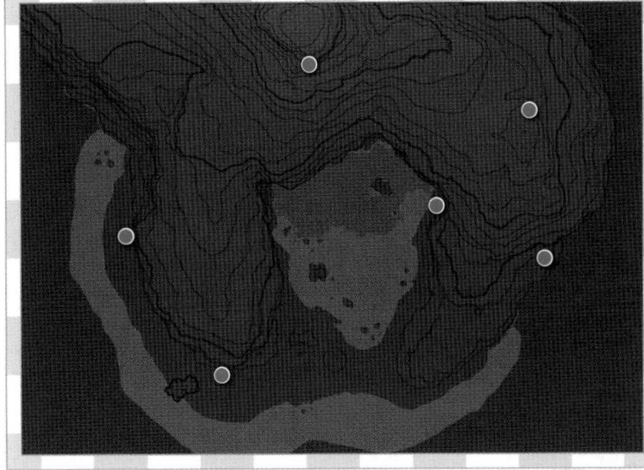
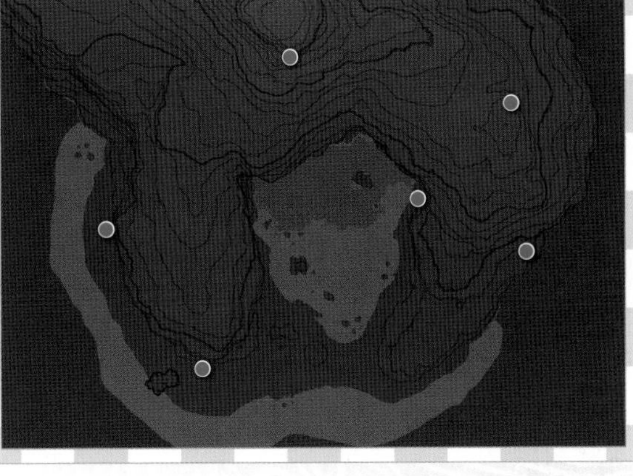

Advanced Ore Collection Spot #2: You can glide to this location, east of Hateno Beach and Deepback Bay, from the Hateno Ancient Tech Lab. There are 24 deposits (including two rare) and a Talus in the pool at the center.

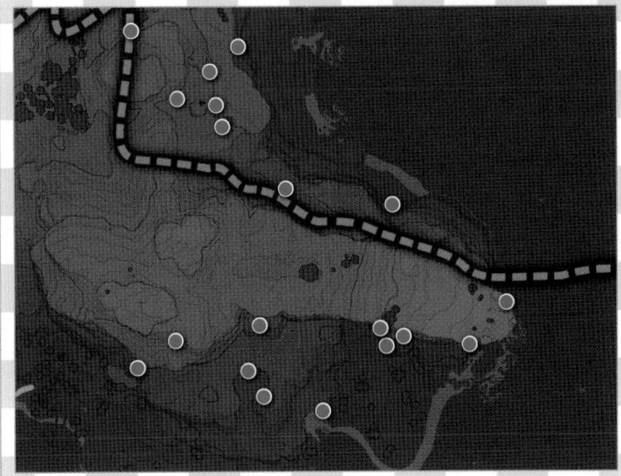

Advanced Ore Collection Spot #3: This is a slower but very profitable farming run. Fast travel to the Muwo Jeem Shrine on Cape Cales (east of Lurelin Village); you'll warp back to it several times while clearing the cliffs beneath it, which are also a ready source of bird eggs. There's a Talus in Gama Cove to the south of the cape's base and, north of that, a cave surrounded by water that is literally packed with ore. In the area with two pools northwest of Cape Cales, the ore actually appears in a giant cave with a Hinox at the center. A little further northwest, the final major ore collection is above, in a cave close to a giant tree.

Amiibo Overview

For those who collect amiibo, *Breath of the Wild* has a wide range of potential bonus treasures. To avoid interfering with the natural difficulty curve of a playthrough, certain rewards – particularly armor sets and weapons – are not available until you leave the Great Plateau. Others remain locked until you free at least one Divine Beast. As a general rule, with the partial exception of Wolf Link, you can scan each applicable amiibo once per day.

COMPATIBLE AMIIBO & REWARDS*

IMAGE	AMIIBO (SERIES)	REWARDS
	Link – Majora's Mask *(The Legend of Zelda)*	Fierce Deity Sword, Fierce Deity Boots, Fierce Deity Armor, Fierce Deity Mask; can also drop swords, arrows and assorted mushrooms.
	Link – Skyward Sword *(The Legend of Zelda)*	Goddess Sword, Trousers of the Sky, Tunic of the Sky, Cap of the Sky; assorted weapons, arrows and shields.
	Wolf Link *(The Legend of Zelda)*	Summons Wolf Link. He will attack enemies on his own and help you find items you're searching for. Wolf Link has three hearts by default, which makes him more suited for less dangerous locales where his powers of detection and distraction are of paramount value. You can spawn him as often as you like, but he will be unavailable for an entire day should he fall to mishap or monster alike. However, it's possible to boost his endurance by excelling in the Cave of Trials in Twilight Princess HD on the Wii U.
	Link – Twilight Princess *(The Legend of Zelda)*	Trousers of Twilight, Tunic of Twilight, Cap of Twilight; assorted weapons, arrows and foodstuffs. Each amiibo also summons Epona on the first scan. She is technically a wild horse at this stage, so you will need to immediately register her at a stable. It may take many scans for her to appear again if you lose her! Epona is unique in that her gallop duration per command is longer than any other horse in Hyrule.
	Link *(Super Smash Bros)*	
	Ganondorf *(Super Smash Bros.)*	Sword of the Six Sages; chest may contain valuable star fragments and Lynel guts, as well as assorted swords.
	Sheik *(Super Smash Bros.)*	Sheik's Mask; chest containing assorted weapons, arrows and food.
	Zelda *(Super Smash Bros.)*	Twilight Bow, plus other potential bow types, high-value gemstones and foodstuffs. Chance to spawn a star fragment. The Twilight Bow cannot spawn until you free one Divine Beast.
	Toon Link *(Super Smash Bros.)*	Trousers of the Wind, Tunic of the Wind, Cap of the Wind, Sea-Breeze Boomerang; chest contains assorted equipment, arrows and foodstuffs.
	Toon Link – The Wind Waker *(30th Anniversary – The Legend of Zelda)*	
	Link – The Legend of Zelda *(30th Anniversary – The Legend of Zelda)*	Trousers of the Hero, Tunic of the Hero, Cap of the Hero, Sword; assorted weapons, arrows and a chance of rupees.

IMAGE	AMIIBO (SERIES)	REWARDS
	Link – Ocarina of Time *(30th Anniversary – The Legend of Zelda)*	Trousers of Time, Tunic of Time, Cap of Time, Biggoron's Sword; chest containing equipment, arrows and foodstuffs. Biggoron's Sword cannot spawn until you leave the Great Plateau.
	Zelda – The Wind Waker *(30th Anniversary – The Legend of Zelda)*	Hero's Shield; chance to drop equipment, gemstones and ingredients. May drop a star fragment.
	Bokoblin *(The Legend of Zelda: Breath of the Wild)*	Can drop Boko weapons, meat and Bokoblin guts.
	Guardian *(The Legend of Zelda: Breath of the Wild)*	Can drop ancient weapons and shields, ancient arrows, and both types of ancient core; can also drop rusty weapons, ancient materials and gemstones.
	Link (Archer) *(The Legend of Zelda: Breath of the Wild)*	Can drop bows, arrows, and a wide variety of foodstuffs.
	Link (Rider) *(The Legend of Zelda: Breath of the Wild)*	Traveler's Bridle, Traveler's Saddle; can also drop swords, arrows and assorted mushrooms.
	Zelda *(The Legend of Zelda: Breath of the Wild)*	Can drop equipment, gems and ingredients; can spawn a star fragment.
	Daruk *(The Legend of Zelda: Breath of the Wild)*	Vah Rudania Divine Helm (Flame Guard); Goron weapon; assorted gemstones.
	Mipha *(The Legend of Zelda: Breath of the Wild)*	Vah Ruta Divine Helm (Swim Speed Up); Zora spear; diamond; assorted fishes.
	Revali *(The Legend of Zelda: Breath of the Wild)*	Vah Medoh Divine Helm (Cold Resistance); Rito bow; diamond; assorted arrows and fruits.
	Urbosa *(The Legend of Zelda: Breath of the Wild)*	Vah Naboris Divine Helm (Shock Resistance); Gerudo sword; Gerudo shield; diamond; assorted meats.

* amiibo not directly related to the *Zelda* universe will drop assorted foodstuffs.

MERCHANTS

Though Link can harvest, scavenge, seize or hunt practically everything he might ever need while exploring Hyrule, the many merchants that he encounters during his travels do, on occasion, offer deals of interest. You are free to pore over the tables that follow and judge every potential purchase yourself, but we would draw your attention to the following opportunities in particular:

- Beedle sells **smotherwing butterflies** at the Wetland Stable and East Akkala Stable. Given the effort of catching these in the Eldin region, this service is almost enough to warrant forgiveness for his incessant beetle-related pestering. *Almost*.
- For **standard arrows**, the 35 rupees per 10 arrows price offered by the Slippery Falcon at Tarrey Town (once open – see page 232), Jini at the Mounted Archery Camp and wandering merchant Botrick in rainy conditions are the best deals you can get.
- Danda in Gerudo Town and the Tarrey Town's Slippery Falcon are by far your best choices for quickly stocking up on **bomb arrows** and **elemental arrows**. However, Danda's bundles of 20 bomb arrows are unique in Hyrule, and remarkably cheap – only Jini at the Mounted Archery Camp technically offers them for less, but his five for 50 rupees deal is only available once per visit.
- Whenever it rains during your visits to the Necluda region, make haste to barter with Teli. He sells a single **ancient core** when the weather is inclement, which – over time – will remove a principal supply bottleneck that might prevent you from purchasing valuable ancient equipment from Cherry in Akkala.
- **Goron spice** and **bird eggs** are second only to dragon body parts in terms of the duration extension they provide to meal-induced status effects. The former can only be purchased from vendors; the latter involves lots of tree-climbing and cliff exploration to gather in the wild. If money is no object, it's a good idea to stockpile them whenever you meet a merchant who sells them.

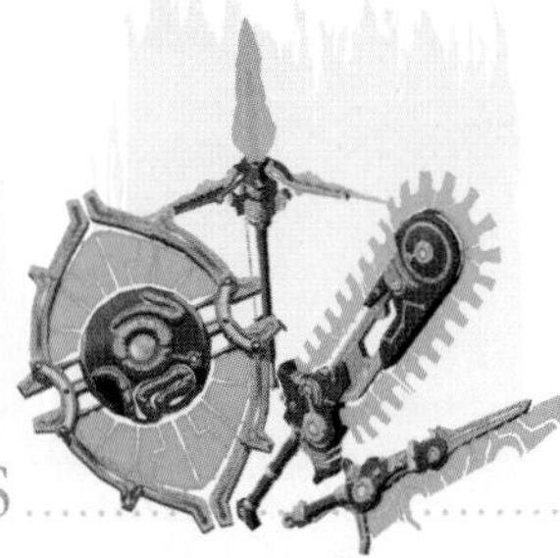

FIXED MERCHANTS

AKKALA ANCIENT TECH LAB (CHERRY)

ITEM	RUPEES	MATERIAL COST
Ancient Arrow	90	Ancient Screw x2, Ancient Shaft x1, Arrow x1
Ancient Arrow x3	250	Ancient Screw x6, Ancient Shaft x3, Arrow x3
Ancient Arrow x5	400	Ancient Spring x5, Ancient Shaft x5, Arrow x5
Ancient Short Sword	1,000	Ancient Spring x15, Ancient Shaft x5, Ancient Core x2
Ancient Shield	1,000	Ancient Gear x10, Ancient Spring x15, Giant Ancient Core x1
Ancient Bladesaw	1,000	Ancient Screw x15, Ancient Shaft x5, Ancient Core x2
Ancient Spear	1,000	Ancient Gear x15, Ancient Shaft x5, Ancient Core x2
Ancient Bow	1,000	Ancient Gear x10, Ancient Spring x15, Giant Ancient Core x1
Ancient Helm	2,000	Ancient Gear x20, Ancient Shaft x5, Ancient Core x3
Ancient Cuirass	2,000	Ancient Gear x20, Ancient Screw x5, Ancient Core x3
Ancient Greaves	2,000	Ancient Gear x20, Ancient Spring x5, Ancient Core x3

GERUDO TOWN

VENDOR	STOCK	RUPEES	QUANTITY
Ardin	**Chillshroom**	16	1
	Ironshroom	20	1
	Razorshroom	20	1
	Sunshroom	16	1
	Zapshroom	16	1
Danda	**Arrow x5**	20	3
	Bomb Arrow x20	600	3
	Fire Arrow x10	140	3
	Ice Arrow x10	140	3
	Shock Arrow x10	140	3
Estan	**Seared Gourmet Steak**	140	1
	Seared Prime Steak	58	1
	Seared Steak	30	1
Fashion Passion	**Gerudo Sirwal**	180	1
	Gerudo Top	180	1
	Gerudo Veil	180	1
Gerudo Secret Club	**Desert Voe Headband**	450	1
	Desert Voe Spaulder	1,300	1
	Desert Voe Trousers	650	1
	Radiant Mask	800*	1
	Radiant Shirt	800*	1
	Radiant Tights	800*	1
Lorn	**Hearty Durian**	60	3
	Hydromelon	16	3
	Voltfruit	16	3
Spera	**Hylian Rice**	12	2
	Rock Salt	12	2
	Tabantha Wheat	12	3
Starlight Memories	**Amber Earrings****	100	-
	Diamond Circlet**	1,500	-
	Opal Earrings**	200	-
	Ruby Circlet**	500	-
	Sapphire Circlet**	800	-
	Topaz Earrings**	500	-

* Three luminous stones are also required to purchase each part of the set.

** A set quantity of the relevant item type must be supplied for each purchase: 10 pieces of amber, 3 diamonds, 8 opals, 3 rubies, 3 sapphires, and 5 pieces of topaz.

FIXED MERCHANTS (CONTINUED)

GORON CITY

VENDOR	STOCK	RUPEES	QUANTITY
Goron Gusto Shop	Cane Sugar	12	3
	Fire Arrow	20	3
	Goron Spice	16	3
	Ice Arrow	20	3
	Rock Salt	12	3
Protein Palace	Roasted Bass	23	1
	Seared Steak	30	1
	Toasty Hylian Shroom	12	1
Ripped and Shredded	Flamebreaker Armor	600	-
	Flamebreaker Boots	700	-
	Flamebreaker Helm	2,000	-

HATENO VILLAGE

VENDOR	STOCK	RUPEES	QUANTITY
East Wind	Arrow x5	20	3
	Bird Egg	12	5
	Bomb Arrow	50	5
	Bomb Arrow x10	350	3
	Endura Shroom	24	2
	Fresh Milk	12	3
	Hearty Truffle	24	2
	Hylian Rice	12	5
Ventest Clothing	Hylian Hood	60	-
	Hylian Trousers	90	-
	Hylian Tunic	120	-
	Soldier's Armor	250	-
	Soldier's Greaves	200	-
	Soldier's Helm	180	-
	Warm Doublet	80	-

KAKARIKO VILLAGE

VENDOR	STOCK	RUPEES	QUANTITY
Curious Quiver	Arrow	5	10
	Arrow x5	20	2
	Fire Arrow	20	10
	Fire Arrow x5	80	2
High Spirits Produce	Bird Egg	12	5
	Bokoblin Guts	80	3
	Goat Butter	12	5
	Swift Carrot	16	12
Enchanted	Hylian Hood	60	-
	Hylian Trousers	90	-
	Hylian Tunic	120	-
	Stealth Chest Guard	700	-
	Stealth Mask	500	-
	Stealth Tights	600	-
Olkin	Fortified Pumpkin	20	8

RITO VILLAGE

VENDOR	STOCK	RUPEES	QUANTITY
Brazen Beak	Snowquill Headdress	1,000	-
	Snowquill Trousers	550	-
	Snowquill Tunic	600	-
Slippery Falcon	Arrow x5	20	3
	Bomb Arrow x5	200	5
	Cane Sugar	12	3
	Goat Butter	12	5
	Sunshroom	16	4
	Tabantha Wheat	12	3

KARA KARA BAZAAR

VENDOR	STOCK	RUPEES	QUANTITY
Emri	Hydromelon	16	7
	Mighty Bananas	20	1
	Palm Fruit	16	1
Maike	Lizalfos Tail	112	1
	Roasted Bass	23	1
	Seared Steak	30	1
Shaillu	Arrow	5	1
	Bomb Arrow	50	1
	Fire Arrow	20	1
	Ice Arrow	20	1
	Shock Arrow	20	1

KOROK FOREST

VENDOR	STOCK	RUPEES	QUANTITY
General Shoppe	Apple	12	1
	Arrow x5	20	3
	Cane Sugar	12	3
	Hearty Radish	32	1
	Hylian Rice	12	3
	Shock Arrow x5	80	3
Spore Store	Hearty Truffle	24	1
	Ironshroom	20	4
	Razorshroom	20	4
	Rushroom	12	4
	Stamella Shroom	20	4

LURELIN VILLAGE

VENDOR	STOCK	RUPEES	QUANTITY
Mubs	Armored Porgy	40	3
	Arrow x5	20	3
	Ironshell Crab	32	3
	Mighty Porgy	40	3
	Octo Balloon	20	3
	Shock Arrow x10	140	3

TARREY TOWN

VENDOR	STOCK	RUPEES	QUANTITY
Ore and More	Diamond	2,000	1
	Ruby	840	1
	Sapphire	1,040	1
	Topaz	720	1
Rhondson Armor	Desert Voe Headband	450	-
	Desert Voe Spaulder	1,300	-
	Desert Voe Trousers	650	-
Slippery Falcon (Tarrey Town Branch)	Ancient Gear	120	1
	Arrow x10	35	5
	Bomb Arrow x10	350	5
	Fire Arrow x10	140	5
	Ice Arrow x10	140	5
	Shock Arrow x10	140	5

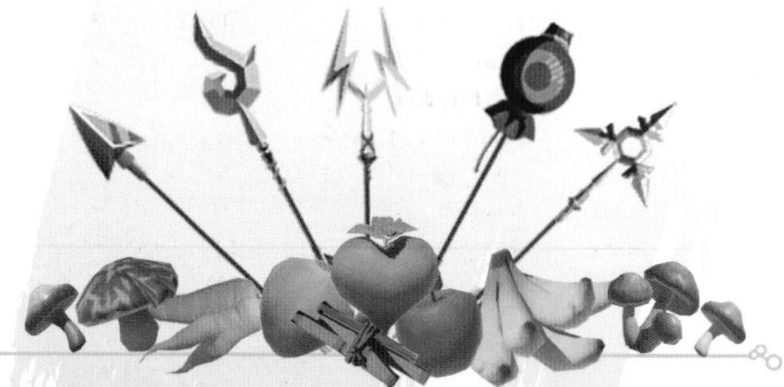

FIXED MERCHANTS (CONTINUED)

ZORA'S DOMAIN

VENDOR	STOCK	RUPEES	QUANTITY
Coral Reef	Arrow x5	20	3
	Chillfin Trout	24	2
	Hylian Rice	12	4
	Ice Arrow	20	5
	Ice Arrow x5	80	3
	Rock Salt	12	4
	Sizzlefin Trout	24	2
	Swift Violet	40	4

GRANTÉ

This special vendor appears once Tarrey Town is complete, but is not a traditional merchant. Instead, he can replace certain items that you might have lost or sold. You must have owned the item in question before, or he will not make it available for sale. The most likely use you will have for his services is to buy a new Hylian Shield after the one found in Hyrule Castle breaks. Note, however, that you can only carry one of these at a time.

GRANTÉ'S SHOP LIST

ITEM	RUPEES
Barbarian Armor	4,000
Barbarian Helm	4,000
Barbarian Leg Wraps	4,000
Climbing Bandana	4,000
Climbing Boots	4,000
Climbing Gear	4,000
Hylian Shield	3,000
Island Lobster Shirt	50
Old Shirt	50
Phantom Ganon Armor	50
Phantom Ganon Greaves	50
Phantom Ganon Skull	50
Ravio's Hood	50

ITEM	RUPEES
Royal Guard Boots	50
Royal Guard Cap	50
Royal Guard Uniform	50
Rubber Armor	4,000
Rubber Helm	4,000
Rubber Tights	4,000
Salvager Headwear	50
Salvager Trousers	50
Salvager Vest	50
Sand Boots	800
Snow Boots	800
Well-Worn Trousers	50
Zant's Helmet	50

BEEDLE

Beedle is found at all stables, and can also be encountered roaming around at Kara Kara Bazaar in the Gerudo Desert. To avoid needless repetition in the table that follows, you should take it as read that he has 20 single arrows in stock at six rupees per piece at each destination. If you own beetles, Beedle will offer you trades in exchange for elixirs. You will need 15 energetic rhino beetles to upgrade the "of the Wind" armor set, so we suggest you decline his offer until you have gathered all you need.

BEEDLE'S SHOP LIST

VENDOR	STOCK	RUPEES	QUANTITY
Dueling Peaks Stable	Arrow x5	30	2
	Hot-Footed Frog	10	3
	Octo Balloon	20	3
	Restless Cricket	10	5
East Akkala Stable	Arrow x10	45	1
	Hearty Radish	32	2
	Smotherwing Butterfly	10	3
	Swift Carrot	16	3
Foothill Stable	Arrow x5	30	2
	Hearty Lizard	100	5
	Tireless Frog	100	5

BEEDLE'S SHOP LIST (CONTINUED)

VENDOR	STOCK	RUPEES	QUANTITY
Gerudo Canyon Stable	Arrow x10	45	2
	Hearty Lizard	100	2
	Warm Darner	10	5
	Winterwing Butterfly	10	5
Highland Stable	Arrow x10	45	1
	Hearty Lizard	100	1
	Octo Balloon	20	5
	Sunset Firefly	10	3
Kara Kara Bazaar	Arrow x10	45	1
	Cold Darner	10	5
	Summerwing Butterfly	10	5
	Tireless Frog	100	3
Lakeside Stable	Arrow x5	30	1
	Hightail Lizard	10	2
	Thunderwing Butterfly	10	3
	Tireless Frog	100	2
Outskirt Stable	Arrow x5	30	2
	Hearty Lizard	100	3
	Hot-Footed Frog	10	3
	Restless Cricket	10	5
Rito Stable	Arrow x10	45	1
	Sunset Firefly	10	3
	Tireless Frog	100	2
	Warm Darner	10	3
Riverside Stable	Arrow x5	30	1
	Electric Darner	10	3
	Thunderwing Butterfly	10	3
	Tireless Frog	100	3
Serenne Stable	Arrow x10	45	1
	Sunset Firefly	10	4
	Tireless Frog	100	2
	Warm Darner	10	4
Snowfield Stable	Arrow x10	45	1
	Summerwing Butterfly	10	3
	Tireless Frog	100	2
	Warm Darner	10	3
South Akkala Stable	Arrow x10	45	1
	Fireproof Lizard	25	2
	Hearty Lizard	100	2
	Hightail Lizard	10	3
Tabantha Bridge Stable	Arrow x10	45	1
	Summerwing Butterfly	10	3
	Thunderwing Butterfly	10	3
	Winterwing Butterfly	10	3
Wetland Stable	Arrow x5	30	1
	Hot-Footed Frog	10	3
	Smotherwing Butterfly	10	3
	Tireless Frog	100	2
Woodland Stable	Arrow x5	30	1
	Cold Darner	10	3
	Hearty Lizard	100	1
	Sunset Firefly	10	3

KILTON

When you first meet this singular individual at Skull Lake in Akkala (see page 342), Kilton's shop appears close to all major settlements in Hyrule at night. His inventory is determined by your progress with the Divine Beasts, and purchased by exchanging monster parts for his very specific form of scrip, called "mon".

KILTON'S SHOP LIST

STORY PROGRESS	STOCK	MON	QUANTITY
No Divine Beasts liberated	Bokoblin Mask	99	-
	Monster Extract	9	5
	Wooden Mop	19	-
One Divine Beast liberated	Moblin Mask	199	-
	Spring-Loaded Hammer	199	-
Two Divine Beasts liberated	Lizalfos Mask	299	-
	Monster Bridle	399	-
	Monster Extract (stock increased)	9	10
	Monster Saddle	299	-
Three Divine Beasts liberated	Lynel Mask	999	-
Four Divine Beasts liberated	Dark Hood	1,999	-
	Dark Trousers	999	-
	Dark Tunic	999	-
	Monster Extract (stock increased)	9	20

WANDERING MERCHANTS

Most commonly found close to stables, but occasionally encountered further afield on the roads that lead to them, many of these itinerant hucksters change their inventory in accordance with the weather: one set of stock when conditions are clear, and another when it is raining or snowing. In the relatively few instances where the cost or quantity of goods available in all conditions varies, the figure for wet or snowy weather is the second, parenthesized total.

AGUS*

STOCK	RUPEES	QUANTITY
Bird Egg	12 (10)	2
Fresh Milk	12 (10)	2
Goat Butter	12 (10)	2

* Between Dueling Peaks and Hateno Village.

BOTRICK*

CONDITIONS	STOCK	RUPEES	QUANTITY
All	Arrow	5	10
	Fire Arrow	20	5
	Fire Arrow x5	80	2 (3)
Dry	Arrow x5	20	3
Wet	Arrow x10	35	3
	Ice Arrow x5	80	3

* On the road north or south of Outskirt Stable.

BUGUT*

CONDITIONS	STOCK	RUPEES	QUANTITY
Dry	Bright-Eyed Crab	40	3
	Energetic Rhino Beetle	150	1
	Stamella Shroom	20	3
	Staminoka Bass	72	1
Wet	Endura Carrot	120	1
	Endura Shroom	24	3
	Tireless Frog	100	1

* Between Kakariko Village and Dueling Peaks Stable.

CAMBO*

CONDITIONS	STOCK	RUPEES	QUANTITY
All	Fortified Pumpkin	20	3
	Raw Meat	32	2 (3)
	Hearty Truffle	24	2
Dry	Swift Carrot	16	3
Wet	Big Hearty Truffle	60	1
	Raw Prime Meat	60	2

* On short road beyond Kakariko Village's south gate, or on the road leading south from Wetland Stable.

CHUMIN*

CONDITIONS	STOCK	RUPEES	QUANTITY
All	Armored Porgy	40	3
	Hearty Durian	60	5
	Mighty Porgy	40	3
	Palm Fruit	16	5
Dry	Bright-Eyed Crab	40	3
Wet	Hearty Blueshell Snail	60	3

* On the roads that link Highland Stable, Lakeside Stable and Lurelin Village.

GARTAN*

STOCK	RUPEES	QUANTITY
Arrow	5	20
Acorn	8	10
Apple	12	10
Restless Cricket	10	5

* Between Gerudo Canyon Stable and Gerudo Town.

GIRO*

CONDITIONS	STOCK	RUPEES	QUANTITY
All	Arrow x5	20	3
	Hearty Truffle	24	2
	Rock Salt	12	5
Dry	Stamella Shroom	20	3
	Swift Carrot	16	3
Wet	Big Hearty Truffle	60	1
	Swift Violet	40	2

* Camped by the giant stone pillar southwest of the Dueling Peaks Tower.

WANDERING MERCHANTS (CONTINUED)

JINI*

CONDITIONS	STOCK	RUPEES	QUANTITY
All	Arrow	5	10
	Arrow x5	20	5
	Arrow x10	35	5
Dry	Bomb Arrow x5	50	5
Wet	Shock Arrow x5	80	3

* At the Mounted Archery Camp; you'll need to be riding a registered horse to barter.

KAIRO*

STOCK	RUPEES	QUANTITY
Amber	60	1
Opal	80	1
Ruby	420	1
Sapphire	520	1
Topaz	360	1

* Paces the road north of Foothill Stable; stops before the first Guardian Stalker.

KANNY*

CONDITIONS	STOCK	RUPEES	QUANTITY
Dry	Chillshroom	16	3
	Stamella Shroom	20	1
	Sunshroom	16	3
	Zapshroom	16	3
Rain/Snow	Big Hearty Truffle	60	1
	Endura Shroom	24	3
	Hearty Truffle	24	2
	Ironshroom	20	3
	Razorshroom	20	3

* Paces the road that leads between Rito Stable, Snowfield Stable and Serenne Stable.

MEZER*

CONDITIONS	STOCK	RUPEES	QUANTITY
All	Raw Meat	32	3
	Rock Salt	12	3
Dry	Raw Bird Drumstick	32	3
	Raw Bird Thigh	60	1
	Raw Prime Meat	60	1
Wet	Raw Bird Thigh	60	3
	Raw Gourmet Meat	140	1
	Raw Prime Meat	60	3

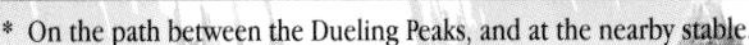

* On the path between the Dueling Peaks, and at the nearby stable.

STAMM*

CONDITIONS	STOCK	RUPEES	QUANTITY
All	Fleet-Lotus Seeds	20	1 (2)
	Sizzlefin Trout	24	1 (2)
Dry	Raw Prime Meat	60	2
	Razorshroom	20	1
Wet	Goron Spice	16	1
	Ironshroom	20	2
	Raw Gourmet Meat	140	2

* On the road east of South Akkala Stable.

TELI*

CONDITIONS	STOCK	RUPEES	QUANTITY
All	Ancient Gear	120	1 (2)
	Ancient Screw	48	1 (2)
	Ancient Spring	60	1 (2)
Wet	Ancient Core	320	1
	Ancient Shaft	160	1

* Between Fort Hateno and Hateno Village.

YAMMO*

CONDITIONS	STOCK	RUPEES	QUANTITY
All	Hylian Rice	14 (12)	5
	Tabantha Wheat	14 (12)	10
Dry	Bird Egg	13	5
	Goat Butter	14	5
Rain/Snow	Cane Sugar	12	5
	Fresh Milk	12	10
	Goron Spice	16	5

* Travels along the road that links Tabantha Bridge Stable, Serenne Stable and Snowfield Stable.

OTHER VENDORS

- Gaile at Foothill Stable sells Level 1 **fireproof elixirs** with a 6:10 duration. You can buy one for 60 rupees, two for 110 rupees, or three for 150 rupees.
- Maypin meanders along the path either side of Gerudo Canyon Stable, offering **warm darners** and **cold darners** for 10 rupees apiece. She stocks three of each.
- In Goron City, Offrak sells Level 1 **fireproof elixirs** (duration 6:30) for 60 rupees.
- Russ can be found by the giant tree on top of the hill north of Zelo Pond. He sells a **wooden shield** for 30 rupees, a **soldier's shield** for 100 rupees, and a **knight's shield** for 300 rupees. Speaking to him triggers a shield surfing tutorial page. He does not restock items that you buy.
- Distinct from other instances of the nefarious "Traveler" that you meet on Hyrule's highways and byways, there are two that pose as merchants: one at the junction east of Floria Bridge en route to Tuft Mountain or Lurelin Village, the other on the road halfway between Zelo Pond and the Soh Kofi Shrine in the north of the Lanayru Wetlands. These sell **mighty bananas** at 99 rupees per piece, with 99 in stock. At that price, however, you will be wise to forgo the opportunity and end the charade by defeating either charlatan posthaste.

MISCELLANY

ELITE HORSES

While most players will be perfectly happy with one of the three unique horses that can be found in Hyrule – the white horse (see page 269), the giant horse (see page 247) and, with the appropriate amiibo, Epona (see page 366) – it is actually possible to catch two wild horses that are arguably superior, including one unique specimen that has the highest possible 5-star speed rating.

To do so, you'll need to visit two very specific places where these particular steeds can spawn: the Taobab Grassland (glide southwest of the Owa Daim shrine on the Great Plateau), and the gentle sloped meadow northwest of Lindor's Brow (the hill north of the Ridgeland Tower).

A trip to the north of the **Taobab Grassland** (which is also the spawn point of the unique giant horse) makes the catching process much easier, as you can identify your target from a position on the surrounding cliffs and glide down to land on it. The drawback to this locale is that you must then ride your new (but decidedly wild) horse all the way to the Highland Stable to register it – a route that will take you past two Lynels and a small horde of mounted Bokoblins before you arrive at the relative safety of the road heading east from the Mounted Archery Camp. If you have the Expansion Pass and the Master Trials DLC pack installed, we advise the use of Majora's Mask (or, failing that, suitable disguises purchased from Kilton) to avoid an unhappy premature end to your journey.

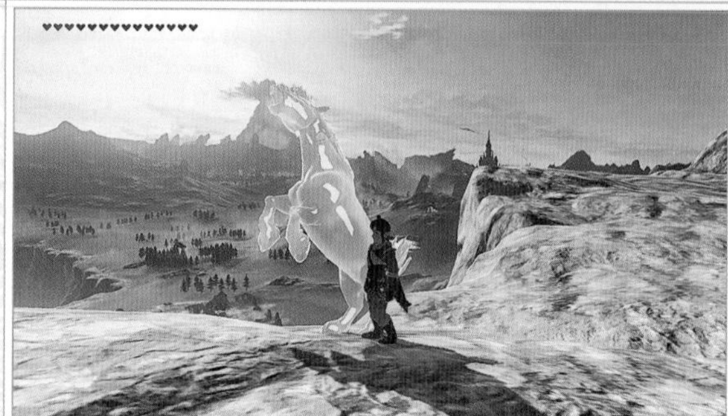

If you opt for the **Lindor's Brow** location, the quickest way to get there is to fast travel to the Maag No'rah Shrine (just north of the Ridgeland Tower) and climb up. If you then look towards Tanagar Canyon, you should see a small herd on the grassland to the northwest. Gliding is not always an option here (unless you have a charge of Revali's Gale available, of course), but there is another trick that you can employ: if you freeze a horse with an ice arrow (using your weakest bow), you will have sufficient time to approach it and prepare to mount the moment it thaws. You can then ride it down the slope north of Lindor's Brow to reach the Serenne Stable.

You cannot know a horse's exact stats until you register it, but there are a few clues that will make your search much easier:

- The horse must have a single body color, though its mane and tail can be of another hue. This should narrow down your choices to no more than a handful of targets at either potential habitat.
- Horses have three primary attributes: strength, speed and stamina. The fastest horse in the game is rated 2/5/3. If you catch one and find that it has a three-part dash gauge, you may well have caught this rare beast. Your first gallop should confirm it – it's *extremely* quick.
- If your horse has a five-part dash gauge, it can be one of two possible types: a 5/3/5 "strong" archetype that is nice to own, but is rendered rather obsolete by the giant horse, or the 4/4/5 "balanced" variety that offers a great blend of survivability, speed and stamina. You'll need to take it to a stable to know for sure.

HORSE TRIVIA

- All horses have an attack rating of 5, with the exception of the giant horse, which has 10 (as befits its monstrous frame). High-speed collisions will kill smaller monsters and animals outright, knock standard monsters from their feet, and can even bowl over Guardians if you angle your approach correctly. Their strength rating, meanwhile, is an approximate measure of their total HP, which can range from 90 to 300.
- Even though the giant horse cannot dash, its long legs make its default gallop surprisingly fast.
- Epona (only available if you have the appropriate amiibo) has two special attributes: she has a gentle temperament (while all other fast horses in Hyrule are classified as "wild"), and has a slightly longer dash duration than any other steed.
- Once you have caught a horse, you can dismount and feed it apples or carrots to increase its bond with Link. To do so, stand in front of the horse while carrying the fruit or vegetables in your hands. Endura Carrots have the unique effect of adding bonus dash gauge portions that are used only when the horse would otherwise be exhausted.
- Horse HP is restored whenever you see a loading screen. If there's a danger that your steed might fall when assailed, fast traveling to any position in Hyrule could save you a trip to the Horse God.
- The in-game lore suggests that the white horse is a descendent of Zelda's steed from 100 years before. The giant horse found at Taobab Grassland, meanwhile, is very similar in stature and coloration to Ganon's horse in Ocarina of Time.

COLISEUM UPGRADES

Unlike other monsters of their ilk in Hyrule, the Bokoblins, Moblins, Lizalfos and single Lynel found in the Coliseum Ruins southwest of Hyrule Field are not upgraded in accordance with the hidden "world level" counter, but by your progress in liberating Divine Beasts.

By default, the minor enemies inside the Coliseum Ruins carry soldier weaponry until you complete two Divine Beast dungeons, at which point their gear is upgraded to knight grade. At three Divine Beasts liberated, they wield royal equipment.

The most interesting upgrade occurs once you complete your final Divine Beast dungeon. After you pass this threshold, the Bokoblins wield fire weapons, the Lizalfos have ice weapons, and the Moblins wield electrical weapons. If you become adept at creeping into the ruins from above and eliminating individuals with sneakstrikes, the Coliseum Ruins can supplement your elemental weapon requirements in late-story play.

The resident Lynel, meanwhile, is upgraded by one level with each Divine Beast liberated after the first. The final version is a Silver Lynel (gold in Master Mode) equipped with a flameblade, a sight you will not see anywhere else in Hyrule.

YIGA CLAN

The quest to free the Divine Beast Vah Naboris in the Gerudo Desert is unique in that it causes a new enemy type to appear in Hyrule: the Yiga Blademaster.

There are two stages to the proliferation of Yiga Clan assassins in Hyrule:

- **1.** Once you complete the Seek Out Impa quest, disguised assassins can appear in fixed positions. You can easily differentiate these from other NPCs you have already talked to, as they have no obvious name tag, and – if you study them closely – are prone to standing in a blatantly suspicious manner. These are very easy to avoid once you have an eye for spotting them.
- **2.** Once you defeat Master Kohga and return the Thunder Helm to Riju, Yiga Footsoldiers and Blademasters can attack Link at any time. The disguised "Traveler" variants that you encounter may also wield a stronger melee weapon.

Yiga assassins are more nuisance than danger once you have Stasis+, but the complications that they potentially introduce to general exploration make a compelling case for leaving Vah Naboris and the Gerudo storyline (from the point at which you actually visit the hideout) until last.

WORLD LEVEL, ENEMY RANKS & ITEM FARMING

There are very specific conditions that determine enemy rank upgrades during a playthrough. The concise explanation of how the system works is that every monster in the accompanying table adds a preset figure to a hidden counter whenever they die – even if Link is not actually the author of their downfall. When this tally reaches certain totals, specific enemies in the world are immediately upgraded by one rank. Though it's not something that you'll ever see happen with your own eyes, the transformation is actually instantaneous, and does not require a Blood Moon to take place.

Perhaps a little surprisingly, standard and blue grades of Bokoblins, Moblins, Lizalfos and their Stal variants are not counted – so they are always fair game, no matter your general approach to combat.

There is one additional rule that will be of huge interest to those who farm monsters and Guardians for equipment and drops: after you kill a particular variety 10 times, that very specific opponent will no longer contribute to the hidden counter. To be perfectly clear, a Guardian Scout III has a different counter to a Guardian Scout IV, just as a Silver Bokoblin is treated separately to a Black Bokoblin.

WORLD LEVEL COUNTER INCREMENTS PER DEATH

COUNTER INCREASE	MONSTER VARIETIES
Maximum	Calamity Ganon, Monk Maz Koshia*
Huge	Fireblight Ganon, Thunderblight Ganon, Waterblight Ganon, Windblight Ganon**
Very Large	Blue-Maned Lynel, Silver Lynel, White-Maned Lynel
Large	Black Hinox, Frost Talus, Guardian Scout IV, Guardian Skywatcher, Guardian Stalker, Guardian Turret, Igneo Talus, Lynel, Molduga, Silver Moblin
Medium	Black Lizalfos, Blue Hinox, Electric Lizalfos, Fire-Breath Lizalfos, Ice-Breath Lizalfos, Guardian Scout III, Silver Bokoblin, Silver Lizalfos, Stalnox, Stone Talus (Luminous), Stone Talus (Rare)
Small	Black Bokoblin, Black Moblin, Blizzrobe, Decayed Guardian, Hinox, Meteo Wizzrobe, Sentry, Stone Talus, Thunder Wizzrobe, Yiga Blademaster
Nominal	Electric Wizzrobe, Fire Wizzrobe, Ice Wizzrobe

* The increment applied for Calamity Ganon and Monk Maz Koshia only occurs after the first instance that you defeat them.

** The four "-blight" bosses only add to the counter when you defeat the incarnations that guard the Divine Beasts. Defeating them in Hyrule Castle has no impact on the world level tally.

MAPS

This chapter features detailed, annotated maps covering the entire kingdom of Hyrule. While the poster that comes with this guide provides a convenient general overview of the continent, the pages that follow are more akin to an atlas – a collection of expanded maps, each dedicated to a specific game area. You can use these as powerful tools to scour every inch of terrain and find all of the game's collectibles.

INTRODUCTION

This chapter offers expanded topographic maps of Hyrule. For each area, you will find detailed annotations revealing the position of all key points of interest and collectibles.

POINTS OF INTEREST

TOWERS are thin, tall structures. When you interact with the terminal at the top of these, you reveal the regional map and a new fast travel position.

SHRINES are self-contained locations that challenge you to solve all sorts of puzzles. Much like towers, they are high-priority targets in terms of exploration, gradually forming a network that enables you to warp to virtually anywhere on the map. Note that a few shrines are exclusive to the Champions' Ballad DLC pack (see page 452) – you can identify them by their unusually tall roof structure.

VILLAGES are hubs where you will find assorted amenities including shops, quest vendors, cooking pots, and goddess statues.

STABLES are smaller settlements where you can register horses that you have tamed in the wild.

ANCIENT TECH LABS are special buildings where you can upgrade your runes or purchase equipment of the Ancient type.

OTHER LANDMARKS are related to main quests or side quests.

COLLECTIBLES

KOROK SEEDS are collectibles that you obtain every time you find a Korok in the wild. The location of all 900 seeds is shown in this chapter. There are various types of mini-challenges that you must solve to reveal Koroks. Each challenge is associated with a specific icon, enabling you to know which kind of puzzle you need to be looking for whenever you approach a seed's location. Any path you might need to follow, where applicable, is represented by a thin line.

KOROK SEED LEGEND

ICON	CHALLENGE TYPE	DESCRIPTION (see page 330 for details)
△	**Rock Pattern**	Small rocks configured in a geometrical pattern, with at least one rock missing that you need to reposition to complete the arrangement.
▲	**Cube Pattern**	Small metal cubes arranged in symmetrical shapes, with one anomaly that you need to fix by repositioning a cube with Magnesis.
●	**Circles**	Objects (such as rocks or water lilies) arranged in a circle. You need to either throw a rock through it, or physically fall through it.
●	**Natural Hiding Spot**	Natural objects that hide a Korok. In most cases, you need to lift small rocks found on elevated spots. Sometimes you first need to remove an obstacle: a destructible wall, an ice block that you must melt…
▲	**Leaves with Fairy Dust**	Leaves with a fairy dust effect that you need to examine, either as they move along a set course, or in a fixed, usually elevated, position such as a spire.
▲	**Race**	A race triggered when you step on a tree stump, requiring you to reach a ring before the countdown ends.
▲	**Food Offering**	Groups of aligned statues with small trays in front of them, requiring you to drop the right type of food on all trays.
▲	**Flower Trails**	Trails of flowers that you need to follow as they appear, or in a logical order.
●	**Archery**	Balloons or acorns (or occasionally other targets) that you have to hit with arrows.
●	**Boulders**	One or more large boulders that need to be moved to specific positions (nearby holes, hollow tree stumps, wells), or arranged in a pattern.
●	**Tree Patterns**	Adjacent trees, one of which has extraneous fruit that needs to be removed to make it look like the others.

TREASURE CHESTS are abundant all over Hyrule. They each contain one item and disappear permanently once opened (with the exception of those on and around Eventide Island, which respawn after every loading screen). If you inadvertently destroy or lose a chest (making it fall into an abyss, for instance), they will reappear on a subsequent visit.

- **Chest Types:** There are five different treasure chest types.
  - **Metal chests** are sometimes found underwater, partly buried in the ground, or on seemingly inaccessible ledges. You can lift them with Magnesis, the rune also being the best way to spot them from a distance.
  - **Wooden chests** can burn, potentially setting ablaze their content. These chests are occasionally found floating on water surfaces: raise a pillar of ice underneath them using Cryonis to plunder them.
  - **Stone chests** are immoveable.
  - **Skull chests** are located in enemy camps. They are initially locked, emitting a purple glow. To open them, you first need to eliminate all local foes.
  - **EX chests** will only appear in your game if you purchase *Breath of the Wild*'s Expansion Pass.
- **Treasure Hunting:** One very useful tool when tracking down chests is the Sheikah sensor. From the Map menu, press Ⓨ and change your current target to treasure chests (assuming you have photographed one with the Camera rune). Every time a chest is detected in the sensor's three-dimensional radius, you can use the visual and audio cues to head toward it. Don't forget that chests are often very well hidden. You might need to adjust the camera angle or interact with the environment to reach them – they can, for example, lie under rock slabs that you can lift with an Octo balloon, behind thorns that you have to burn, under piles of leaves, behind waterfalls, and so forth.
- **Master Mode:** A number of chests are exclusive to Master Mode (unlocked by purchasing the game's Expansion Pass). These chests are typically found on well-defended Sky Octorok platforms (see page 422). They tend to contain high-value items, particularly if you open them early on in the adventure.
- **Chest Evolution:** Certain chests are affected by the "world level" (see page 373). This means that the pieces of equipment they contain improve as you progress in the game. They can either gain bonuses (such as increased attack for weapons), or turn into better items based on the following evolution lines:
  - "Traveler's" equipment ▷ "Soldier's" equipment ▷ "Knight's" equipment ▷ "Royal" equipment
  - Eightfold Longblade ▷ Edge of Duality
  - Cobble Crusher ▷ Stone Smasher
  - Zora Spear ▷ Silverscale Spear
  - Swallow Bow ▷ Falcon Bow
  - Gerudo Scimitar ▷ Moonlight Scimitar
  - Gerudo Shield ▷ Radiant Shield
  - Ice Rod ▷ Blizzard Rod
  - Lightning Rod ▷ Thunderstorm Rod
  - Fire Rod ▷ Meteor Rod
- **Chest Icons:** *Breath of the Wild* features well over 1,300 chests. Many of these yield common loot, such as low-value materials or rupees. To help you easily identify the ones with the best contents, we have clearly flagged them with specific icons. Broadly speaking, this includes items worth 200 rupees or more, unique pieces of armor, rare material such as Star Fragments and dragon parts, as well as powerful equipment that is upgraded as you progress in the game.

TREASURE CHEST LEGEND

ICON	ICON TYPE
	Common Loot
	Master Mode Chest
	Gold Rupee
	High-Value Gemstone
	Rare Material
	Fire-Elemental Weapon
	Ice-Elemental Weapon
	Lightning-Elemental Weapon
	Ancient Arrow
	Magic Arrow Bundle
	Notable One-Handed Weapon
	Notable Two-Handed Weapon
	Notable Spear
	Notable Bow
	Notable Shield
	Key Item
	Piece of Armor

FOOTNOTES

For the more hard-to-find Korok seeds and treasure chests, you will see footnotes throughout this chapter revealing where they are hidden and/or what needs to be achieved to reach them. You can easily connect a collectible position to its associated footnote by matching the numbered icon next to it. Note that these icons are color-coded: green for chests (◉), purple for Korok seeds (◉).

PAGE 384
ELDIN (WEST)

PAGE 385
ELDIN (EAST)

PAGE 386
AKKALA

PAGE 391
LANAYRU (WEST)

PAGE 392
LANAYRU (CENTER)

PAGE 393
LANAYRU (EAST)

PAGE 398
DUELING PEAKS

PAGE 399
HATENO (WEST)

PAGE 400
HATENO (EAST)

PAGE 405
FARON (WEST)

PAGE 406
FARON (EAST)

PAGE 407
NECLUDA SEA

The atlas that begins overleaf consists of 28 pages, each featuring a map corresponding to a portion of Hyrule. This overview offers a visual index of those 28 maps. If you are currently exploring a specific region, you can use this to jump immediately to the relevant page.

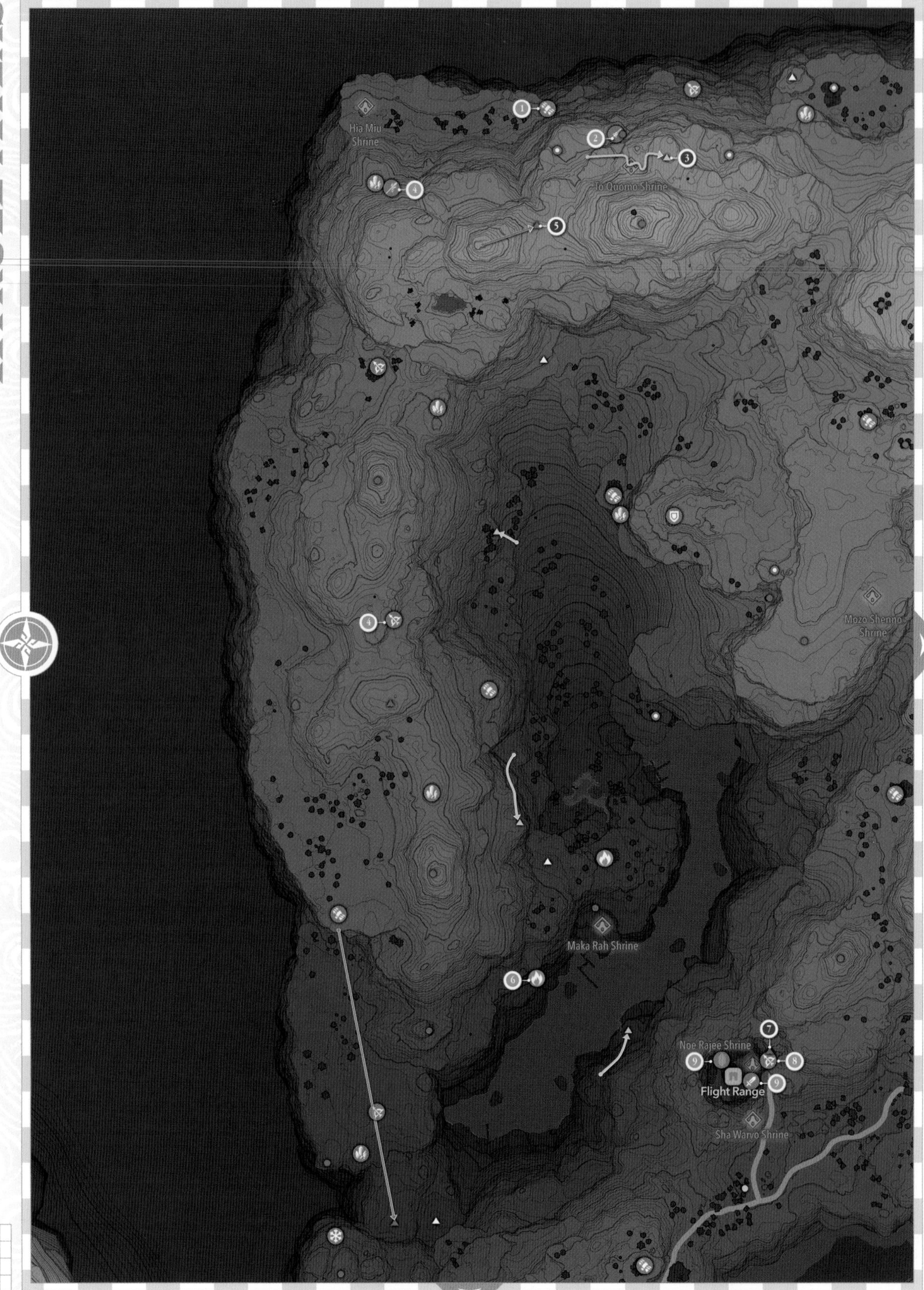

PAGE 387 – TABANTHA (WEST)

1. On the bottom ledge, inside the biggest ice block.
2. In the middle ice block.
3. In the cave where the To Quomo Shrine lies. The first flower grows at the base of the Great Skeleton spine.
4. Behind destructible rocks.
5. Requires you to shield-surf.
6. Halfway up the cliff, behind destructible rocks.
7. On the rooftop of the Flight Range's hut.
8. Reward for passing Teba's archery test during the main adventure.
9. Underwater.

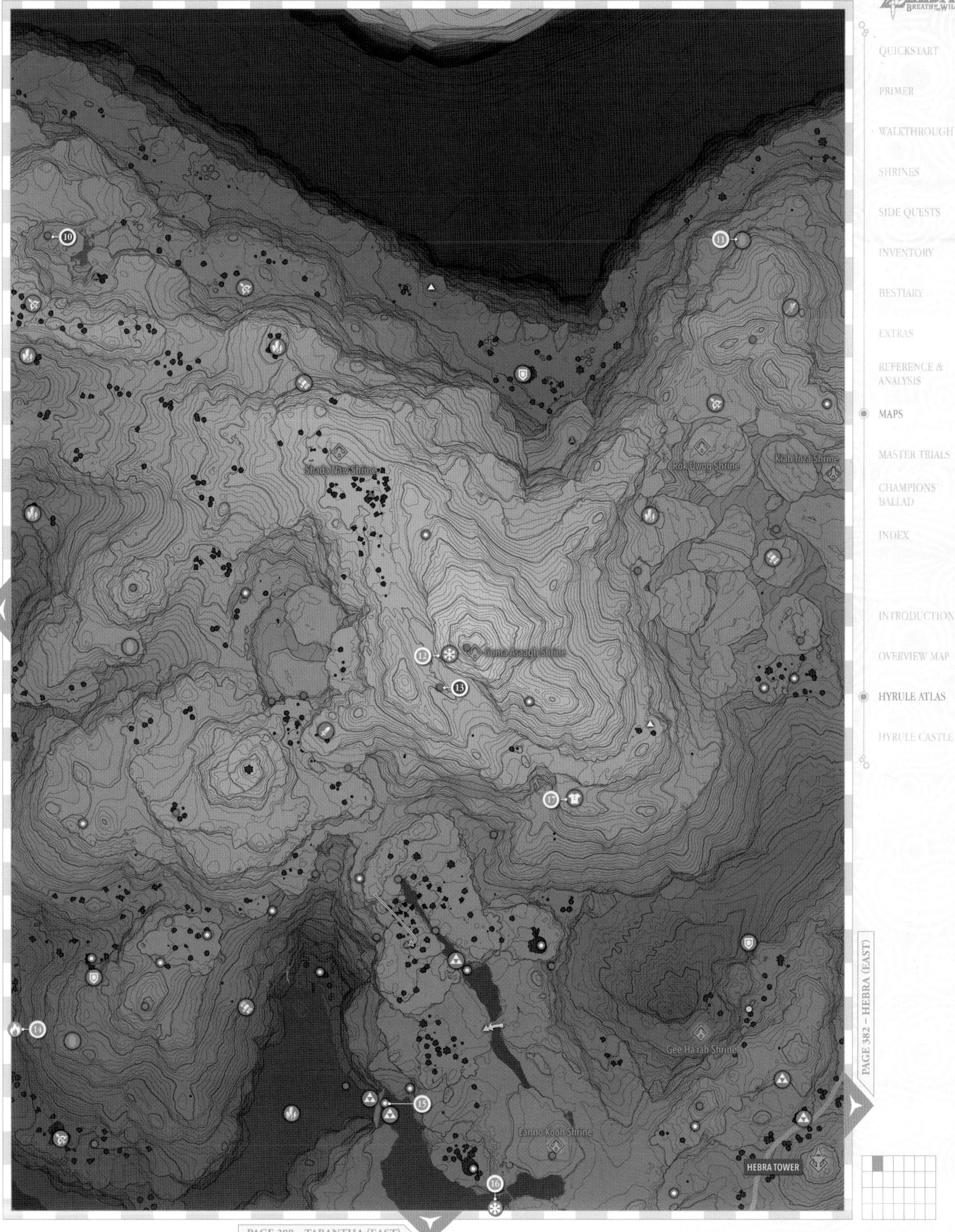

PAGE 382 – HEBRA (EAST)

PAGE 388 – TABANTHA (EAST)

10. Walk to the west end of the hot spring and clear the pile of leaves to reveal a rock.
11. Behind destructible rocks.
12. In the large ice block.
13. Under a stone hidden beneath two angled rock formations.
14. Inside the house.
15. On an intermediate ledge behind the waterfall, behind destructible rocks.
16. Master Mode only.
17. Only at night, with the Xenoblade Chronicles 2 side quest activated.

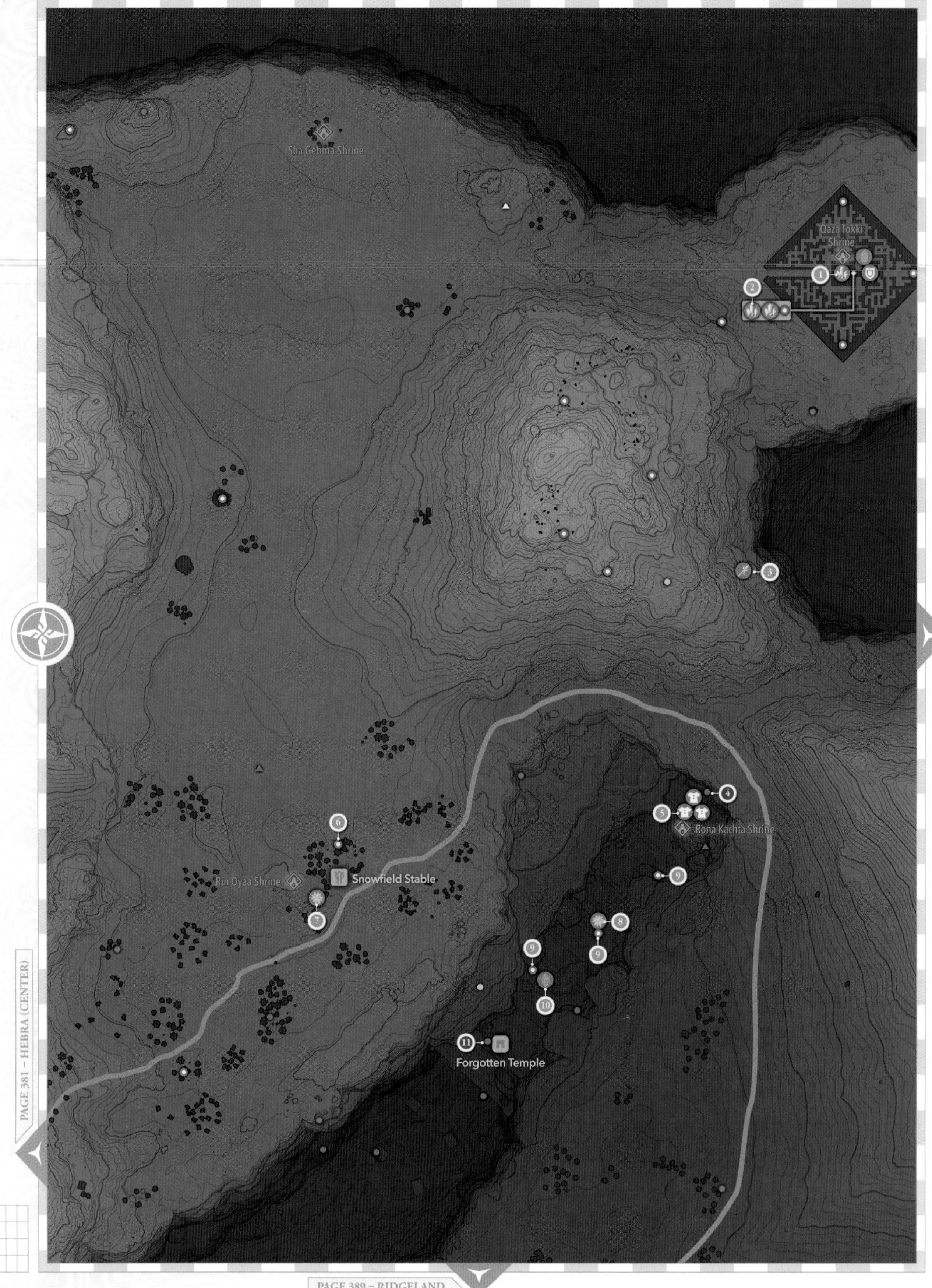

PAGE 381 – HEBRA (CENTER)

PAGE 389 – RIDGELAND

1. At the top of the structure.
2. In a secret room just west of the shrine.
3. Behind destructible rocks.
4. Inside the Forgotten Temple, on the ledge behind the goddess statue's head.
5. Only after clearing all 120 shrines.
6. Only after feeding the grey dog to the north of the stable.
7. Only after feeding the dog next to the cooking pot at the nearby stable.
8. Inside the Forgotten Temple, in a small recess hidden at the base of the final updraft.
9. Inside the Forgotten Temple, on the floor.
10. Inside the Forgotten Temple, in a small recess hidden at the base of the second updraft.
11. Above the Forgotten Temple's entrance, on the left side of the blocked archway.

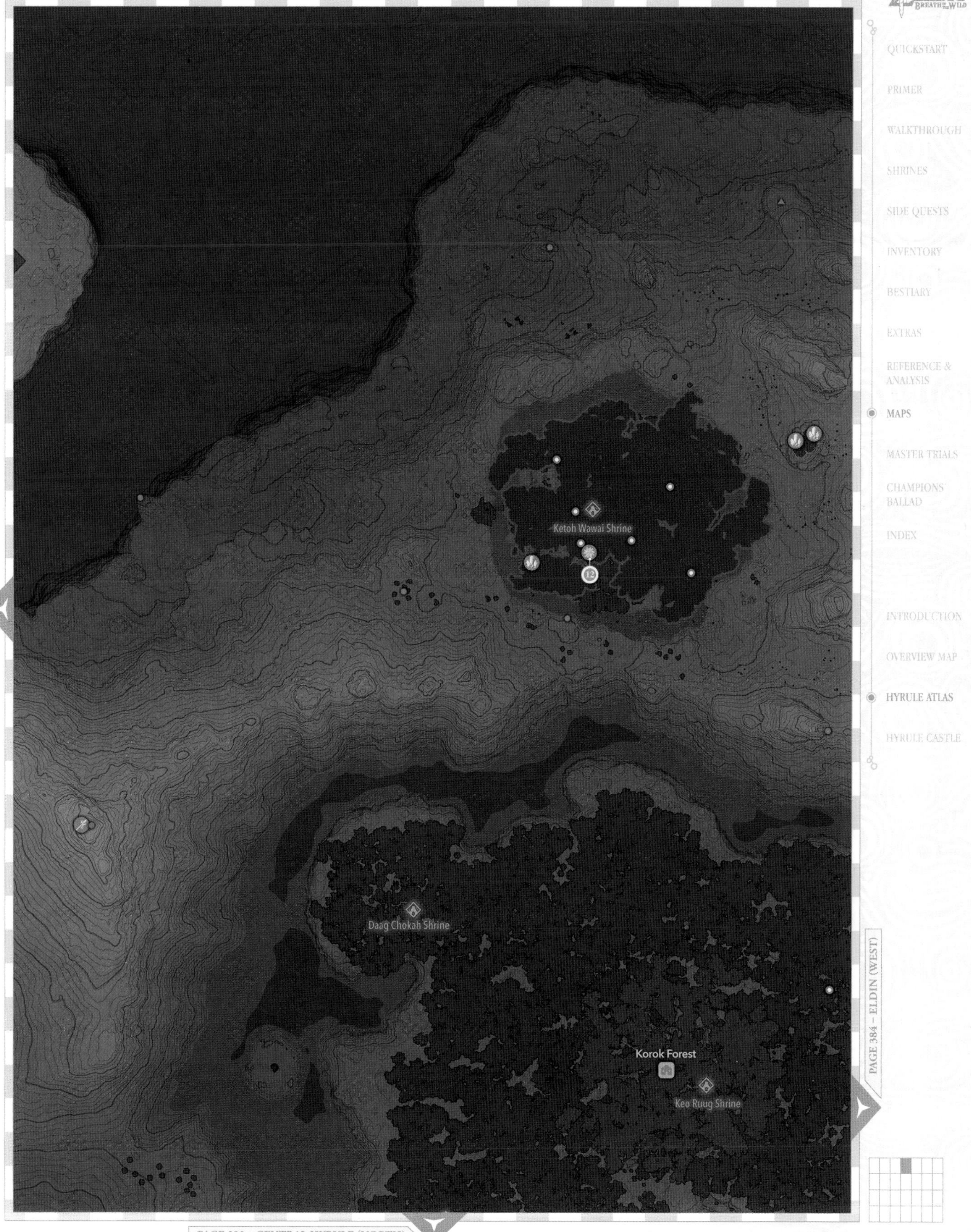

PAGE 384 – ELDIN (WEST)

PAGE 390 – CENTRAL HYRULE (NORTH)

12 Atop the low stone ruins.

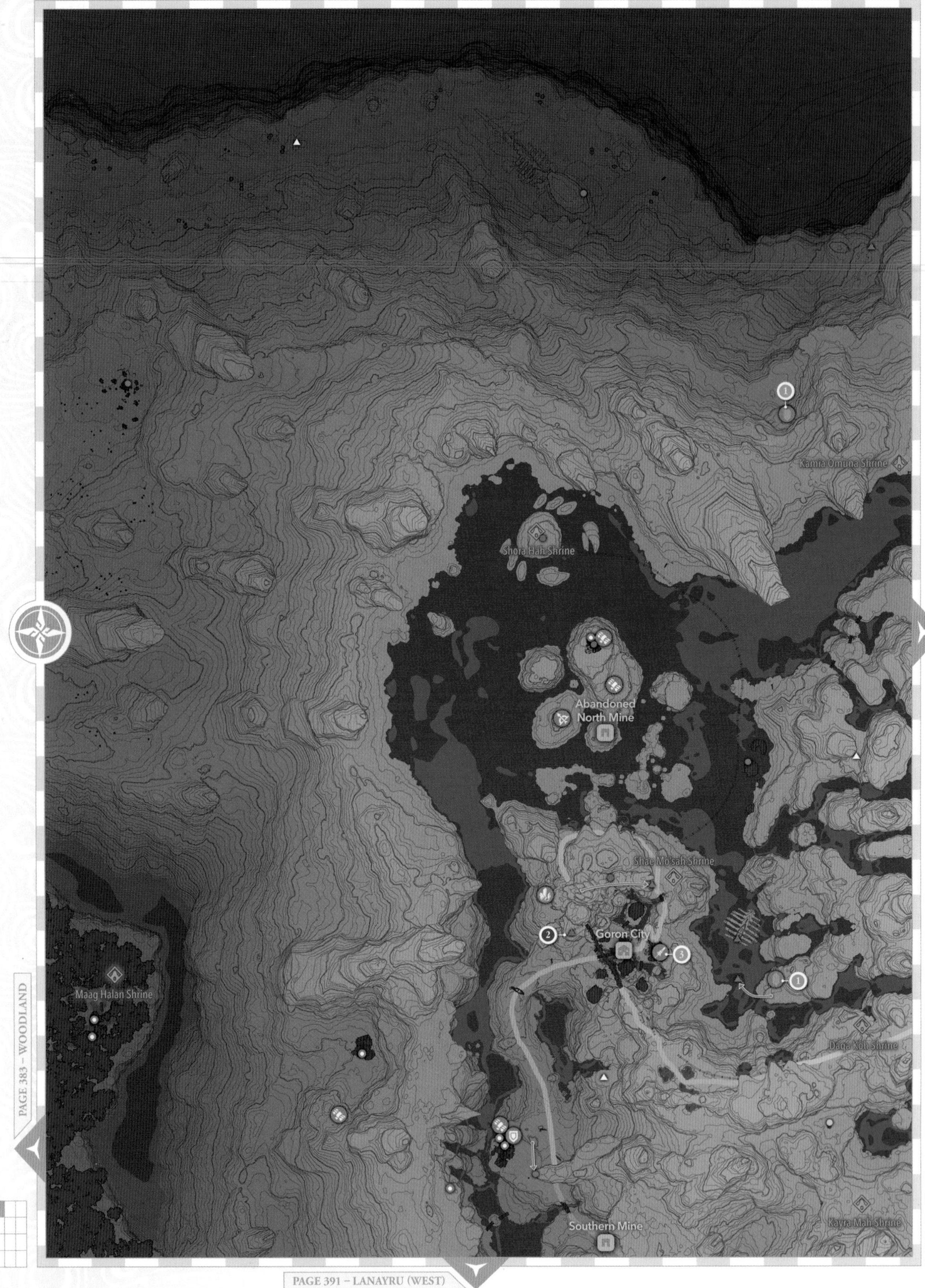

PAGE 383 – WOODLAND

PAGE 391 – LANAYRU (WEST)

1. Behind destructible rocks.
2. Inside the mouth of the Goron statue.
3. Reward for clearing Divine Beast Vah Rudania.

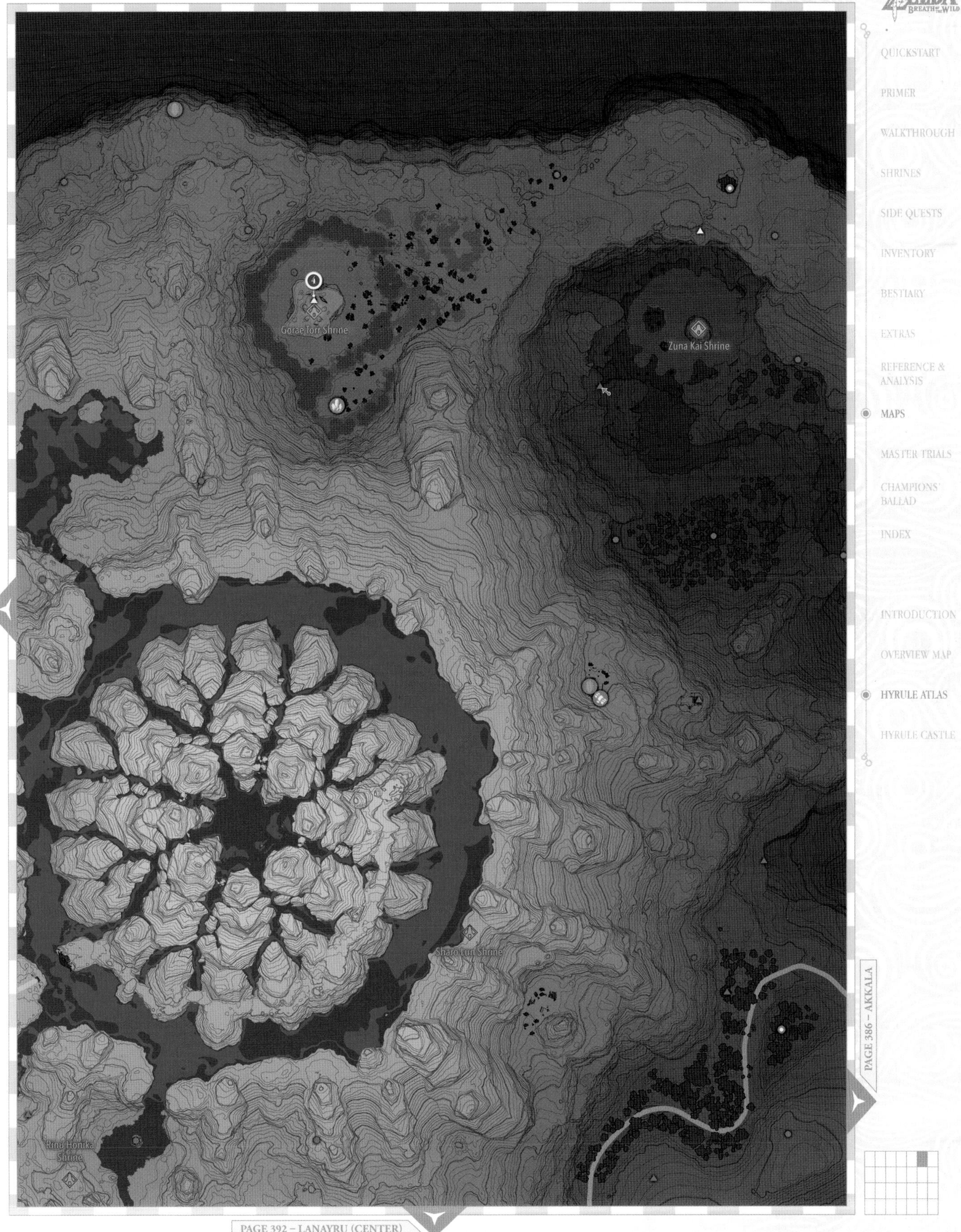

PAGE 386 – AKKALA

PAGE 392 – LANAYRU (CENTER)

(4) Five pillars surround the shrine, each with a rock on top of it. You need to move the odd rock to the opposite edge of its pillar, in the highest possible spot, matching the layout of the other pillars.

1. At ground level, behind a metal cube.
2. In a giant underground chamber accessible via an opening directly in front of the Tu Ka'loh Shrine after completing it.
3. In a giant underground chamber accessible via an opening directly in front of the Tu Ka'loh Shrine after completing it (Expansion Pass required).
4. Only at night, with the Xenoblade Chronicles 2 side quest activated.
5. Only after feeding the dog at the nearby stable.

TABANTHA (WEST)

PAGE 380 – HEBRA (WEST)

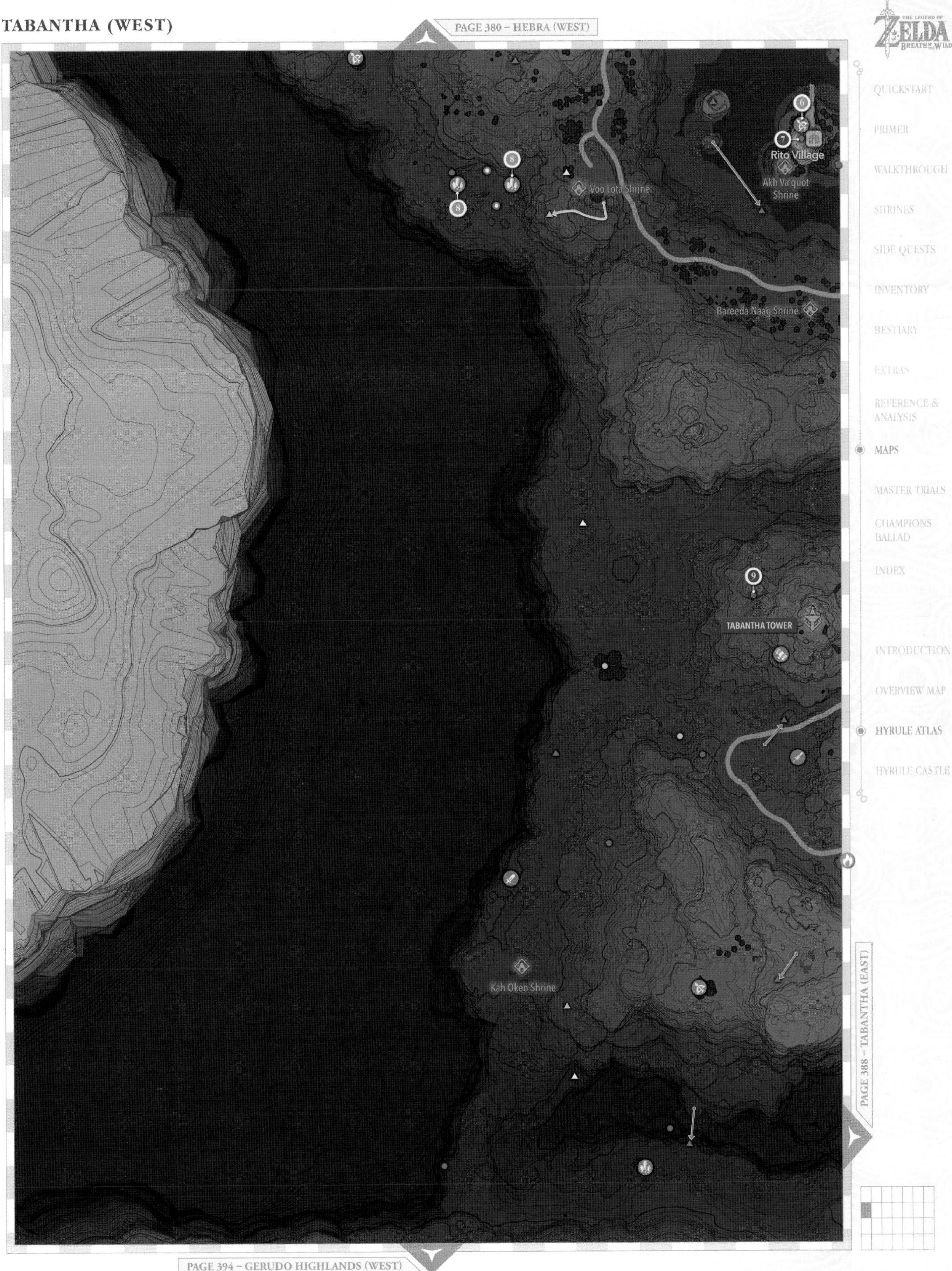

PAGE 388 – TABANTHA (EAST)

PAGE 394 – GERUDO HIGHLANDS (WEST)

6. Reward for clearing Divine Beast Vah Medoh.
7. Shoot the balloon near the top of Rito Village's peak.
8. In the bog.
9. Under a rock overhang. Shoot the glowing eyeball to clear the Malice goo.

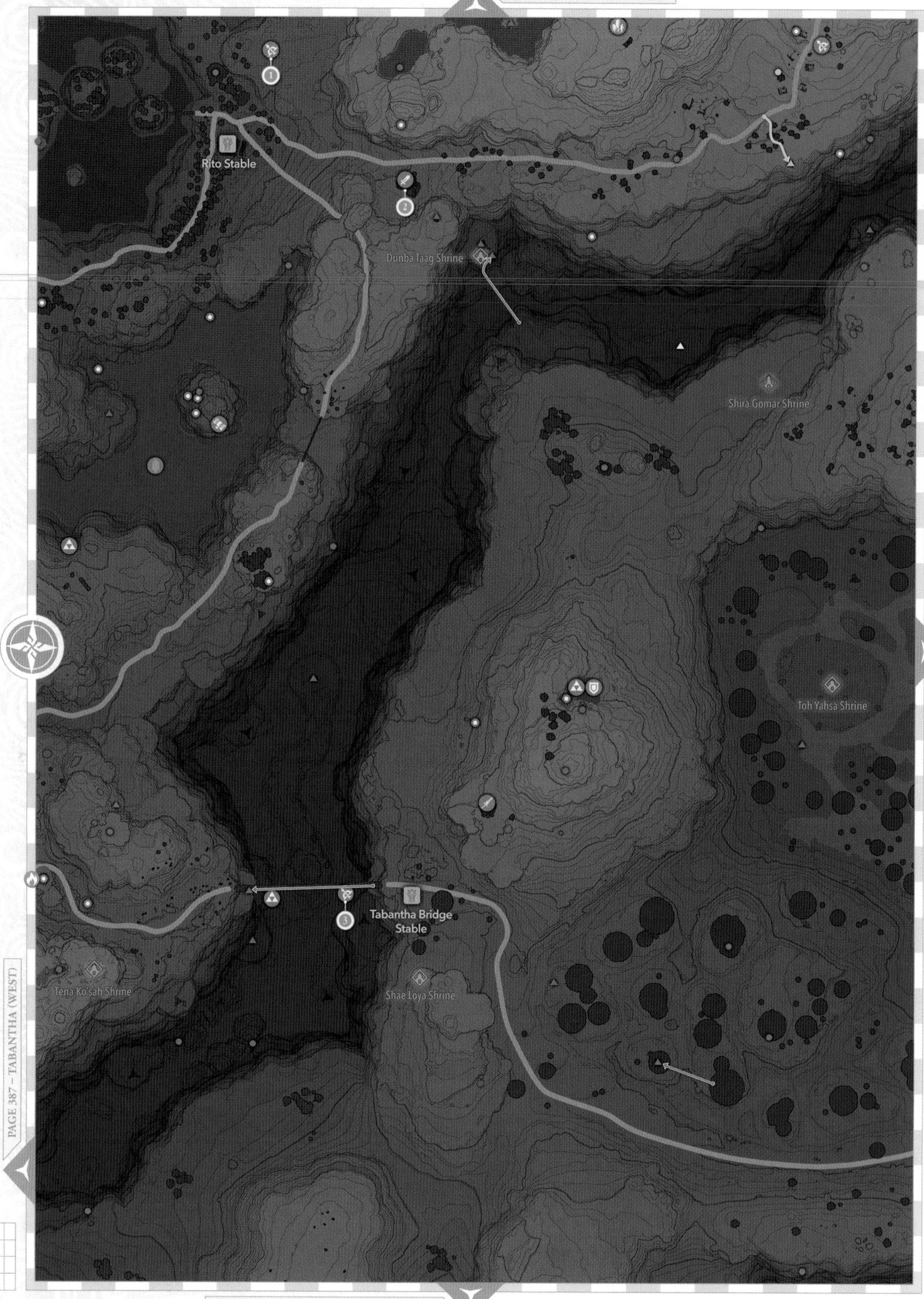

1. At the top of the tall pillar.
2. On the top platform of the enemy camp.
3. Master Mode only.

PAGE 382 – HEBRA (EAST)

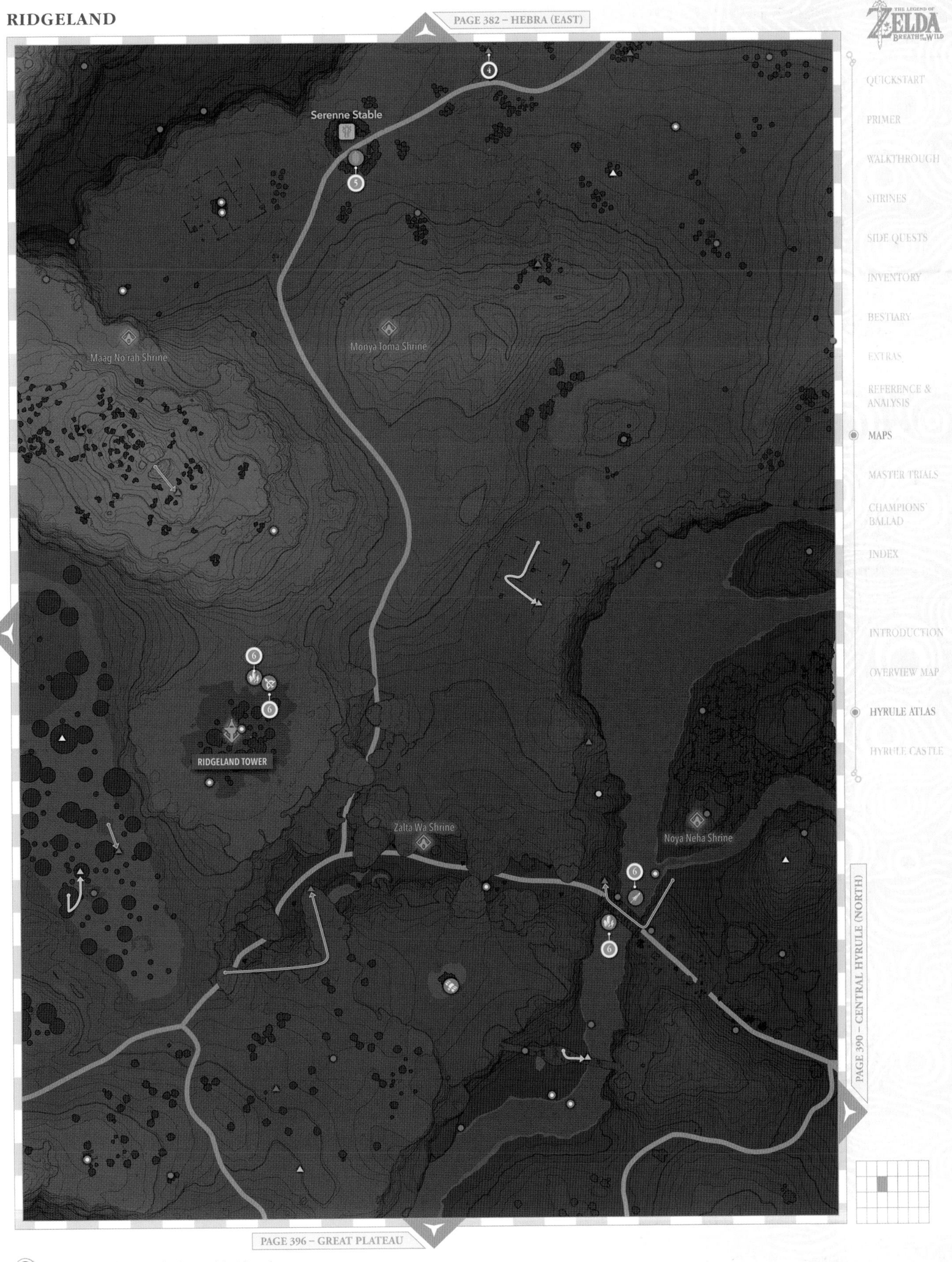

PAGE 390 – CENTRAL HYRULE (NORTH)

PAGE 396 – GREAT PLATEAU

4. Jump above the three wooden fences while riding a horse.
5. Only after feeding the black dog.
6. Master Mode only.

CENTRAL HYRULE (NORTH)

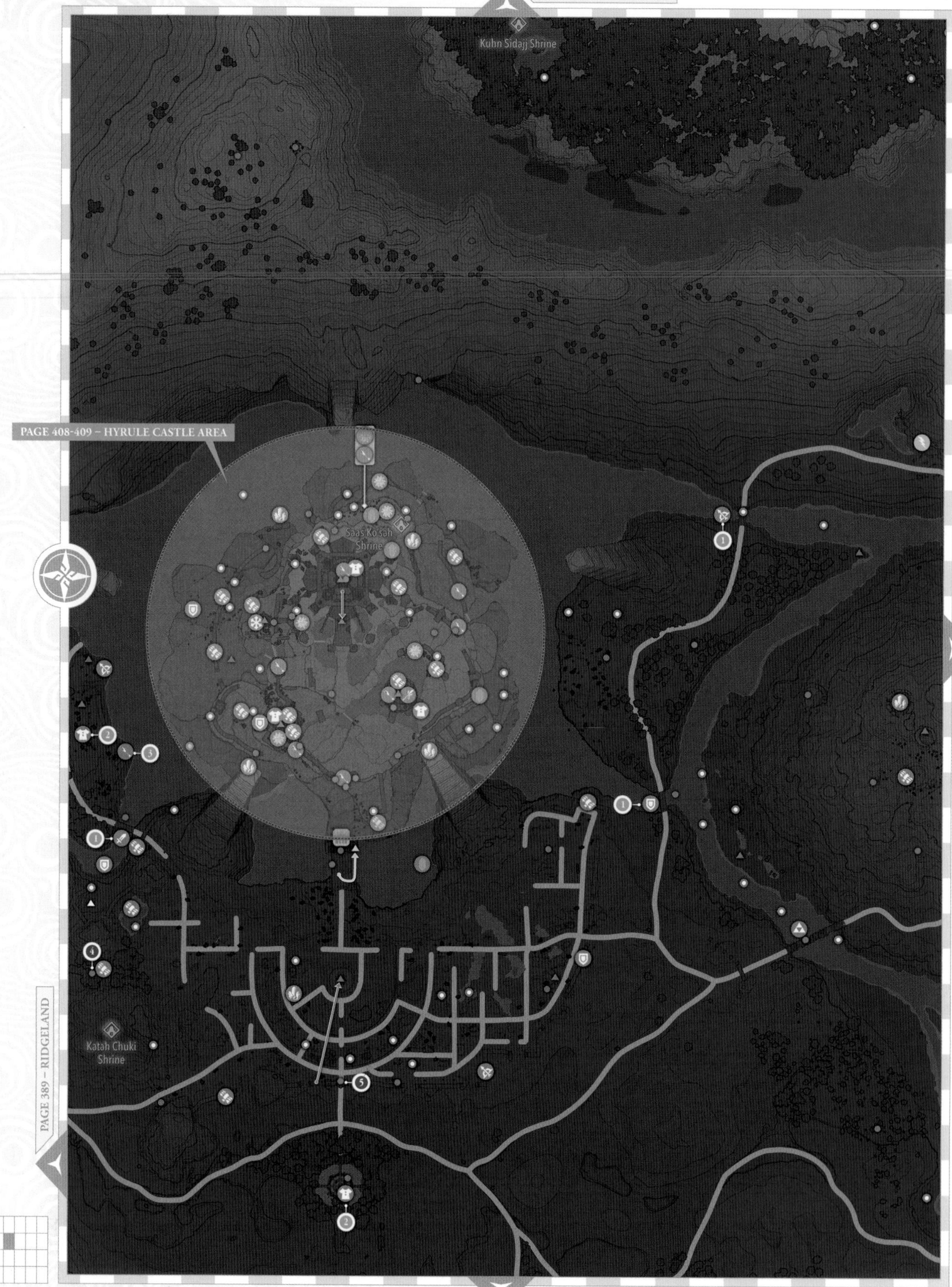

1. Master Mode only.
2. Expansion Pass required.
3. On the fortified wall.
4. Shoot the balloon in the tree just west of the tower.
5. Shoot the Triforce emblem on the north side of the wall, above the gate.

PAGE 384 – ELDIN (WEST)

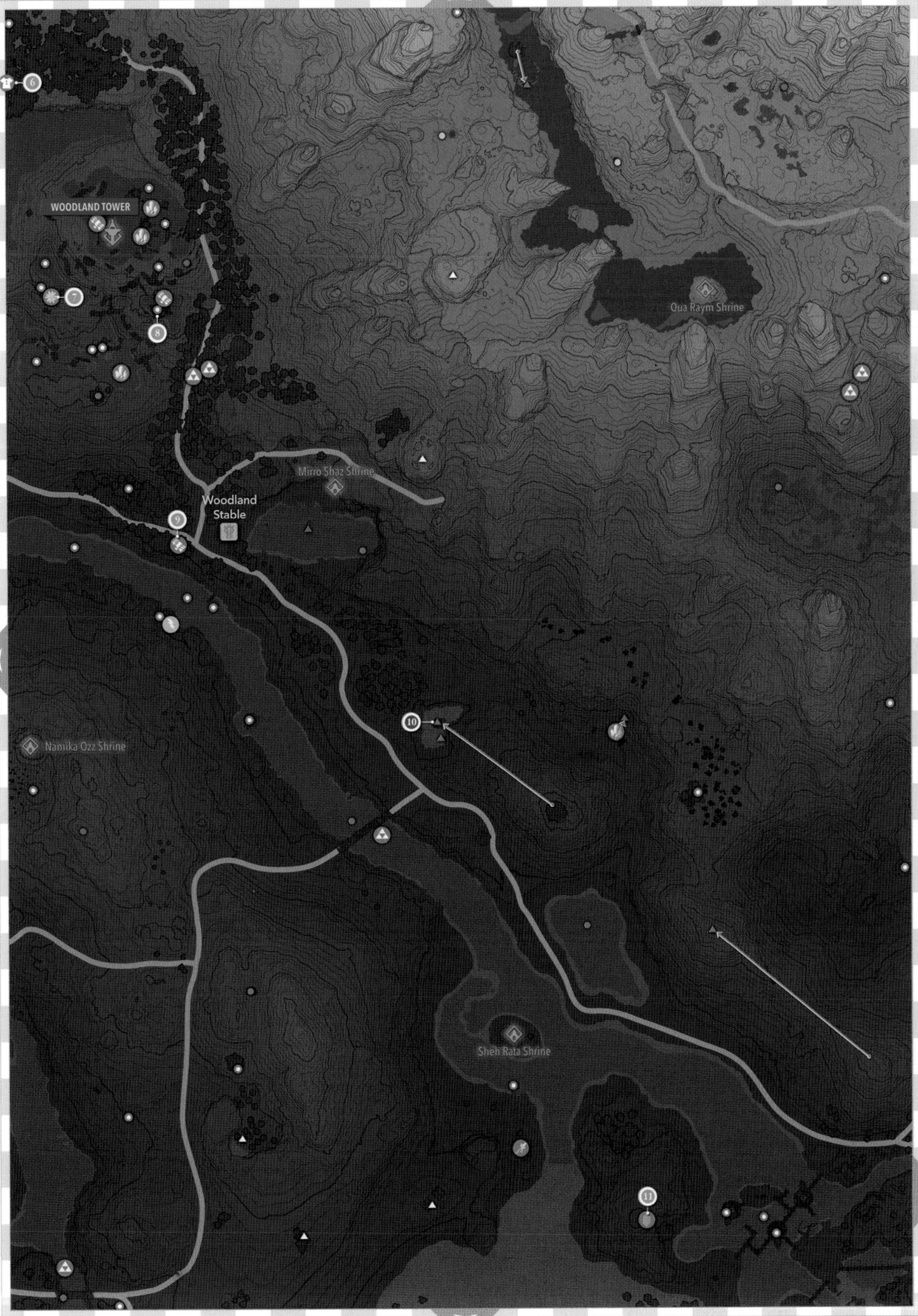

PAGE 392 – LANAYRU (CENTER)

PAGE 398 – DUELING PEAKS

6 Expansion Pass required.

7 In the bog.

8 On the top platform of the enemy camp.

9 Only after feeding the dog at the nearby stable.

10 The starting point is at the top of the large tree. You then need to shield-surf at maximum speed to the ring target.

11 Inside a cavern.

PAGE 385 – ELDIN (EAST)

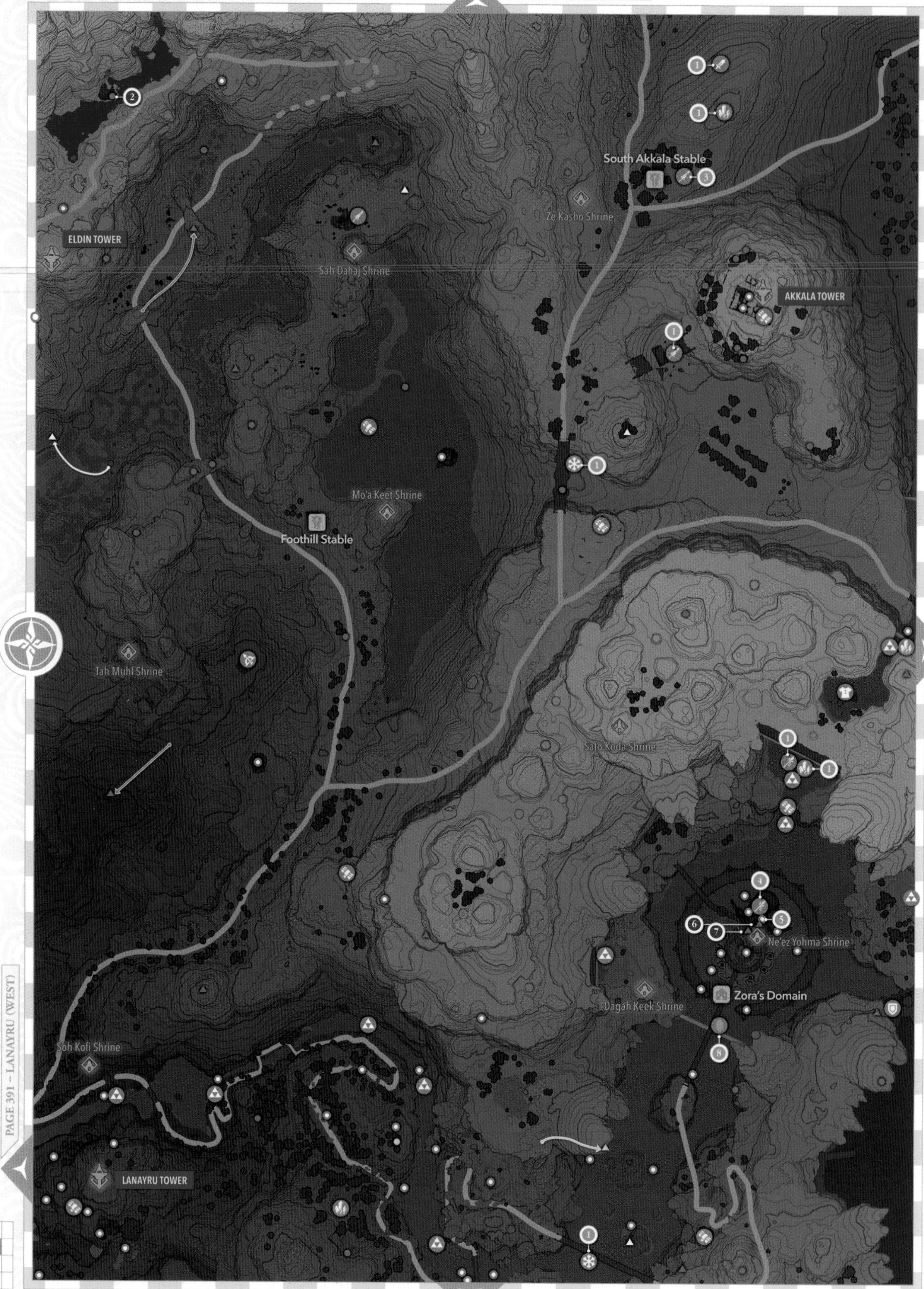

PAGE 391 – LANAYRU (WEST)

PAGE 399 – HATENO (WEST)

1. Master Mode only.
2. From the pinwheel inside the skull-shaped structure, aim through the eye to pop the balloon far to the southeast. A bow with long range will make the process much easier.
3. Only after feeding the dog at the nearby stable.
4. Reward for clearing Divine Beast Vah Ruta.
5. At the base of the tail of the giant fish above the throne room.
6. Inside the flower on the head of the fish statue, above the throne room.
7. On the tip of the fish statue's tail, at the very top of Zora's Domain.
8. Behind the base of the waterfall.

PAGE 386 – AKKALA

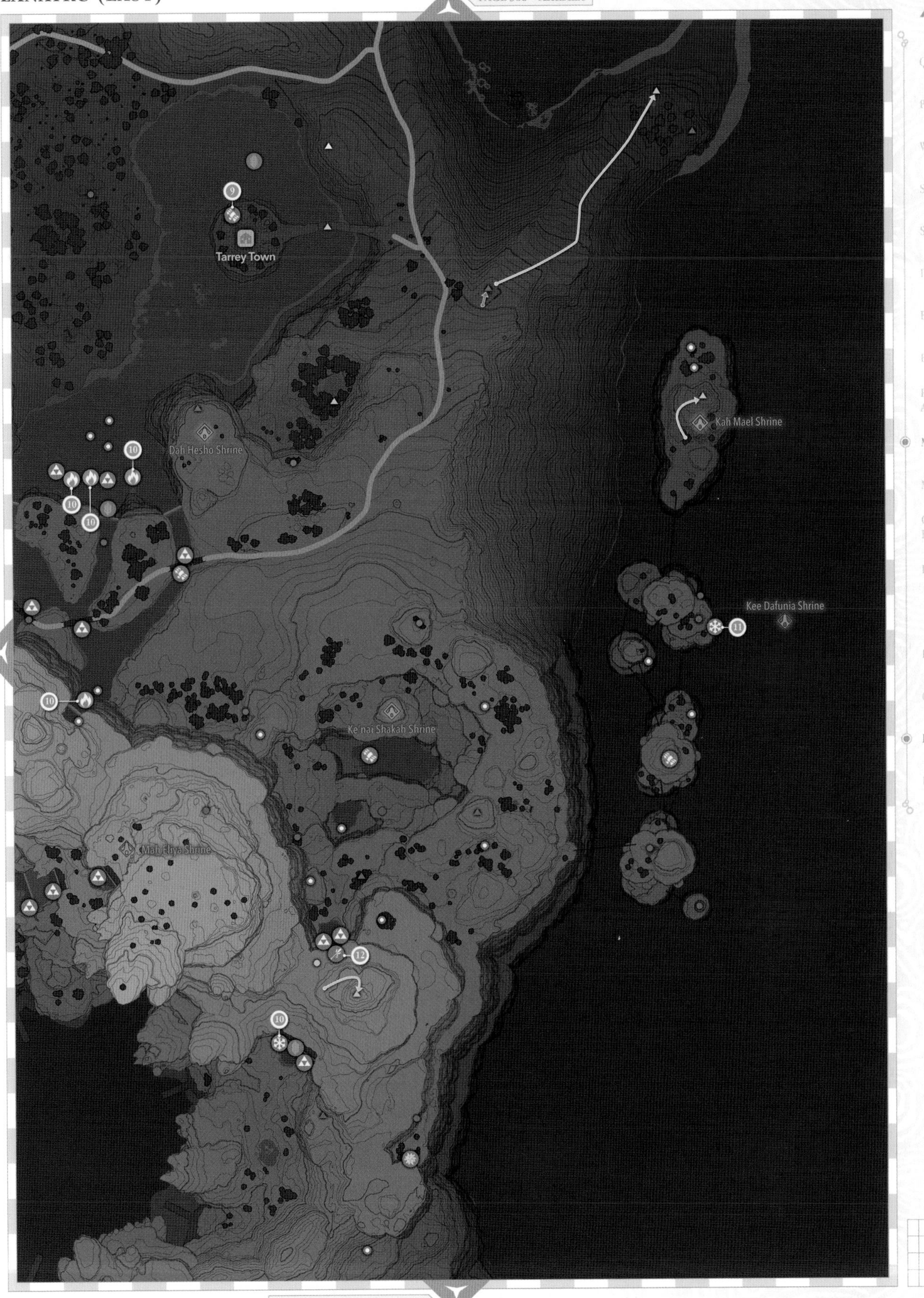

PAGE 400 – HATENO (EAST)

(9) Feed the black dog behind the house (only after recruiting Fyson during the "From the Ground Up" side quest).

(10) Master Mode only.

(11) Behind destructible rocks.

(12) Behind the waterfall.

PAGE 387 – TABANTHA (WEST)

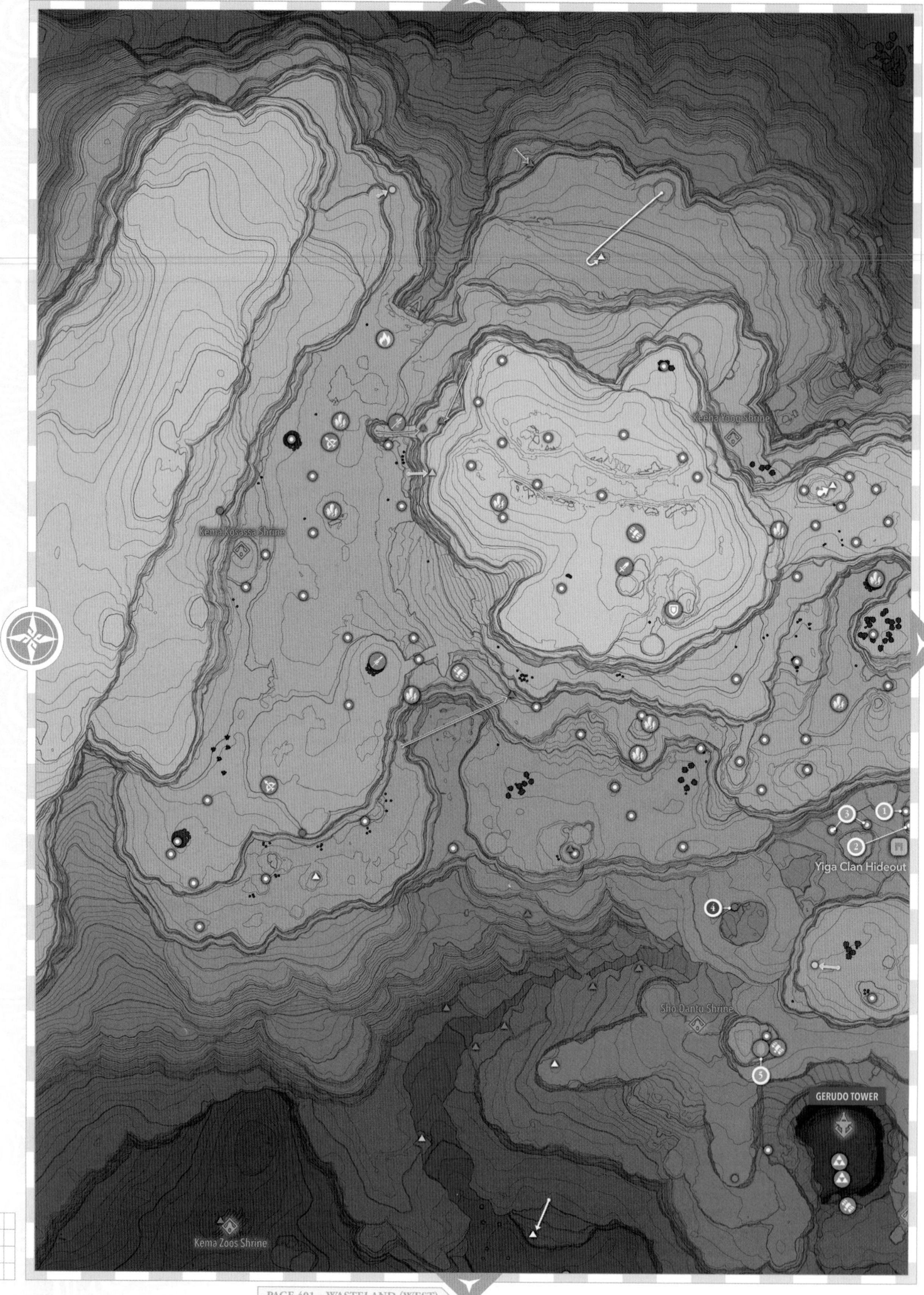

PAGE 401 – WASTELAND (WEST)

1. In the Yiga Clan Hideout's main room, next to the pile of bananas.
2. In the Yiga Clan Hideout's main room, atop the central pillar.
3. In a hidden recess in the Yiga Clan Hideout's entrance chamber.
4. On a small elevated ledge in the rock overhang's large round hole.
5. In a cave blocked by rocks that can be moved with Stasis, at the base of the rocky outcrop.

GERUDO HIGHLANDS (EAST)

PAGE 388 – TABANTHA (EAST)

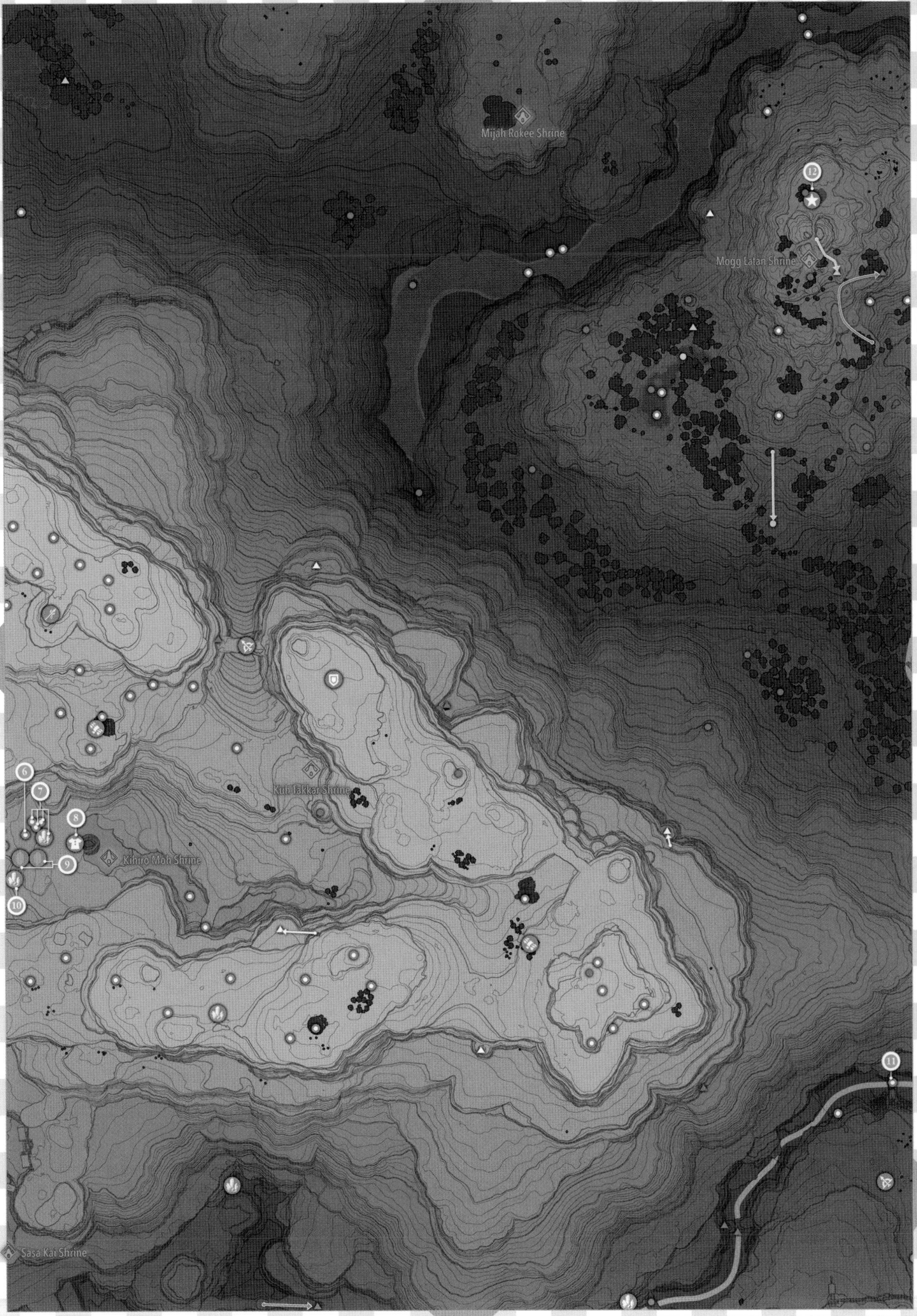

Mijah Rokee Shrine

Mogg Latan Shrine

Kuh Takkar Shrine

Kihiro Moh Shrine

Sasa Kai Shrine

PAGE 396 – GREAT PLATEAU

PAGE 402 – WASTELAND (CENTER)

6. In the Yiga Clan Hideout's main room, above the exit.
7. In the Yiga Clan Hideout's final room.
8. Reward for defeating Master Kohga.
9. In the Yiga Clan Hideout's main room, behind the flammable wall covering.
10. In the Yiga Clan Hideout's second room.
11. Only after starting the "Missing in Action" side quest.
12. Expansion Pass required.

PAGE 389 – RIDGELAND

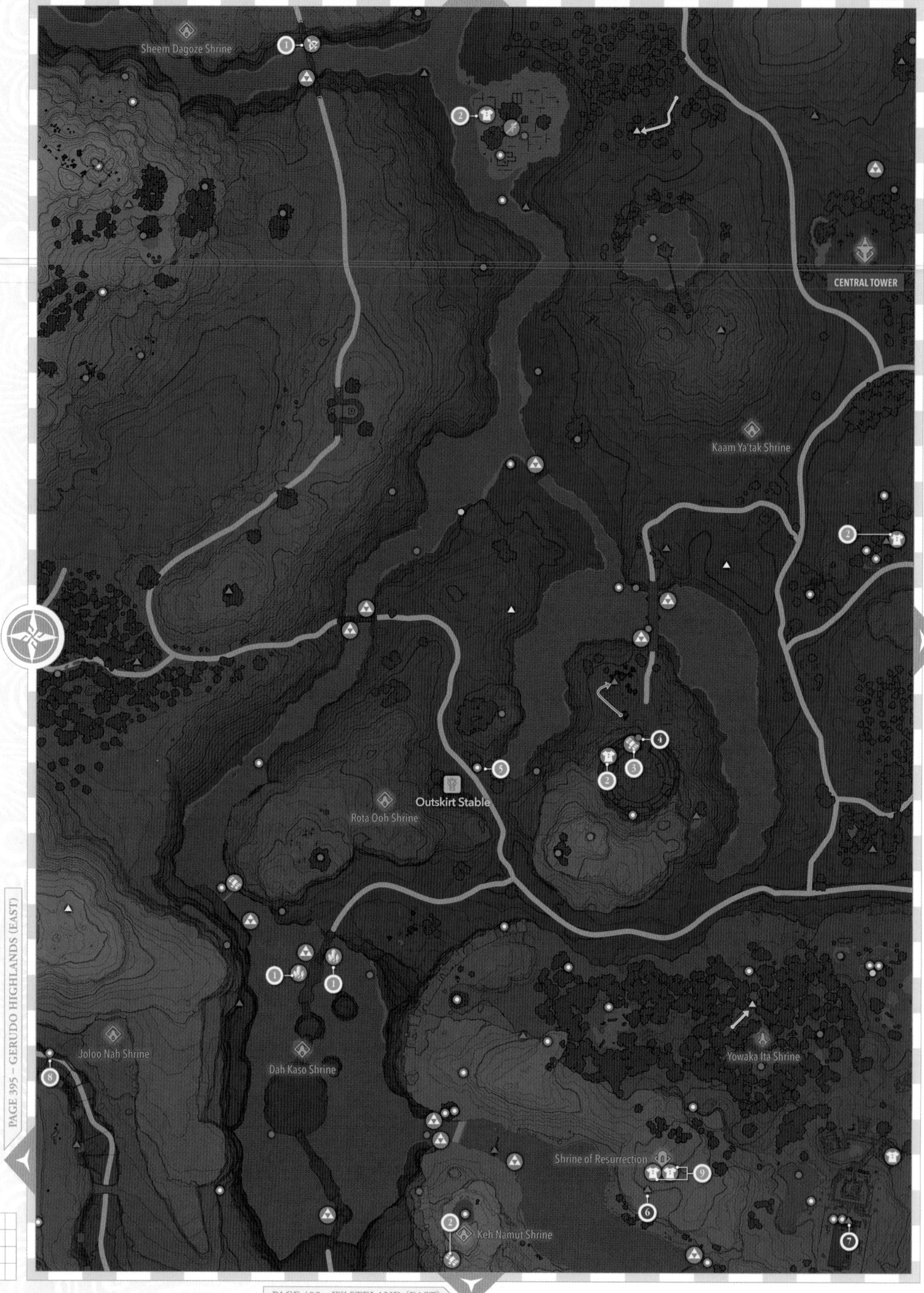

PAGE 395 – GERUDO HIGHLANDS (EAST)

PAGE 403 – WASTELAND (EAST)

1. Master Mode only.
2. Expansion Pass required.
3. At the top of the Coliseum.
4. Under a rock on a small elevated ledge, above the Coliseum's entrance.
5. Only after feeding the dog at the nearby stable.
6. You can only obtain this seed inside the Shrine of Resurrection after leaving the Great Plateau.
7. At the top of the Temple of Time's spire.
8. Only after starting the "Missing in Action" side quest.
9. Inside the Shrine of Resurrection.

PAGE 390 – CENTRAL HYRULE (NORTH)

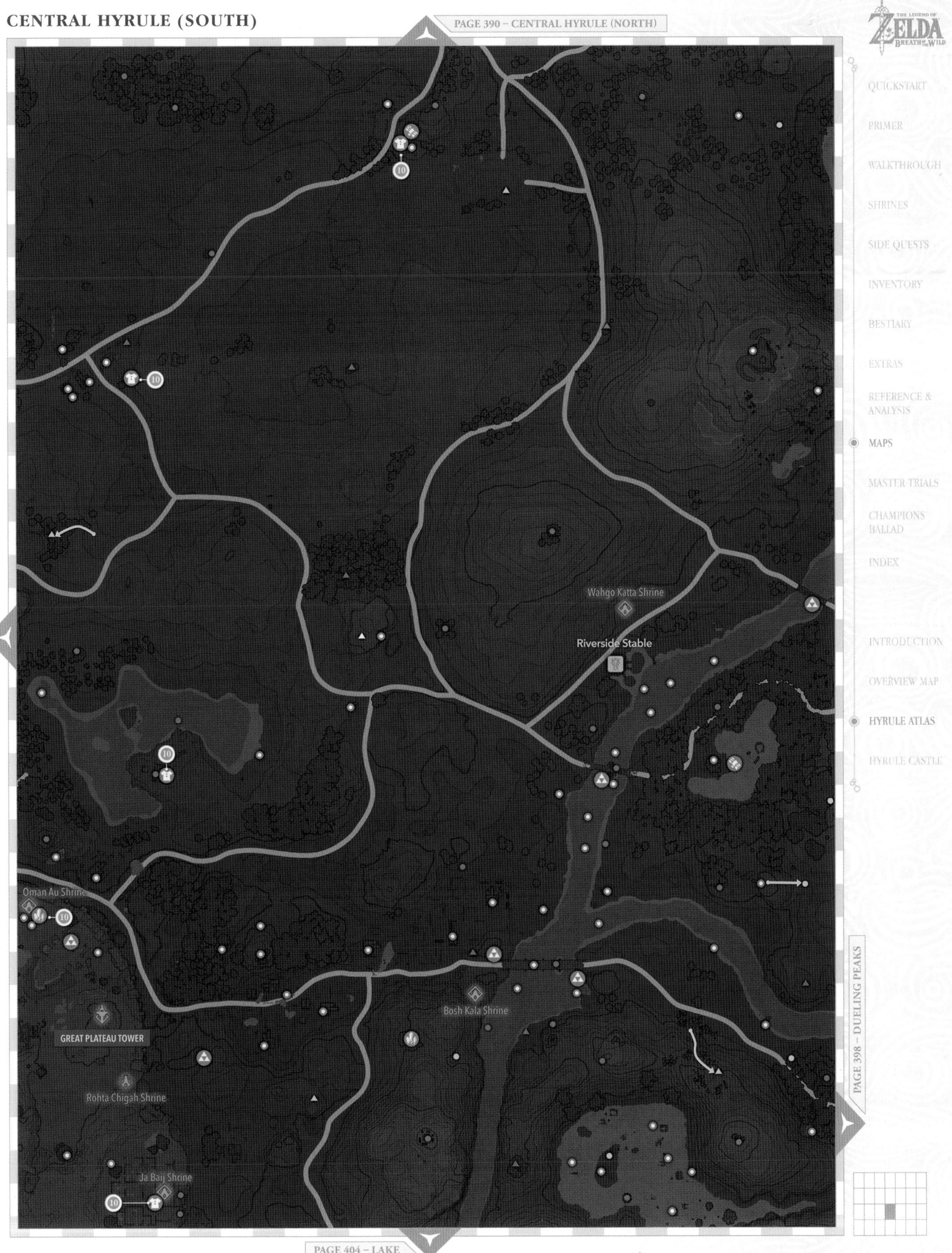

PAGE 398 – DUELING PEAKS

PAGE 404 – LAKE

(10) Expansion Pass required.

DUELING PEAKS

PAGE 391 – LANAYRU (WEST)

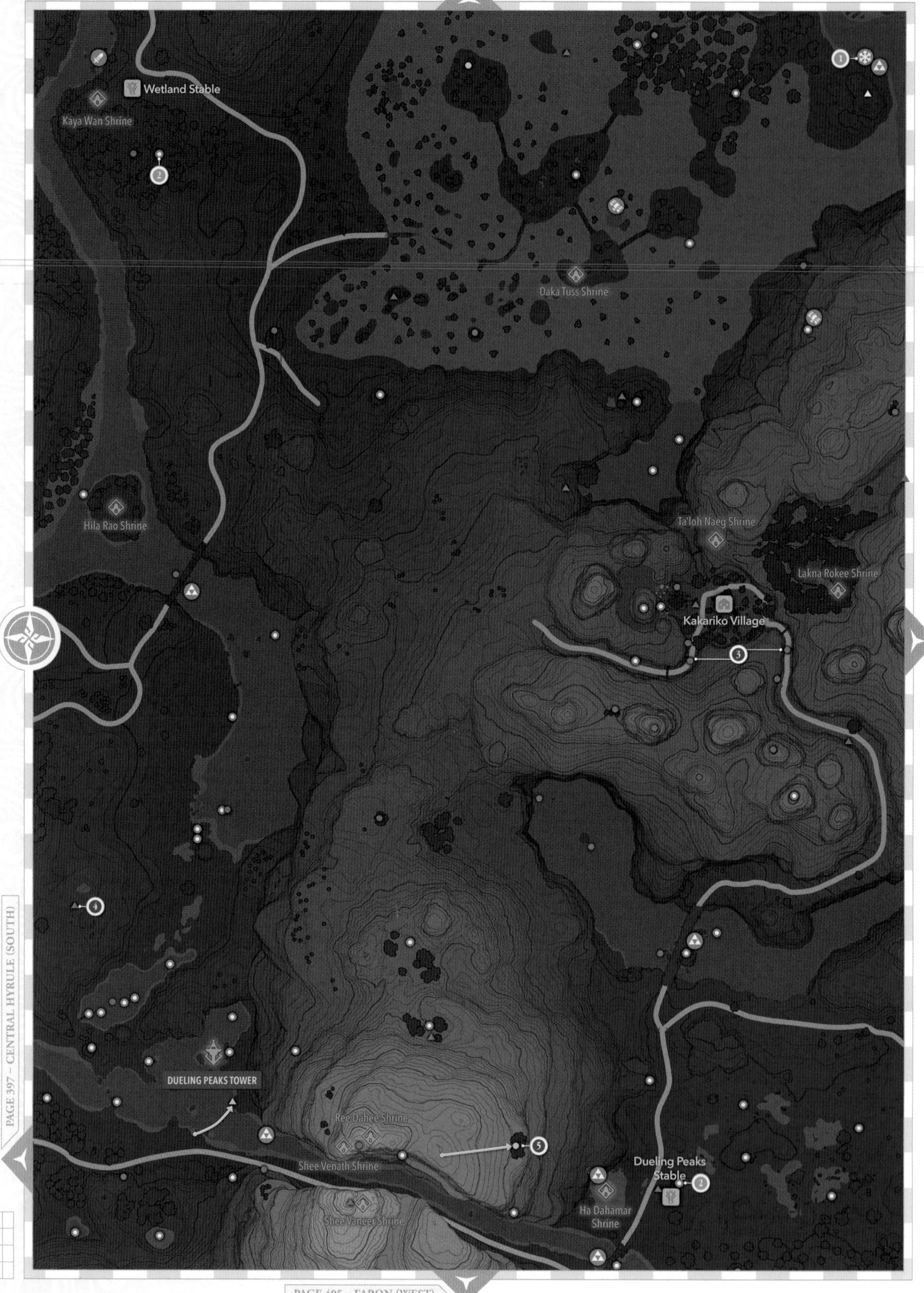

PAGE 397 – CENTRAL HYRULE (SOUTH)

PAGE 405 – FARON (WEST)

1. Master Mode only.
2. Only after feeding the dog at the nearby stable.
3. Shoot an arrow at the eye symbol on the south side of the village's wooden gate.
4. Jump above the three wooden fences while riding a horse.
5. Push one of the boulders at the top of the peak so that it rolls between the two trees down the hill.

PAGE 392 – LANAYRU (CENTER)

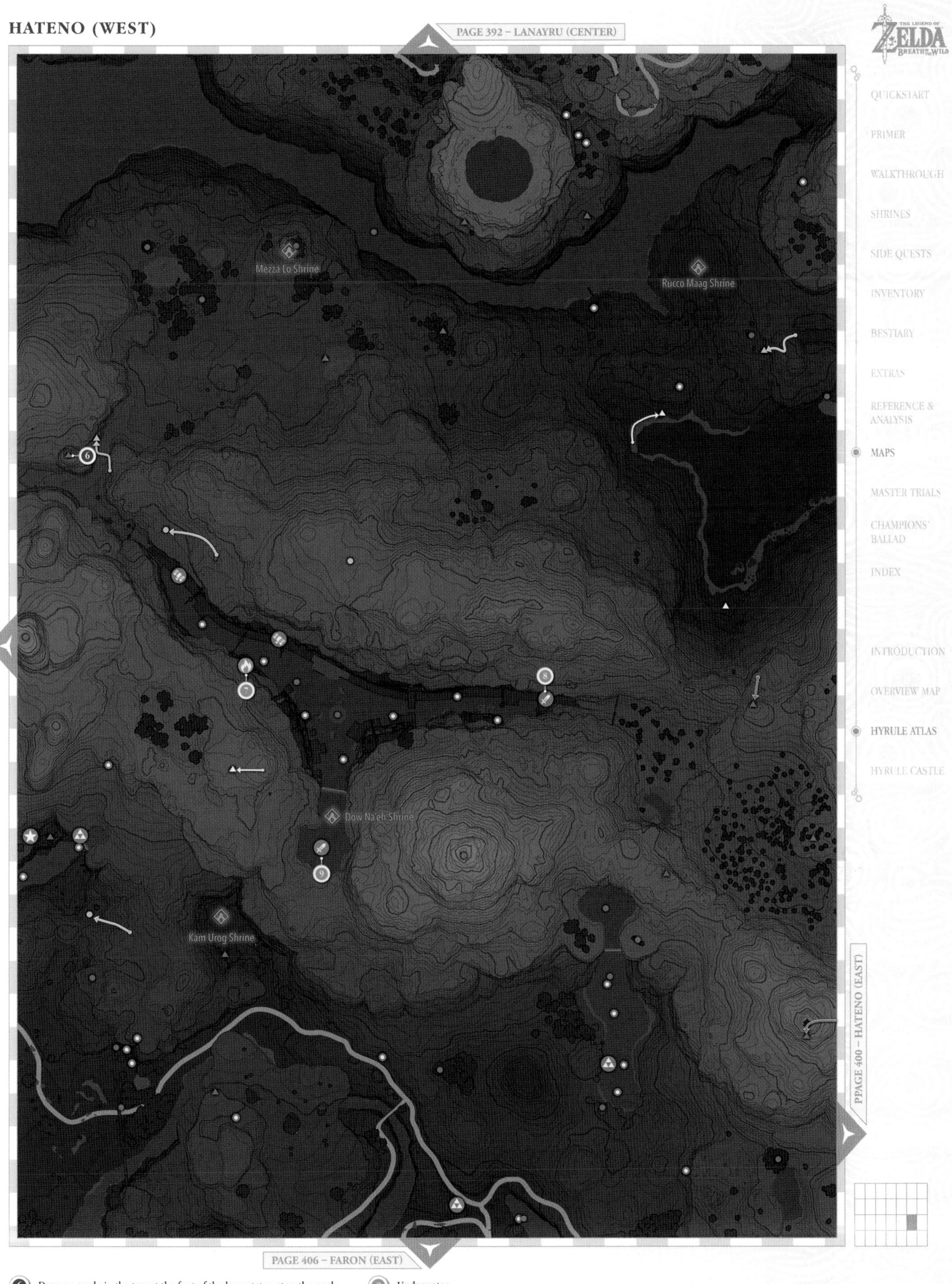

PPAGE 400 – HATENO (EAST)

PAGE 406 – FARON (EAST)

6. Drop an apple in the tray at the foot of the lone statue atop the peak.
7. Behind the tree.
8. Underwater.
9. Master Mode only.

HATENO (EAST)

PAGE 393 – LANAYRU (EAST)

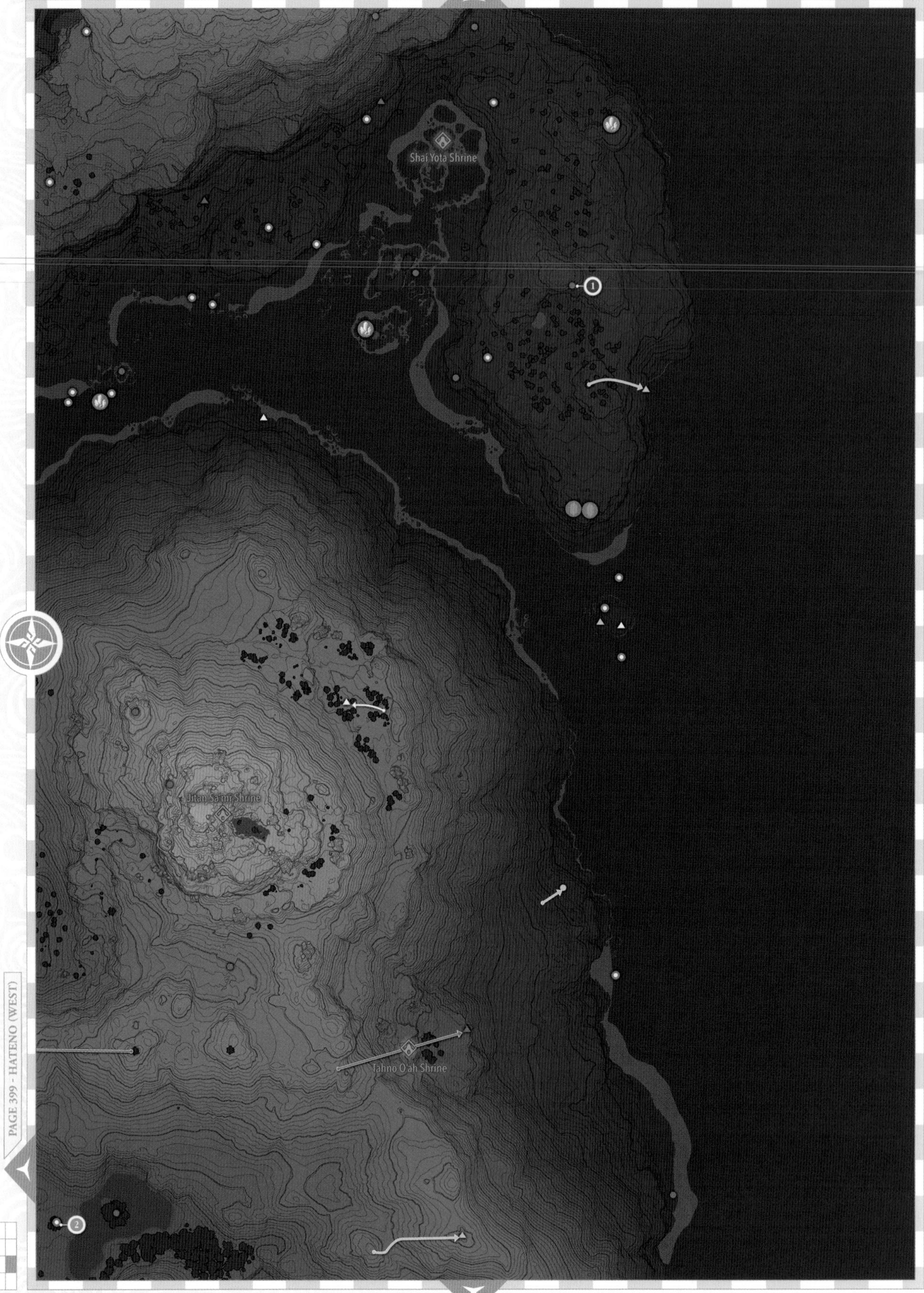

PAGE 399 – HATENO (WEST)

PAGE 407 – NECLUDA SEA

1. Pop the balloon under the big stone arch.
2. Only after feeding the black and white dog at the nearby farm.

PAGE 394 – GERUDO HIGHLANDS (WEST)

Takama Shiri Shrine

Tho Kayu Shrine

Daqo Chisay Shrine

Gerudo Town

Raqa Zunzo Shrine

Hawa Koth Shrine

PAGE 402 – WASTELAND (CENTER)

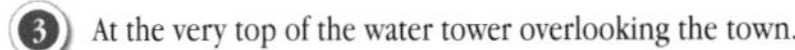

3 At the very top of the water tower overlooking the town.

4 Reward for clearing Divine Beast Vah Naboris.

WASTELAND (CENTER)

PAGE 395 – GERUDO HIGHLANDS (EAST)

PPAGE 401 – WASTELAND (WEST)

1. Reward for completing the "Rushroom Rush!" side quest.
2. Only after feeding the dog at the nearby stable.
3. Only after feeding the local dog.
4. Shoot the balloon hidden between the statue's arms.
5. At the top of the southernmost statue.

PAGE 396 – GREAT PLATEAU

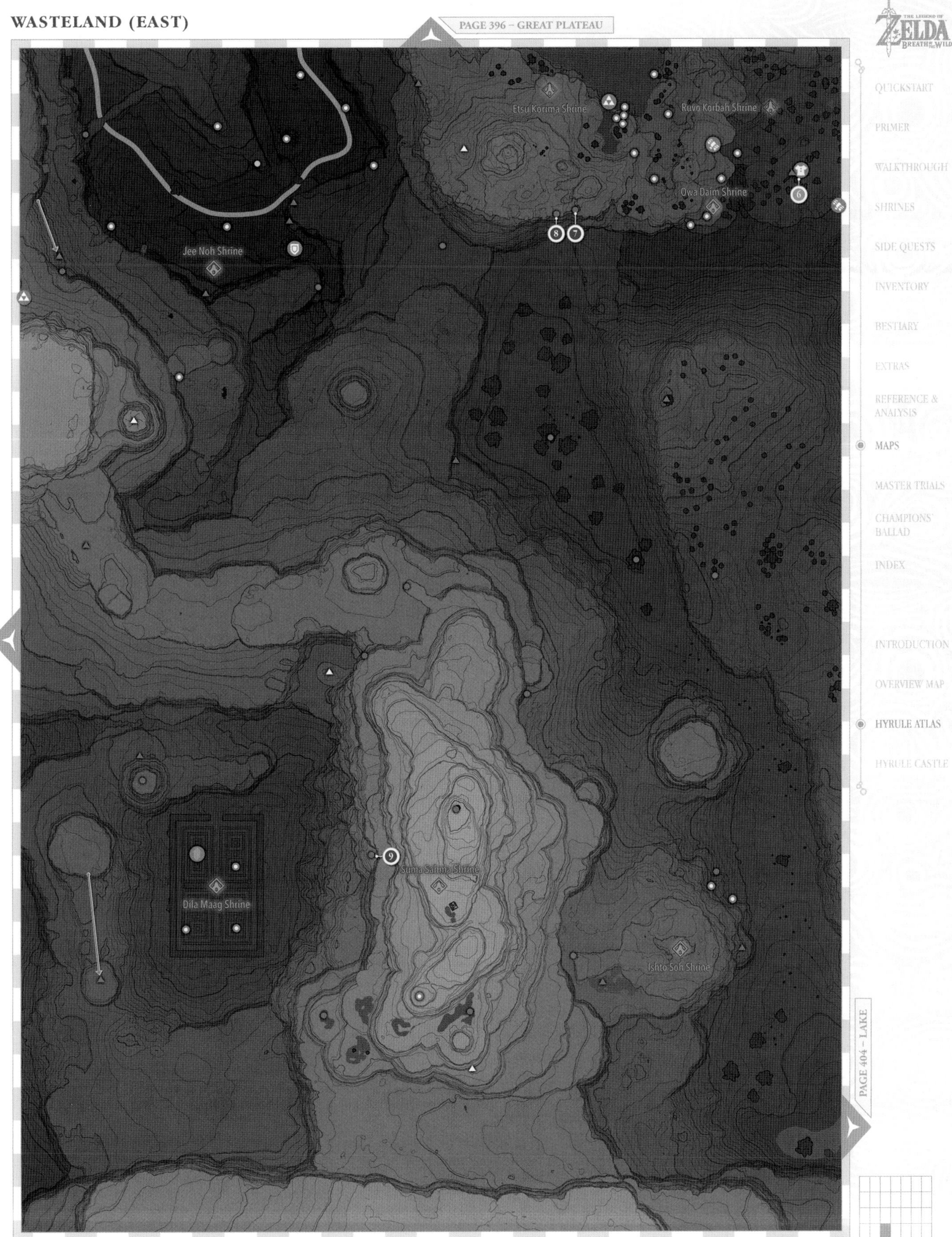

PAGE 404 – LAKE

6. Only after obtaining the Paraglider; not available if the old man gave you the item earlier.
7. By the easternmost end of the Great Plateau's fortified wall.
8. On a cliff ledge overlooking the Taobab Grasslands, in front of one of the fortification's arches.
9. On a small cliff ledge overlooking the labyrinth, easily accessed by gliding down from the Suma Sahma Shrine.

LAKE

PAGE 397 – CENTRAL HYRULE (SOUTH)

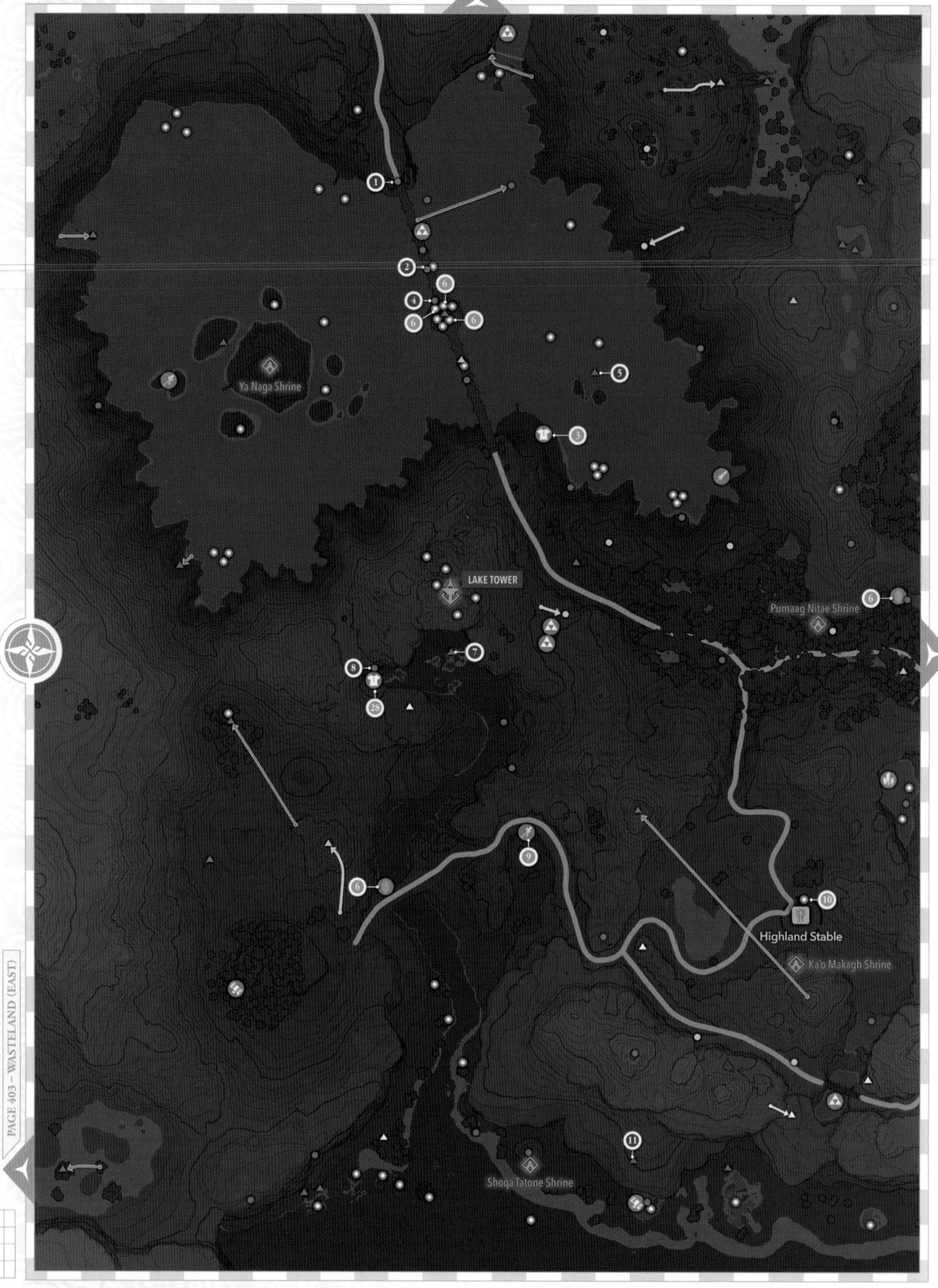

PAGE 403 – WASTELAND (EAST)

1. Light the torch at the top of both towers.
2. Shoot the balloon inside the broken pillar, under the bridge.
3. Only at night, with the Xenoblade Chronicles 2 side quest activated
4. Pick up the tree branch on the pillar's narrow ledge.
5. Raise a pillar of ice from which you can grab the lone metal cube with Magnesis to complete the puzzle.
6. Underwater.
7. Grab the underwater metal cube with Magnesis (angling the camera vertically), then use ice pillars to take it to the twin structure on the north cliff.
8. On a small ledge halfway up the cliff.
9. Behind destructible rocks.
10. Only after feeding the dog at the nearby stable.
11. Underneath the rock overhang.
12. Knock down one of the three trees to create a bridge across the bog.
13. Cast Stasis on the boulder atop the pillar and hit it with a bomb arrow to make it fall in the southwest corner of the ruins.
14. You need to place the underwater boulder on the empty rock. Cast Stasis on the one it is chained to, then use Magnesis.
15. Master Mode only.

PAGE 398 – DUELING PEAKS

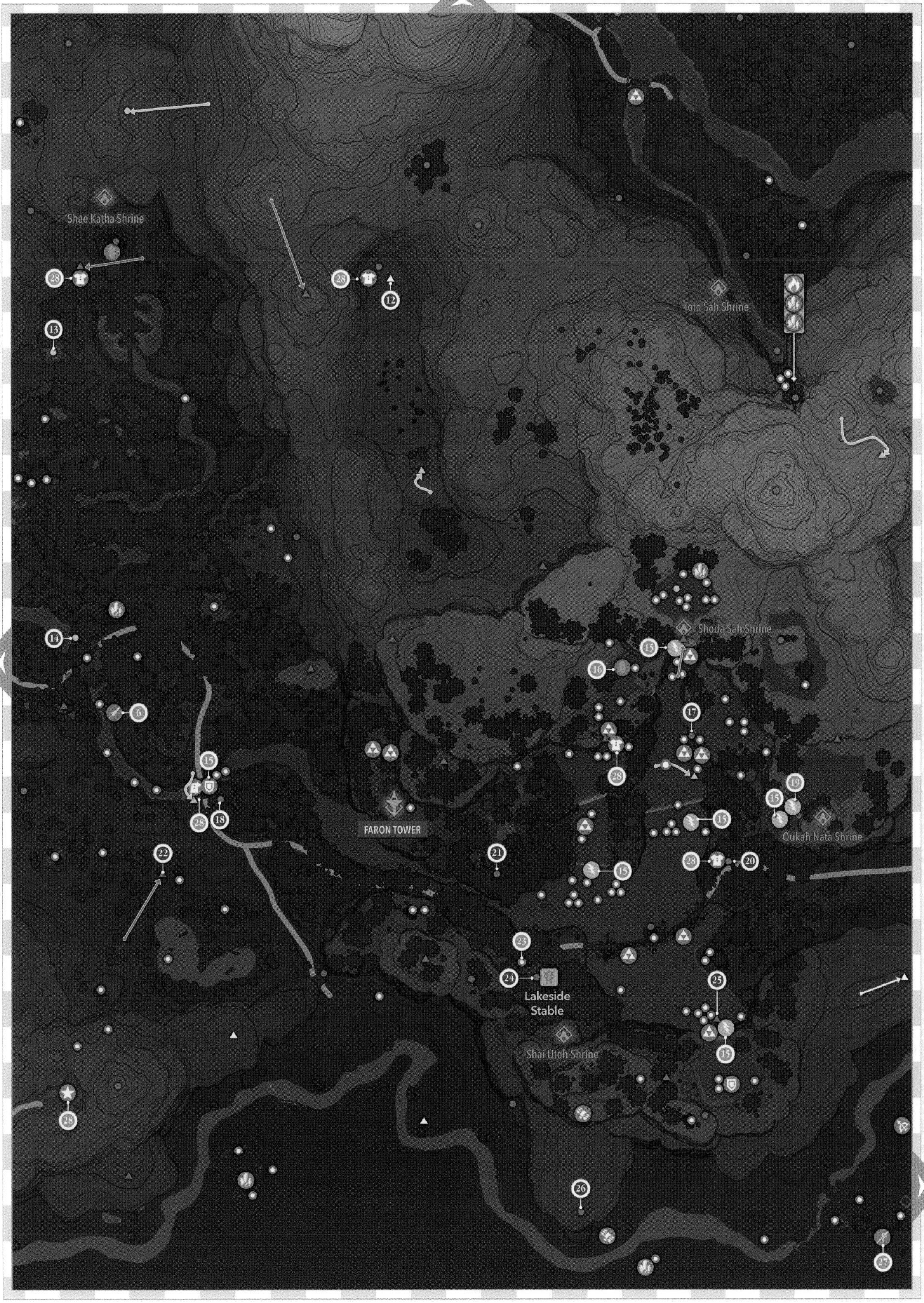

PAGE 406 – FARON (EAST)

16 Under a boulder.

17 On the small ledge halfway up the waterfall.

18 Shoot the balloon in the palm tree from the top of the cliff to the east.

19 On an intermediate ledge behind the waterfall.

20 Shoot the luminous stone to dislodge it from the middle statue's eye.

21 From the pinwheel at the top of the large tree stump, you have three balloons to shoot: two through the leaves (east and west), one close to the ground (north).

22 Climb to the top of the tallest pillar to the southwest (just west of Herin Lake) to begin the race.

23 Only after feeding the dog at the nearby stable.

24 Shoot a fire arrow to burn the goatee of the horse structure above the Lakeside Stable.

25 Raise pillars of ice at the base of the waterfall. The cube is behind the waterfall, with the two structures on the sides.

26 Shoot the balloon underneath the rock overhang.

27 On the top platform of the enemy camp.

28 Expansion Pass required.

PAGE 399 – HATENO (WEST)

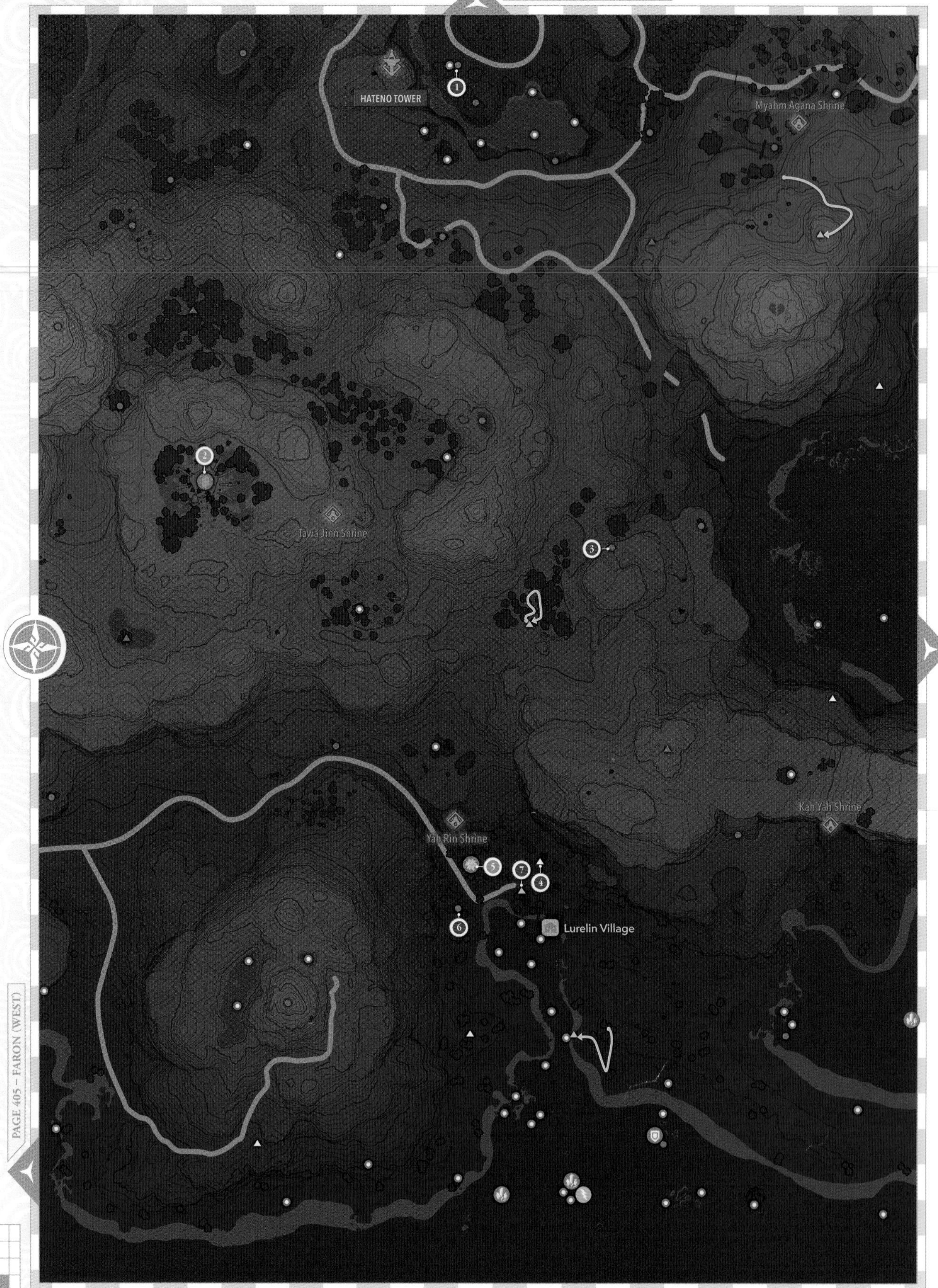

PAGE 405 – FARON (WEST)

1. Shoot the 10 wooden targets scattered around the equestrian riding course, then pop the balloon that appears above the cabin on the west side of the loop.
2. Buried under the Hinox.
3. Pick up the rock in the small cave with luminous stone deposits, at the foot of the large tree.
4. Move a rock right next to the building and attach two Octo balloons to it; once the rock is high enough, cast Stasis on it and shoot a single bomb arrow to make it fall on the deck, enabling you to complete the triangle pattern.
5. Only after feeding the nearby dog (on the main road next to the beach).
6. Shoot the apple positioned between palm fruits at the top of the tree on the westernmost hut.
7. Above the inn.

PAGE 400 – HATENO (EAST)

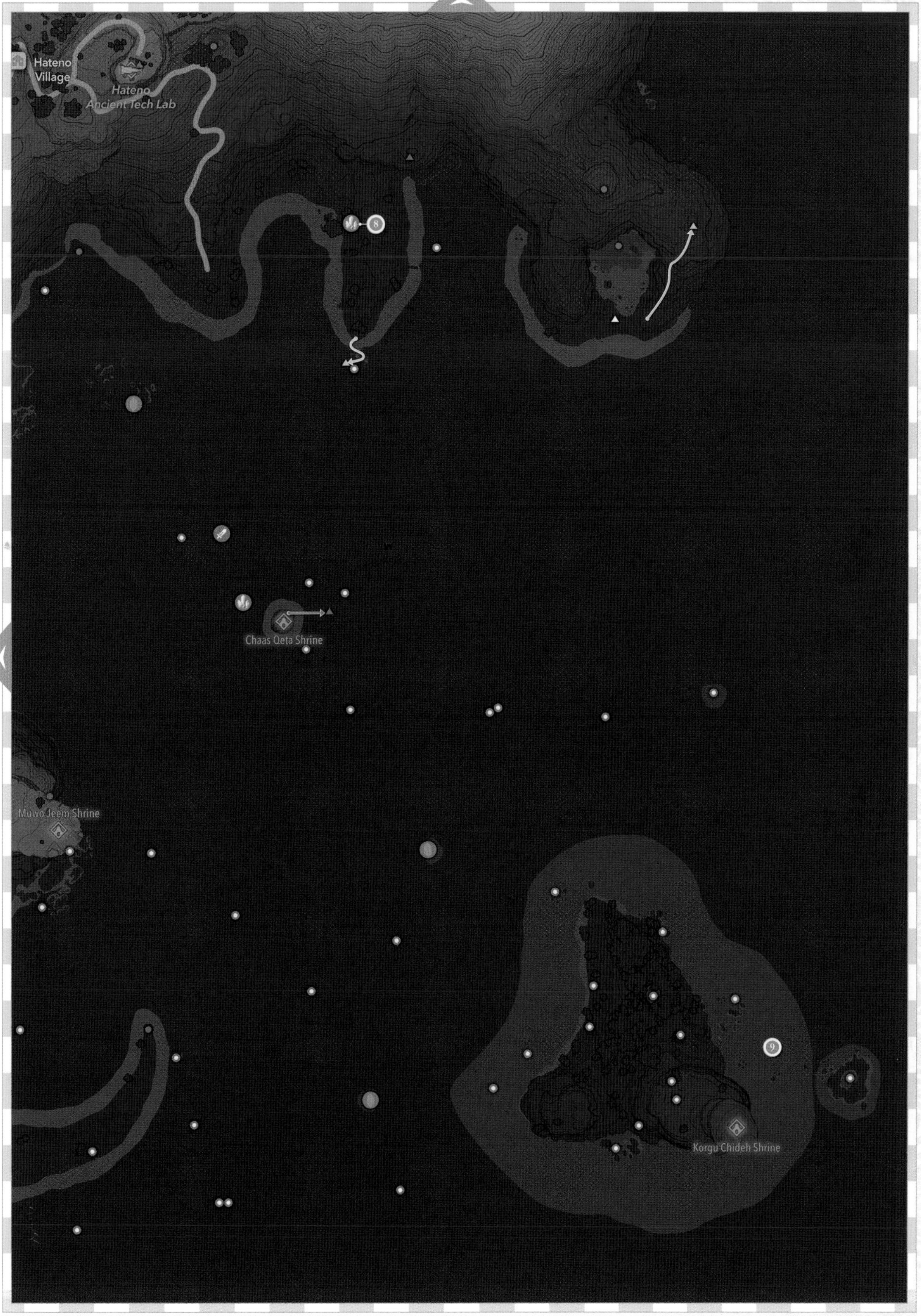

Hateno Village
Hateno Ancient Tech Lab
Chaas Qeta Shrine
Muwo Jeem Shrine
Korgu Chideh Shrine

8. Only after you begin the side quest entitled "The Sheep Rustlers".

9. The chests on (and around) Eventide Island respawn after every loading screen.

HYRULE CASTLE

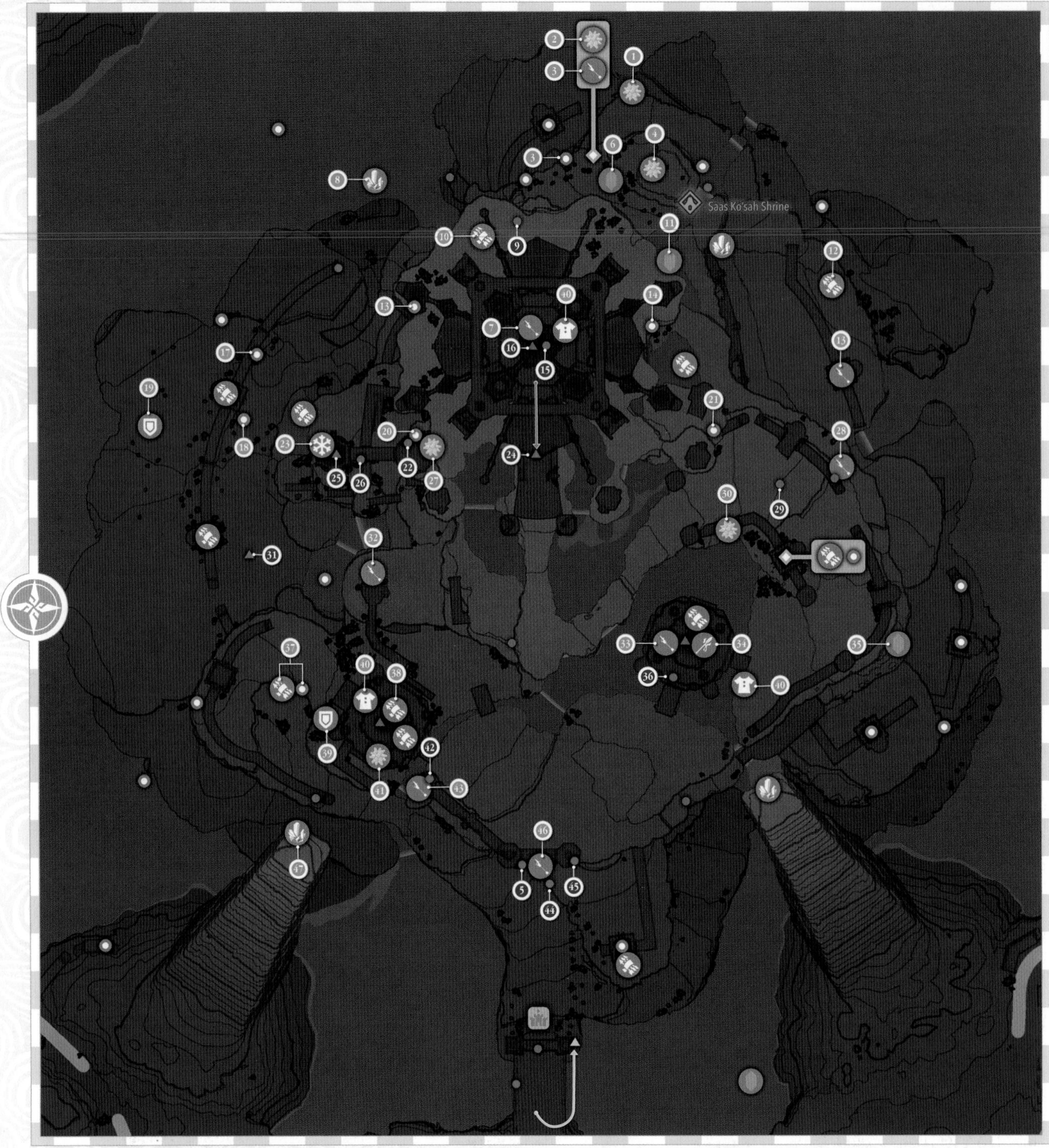

Hyrule Castle is one of the densest areas in the game in terms of collectible items. It also happens to be a location with a very complex layout, featuring multiple floor levels and a whole network of indoor and outdoor passages. This section will help you make sense of its mind-boggling structure, using the names of key rooms inside the castle as handy reference points.

If this is your first time exploring the fortress, feel free to consult our "grand tour" on page 106 – this charts a straightforward path through the dungeon, enabling you to loot its most valuable treasures, including powerful weapons and equipment.

1. At the base of a low cliff, behind destructible rocks.
2. In the Docks, underwater, next to the pier.
3. In the Docks, floating on the water next to the pier (use Cryonis).
4. Under a rock slab.
5. Shoot an arrow at the Triforce emblem built into the Observation Room's balcony.
6. In the Docks, underwater, next to the pier.
7. Near the top of Castle Hyrule belltower.
8. Underwater.
9. Behind destructible rocks, on a cliff ledge just below the Sanctum.
10. On a ledge on the cliff, behind destructible rocks.
11. In the King's Study.
12. Near the cart at the entrance to the East Passage.
13. At the top of the watchtower.
14. In the Library, in a secret passage behind the west metal bookcase.
15. In the castle's tallest tower, shoot the balloon hidden above the bell.
16. At the very top of the spire at the pinnacle of Hyrule Castle.
17. In the Lockup (activate the lever and destroy the wall from the adjacent cell).

18 In the Lockup, to the left, just before reaching the Stalnox's cell.

19 Reward for defeating the Stalnox in the Lockup.

20 In Princess Zelda's Room.

21 In the Library, on the intermediate landing on the south side.

22 On the balcony outside Princess Zelda's Room.

23 On the upper level beams of the Elevator Shaft.

24 The starting point is located on a ledge directly above the Sanctum's main entrance.

25 At the top of the spire above Zelda's Study.

26 In the Elevator Shaft, on a wooden ledge on the south wall, opposite the top of the waterfall.

27 In the Elevator Shaft, behind a destructible wall in the intermediate room.

28 Underwater, above the waterfall.

29 In the East Passage, inside the largest ice block.

30 In a small recess at the top of the East Passage's vertical shaft.

31 In the West Passage's main room, drop a Bird Egg at the foot of the statue to complete the food-offering pattern.

32 In the castle's west corridor, to the right of the staircase.

33 Inside the Second Gatehouse, as a reward for defeating the Lynel.

34 In the Second Gatehouse's attic.

35 On a cliff, behind destructible rocks.

36 Immediately after leaving the Armory, destroy the breakable wall on your right and shoot the acorn hanging from the ceiling in the hidden room.

37 In the Guards' Chamber, on the upper deck.

38 Inside the First Gatehouse, as a reward for defeating the Lynel.

39 In the Guards' Chamber, under the second set of stairs.

40 Expansion Pass required.

41 In the Guards' Chamber, under the first set of stairs.

42 Behind a destructible wall opposite the Guards' Chamber entrance, shoot the acorn hanging from the ceiling.

43 In the castle's south corridor, in a secret room opposite the Guards' Chamber entrance.

44 Shoot the distant balloon from the pinwheel on the Observation Room's balcony; a bow with long range, such as the Falcon Bow, makes the aiming process much easier.

45 Shoot the balloons through the Malice from the pinwheel at the top of the watchtower, above the Observation Room.

46 On the Observation Room's balcony.

47 At the West Passage's south entrance.

CASTLE: INTERIOR

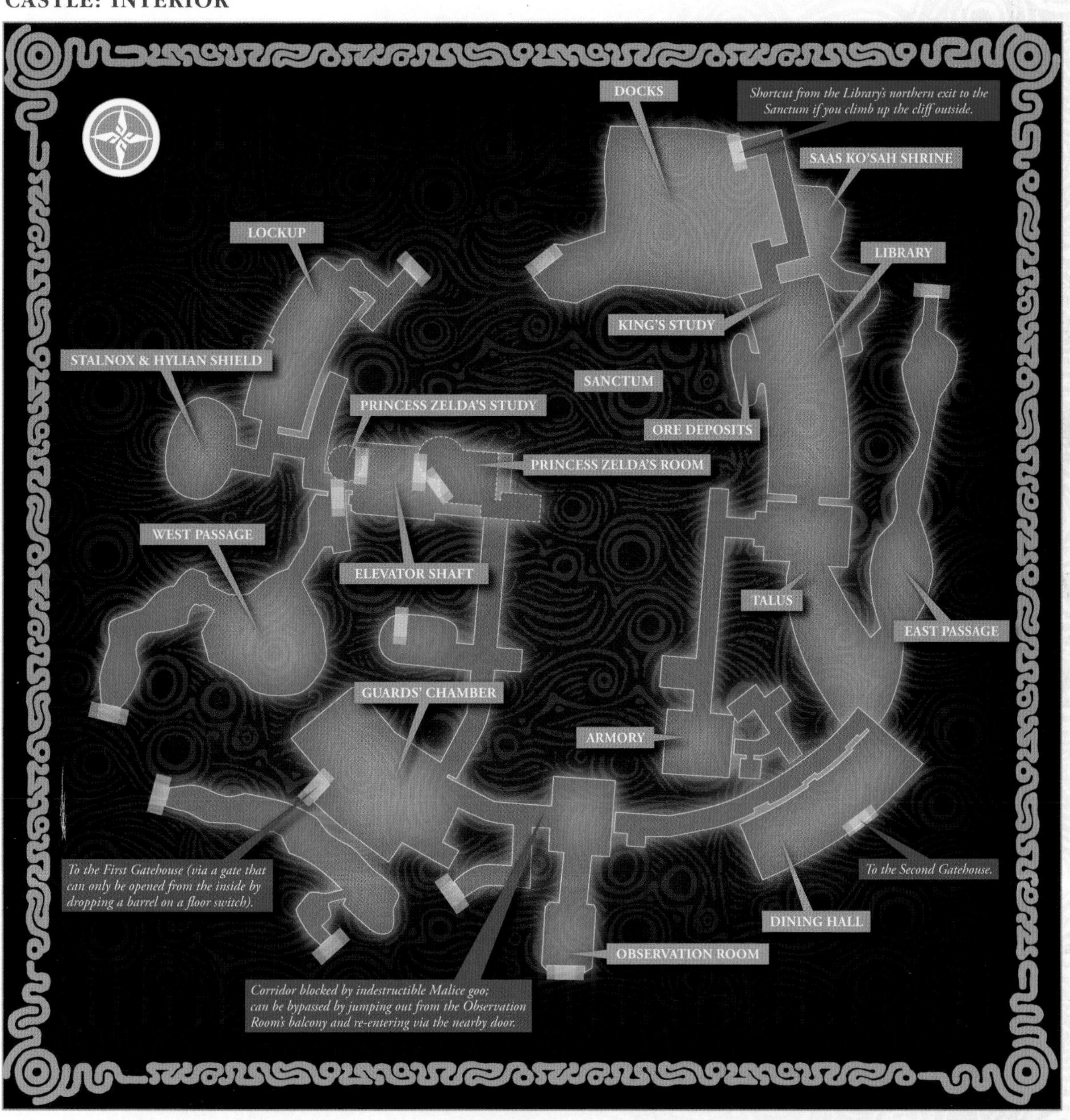

The Master Trials

The first expansion for *Breath of the Wild* introduces new side quests and loot, the Master Mode difficulty setting, and a special challenge known as Trial of the Sword where Link must defeat successive groups of enemies in order to obtain upgrades for the Master Sword. In this chapter, we'll show you how to get the most out of the many new features in this Expansion Pass exclusive download.

Overview Map

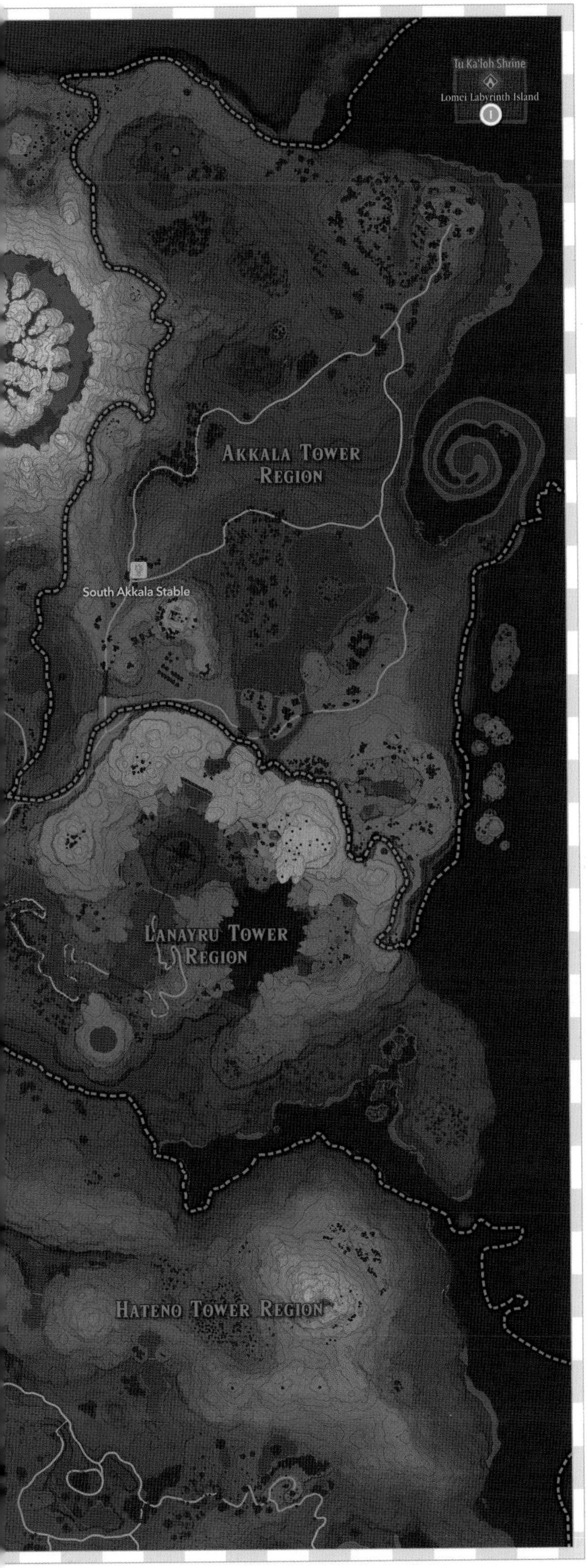

This map shows the position of the Master Trials' main points of interest. The corresponding side quests are detailed in the pages that follow.

REWARD LIST

ICON	NAME	REWARD
A	EX TREASURE CHEST	Ruby
B	EX TREASURE CHEST	Nintendo Switch Shirt
C	EX TREASURE CHEST	Bomb Arrow x5
D	EX TREASURE: ANCIENT MASK	Majora's Mask (most enemies ignore Link)
E1	EX TREASURE: PHANTASMA	Phantom set (Attack Up)
E2		
E3		
F1	EX TREASURE: FAIRY CLOTHES	Tingle's Fairy Clothes (Night Speed Up)
F2		
F3		
G	EX TREASURE: TWILIGHT RELIC	Midna's Helmet (Guardian Resist Up)
H	EX STRANGE MASK RUMORS	Korok Mask (Korok seed sensor)
I	EX TELEPORTATION RUMORS	Travel Medallion (create your own fast travel location)

BONUS CHESTS

These three treasure chests appear on the Great Plateau for all Expansion Pass owners to collect.

- **A** Found next to the Oman Au shrine, to the left of the entrance.
- **B** On top of a wall found a few strides southwest of the Ja Baij shrine.
- **C** Southwest of Keh Namut shrine; it's clearly visible on top of a section of the Plateau's outer wall.

USEFUL FAST TRAVEL POSITIONS

In a new playthrough where you may not wish to tangle with Hyrule Field's high-level enemies (especially Guardian Stalkers in Master Mode) while searching for EX treasure chests, we suggest that you visit the Kaam Ya'tak and Wahgo Katta shrines to create fast travel positions. These will be extremely convenient while you collect the items in and around Hyrule Field.

Side Quests

The Master Trials DLC introduces a selection of new equipment with varied and interesting applications. These are found in special EX treasure chests hidden in lesser-travelled (and usually dangerous) areas of Hyrule (see the map on the previous page).

First Steps

You can begin your search for the exclusive Master Trials items once you complete the opening section of the story and leave the Great Plateau. If you are returning to an existing save point where you have progressed further into the adventure, the quests are available immediately.

If you would like to hunt for the items without assistance, you will first need to find three documents that offer the necessary clues (see the screenshots below). If you intend to use our guidance to head straight for the objects that most interest you, these initial quest steps are purely optional.

It's worth noting that all armor pieces that you can obtain cannot be upgraded at Great Fairy Fountains. Their primary function is either to offer a discretional difficulty reduction during the early stages of the story, or a specific, situational benefit as and when required. However, their low armor ratings become quite a significant disadvantage later in the adventure.

DOCUMENT #1: To formally begin the EX Treasure side quests that lead to new apparel for Link, head to the Outpost Ruins directly east of the Great Plateau Tower; the main road leading to the Dueling Peaks Stable passes through the middle of this location, so it's easy to find. Once you arrive, enter the large ruined building in the southwest to find **Misko's EX Journal**.

DOCUMENTS #2 AND #3: To obtain the clue for the EX Strange Mask Rumors side quest, read the **Super Rumor Mill V1** book found at Woodland Stable. The opening part of the EX Teleportation Rumors! quest is to peruse **Super Rumor Mill V2** at South Akkala Stable; both appear on tables inside the main building.

EX Treasure: Ancient Mask

D

"The ancient mask lies at the ruins where soldiers gathered. From there, the waters of Lake Kolomo are visible."

Head to the south side of the main building at Kolomo Garrison Ruins; you can easily reach this by gliding to the north from the Oman Au shrine on the Great Plateau. Activate Magnesis to identify the EX chest, then pull it from the ground.

Majora's Mask makes a guest appearance from the (much-celebrated) Zelda adventure of the same name. *In Breath of the Wild*, it causes most weapon-bearing monsters (Bokoblins, Moblins, Lizalfos, and the Stal versions of all three) to ignore Link. Even Lynels will pay no real heed to him at the far extent of their detection range unless he does something broadly provocative – such as drawing a weapon, readying a rune power, or lingering within their sightline for too long. Majora's Mask is, in effect, a piece of headgear that offers the combined effects of Kilton's special monster masks.

Naturally, having this power at your disposal has a profound effect on the overall *Breath of the Wild* difficulty level, and is something that we advise that you use sparingly. It is, however, extremely useful when your sole focus is on resource gathering: it can even make sorties into Hyrule Castle fairly trivial if you know how to avoid the hazards (principally Guardians) that it does not ward against. It also makes it easy to stroll into heavily guarded monster encampments and avail yourself of unlocked treasure chests – or even those sealed until all potential combatants are slain, if you make judiciously cynical use of sneakstrikes and environmental deaths. However, you cannot enjoy its effects if you equip it during open combat: most monsters may be gullible, but they're not *that* stupid.

In Master Mode, Majora's Mask is a near-necessity if you plan to make regular long journeys on horseback. The monsters armed with bows and powerful arrows on floating platforms close to major highways (especially pertinent by river or ravine crossings) will only serve to fill the coffers of the Horse Fairy if you do not.

EX TREASURE: PHANTASMA

"Armor worn by fierce phantoms, feared even by heroes, is hidden in the ruins of Hyrule Field."

As with Majora's Mask, the Phantom set is hidden in Hyrule Field and has a profound effect on *Breath of the Wild*'s difficulty level. The 50% damage bonus that the full set offers – not to mention noteworthy resistance to injury if obtained shortly after leaving the Great Plateau – means that it makes Link almost imperiously powerful in Normal Mode. In Master Mode, should you diligently acquire competitively powerful weapons, it evens out the early difficulty level.

Long-term, the Phantom set becomes less effective with the gradual difficulty increase that takes place as you complete Divine Beasts and defeat Hyrule's many monsters, and is ultimately superseded by the Barbarian set (which can be upgraded for increased defense, and also decreases the stamina cost of charged attacks).

The Phantom set has a special property: NPCs will regularly be startled, shout with alarm or cower when Link approaches them while wearing it.

PHANTOM ARMOR

E2

"...at ceremonial grounds where royal guards are honored..."

By far the most difficult set piece to obtain without attracting attention from the numerous Guardians of Hyrule Field, the **Phantom Armor** is found in the first inner ring of water at the south edge of the Sacred Ground Ruins. The most practical approach is to unlock the Central Tower (see page 216), glide to the northeast, then crouch down on the final seconds of the approach to avoid detection by the Guardian Stalkers to the north and east. Alternatively, you can usually arrive at the Passeri Greenbelt without incident by travelling almost directly northwest from the Wahgo Katta shrine.

PHANTOM HELMET

E1

"...at a battleground where brave souls tested their skill..."

The chest containing the **Phantom Helmet** is concealed right next to the inner wall in the northwest of the main Coliseum Ruins arena, on the ground floor. Save your progress at the main entrance, then sneak in and head to the right, hugging the inner perimeter (and making use of the first pillar) to avoid the attention of the Lynel that stalks this area. A stealth approach is much easier if it is raining, and doubly so if you have Majora's Mask equipped.

E3

"...and at the ruins where the soldiers of Hyrule gathered."

The **Phantom Greaves** are found in a partially buried chest at the southeast edge of the Hyrule Garrison Ruins, next to a ruined Guardian. The only sensible way to reach it without provoking the Guardian Stalkers patrolling to the northeast and west (not to mention the mounted Bokoblins that range to the north) is to approach directly from the south.

EX TREASURE: FAIRY CLOTHES

"The green garments of the man who wished to be a fairy are hidden in the ruins of Hyrule Field."

A tribute to the most... *distinctive* character in the Zelda canon, this armor set is also found on Hyrule Field. It offers a token armor rating of 2 per garment. Its true power is only gained when you wear all three parts, which unlocks the Night Speed+ set bonus. This increases Link's movement speed (both running and sprinting) when the sun goes down, which is handy for effortlessly outpacing Stals and expediting impromptu diversions to collect star fragments until you can later upgrade to the superior Stealth set.

Funnily enough, the full Fairy Clothes set has a secret secondary effect: as with the Phantom garb, NPCs will react with alarm or fear when Link approaches them, though it does not affect their behavior during interactions.

TINGLE'S HOOD

F1

"...at the ruins where trade flourished..."

Tingle's Hood is found in a pile of rubble at the Exchange Ruins, a short walk southeast of Kaam Ya'tak shrine and northeast of the Coliseum Ruins. There is a Korok seed directly next to it.

TINGLE'S SHIRT

F2

"...at the ruins where sinners were imprisoned..."

Tingle's Shirt can be collected at Castle Town Prison, located on the island directly west of Hyrule Castle. Unlock the nearby Noya Neha shrine (see page 170) if you have yet to do so, then use the forest canopy to stay out of sight of Skywatchers as you head east. Slow down as you draw close to the destination: a Guardian Stalker patrols the exact area where the chest is found. Either destroy it, or bide your time and run in to pull the chest out of the ground with Magnesis, open it, then fast travel to anywhere else.

TINGLE'S TIGHTS

F3

"...and at the village ruins next to farmland where many people once gathered."

Start at Wahgo Katta shrine and head northwest over Whistling Hill, then change bearing at the bottom of the opposite slope to travel directly north: this will take you to Mabe Village Ruins. As you cross the plain, ignore the first building to your right – this is the Ranch Ruins, where a Guardian Stalker patrols. On arrival at the south of the village, approach the disabled Guardian and move behind it to find the chest containing **Tingle's Tights** hidden beneath.

EX TREASURE: TWILIGHT RELIC

"The princess of twilight, whose stories are handed down alongside those of the Hero of Twilight... Her helmet can be found at the temple ruins soaked in the waters of Regencia River."

This special headgear offers a modest (but, in the early game, competitive) 7 armor and one increment of the Guardian Resist Up buff. It's useful for Test of Strength shrines and other Guardian encounters before you obtain the Ancient set.

Starting at the Kaam Ya'tak shrine, head northwest and follow the bank of the Regencia River to arrive at the Sage Temple Ruins. The chest containing **Midna's Helmet** (the facegear worn by Link's companion in *Twilight Princess*) can be found in a pile of rubble close to the south wall of the northwest building. To avoid confrontations, either cross the river in advance and approach the chest from the west, or skirt around the ruins to arrive from the north.

EX STRANGE MASK RUMORS

"Some say the treasure chest containing this mask is hidden in a tree hollow in a forest that makes people lose their way."

If you'd like to optimize your inventory expansion progress from an early point in the adventure, but don't want to embark on methodical join-the-dots expeditions to find the elusive woodland folk, the Korok Mask is a solid compromise. Though its armor rating is nominal, it vibrates and emits fairy dust particles (as well as the Korok's signature sound) whenever a Korok can be found in the vicinity; at that point, you can stop and scan your surroundings for the obvious point of incongruity that marks their hiding spot. If you wear it whenever you are exploring or gathering resources, you'll be surprised at how many Korok seeds you accumulate without really trying.

It's something of a hike to pick up the Korok Mask early in the story, after leaving the Great Plateau, but the journey will also enable you to unlock fast travel positions close to three stables that you will be grateful for later. From the Great Plateau Tower, glide northeast over the Forest of Time and continue until you reach the Riverside Stable. Cross the Hylia River via Horwell Bridge to the east, then take a left at the next junction and follow the road north to arrive at Wetland Stable. Woodland Stable is almost directly to the north, with a cross-country ramble and river crossing faster than following the main road. The final leg of the journey is to follow the road north until you enter the Lost Woods.

Once inside the Lost Woods, follow the burning braziers to complete the first part of navigating the maze (see page 102). When you arrive at two parallel braziers, take several steps to the west, then head directly south. Pass between the two trees, then examine a third just beyond; the chest containing the **Korok Mask** is found in its "mouth". It's worth taking the time to continue to the Korok Forest afterwards (remember: the direction that the embers are blown from a lit torch points the way) as you can unlock the Keo Ruug shrine for quick access to inventory upgrades later.

EX TELEPORTATION RUMORS

1

"I hear the treasure chest containing this tool is located beneath a labyrinth in northeast Akkala."

Unlike other Master Trials items, obtaining the **Travel Medallion** is quite a substantial undertaking on a new playthrough. It is hidden on Lomei Labyrinth Island, located in the far northeast of Hyrule, and you must navigate the complete maze and reach the Tu Ka'loh shrine to find it.

Unless you are an experienced and reasonably adept player, you may wish to make a little progress in the main storyline and develop Link before you set out to collect it (you will need at least three extra Stamina Vessels just to reach the shrine). If you are sufficiently confident to evade or escape the labyrinth's denizens, though, the set-piece that awaits in a chamber beneath the shrine can actually be completed without conflict.

In addition to the sheer usefulness of always having a manual fast travel position that you can designate within seconds, the Travel Medallion also offers the following advantages:

- You can only have one "travel gate" at a time, but you can establish this practically anywhere in Hyrule. From the Inventory menu, scroll to the Key Items tab, highlight the Travel Medallion, then press Ⓐ and select "Place". You can then journey to the travel gate in the same way as you warp to shrines and towers – just select it from the map screen.
- The Travel Medallion is *extraordinarily* useful for opportunistic resource gathering. In those common instances where you suddenly notice a valuable collection of ore deposits far below after a long ascent, or espy something hitherto unseen that you'd like to investigate, you can use it to effectively "bookmark" your journey and return after dealing with whatever caught your eye. This also applies to valuable star fragments: once you have the Travel Medallion, you can throw down a fast travel point at your current position and head off to collect one, then resume your previous trek after a short load break.
- When you arrive at locations to complete time-sensitive activities where there's a potentially long wait until you can begin (such as the Sasa Kai and Dako Tah shrine quests in the Gerudo region), creating a fast travel point enables you to continue with other activities until you reach the appropriate hour.
- Dragon part collection becomes far less time-consuming, and therefore hugely lucrative. Once you learn their spawn spots and routines, placing a fast travel point in a smart location for farming (see page 363) transforms a potential time-sink into a routine opportunity to gather high-level materials.
- As experienced players will already know, Hyrule Castle is full of high-level items. If you place a travel gate in a suitable location within its boundaries, you can warp there whenever you wish (though only from outside the castle) to plunder its resources.

1

If you have yet to reach the Tu Ka'loh shrine, follow our guidance on page 213 to find it, then interact with the terminal to activate it as a fast travel position. After you clear it, you will immediately notice a hole in the ground with a perpetual updraft directly in front of the shrine. Once ready, drop through the opening and use the paraglider to break your fall before you reach the ground.

2

You don't need to be blessed with bountiful intuition to immediately realize that this giant chamber filled with seemingly dead Guardians is a terrible, terrible trap. What might not be immediately apparent is that there are actually two treasure chests in this room, and that the one prominently visible on the slightly elevated platform at the center does *not* contain the prize you came for. It does, however, immediately activate dormant Guardians that surround your position, so make sure you steer clear of it for now.

3

There are also two Guardian Stalkers that will activate when you approach them: one in the far southwest, and a second east of the central chest. You do not need to awaken them, however, as the chest with the **Travel Medallion** inside is found close to the center of the far south wall. Opening this does not trigger any Guardians. This then leaves you free to plunder the central chest (which, with a certain irony, contains a Diamond Circlet that offers the Guardian Resist perk) and immediately fast travel elsewhere to avoid the resultant onslaught.

MASTER MODE

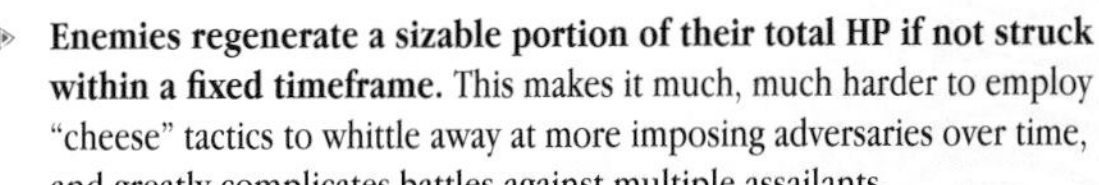

Designed to offer a heightened challenge, Master Mode primarily increases combat difficulty – but there's much more to this new way of playing than you might initially suspect. The need to avoid battles against foes that you are ill-equipped to fight adds a new tension to exploration and encourages a more creative approach to sections of the adventure that you have faced before.

Master Mode has its own save slots, so will not overwrite your existing Normal Mode progress. However, you are limited to a single manual save and an autosave slot. This means that if you commit to a risky or foolish actions, you will not have numerous prior restore points to call upon in your remorse should things go awry.

DIFFERENCES FROM NORMAL MODE

The fundamental Master Mode changes are as follows:

- **Enemies with distinct color-coded ranks are universally upgraded by one level.** For example, the red Bokoblins that you would expect to encounter on the Great Plateau are blue Bokoblins in Master Mode. However, the weapons that they wield (and, therefore, drop) remain consistent with their Normal Mode equipment. In short, they are harder to defeat and generally yield low-quality weapons, so you should pick your battles wisely.

- **There is a new ultimate gold tier for Bokoblins, Moblins, Lizalfos and Lynels.** These foes are functionally similar to their silver variants, but have deeper HP pools and greater resistance to elemental damage. You will not encounter these until you advance the global "world level" difficulty by slaying monsters and bosses (see page 373).

- **Enemies regenerate a sizable portion of their total HP if not struck within a fixed timeframe.** This makes it much, much harder to employ "cheese" tactics to whittle away at more imposing adversaries over time, and greatly complicates battles against multiple assailants.

- **All Guardian variants are more powerful.** The larger models that employ the distinctive beam attack can now attempt to foil your deflection attempts with a new firing delay. The Scouts are more aggressive and resilient, increasing the potential difficulty of any shrine where they are encountered – especially those that you visit early in the adventure.

- **Monsters have an extended detection range.** The existing universal rules (tall grass and foliage mostly conceal Link; rain muffles his footsteps and reduces visibility; enemies cannot see through solid cover) still apply. However, potential antagonists have an improved ability to recognize him as an enemy over greater distances.

- **New floating platforms held aloft by Sky Octoroks introduce both risks and rewards.** Found throughout Hyrule, usually close to crossings and cliffs, these are generally occupied by enemy snipers equipped with powerful arrows, and are also home to treasure chests containing advanced weaponry and other high-level rewards.

GENERAL ADVICE

Broadly speaking, Master Mode does not alter the essential steps required to complete *Breath of the Wild*: the difficulty increase is only experienced when you encounter enemies. Over the few pages that follow, we'll detail various ways that you can cope (and even thrive) during your journey through this more perilous version of Hyrule.

MANUAL DIFFICULTY MANAGEMENT

Once you leave the Great Plateau, you are free to collect the new armor and equipment introduced in the Master Trials DLC (see page 413). Two of the new additions are particularly relevant to a Master Mode playthrough.

- The **Phantom Armor** provides a 50% total damage increase when Link wears the full set, enabling you to eliminate enemies more quickly, and with reduced material costs in terms of weapon degradation. What's more, the 24 total defense rating that all three pieces provide is unparalleled until you have unlocked at least two Fairy Fountains and taken the steps necessary to acquire other garb and upgrade materials. In short, it adjusts the early difficulty scaling of Master Mode combat from murderous to mostly manageable. Its usefulness wanes as you make meaningful story progress, or make extended expeditions into areas that require environmental protection. It is ultimately superseded by the Barbarian set later in the adventure.

- If the Phantom Armor pulls a few fangs from Master Mode's foreboding maw, **Majora's Mask** renders it effectively toothless. Wearing it essentially activates "easy mode", where the majority of weapon-bearing enemies (sub-bosses excepted) will treat Link as no more than a curiosity. You are even free to stroll into encampments and pilfer weapons and chest contents without arousing the ire of their denizens. This headgear is therefore best used sparingly.

SURVIVAL TIPS

- Discretion is the better part of valor in Master Mode. You don't need to fight everything, and will rarely profit by doing so. The best survival advice we could offer is to slay as few enemies as possible, as this will delay the instances where certain monsters are upgraded in rank after you reach hidden kill count thresholds. Minor enemies such as Keese and Chuchus, however, are fair game.

- Purchase the Stasis+ and Remote Bombs+ upgrades from the Hateno Tech Lab as soon as you can; see page 359 for advice on quickly farming Guardian tech. The former greatly simplifies encounters with tough targets (and has useful stealth applications), while the latter makes alternating between the two bomb types a viable combat tactic, and saves you time by reducing cooldown delays. You should definitely upgrade both runes before you enter the Trial of the Sword.

- Hestu's inventory expansions are a must, as having more weapon slots enables you to accumulate a varied and powerful arsenal. The locations of the Korok seeds required to unlock extra slots are documented on the poster included with this guide, and in the Maps chapter that starts on page 374.

- If you perhaps neglected advanced meal and elixir creation in Normal Mode, you'll find the buffs they offer extremely useful in Master Mode – especially when the time comes to start tackling adversaries such as Lynels. See page 356 for an advanced guide to preparing buffs and restoratives at cooking pots.

- It will be second-nature to most experienced *Breath of the Wild* players, but it's a good idea to explore Hyrule and unlock shrine and tower fast travel positions to build a network of locations that you can warp to in order to farm regional resources when required. Unlocking Faron Tower, for example, will enable you to regularly collect over 30 hearty durians within a matter of minutes. We offer further advice on resource farming on page 354.

- Avoid enemies that you do not need to fight, especially groups, but take opportunities to eliminate isolated foes who offer valuable resource drops that you can later use to upgrade armor. One benefit of Master Mode is that you obtain early access to certain crafting materials you would ordinarily find in short supply early in a Normal Mode playthrough.

- Sneakstrikes can inflict massive damage in return for a negligible weapon durability cost, so try to engineer stealth attacks whenever possible. It's a good idea to carry (and preserve) at least one heavy weapon with 30+ damage at all times purely for this purpose. In open combat, don't forget that it's possible to maneuver Link behind opponents (especially slow-moving Moblins) to secure rear attack damage bonuses when they commit to certain actions. A consistent way to engineer back-attacks is to drop a Remote Bomb; as your opponent reacts to this action, move behind them to strike.

- Having at least one fire and lightning elemental weapon in your inventory is useful, but you should ensure that you carry at least two or three ice weapons at all times. Ice-imbued swords and spears (the latter being preferable for their range advantage) freeze most enemies, with the subsequent hit – ideally with your most powerful weapon – carrying a x3 damage multiplier. Refer to page 358 to find out where you can discover elemental weapons.

- When you can, employ cheap and easy environmental kills. The humble Boko Leaf, overlooked in most Normal Mode playthroughs, is incredibly effective at propelling susceptible enemies over cliffs and into deep water. And, as long as you don't inadvertently strike enemies, a single leaf will last for as long as you need it.

- All Guardian variants that employ the targeted laser beam can now foil your attempts to use the traditional audiovisual deflect cues by delaying the shot by a second or two. You can compensate for this by waiting for a beat before repeating the Perfect Guard attempt. It will take practice to master this, but there is no shortage of training opportunities in Hyrule Field.

- The Guardian Scouts encountered in shrines are more dangerous. Those that employ melee weapons (regularly encountered in Test of Strength shrines) are functionally identical, but the Guardian Scout I gains an entirely new dimension in Master Mode. They are extremely evasive, so have a fast weapon at the ready (ideally a polearm for the perfect blend of speed and reach) to strike and shoot arrows in their eye to cancel their laser attacks.

- There is a simple way to carry up to 11 fairies at a time. Collect three or four at a Great Fairy Fountain, then warp to another one. Fairies will initially not spawn if Link is carrying three or more, but you can game the system: open your inventory and have Link hold your current fairies in his hands. This technically removes them from your inventory, causing new fairies to appear at the fountain. Put your fairies away with Ⓑ, collect the new ones, and you can then repeat this trick until you have a full stock of 11.

GOLD ENEMIES

Though you are unlikely to see them for many hours, there are four new gold-tier enemies that you can encounter later in the story. These opponents are incredibly strong, so be sure that you have the necessary weapons (and ideally start with a sneakstrike) should you decide to tackle them. As with silver-grade enemies, they might drop high-value loot (such as star fragments) when they fall.

VARIANT	HP
GOLD BOKOBLIN	1,080
GOLD MOBLIN	1,620
GOLD LIZALFOS	1,296
GOLD LYNEL	7,500

WALKTHROUGH ADDENDUM

All main story missions and side quests are essentially identical in Master Mode, with increased enemy difficulty (and, on occasion, the added complication of snipers on Sky Octorok platforms) only serving to heighten the potential challenge.

Our Walkthrough chapter is equally relevant to a Master Mode playthrough. There are, however, two main junctures early in the adventure where you will benefit from additional advice.

PROLOGUE: THE GREAT PLATEAU (PAGE 36)

With all Bokoblins on the Plateau elevated to blue grade (and a couple promoted to black), but still carrying low-level weapons, we strongly advise that you avoid combat unless you can end it immediately with a sneakstrike. See page 396 for a map of treasure chests on the Great Plateau, and take the time to plunder those that will provide you with a solid collection of strong melee weapons, bows and arrows while you tour the four shrines.

There is a Lynel situated on the plains southeast of the Temple of Time, so pay this an extremely wide berth. There isn't a single Bokoblin that you can't avoid by taking a different route, and even those that block your path to the Great Plateau Tower close to the start can be bypassed with a well-timed sprint.

A word of warning: the Guardian Scouts encountered in the Keh Namut and Oman Au shrines will be a shock to the system if you're accustomed to dispatching them with one-shot kills in Normal Mode. If you neglect to collect decent weapons before you encounter them, you may find them surprisingly hard to beat. Try to lure them around corners and strike with fast weapons before they can attempt to hit Link with their ranged attack. Runes can also prove very useful.

SEEK OUT IMPA (PAGE 44)

If you intend to make a "story complete" playthrough (120 shrines, all Captured Memories, all four Divine Beasts) or the gargantuan undertaking of a true 100% playthrough, you may wish to keep your kill count to a minimum and leave the Divine Beasts until you have completed all other activities.

Breath of the Wild has a hidden score counter that keeps a tally of Link's combat victories against qualifying enemies (broadly, all weapon-bearing foes, sub-bosses and bosses). When this score reaches set thresholds, assorted hostiles in the game world are elevated by one rank – from blue to black, black to silver, and – eventually – from silver to gold. Eliminating annoying Stals at night or killing the occasional Bokoblin or Moblin won't make much of a difference, but any meaningful depopulation of sub-bosses or victories against the Blight bosses will lead to fairly significant increments in the hidden "world level" tally (see page 373).

This secret variable is both a blessing and a curse, though, because it also gradually leads to better loot from both monster drops and applicable chests.

If you would prefer an easy life, we suggest that you leave all optional sub-boss encounters and the Divine Beast dungeons until you have completed all other activities on your playthrough itinerary (such as towers, shrines, side quests and general exploration) and are ready to focus on the main story path that leads to the final showdown with Ganon. While you're free to advance most of the regional main quests without any unforeseen consequences, you may also benefit by leaving the Yiga Clan portion of the Gerudo questline until later – completing it could increase the number of ambushes you'll face while traveling.

Alternatively, you can make it your mission to eliminate every hostile that you encounter... and reap the rewards while enjoying the challenge of experiencing Hyrule at its most hostile. The choice, of course, is yours to make.

SKY OCTOROK PLATFORMS

Exclusive to Master Mode, Sky Octorok platforms are one of the keys to dealing with the greater difficulty of combat. Unlike standard enemies, the sentries (and chests) found on these platforms tend to offer items that you wouldn't usually expect to obtain until much, much later in the story. Better still, the melee weapons, bows and shields you collect are often enchanted.

Making regular stops to raid Sky Octorok platforms when you find them will leave Link equipped to deal with almost any enemy. The chests do not respawn once opened, but – as the map here clearly attests – are sufficiently plentiful that you can overcome everything that Master Mode throws at you until monsters generally start to carry better weapons.

GENERAL TIPS AND OBSERVATIONS

- The monsters that occupy most platforms have a very long detection range. They wield bows with magic arrows (including bomb arrows) or, less commonly, elemental rods.
- Many platforms are, in a sense, puzzles: figuring out how to obtain their loot without undue effort or injury is surprisingly enjoyable. Some are quite ingenious and playful.
- The obvious, brute-force solution is to shoot the Sky Octoroks. However, some chests are situated where they will fall to inaccessible positions.
- Some enemies can carry valuable arrows and top-quality bows. Where possible, try to kill them in a way that doesn't propel them from the platform where such items may be lost – for example, try to engineer it so that their bodies rebound from the ropes, chests or Sky Octoroks. Once you have the Travel Medallion (see page 418), you can optionally create a useful travel point before you engage sentries, float down to claim their loot, then warp back and head to the platforms to claim the other prizes.
- Approaching via a high vantage point is always beneficial; from below or on a similar level, there's a far greater risk of detection. The sentries behave in an identical way to marksmen on guard towers, shifting their body position/view cone at regular intervals. If you have a sufficiently powerful bow, a single headshot will suffice. We strongly advise that you keep a Falcon Bow (or another variety defined by its long range) at hand to hit more distant targets.
- The Sky Octoroks will detect you as you move closer, but don't worry – they will not alert nearby monsters, and cannot attack.
- Explosions or high-powered attacks that slam the wooden platforms with heavy weapons will break them. This can include sneakstrikes with heavy weapons. Smashed platforms are replenished if you move a sufficient distance away or fast travel. The sentries only reappear every Blood Moon, as per the universal rules.
- Multiple platforms are "connected" in the sense that if a sentry sounds the alarm on one, they may all move up to new elevations. Beware of hidden platforms that may contain snipers! While standing on an unoccupied platform in its lower position, Link can whistle to make it rise. It will return to its lower position after a set interval of time, or should you move a sufficient distance away. Note that all platforms in the current group will also rise when you do this – even if they still have enemies on board.
- With platforms suspended by four Sky Octoroks, you can safely shoot one without having the entire platform become unstable. A fringe benefit of this is that it makes the platform hang slightly lower. When you find instances where a platform is *just* out of easy jumping range, this can be the solution.
- If you want to get a metal chest, and it's an even vaguely technical jump to reach the platform, grab it with Magnesis.
- Platforms are subject to *Breath of the Wild*'s physics engine. If a dragon passes by close to a floating platform, it may well be blown to a new position. If they fall into water, they will float, and drift in prevailing currents. The same applies to the chests that you find on them: metal containers will sink, but wooden boxes will bob on the surface, enabling you to plunder them after placing a Cryonis pillar.

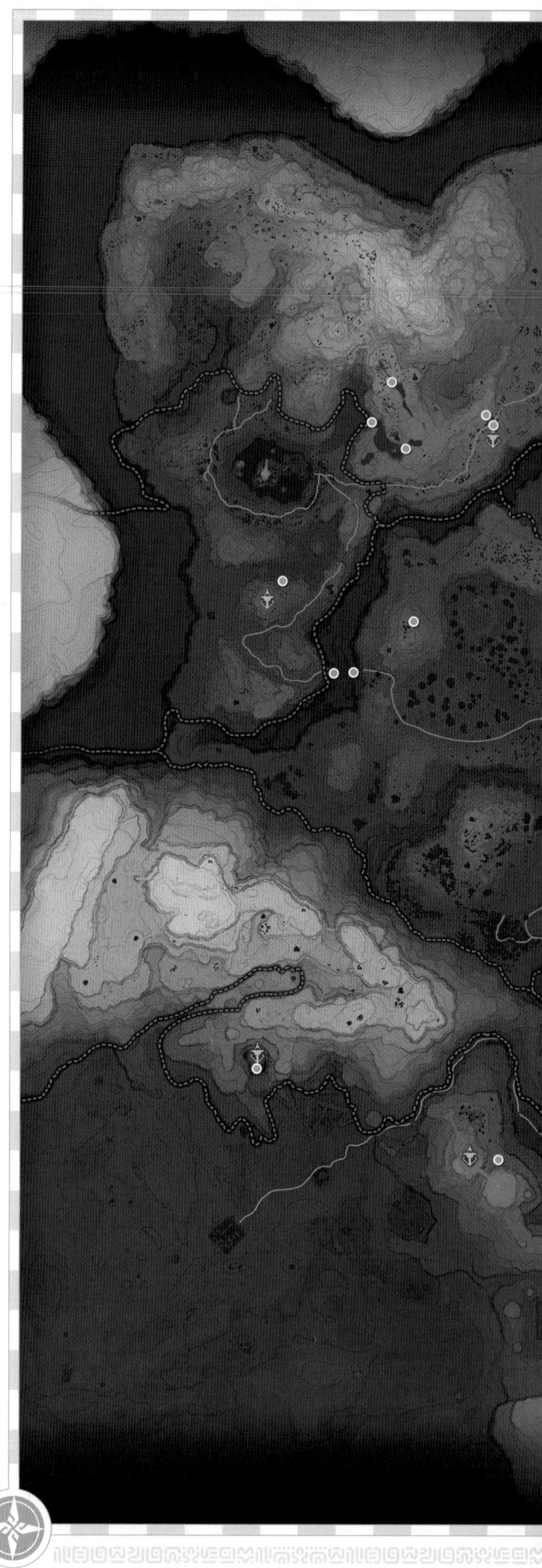

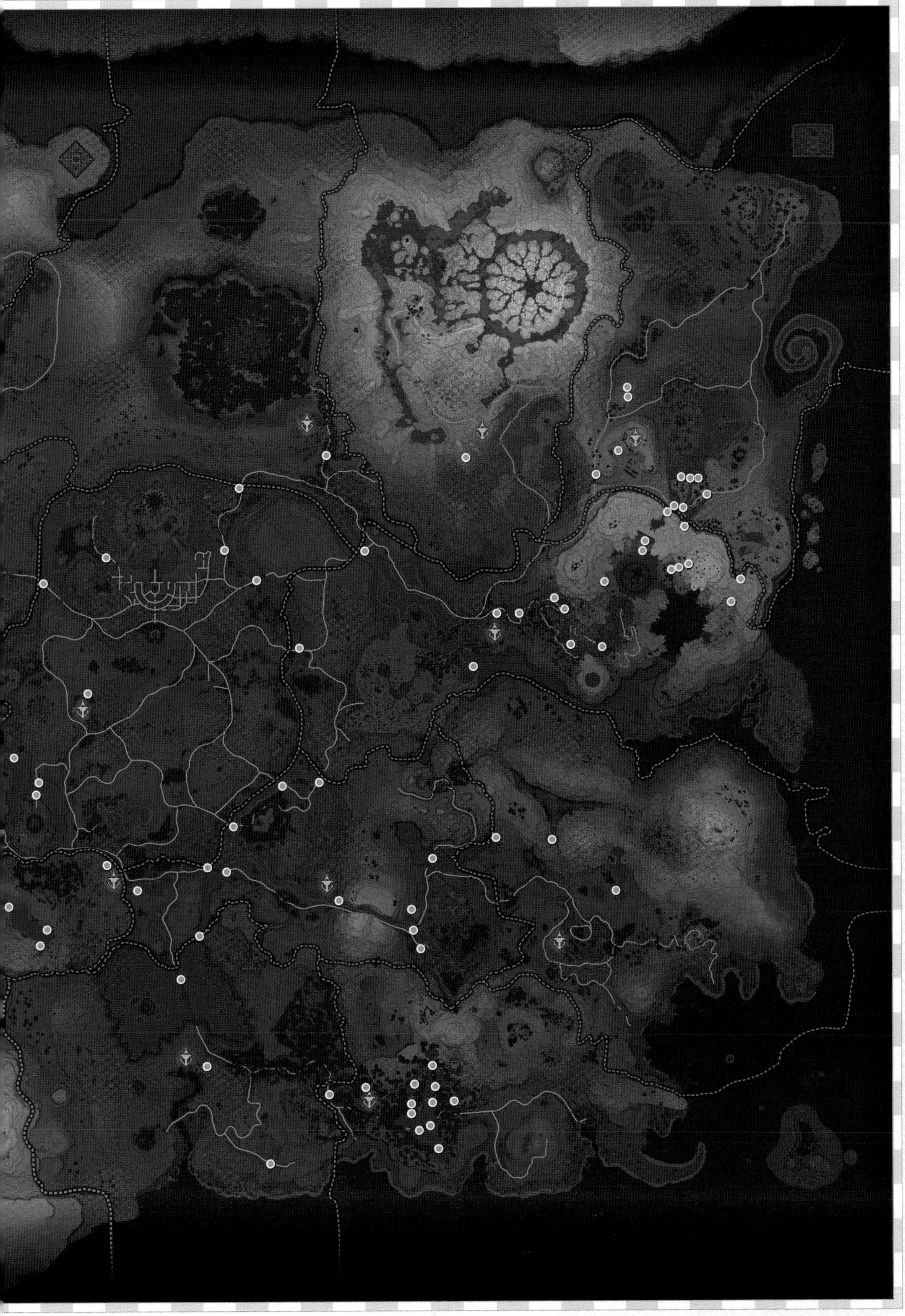

TRIAL OF THE SWORD

Designed as a late-story test of wits, composure and pure combat prowess, but available from the moment Link claims the Master Sword, Trial of the Sword is home to some of the most difficult battles you can face in *Breath of the Wild* – especially when played in Master Mode.

THE BASICS

To unlock Trial of the Sword, Link must first acquire at least 13 red hearts – yellow temporary hearts do not count – and pull the Master Sword from its pedestal at the heart of the Korok Forest (see page 100).

At this point, fast travel to any other location to obtain a message about the availability of the Trial. If you are returning to an existing save file after installing the Master Trials DLC, where Link already has the Master Sword, you'll encounter this message when you resume your playthrough.

As you approach the Great Deku Tree on your next visit to the Korok Forest, a cutscene will play. When that ends, approach the Master Sword slot and press Ⓐ to begin. There is, however, one last condition that may delay your entry: if the Master Sword is out of energy, you must first wait for the recharge timer to elapse.

Link begins each set of Trials without weapons, equipment or consumables. Any Champion abilities acquired are sealed (as is the Travel Medallion). Your only resources at the start are the Sheikah Slate rune powers, and the paraglider. Everything else you must scavenge from within the arenas that you fight in, or wrest from hostile owners.

Trial of the Sword consists of three separate segments: the Beginning Trials (12 floors), the Middle Trials (16 floors) and the Final Trials (23 floors). You must guide Link safely through the Beginning Trials to unlock the Middle Trials, and then conquer the latter to make the Final Trials available.

Link obtains an incremental +10 attack upgrade for the Master Sword on successful completion of each segment, and is then returned to the Korok Forest. Once the Master Sword has recovered its full strength, its attack power is permanently set at 60.

Saving is not possible during Trials: each of the three segments must be beaten within a single sitting. The consequences for failure, or quitting an uncompleted segment, are entirely unforgiving: Link is immediately returned to Hyrule, and all progress in that Trial is reset. You must start from scratch on your next attempt. However, there is no time limit on each floor, so you are free to reconnoiter, plan, and then execute your favored strategy – even if that approach is arduously slow but almost completely safe.

Once all enemies on a floor have been dispatched, an exit portal will activate. There is no need to rush for this – it's always wise to scour the area for useful items before you depart. When you are ready, you can approach it and press Ⓐ to proceed.

The Trial segments are divided by monster-free rest areas that feature a cooking pot where you can prepare meals with gathered ingredients to restore lost hearts and gain status effects.

PREPARATION

Though you only need 13 hearts to begin, we strongly advise that you spend more time on developing Link before you enter the Trials.

- The more hearts you have, the better Link's chances of survival will be. As you do not have the advanced armors that you acquire during the course of the main story, you cannot haphazardly trade or tank hits in combat.
- You begin the Trials with the same amount of weapon, bow and shield inventory slots that you enter with. Melee weapon slots are essential: you should have at least 15, which will enable you to collect and keep weapons to cover multiple scenarios (see page 330).
- Having three full stamina wheels is hugely advantageous, especially once you unlock the Middle Trials, as this will enable you to make full use of slo-mo aerial archery and charged melee attacks.
- The upgrades for Stasis and the Remote Bombs are categorically necessary (see page 229). You will put yourself at a massive disadvantage if you do not have them.
- Link carries his current status into each Trials session. If you have any depleted hearts, always speak to Pepp by the bed inside the Great Deku Tree for a free rest before you begin.

Interestingly, status effects are also carried into the Trials. This means that you can prepare and consume a high-level meal beforehand to gain a buff that will give Link an edge for as long as it lasts. The most appropriate concoctions are as follows:

- Four razorshrooms (or other ingredients that boost attack) and a Dragon's Horn will lead to a dish that will imbue Link with the maximum possible Attack Up boost for half an hour. This is incredibly effective in Master Mode, where the principal challenge (especially in the Beginning and Middle Trials) is inflicting sufficient damage to dispatch upgraded enemies without eating through limited melee weapons at an unsustainable rate.
- You can gain a slight additional survivability boost by cooking five endura carrots to get enduring fried wild greens. This gives two bonus stamina wheels.
- A final (though less important) step is to cook hearty durians to gain the full 30 hearts.

Refer to page 356 to learn how to quickly farm the ingredients detailed above.

USEFUL TIPS

- Remote Bombs represent "free" kills on weaker enemies, enabling you to preserve melee weapons and your stock of arrows; don't forget that you can alternate between the two types to maintain a barrage and effectively bypass the individual cooldown periods. Whenever there is a heavy metal object within reach, you can activate Magnesis to employ it as a cudgel or drop it from a great height.
- Trees yield wood bundles, Korok leaves, branches and acorns. You can roast acorns for emergency heart refills, and even cook each bundle of wood individually at Rest Areas to obtain rock-hard food that heals a quarter of a heart if your survival prospects are truly bleak.
- Smash *all* crates and barrels to obtain arrows and food; try to avoid scenarios where they are set ablaze, as this will burn or roast the items inside. The contents (and quantities) are variable: sometimes you're lucky, other times less so. With containers that drop arrows, it's a roll of the dice as to whether they yield one, five or 10. Treasure chest contents, however, are always the same. Unless it's a dire emergency, save all food that you can cook for rest areas, where you can prepare meals that offer far superior healing returns and buffs.
- Unlike in Hyrule, cutting grass does not yield items, critters or fairies. Monsters drop their weapons, if they have them, and nothing else. Fairies can only be obtained at rest areas: as always, crouch-walk quietly toward them to collect them; any noise you make will scare them away.
- Fight with wit and caution: don't rely on brute force strategies. Where possible, always look to lure monsters away from their allies and dispatch them in a position of your choosing. If there is an environmental kill opportunity, use it.

MASTER MODE

The global Master Mode rules that are applied to all other activities in Hyrule also apply in Trial of the Sword: all foes of note can regenerate health, while the opponents you face are all one rank higher (where applicable).

These conditions can transform Trial of the Sword into a pitilessly difficult experience unless you use critical advanced strategies. If you are less than proficient at the following key skills, we suggest that you strip Link down to his undergarments (for an authentic simulation of the Trial of the Sword experience) and practice them against strong foes beforehand.

- Aerial archery is an absolute must. You only need a slight downhill incline or short direct drop in front of Link to activate the slow motion effect with practice, which can enable you to land multiple midair critical hits in rapid succession.
- The ability to target and inflict Stasis+ immediately, and with great accuracy, is profoundly advantageous. One oft-overlooked application of it is that you can use it on sentries from a fair distance and then just sprint directly through their sightlines; it's also a way to safely set up stealth attacks.
- Practice and master the art of defeating single enemies with perpetual sneakstrikes. Bokoblins, Moblins and Lizalfos always jump to their feet and then turn to face the direction that a sneakstrike was landed from. It may seem slightly counter-intuitive, but they cannot see Link if you stay close and move behind them just after the blow is landed. This means that when they turn to face the origin of the prior blow, you can trigger another sneakstrike prompt. It's a great trick to have in your repertoire in general, and is also the most reliable way to beat notoriously hard floors. When required, you can employ single arrows to carefully lure opponents to more suitable ambush positions.
- Escape is an option in most arenas, and is preferable to engaging multiple opponents.

USING THE WALKTHROUGHS

Our strategies generally err on the side of caution, outlining approaches that will work for all readers – not just experienced and capable players. If you're confident, you'll know exactly when you can charge in and dispatch enemies without any measure of ceremony or unwarranted caution.

There is no mini-map in the Trials, but you can determine the direction that Link is facing by opening up the main map. With only a handful of minor exceptions, Link faces directly north when he materializes on each floor.

There are certain instances where specific tools, if saved until the right moment, can make a difficult fight *much* easier. We highlight these with footnotes beneath the overview tables.

If you don't care about spoilers, we suggest that you browse all walkthrough entries for the Trials section you are due to undertake before you begin. This will give you a clear sense of what you must accomplish, and which items will be most critical to your survival.

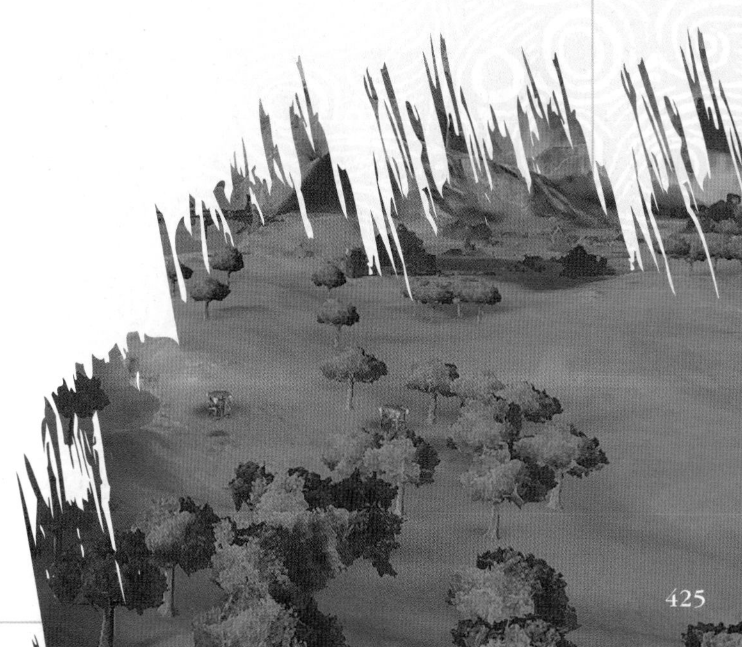

BEGINNING TRIALS

The first Trial of the Sword consists of 12 floors, with a rest area on the seventh. Floor 10 is an infamous difficulty spike in Master Mode.

Floor 01

OVERVIEW

Enemies	Bokoblin x3	
Equipment	Tree Branch x2, Boko Club, Boko Spear, Woodcutter's Axe, Boko Shield	*Master Mode only:* Rusty Broadsword, Rusty Halberd, Rusty Claymore, Rusty Shield, Extra Boko Spear
Noteworthy Items	Seared Steak, assorted food items in the barrels and crates close to the camp	*Master Mode only:* Bird Egg x2 in the large tree closest to the center

WALKTHROUGH: The three Bokoblins are gathered around a campfire to the northeast. Sneak to their position, ready a Remote Bomb, then step out into the open and throw it at their collection of weapons when they rush to arm themselves. The detonation should eliminate all three at once.

MASTER MODE NOTES: The fight is much easier if you can grab the enemy weapons by the log and just beyond the campfire before the Blue Bokoblins can reach them. From your starting position, sneak to the giant tree and whistle while concealed behind the trunk. Climb the tree before your opponents close in, then jump and glide over their heads; if you time it right, you can collect most (or even all) of the weapons for yourself. If you fight the Bokoblins individually, note that you can alternate between both bomb types to defeat them, thereby preserving weapon durability.

Floor 02

OVERVIEW

Enemies	Bokoblin x4, Large Fire Chuchu	
Equipment	Traveler's Sword, Traveler's Shield, Boko Bow x2, Boko Bat	*Master Mode only:* Iron Sledgehammer*, Wooden Bow, Boko Club * Save this for Floor 06 on Master Mode.
Noteworthy Items	Arrows and food items in the crates on the elevated platform; arrows in the barrels next to the guard tower	

WALKTHROUGH: You can reach the main treehouse platform by gliding from one of the nearby trees, or using an updraft caused by the Fire Chuchu. If you don't wish to engage the main trio all at once, feel free to bowl at least one down to the lower level with a Korok leaf.

MASTER MODE NOTES: Deal with the lone archer first, then smash the barrels beside its tower to gain arrows. The Bokoblins on the tree fort platform are unlikely to leave it voluntarily. You can exploit this to sequentially knock individuals down, then lure them a safe distance away before you fight.

Floor 03

OVERVIEW

Enemies	Chuchu, Fire Chuchu x4, Large Fire Chuchu x4
Equipment	Boomerang
Noteworthy Items	Fire arrow x5

WALKTHROUGH: The Chuchus spawn in three waves and can be easily dispatched with Remote Bombs. The challenge lies in leading individual Fire Chuchus close to the south and north walls, where you can use updrafts caused by burning grass to reach two treasure chests in otherwise inaccessible positions. Try to face the platforms on takeoff, as the gusts only offer limited elevation.

Floor 04

OVERVIEW

Enemies	Bokoblin x5, Blue Bokoblin x2	
Equipment	Soldier's Broadsword, Soldier's Shield, Spiked Boko Bat, Boko Spear, Spiked Boko Bow, Traveler's Bow, Boko Club, Traveler's Spear	*Master Mode only:* Extra Spiked Boko Bat, Rusty Broadsword, Rusty Shield
Noteworthy Items	Fire arrows in the barrels next to the sniper; assorted food and arrows in the crates; Bird Egg x2 in the large tree to the northwest	

WALKTHROUGH: As soon as the level begins, crouch down and creep behind the tree to your right before an archer equipped with fire arrows detects Link. Work on gradually eliminating the Bokoblins individually from the bottom of the camp to the top. When you arrive at the upper reaches, look for a spear-wielding Bokoblin on the watch platform accessed separately via a long ladder. By far the most sensible way to deal with him is to use a fire arrow to ignite the explosive barrels right next to him.

MASTER MODE NOTES: Try to deal with at least the first three Bokoblins (two Blues in the lower reaches of the treehouse, then one Black) with sneakstrikes. Lure the second Black Bokoblin down and dispatch him carefully; wait for clear openings, and don't get drawn into trading hits.

Floor 05

OVERVIEW

Enemies	Moblin x2, Blue Bokoblin x3	
Equipment	Moblin Club, Moblin Spear, Spiked Boko Bat, Spiked Boko Club, Spiked Boko Spear, Spiked Boko Shield	*Master Mode only:* Woodcutter's Axe, Spiked Moblin Club, Extra Spiked Boko Bat, Extra Spiked Boko Spear
Noteworthy Items	Arrows and food in the two barrels and four crates inside the skull cave	

WALKTHROUGH: Crouch as soon as Link fully materializes, then move into cover. Lure the Moblins patrolling either side of the skull cave to the southeast and southwest corners respectively for quick kills that won't alert their allies. Detonating the explosive barrels by the Bokoblins will destroy perishable collectibles in the vicinity, so it's better to use arrows to lure individuals out and fight them one by one.

MASTER MODE NOTES: In the event that you alert more than one Black Bokoblin at once, it's prudent to sprint until you lose all but a single pursuer.

Floor 06

WALKTHROUGH: If you're playing Trial of the Sword, you shouldn't need to be told how to fight a Stone Talus (see page 314 otherwise). On Master Mode, though, your adversary's attacks can be deadly – so a quick finish will be beneficial. Use the sledgehammer found on Floor 02 to optimize your damage output.

OVERVIEW

Opponent	Stone Talus
Equipment	*Master Mode only:* Rusty Claymore x3

Floor 07: Rest Area

WALKTHROUGH: Plunder this peaceful space of its treasures, then use the pot to prepare meals (refer to page 296 for a comprehensive guide to cooking). There's no need to be frugal: you won't get another chance to do so before the end of the Beginning Trials.

MASTER MODE NOTES: If you are taking things very carefully, your pre-Trials Attack Up boost will likely expire before you arrive at the all-important Floor 10. Unless you have been desperately unlucky with item drops from crates, you should have sufficient razorshrooms and/or mighty bananas (exactly four in any ratio) to prepare a meal that will offer a new Level 3 Attack Up buff; add a bird egg to maximize the duration. Save this dish until you need it!

OVERVIEW

Equipment	Eightfold Blade, Serpentine Spear, Shield of the Mind's Eye, Torch
Noteworthy Items	Fairy, Razorshroom x2, Ironshroom x2, Armored Carp x3, Apples x2, plus arrows (including fire arrows) and food in the wooden crates

Floor 08

OVERVIEW

Enemies	Lizalfos x2, Blue Lizalfos x2, Large Electric Chuchu	
Equipment	Lizal Boomerang, Lizal Bow*, Throwing Spear, Boko Spear x4 * Preserve this for Floors 11 and 12 if you can.	*Master Mode only:* Fishing Harpoon, Lizal Spear
Noteworthy Items	Roasted Bass x3, two wooden crates with items inside, metal treasure chest in the northwest containing arrows x10	

WALKTHROUGH: The best approach is to tackle the enemies here in a counter-clockwise progression. Bait the first Lizalfos into attacking without alerting the archer to the northwest, then eliminate the latter with a headshot. The southwest island has a convenient raised area on the northern edge that enables you to move onto dry land and wait out of sight. If you're confident, you can alert the two Lizalfos and then shoot the Electric Chuchu to disable and disarm them as they run past it, then grab their weapons to greatly simplify the fight.

MASTER MODE NOTES: Unless you are extremely fortunate, the Blue Lizalfos archer on the rocks to the northeast will detect and fire on Link while you engage his ally directly north of your starting position. This is not a huge threat if you keep the fight close to the outer wall. Stasis+ will make your life easier. The two Black Lizalfos on the southwest island can be deadly if fought as a pair, so the best strategy is to separate them. Land on the north edge of their island and cast Stasis+ on one, then lead the second to the northeast land area, where you can pin it against a wall and stun-lock it.

Floor 09

OVERVIEW

Enemies	Water Octorok x2, Electric Wizzrobe	
Equipment	Lightning Rod	*Master Mode only:* Silver Bow* in treasure chest to the northwest * Save this for Floors 10 and 11.
Noteworthy Items	Arrow x10 in treasure chest	

WALKTHROUGH: You begin on an island in the south of the arena. Immediately turn right and dodge the Water Octorok's opening salvo. Burst it with an arrow, then use a Cryonis pillar to elevate the clearly visible treasure chest in the southwest. Climb the tall rock spire and eliminate the second Water Octorok to the north. The quickest way to deal with the Wizzrobe is to wait until it moves relatively close, then glide down and hit it with a volley of slow-mo arrow headshots. You can then finish it off with a melee weapon.

MASTER MODE NOTES: Despite the Lightning Rod, this is actually a Thunder Wizzrobe. The extra hit points can make this a frustrating encounter if you lose your cool, because melee weapons will often knock your opponent into the water – which causes it to immediately disappear and, of course, begin healing. The solution is to only use arrows, employ Stasis+ to secure multiple headshots, and work to keep your opponent on solid ground. Placing three Cryonis pillars around the island (as close to land as you can manage) will enable you to subject your opponent to slow-motion headshot barrages.

Floor 10

OVERVIEW

Enemies	Blue Lizalfos, Black Lizalfos x2	
Equipment	Lizal Bow, Lizal Spear, Lizal Boomerang, Lizal Shield	*Master Mode only:* Soldier's Bow (in a treasure chest close to the west wall), Enhanced Lizal Spear (embedded in the giant fish skull; use Magnesis)
Noteworthy Items	Four breakable crates yielding arrows, and two barrels with foodstuffs	

WALKTHROUGH: The Blue Lizalfos directly ahead as Link arrives will recognize him almost immediately. Without hesitation, freeze it with Stasis+ and shower it with a volley of arrows aimed at the head; if it has even a second to blow its horn and alert its companions, this battle will become very unpleasant. Once the first Lizalfos falls, the two that remain will be looking out over the water in opposite directions. At this point, we suggest that you use this opportunity to try out the special sneakstrike strategy that we detail in the Master Mode notes. If any equipment should fall into the depths, note that you can retrieve it with Magnesis once the battle ends.

MASTER MODE NOTES: Many have opined that this is the single hardest floor in the entire Trial of the Sword. Killing the first Lizalfos before it can blow its horn is an absolutely critical step on Master Mode, but it's not the end of this Trials run if you fail: just focus on killing the archer, then escape by any means necessary – ideally via pre-placed Cryonis pillars to avoid the risk of drowning. You can then wait for the last two Lizalfos to face away from each other before you begin the next step.

If your pre-Trials Attack Up meal boost has expired, now would be a very good time to eat the Mighty dish you prepared at the rest area. As detailed on page 425, certain monsters are vulnerable to a strategy whereby you inflict a sneakstrike, then move 180 degrees around them and inflict another sneakstrike when the prompt appears – and repeat as often as necessary. The only flaw in using this approach here is that an individual blow with a strong weapon in the direction of the ramp might propel a Lizalfos into the water, breaking stealth and causing it to heal almost instantly. You can fine-tune the strategy, however, by using a weapon with less power (such as a polearm) while facing the water, and the heavy-hitting spiked Moblin club when you face the main platform, adjusting as required. One important extra tip: should a weapon go into critical durability status, *stop using it immediately*. Anything that might accidentally propel a Lizalfos into the water is to be avoided at all costs.

Floor 11

OVERVIEW

Enemies	Bokoblin x6, Blue Bokoblin, Black Bokoblin, Black Moblin
Equipment	Spiked Boko Bow x4, Spiked Boko Bat, Spiked Boko Spear, Dragonbone Boko Club, Dragonbone Boko Shield, Soldier's Broadsword, Soldier's Spear; *Master Mode only:* Silver Longsword, Zora Spear
Noteworthy Items	Fire arrow x10 and shock arrow x10 in treasure chests; assorted arrows and foodstuffs in wooden crates

WALKTHROUGH: The raft to your right is, for the avoidance of all doubt, a trap that will serve only to deliver Link into an extremely difficult test of marksmanship. Instead, create a Cryonis causeway to move sufficiently close to eliminate the four archers with headshots. Should they detect and target Link, just drop behind your current pillar when they fire. By the time you climb back up, you should have time to release at least a couple of shots before they can aim and fire again. There is a treasure chest on an elevated platform on the east side; use Magnesis to grab it and obtain the fire arrows inside. At the center of the rocks to the west, you can obtain 10 shock arrows from a second treasure chest.

Bokoblins and Moblins drown if they fall into water, so the quickest way to complete the level is to hit them with bow headshots when they are close to a ledge, or freeze them with Stasis+ and propel them to a watery grave with a melee weapon. You can later retrieve metal weapons that fall into the depths with Magnesis, while the dragonbone gear carried by the Moblin will float. Break open the available crates for supplies, then head for the exit portal. If you are playing on Master Mode, don't forget to look up at the skull above to find additional weapons.

Floor 12

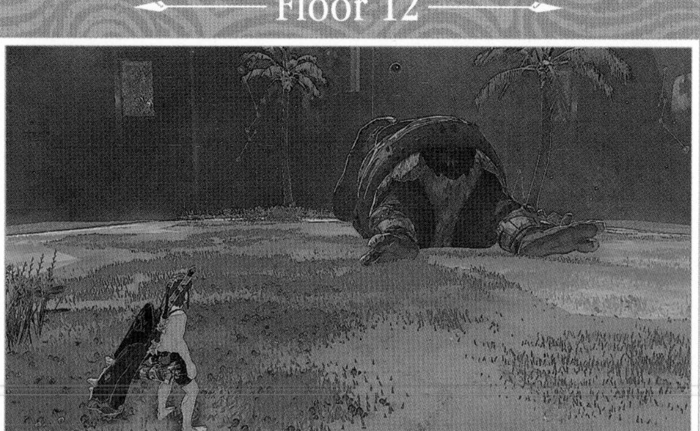

OVERVIEW

Enemies	Blue Hinox
Equipment	Knight's Broadsword, Knight's Bow, Knight's Shield
Noteworthy Items	Palm Fruit from the trees

WALKTHROUGH: If you'd prefer to take no chances, chop down the trees before you engage the Hinox (see page 316). Other than that, this is a fairly standard encounter against this sub-boss variety, with plenty of space to escape into. The monster wears shin guards, so be careful to always direct your melee attacks at the torso (locking-on helps here). Don't take any risks on a Master Mode playthrough: use Stasis+ to set up eye shots and always back off as soon as the creature begins to stand.

There is no need to gather items before you head for the exit portal, as you will be losing all accumulated items once you leave. After the cutscene, follow the Sword Monk's instructions and take the Master Sword to unlock the first power increment.

MIDDLE TRIALS

The first two sets of Trials in this sequence complicate matters by introducing environmental considerations, while the final stretch pits Link against challenging combinations of the minor Guardians.

Floor 01

OVERVIEW

Enemies	Bokoblin x5	
Equipment	Boko Spear, Boko Club, Boko Bow, Woodcutter's Axe, Spiked Boko Spear, Spiked Boko Club, Soldier's Bow x2, Soldier's Broadsword, Spiked Boko Shield	*Master Mode only:* Extra Spiked Boko Spear, Spiked Boko Bow
Noteworthy Items	Foodstuffs and arrows in the numerous crates and barrels, including fire arrows* on the north platform	

* Two or three of these will simplify Floor 15 on Master Mode.

WALKTHROUGH: Jump into the updraft and open the paraglider to float to the upper platform to the east (look for the two wooden crates), where you can easily evade incoming arrows. Collect the Boko Spear.

With a precious weapon in hand, float over to the platform to the west and grab the Boko Club, then defeat the two Bokoblins there. This will give you sufficient resources to finish off the enemies that remain without complications. Before you leave, use fire arrows to burn the wooden platforms high on the east and north walls to access two treasure chests.

MASTER MODE NOTES: Head straight for the north platform and, while dodging incoming arrows, grab the Spiked Boko Spear and Spiked Boko Bow, then immediately take off for the western platform. Your priority here is to kill the Bokoblin carrying the woodcutter's axe to claim his essential weapon. Once you have it, you can smash containers to gather arrows. The remaining Blue Bokoblins will fall quickly to headshots, which are simple to land while riding updrafts. Try not to knock them over the ledges: weapons are important at this stage, especially bows.

Floor 02

OVERVIEW

Enemies	Bokoblin x2, Blue Bokoblin, Fire Wizzrobe, Meteo Wizzrobe
Equipment	Soldier's Spear, Soldier's Broadsword, Soldier's Shield, Spiked Boko Bow, Fire Rod, Meteor Rod, Feathered Edge
Noteworthy Items	Food and arrows in assorted wooden crates

WALKTHROUGH: There are two Bokoblins to your left on the starting platform, so be ready to deal with them immediately. Ideally, you should dispatch both without knocking them from the ledge and losing their weapons. Ride the updraft to reach the platform above in the southwest and eliminate the Bokoblin archer, then smash the crates to obtain arrows.

The final two enemies are a Fire Wizzrobe to the east, and a Meteo Wizzrobe to the north. Attempting to obtain their weapons is a very technical and risky process, especially with the Meteo Wizzrobe. The two magical rods are not worth an early death or a large investment of arrows. It's probably better to just commit their owners to the void with a well-timed headshot each. Before you leave, burn the wooden platform in the northeast corner to obtain a Feathered Edge.

MASTER MODE NOTES: Deal with the Wizzrobes first to be safe, taking care to ensure that they are above a drop before you make the headshot. The Black Bokoblin isn't worth the trouble to fight, so just knock him over the edge.

Floor 03

OVERVIEW

Enemies	Bokoblin x5, Blue Bokoblin x2
Equipment	Feathered Spear, Enhanced Lizal Spear, Spiked Boko Bow x2, Phrenic Bow, Lizal Forked Boomerang, Reinforced Lizal Shield Boko Bow
Noteworthy Items	Foodstuffs and assorted arrows (including bomb arrows*, ice arrows** and shock arrows) in the crates and barrels

* On Master Mode, try to keep the bomb arrows for Floor 10.
** Save the ice arrows for Floors 07 and 08.

WALKTHROUGH: This room is filled with Bokoblin archers, who will raise the alarm and nock their bows the moment Link arrives. The only space that offers respite is in the corner behind the wall on the platform in the southwest of the area – so take off and head there immediately. Directly above, you'll notice a platform suspended by balloons; shoot the one closest to the west wall to cause the treasure chest to slide off to a position where you can dash over and grab the feathered spear inside.

The safest strategy is to fly out and eliminate one archer at a time with slo-mo headshots (or burst balloons for the central target) with a soldier's bow obtained on the first floor, then return to the hiding spot to recover before your next sortie. Finish off the Bokoblins armed with melee weapons by whatever means you see fit.

MASTER MODE NOTES: If you eliminate the archer on the floating platform and the Blue Bokoblins first, you can deal with the Black Bokoblins with multiple sneakstrikes, maximizing your possible weapon gains. Stay on the move and make the most of slow motion to minimize the risk of being hit by an arrow.

Floor 04

OVERVIEW

Opponent	Decayed Guardian
Equipment	Knight's Shield, Soldier's Bow
Noteworthy Items	Numerous arrows in the wooden crates

WALKTHROUGH: Link materializes on this floor with a Decayed Guardian staring directly at him from the upper platform to the north. If you're supremely confident, just wait and deflect the first beam back for an instant kill. Alternatively, paraglide to the lower platform to the north, below the Guardian – the one place in this arena where it cannot target you. When you are ready to attack, hit its eye with an arrow to cancel its laser attack, then assail it with melee blows.

With the chest floating above the southeast platform, pop two balloons and wait for it to fall for a short distance, then employ Stasis+ on the chest before hitting the final balloon to ensure that it drops safely. Use a fire arrow to burn the wooden ledge to the southwest to access a second treasure chest.

Floor 05: Rest Area

WALKTHROUGH: Collect the fairy in the north of the garden, then gather everything you need and prepare meals. On Master Mode, where you will still have the Attack Up boost applied before entering these Trials, save key ingredients collected so far, such as razorshrooms or ironshrooms, in the hope of gaining enough for max-level buffs over the next five floors.

OVERVIEW

Equipment	Knight's Broadsword, Hylian Trousers, Falcon Bow, Woodcutter's Axe, Torch
Noteworthy Items	Fairy, Hyrule Bass x3, Ironshroom x2, Hylian Shroom x2, Apple x2; assorted foodstuffs and arrows in the crates

Floor 06

OVERVIEW

Enemies	Fire Keese x5, Large Electric Chuchu
Noteworthy Items	Wood (and associated drops) from the smaller trees

WALKTHROUGH: A supremely simple room, as long as the darkness and over-confidence don't lead to mistakes. Equip a spear and entice the five Fire Keese within range for easy kills; bombs also suffice. Dispatch the Large Electric Chuchu with an arrow. Once all enemies are dead, the room will be illuminated: a feature repeated in the four arenas that follow.

Floor 07

OVERVIEW

Enemies	Blue Lizalfos x2, Fire-Breath Lizalfos x2
Equipment	Enhanced Lizal Spear, Forest Dweller's Spear, Flameblade, Strengthened Lizal Bow, Torch
Noteworthy Items	Food and fire arrows in the crates inside the skull cave

WALKTHROUGH: The two shadowy figures you can dimly see to the north, outside the skull cave, are Fire-Breath Lizalfos. Equip ice arrows, then entice them individually to the illuminated start position for easy kills; note, however, that Stasis+ will negate the instant kill effect. You ideally need to save at least one ice arrow for the next floor, so pick your shots carefully.

Don't underestimate the two Lizalfos that remain: one has fire arrows and a strong bow, while the other wields a flameblade. You can obviously shoot the rope to drop the lantern onto the skull cave floor, killing them immediately as it detonates the surrounding explosive barrels, but you'll lose items from the crates inside. If you alternatively snipe with standard arrows from afar, you can actually kill the targets before they see Link.

MASTER MODE NOTES: If you were unlucky enough to only obtain two ice arrows earlier, it would be wiser to save them for a target on the far more difficult floor that follows. Detonating the explosive barrels will not always help with the two final targets. Lure the Black Lizalfos with the flameblade out first, fighting him by the start area, then creep in for a sneakstrike on the second.

Floor 08

OVERVIEW

Enemies	Blue Bokoblin x2, Black Bokoblin x1, Meteo Wizzrobe	
Equipment	Meteor Rod, Soldier's Broadsword, Solder's Shield, Dragonbone Boko Club, Dragonbone Boko Bat, Rusty Broadsword x2, Rusty Halberd, Rusty Shield, Torch x2	*Master Mode only:* Soldier's Claymore, Soldier's Spear
Noteworthy Items	Seared Steak; four wooden crates close to the campfire containing food and arrows	

Floor 08 (Continued)

WALKTHROUGH: Climb the south wall of the building to your right when you arrive to get a good overview of the area. There is a camp with three Bokoblins on the east side of the room, and a Meteo Wizzrobe dancing in circles over to the east. Eliminate the latter with an ice arrow.

To defeat the Bokoblins, you should fire single arrows towards the ground at just the right range to lure individuals away from the others (look out for the tell-tale "?" icon) to engage them separately. Don't worry about wasting ammunition: you can retrieve your arrows later. Keep the fights to the reasonably well-illuminated area around the arrival point, then use a sneakstrike for the final Bokoblin.

MASTER MODE NOTES: This floor is the difficulty peak for the Middle Trials unless you play it very, *very* carefully. Use the same strategy as Normal Mode, but try to leave the Silver Bokoblin (identify him with the Camera from on top of the wall) until last, when you can defeat him with multiple consecutive sneakstrikes. If more than one enemy should charge, escape at all costs.

Floor 09

OVERVIEW

Opponent	Decayed Guardian
Equipment	Torch x2, Rusty Broadsword, Rusty Shield
Noteworthy Items	Crates containing arrows

WALKTHROUGH: Move towards the wall directly in front of Link's start position and adjust the camera to take stock of this floor's sole enemy beyond it: a Decayed Guardian. As with the earlier encounter, your strategy should be informed by your proficiencies: a shield deflect if you excel at them, or, if not, an arrow to the eye, followed by Stasis+, topped off with a melee assault from behind.

Floor 10

OVERVIEW

Opponent	Black Hinox
Equipment	Knight's Broadsword, Knight's Bow, Thunderstorm Rod, Rusty Halberd, Rusty Claymore, Torch x2
Noteworthy Items	Barrels containing arrows in the southwest tower

WALKTHROUGH: If you've conquered the similar encounter in Thyphlo Ruins to reach the Ketoh Wawai shrine, you know what to expect here. The darkness and sheer insistent pursuit of the Hinox can be intimidating, but you have enough room to maneuver. The important thing is to minimize the amount of time that your opponent remains on its feet by landing eye shots. Freezing the monster with Stasis+ makes this process much easier.

MASTER MODE NOTES: If you're running low on suitable weapons, run between the Hinox's legs after a critical hit on its eye to collect the knight's broadsword. If it should uproot a tree, you cannot risk the blow that will inevitably follow in such a cramped battleground: blow the trunk up with a bomb arrow as soon as the Hinox wields it. Assuming you use Stasis+ for eye shots each time, it should always recharge no more than a few seconds after the Hinox is back on its feet. If you're in danger of being trapped, use the meteor rod to set a wooden shin guard on fire.

Floor 11: Rest Area

WALKTHROUGH: Begin your final period of respite during the Middle Trials by collecting the two Fairies. The Hylian tunic will add to the (admittedly marginal) damage resistance conferred by the Hylian trousers collected in the first rest area, but your primary goal should still be to *avoid being hit at all.* Once you have collected everything and prepared meals, head to the warp point to make a start on the final five floors.

MASTER MODE NOTES: Don't forget to cook up razorshrooms and mighty bananas to be able to refresh your Attack Up boost should it have expired.

OVERVIEW

Equipment	Hylian Tunic, Forest Dweller's Sword, Forest Dweller's Spear
Noteworthy Items	Fairy x2, Ironshroom x2, Hyrule Bass x3, Endura Shroom x2, Apple x2; arrows and assorted foodstuffs in the four crates

Floor 12

OVERVIEW

Enemies	Guardian Scout x6
Noteworthy Items	Arrow x10

WALKTHROUGH: Stay on the move! The six stationary Guardian Scouts will all fire intermittently at different intervals, but their laser bolts are easy to evade. If you equip the soldier's bow, strengthened Lizal bow or knight's bow, they will each fall to a single arrow. Use a Cryonis pillar to reach the treasure chest before you depart.

MASTER MODE NOTES: Greater caution is required here. As soon as you gain control, create a barricade of three Cryonis pillars to work behind, then focus on firing at one target at a time.

Floor 13

OVERVIEW

Enemies	Guardian Scout II x3
Equipment	Guardian Sword, Guardian Spear, Ancient Battle Axe, Duplex Bow

WALKTHROUGH: Individually, these Guardian Scout models are nothing to fear – but if you're overconfident on this floor and rush into the center, you will quickly find yourself surrounded by all three. From the start, run out of sight of the first target directly ahead, escape the chasing pack, then try to lure each one to corners far from the others; when they are not aware of Link, the unoccupied Guardians will enter their dormant state.

Before you depart, visit the northwest corner of the room and use Magnesis to pull a metal block from the nearby wall; there's a treasure chest behind it.

MASTER MODE NOTES: These opponents are damage sponges on the higher difficulty level. To save your resources, the metal cube in the northwest of the arena can be employed to grind out three victories. It's most effective when you get a really good swing or drop it from a great height (which is easier to achieve after freezing your target with Stasis+).

Floor 14

OVERVIEW

Enemies	Guardian Scout I x4, Guardian Scout II x2
Equipment	Guardian Sword x2, Guardian Shield x2, Eightfold Longblade

WALKTHROUGH: Once Link materializes, stay close to the south wall and eliminate the four Scouts on the raised platforms with arrows; if you remain in your starting position, the two Guardian Scout II models won't activate and engage. This is critical on Master Mode. When you have dealt with the first targets, bait a single Guardian Scout II into attacking. Cast Stasis+ when it reaches your position, then use a heavy weapon (the woodcutter's axe, as suggested earlier, works well) to propel it to instant death in the water. Repeat for the second Guardian. Retrieve and open the metal treasure chest from the northeast pool before you leave.

Floor 15

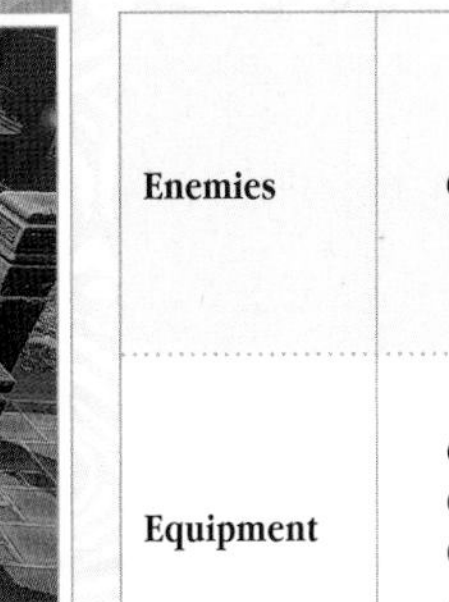

OVERVIEW

Enemies	Guardian Scout II x2
Equipment	Guardian Sword+, Guardian Shield+, Guardian Spear, Ancient Battle Axe

WALKTHROUGH: Fighting both Guardian Scouts at once disrupts your instincts, and their sheer speed and insistence may force a constant retreat – which leaves you vulnerable to simultaneous bouts of their spin attacks.

The best strategy is to lead them to one of the patches of leaves close to the west, north and east walls. If you set these ablaze with a fire arrow (or the meteor rod or flameblade) while the Guardians are on top, you can then jump and ride the updraft to reach the closest elevated platform. From there, equip the duplex bow found on Floor 13 and rain down arrows on a single target to destroy it quickly; bomb arrows, if you have any, are naturally the best. When only one Guardian remains, the fight is effectively over.

Floor 16

OVERVIEW

Opponent	Guardian Scout IV
Equipment	Guardian Sword+, Guardian Spear+, Ancient Battle Axe+

WALKTHROUGH: Though it's never an opponent to underestimate, the Guardian Scout IV (equivalent to those encountered in "Major Test of Strength" shrines) should not disturb the composure of an experienced *Breath of the Wild* player.

There's nothing in this fight that you haven't seen many times before, so just focus on safe, measured attacking salvos with the better Guardian weapons acquired over previous floors. This is the final battle of the Middle Trials, so there's no need to conserve anything. Remember that you can always interrupt or stun the Guardian with Stasis+, or any shock or fire weapons that you still have to hand. When the fight ends, leave the arena and make your way up the two flights of stairs to claim the second power increment for the Master Sword.

FINAL TRIALS

If you know where to find this segment's most important resources, and when to use them, the Final Trials are not unduly difficult. Ancient arrows are the key to beating its last sequence of floors with relatively little danger.

Floor 01

OVERVIEW

Enemies	Stalkoblin x4
Equipment	Bokoblin Arm x4, Spiked Boko Bow, Spiked Boko Spear, Spiked Boko Bat, Spiked Boko Club, Rusty Halberd*, Rusty Claymore*, Rusty Broadsword*, Spiked Boko Shield, Rusty Shield* * You can save these (and other "rusty" implements found later) for recycling via a Rock Octorok on Floor 07, though it's not strictly necessary.
Noteworthy Items	Two wooden crates containing arrows

WALKTHROUGH: The fight in this first room is entirely straightforward: hit a Stalkoblin with a bomb explosion, then use disposable Bokoblin arms to defeat the four remaining monsters.

This floor and the four that follow are complicated by constant thunderstorms. While it's fine to collect metal equipment (unless you see the telltale sparks that indicate an imminent lightning strike as you approach), you should try to not have metal weapons, shields or bows equipped for more than a few seconds at a time.

Floor 02

OVERVIEW

Enemies	Electric Keese x2, Stalizalfos x3
Equipment	Spiked Boko Spear x2, Lizalfos Arm x3, Lizal Forked Boomerang, Reinforced Lizal Shield, Royal Guard's Sword* * Save this powerful weapon for sneakstrikes – especially on Floors 10, 14 and 15.
Noteworthy Items	Three crates containing food and arrows

WALKTHROUGH: Use bombs or the spiked Boko spear collected on the previous floor to hit the Electric Keese from safe range. The three Stalizalfos will not emerge until you enter the skull cave. Draw them to the entrance to avoid mishaps with the explosive barrels, but eliminate the target carrying a metal boomerang and shield first (and then immediately collect both) to prevent lightning strikes. There is a buried metal treasure chest on the west side of the arena containing a royal guard's sword that will be hugely useful later.

Floor 03

OVERVIEW

Enemies	Large Electric Chuchu x2, Stalmoblin x5
Equipment	Spiked Moblin Spear, Spiked Moblin Club, Dragon Bone Boko Bow, Moblin Arm x5, Knight's Bow, Knight's Shield
Noteworthy Items	Two barrels containing arrows on the main platform.

WALKTHROUGH: Dispatch the Electric Chuchu, then head up the ramp into the base; the five Stalmoblins will appear below when you open the closest treasure chest. If they don't all emerge at once, circle the camp in a search for bone piles. The second treasure chest can be carefully relocated from its inaccessible perch with Magnesis.

Floor 04

OVERVIEW

Enemies	Mounted Stalkoblin x8
Equipment	Boko Spear x2, Dragonbone Boko Spear, Dragonbone Boko Club, Dragonbone Boko Bat, Boko Bow, Spiked Boko Bow x2, Rusty Broadsword x2, Rusty Halberd, Rusty Shield, Rusty Claymore, Bokoblin Arm x8
Noteworthy Items	Crates containing arrows (including shock arrows)

WALKTHROUGH: Turn to your left when you gain control of Link and prepare a Remote Bomb to greet the first Bokoblin cavalry charge. The monsters with melee weapons are simple to dismount and dispatch, but the three archers can be elusive once they engage. Mount a Stalhorse and leap from the saddle while galloping, then immediately aim with a bow to hit them with slow-motion headshots. Drop any monster limbs that you may be carrying before you leave – you won't need them.

Floor 05

WALKTHROUGH: Standard Stalnox strategies apply here, though you should be wary of lightning strikes whenever you down the sub-boss and run in for melee strikes – be attentive for the usual audio and visual cues.

OVERVIEW

Opponent	Stalnox	
Equipment	Flamespear, Great Frostblade, Thunderblade	*Master Mode only:* Royal Guard's Sword
Noteworthy Items	Metal crates containing arrows; frost arrows in a buried metal treasure chest in the southwest	

The flamespear, great frostblade and frost arrows are necessary for an easy run through otherwise-challenging later floors. On a first playthrough, we suggest that you use them only as and when directed by this walkthrough.

Floor 06: Rest Area

WALKTHROUGH: Catch the fairy and collect everything of use before visiting the pot to cook. Each hearty truffle offers a full heal and a bonus heart when cooked individually. Equip the flamebreaker boots and swap out any flammable weapons, shields and bows before you depart: the next five floors all have a constant Level 1 flame effect active.

The bundle of ancient arrows here is the first of three that you can find in the Final Trials. These can be employed to eliminate all mortal enemies with a single hit, and Guardians with a critical hit. We'll let you know when it's a good time to use them.

OVERVIEW

Equipment	Double Axe, Flamebreaker Boots, Knight's Bow, Ancient Arrow x3, Torch	
Noteworthy Items	Fairy, Razorshroom x2, Hearty Truffle x2, Apple x2, Armored Carp x3, four crates containing food and arrows	*Master Mode only:* Extra Fairy

Floor 07

OVERVIEW

Enemies	Large Fire Chuchu, Igneo Pebblit x2, Rock Octorok
Equipment	Rusty Claymore

WALKTHROUGH: Use Remote Bombs to eliminate the Chuchu and Pebblits, then consecutively feed the rusty weapons you have carried this far (and the rusty claymore found in this area) to the Rock Octorok. These will damage Link if they strike him when the Octorok spits them back, so stand at a safe distance and catch them with Magnesis.

Incidentally, to put your mind at rest, falling into the lava in this stage of the Final Trials is not instantly fatal – but Link *will* lose valuable hearts.

Floor 08

OVERVIEW

Enemies	Fire-Breath Lizalfos x3
Equipment	Strengthened Lizal Bow x3
Noteworthy Items	Two metal crates containing fire arrows and random roasted food

WALKTHROUGH: The three Lizalfos will die with a single swing of the great frostblade, so use the updrafts to reach each of them in sequence. As they fire elemental arrows, start with the one on the highest rock spire. To be extra careful, approach the final two when they face away. You should note that they are immune to lava, so don't use other weapons.

Floor 09

OVERVIEW

Enemies	Meteo Wizzrobe, Blue Moblin, Fire-Breath Lizalfos x2
Equipment	Meteor Rod*, Iron Sledgehammer**, Enhanced Lizal Spear, Lizal Forked Boomerang, Reinforced Lizal Shield * Save this for Floors 13 to 17. ** Save this for Floor 11.
Noteworthy Items	Arrows and roasted food in the metal containers inside the skull cave

WALKTHROUGH: Dispatch the Meteo Wizzrobe with an ice arrow (or a standard arrow headshot followed by a swing of the great frostblade when it lands), then vaporize the two fire-spewing Lizalfos inside the cave in the same way. The Moblin wields an iron sledgehammer that gives it a lot of range; you may wish to start by disarming it with the thunderblade or escape and return afterwards to kill it with sneakstrikes.

Floor 10

OVERVIEW

Enemies	Fire-Breath Lizalfos, Black Moblin x3
Equipment	Strengthened Lizal Bow, Steel Lizal Bow, Royal Guard's Spear, Knight's Claymore, Ancient Arrow x3
Noteworthy Items	Baked food and arrows (including fire arrows*) in the metal crates * Save these for Floors 13 to 17.

WALKTHROUGH: Link faces the camp to the northwest at the start of this floor. Turn to the north and watch the Fire-Breath Lizalfos; when he turns away, glide via the updraft to reach him, then land and strike with the great frostblade. Crouch down immediately afterwards to avoid detection by the three Moblins in the center.

Moblins will die instantly if propelled into the lava, which is the most obvious solution, but you'll almost certainly lose their weapons. A better strategy is to briefly immobilize the closest Moblin with Stasis+ from afar, then immediately glide over from the northernmost updraft, angling your approach to land safely by the upright metal beam. From there, you can attempt to defeat all three with sneakstrikes; use the royal guard's sword found much earlier for maximum damage. Stasis+ will help to give brief windows where you can move through cones of vision to get into position. If you are detected, drop down to the rock below the camp and wait for any alerted foes to return to their original positions.

A metal treasure chest containing the second bundle of three ancient arrows can be retrieved from the lava just east of the camp with Magnesis. Don't forget to claim them before you depart!

MASTER MODE NOTES: Use Magnesis and the metal block found in the lava close to the camp to defeat the Moblins. If this is too much trouble, just knock them into the lava – their weapons are not worth the durability (and time!) you would need to expend to defeat them with sneakstrikes.

Floor 11

OVERVIEW

Opponent	Igneo Talus
Noteworthy Items	Metal crates containing arrows

WALKTHROUGH: If you stay clear of the dormant Igneo Talus at the center of the room, you can blow up three rock piles to reveal updrafts before the fight begins; place the Remote Bombs on the far side of each one to be doubly safe.

Hit the legs or body once with the great frostblade to cool it down, then climb up before it rises and start your assault on the weak spot. A charged spin attack with the iron sledgehammer (if you acquired it from Floor 09) will enable you to defeat this opponent within a single attack cycle.

Floor 12: Rest Area

OVERVIEW		
Equipment	Hylian Tunic, Stone Smasher*, Royal Guard's Shield * Save this for Floor 16.	
Noteworthy Items	Fairy x2, Stamella Shroom x2, Silent Shroom, Apple x2, Hearty Radish, Sizzlefin Trout x3, Spicy Pepper x6, arrows and food in the wooden crates	*Master Mode only:* Extra Fairy

WALKTHROUGH: After collecting the local fairies, cook the hearty radish on its own for another full HP recovery meal. Floors 13 to 17 take place in icy arenas where Link will incur continual damage unless protected by Level 1 cold resistance, which is why this rest area is stocked with spicy peppers and sizzlefin trout. If you're taking things slowly and carefully, you may need multiple cold-resistance meals to be safe: cook spicy peppers and sizzlefin trout together or with any neutral foodstuffs that you have at hand (just make sure you don't combine any added effects, as they will cancel each other). Should you ever run out of options to fight the cold temperatures, don't forget that you can equip a fire-elemental weapon to temporarily get warm.

MASTER MODE NOTES: A cold-resistance status effect would mean forgoing a more valuable offense boost that you may already have (if you followed our pre-loading tip) or intend to prepare at the cooking pot. There is a way to avoid persistent cold damage – which is, of course, to equip the meteor rod or flamespear. This means that you will also need to swap them in every few seconds during combat to reset the timer that starts when Link is sufficiently chilled, which is a distraction and a nuisance. But you have to weigh that inconvenience against the huge benefit of an Attack Up buff in a series of floors that feature multiple Silver and Gold enemies.

Floor 13

OVERVIEW		
Enemies	Frost Pebblit x2, Large Ice Chuchu, Blue Bokoblin x2, Black Bokoblin	
Equipment	Lizal Tri-Boomerang, Spiked Boko Spear, Spiked Boko Bow, Steel Lizal Shield	*Master Mode only:* Dragonbone Boko Spear, Royal Spear
Noteworthy Items	Bomb arrows x5 in the treasure chest; food in the two crates by the camp (collect the meat before it freezes)	

WALKTHROUGH: Unless you are following the alternative Master Mode strategy detailed previously, eat a cold-resistance meal once Link materializes. You can eliminate the two Frost Pebblits with Remote Bombs, then hit the Ice Chuchu with a standard arrow without disturbing the Bokoblins at the camp to the northwest.

If you have a plentiful supply of standard arrows (and you should at this stage), leap from the prominent hill and dispatch at least two of the three Bokoblins with slow-motion headshots; target the Blues first.

Equip the flamespear or meteor rod to melt the ice block on the east side of the hill to reveal a treasure chest, but don't waste irreplaceable durability by striking it: just stand close and wait.

MASTER MODE NOTES: Take the time to fight the Bokoblins individually, leaving the Silver until last; kill it with multiple sneakstrikes.

Floor 14

WALKTHROUGH: Creep to the cover available to your right after arrival to avoid detection by the Bokoblin above. Make your way carefully to the north and take out the two Chuchus with arrows; when the Ice-Breath Lizalfos moves to investigate, approach and dispatch it with a single stab of the flamespear.

Head up the ramp into the base and use sneakstrikes to deal with the first two Bokoblins. As moving in the open risks detection by the Silver Moblin above, you can deal with the third by casting Stasis+ and then hitting it with a single headshot if using the steel Lizal bow, or two headshots with any other available bow.

Fighting the Silver Moblin in a straight duel is dangerous and risks using up several very good weapons. Use Stasis+ to safely get behind it, then employ the multiple sneakstrike technique (see page 425) to beat it without undue effort.

OVERVIEW

Enemies	Blue Bokoblin x3, Silver Moblin, Ice-Breath Lizalfos, Large Ice Chuchu x2	
Equipment	Forked Lizal Spear, Dragonbone Boko Bat, Dragonbone Moblin Club, Dragonbone Boko Club, Dragonbone Boko Shield, Dragon Bone Boko Bow, Ancient Arrow x3	*Master Mode only:* Extra Forked Lizal Spear, Extra Dragon Bone Boko Bow, Royal Claymore, Royal Sword
Noteworthy Items	Three crates containing arrows (including ice arrows)	

The ice blocks in the northwest and southeast block updrafts; a third in the northeast conceals a treasure chest containing the final bundle of three ancient arrows.

MASTER MODE NOTES: The same strategy applies, but you'll need to ensure that you use strong weapons to kill the first two Bokoblins with a single sneakstrike. With the third, arrows won't suffice for a quick kill, so either drop down and finish it below, or risk a sneakstrike and escape from the Gold Moblin if required. That last foe will take a lot of sneakstrikes to defeat – but it's cheaper than a standard fight. If you struggle too much, an ancient arrow will make short work of it.

Floor 15

WALKTHROUGH: The priority at the start here is to deal with the Blizzrobe and Black Moblin without alerting the Bokoblins. Time is of the essence with the Wizzrobe: if you delay too long, it tends to move further and further to the north. The quickest solution is to immediately climb the tower to your right, jump off and hit it with a carefully aimed slow-motion fire arrow; you can then glide or drop to safety behind the wall.

The Moblin, unless disturbed, walks counterclockwise circuits of the stone pillar to the west. If you time your approach very carefully, you can use Stasis+ to get directly behind it and set up a multiple sneakstrike kill. Should this fail, lure it to the south and defeat it there. It is unarmed, so less dangerous than usual.

With the Bokoblins, jump down from either the southeast or north tower and dispatch both Blue Bokoblins with slow-motion headshots; you just need a single headshot on the Silver Bokoblin to stun it. Quickly land and grab the available weapons from the log beside the fire (ensure you have free inventory space beforehand). You can then either defeat the final foe with standard tactics, or escape and return to finish it off with sneakstrikes.

OVERVIEW

Enemies	Black Moblin, Blue Bokoblin x2, Silver Bokoblin, Blizzrobe	
Equipment	Blizzard Rod*, Knight's Broadsword, Knight's Halberd, Knight's Bow, Knight's Shield * Save this weapon for Floor 23, where its crowd-control applications can be a real life-saver.	*Master Mode only:* Royal Claymore, Royal Sword
Noteworthy Items	Arrows and food in the two crates and two barrels	

MASTER MODE NOTES: This is one of the more difficult floors in the Final Trials. If the Gold Bokoblin fills you with dread, he's a perfectly valid candidate for an ancient arrow one-shot kill, though you really need to keep these for the final few floors. The royal claymore exclusive to Master Mode is found leaning against the tower where the Silver Moblin patrols: be sure to claim this before any monster does.

Floor 16

OVERVIEW

Opponent	Frost Talus

WALKTHROUGH: With the meteor rod and stone smasher collected earlier, you can complete this floor in less than 30 seconds. Wait until the Frost Talus stands, then target its body with fireballs. Cast Stasis+ when it hits the ground, then climb on and assail the weak spot; with the stone smasher and a quick mount, you can defeat your opponent before it can dislodge Link, even in Master Mode, though opting for two cycles instead is a reasonable precaution. Ignore the two ice blocks: they simply cover updraft vents that you have no need for.

Floor 17

OVERVIEW

Opponent	Blue-Maned Lynel	
Equipment	Mighty Lynel Bow, Mighty Lynel Sword, Mighty Lynel Shield	*Master Mode only:* Savage Lynel Crusher, Savage Lynel Spear
Noteworthy Items	Bomb Arrow x5	

WALKTHROUGH: If you're practiced at defeating Lynels, you may wish to engage this specimen in a fair fight. Should an attempted battle not go as planned, you always have the option to stick it with an ancient arrow to end the danger immediately. You forgo the opportunity to take its weapons, of course, but that's a small price to pay at this stage in the Final Trials.

The benefit of defeating the Lynel without using the available one-hit kill is that you get to keep its three-shot bow. This means that you will not need to target Guardian weak points to slay them with the ancient arrows on the final four floors, as you can just get in close and let loose (three body shots are instantly fatal). This is by no means necessary, though. We would opine that only one ancient arrow could be regarded as essential, and that's the one used to kill another Lynel on the final floor. If in doubt, read ahead to make a more informed decision.

However the battle ends, melt the ice block in the northeast corner to obtain bomb arrows.

Floor 18: Rest Area

WALKTHROUGH: If you have more than two fairies in your inventory, the ones that usually appear here will not spawn. The hearty bass in the pool can be cooked individually for three meals that restore full health. If you have mighty bananas and razorshrooms, cook four in any combination (plus a suitable high-grade meat if you have one to extend the effect duration) to create a dish that maximizes Link's attack power. The ironshrooms here and armored carp from the first rest area (if you still have them) can be used to create a full defense buff that isn't strictly essential, but might prove useful in an emergency. You can then cook everything else, as there's no cause to hoard ingredients at this stage: the final five floors await…

OVERVIEW

Equipment	Royal Broadsword, Royal Shield, Royal Bow
Noteworthy Items	Fairy x3, Ironshroom x2, Stamella Shroom x2, Apple x2, Hearty Bass x3; arrows and food in the four crates

Floor 19

OVERVIEW

Enemies	Decayed Guardian x6
Equipment	Knight's Shield

WALKTHROUGH: The least dangerous way to complete this floor is to destroy the Decayed Guardians with melee attacks in a specific order, employing shots to their vulnerable eyes to forestall beam attacks if required. When Link materializes, turn left and start with the Decayed Guardian almost directly behind him. The strategy is then to deal with the rest in a clockwise progression. The Guardian on the north wall will automatically activate when you approach the second, but you can easily stay out of sight behind Guardian #2 as you destroy it. Quickly sprint to Guardian #3 to the north, get behind it, and repeat.

You now need to deal with Guardian #4 on the north wall. Cast Stasis+ and hit its eye with an arrow to confuse it while you cross the open terrain (note that the intervening tree would provide no protection at all should it fire, so don't try to hide).

Guardian #6 in the southeast corner will activate as you approach the still-dormant Guardian #5 midway along the east wall, but your next target provides ample cover on the approach. When the penultimate target falls, use Stasis+ and an arrow again to stun the final Guardian, then get in close and finish the fight. If you have need of a shield, open the buried treasure chest in the southwest corner before you proceed.

Floor 20

OVERVIEW

Opponent	Guardian Stalker
Noteworthy Items	Three wooden containers at the central fountain containing arrows

WALKTHROUGH: The tall grass and ruined fountain provide ample cover as you carefully approach the Guardian Stalker. Your tactics should be determined by what you're best at. If shield deflects are your forte, this is a simple floor. If you're more inclined to get in close and slash the legs of Stalkers – especially on Master Mode – that's also a valid course of action.

Naturally, a single ancient arrow aimed at the eye is instantly lethal. There are six major targets left on the remaining floors, three of which most readers may prefer to eliminate with ancient arrows (a Skywatcher each on 21 and 22, then a Lynel on 23). You may choose to use one here for an easy kill or keep it for later (in case you miss a shot, for example): it's your call.

Floor 21

OVERVIEW

Opponent	Guardian Skywatcher
Noteworthy Items	Bomb Arrow x5 in the treasure chest, standard arrows in the wooden containers

WALKTHROUGH: The Guardian Skywatcher will not engage you unless you move into its detection range, so make a quick dash for the tower to the southwest (left of your start position). Stasis+ (or slow motion after jumping from a suitable height) and an ancient arrow to the eye is clearly the most practical option, but another method is to climb a tower and destroy its propellers with bomb arrows if you still have them; there are five more in the treasure chest on top of the central tower if needed. It takes three shots per propeller to send the Skywatcher plummeting to the ground, which renders it functionally helpless unless you are unfortunate enough for it land upright.

If you're one of the rare few to have mastered the art of deflecting their beams with great accuracy, feel free to ignore the above advice.

Floor 22

OVERVIEW

Enemies	Guardian Stalker, Guardian Skywatcher, Guardian Turret
Equipment	Royal Shield, Royal Bow
Noteworthy Items	Food and arrows in the destructible containers

WALKTHROUGH: If you linger in the open at the start point, the Skywatcher may detect Link as it completes its first circuit of the central structure. You can make it to the safety of the building if you sprint there immediately.

It's in your interest to act decisively here. The Guardian Stalker should stay in the northwest for now, so head out and engage the Skywatcher first when it flies to the south of the building; this target is definitely worth an ancient arrow.

If you then lure the Stalker to the same area, you can finish it off in any way you prefer without worrying about the Guardian Turret high on the northeast tower. You only really need one melee weapon for the final floor if you prudently kill the Lynel there with an ancient arrow, so a straightforward engagement (or shield reflects, of course) will conserve your most deadly resource for where it may matter most.

Climb the north wall of the Guardian Turret's tower to destroy it. Melee weapons work well here. There's a risk of the "reflex" blasts that Guardians occasionally fire when assailed from close range. As long as you stay behind it, though, you should be fine to just pummel away.

Floor 23

OVERVIEW

Enemies	White-Maned Lynel, Guardian Turret, Mounted Bokoblin x8 (x9 on Master Mode)
Equipment	Royal Broadsword, Lizal Tri-Boomerang x2, Forked Lizal Spear x2, Knight's Halberd, Royal Shield, Steel Lizal Shield, Knight's Claymore, Dragonbone Moblin Club, Stone Smasher, Savage Lynel Spear, Savage Lynel Bow
Noteworthy Items	Bomb Arrow x5 in the treasure chest

WALKTHROUGH: As soon as you gain control of Link, identify the Lynel and hit it with an ancient arrow without pause or ceremony. You will then be in the *comparatively very safe* position of only having a horde of mounted Bokoblins bear down on you while a Guardian Turret targets from on high.

The blizzard rod obtained earlier can be used to freeze charging Bokoblins if required; a single blow can freeze the entire horde, making it easy to shatter them all with your most powerful weapon. Sprint towards the Guardian Turret if required: it cannot fire on you within a fair radius once you approach the base of its tower, which enables you to pick off the Bokoblins on your terms. The final combat action of the Final Trials is to scale the tower and dispatch the Guardian.

Spare a sympathetic thought for those unfortunate players who arrived here on Master Mode without ancient arrows, then head to the exit portal. Congratulations! Draw the Master Sword from its slot at the top of the third staircase to claim the final upgrade and return to Hyrule.

The Champions' Ballad

Breath of the Wild's second downloadable expansion features new side quests and a substantial main quest story that leads Link on a journey through unexplored shrines to reach a fifth Divine Beast. This chapter will guide you through all of these new challenges and show you how to obtain every reward.

Overview Map

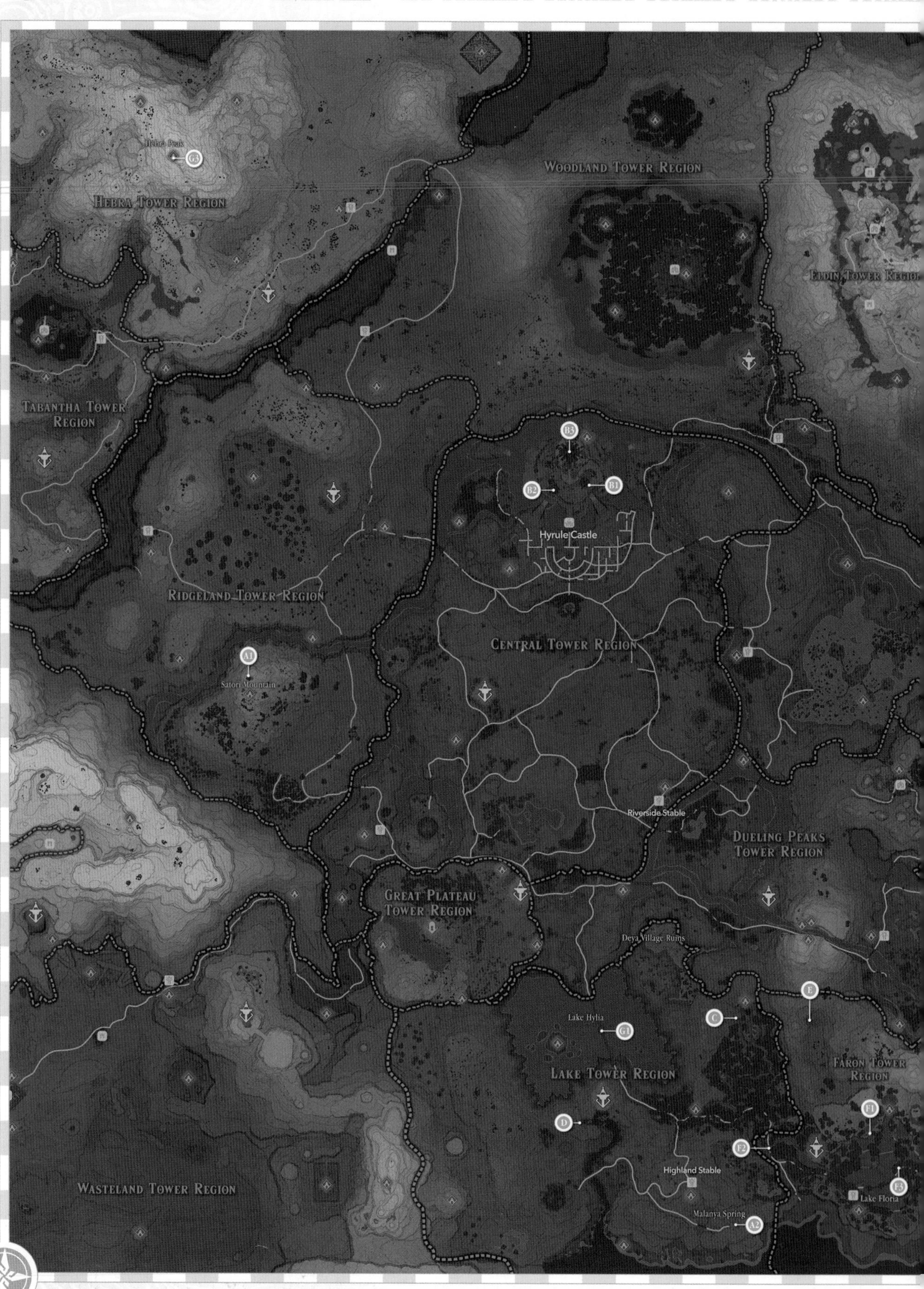

The overview map shows the locations of the main points of interest in the Champions' Ballad storyline.

REWARD LIST

ICON	NAME	REWARD
A1, A2	EX ANCIENT HORSE RUMORS	Ancient Bridle (longer-lasting gallop) and Ancient Saddle (your horse can warp to you)
B1, B2, B3	EX ROYAL GUARD RUMORS	Royal Guard set (Charge Atk. Stamina Up)
C	EX TREASURE: MERCHANT'S HOOD	Ravio's Hood (sideways climbing speed increased)
D	EX TREASURE: GARB OF WINDS	Island Lobster Shirt (Heat Resistance)
E	EX TREASURE: USURPER KING	Zant's Helmet (Unfreezable)
F1, F2, F3	EX TREASURE: DARK ARMOR	Phantom Ganon set (Stealth Up, Stal Disguise, Bone Atk. Up)
G1, G2, G3	XENOBLADE CHRONICLES 2	Salvager set (Swim Speed Up, Swim Dash Stamina Up)

BONUS FEATURES

A software update released shortly before the Champions' Ballad expansion adds a few additional features for everyone to enjoy, irrespective of Expansion Pass ownership.

- Four new champion amiibo are available. As with all other figures, you can scan each of them once per day to obtain items randomly selected from a list of possible rewards. When equipped with the Ancient Cuirass and Ancient Greaves, note that the Divine Helms additionally offer the Ancient Proficiency set bonus.

AMIIBO (SERIES)	POSSIBLE REWARDS
Mipha (*Breath of the Wild*)	Vah Ruta Divine Helm (Swim Speed Up); Zora spear; diamond; assorted fishes.
Urbosa (*Breath of the Wild*)	Vah Naboris Divine Helm (Shock Resistance); Gerudo sword; Gerudo shield; diamond; assorted meats.
Daruk (*Breath of the Wild*)	Vah Rudania Divine Helm (Flame Guard); Goron weapon; assorted gemstones.
Revali (*Breath of the Wild*)	Vah Medoh Divine Helm (Cold Resistance); Rito bow; diamond; assorted arrows and fruits.

- A Xenoblade Chronicles 2 themed armor is offered as a reward for completing a new side quest, which involves finding the impact sites of three meteorites at night – see page 451 for details.

- You can now re-acquire the armor pieces exclusive to The Master Trials DLC should you have accidentally sold them. As with all other items that you can only obtain once by normal means (such as the Hylian shield), they become available for purchase in Granté's shop in Tarrey Town after you collect them for the first time. Granté appears on the terrace of the building to the right of the settlement's entrance after you complete the "From the Ground Up" side quest (see page 232).

SIDE QUESTS

Much like The Master Trials, The Champions' Ballad DLC introduces new equipment found in special EX treasure chests. Many of these containers are located in the Faron region: see the map on the previous page for a concise overview of their locations.

FIRST STEPS

All EX treasure chests exclusive to the Champions' Ballad can be opened as soon as you complete the main story prologue and leave the Great Plateau. They are generally hidden, either underwater or partly buried in the ground. As the containers are metal, make use of Magnesis to locate them more easily.

If you would prefer to hunt for these items on your own, you will first need to find three documents that offer clues as to the whereabouts of each EX chest. This is a purely optional step: the treasures are available to collect whether you read them or not.

MISKO'S EX JOURNAL 2: Finding this document formally begins the EX Treasure side quests that lead to new apparel for Link. Head to Deya Village Ruins, to the east of the Great Plateau, just across the Hylia River. The journal is hidden under the collapsed wall of a derelict house.

SUPER RUMOR MILL V3 & SUPER RUMOR MILL V4: Both of these appear on tables inside stable buildings – the former at the Highland Stable and the latter at the Riverside Stable.

EX ANCIENT HORSE RUMORS

This side quest leads to special equipment that can greatly optimize the way that you use horses to navigate Hyrule.

- The **Ancient Bridle** will add two spur icons to your horse's dash gauge, increasing the number of times you can make a horse gallop at full speed. A horse with a stamina attribute of 2, for example, can normally be spurred twice, which is represented by two spur icons on your screen. With this bridle equipped, you obtain two extra spurs – extending the gauge to four. The bonus icons appear in blue, the color of Ancient technology.
- The **Ancient Saddle** enables you to warp your horse to your current position with ✚ irrespective of its current location. Essentially, it grants you a much-improved version of your whistle command. Common-sense restrictions apply, of course: you cannot teleport your horse to places that they cannot physically reach, such as the Gerudo Desert, or upper floors of buildings.

To equip these items on your mount, talk to the woman feeding the horses at one of the following four stables: Highland Stable, Outskirt Stable, Woodland Stable, or South Akkala Stable. She will only do so if your bond with the horse in question is at its maximum value, though. Apples are a quick and affordable way to buy a horse's affection if you're in a hurry.

ANCIENT BRIDLE

A1

"The bridle is south of Hyrule Ridge, under the cherry blossom tree at the mountain where creatures gather."

Head to the top of Satori Mountain, to the south of Hyrule Ridge. You will find this chest buried at the foot of the cherry tree that grows there. Activate Magnesis to pull it out of the ground.

ANCIENT SADDLE

A2

"The saddle is at a mysterious spring where a horse spirit resides."

This item is hidden at Malanya Spring, to the southeast of the Highland Stable, just behind the Horse God's fountain. It is partly buried in the ground so you will need to lift it with Magnesis.

EX ROYAL GUARD RUMORS

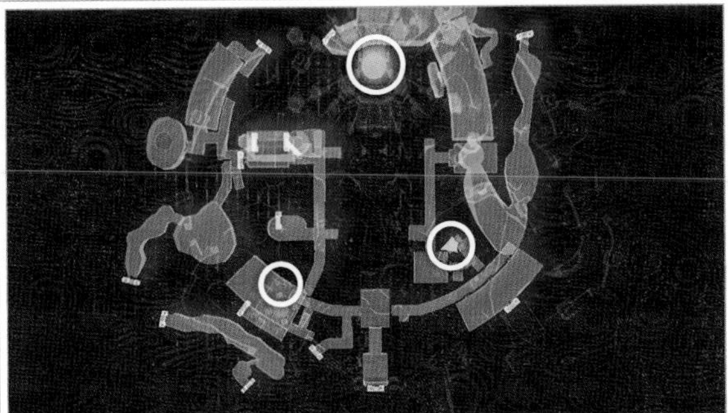

This quest offers you a chance to obtain the official **outfit of Hyrule's Royal Guard**. All three pieces are found inside Hyrule Castle and have a defense value of 4. If you equip them at the same time, you will trigger the Charge Atk. Stamina Up set bonus, which reduces stamina consumption when Link performs charged attacks. If you would like information on how to get into the castle, and what you can expect when you arrive, refer to the tour that we provide on page 106.

ROYAL GUARD UNIFORM

B1 *"Near the Dining Hall."*

This treasure chest is found in a small room initially blocked by destructible rocks, on your left as you walk from the Armory to the Dining Hall.

ROYAL GUARD BOOTS

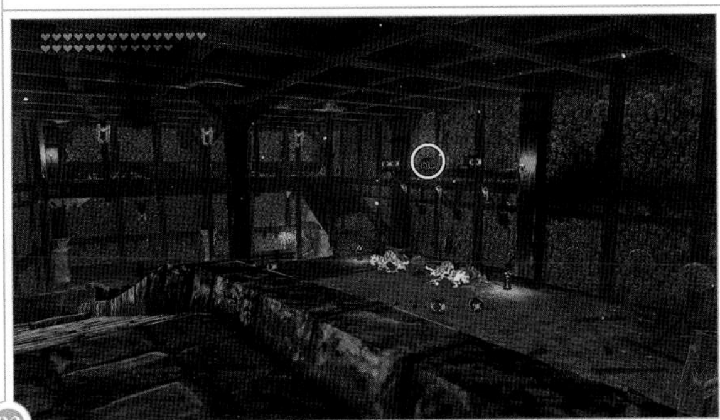

B2 *"Near the Guards' Chamber."*

This chest lies on a wooden ledge above the Lizalfos in the Guards' Chamber.

ROYAL GUARD CAP

B3 *"On the second floor."*

Head to the room above the Sanctum to reach this treasure chest.

EX TREASURE: MERCHANT'S HOOD

C *"The traveling merchant's hood is in the right hand of the dragon that consumes the Spring of Courage at Dracozu Lake."*

Head to the Spring of Courage, just southwest of the Dueling Peaks. A dragon statue stands at the spring's entrance. Climb into its right paw to find a hidden chest; dislodge it with Magnesis.

Ravio's Hood is a replica of the mask worn by Ravio, one of the key protagonists in *A Link Between Worlds*. It provides a token defense rating of 2, but it offers a secret perk that is not immediately apparent: wearing this headgear dramatically increases Link's sideways climbing speed. This subtle bonus pays homage to Link's ability to merge into walls and move laterally in *A Link Between Worlds*.

EX TREASURE: GARB OF WINDS

D

"The blue garb of the hero who controlled the wind and traveled the ocean is where the Menoat River was born."

Make your way to Cora Lake, a short walk to the south of the Lake Tower. Standing on the westernmost rock, use Cryonis to raise a pillar of ice just in front of the cave from which the river is flowing. Climb on it and look down with Magnesis turned on: you will see the chest underwater, on the riverbed.

The **Island Lobster Shirt** is the signature shirt worn by Link in *The Wind Waker*. Once equipped, it provides a Level 1 heat resistance added effect, which can be useful during your early forays into the Gerudo Desert.

EX TREASURE: DARK ARMOR

A reference to Ganon, the Great King of Evil himself, the **Phantom Ganon set** offers a token armor rating of 4 per garment. Each of its parts also confers one level of the Stealth Up effect. Early in the adventure, this means that you can enjoy the maximum Level 3 bonus without having to purchase the relatively expensive Stealth outfit from the shop in Kakariko Village. Among many other applications, this enables you to approach monsters quietly from behind for easy sneak attacks, or to collect little critters such as lizards or fairies without needing to crouch-walk.

If you wear the complete outfit, Link enjoys a set bonus that confers two further added effects: Stal Disguise (minor Stal monsters will not automatically attack Link) and Bone Atk. Up (increased damage for Dragonbone weapons, a very useful perk during the early-to-middle sections of the main storyline when such weapons are commonplace). NPCs will also react with alarm when Link approaches them, though their behavior during interactions remains unchanged.

EX TREASURE: USURPER KING

E

"The helm of the self-proclaimed King of Shadows is in the swamp of the valley of dead trees, south of Dueling Peaks."

Head to Tobio's Hollow, the narrow valley filled with dead trees, directly south of Dueling Peaks. You will find a swamp at the northern tip of this location, with a few rock platforms surrounded by a bog. Raise a few pillars of ice with Cryonis to reach the rock with two dead trees: the chest is buried between them.

With an armor rating of three, **Zant's Helmet** isn't particularly useful in terms of raw defense. What makes it really stand out is the Unfreezable effect that it grants to Link. Until you can upgrade a full Snowquill armor set to Level 2, this is the only way for Link to resist the frozen status effect caused by various ice-imbued enemies and weapons. When facing an Ice-Breath Lizalfos, for instance, this can prove invaluable. This helmet was originally worn by the Usurper King, Zant, one of Link's antagonists in *Twilight Princess*.

PHANTOM GANON SKULL

F1

"At the bottom of the highest of three waterfalls north of Lake Floria."

This treasure hunt takes place at Corta Lake, to the northeast of the Faron Tower. Use Magnesis to scan the bottom of the waterfall at the south end of the lake and you will see a chest on the riverbed. If you arrive from Lake Floria to the south and have the Zora armor, you can swim up the two westernmost waterfalls to reach this destination (at the base of third waterfall) in mere seconds.

PHANTOM GANON ARMOR

F2 *"In the Floria River at the bridge between the small waterfalls."*

This chest is hidden underneath Sarjon Bridge, directly to the west of the Faron Tower. Activate Magnesis in advance to identify it from a distance – it's between two pillars.

PHANTOM GANON GREAVES

F3 *"At the broken stone bird of Ebara Forest."*

You will find this treasure in Ebara Forest, on the east shore of Lake Floria. Look for three large bird statues at the eastern end of the Floria Bridge. One of them has been decapitated: the chest is buried at its base. It's covered with grass; use Magnesis to identify it.

XENOBLADE CHRONICLES 2

A tie-in with Xenoblade Chronicles 2, the pieces of the **Salvager armor set** *can be obtained only at night.* Head to the correct locations, look for red shooting stars in the night sky, and make your way to their impact sites (clearly marked by a red aura) to find a treasure chest.

Each part of this set offers a defense value of 5 and provides the Swim Speed Up added effect. You additionally enjoy the Swim Dash Stamina Up set bonus if you equip the complete outfit, making this useful for exploring areas with large bodies of water at an early stage in the storyline. It is later superseded by the superior Zora armor, which also enables Link to ascend waterfalls and to perform a spin attack while swimming.

SALVAGER VEST

G2 *"The eastern sky from the skull's left eye."*

Warp to the Zuna Kai shrine at Skull Lake, in the north of the Akkala region. Look toward the east and observe the night sky. You should see a red meteorite appear after a few seconds. Glide to its impact site to find the treasure chest.

SALVAGER HEADWEAR

G1 *"The southern sky from the middle of the largest bridge."*

Stand near the fountain at the middle of the Bridge of Hylia that spans Lake Hylia, directly southeast of the Great Plateau. Look up and to the south and you will soon spot a red meteorite that lands on the lake's shore, just east of the bridge's southern end.

SALVAGER TROUSERS

G3 *"The southeastern sky from the peak of the tall, pierced snowy mountain."*

Climb to the top of Hebra Peak (the tall mountain where the Goma Asaagh shrine is found inside a cave) at nighttime. Look to the southeast until you spot the red meteorite. Glide to its impact site on a small plateau down below to retrieve your treasure.

MAIN QUESTS

The new quests introduced by The Champions' Ballad can only be accessed if you have purchased the Expansion Pass, **but remain locked until you have liberated all four Divine Beasts in the main storyline**.

EX THE CHAMPIONS' BALLAD: OPENING TRIAL

Once you have freed all four Divine Beasts in the central storyline, or should you return to a previous save with that milestone accomplished, a short cutscene will introduce the new main quest. This invites you to return to the Shrine of Resurrection on the Great Plateau.

Puzzle-solving, exploration and tactical combat are the primary focus of this new adventure. This means that Master Mode shouldn't be noticeably more difficult than Normal for relatively experienced players – though boss battles do require greater confidence and precision.

Once inside the Shrine of Resurrection, interact with the terminal where you originally acquired the Sheikah Slate. This causes four markers to appear on the Great Plateau, and provides a very specific weapon for Link to use: the One-Hit Obliterator. Your first assignment in this extensive quest line begins once you pick it up.

Your goal in the opening trial is to find and clear four new shrines, which we cover over the pages that follow. To do so, you will first need to reveal them by defeating the enemies that guard each site.

THE ONE-HIT OBLITERATOR

The One-Hit Obliterator defeats enemies with a single blow, but enforces an equivalent burden of peril upon Link: his health is reduced to a quarter of a heart, making him vulnerable to any act of aggression that he cannot block or evade. The weapon briefly loses its lethal power after two consecutive uses, at which point its blue glow disappears. In these instances, you must wait a few seconds for it to recharge and regain its effectiveness. As soon as the blue hue is restored, the cooldown is over and you can resume your attack.

Once you have picked it up, the One-Hit Obliterator cannot be dropped or exchanged for another melee weapon. You must use it exclusively until you complete this opening trial, or quit the endeavor by leaving the Great Plateau.

The fact that a single hit will floor Link means that you can't afford to rush; you should also make liberal use of the save function prior to primary confrontations. The following advice will help:

- While approaching each of the four heavily guarded monster bases, your priority is to avoid detection: having to manage a group of foes with a bare quarter of a heart holding Link upright is not an enticing prospect. Aim to sneak up and eliminate lone enemies from behind. This feat is much easier if you equip the Stealth or Phantom Ganon outfits (or consume appropriate meals). We cannot emphasize enough how beneficial a maximum Level 3 stealth bonus will be. In some instances, you will need to lure individuals away from their allies; use judiciously targeted arrows fired at the ground to entice your chosen quarry to an ambush position of your preference.
- The fact that your weapon has a strict cooldown restriction means that you need to be methodical. You can, however, defeat multiple foes with a single blow by performing an area-of-effect technique – for example, charged attacks and jump slashes. All enemies caught within the radius will be killed instantly.
- When stealth is not a viable option, consider hit-and-run tactics: sprint or, even better, glide into the fray to eliminate a target or two, then immediately escape. As soon as your pursuers give up, repeat the process. This can work especially well if you begin each sortie from an elevated vantage point, where you are more likely to take adversaries completely by surprise.
- If combat is not your strong suit and you struggle to clear groups of enemies guarding each of the four bases, equipping Majora's Mask (see page 414) is an option. This rather spoils the challenge of this opening trial, though, so it's best considered as a last resort.
- Last but not least, pay close attention to environmental hazards. Spikes, thorns, and even the briefest lick of flame can be instantly lethal when you have only a quarter of a heart.

YOWAKA ITA SHRINE

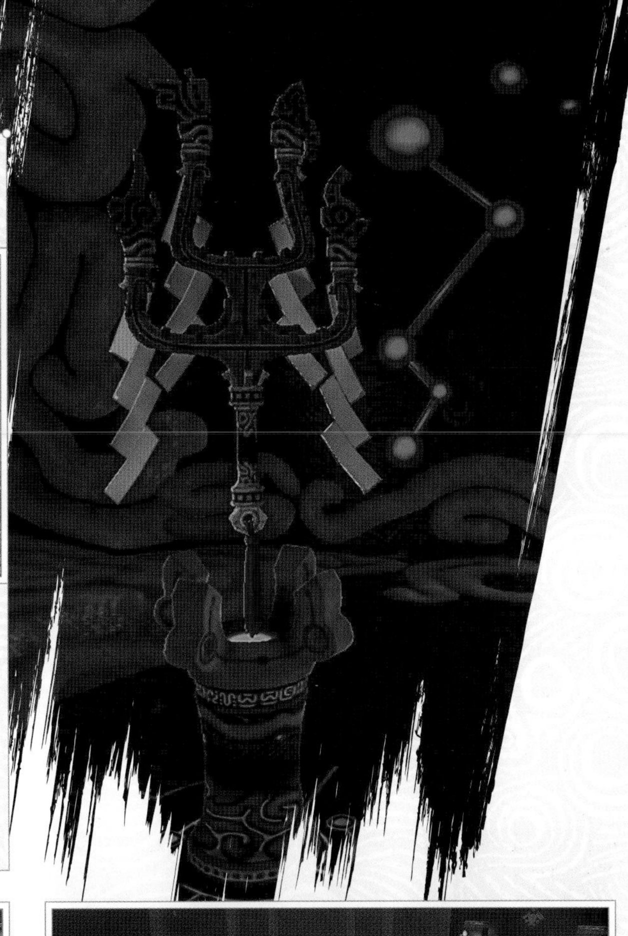

APPROACH: From the Shrine of Resurrection's cave entrance, you can glide directly to the marker at the heart of the Forest of Spirits, where you will encounter a large group of Bokoblins. If you make your approach from the southwest, you will be able to start with the two sentries stationed on trees, who can detect you from a great distance. Be mindful of the swarm of Keese, too: arrows can be a reliable way to get rid of them in advance. If you are spotted, retreat immediately and make a new approach after your pursuers return to their usual routine. Once they are all dead, the Yowaka Ita Shrine appears.

1

Make your way to the other end of the chamber, avoiding the boulders and hazards that roll down the initial slope. Once on the second platform, pick up the scoop with Magnesis. Your goal is to catch three objects: a small orb, a large orb, and a treasure chest. Position the scoop in the general direction of each incoming target and you will soon get an approximate sense of the trajectories they follow, which can vary every time. You need to take both their speed and their height into account, and react accordingly.

2

When you catch an object in the scoop, carefully bring it to your position and drop it on the platform. The chest yields five bomb arrows. Drop or push the large orb into the concave slot by the nearby gate to reach a second chest that contains a phrenic bow.

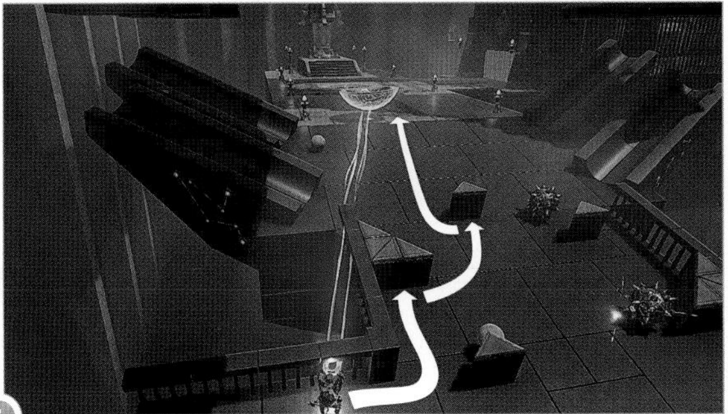

3

The small orb needs to be taken back to the slot you passed earlier. The safest way to deliver it safely beyond the hazards is to leave it in the scoop and carefully place it on the first platform beyond the slope; Magnesis offers just enough distance for you to set the scoop down carefully after you cross the bridge and press up against the wall. Alternatively, you can carry it manually and make timed runs to avoid the rolling objects.

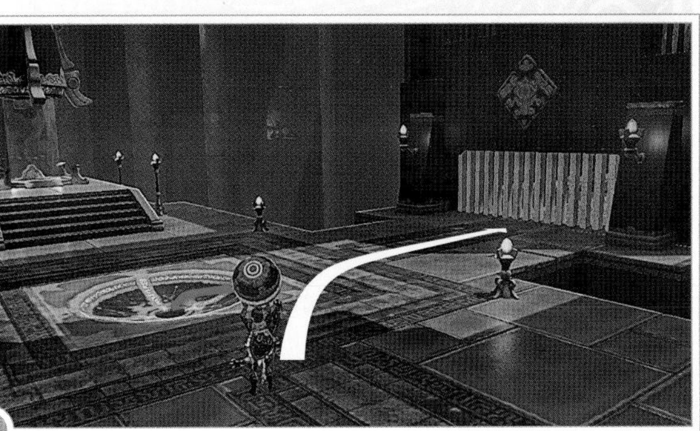

4

Once the small orb rolls into position, the gate leading to the altar opens.

ROHTA CHIGAH SHRINE

APPROACH: The location highlighted by the marker to the south of the Great Plateau Tower is home to a large group of Lizalfos and a Decayed Guardian. The archers complicate matters significantly, as any patch of grass that is set ablaze by their fire arrows (let alone barrel explosions) can potentially kill Link instantly. You should therefore aim to remain out of sight and methodically eliminate each foe without being detected. Approaching the base from the south to sneakily dispatch the archers and the Guardian first can be a sound option. If you are spotted or threatened by multiple targets at once, don't take any chances: flee the scene and return once your pursuers lose track of you.

1

Once inside the shrine, gaining access to the treasure chest (which contains a forest dweller's shield) on the wall to your right involves employing Magnesis to position the three metal objects as shown in this picture: the metal cube at the foot of the alcove where the chest rests, perfectly aligned on the square-shaped spiked platform beneath, with the two metal slabs acting as a bridge to the cube.

2

Once the chest contents are yours, move the two slabs to form another bridge, this time enabling you to leave the room.

3

In the next section you have to navigate cogwheels and conveyor belts, with dangerous spikes leaving you with little room to maneuver. The key is to move with care, always taking into account the direction in which Link is being (or soon will be) pushed. Stasis can make the tricky final spike-lined corridor a little easier.

4

In the third segment of this shrine, three spiked boulders are hanging from chains, swinging wildly across the chasm. Your goal is to glide down to the far side without touching them. The most consistent way to achieve this is to freeze the closest boulder with Stasis to automatically secure a good take-off, then adjust your course as you glide down to avoid the two other boulders.

5

The final stretch begins once you step on the floor switch. This triggers a spiked block that starts moving behind you, forcing you to run toward the altar at the opposite end. Carefully navigate the spikes that jut out from all sides, climb on top of the second rock cube, then walk to either side of the third one. Just before the end, you will need to jump to the top of a block that protrudes from the wall on the right; from there, hop down to the platform and approach the altar.

RUVO KORBAH SHRINE

APPROACH: The difficulty ramps up at the marker to the south of the Temple of Time. This location features assorted Lizalfos, Moblins, and Bokoblins, some of which are riding horses. Consider using the hill on which the Temple of Time is built as a staging post: glide toward your enemies and eliminate one or two with a jump slash, beat a hasty retreat before returning to your original position, then repeat until all targets have been eliminated.

1

Inside the Ruvo Korbah Shrine, a Guardian Scout IV awaits. As imposing as it may seem, the power of your weapon makes this a relatively trivial encounter. Hold your shield aloft to block the customary opening laser salvo, then dispatch it with a combo or a counter.

2

The treasure chest in the next room contains 10 bomb arrows. Stand on the floor switch at the top of the steps, then backtrack to the main room and drop into the elevator shaft shown in the brief cutscene.

3

Follow the path to your left and eliminate the Guardian Scout on the way. More Scouts roam in the area: proceed cautiously, being careful to destroy them one by one. Keep your shield at the ready at all times.

4

From the downward stairs, you have one more Scout within immediate reach, with another standing watch on the above floor. Briefly dart out and eliminate the former, then hide behind a wall. Next, bait a shot by the second Scout, then jump to the top of the ladder and hold your shield aloft as you walk to its position to dispatch it. You will find a small key in the nearby treasure chest: use it to open the locked door. Before you do, though, consider making a short detour: the corridor that was guarded by the first Scout leads to another treasure chest that contains a giant ancient core.

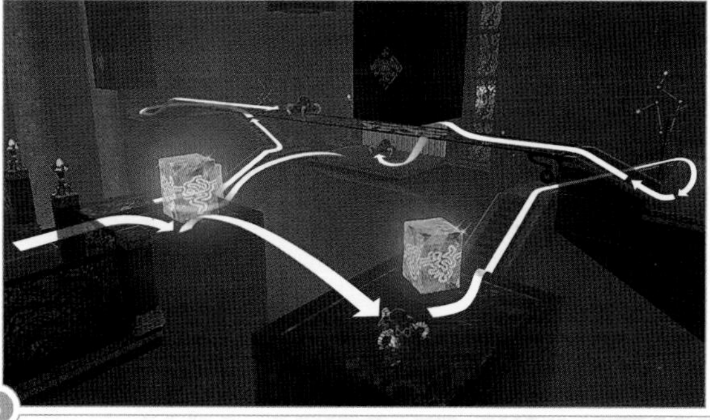

5

Before you set foot in the next room, raise one block of ice with Cryonis in each of the three small pools, preferably in any corner. These will enable you to shield yourself from the laser beams of the four Guardian Scouts that will appear once you press forward. With this precaution taken, you have two options: the first one is to methodically eliminate your enemies with arrows from your starting position, even throwing in a few bomb arrows if you wish to expedite the process. Alternatively, you can glide down to one of the lower pools and eliminate a first adversary, then use the three pillars and ornate fences as cover as you approach and disable each opponent. The Scout on the long bridge has a shield, so it makes sense to deal with it last. Once all foes are down, the path to the altar opens.

ETSU KORIMA SHRINE

APPROACH: The marker on Mount Hylia is in an area where cold resistance gear (or an equivalent temporary buff) will be essential. The monsters guarding this site include Moblins, Lizalfos, and a Blizzrobe. The best solution is to climb to the upper reaches of Mount Hylia. From here, you can easily eliminate the Blizzrobe and Ice-Breath Lizalfos with fire arrows. The remaining targets can be dispatched with aerial attacks: glide to them and unleash a jump slash from above. With any luck, the impact will eliminate multiple creatures. As soon as you touch the ground, flee and climb back to your vantage point on Mount Hylia. Repeat this maneuver until no threat remains. Note that you can easily dispatch Ice Keese and Chuchus from a safe distance with bombs or arrows.

1

The first room inside this dimly lit shrine is home to multiple laser beams. Weave between the vertical lines, crouch-walk under the three horizontal lines, then run past the final laser once it moves above or below your position. If you find the ambient darkness disorienting, note that you can activate the Stasis rune to marginally improve visibility and get a better sense of your surroundings.

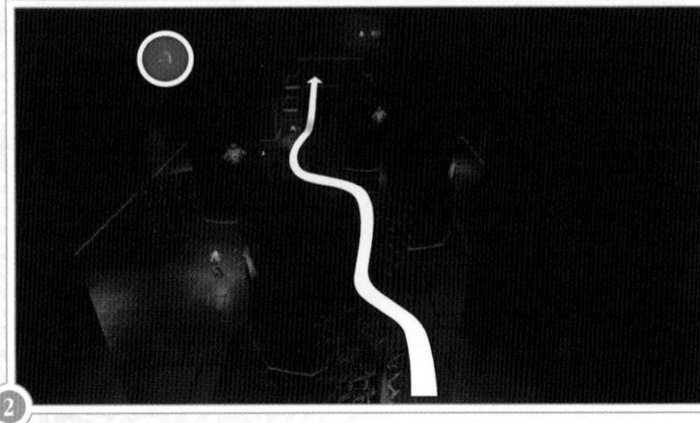

2

In the next room, you must navigate through spiked structures that slowly rotate; they're akin to revolving doors, and shouldn't pose any problems. There is a chest on a wooden ledge to your left just before you leave the room. Set the leaves beneath it ablaze to make it fall to you – it contains a gold rupee.

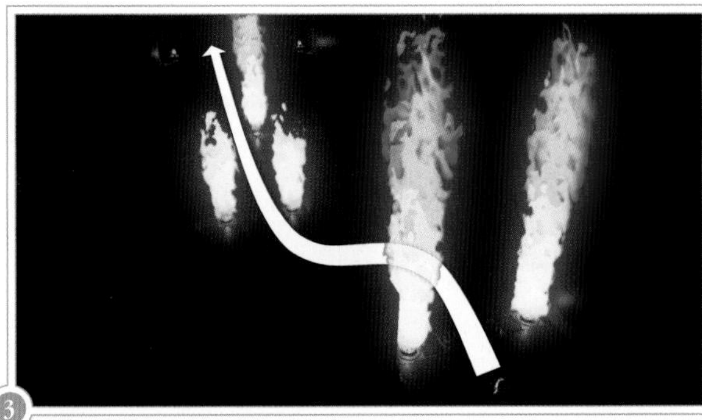

3

You will arrive at a corridor where pillars of flame are fired from jets on the floor. Some of these are intermittent, and activate at predictable intervals; wait, watch, and then make timely dashes to pass these obstacles. Alternatively, you can walk straight through with the Fireproof effect active. Finally, you will encounter three Guardian Scouts. You should be able to dispatch the closest one stealthily. Use the various barriers (especially the low raised platform just inside the entrance) as cover from laser bolts while you eliminate the other two. The altar awaits at the top of the steps.

THE FOUR SONG QUESTS

Clearing all four shrines completes the introductory trial on the Great Plateau. Link's One-Hit Obliterator vanishes, restoring access to your full arsenal. Four markers now appear on the world map, each leading to a pedestal surrounded by three pillars. Each of the pillars features a small map portion. Your goal is to discover which location on the world map each one refers to, then head there and fulfill a specific objective to reveal a shrine. Note that you are free to tackle these challenges in whichever order you prefer.

After you clear all three shrines associated with a specific champion you can fast travel to the corresponding Divine Beast, where you will face the regional Blight Ganon once again. This time, however, your inventory will replicate the tools that the champions had at their disposal when they faced these monsters 100 years previously. Interestingly, status effects are carried into these battles. If, for instance, you consume a meal granting a Level 3 Attack Up bonus prior to an encounter, this will give Link a significant edge (which can prove particularly welcome on Master Mode).

Defeating a Blight Ganon unlocks the respective Champion's "+" ability, which drastically reduces the cooldown for the following valuable perks.

CHAMPION POWER COOLDOWNS

ICON	NAME	ORIGINAL COOLDOWN	"+" COOLDOWN
	Mipha's Grace	24 minutes	8 minutes
	Urbosa's Fury	12 minutes	4 minutes
	Revali's Gale	6 minutes	2 minutes
	Daruk's Protection	18 minutes	6 minutes

If you wish, you can subsequently return to the Divine Beasts and face each boss again. Each further victory triggers a new line of dialog by the champion in question (up to a maximum of six), which eventually allude to the existence of their personal diaries. These documents offer additional insights into each champion's story. They can be found in the following locations:

- **Mipha's Diary:** On a small table close to King Dorephan's throne in Zora's Domain.
- **Urbosa's Diary:** In Riju's room in Gerudo Town, above the throne room.
- **Revali's Diary:** In Teba's hut in Rito Village.
- **Daruk's Diary:** In Yunobo's house in Goron City.

EX CHAMPION MIPHA'S SONG

Mipha's pedestal is found on Ja'Abu Ridge, just south of the East Reservoir Lake. This map shows its location, as well as those of the three associated shrines that become available after you visit the pedestal for the first time.

AREA MAP

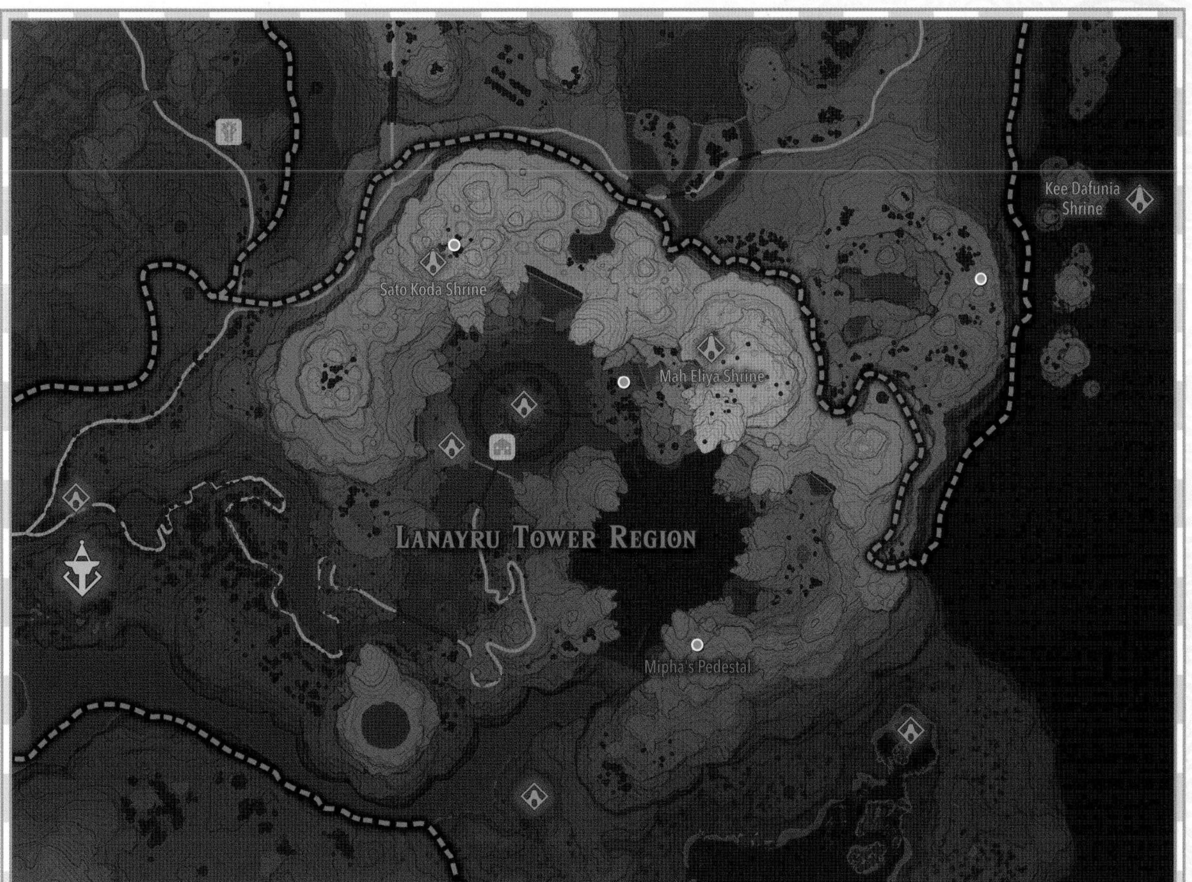

SATO KODA SHRINE

LOCATION: This shrine is hidden in Upland Zorana, just north of Zora's Domain. To reveal it, you first need to destroy the three Guardian Skywatchers and the Guardian Turret in the area. The Skywatchers, as ever, are redoubtable opponents; we advise that you vaporize them instantly by hitting their blue eye with an ancient arrow. Failing that, aerial slo-mo barrages of bomb arrows also work well to destroy their propellers. Once condemned to the ground, they are far less trouble to deal with.

1 Your goal in this shrine is to guide the orb to the floor switch at the bottom of the structure. This puzzle may seem confounding at first, but it actually has a surprisingly simple solution. Standing at the edge of the top platform, summon two blocks of ice with Cryonis in the positions illustrated in the accompanying screenshot. This is sufficient to carry the ball into a launcher, which automates the final part of the journey. Once it ultimately lands in the concave slot, the way to the altar opens up.

2 Before you leave the shrine, don't forget to open the treasure chest. You can reach it by building an improvised set of steps made with ice blocks. It contains a giant ancient core.

KEE DAFUNIA SHRINE

LOCATION: Before you begin this challenge, make sure that you at least have a fire weapon in your inventory; see page 358 if you do not have one to hand. To reveal this shrine, head to the cliffs facing the four islands in the easternmost part of the Lanayru region. Look for the smoke of a campfire and you will find Muzu nearby. Use the fire to wait until morning (05:00 AM). As soon as Link wakes up, run to the east, in the direction of the rising sun, and glide between Ankel Island and Knuckel Island. You will soon notice a ring of light just above the sea. The shrine appears if you can pass through the ring – either gliding or swimming – before it disappears at approximately 06:10 AM.

1

Start by melting the two large ice cubes that block your progression into the main room. You can do so by standing next to them with a fire weapon equipped, or – much faster – by shooting fire arrows. Switch back to a standard weapon once you're done. If you have no fire-imbued tool in your arsenal, you can alternatively propel the cubes away by hitting them multiple times while they are frozen with Stasis. You could also use the torch close to the shrine's entrance, but you cannot sprint or jump while it is lit, making it a rather unpractical option.

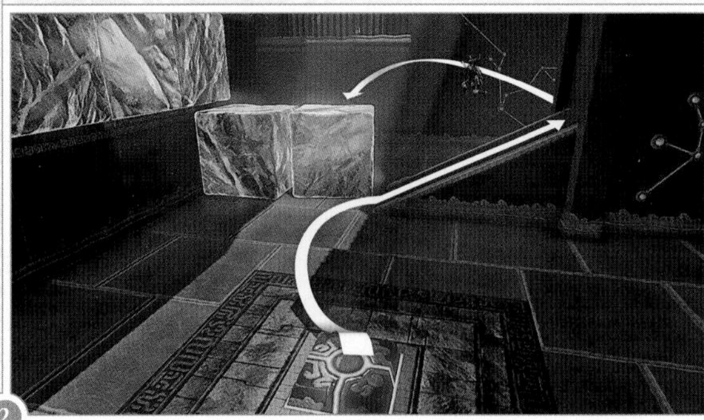

2

Walk to a floor switch on either side of the room, and step on it to make a large cube fall down the nearby ramp. Do this again to make a second cube fall from the same ramp. Both cubes need to be aligned, forming a bridge between the ramp and the central platform. If they are not, note that you can realign them with Stasis, or even make the one closest to the ramp melt a little bit, thereby making it more accessible. Now walk to the top of the corresponding ramp. From here, sprint and immediately glide so as to reach the top of the closest cube.

3

Position Link against the central platform, which is entirely covered with ice cubes. Equip your fire weapon to start making all nearby cubes melt. As soon as there is enough space for Link to hop on the platform, do so. Keep the melting process going until the cubes near you are small enough that you can pick them up. As soon as this is the case (pay attention to the onscreen prompt), switch to a different weapon, then arrange the melted cubes as stepping stones to reach the top of the structure. If you do not have a fire weapon, note that you can shoot arrows through the torches on the ground to achieve a similar result.

4

Before you move on to the next step, melt the cubes located beneath the upper walkway. This will reveal a hidden alcove where a chest containing a frostblade can be found.

5

Once on the top platform, melt the only cube available. As soon as it is small enough for Link to pick up, unequip your weapon. Take the cube to the small pool beyond and throw it or push it beneath the low gate. Finally, position it against the wall at the far end and raise a pillar of ice with Cryonis right underneath it. This will enable you to climb up and reach the altar.

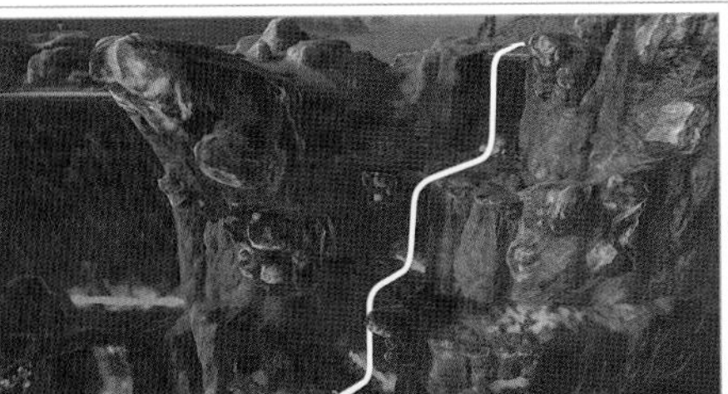

MAH ELIYA SHRINE

LOCATION: This shrine awaits on Ploymus Mountain. You can discover it by heading to Mikau Lake, at the foot of the three waterfalls to the east of Zora's Domain. You will see a blue ring, similar to those encountered in Korok seed challenges of the "race" variety. Run through the ring to begin the trial. Your goal is to swim through the rings that appear consecutively before the countdown expires. With the full Zora armor set equipped (see page 284), you should easily reach the final gate in time.

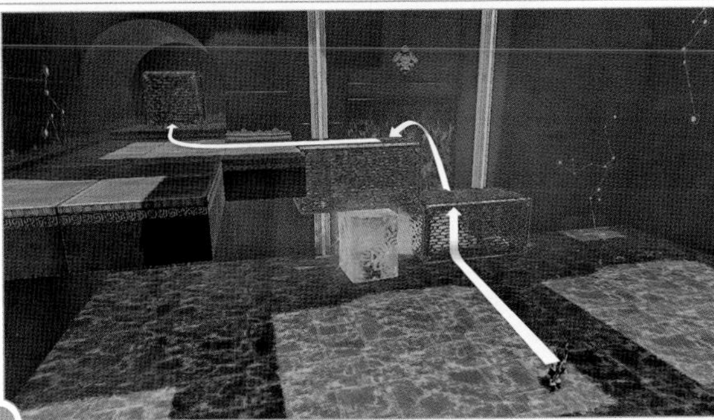

1 Use Cryonis to raise an ice pillar beneath the climbable rectangular block on the left to create a route to the platform above, where you will find a metal cube that you can grab with Magnesis. Drop it down to the ground floor and shatter the first pillar of ice.

2 Now raise a new pillar of ice, this time beneath both rectangular blocks to elevate them simultaneously. Grab the metal cube with Magnesis and use it to lift the right-hand rectangular block. Carefully position the cube so that it rests on the left-hand block while supporting the right-hand block, as shown in the above picture.

3 You can now raise a horizontal ice pillar in the top-right corner of the waterfall, as high as possible. This ejects the metal cube, while maintaining the right-hand rectangular block in its elevated position.

4 Climb on top of the pillar of ice at the bottom of the structure. From here, grab the metal cube with Magnesis and use it to raise the left-hand rectangular block to its maximum height. Carefully adjust the cube so that it rests on the right-hand block while also supporting the block on the left.

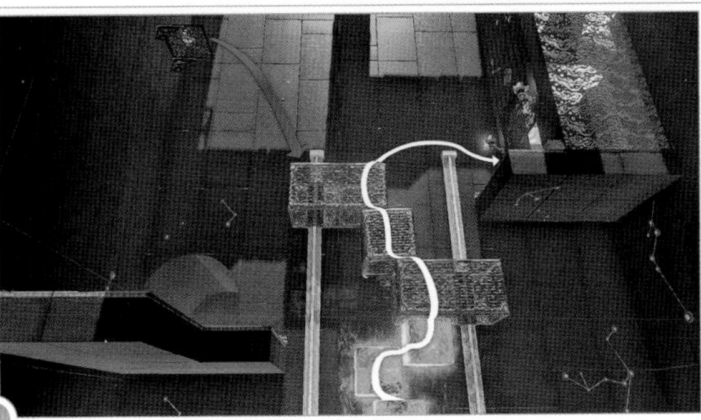

5 Finally, create a horizontal pillar of ice between the two existing pillars and climb to the top of the improvised structure. From here, you can grab the treasure chest on the ledge above with Magnesis (it contains a royal shield). With that done, glide to the platform in the opposite direction to reach the altar.

WATERBLIGHT GANON

After clearing Mipha's three shrines, fast travel to Divine Beast Vah Ruta for a new showdown against Waterblight Ganon. The battle plays out in the same manner as when you cleared the Divine Beast, with one key difference: you only have 10 arrows available, so you absolutely need to make each one count.

- During the first phase, focus exclusively on melee combat, making the most of your spear's reach. Sprint away whenever your foe prepares his shockwave attack, but remain very aggressive at close range for the rest of the time.
- Once the second phase begins, raise a pillar of ice with Cryonis; you can then climb on top of it, and from there jump towards the boss and immediately pull out your bow. The slow-motion effect makes it much easier to align three eye shots in a row, which stuns the monster, offering a chance to unleash at least two full melee combos if you're fast. Repeat this twice (requiring nine of your 10 arrows in total) and you will emerge victorious very quickly.
- On Master Mode, the very same strategy applies, though you need to act with great efficiency to avoid a situation where your opponent's health bar regenerates.

EX CHAMPION URBOSA'S SONG

Urbosa's pedestal is found on the tallest rocky outcrop of the East Gerudo Mesa, just southeast of Divine Beast Vah Naboris. This map shows its position, as well as those of its three associated shrines that become available after you visit the pedestal.

AREA MAP

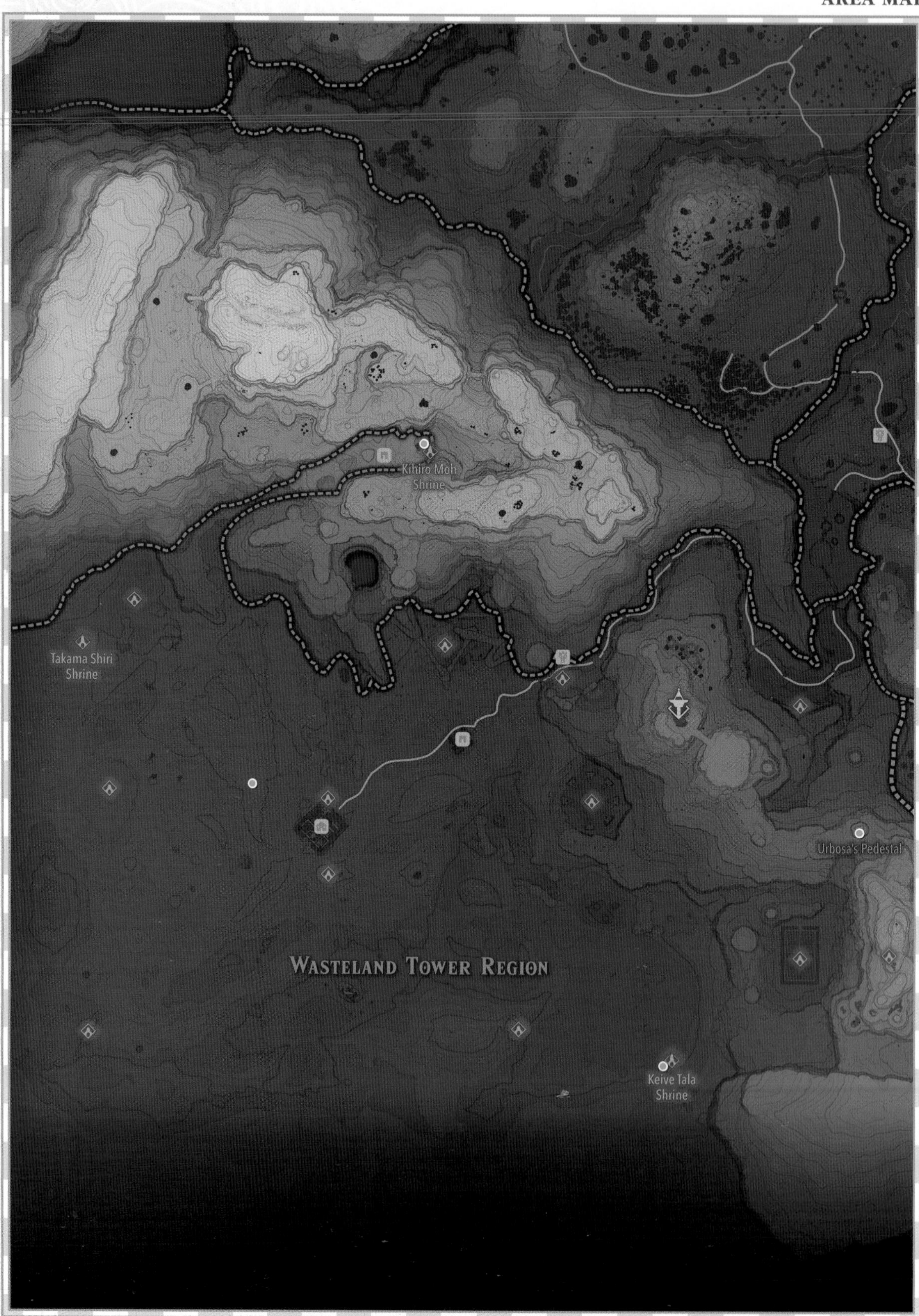

KEIVE TALA SHRINE

LOCATION: This shrine is located in the East Barrens, in the far southeast of the Gerudo Desert. To reveal it, you will need to defeat a sub-boss who roams in the area: Molduking. Standard tactics apply against this Molduga (see page 318), though you should note that it is extremely weak to electricity. If you hit it with a great thunderblade's spinning attack while it is stunned, you will deal tremendous amounts of damage.

1

The idea here is to complete the electrical circuit along the wall to raise the barrier blocking access to the altar. Using Magnesis, grab the first small metal cube in the alcove to your right, and drop it between the two small chained boulders. This electrifies the first segment of this shrine's circuit. Grab the second small metal cube and move it so that it connects the electrode to the circuit. This causes the adjacent elevator to move upwards: once the elevator reaches its top position, move the cube away from the electrode and drop it on the elevator so that the electrical current flows to the next segment.

2

Now grab the large boulder hanging from the chain with Magnesis, and drop it on the other side of the beam protruding from the wall. Switch to Cryonis and raise a pillar of ice just beyond the second beam. Drop the final large metal cube on top of this pillar: with the circuit complete, the barrier will rise, opening the way to the altar.

3

Before you leave this shrine, consider interacting with the device on the right if you wish to open the sole treasure chest. Your goal here is to align the four moving tiles so that they form a line and carry the current over the void. To do so, you need to hit the crystals with the laser beam using the gyroscopic functionality of your controller. Make very gentle movements to avoid accidentally reactivating a tile that you have already fixed into the correct position, particularly when dealing with the fast-moving ones. Once the connection is firmly established, the nearby barrier will rise. The chest contains a radiant shield.

KIHIRO MOH SHRINE

LOCATION: The marker for this trial points to the back entrance of the Yiga Clan Hideout, in the arena where you fought Master Kohga during the main adventure. Your task here is to return to the storage room filled with bananas, at the end of the walkway overlooking the hideout's main room, where you will find an orb that you need to take back outside. Yiga soldiers guard the area, though, so you will either need to sneak out with the orb above your head (a Level 3 stealth bonus obviously helps here), or defeat them first (Urbosa's Fury will be of obvious benefit). Both options should pose little challenge at this very late stage in your progression. Once you are back in the open-air arena, throw the orb into the large hole where Master Kohga once fell to his doom to reveal the shrine.

1

The key to solving this puzzle is to identify how many orbs of each color are contained inside the cage in the adjacent room. To count them, you need to interact with the device on the central platform and rotate the cage using the gyroscopic features of your controller, slowly adjusting the view from various angles. Once you know the answers, drop each colored orb in the relevant concave slot, their value ranging from 1 (for those closest to the locked gate) to 5 (for those closest to the shrine entrance). The correct configuration is shown in the above picture: pink = 1, green = 2, yellow = 2, purple = 4.

2

Before you complete the shrine, you will notice three large concave slots in the area to your right, each with an associated value (one, two, or three). Your goal here is to fill the correct pedestal with one of the colorless metallic balls that are also trapped inside the container. You can release these by rotating the object once again, this time leaving it in a position whereby its metallic tip (on the side opposite the Sheikah eye symbol) faces down. Now approach the cage and open it with Magnesis: the orbs will pour out. You will notice that there are three metal balls. Grab one of them with Magnesis and drop it in the right-hand slot (representing three, the number of metallic balls) to raise the barrier. The chest contains a thunderspear.

TAKAMA SHIRI SHRINE

LOCATION: To reveal this shrine, you will first need to offer an exhibition of your sand-seal racing skills. Rent a sand seal and head to the northwest of Gerudo Town. You will soon notice a blue ring in the distance, roughly midway between the village and the West Barrens. Once you go through the ring, another appears; complete the course before the countdown elapses. The path to follow is very linear. Just be sure to dash at all times and steer clear of the few hazards that appear on the course. The shrine appears once you reach the final ring.

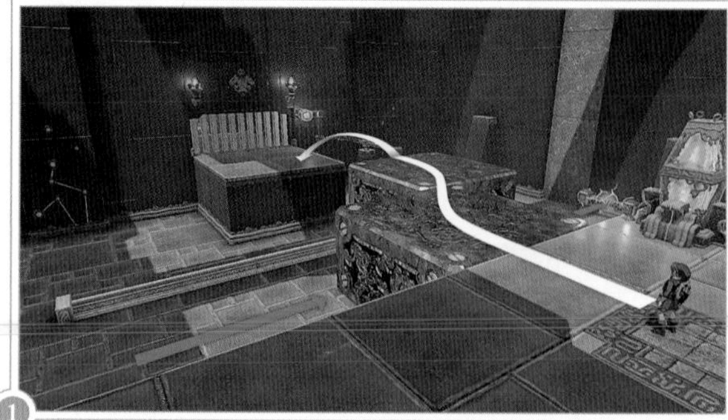

1

In the first room, you need to reach the platform with the locked gate before you worry about restoring the power. Move the closest metal block to the right, but not quite all the way; you can then reach the opposite platform. Turn around and move the same block all the way to the green crystal. Once the electricity flows, the barrier will be raised.

2

In the second room, grab the second block closest to your position with Magnesis and push it away, aligning it with the end of the walkway to your right – your next destination. From here, move the two blocks on the opposite side toward the locked gate to disrupt the electrical connection. This enables you to cross to the platform with the green crystal.

3

Turn around and move the block closest to the green crystal to restore the power, as illustrated here. In short, this block and the one on the other rail should now form a bridge between the crystal and the walkway. The third block, however, should still be in the corner by the door, isolated from the others – use it as a stepping stone to jump through the now-open door.

4

In the final room, adjust the metal cubes so that they form a pyramid, as shown in the above picture. Your goal is to direct the electricity to the segment on your left. This gives you access to the chest hidden in the corridor behind the back wall, which contains a royal bow. When you're done, align the three climbable blocks vertically in a central position. This enables you to climb to the upper floor. Head to the walkway above the room's entrance.

5

Finally, move the blocks to reproduce the configuration shown in this picture. The idea is to conduct the current from the green crystal in the lower right to the cable at the top left. The blocks on the bottom rail should be as far right as they can go; those on the middle rail should be adjusted diagonally; the left-hand block on the top rail should be moved to the far left, and the other one to the far right. This enables you to climb to the now-open gate via the non-electrified metal block in the upper-right.

THUNDERBLIGHT GANON

After clearing the three shrines related to Urbosa, fast travel to Divine Beast Vah Naboris. You can find a complete breakdown of the boss battle against Thunderblight Ganon on page 74. The key for a swift resolution is to perform a perfect dodge backflip every time the creature unleashes its zigzag attack, and follow up with full flurry rush combos. This is especially important during the second phase, where the monster's electricity-infused blows can otherwise prove extremely annoying. Remember: the correct timing to execute your backflip is when the monster warps to your right, poised to strike.

We suggest you fight the entire battle with the Scimitar of the Seven, as this enables you to wield your shield simultaneously. Avoid wasting your blade's precious durability on the boss's shield at all costs: if it breaks, you will have to use the two-handed edge of duality, making it harder to defend when required.

If you play on Master Mode, you positively *need* to consistently counter each zigzag attack with a flurry rush and a follow-up combo. Each time you fail, the beast's health will regenerate at an alarming rate, extending the confrontation.

EX CHAMPION REVALI'S SONG

Revali's pedestal is found on Cuho Mountain. It is easily accessed by gliding northward from the Tabantha Tower. This map shows its position, as well as the three associated shrines that you can conquer after you visit the pedestal for the first time.

AREA MAP

Kiah Toza Shrine
Hebra Tower Region
Noe Rajee Shrine
Shira Gomar Shrine
Revali's Pedestal
Tabantha Tower Region

KIAH TOZA SHRINE

LOCATION: To reveal this shrine, head to the west side of Hebra Peak. You will spot a blue ring right outside Goma Asaagh Shrine: shield-surf through it (see page 335) and keep sliding down the slope as fast as possible, holding Ⓛ forward. You will need to glide across a chasm after the second ring, but don't linger in the air and resume shield-surfing as soon as you are on the other side to maintain maximum speed. Once you go through the final ring at the end of the surfing course, the shrine appears nearby.

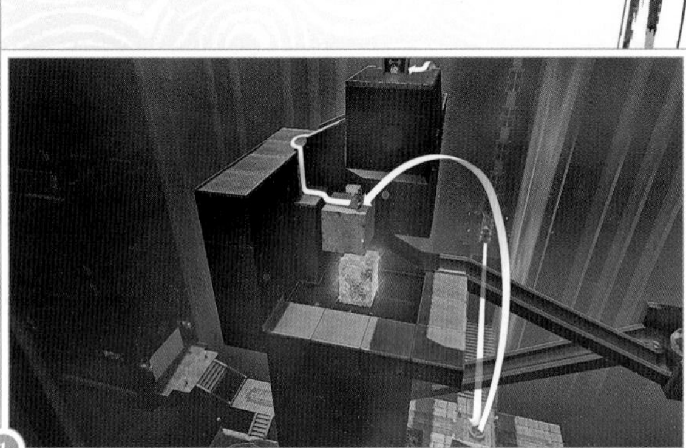

1

In this shrine, you need to use your wits and a variety of tools to shepherd a large orb on a very specific path through the apparatus in front of you. Start by riding the updraft as high as it goes, then glide around the corner to the right to land on a stone block affixed to a vertical rail on the nearby wall. From here, look down at the shallow water and raise a pillar of ice with Cryonis to lift the block, providing access to the nearby ladder. The chest at the top of the structure contains a falcon bow.

2

You now need to make advanced preparations to guide the rolling orb on the correct path. First, glide down to the middle section of the tower: land close to the metal blocks and a floor switch. The metal blocks on horizontal rails must be moved directly next to each other to create a barrier that guides the orb to the left; you can then reposition the two metal platforms to make a bridge. Next, drop to the bottom of the tower and create two horizontal pillars of ice on the water wall to form steps that will eventually guide the orb to the final ramp.

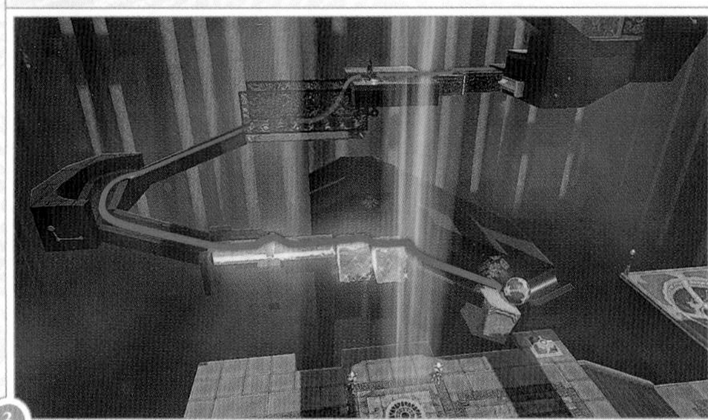

3

Ride the updraft and land on the floor switch close to the metal blocks. This changes the direction of the nearby conveyor belt. Wait until the orb has rolled over it, then cast Stasis on the rotating slab further down the slope to stabilize it. The orb should then roll safely into place in the launcher below.

4

Finally, step on the floor switch by the launcher to propel the orb to its slot. This opens the gate leading to the altar.

NOE RAJEE SHRINE

LOCATION: This trial takes place at the Flight Range; ensure that you have a healthy stock of arrows and at least a handful of bomb arrows before you begin. Your goal is to destroy four blue targets within a fraction of a second – which, naturally, involves gliding into position and hitting the required number within a single slow-motion sequence. To make this challenge much easier, equip a bow with superior range – such as the falcon bow, or the swallow bow available at the Flight Range. From your starting position on the wooden ledge where Tulin usually stands, there are actually four targets right in front of you that make ideal candidates. Catch the updraft and aim at each target one after the other; you will need to aim a little higher for the two on the far cliff. Once you complete the challenge, the shrine will appear.

1

Hit the crystal in front of your starting position to create an updraft, and ride this to the platform above. This huge chamber features a rotating tower structure in its center. Your goal is to strike four crystals – one on each side of the tower – to activate additional fans, whose updrafts will enable you to reach the altar at the very top. The best crystal to begin with is the one concealed behind destructible stone blocks. From your vantage point, destroy these obstructions with a bomb arrow. The explosion might trigger the crystal; if not, hit it with a second arrow.

2

The next crystal is found in an alcove behind a fence, preventing you from reaching it physically. Glide close to it, adjusting your height as required. Once you have it in sight, hit it with an arrow.

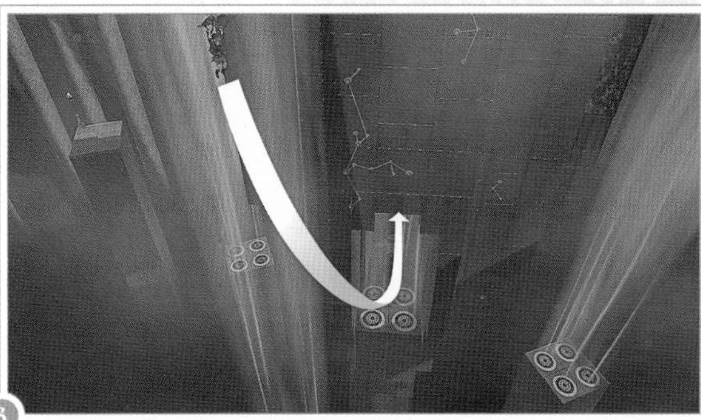

3

The next face of the tower features an opening at its base. Glide inside and you will find more fans generating an updraft in the tower's inner shaft. Ride this to the top and fire an arrow at the crystal.

4

The final crystal is hidden behind a door, which opens only when the fan just outside it is activated by an updraft. Get into position in advance. Just before the fan is about to start spinning, make a controlled descent and shoot at the crystal through the door while it is open.

5

Once all four crystals have been activated, you can ride the new updrafts in a counterclockwise direction to reach the top of the tower. Before you head to the altar, you may wish to open the treasure chest that rests on the opposite side of the chamber. To reach it, you need to glide to the far side of the pillar, where you will find an opening with an updraft just inside. The chest contains a Shield of the Mind's Eye.

SHIRA GOMAR SHRINE

LOCATION: Head to the plateau that overlooks Tanagar Canyon, to the southwest of Hebra Tower (directly east of the Dunba Taag Shrine). You will find a campfire with a Rito there: use this to wait until night. Now walk to the edge of the canyon and look to the northeast. Dinraal will appear and fly in your direction, though you should note that this can occasionally take a few minutes. Once he is close, catch the updrafts he generates to glide towards the dragon's head. Hit the creature's glowing horn with an arrow to reveal the shrine across the canyon.

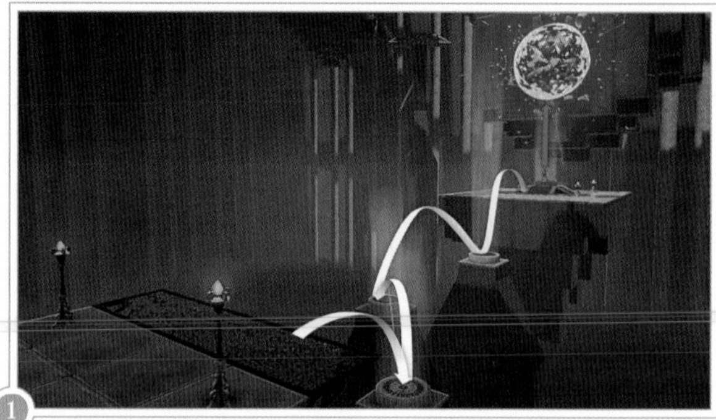

1

Navigate the updrafts to reach the platform across the chasm. Drop a bomb on the fan and detonate it as it floats close to the destructible rocks above. You can then glide through this new opening.

2

Drop a round bomb in the small pipe and, once again, detonate it once it moves close to the destructible blocks. When the path is clear, ride the sequence of updrafts to reach a rotating platform.

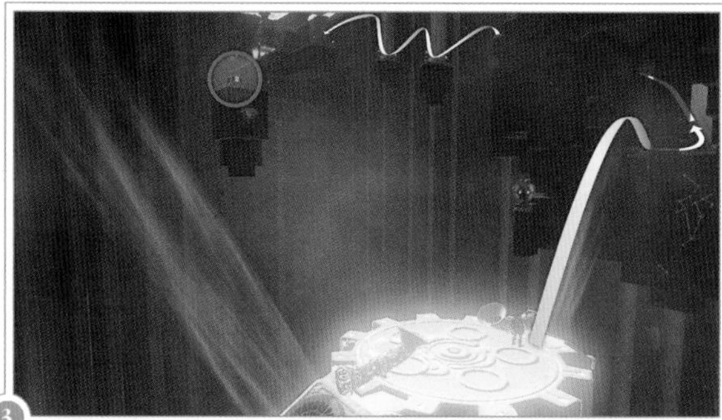

3

Wait until either updraft is blowing directly towards the next set of destructible rocks, then freeze the platform with Stasis at that precise moment. Quickly drop a round bomb into the pipe and detonate it once it reaches the stone blocks to clear a path. You may have just enough time to jump into the updraft and glide through the opening; if not, repeat the previous Stasis maneuver when one of the two fans is facing in the appropriate direction. You can then ride a sequence of updrafts to reach the altar. If you look to your left during the final approach, you will see a treasure chest on an isolated pillar; this contains 10 bomb arrows.

WINDBLIGHT GANON

After clearing Revali's three shrines, fast travel to Divine Beast Vah Medoh. If you would like tips on how to defeat Windblight Ganon, turn to page 84. You do not have a shield in your inventory in this alternative version of the fight, so be ready to sprint away when the boss fires its laser beams at you, or hide behind solid objects.

There are two tactics that can significantly abbreviate this encounter. Firstly, rush to your adversary whenever it hovers at ground level. You are mostly safe if you stand underneath it, enabling you to unleash a powerful barrage of melee attacks. Secondly, ride any of the updrafts available in the area when your foe moves high in the air. The slow-motion effect you enjoy during airborne aiming makes it far easier to hit the boss's blue eye three times in succession, which stuns it.

Your sword will eventually break, but you should still have plenty of arrows to finish off your opponent – including bomb arrows that deal significant damage when fired with the duplex bow. This strategy works perfectly well on Master Mode too, though you need to keep your opponent under a steady barrage of arrows to prevent its health from regenerating.

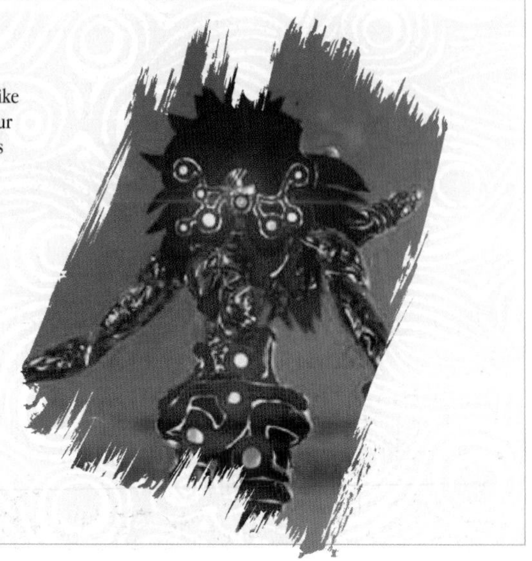

EX CHAMPION DARUK'S SONG

Daruk's pedestal lies on the mountains southwest of Goron City. This map shows its position, as well as the locations of the three associated shrines that are unlocked once you visit the pedestal for the first time.

AREA MAP

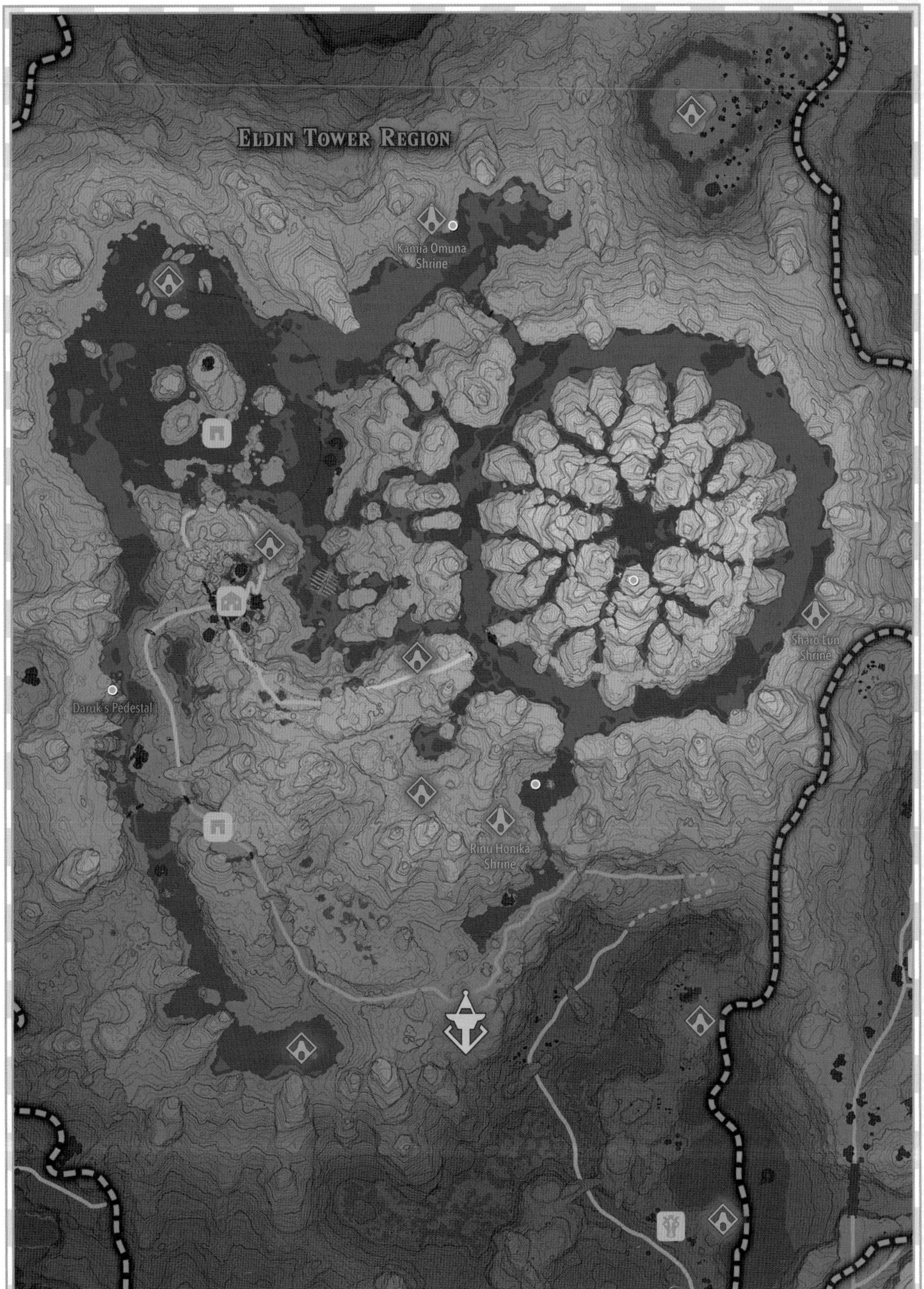

RINU HONIKA SHRINE

LOCATION: You will greatly benefit by equipping a full flamebreaker outfit upgraded to Level 2 (see page 282), as the fireproof effect is useful both outside and inside the shrine. Head to Darb Pond, directly south of Death Mountain. Look closely and you will spot a glowing ring in the middle of the lava. Your goal is to stand within that ring. The solution is to use Magnesis on the two nearby metal cubes to create a bridge from the shore to the ring; the four rocks submerged in the lava can be repositioned with a metal cube. Once you have a solid base beneath the ring, all you have to do is leap to it, or glide from the cliff overlooking the area where the Gorons offer their encouragement. This causes the shrine to appear on the nearby hill.

1

If you have the fireproof effect active, you can walk straight through the flames without a care in the world – skip to step 4. Otherwise you will need to find unique solutions for each fiery obstruction. The initial instance is entirely obvious: crouch-walk underneath the first collection of flame jets. For the next set, blow up the destructible rock at the base of the pillar on your left to displace the fire-spewing nozzle.

2

Next, look to your right and grab the metal cube at the base of the wall with Magnesis. Move it up to your position and you can use it as a shield that will protect Link as he side-steps past the flames.

3

When you reach the bottom of the stairs, drop the cube on the solid platform just ahead. Hop over to this position, then raise a second cube from the lava. You can now position them inside the wall of flames. The idea is to have a base cube in the center, but the upper cube adjacent to the wall – thereby forming an arch that offers safe passage to the opposite side.

4

Look to your right immediately after you clear the wall of flames. A treasure chest (which contains a stone smasher) rests on a platform. Drop a metal cube into the lava to reach it. From the chest, you can glide directly back to the main platform.

5

If you have the fireproof effect active, you can head directly to the altar. If not, interact with the terminal to gain control of the platform. Using the gyroscopic features of your controller, turn the platform upside down and align the vertical pillars to block the flames before you proceed.

KAMIA OMUNA SHRINE

LOCATION: Head to the northern shore of Lake Darman, to the northwest of Death Mountain. You will notice what appears to be a glowing boulder in the lava. This is, in fact, an Igneo Talus Titan – a giant variant of the monster. There is a constant updraft in the entire area, which you can use both to avoid your foe's projectiles and to reach its body after you have cooled it down with an ice arrow. Make sure you have plenty of these in your inventory before you begin this challenge, as well as maximum Flame Guard protection and a powerful two-handed weapon. Your strategy should be to hit the monster's body with an ice arrow while riding the updraft, then drop on top of it and perform a spinning charged attack to shatter the weak point as quickly as you can. Don't forget to fly away as soon as the boss dies – or when it is about to recover if you fail to finish it off in a single assault. After the giant falls, the shrine will appear on the shore.

1

From the entrance, head to the canon to your left. Drop a round bomb inside, then strike the crystal to make the device rotate. Detonate the bomb once the canon is aligned with the target on the wall.

2

A second target moves up and down on the far wall. The target makes stops in three areas: top, middle, and bottom. You can hit it with the cannon while it is in the middle position.

3

If you wish to claim the diamond inside the treasure chest to the far right of the distant wall, you must destroy the ledge on which it rests. This will cause it to fall into the cage below, where you can retrieve it using Magnesis. The easiest way to align your shot is to drop your bomb into the canon while it is at its maximum rightmost rotation. Activate the crystal, then immediately detonate the explosive.

4

There are two more targets to hit further into the chamber before you can reach the altar. First, interact with the terminal and use the gyroscopic functions of your controller to align the rotating structure so that the target faces the canon, as illustrated here. As before, detonate your bomb to fire the canon as it rotates to hit the target. After a successful strike, a final target is revealed in the background.

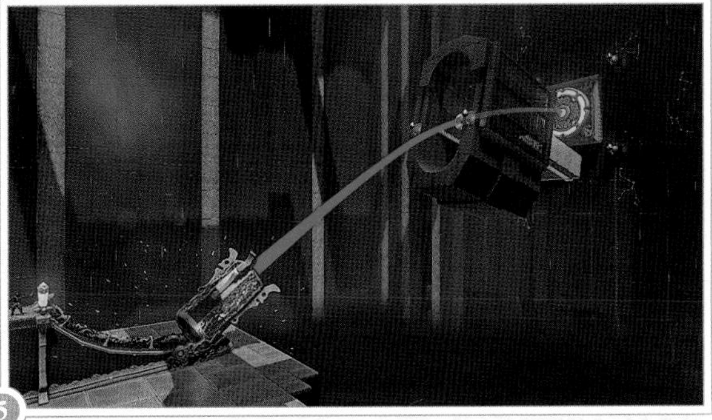

5

This time, you need to fire your projectile ***through*** the rotating structure. Return to the terminal and realign the obstruction as shown in the above picture, creating an opening for the orb to travel through. You then have a clear shot to the target which, once activated, opens the gate leading to the altar.

SHARO LUN SHRINE

LOCATION: As always in this region, ensure that you have suitable Level 2 flame guard protection. A maximum-capacity stamina wheel is also strongly recommended for this challenge. When you're ready, warp to the Divine Beast atop Death Mountain. Your starting point is the blue ring at the top of the peak just southeast of where Vah Rudania stands. The moment you walk through it, a race against time begins. As usual, move from one waypoint to the next until you hit the final ring which reveals the shrine. The first couple of rings pose no challenge. Shortly afterwards, however, you begin a long descent where you need to regularly put away the paraglider to "skydive", then quickly resume gliding to pass through the next target. This is far less difficult than it initially seems.

1

This shrine features climbable blocks that are conveyed along set courses. Jump to grab a block as it arrives, then position Link on the right-hand side to avoid the first set of flames. As soon as you pass this first hazard, traverse to the left side to shelter from the next set of flame jets; after that, climb on top of the block. If you have the fireproof effect active, you can situate Link wherever you please – the jets will have no effect. When you arrive close to the platform, glide down before the block plunges into the abyss.

2

For the next corridor, remain on any side of the block until you clear the spiked obstacles, then immediately climb on top. Guardian Scouts will spawn in sequence on the ledges: left, then right, then left again. Eliminate them with arrows as quickly as you can. Climb down to any side of the block before you reach the next spiked obstacle, then drop down once you arrive at the next walkway.

3

In the third part of this shrine, climb onto a block once again. As you approach the waterfall, create a horizontal pillar of ice so that you can jump to the nearby ledge. Create a second pillar of ice between this ledge and the next one. This will cause the chest that falls at regular intervals to bounce off it: grab it with Magnesis and open it to obtain a great flameblade. Wait on the platform closest to the flame jets until a block moves into position, then glide down to it.

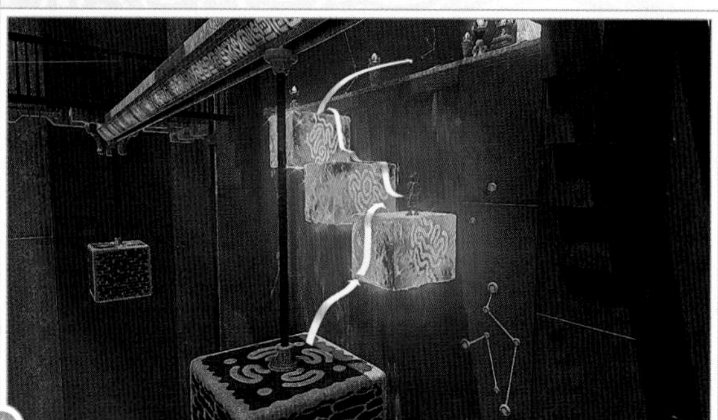

4

Finally, create a horizontal ice pillar as you approach another waterfall, positioned so that Link can easily jump to it as the moving block passes by. From here, create additional ice pillars to reach the platform above.

FIREBLIGHT GANON

After clearing the three shrines related to Daruk, fast travel to Divine Beast Vah Rudania; see page 95 for a detailed description of how this battle unfolds. You have a very limited quantity of arrows at your disposal, so brute force is the best plan.

Rush to your enemy, standing right under its body (where you are out of reach of most of its blows), and then unleash a devastating multi-hit spinning attack. It's actually possible to end both phases of the fight with a single, extended combo. Don't forget to throw a bomb at the boss when it summons a force field: detonate it to stun the monstrosity, then resume your melee onslaught for a swift conclusion. This strategy works perfectly well on Master Mode too, making it one of the easier boss battles.

EX THE CHAMPIONS' BALLAD: FINAL TRIAL

After you have completed all four song quests, you unlock the final trial of the Champions' Ballad. Fast travel back to the Shrine of Resurrection and interact with the terminal to enter a new dungeon.

1 **Guidance Stone & Divine Beast Controls:** From the entrance, walk straight forward until you find the Guidance Stone in the large central chamber; you will need to eliminate a Guardian Scout on the way. As with other Divine Beasts, interacting with this device provides you with the dungeon's 3D map and gives you a measure of control over the leviathan. In this instance, you command the direction of the rotation of the giant cogwheels found throughout the dungeon. Use these controls immediately to set the cogwheels in motion: from the Map menu, press Ⓐ then Ⓑ. Note how a colored glow (orange or blue) is associated to each direction: this is replicated on all the cogwheels that are affected by these controls. Your goal is to activate the dungeon's four terminals – each found in a specific themed wing connected to the central chamber.

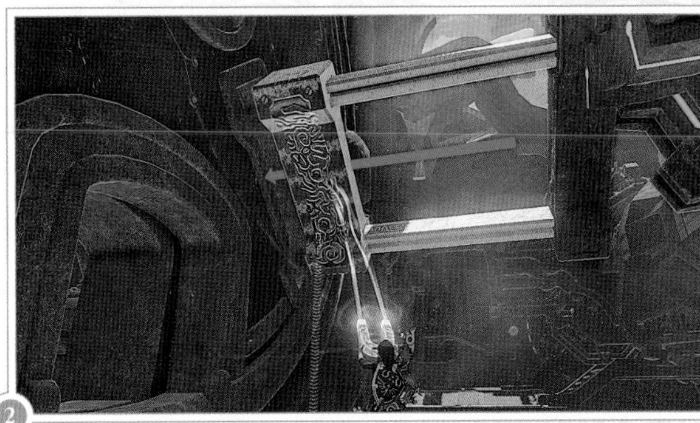

2 **Electricity-Themed Wing:** With the dungeon's entrance behind you, head to the ramp on your left. A large cogwheel with a metal piece attached to it revolves around a central axis. Wait until the metal piece moves within Magnesis range, then grab it and slide it along the rails all the way to the wall. Keep pushing sideways so that the metal piece enters a corresponding slot. This causes the wall to rotate like a disc, which activates a rotating device in the room beyond the doorway.

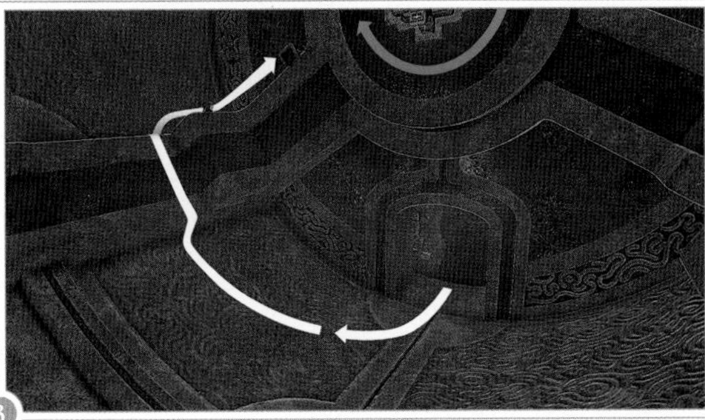

3 **First Treasure Chest (Electricity-Themed Wing):** Once inside the electricity-themed wing, make sure the direction of the cogwheels is set to blue. Turn around and look at the rotating structure that surrounds the doorway: three "arms" revolve around a central green crystal. Identify the arm with a treasure chest and, once it passes in front of the entrance doorway, move to it and let the rotation do its work until you can approach the chest, which contains a Gerudo scimitar.

4 You now need to reach the walkway on the right side of the room. Ride a rotating arm up to it, then climb up the stairs. From the top of the stairs, you can grab a metal piece attached to the ceiling with Magnesis.

5 **First Terminal (Electricity-Themed Wing):** Drop down to the ground floor with the metal piece, and insert it into the dedicated slot. Now wait until the larger metal block moves within Magnesis range. Grab it and move it along its rail so that it comes into contact with the small metal piece, thus triggering the rotation of the three arms on the opposite side of the room (note that the color associated with the cogwheels still needs to be blue). Wait until the now-open gate leading to the terminal reaches the bottom part of its rotation, then sprint to the device and activate it.

6 **Lava-Themed Wing:** Return to the central chamber and eliminate the handful of Guardian Scouts that have appeared, then set the direction of the cogwheels so that they have an orange glow. With the "electricity wing" directly behind you, jump on one of the teeth of the moving cogwheel as it emerges from the lava. This will deliver you to the nearby ledge, from which you can access an opening to the lava-themed wing of the dungeon.

7

When you reach the rotating pillar covered with spikes, toggle the direction of the cogwheels from the map menu (the glow should be blue). You can now slowly make your way across the pillar by carefully negotiating a diagonal path between the spikes to reach the platform on the far side. Once there, wait for a vertical flame jet to stop before jumping over the gap.

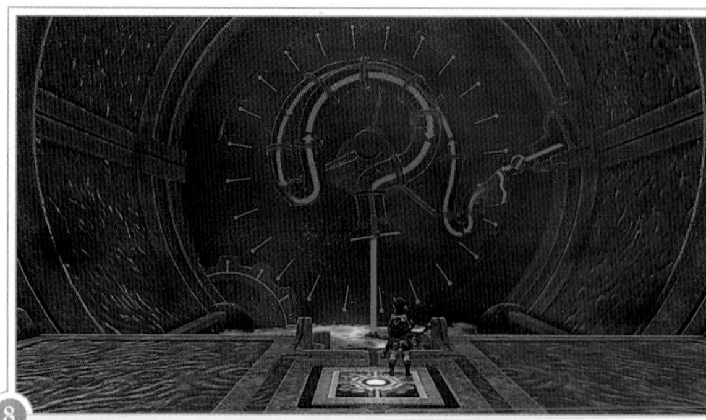

8

Before you interact with the floor switch, change the direction of the cogwheels (back to orange). If you look at the far wall, you will see a winding pipe apparatus, and an orb trapped behind a gate on the right side. Step on the switch just as the end of the pipe is about to be aligned with the fenced gate: this causes the orb to roll inside. As the orb progresses through the little maze, you will need to change the direction of the cogwheels twice – in both instances after the orb moves past a "hairpin" bend. This will ensure the orb comes out through the other end of the pipe. If you struggle with this, pay attention to the ball's direction of travel: when it starts moving backwards, this is your cue to change the cogwheel direction in the menu.

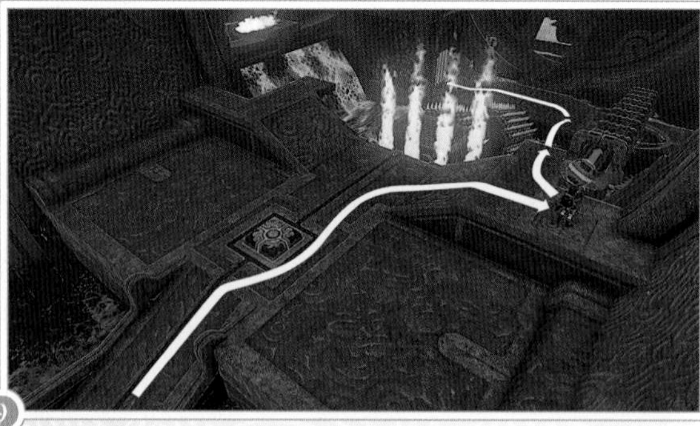

9

Second Terminal (Lava-Themed Wing): Pick up the orb when it drops from the pipe, walk up the ramp, and deposit it in the slanted caged track. The orb will roll down to the concave slot below, which opens the gate to the terminal.

10

Second Treasure Chest (Lava-Themed Wing): You now need to go through the rotating "disc" wall to return to the central chamber. Just as you arrive in the doorway, stop and allow the rotation to deliver Link to an elevated position from which you can glide to the nearby treasure chest close to the right-hand wall. This contains a cobble crusher.

11

Third Treasure Chest (Central Chamber): Return to the opening in the disc wall and, once again, stand just inside to ride it upwards. This time, face into the central chamber. Once you have sufficient elevation, glide from the doorway to the hexagonal beam, then turn left. There is a treasure chest directly ahead; freeze the spinning structure when either of its "windows" is aligned with the chest to claim the Gerudo shield it contains.

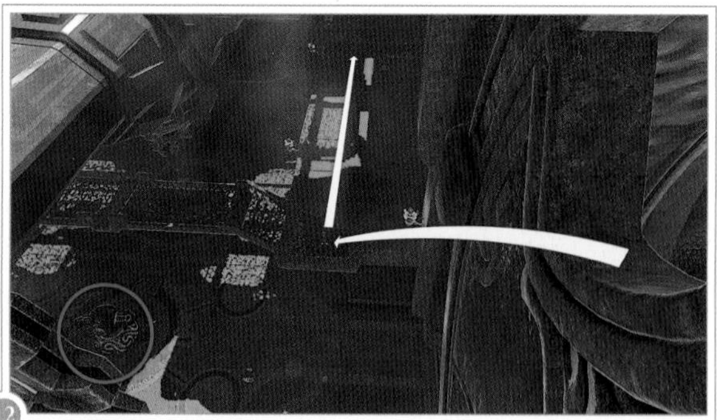

12

Repeat the exact same process one more time, standing inside the doorway leading to the lava-themed room so that the rotation takes you to the very top, then glide from there to the bridge that runs across the other side of the central chamber. You will notice that a Guardian Turret now stands guard in the middle of the room. After you land on the bridge, you can easily defeat it with arrows aimed at its blue eye. Once you're ready, and with the dungeon entrance behind you, head for the door on your right.

13

Fourth Treasure Chest (Central Chamber): Before you reach the door, climb to the top of the nearby ladder, take a few steps up the ramp, and turn around. Grab the treasure chest on the ledge with Magnesis; it contains five bomb arrows.

14

Wind-Themed Wing: From the exact same position, use Magnesis again, this time to take hold of the metal piece that protrudes from the ledge where you found the chest. Move the piece upwards and insert it into the slot on the (currently stationary) cogwheel. You can then use Magnesis on the metal square shaft directly opposite the piece you placed moments before. Move it sideways so that it locks into position. This powers up the wind-themed wing, which you can now enter via the rotating doorway below your position.

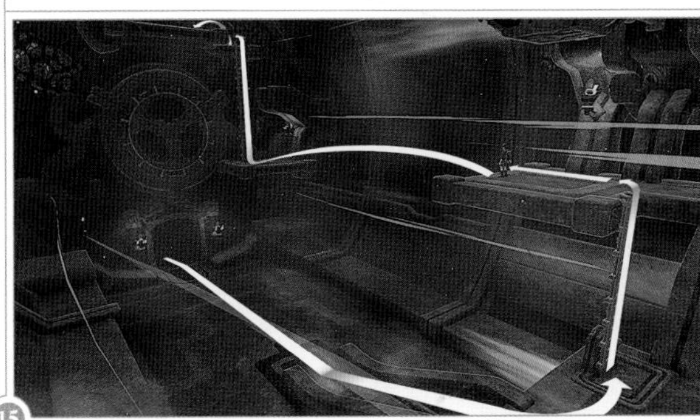

15

Run up the stairs in the middle of the room, then climb up the ladder. Ensure that the cogwheels are in their blue state (if not, change their rotation via the Map menu), then glide from the platform to the long ladder above the entrance – the wind generated by the large fan at the back of the room will assist your flight. Climb to the top platform then turn around.

16

Third Terminal & Fifth Treasure Chest (Wind-Themed Wing): Change the direction of the cogwheels via the Map menu. Their glow should now be orange, which reverses the direction of the wind in the room. Wait until the floating platform reaches the right half of its course, then quickly glide to it. From here, you can freeze the fan with Stasis, before gliding to the terminal. Once you have activated it, cast Stasis once again on the fan and drop down to the ground to find a treasure chest directly behind the device. Defeat the Scout that guards it to obtain a swallow bow. You may then need to stop the fan one more time to safely return to the central chamber.

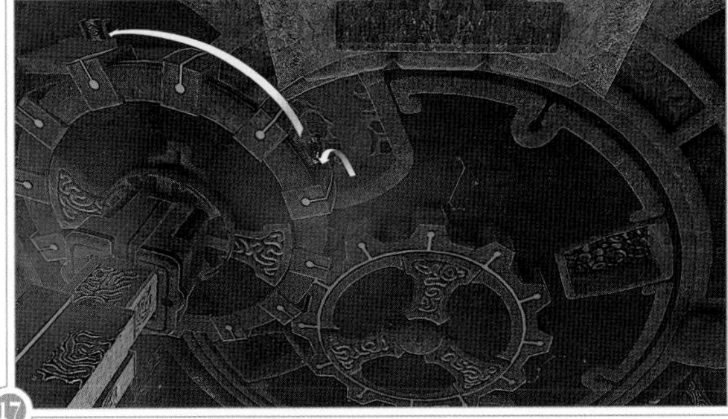

17

Sixth Treasure Chest (Central Chamber): There is a well-hidden chest that you can reach on your way out of the wind-themed wing. To access it, stand in the middle of the doorway leading to that wing and let the rotation take you to its topmost position, as shown in the above picture. From here, you can leap to the adjacent cogwheel; if the cogwheel direction is set to orange, its rotation will take you straight to the chest (which contains a diamond).

18

Back in front of the entrance to the wind-themed wing, cross the bridge and climb up the ladder on the other side. Note that a Guardian Skywatcher will now patrol the central chamber. It's not mandatory that you engage it, but note that it will complicate matters when you return here later. If you have ancient arrows to spare, it's worth your while to disable it immediately.

19

Water-Themed Wing: The walkway where you end up at the top of the ladder overlooks a suspended platform. Double-check that the cogwheels are set to orange, then look up. If you turn on Stasis, you will notice that the small cogwheel just above you features stone teeth. These slide along a rail under the effect of gravity, preventing them from setting a lever in motion. Cast Stasis on one of these teeth just as it is set to connect with the lever: the lever will be activated, temporarily raising the suspended platform. Jump to the doorway above before Stasis ends to enter the water-themed wing.

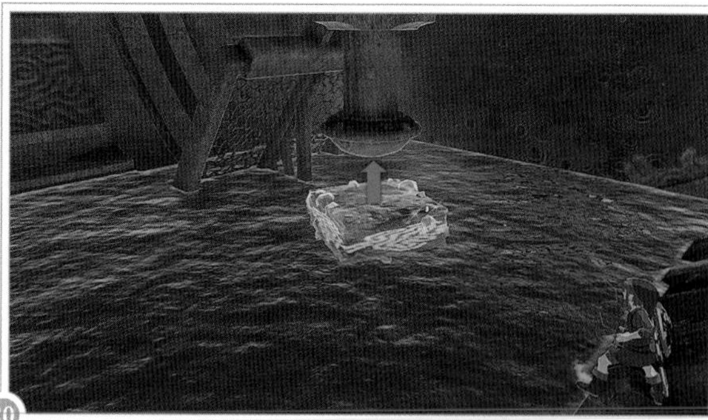

20

Raise a pillar of ice right underneath the pressure switch. This causes the entire arm that the switch is part of to start rotating. Change the direction of the cogwheels one more time (their glow should be back to blue now) and float over to the rotating platform while it is in its lower vertical position to take a ride to the walkway on the left, which provides access to the second half of the room.

21

Seventh Treasure Chest (Water-Themed Wing): Cast Stasis on the giant faucet then hit it multiple times so that it spins in a clockwise direction. This stops the flow of water. Once the water level descends, you can open the treasure chest against the far wall: it contains a Zora spear.

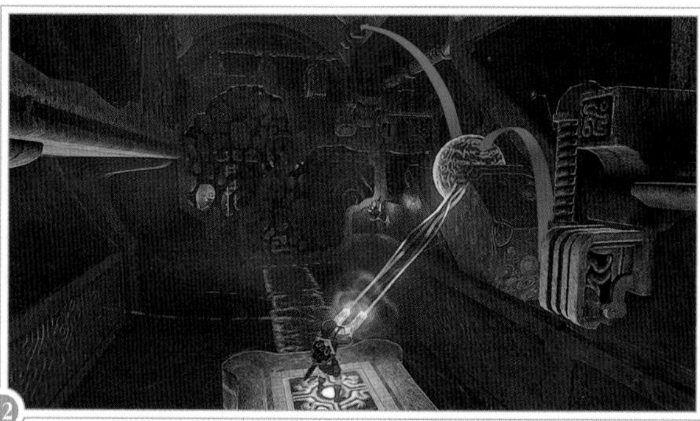

22

Head through the opening and continue until you reach a floor switch; step on this to reveal a metal ball stuck behind a launcher. Grab the ball with Magnesis and drop it on the opposite side of the device. Now step off the switch, then back on again: propelled by the launcher, the ball will hit the faucet in the distance, which refills the room with water.

23

Fourth Terminal (Water-Themed Wing): Raise a block of ice with Cryonis at the foot of the steps that lead to the terminal. Activating the device opens the nearby gate, enabling you to return to the central chamber.

24

Climb back up the nearby ladder, then make your way to the central platform just above. You will need to eliminate a Guardian Scout patrolling the area; if you opted not to deal with the Skywatcher earlier, it may involve itself during this battle. After dealing with the Guardian Scout, walk to the rotating cogwheel at the end of that platform. Grab it with Magnesis, then push it so that it slots into the gate beyond. This opens the path to a final altar. Make sure you are totally prepared before you interact with it, as doing so triggers the closing boss battle of the Champions' Ballad.

BOSS: MONK MAZ KOSHIA

The fight against Monk Maz Koshia has multiple phases, each with a unique pattern. This can be a brutal battle if you approach it too casually, so make the best possible preparations – especially if you are playing on Master Mode. The highest damage output can be achieved by combining the Ancient Proficiency set bonus (bestowed by the Ancient armor set) with a food-induced Level 3 Attack Up bonus, and with Link wielding powerful Guardian/Ancient weaponry. Turn to page 360 for further details.

Having plenty of meals that restore your entire health bar is also highly recommended. Note that you can warp to any location via the Map menu and return later if you don't feel ready. To return, interact with the terminal in the Shrine of Resurrection.

The following tactics are applicable to both Normal Mode and Master Mode; the battle plays out identically in the latter, but naturally requires more precise timing and greater consistency in execution.

FIRST PHASE

During the opening phase, Monk Maz Koshia employs Yiga-style tactics. Memorizing the cues that foreshadow each attack type here is important, as your opponent will reuse them in later phases.

Whenever the boss vanishes in a cloud of smoke and jumps high in the air, he is ready to fire an elemental arrow at you. Sprint or leap sideways to avoid the projectile, then rush to the spot where he will land. This is a very safe opportunity to unleash a full combo and make a dent in your opponent's life gauge.

Every time you see Monk Maz Koshia focusing with a circular red aura around his head, be prepared to evade his imminent aerial assault. This technique cannot be blocked, so you either need to sprint away or perform a backflip. A perfect dodge is possible if you execute the move in advance, while your enemy is still high in the air.

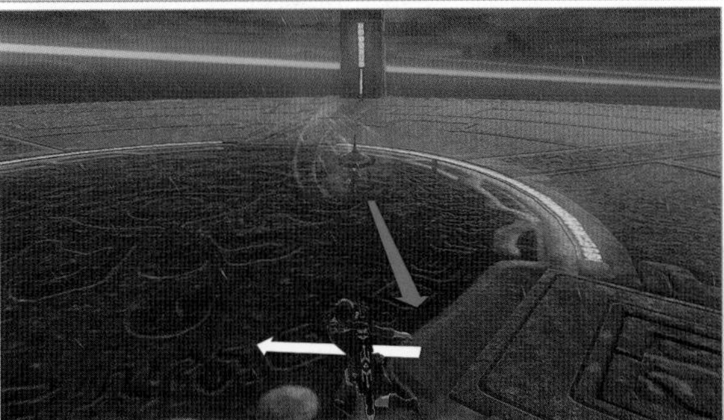

When your foe dashes straight in your direction, he performs a simple but powerful melee attack. Counter this with a perfect guard or perfect dodge to inflict heavy damage.

After sustaining several meaningful blows, Monk Maz Koshia will begin to employ the signature zigzag attack of Thunderblight Ganon. Try to perform a perfect dodge backflip in order to punish him with a flurry rush follow-up.

Your enemy will also use a signature technique employed by Yiga Blademasters: he sends a small geyser in your direction, from which a rock spike will eventually emerge. Leap vertically and open your paraglider to ride the accompanying updraft to escape, then hit your target's eye with an arrow during your flight to stun him and follow up with a melee combo. If you're exceptionally swift and composed, you can even cancel the geyser attack by landing an eye shot on your opponent while he's in the process of preparing it.

SECOND PHASE

Once he loses approximately 25% of his health, Monk Maz Koshia starts to regularly summon multiple clones, who will all attack you simultaneously using the various techniques from the first phase.

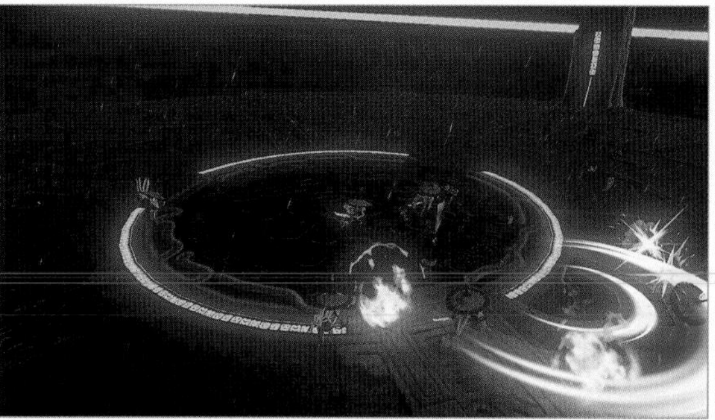

Facing so many targets can and will make the battle very hectic: efficient crowd control is of the utmost importance. Area-of-effect abilities that can eliminate several targets at once are especially useful. These include charged attacks, multi-arrow bow shots, bomb explosions, and Urbosa's Fury.

All clones are eliminated with a single hit. Your principal foe will tellingly remain in place after a blow; note that his doppelgangers are disabled while you strike him. The moment you identify the true target, attack relentlessly.

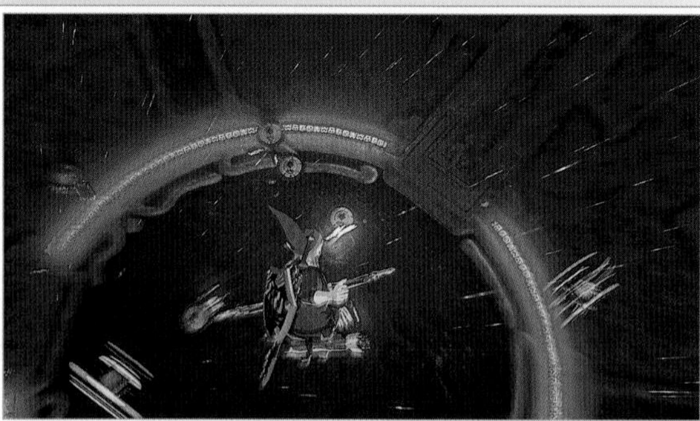

A creative and extremely reliable solution for surviving the chaos caused by the clones is to unleash an updraft with Revali's Gale. Take out your bow while high in the air, then pepper your targets with arrows until you find the real boss.

Every time you inflict a full combo on the actual boss, he will re-summon his clones and deploy them in a circular or linear formation. They can randomly fire elemental arrows, dash toward you and execute a slash attack, or perform their aerial diving technique. As a rule, the best defense is to stay on the move and sprint away when the clones are homing in on you. Usually, they perform three of these group maneuvers in a row. The real Monk Maz Koshia remains briefly alone and idle after each assault – don't miss the opportunity to identify and pummel him.

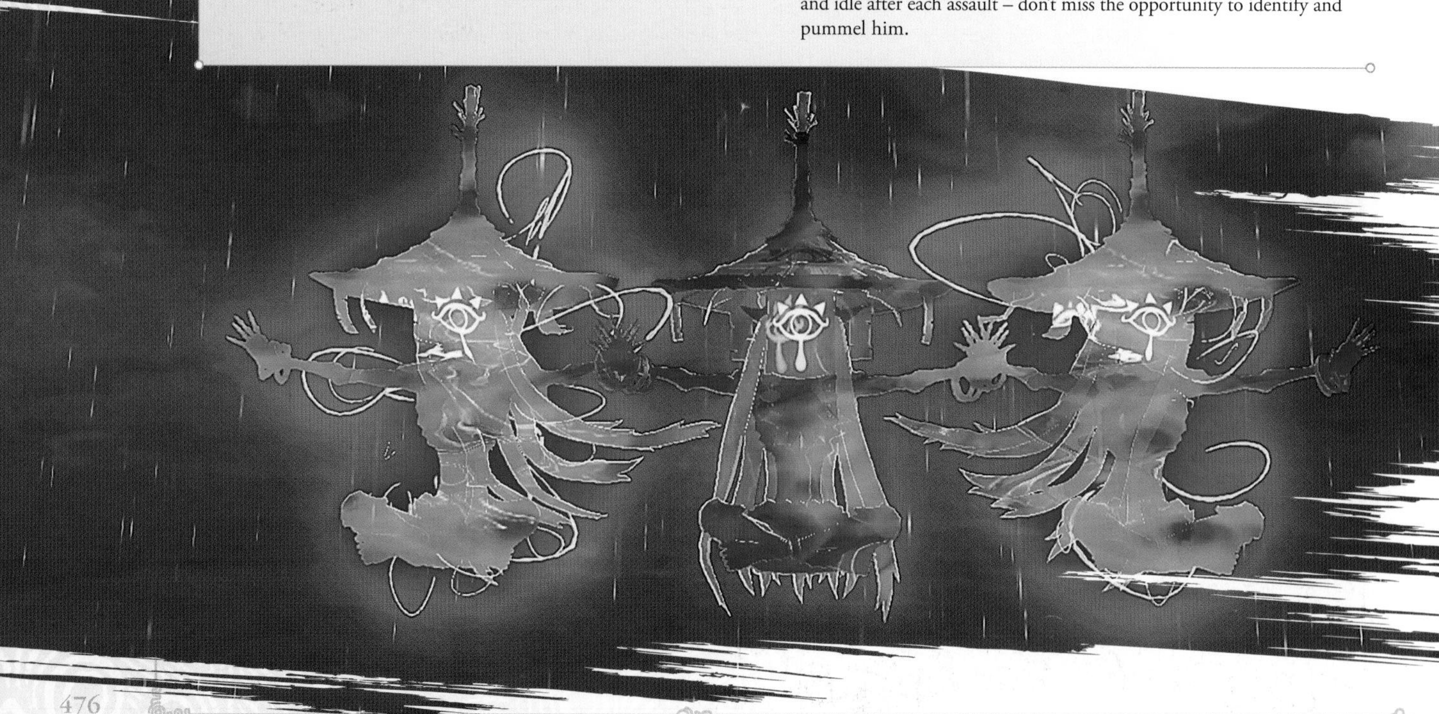

THIRD PHASE

With his health bar depleted by half, Monk Maz Koshia transforms into a giant version of himself.

At first, Monk Maz Koshia levitates above the arena and performs various moves. In one of them, he targets Link with a Guardian-style laser attack. Either sprint away from the point of impact, or deflect the beam back with a well-timed perfect guard (or simply by holding your shield aloft if you own an ancient shield purchased from Akkala Ancient Tech Lab). Note that you cannot interrupt the firing process, even with critical hits to the eye.

The giant version of the boss will also execute the geyser attack. Use the updraft to glide away, then immediately shoot an arrow at your opponent's eye to stun him. Ancient arrows deal massive damage here when combined with a powerful multi-shot bow – a few of these fired during a single slow-motion sequence can be a supremely effective way of shortening the confrontation on Master Mode. You can then attack your foe at close range while he is incapacitated.

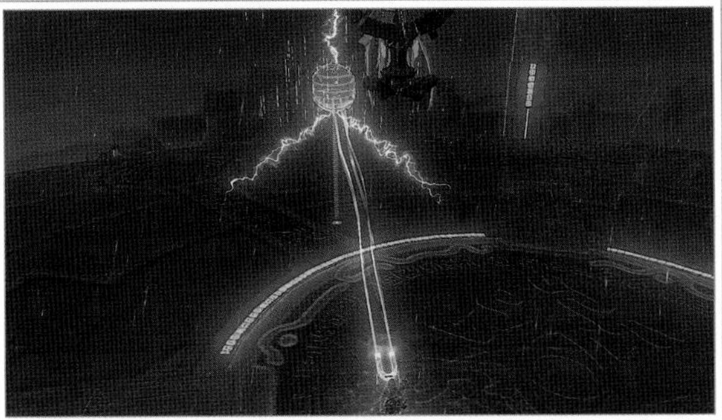

Monk Maz Koshia often summons multiple spiked metallic boulders, hurling them at you or making them roll around by tilting the entire arena. Either take evasive maneuvers, or grab one with Magnesis and use it as a shield against the other hazards. If you see flashes of electricity appearing around the orbs, pick one up with Magnesis and move it to the boss's position to electrocute him, just as you did against Thunderblight Ganon. You can follow this up with another melee combo.

Once Monk Maz Koshia has a quarter of his health left, he stops levitating and resumes the fight on his feet. He employs various techniques from the previous phases, including the red laser beam and the ability to summon clones. He will also attempt to stomp Link, Hinox-like, at close range. He is relatively slow in this attack state, though, so take the opportunity to rush to him and attack his legs with your most powerful weapons. You can even risk a charged spinning attack with your best two-handed weapon here. A fully upgraded and well-equipped Link can finish off the boss in almost no time at all.

REWARDS

Your main reward for completing the Champions' Ballad is your very own Divine Beast: a motorcycle called Master Cycle Zero.

- This ancient relic is available as a new rune. After selecting it with ✚, press L then A to summon it.
- Mount and dismount with A and B respectively; accelerate with A and brake with B. You can perform small jumps with L or jump off the vehicle with X. Your weapons are available with the usual commands.

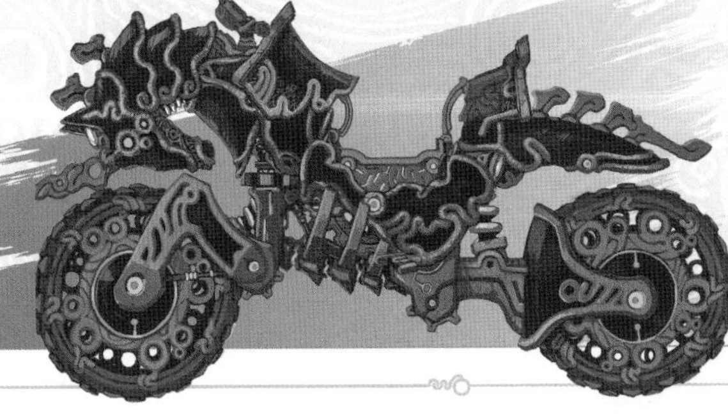

- The motorbike cannot function in certain areas, most notably sand dunes. If you attempt to ride it over incompatible terrain, it will vanish into thin air.
- Master Cycle Zero consumes fuel, as indicated by the gauge that appears at the top-left of the mini-map. Whenever this drops low, simply insert materials in the motorcycle, just like you drop ingredients in a cooking pot. You should ideally sacrifice abundant items that you have no real use for. Even five modest apples or a handful of the most common monster parts will refill a substantial portion of the gauge.

In addition to Master Cycle Zero, defeating Monk Maz Koshia rewards you with a unique picture. If you take this to Link's fully upgraded house (read about the Hylian Homeowner side quest on page 231), you will be given the opportunity to display it on the wall next to Link's bed.

Note that you can revisit the dungeon and fight further bouts against Monk Maz Koshia at your leisure. To do so, warp to the fifth Divine Beast via the Shrine of Resurrection, then approach the altar once again.

CONCEPT ART

This section offers a concept art tour of assorted characters, monsters, locales, and animals encountered in *Breath of the Wild*, with a variety of illustrations offering visual insights on the development process behind the game.

LINK

PRINCESS ZELDA

OLD MAN

・立派で精悍なヒゲ.
・太っていながらも
鍛えられた体.
・意志の強い目.
二重まぶた
・60才くらい
・ボロく.毛羽立っている服、
・ちょっと高貴さをにおわせる
金属かざり.
・ボロのブーツ・手袋を皮で補強し
皮ヒモでしばっている.
カンテラ付き
桜の木の杖

MIPHA
THE ZORA CHAMPION

URBOSA
THE GERUDO CHAMPION

REVALI
THE RITO CHAMPION

DARUK
THE GORON CHAMPION

WILDLIFE

◀DEER
SPARROWS▶
■平地
■熱帯
■水辺
■寒冷地
【マス】
耐寒
耐暑
帯電
・耐寒
山、岩場のイメージ
顔
正面
羽の
イメージ
横向き
DARNERS
BEETLES
TROUTS
WOLVES▶

MONSTERS

フィールド上に落ちているものを拾って乗せている。
何を乗せているかは場所によって変わります。

OCTOROKS ▶

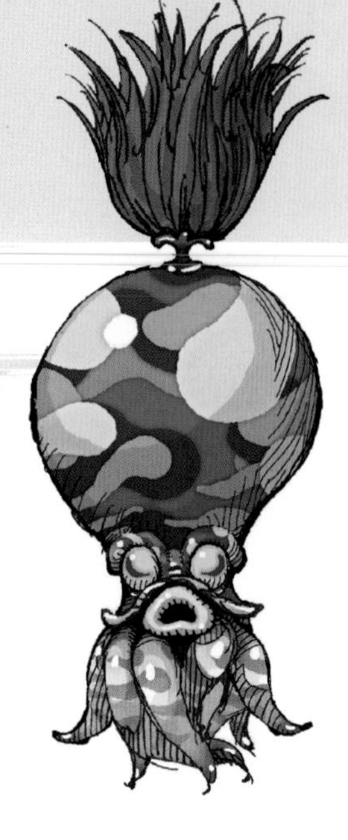

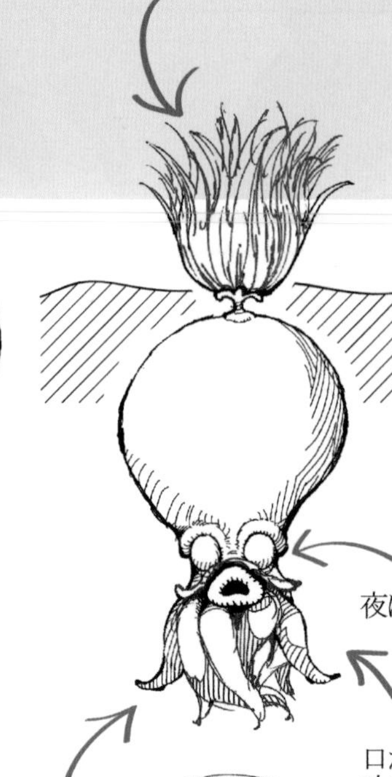

夜は目が光る

口から岩とか
吐いてくる。

平野・森

平野や森の茂みなどに隠れている。頭には木の枝とかキノコとか乗せてるかも。

川・海

川や海に生息しているオクタロック。頭上に葦を乗せて擬態している。時折アヒルを載せることもあるかも。

砂漠

砂漠版のオクタロック。砂漠の中を泳いでいて、宝箱だと思って近づいたら襲われる。

- 雨が降ると普段より凶暴になる。
- 擬態を見破って先制攻撃すると、びっくりしてピヨる。
- そんなに賢くないのでプレイヤーを発見しても見失うとすぐ忘れる。

BOKOBLINS ▶

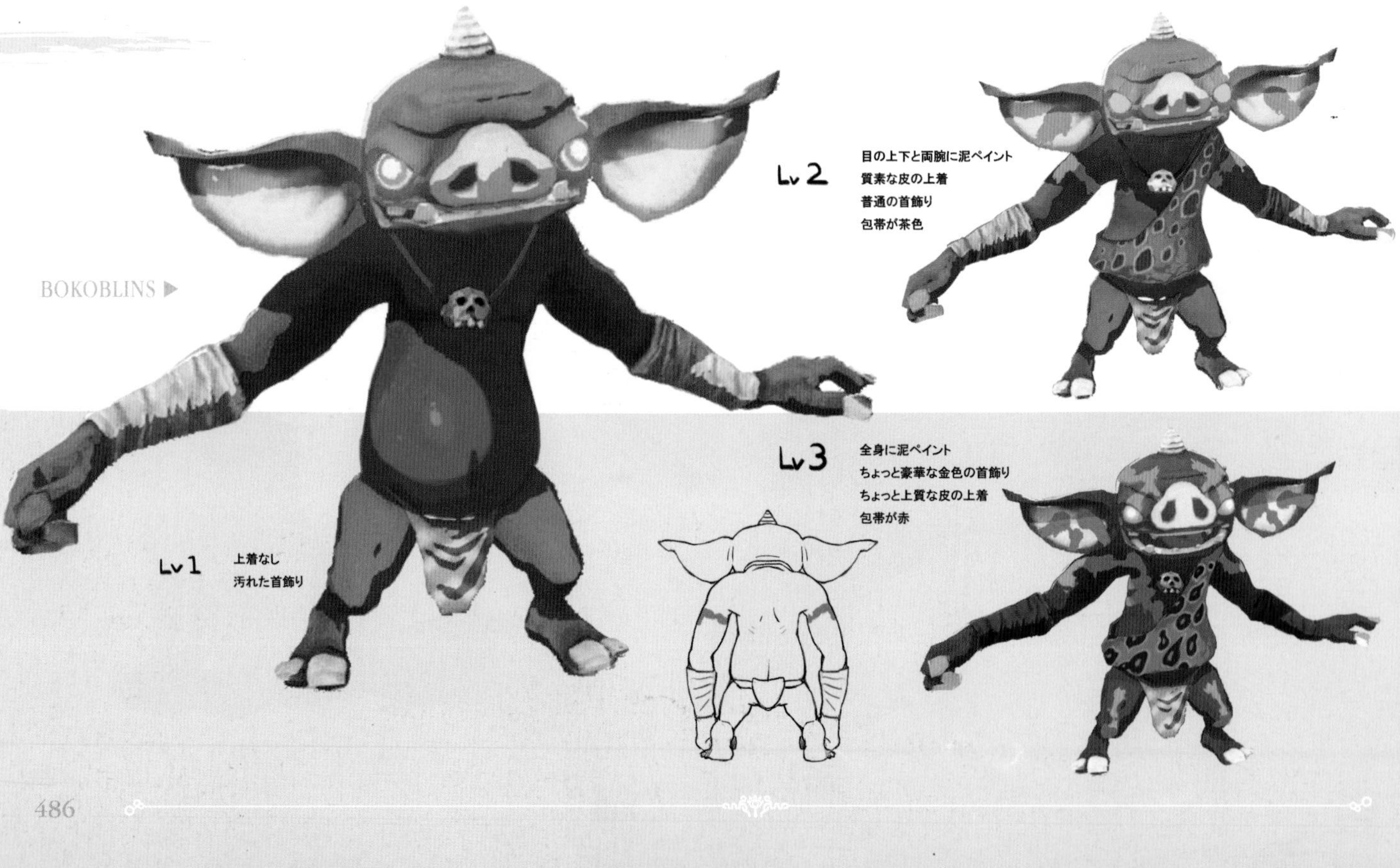

Lv 2
目の上下と両腕に泥ペイント
質素な皮の上着
普通の首飾り
包帯が茶色

Lv 3
全身に泥ペイント
ちょっと豪華な金色の首飾り
ちょっと上質な皮の上着
包帯が赤

Lv 1
上着なし
汚れた首飾り

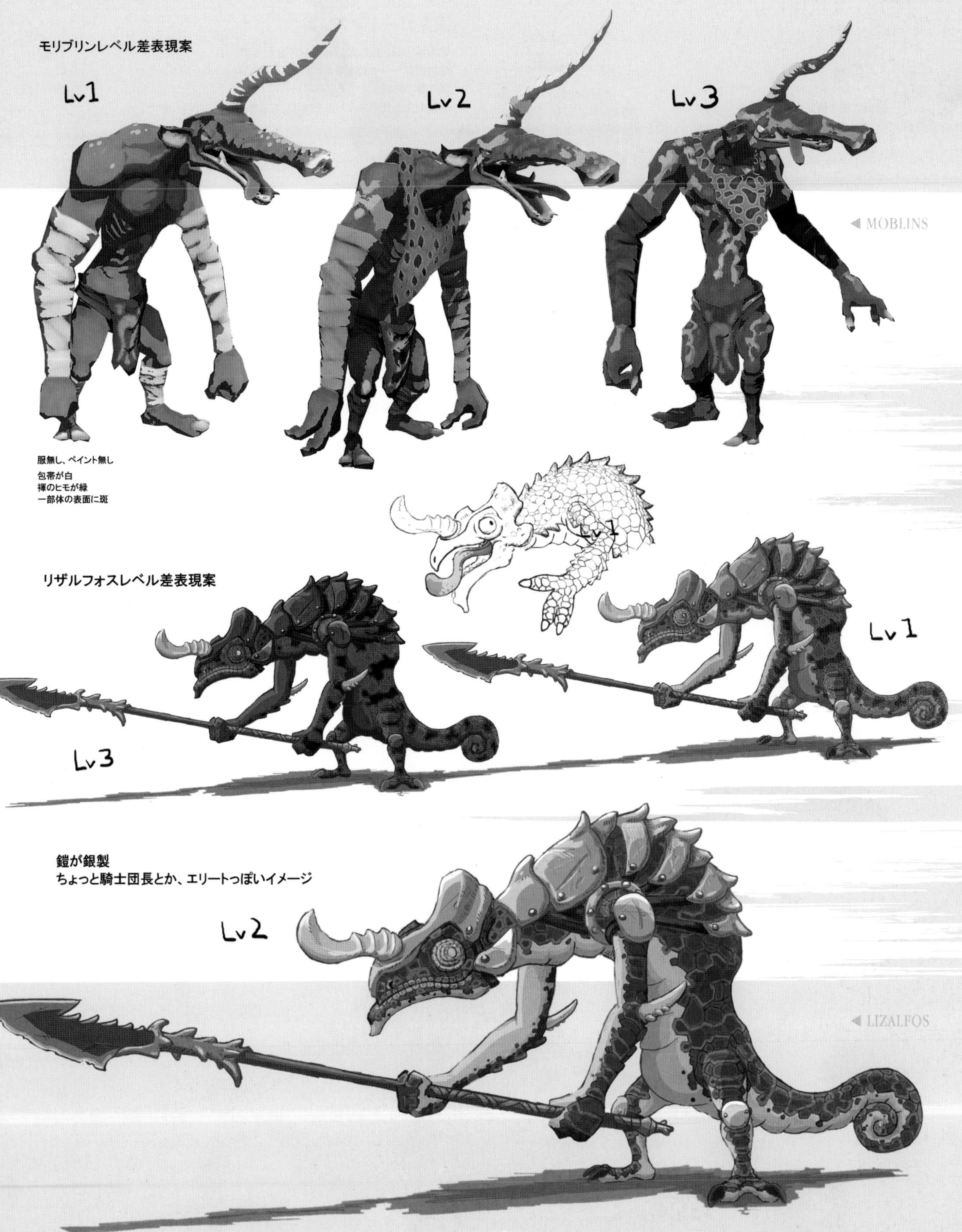

◀ MOBLINS

◀ LIZALFOS

固定ガーディアン案

首の横回転と頭の縦回転の組み合わせで
全方向のサーチ範囲をカバーをします
更に首が伸縮します
攻撃対象を発見すると首を伸ばして迎撃モードに移行します

地面に杭で固定されています

頭部横から

GUARDIAN TURRETS ▶

首パーツを伸ばした状態

グロー箇所

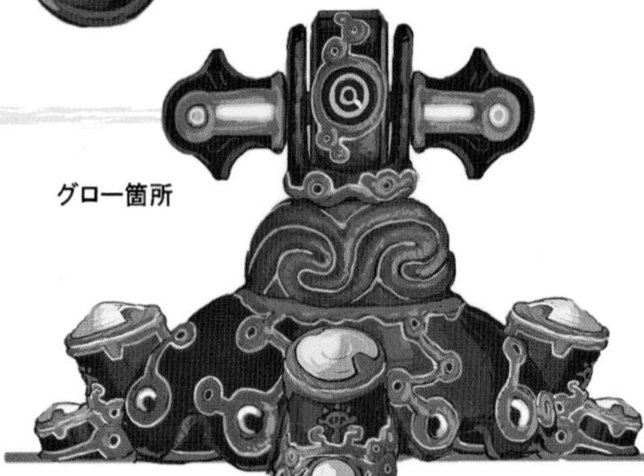

底面

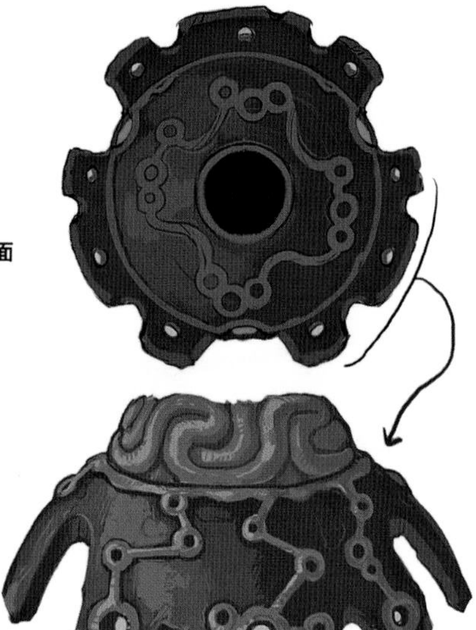

伸縮パーツ収納鞘部分の天面にシーカーマーク

GUARDIAN SCOUT ▶

TALUS ▶

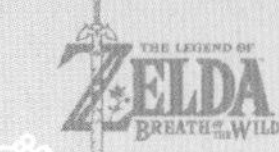

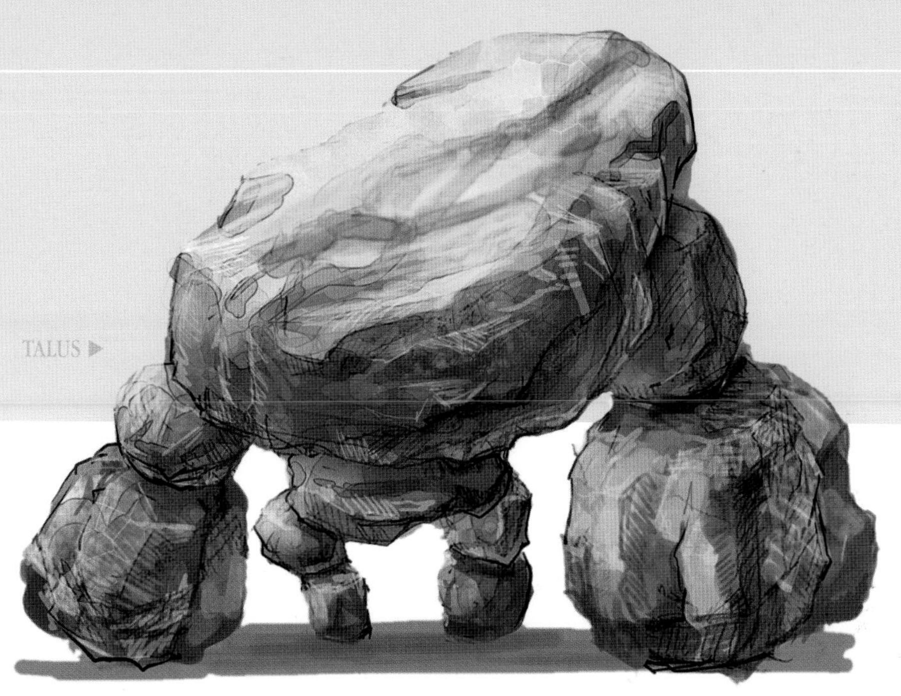

ライネル案　Lv 1

筋骨隆々な半馬の獣人です
狂暴ながらも気高い性格で弱い者は相手にしません
金属の加工技術も高いのですが
荒っぽいセンスなので打ちっぱなしです
多くの決闘や戦いなどを潜り抜けてきたので
体には多数の古傷があります
追いつめられると理性が失われ、本能のままに相手に襲い掛かります

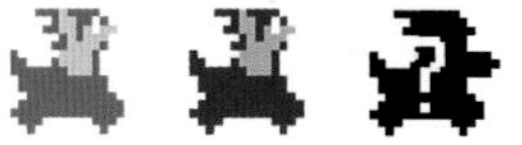

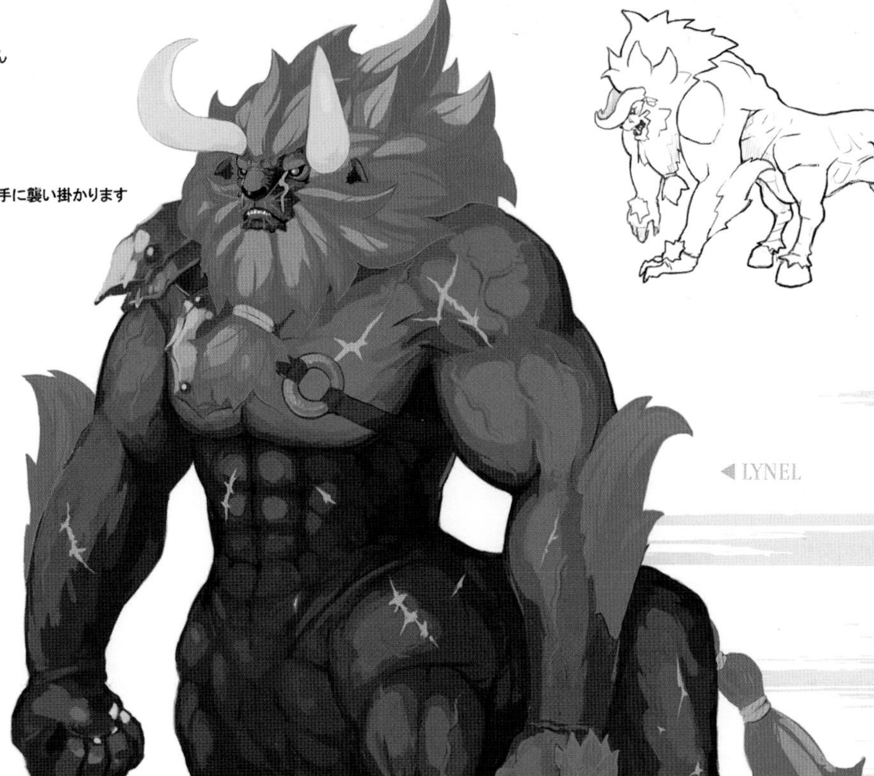

◀ LYNEL

鎧は胸当てのみ
鉄製

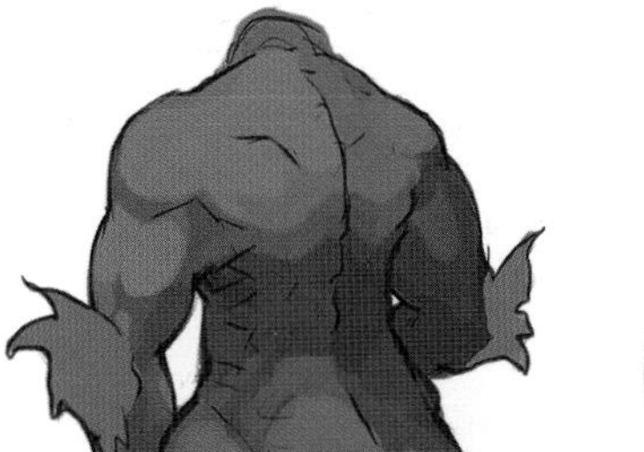

背中側

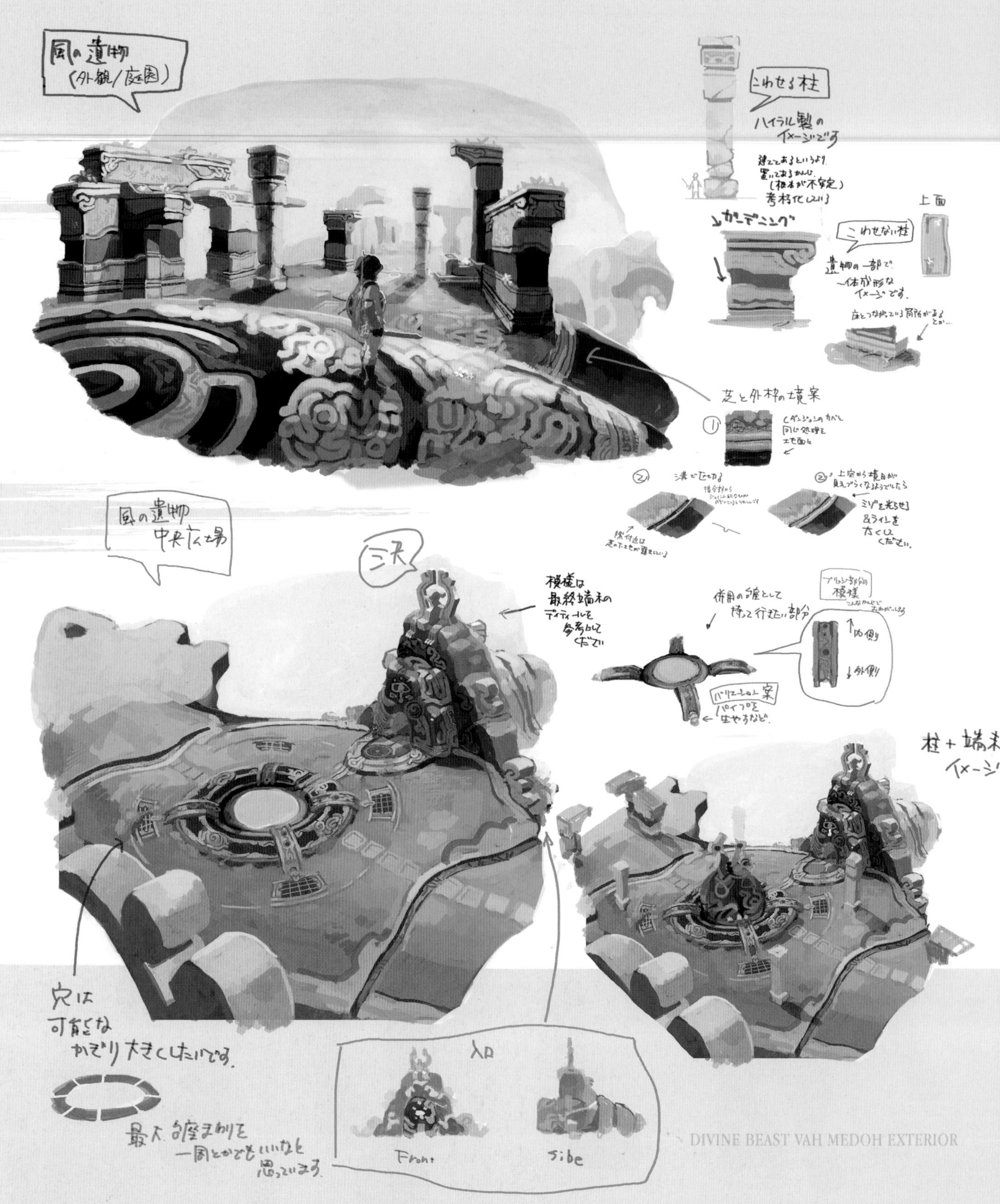

DIVINE BEAST VAH MEDOH EXTERIOR

FAST TRAVEL PEDESTAL

ダンジョンOBJ / ワープ端末

Cダンジョン用

※現モデルと同じ大きさ。

神獣用

中央の盤少し盛りあがっています

※ひとまわり大きくしてください。(現モデルより)

設置イメージ

HYRULE & DUNGEONS
(CONTINUED)

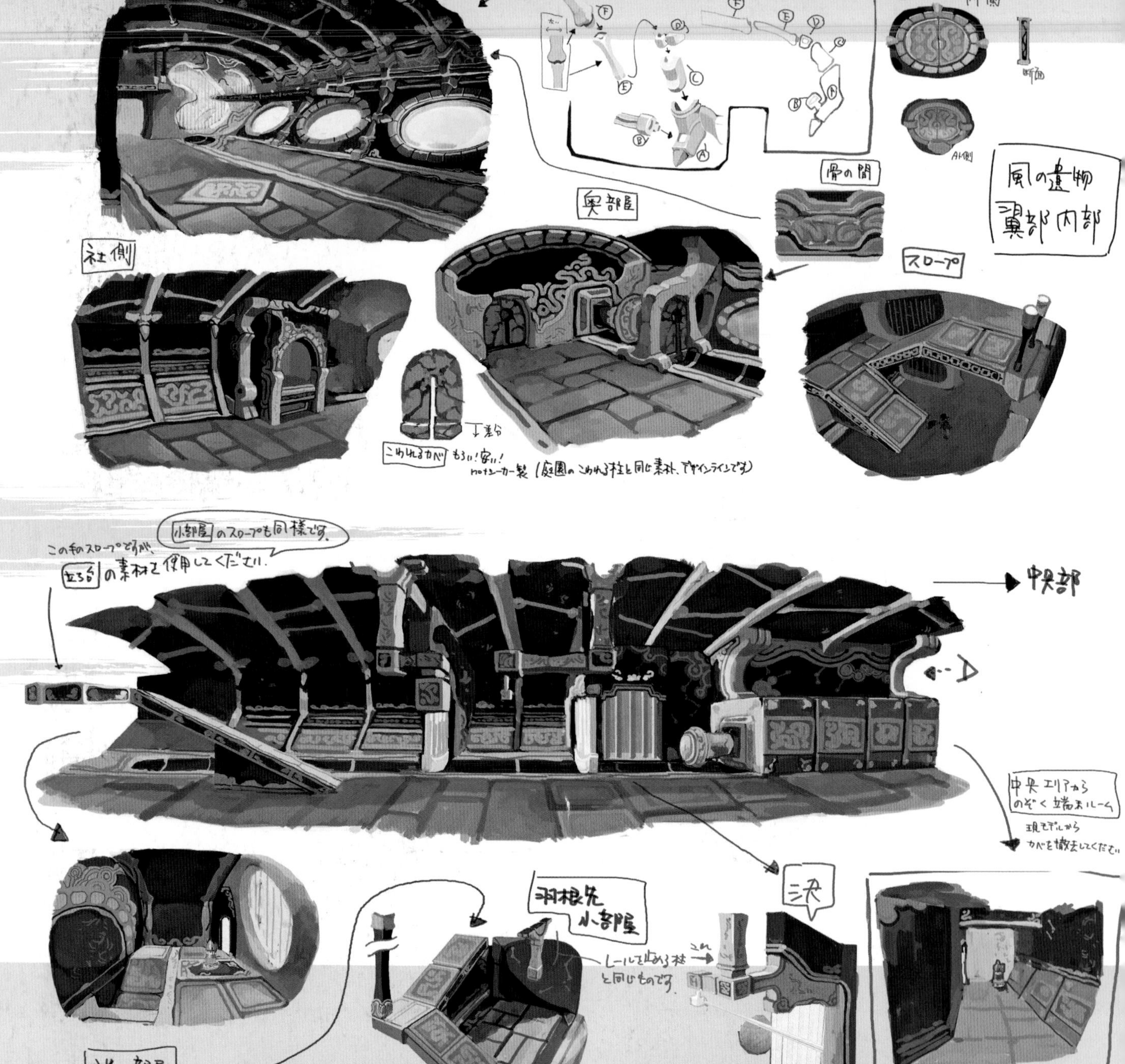

DIVINE BEAST VAH MEDOH INTERIOR

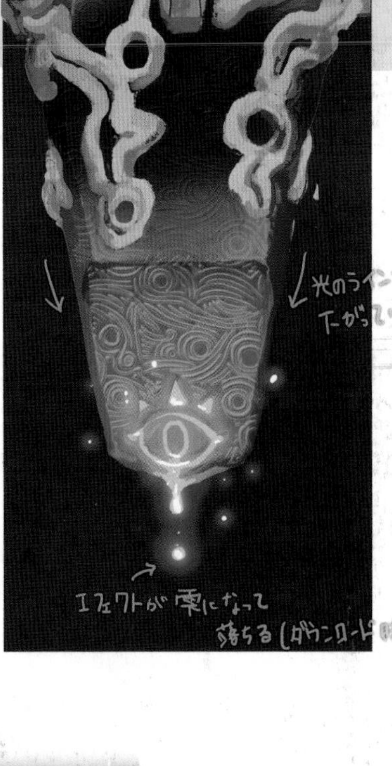
エフェクトイメージ
光のラインが下がっていく
エフェクトが雫になって落ちる（ダウンロード時）

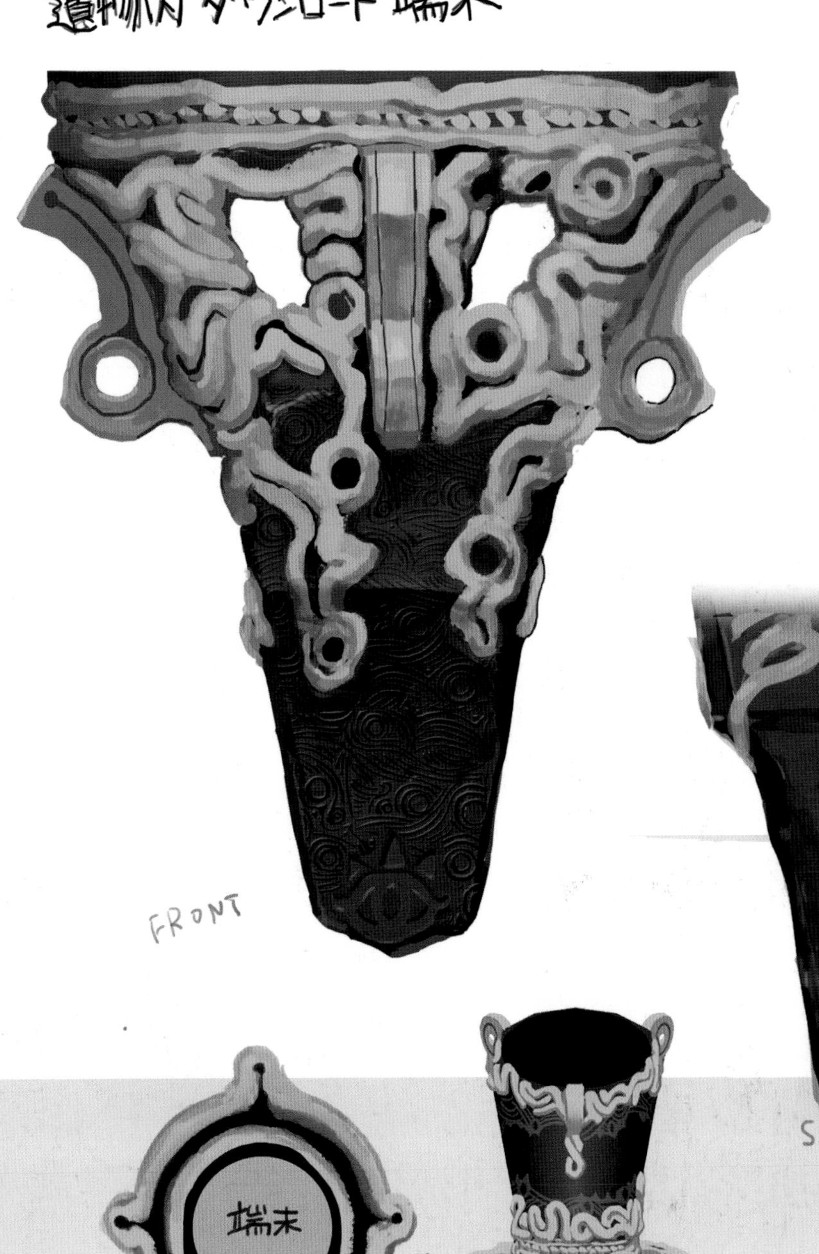
遺物内 ダウンロード端末
FRONT
SIDE
端末

◀ TERMINALS

EXPANSION PASS ARTWORK GALLERY

This section offers a concept art tour of some of the key features in *Breath of the Wild*'s two DLC packs, focusing primarily on unlockable items and notable protagonists.

Majora's Mask

Midna's Helmet

Tingle's Set

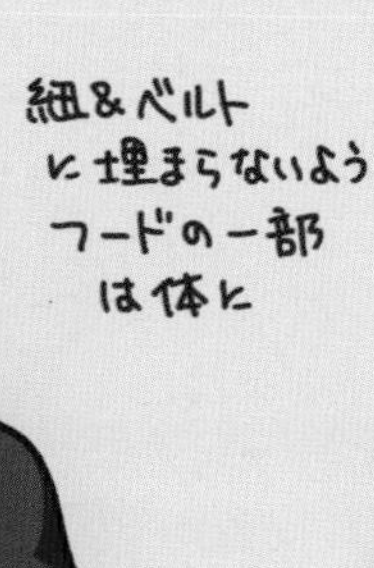

バックル

風車OFF

Korok Mask

Phantom Set

ファントム装備

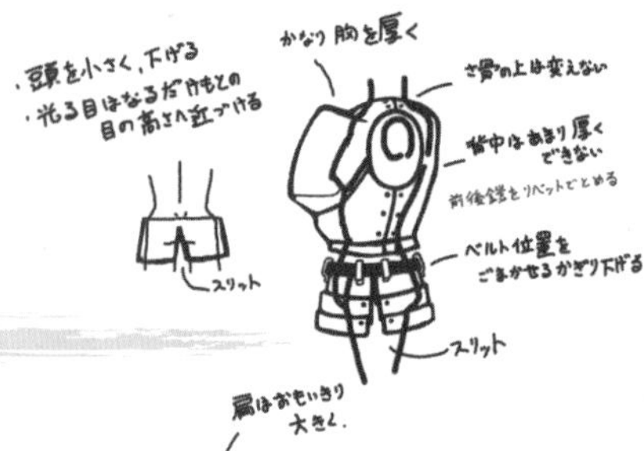

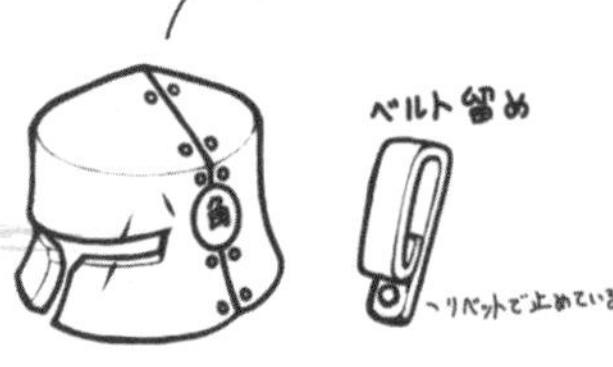

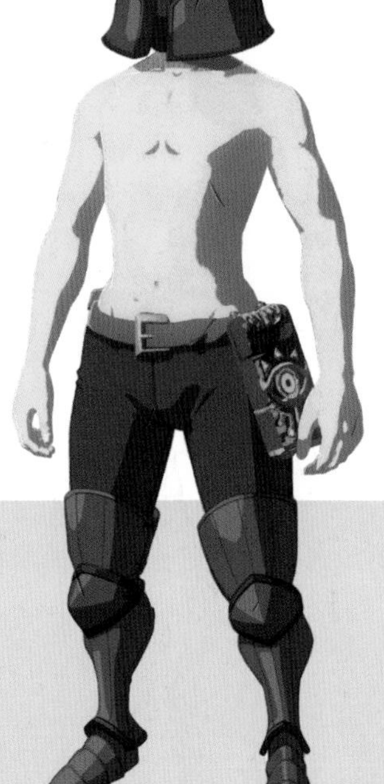

Royal Guard Set

Phantom Ganon Set

Ravio's Hood

Zant's Helmet

Island Lobster Shirt

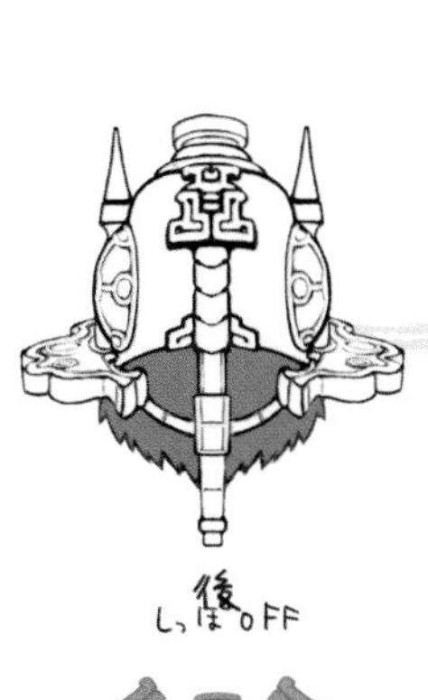

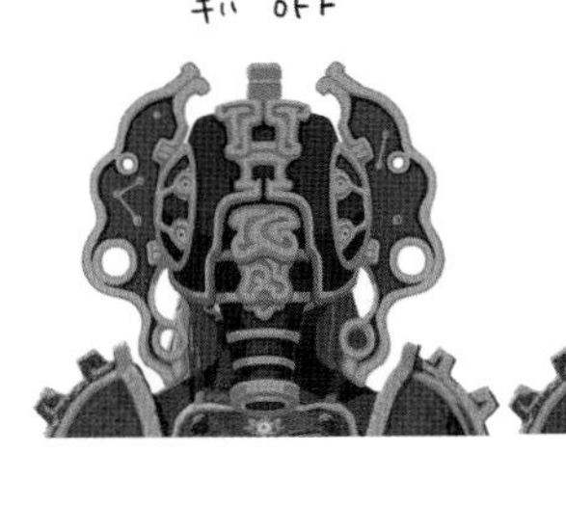

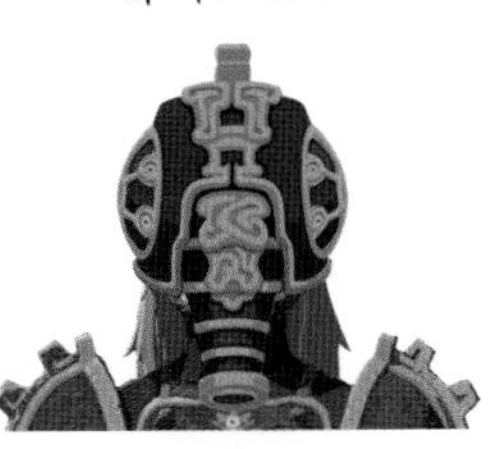

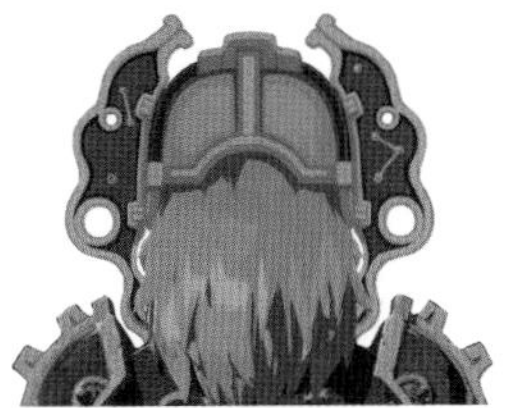

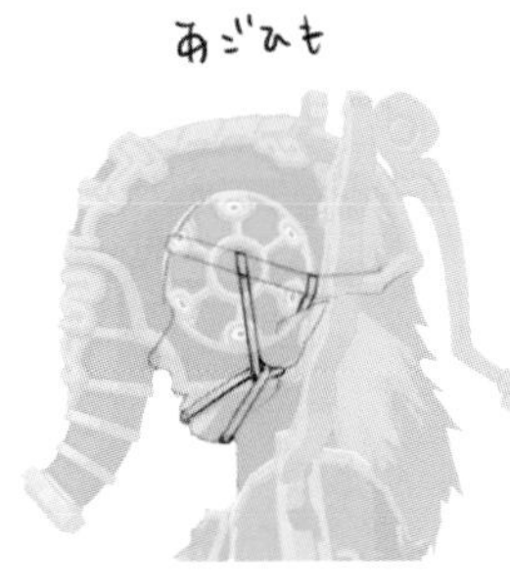

Vah Ruta Divine Helm

ゾーラ神獣装備

Vah Rudania Divine Helm

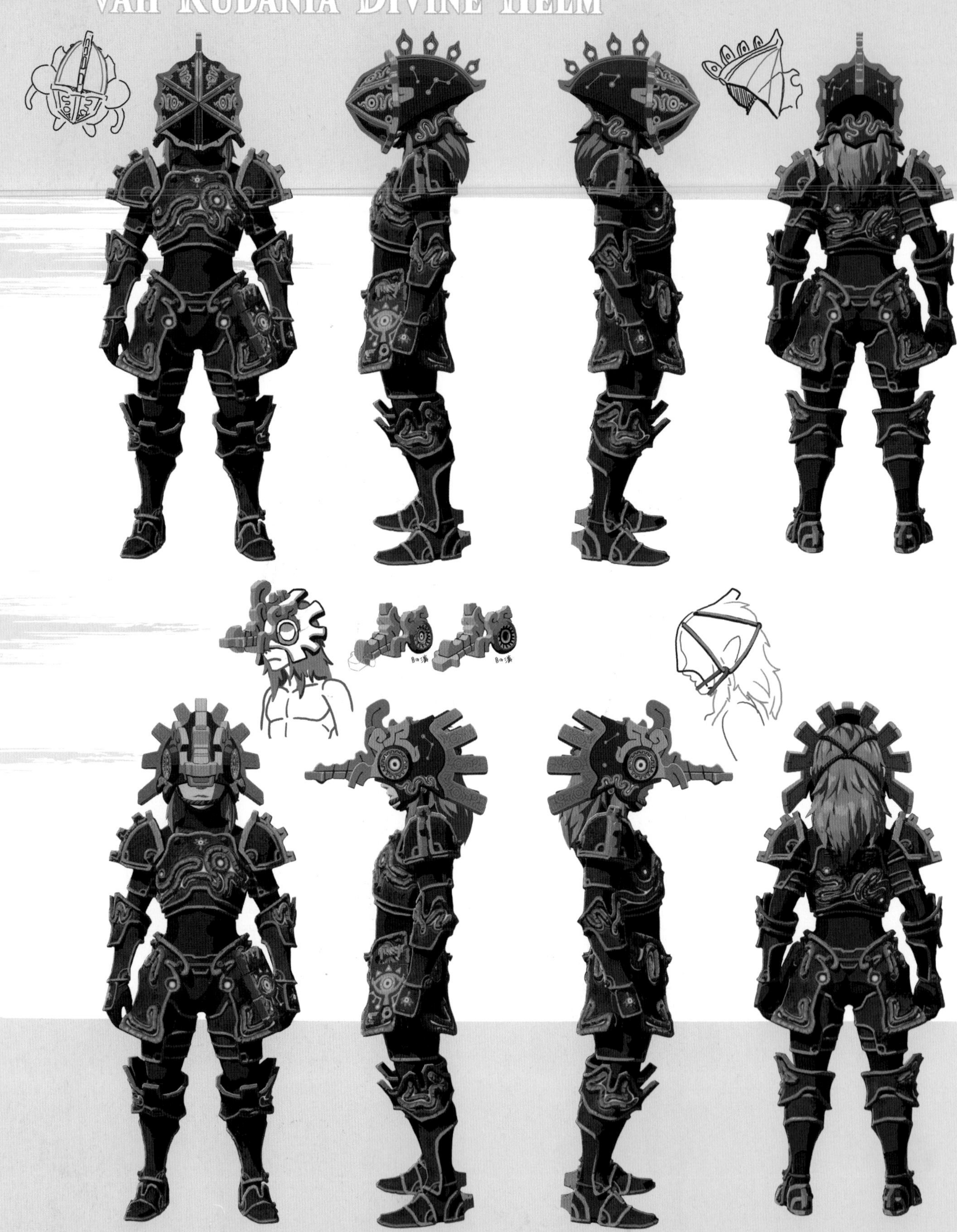

Vah Medoh Divine Helm

Vah Naboris Divine Helm

Ancient Bridle & Ancient Saddle

Master Cycle Zero

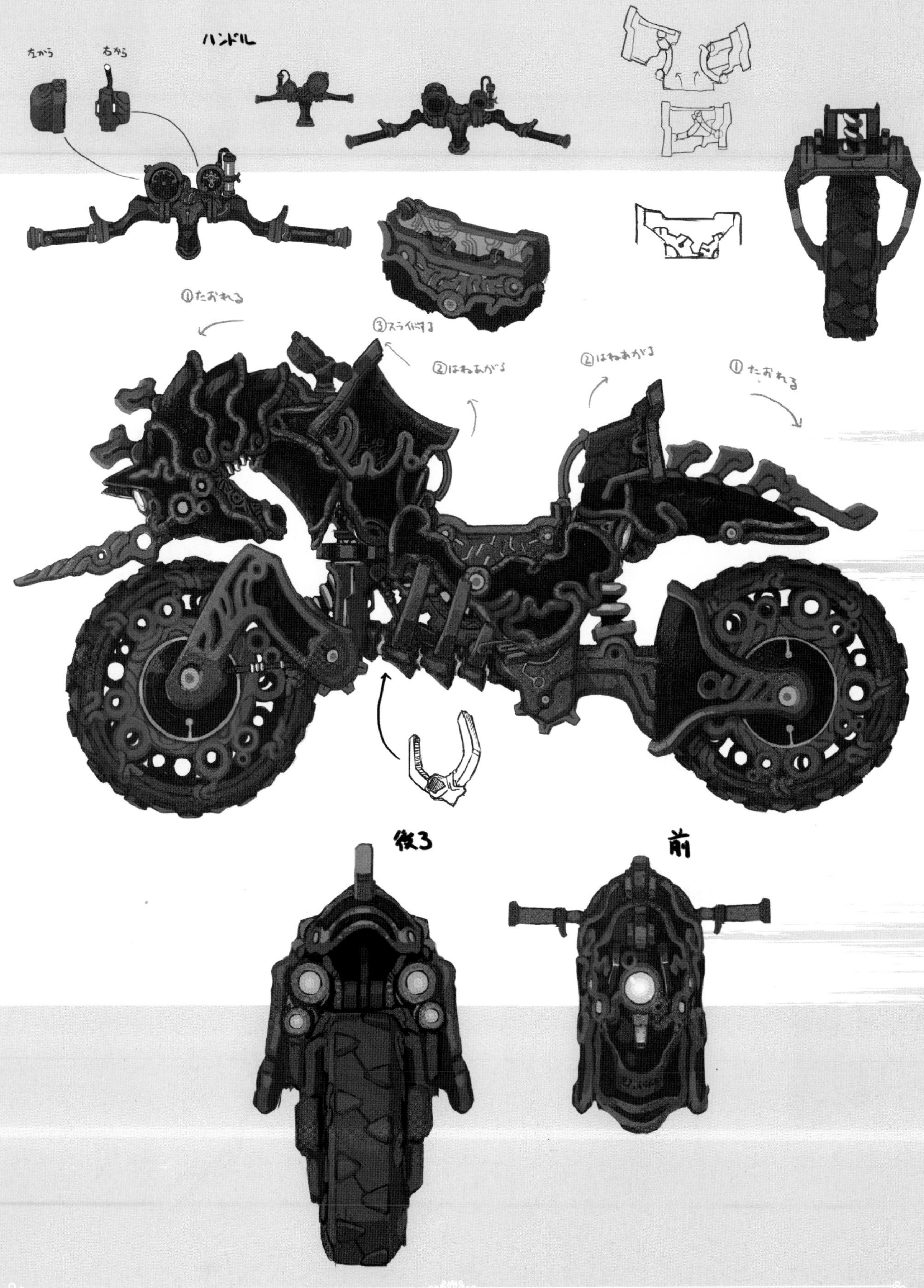

ハンドル

左から

右から

①たおれる

③スライドする

②はねあがる

②はねあがる

① たおれる

後ろ

前

One-Hit Obliterator

PRINCESS ZELDA

CHAMPION MIPHA

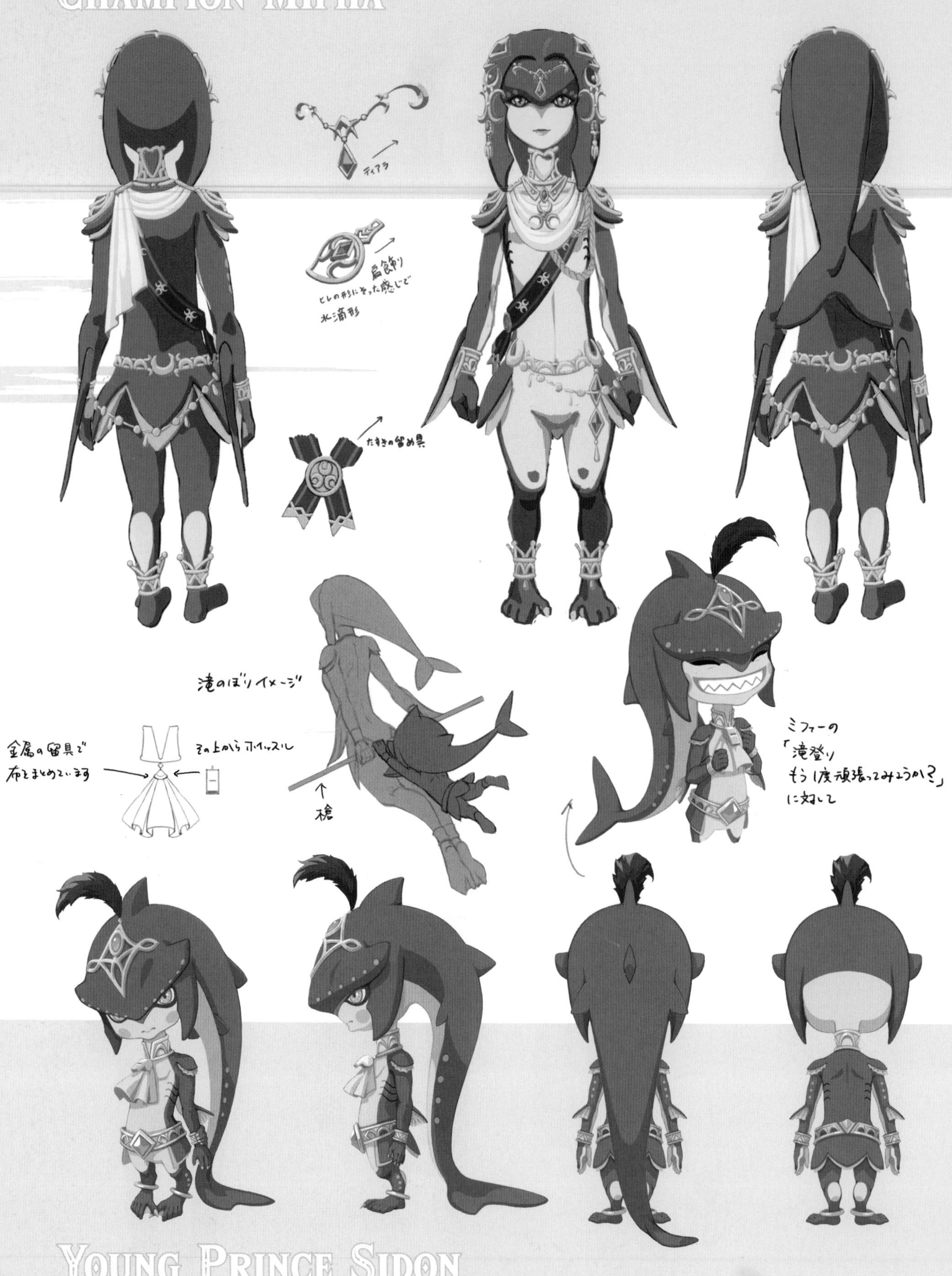

YOUNG PRINCE SIDON

Champion Urbosa

ルージュの額のと
同じデザイン
宝石はなし

冠の中心

ゲルドマークを
ラインで描く

Champion Daruk

Champion Revali

A Hylian Maid

INDEX

If you are looking for specific information, this alphabetical listing is just what you need. To avoid potential spoilers, note that critical page references are written in red.

CREDITS

The Complete Official Guide to *The Legend of Zelda: Breath of the Wild* is a Piggyback Interactive Limited production.

PIGGYBACK

Publishers:	Louie Beatty, Vincent Pargney
Project Leads:	Simone Dorn, Matthias Loges, Carsten Ostermann
Editorial Director:	Mathieu Daujam
Co-Authors:	Tony Gao, James Price
Support:	Hirofumi Yamada, David Schunk, Claude-Olivier Eliçabe
Finance Director:	Anskje Kirschner
Logistics:	Angela Kosik
Sales & Marketing:	Debra Kempker
Art Directors:	Jeanette Killmann & Martin C. Schneider (Glorienschein)
Designers:	Christian Runkel, Christian Schmal

ENGLISH VERSION

Sub-Editing:	Maura Sutton

FRENCH VERSION

Editors:	Claude-Olivier Eliçabe, Mathieu Daujam

GERMAN VERSION

Editor:	Klaus-Dieter Hartwig
Sub-Editing:	Barbara Bode

ITALIAN VERSION

	Marco Auletta, Filippo Facchetti, Lisa Franchini (Synthesis)
Localization Manager:	Emanuele Scichilone (Synthesis)

SPANISH VERSION

Carolin Schneider, Camila Groth Ibarra, Beatriz Tirado, Isabel Merino Bodes, Abel Funcia, José Manuel Gallardo, Marco Antonio Fernández Lago (Synthesis)

PREPRINT

Tino Bordusa, Dietmar Bormann, Larissa Bormann, Katharina Börner, Nicole Hannowsky, Ilse Hüttner, Anke Mattke, Frauke Müffelmann, Ralf Müller-Hensmann, Petra Reidath, Stefan Reiter, Arwed Scibba, Rabea Tilch, Anke Wedemeier, Torsten Wedemeier, Katja Wolf (AlsterWerk)

Thank you for your dedicated support throughout as well as your contributions!

NINTENDO

Eiji Aonuma
Hidemaro Fujibayashi
Yusuke Yamasoto
Makoto Miyanaga
Chiko Bird
Nate Bihldorff
Ryan Kelley
Billy Carroll
Zac Evans
Jeremy Krueger-Pack
Emiko Ohmori
Melena Jankanish
Kevin Williams

...and all the Development Team

NOA TEXT REVIEWERS

Alec Mohs-Hale, Benjamin Nutu, Cassandra Dillhoff, Charles Clute, Chelsea Staab, Clinton Newcombe, Connor McLoughlin, Dylan Rondeau, Eric Compton, Garrett Higgins, Gary Meads, Jack Malametz, Krystle Russell, Mairo Small, Mark Glass, Micah Kenworthy, Ondrej Lang, Taylor Simmons, Tom Hanusa

978-1-911015-48-2 (Expanded Edition | North America)
Printed in the United States of America.

978-1-911015-49-9 (Expanded Edition | Europe)
Printed in Germany.